PRINCIPLES OF ECONOMICS
FIFTH EDITION

Bob Rabboh, Ph.D. and Ronald J. Bartson, Ph.D.

Cover Art: "Silhouette" © Mary McCarthy.

Copyright © 1996 by Simon & Schuster Custom Publishing.
Copyright © 1999 by Pearson Custom Publishing.
All rights reserved.

Permission in writing must be obtained from the publisher before any part of this work may be reproduced or transmitted in any form or by any means, electronic or mechanical, including photocopying and recording, or by any information storage or retrieval system.

Printed in the United States of America

10 9 8 7 6 5 4 3 2 1

ISBN 0-536-02794-3
BA 990403

PEARSON CUSTOM PUBLISHING
160 Gould Street/Needham Heights, MA 02494
A Pearson Education Company

Contents

About the Authors xvii
Preface xix

Chapter 1   Economics—An Introduction 1
Learning Objectives 1
    Social Sciences 2
    Economics 2
    Macro vs. Micro 3
    Positive and Normative Economics 4
    The Economic Approach 4
    Ceteris Paribus 10
    Common Fallacies 10
    Cause and Effect Fallacy 10
    The Composition Fallacy 11
The Nobel Prize 11
Presentation Tools 12
    Slope 18
    45° Line 21
Mastering Economics 22
    An Overview of Economics 22
    The Fields of Economics 23
    Economics Statistics 24
    Career Opportunities Available to an Economics Major 25
    Employment Opportunities for Economists—1995 to 2005 25
Chapter 1 Key Concepts 27
Discussion Questions 28
1.1 Learning Practice 28
Solutions 29

Chapter 2   The Basics of Scarcity 31
Learning Objectives 31
Introduction 32
    Scarcity 32
    Choices 34
Production Possibilities—Macro 34
    Opportunity Costs 37
    Opportunity Costs—Personal 38
    Production Possibilities Graph 38
    Marginal Rate of Transformation 41
    Economic Growth 42

Production Possibilities—Micro 43
Efficiency 44
Economic Systems 46
      Arabic Tradition & Muslims: An Overview 47
      Mixed Market Structure 49
Chapter Summary 49
Chapter 2 Key Concepts 51
Discussion Questions 52
2.1 Learning Practice 52
Solutions 53

Chapter 3 The Market 55

Learning Objectives 55
An Introduction to the Market 56
Demand and Supply 56
Individual Demand 56
    Graphing Individual Demand 58
    Changes in Individual Demand 60
Market Demand 64
Firm's Supply 66
    Graphing a Firm's Supply 67
    Changes in a Firm's Supply 69
Market Supply 72
Equilibrium 74
Changes in the Market Price 79
Causes of Changes in Supply and Demand 83
    Quantity Demanded and Demand 84
    Quantity Supplied and Supply 84
Price Controls 85
    Price Floor 85
    Minimum Wages 86
    Agricultural Prices 86
    Price Ceiling 87
    Price Freeze 88
Take-A-Note 88
    1. Price Floors and Price Ceilings 88
    2. The Law of Demand 88
    3. The Law of Supply 88
    4. Changes in Demand and Supply 89
Chapter Summary 90
Chapter 3 Key Concepts 91
Discussion Questions 92
3.1 Learning Practice 93
Solutions 94
3.2 Learning Practice 95

Chapter 4 Elasticity 97

Learning Objectives 97
Elasticity 98
Price Elasticity of Demand 98
Types of Elasticity 100
    Relatively Elastic 100
    Relatively Inelastic 101
    Characteristics 103
    Unitary Elastic 104
    Perfectly Elastic Demand 105
    Perfectly Inelastic Demand 107
    Summary 108
    Slope 110
Income Elasticity of Demand 111
    Income Elasticity 112
    Normal Goods 113
    Luxury Items 114
    Neutral Good 115
Cross Elasticity of Demand 115
    Complementary Good 117
    Substitute Good 117
    Independent Good 118
Price Elasticity of Supply 119
    Relatively Elastic Supply 120
    Total Revenue Method 121
    Elasticity and Total Revenue 122
    Relatively Inelastic Supply 122
    Perfectly Elastic Supply 123
    Perfectly Inelastic Supply 124
    Unitary Elastic Supply 126
Elasticity Along the Demand Curve 127
Take-A-Note 129
Elasticity 129
    Types of Elasticity 129
    The Cross Elasticity of Demand 130
Chapter Summary 131
Chapter 4 Key Concepts 133
Discussion Questions 134
4.1 Learning Practice 134
Solutions 136
4.2 Learning Practice 137
4.3 Learning Practice 137

Chapter 5 The Foundation of Consumer Choice 139

Learning Objectives 139
Introduction 140
    The Rational Consumer 140
    Total Utility and Marginal Utility 140
    Principle of Diminishing Marginal Utility (DMU) 141
    Total and Marginal Utility Graphically 142
    Utility Consumer Behavior 143
    Maximizing Total Utility 143
    Disutility (DU) 145
    The Diamond-Water Paradox 146
    Indifference Curve Analysis 146
    Marginal Rates of Substitution (MRS) 150
    Characteristics of Indifference Curves 151
    Budget Constraints 154
    The Consumer's Maximization of Utility 156
    Derivation of the Demand Curve 158
5.3 Learning Practice 160
Solutions 161
5.4 Learning Practice 161
5.5 Learning Practice 162
5.6 Learning Practice 162
5.7 Learning Practice 162
5.8 Diminishing Marginal Utility (DMU) 163
Dozen Donut Holes 163
5.9 Learning Practice 164
Take-A-Note 164
    Choosing Between Goods 164
    Diamond—Water Paradox 164
Chapter Summary 165
Chapter 5 Key Concepts 166
Discussion Questions 166

Chapter 6 The Firm and Costs of Production 167

Learning Objectives 167
The Firm 168
    Financial Concerns of the Firm 168
Types of Business Forms 168
    Sole Proprietorship 168
    Partnership 168
    Corporation 169
Corporate Finance: Stocks and Bonds 170

      Bonds 170
      Common and Preferred Stocks 170
      Methods of Raising Financial Capital 171

Choices Open to the Firm in Production:
    Economic Time Periods 171
      Sunk Cost 172
      Explicit Costs (Accounting Costs or Money Outlay) 172
      Implicit Costs 172
      Opportunity Cost 172

Types of Profit 172
      Accounting Profit and Economic Profit, Marginal Revenue and Total Revenue 173

Short Run Costs 173
    Total Fixed Costs 173
    Total Variable Costs 174

Short-Run Cost Curves 175
    Short Run Cost Curves (TFC, TVC and TC curves) 175

Marginal Cost, Average Fixed Cost, Average Variable Cost,
    and Average Total Cost Curves 177
      Shapes of Individual Cost Curves in the Short Run 178

Relationships Between Cost Concepts in the Short Run 179
      Principle of Diminishing Returns 180

To Produce or Not to Produce? 180
      Break Even and Shut Down Situations 180

Calculation of Business Profits and Losses 181

Cost Analysis and Behavior:
    Production and Costs in the Long Run 181

Economies and Diseconomies of Scale
    and Constant Returns to Scale 183
      Diseconomies of Scale 183
      Constant Returns to Scale 184

Chapter Summary 186
6.13 Learning Practice 187
6.14 Learning Practice 188
    Examples 189
6.16 Learning Practice: Distinguishing Opportunity
    Costs and Sunk Costs 189
6.17 Learning Practice and Solutions 190
Take-A-Note 191
    The Average-Marginal Relationship 191
    A Firm's Cost 191
6.18 Learning Practice 192
    Hypothetical Cost Schedules for an Individual Firm in the Short Run 192
6.19 Learning Practice 193

6.20 Learning Practice 193
6.21 Learning Practice 194
Key Concepts 195
Discussion Questions 196

Chapter 7   How Markets Function: Pure Competition 197

Learning Objectives 197
Market Structures 198
Characteristics of Pure Competition 198
    Demand, Cost, Revenue, and the Profit Maximization Output 200
    The Competitive Firm's Short Run Supply Curve 202
    Industry Supply Curve 202
    Profit Maximization Principle: Unit Cost Minus Unit Revenue 203
    Short Run Profit Maximization Under Pure Competition 203
    Profit Rule 204
    Short Run Equilibrium of the Competitive Firm 205
    Purely Competitive Firm in the Long Run Equilibrium 208
    Profits in a Competitive Industry:
        How Much Profit Is Earned in a Competitive Industry? 209
    Economics of Agriculture 209
    Advantages and Disadvantages in a Purely Competitive Market 210
Chapter Summary 211
Chapter 7   Key Concepts 212
Take-A-Note 212
What Is Pure Competition? 212
Discussion Questions 213
7.13 Learning Practice and Solutions 214
7.14 Learning Practice 214

Chapter 8   Pure Monopoly 217

Learning Objectives 217
Introduction 218
    Monopoly 218
Characteristics 218
    Price, Output, Marginal Revenue, and Total Revenue under Monopoly 220
    Demand-Marginal Revenue Curve Under a Monopolist 220
    Demand Curves for a Monopolist and Pure Competitive Firms Compared 222
    Supply Curve of the Monopolist 222
    Monopoly and Price Elasticity of Demand 222
    Price Searcher 224
    Non-Price Competition 224
    Short Run Output—Marginal Revenue and Marginal Cost 224
    Monopoly Profits and Loss and Breaking Even 225

An Example of a Monopolist Breaking Even and Making a Profit 226
An Example of a Monopolist Making a Loss 227
Long Run Equilibrium of Monopoly 227
Characteristics of Monopoly 228
Price Discrimination 229
Dumping 230
Market Power 232
How Is Monopoly Created? 233
Resource Allocations 234
Deadweight Loss of Monopoly 235
Facts About Monopoly 235
Price, Marginal Revenue, Marginal Cost and Profit 235
Detroit Edison 236
Regulating a Natural Monopoly 236
Public Ownership of Monopoly: The Post Office 236
Chapter Summary 237
Take-A-Note 238
Why Monopolies Arise? 238
Questions and Answers 238
Chapter 8   Key Concepts 239
Discussion Questions 240
8.19 Learning Practice:
Monopolistic Firm: Short Run Position 241
8.20 Learning Practice and Solutions:
Monopoly Price, Output and Supply Curve 241
8.21 Learning Practice 242

CHAPTER 9   MONOPOLISTIC COMPETITION 243
Learning Objectives 243
Monopolistic Competition 244
Product Differentiation 244
Numerous Rivals 244
Freedom of Entry and Exit 245
Non-Price Competition 245
Consequences of Advertising 246
Supply Curve 247
Short-Run Conditions: Profits and Loss 248
Long Run Equilibrium Condition in the Monopolistic Competition 250
The Meaning of Zero Profits in Industry 250
Monopolistic Competition and Monopoly Compared 251
Evaluating Monopolistic Competition 252
Restaurants 254
Chapter Summary 254

Key Concepts 255
Discussion Questions 255
Practice Questions and Problems 256
9.1 Learning Practice 256
9.2 Learning Practice 257
9.3 Learning Practice 258

Chapter 10 Oligopoly 259

Learning Objectives 259
Introduction 260
    Interdependence 260
    Price Rigidity 261
Mergers, Collusion, and Cartel 261
    Mergers 261
    Collusion 262
    Cartel 263
    Oligopoly in the Long Run Equilibrium 264
    Potential Entry to an Oligopolistic Industry 265
Oligopoly Models 265
    Kinked Demand Curve Model 265
Pricing Policies 266
    Why Do Oligopolistic Firms Exist? 267
    The Dominant-Firm Industry 267
    General Motors 267
    Game Theory 268
    Cournot Model 268
    Prisoner's Dilemma 269
    Miscellaneous 270
Chapter Summary 271
Chapter 10 Key Concepts 272
Discussion Questions 273
10.1 Learning Practice 274
Solutions 274
10.2 Learning Practice and Solutions 274
10.3 Learning Practice 276
Solutions 277
A Comparison of Various Market Structures 278

Chapter 11 Labor Markets, Wages & Unions 279

Learning Objectives 279
Introduction 280

- Competitive Labor Market 280
- The Average, Marginal and Total Products of Labor 282
  - Average Product of Labor (APL) 282
  - Total Product of Labor (TPL) 282
  - Marginal Product of Labor (MPL) 283
  - Equilibrium Quantity of Labor—Monopsony 283
  - Characteristics of Monopsony 285
  - Monopsony in the Market for Nurses 285
- Labor Unions 286
  - Evolution of the Labor Movement in the United States 286
  - Pre-Civil War 287
  - Post-Civil War 288
  - American Federation of Labor 288
  - Congress of Industrial Organization (CIO) 289
  - AFL-CIO Merger 289
- Unions and Legislations 289
  - Public Policy of the 19th Century 289
  - Clayton Act 290
  - Norris-LaGuardia Act 290
  - Wagner Act 290
  - Taft-Hartley Act 290
  - Landrum-Griffin Act 290
  - Civil Rights Act 291
  - Types of Labor Unions 292
- Laborers and Wages: Approaches to Increase Wages 292
  - Collective Bargaining and Wage Rates 292
- Equilibrium in a Competitive Labor Market 293
  - Effect of a Single Union on Wage Rates and Employment 295
  - Wage Differentials 295
  - Summary of Wage Differentials 296
  - German Workers vs. Ethiopians 296
  - Actions to Decrease Wage Differentials in the U.S. 296
- Determinants of Income 297
- Legislations Concerning Labor 297
- Discrimination and Immigration 299
  - Discrimination 299
  - Racial Discrimination 299
  - Immigration 299
  - Concerns and Benefits from Immigrants 300
  - Factors Affecting the Demand for Labor 300
- Chapter Summary 301

Chapter 11 Key Concepts 303
Discussion Questions 304
11.1 Learning Practice and Solutions 305
11.2 Learning Practice 305
11.3 Learning Practice and Solutions 306
11.3 Learning Practice—Purely Competitive Labor Market 307

CHAPTER 12 REGULATION AND ANTITRUST POLICY 309

Learning Objectives 309
Introduction 310
The Regulatory Process 310
    Analysis of Regulation 311
    Rationale for Regulation 311
    Rent Control in a Large City: Is This a Good Idea? 312
    Price Controls: Agricultural Price Support 312
    Minimum Wage Controversy 313
Deregulation 314
Antitrust Philosophy 315
    Basic Antitrust Laws 316
    Sherman Act 316
    Clayton Act 317
    The Robinson-Patman Act 319
    The Federal Trade Commission Act 320
Exemptions from Antitrust Laws 320
    Anti-Monopoly Legislation 320
    New-Wave Regulation 321
Health and Safety Regulation 321
    How Are the Antitrust Statutes Interpreted and Enforced? 322
    The Effectiveness of the Antitrust Laws 323
    Bringing Professions Under Antitrust Laws: Good or Bad Idea? 323
    Social Regulation 323
Chapter Summary 324
Take-A-Note 325
    Federal Trade Commision (FTC) 1914 325
    The Clayton Act (1914) 325
    The Robinson-Patman Act (1936) 326
Chapter 12 Key Concepts 326
Discussion Questions 327

CHAPTER 13 EXTERNALITIES 329

Learning Objectives 329
Introduction 330
    Market Success 330

Marginal Cost	330
Marginal Benefit (MB)	331
Economic Efficiency	332
Market Failure	333
Environmental Quality	333

Externalities: Positive and Negative 333
    Collective Consumption of Goods as a Source of Inefficiency 334
    Marginal Private Benefits (MPB) Vs. Marginal Social Benefits (MSB) 335
    Marginal Private Costs (MPC) Vs. Marginal Social Costs (MSC) 335

Cost-Benefit Analysis 336
    Example 1—The Consumption of Fertilizer 336
    Example 2—The Production of Electricity 336
    Example 3—The Production and Consumption of Automobiles 337
    Example 4—Sex Education 338

Pollution: The Problem 339
    Prices 339
    Resources 340
    Sources of Pollution 341
    Summary of Major Sources of Pollution 341

Health and Safety 342
Long Term Effects of Air Pollution 342
Solutions 342
    Internalizing 342
    Direct Regulation 345
    Assignment of Property Rights 345

Take-A-Note 347
    Externalties: Positive and Negative 347

Chapter Summary 347
Chapter 13 Key Concepts 348
Discussion Questions 349

CHAPTER 14 GLOBAL PERSPECTIVES: INTERNATIONAL TRADE AND PROTECTIONISM 351

Learning Objectives 351
Scope of International Trade 352
    Terms of Trade 353
International Trade: Free-Trade Theory 353
    a. Absolute Advantage 354

- b. Comparative Advantage 355
  - Example 1: 355
  - Example 2: 355
  - Example 3: 356
  - Advantages to a Country that Engages in International Trade 356
- Reasons for Trade 356
  - a. Cost Advantage 357
  - b. Variety of Goods 357
  - c. Greater Choice 357
  - d. Expansion of Markets for Domestic Goods 357
  - e. Political Reasons 357
- Protectionism Theory 358
- Why Do Nations Restrict Trade? 359
  - Consequences of a Tariff 360
- Foreign Exchange Markets 363
  - a. The Spot Market 363
  - b. The Forward Market 363
- Foreign Exchange and Foreign Exchange Rates 364
  - Changes in Demand and Supply of Currency 364
- The Gold Standard 367
- Bretton Woods System 368
- Exchange Rates 368
  - a. Fixed Exchange Rate (FER) 368
  - Arguments For and Against the Fixed Exchange Rate System 368
  - b. Flexible Exchange vs. Managed Floating Exchange Rates 368
- Determination of Exchange Rate 370
- Factors Affecting Exchange: Why Do Exchange Rates Vary? 371
  - Shifts in Exchange Rates: Devaluation and Revaluation 371
  - Devaluation 371
  - Revaluation 372
  - Depreciation and Appreciation of the U.S. Dollar 372
- Developed vs. Developing Countries 373
  - Less Developed Countries 373
  - Areas 373
- Barriers to Doing Business in Less Developed Countries (LDC) 373
  - Political 373
  - Excessive Government Intervention in Business 374
  - Restrictions on Majority Ownership 375
  - Exchange and Remittance Controls 375
  - Economic Barriers 375
  - Nationalization and Expropriation 376

Trade Policy	377
Communication	377
Distribution Infrastructure	378
Recruiting Locals	378
Training	378
Foreign Corrupt Practices Act (FCPA)	379
Antitrust	379
What Makes a Country Poor?	379
Major Characteristics of Less Developed Countries (LDCs)	380
14.1 Learning Practice and Solutions	381
14.2 Learning Practice and Solutions	381
Chapter Summary	381
Chapter 14 Key Concepts	382
Discussion Questions	384
14.2 Learning Practice	385

Chapter 15 Government: Taxation and the Economy 387

Learning Objectives	387
Government, Taxation, and the Economy	388
Government and Mixed Economy	388
Functions	388
a. Allocation Function	388
b. Distribution Function and the Lorenz Curve	389
The Lorenz Curve	389
Poverty and Inequality	390
Helping the Poor—Investment in Human Capital	390
Primary Causes of Poverty	390
How Does the Government Try to Reduce Poverty?	391
Tax Policy	391
Why Has *Inequality* Been Growing in the United States?	391
c. Stabilization Function	392
Government Goals	392
Economic Growth	393
Determinants of Economic Growth	393
Basic Factors Determining Level of Development and Rate of Growth	393
Growth Size	394
Government Revenues	394
Borrowing	397
The Burden of the Government Debt on Future Generations	397
Fair Tax	397
Negative Income Tax	398
Negative Income Tax (NIT): Another Approach	399

- Example 1. 399
- Example 2. 399
- Example 3. 399
- Example 4. 399
- Example 5. 399
- Example 6. 399

Uses of Taxes 400
- Tax Computation Form 400
- Direct—Indirect 400
- General—Specific 401
- Tax Base 401

Taxation in the United States 401
- Income Taxes 401
- State Income Taxes 401
- Sales/Use Tax 401
- Property Taxes 402
- Other Taxes 402

Federal & State Expenditures 402
- a. Federal Government Expenditures 402
- b. State and Local Revenues and Expenditures 402
- c. Revenues & Expenditures for the State of Michigan 403

The Economic System of the United States 404
- a. Private Enterprises 404
- b. Large Corporations 404
- c. Small Enterprises 404
- d. Government 404
- e. Public Finance 405
- f. Economic Stabilization Policies 405
- g. Government Regulation and Control of Business 406
- h. Social Regulations 406
- i. The National Debt 406
- j. Merchandise Trade 406
- k. Foreign Direct Investment 407
- l. Strengths of the U.S. Economy 408

Chapter Summary 408
Chapter 15   Key Concepts 409
Discussion Questions 411

INDEX 413

About the Authors

Dr. Bob A. Rabboh earned his M.A. in Economics from the University of Detroit and his Ph.D. from Howard University. He is currently on the faculty of the Department of Social Sciences at Detroit College of Business in Dearborn, Michigan. He is adjunct faculty at Central Michigan University and graduate advisor in the off-campus programs, Wayne University and Henry Ford Community College. In addition to teaching a variety of courses at the aforementioned institutions, he has served as an international trade consultant with the international economics and research Inc. in Washington, D.C. He has published economics and international business textbooks and taught graduate courses in the Republic of Taiwan. In addition to his teaching, he serves as a consultant to the International Business Leaders Association.

Ronald J. Bartson, Ph.D. is a professor of Economics and Statistics at the Detroit College of Business in Dearborn, Michigan. He received his B.A. and M.A. from the University of Detroit and his Ph.D. from Wayne State University. He also teaches for Baker College and Central Michigan University. From 1983 to 1993, Dr. Bartson served as the Chairperson of the Social Science Department at Detroit College of Business. From 1987 to 1993, he served as the Director of Student Activities. Today, Dr. Bartson also teaches research classes and serves as a Monitor in the off-campus graduate program of Central Michigan University evaluating the students' integrative projects.

Preface

The challenge in writing about economic principles is in demonstrating the power of economics as a tool for understanding society. Questions have been raised dealing with sequencing of economic principles as to whether or not macroeconomics should precede microeconomics, or vice versa. To many, logic to providing a macroeconomics sequence followed by a micro, illustrations of an overview of the level of national output prior to analyzing and explaining its components. There is also a solid argument that numerous students take only one semester of two semester principle steps. However, macroeconomics is possibly more adequate in understanding current economic issues.

Economics is simply about how we make decisions and what to do when we can't do it all. In order to make a choice about anything you need a few tools. Studying economics can provide you with a set of rules that will be helpful in making decisions, in both your personal and professional life. Most students who take economics end up taking some accounting and statistics. It should come as no great surprise that these areas also provide you with important tools to put in your decision-making tool kit.

A wide variety of businesses and government agencies hire economists. A brief list includes financial institutions (from banks to brokerage houses to insurance companies), medium-sized businesses and multinational corporations and consulting firms.

An economics degree isn't just for students who aspire to be economists. The field is useful to those who intend to enter the business world, perhaps as entrepreneurs. It is also good preparation for graduate work in business (M.B.A) and economics (M.A. or Ph.D.), or the law, and in a variety of professional programs, such as public administration and urban planning.

The writing style throughout this book reflects my personal convictions:

- The easier the reading, the more it will be read and the better it will be understood—the task at hand is tough enough without compounding it by couching the explanation in language unfamiliar to the student.

- Scholarly prose is not an efficient medium for the transmission of deep, basic thoughts to students—there is no idea so deep, no theory so rigorous that it cannot be explained in simple English.

In short, I believe that learning can be (and whenever possible should be) fun. In this book, I have tried my best to make it that.

Students have generally found economics a difficult subject to understand and learn they continue to remain perplexed as a result of the numerous conditions that must often be remembered and correlated in solving a problem. In doing the exercise by themselves, students find that they are required to devote considerably more time to economics than to other subjects of comparable credits, because they are uncertain with regard to the selection and application of the theorems and principles involved.

If our students can find elements of the concepts presented here that have no practical use, we promise to delete the material from the course, and award them bonus points on their next exam.

We seek to achieve a usable level of economic literacy for those students who do not go beyond the principles course, as well as a viable foundation of economic understanding for those who will pursue intermediate economic courses.

Bob A. Rabboh, Ph.D
Professor of Economics

Ronald J. Bartson, Ph.D
Professor of Economics and Statistics

CHAPTER 1

Economics– An Introduction

LEARNING OBJECTIVES

After reading this chapter, you should be able to:
1. Identify economics as a social science.
2. Define economics.
3. Distinguish between macroeconomics and microeconomics.
4. Distinguish between positive and normative economics.
5. Identify the fields of economics.
6. Explain the statistical approach to developing economic theory.
7. Explain how economists build models.
8. Identify the tools an economist uses to present ideas.
9. Explain the concept of *ceteris paribus*.
10. Explain the common fallacies in applying theory.
11. Read a table and a graph.
12. Identify the sources of economics statistics.
13. Explain the concept of a function.
14. Explain the importance of functions to economics.
15. Explain the concept of the slope of a line.

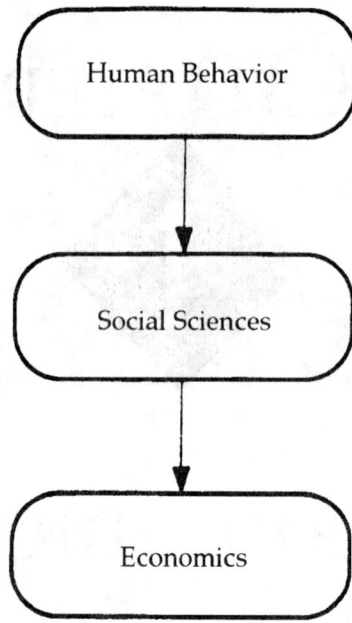

The Derivation of Economics

Social Sciences

The social sciences deal with the behavior of people in society and, thus, include anthropology, economics, geography, history, law, political science, psychiatry, psychology, sociology, and statistics. Social science formulates theories concerning group behavior, usually in an understandable manner and in a way that the theories can be tested against fact. While this book is concerned with economics, all the social sciences are involved since each, by itself, represents an explanation of only a part of human behavior.

Economics

Economics is defined as the study of how individuals and societies satisfy their material needs and wants in a world characterized by scarcity. People have unlimited needs and wants, but the resources do not exist to satisfy all of them. As a result, choices have to be made. Economics is the study of how the choices are made, how scarce resources are funneled into the chosen uses, and how this can best be done.

Economists observe the world around them and collect information to describe their observations. They summarize and present this information in tables, graphs, and written texts. This technique is sometimes called descriptive statistics. Economists develop explanations, or theories, of how an economic system works, and identify the main elements of the system. They develop theories of how individuals and societies interact in order to satisfy their needs and wants. Economists both develop new theories and borrow theories from the other social sciences. For example, since they are observing society and individuals in regard to needs and wants, economists will investigate ideas from sociology and psychology. The theories developed by the economists are used to explain the causes and effects of the description observations. This book is concerned with economic theory, especially that theory that explains the American economic system.

Macro vs. Micro

Economics, as a social science, has been divided into two main branches: macroeconomics and microeconomics (see Figure 1.1). Macroeconomics is the study of the overall system by which a country, or a group of people, conduct their affairs regarding prices, employment, income, and money. Macroeconomics deals with how the whole economy functions. It deals with how prices are determined and how prices, or changes in prices, impact on the economy. Macroeconomics studies the employment needs of a country and the impact upon the economy and individuals when unemployment exists. It studies the causes of unemployment and the solutions to either eliminate unemployment or to reduce the hardships joblessness imposes on people and the system as a whole.

Macroeconomics studies the sources of total income for individuals, businesses and the government. It presents what these different groups spend their income on. Macroeconomics is the study of how one group can impact on the income of another. For example, individuals buying less during the Christmas-gift season will cause business incomes to drop. As a result, less people may be employed, thus reducing the income of the individuals involved. Since both business and individual incomes have dropped, tax collections will be reduced. As a result, the income of the government will drop.

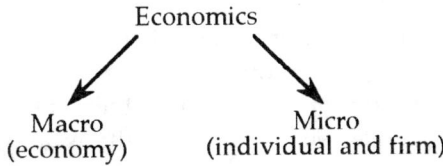

Figure 1.1
Economics is Divided into Macro and Micro

Macroeconomics is also the study of money and the financial institutions which deal with money. Incomes and prices are expressed in terms of money. For example, a person may have a salary of 2,500 dollars a month and a hamburger may cost 1.89 dollars. Both individuals and businesses may have more revenue than expenses and may seek help in putting the surplus to use. Individuals, businesses, and the government all borrow to cover expenses in excess of income. The financial institutions, which assist in handling surpluses and borrowing, play an important role in the economy.

Macroeconomics is the study of how the major components of an economy, individuals, businesses, government, and financial institutions, interact and impact on each other.

In contrast, microeconomics is concerned with how single businesses or individuals produce or spend. It is the study of how a business firm decides what to produce, what price to charge, and what combinations of materials, labor, and machinery will result in the greatest benefit to the firm.

Microeconomics is the study of the various types of industries that exist: namely, monopolies, oligopolies, monopolistically competitive firms, and perfectly competitive firms. It deals, mainly, with how these different types of industries make decisions and the impact upon the firm. For example, a small group of firms may decide to all charge the same price. Since the price selected will probably be a high price, the impact upon the firms will be greater revenue and less costs since competition has been reduced. Microeconomics is the study of the theory of the firm.

In microeconomics, the individual is studied to determine which products he or she will purchase. The individual will try to buy so as to achieve the most utility for the money spent. Microeconomics identifies those variables which lead the individual to buy or not to buy and which determine how much he or she will buy.

While there is a distinction made between macroeconomics and microeconomics, the variables of each impact upon the other. A firm's decision to raise its price, a micro variable, may lead other firms to raise prices. As a result, inflation, a macroeconomic variable, may develop. The economy could be experiencing an increase in unemployment, a macroeconomic variable. As a result, the owners of a shoe store chain decide not to raise the prices of shoes, a microeconomic variable.

Positive and Normative Economics

Positive economics attempts to analyze the actions of individuals, businesses, and government in the economy without making judgments as to whether the results of these actions are good or bad.

The Clinton Administration proposed a program of universal medical coverage for all Americans. Positive economics would present the main points of the program, discuss the costs and the benefits to various sectors of the economy, and discuss its impact. The following questions would be addressed. Who would benefit? Who would lose? Who would pay? Who would handle the program? What would be the effect upon the medical profession? What would be the effect on the insurance companies?

Normative economics analyzes the outcomes of the actions and makes a judgment that the results are either good or bad. As regards a program of universal health coverage, the following statements would be examples of normative economics. The program would be bad since it would result in a lessening in the quality of medical care due to government control of prices. The program would be bad since it would discourage people from entering the medical profession. The program would be good since people without medical coverage would be able to take advantage of medical care without having to worry about how they are going to pay for it. The program would be good because the population would be healthier and able to participate more in the economy.

It is difficult to completely separate positive and normative economics and at times analysis must include both. A candidate for political office may have the position that a program of universal medical coverage is not in the best interests of the country. The candidate should also be able to present sound economic evidence to support the position. Our background, political-cultural-economic-educational, affects how we see the world and the consequences of certain actions. We should always attempt to remove our personal interpretations and base our recommendations for the economy on sound economic logic.

As another example, there is a debate about a constitutional amendment to require the national government to achieve a balanced budget. The government's expenses cannot exceed tax revenue. Normative economics would state that the amendment should be passed and the balance should be achieved by reducing government expenditures for the good of the country. Positive economics would examine the areas of government expenditure and the results of reducing government expenditures. Positive economics would examine the sources of government revenue and the results of increasing taxes. Positive economics would examine the consequences to the power of the government to solve economic problems under the constraint of such an amendment. Positive economics would discuss the amendment and the results objectively without stating what is good or what is bad.

The Economic Approach

Many men and women suffer from migraine headaches. There are various medicines available to relieve these headaches, but researchers are always looking for better ones. After the researchers have developed a new medicine, they will conduct an experiment to determine whether or not it will be effective. They will contact doctors who treat such ailments and elicit, from their patients, volunteers for the experiment. All the patients represent the population of the study. From this population, the researchers will select two different groups. One group will receive the new medicine, while the other group is given a placebo. A placebo has no medicinal value at all. The group given the placebo is called the control group. The researchers will very carefully monitor the two groups and compare results at the end of the experiment. At that time, a decision will be made regarding the value of the new medicine. The researchers are able to conduct a very controlled experiment and make a decision.

In the social sciences, such as economics, it is not possible to conduct such controlled experiments. In order to determine the reaction to a tax reduction, the following would be done in an experimental method. Two groups of volunteers would be selected. One group would be given a tax cut; the other would not be given the cut. Both groups would be monitored for a length of time and then the results would be studied. This would be very difficult to do in the large economic systems that exist with the restrictions imposed by political systems.

The experimental method, as presented, can be summarized by Figure 1.2.

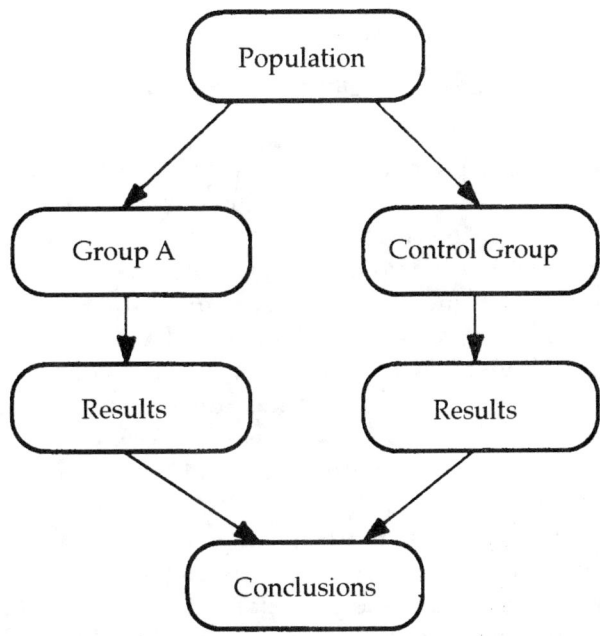

Figure 1.2
The Experimental Method

Instead of using the experimental approach, the economist develops ideas from data that has been collected and from models that he or she has developed. The first can be called a statistical approach, and the second, a model-building approach.

The format of the statistical approach can be summarized by Figure 1.3.

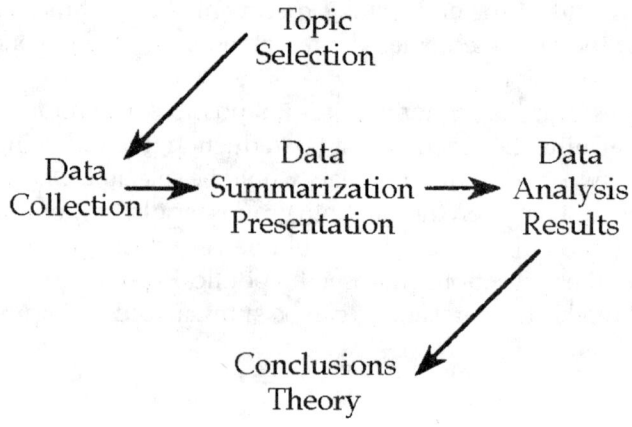

Figure 1.3
The Statistical Method—Inductive Approach

As an example of the statistical method, let us assume we are interested in determining whether or not a change in the price of one item can affect the quantity sold of a related product, sometimes called a complement. Assume further that the main concern to us is the peanut butter and jelly sandwich, for which there are three ingredients: peanut butter, jelly, and bread. These three ingredients are complements since they are used together to make this sandwich. The topic is whether a change in the price of one product will affect the quantity demanded of another, but related, item. We choose the items peanut butter and jelly to draw our conclusion.

Over a period of time, we would collect data regarding the prices of peanut butter at various supermarkets and quantities of jelly sold in those markets. Using various tools, explained in the next section, we would test the data to determine if a relationship exists. Let us assume we find a relationship and that the relationship is such that as the price moves in one direction, the quantity moves in the other direction. Using inductive reasoning, we could conclude that an increase in the price of a good will result in the quantity sold of a complement good to decrease. We could also reverse this and state that a decrease in the price of an item will result in the quantity sold of a complement good to increase. We have formulated an economic theory of prices and complement goods using a statistical approach.

In the previous example, we conducted a statistical study in which we collected data and then developed our theory using inductive reasoning. Inductive reasoning refers to drawing conclusions from particular facts or from individual cases. Instead, we could have used a statistical approach, using deductive reasoning, which is from the general principle to the specific results. Figure 1.4 represents this approach.

Hypothesis
Proposed Theory

↓

Deductive
Reasoning

↓

Results of
Proposed Theory

↓

Compared With
Actual Statistics

↓

Conclusions

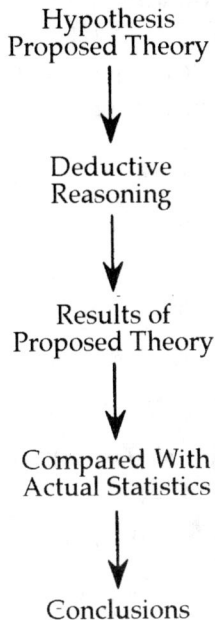

Figure 1.4
The Statistical Method—Deductive Approach

Figure 1.4 represents the deductive approach. Let us assume we have a hypothesis that the amount of household spending is related to the educational level of the head of the household. In other words, we are theorizing that household spending is a function of the educational level of the head of the household. This represents one hypothesis.

Using our hypothesis, we reason that households will have different levels of spending since the heads have different levels of education. We, furthermore, reason that the greater the level of education of the head, the greater will be the level of spending.

In order to test our hypothesis, we would select a sample of households. In this sample would be households headed by persons with less than a high school education, by persons with a high school education, by persons with a college education, and by persons with an advanced college education. We would then collect information regarding the level of spending in these various households.

The next step is to determine if the actual results from the sample match the results from our hypothesis. If the results match, we have shown our hypothesis is correct. If the results do not match, we could correct our hypothesis. It would not be correct to seek data that only supports our hypothesis. Figure 1.5 represents a possible model-building approach.

Hypothesis
Assumptions Variables Definition Model
Analysis
Reasoning
Conclusions
Theory

Figure 1.5
The Model-Building Approach

Many economists develop theory by building models or model economies. To illustrate this method, we develop the following model.

1. The hypothesis we wish to test is "Countries will benefit if they specialize in certain products in which they have an advantage and trade those for products in which other countries have the advantage."

2. Since there are many variables involved, we must develop a model world economy which is simple and can be discussed easily. In order to do this, we make a set of assumptions like the following.

   a. There are only two (2) countries in the world: the U.S.A. and Russia.

   b. There are only two (2) products available for sale: bread and caviar.

   c. A work week is defined as forty (40) hours in each country.

   d. Currently, both products are produced in both countries with workers dividing the work time equally among the products.

   e. Currently, there is no trade between the two countries.

   f. Table 1.1 represents the number of hours it takes a worker in each country to produce one unit of the product.

Table 1.1
Labor Hours

Product	U.S.A.	Russia
Bread	4	8
Caviar	6	4

The variables we have selected are bread, caviar, and labor time. We will define bread as loaves of bread. Caviar will represent jars of caviar. Labor time is defined as the number of hours it takes a worker to produce one unit of the product. To illustrate this, it takes a worker 4 hours of labor in the U.S.A. to produce a loaf of bread and 6 hours to produce a jar of caviar. In Russia, it takes a worker 8 hours of labor to produce a loaf of bread and 4 hours to produce a jar of caviar.

In both countries, workers spend 40 hours a week producing. Half the time, 20 hours, is spent producing each product. We have developed a simple world economy which we will use as our model to develop theory.

3. The next step is to analyze the implications of our model. Based on assumption (f), we could develop Table 1.2, which represents the number of items a worker can produce in 40 hours.

Table 1.2
Products Per 40 Hours

Product	U.S.A.	Russia
Bread	5	2 1/2
Caviar	3 1/3	5

In assumption (d), we stated each worker spends half of the time producing each product. If 20 hours a week is spent producing bread, and if in the U.S.A. a worker takes 4 hours to produce a loaf, a worker can produce 5 loaves a week (20/4 = 5). If 20 hours are spent producing caviar, and if a worker in the U.S.A. takes 6 hours to produce a jar, a worker can produce 3 1/3 jars a week (20/6 = 3 1/3). If a worker in Russia takes 8 hours to produce a loaf of bread, a worker can produce 2 1/2 loaves a week. (20/8 = 2 1/2). A worker in Russia could produce 5 jars of caviar a week, assuming it takes 4 hours (20/4 = 5). The world's total production can be summarized by Table 1.3.

Table 1.3
Total World Production

Product	U.S.A.	Russia	Total
Bread	5	2 1/2	7 1/2
Caviar	3 1/3	5	8 1/3

Thus, if workers divide their work time evenly and produce both products, the world's production will be 7 1/2 loaves of bread per worker per week, and 8 1/3 jars of caviar per worker per week.

4. The next step is to test our hypothesis within the constraints of the model. The hypothesis is "Countries will benefit if they specialize in certain products in which they have an advantage, and if they trade those for products in which other countries have the advantage."

Since a U.S.A. worker can produce more bread per week, the U.S.A. would have an advantage in producing bread. Likewise, Russia would have the advantage in producing caviar. If the U.S.A. worker specializes in producing bread, and the Russian worker specializes in producing caviar, the following will result: Now working 40 hours a week, the U.S.A. worker will produce 10 loaves of bread (40/4 = 10); and the Russian worker will produce 10 jars of caviar (40/4 = 10). Total world production is now 10 loaves of bread per worker per week, and 10 jars of caviar per worker per week (See Table 1.4).

Table 1.4
Production Under Specialization

Product	U.S.A.	Russia	Total
Bread	10	0	10
Caviar	0	10	10

5. We are now ready to draw conclusions and present our hypothesis as a theory. The table demonstrates that world production has increased due to specialization of bread in the U.S.A. and caviar in Russia. Since the U.S.A. no longer produces caviar, it will have to trade with Russia. Likewise, Russia will have to trade with the U.S.A. for bread.

The economist, thus, develops his theories by collecting data to test the hypothesis and by developing simplified models of the world. The economist uses facts, hypotheses, and logic to develop theories. The above example is very similar to how Adam Smith developed the Free-Trade Theory of International Trade, which is covered in a later chapter.

Ceteris Paribus

Economics deals with dependent variables such as: the quantity of a good that will be demanded by the market, the quantity of a good that will be supplied to the market, the amount of money that a person will spend, the amount of money a person will save, the amount of profit a business will reinvest into the firm, the amount of money borrowed by consumers, by businesses, and by the government.

A variable is something that changes over time. A person may spend more this year than last year. The consumers may buy more chicken this week than last week. The government may borrow more money this year than last year. The change in a dependent variable is the result of changes in other variables usually called independent variables.

Economics attempts to explain the logic behind the change. Why did the person spend more this year than last year? Why did the consumers buy more chicken this week than last week? Why did the government borrow more this year than last year?

There are obviously many independent variables which explain the change in these variables. It would be impossible to discuss all of the reasons even if they could all be identified. Economists identify what the main independent variables are for the change and leave out the others. The term for this reasoning is *ceteris paribus* which means "all else equal."

A person spent more this year than last since the person had a higher income this year than last year. More chicken was sold this week than last week since the price was lower this week than last week. The government borrowed more this year than last year since the T-bill rate was higher this year than last year.

There are many other variables that could have affected the differences, but there is no time to discuss all of them. The main independent variables are identified and analyzed. The student should then be able to understand how independent variables can affect change in the dependent variable and be able to identify other variables which could affect the dependent variable.

As examples, a person may spend more this year than last year since the person became a parent and must now support a child, thus family size could be a variable. A person may buy more chicken this week than last week since the government released a study indicating the negative effect on health of eating too much red meat, thus personal preference could be a variable. The government may borrow more this year than last year since Congress reduced the federal income-tax rates, thus tax rates could be a variable.

Common Fallacies

There are two errors of logic that must be considered in developing an explanation of economic activity. Economists refer to these errors as: the cause and effect fallacy and the composition fallacy.

Cause and Effect Fallacy

This error results when a statement is made that one variable causes another when in fact this is not the case. To state that two variables are related does not mean that the one variable causes the other variable.

In macroeconomics there is a relationship between disposable personal income and the amount of money a person will spend. There is no statement that the one causes the other but that they are related. A third variable, such as increased confidence in the economy, may have caused both to increase.

In microeconomics there is a relationship between the price of an item and the quantity that is demanded of the item. If the price of the item drops, the quantity demanded of the item increases. Such a relationship exists, but economists are cautious and do not state that the change in the price of the item caused the change in the quantity demanded of the item. An increase in the supply of the item and an advertising campaign could account for the drop in price and the increase in the quantity demanded.

Economists try to develop a logical explanation of the relationship instead of stating a causal relationship. With the drop in the price of an item, an economist could theorize that the real purchasing power of the consumer has increased leading to a greater quantity demanded. Since the price of this item is now less, consumers substitute this item for similar items. The cause for the increase in the quantity demanded may be the increased purchasing power of the consumers.

The Composition Fallacy

The composition fallacy occurs when a statement is made that what applies to a small group applies to a larger group when this is not necessarily true.

In recent years the number of foreign cars purchased in the United States has been increasing. This has impacted on the number of domestic cars sold and has reduced earnings and employment of the United States automobile companies. The automobile companies and the employees of these companies have been negatively affected. To say that the whole economy has been negatively affected could be a composition fallacy.

It could be that the increased sales of foreign automobiles increased foreign incomes and foreign purchases of other American goods. This would mean that other industries have been positively affected by the increase in foreign automobile sales.

In every situation there are winners and losers. To say, that if one loses the whole loses, is not necessarily true. An economist has to look at the whole picture to determine the effects on the whole economy.

THE NOBEL PRIZE

The Nobel Prize was first awarded in 1901 by the Nobel Committee established by the Swedish Royal Academy to acknowledge major contributions of people to peace, physics, chemistry, literature, and medicine. In 1969 an award for major contributions to economics was established. Economics is the only social science for which there is a specific award. The 1994 award included a $930,000 cash prize which the winners shared. The prize is paid by the Bank of Sweden in Stockholm. In the period from 1969 to 1994 the award was won by Americans 19 of the 26 times the award was given.

By examining some of the winners and their contributions to economics, one can see the importance of developing theory in the social sciences.

In 1976 the Nobel Prize for Economics was awarded to Milton Friedman. Dr. Friedman is a retired professor from the University of Chicago. Dr. Friedman has made many contributions to economic theory. Among these contributions is a discussion of the natural rate of unemployment and its effect on inflation.

According to the Phillips Curve there is a trade-off between unemployment and inflation. Low unemployment means high inflation. High unemployment means low inflation. Friedman developed the theory that the Phillips Curve is vertical at some rate of unemployment called the natural rate of unemployment. The natural rate of unemployment is the sum of the frictional and structural rates of unemployment.

The meaning of the theory is that inflation results only when the actual unemployment rate is less than the natural rate of unemployment. The low rate of unemployment results in higher wages, higher costs, and higher prices. This leads to a lower level of production and unemployment will rise back to the natural rate of unemployment. The natural rate of unemployment and the Phillips Curve will be discussed in the *Principles of Macroeconomics* text in the section on unemployment.

In 1994 the winners were John C. Harsanyi, John F. Nash, and Reinhard Selton. Harsanyi is a retired professor from the University of California in Berkeley. Nash is a researcher at Princeton University, and Selton teaches at the University of Bonn in Germany.

The winners were chosen because of their contributions to the field of game theory. Game theory covers how strategies used in games like poker and chess can explain economic and financial behavior. In economic game theory each firm has a strategy of operation based on the rival firms' strategies. It is like in a chess game where a player decides on a certain move after considering what the other player might do if that move is made. In poker each player has to decide what the other players will do based on their bidding. Does the player have the cards or is the player bluffing? Game theory attempts to forecast what an opponent is most likely to do considering all the options open to the opponent.

Nash developed a concept of equilibrium in game theory. Equilibrium would be at that point where each opponent has made their best possible play given what the opponent is doing.

Game theory will be covered in *Principles of Microeconomics* in the section on oligopoly.

PRESENTATION TOOLS

To present data and theories, the economist uses various tools, such as: tables, graphs, functional relationships, and written texts. Tables and graphs are used to summarize, organize, and present data in a more understandable form. Table 1.5 is an example which shows the principle of demand. It shows various possible prices for an orange and how many Susan would be willing to buy at each of the prices.

Table 1.5
Susan's Demand for Oranges

Price	Quantity
1.00	2
.75	3
.50	4
.25	8
.05	15

A graph is a diagram which represents the successive changes in the value of the quantity of the variable being presented over a period of time. The four main types of graphs are bar graphs, line graphs, pictograms, and pie charts.

A bar graph uses the height or length of a bar to represent the value of the variable. The first example, Figure 1.6, is a vertical bar chart since the bars are vertical to the bottom line.

By reading the height of each bar against the percentage marks, we can determine the unemployment rate in Metropolis in any one year, such as about 11 percent in 1991. We are also able to see that the unemployment rate fell each year to 5 percent in 1994.

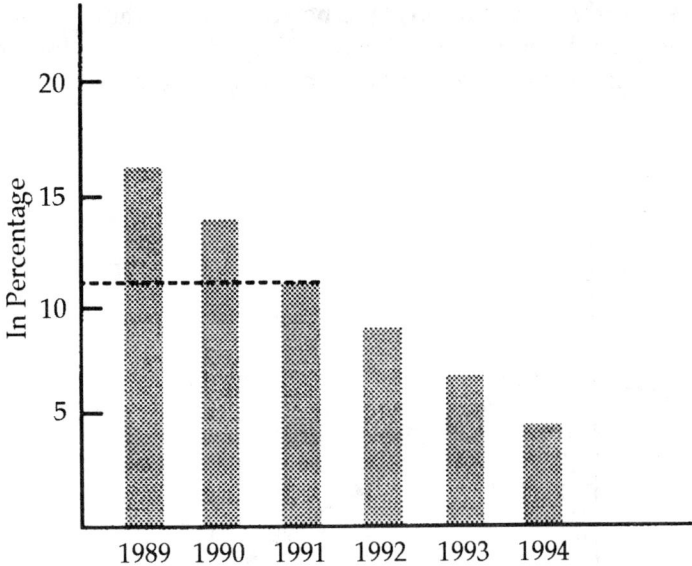

Figure 1.6
Unemployment Rate for Metropolis 1989–1994

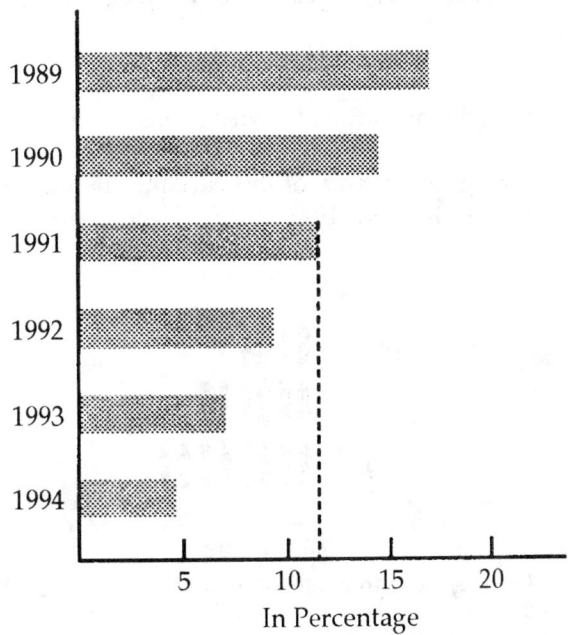

Figure 1.7
Unemployment Rate for Metropolis 1989–1994

The same information can be presented by placing the years vertically and the percentages horizontally. The length of the bar would then represent the value of the variables. Figure 1.7 shows this format. Reading down from the bar for 1991, we note that the unemployment rate is 11 percent.

Figure 1.8 shows how this information could be presented in the form of a line graph. For this type of graph, time is usually plotted horizontally. To read the unemployment rate for 1991, for example, read across from the dot above 1991 to about 11 percent.

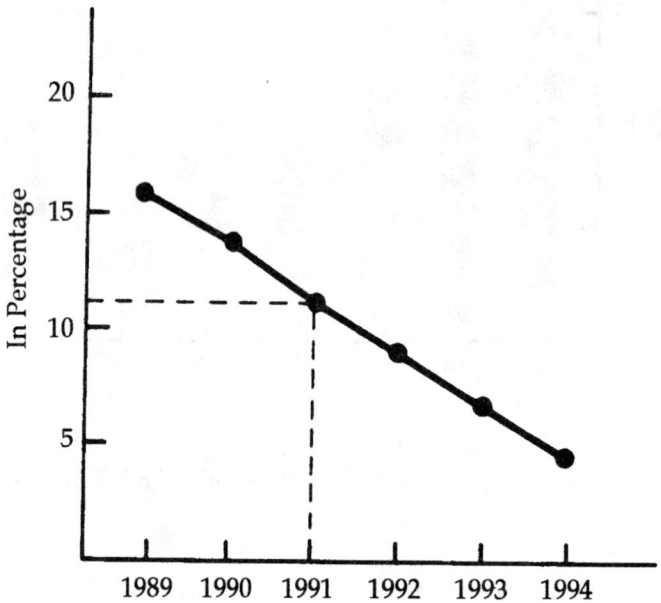

Figure 1.8
Unemployment Rate for Metropolis 1989–1994

A pictogram uses a drawing, or picture, of the variables being presented. Figure 1.9 represents the employment in Metropolis from 1991 to 1993. Each "person" represents 10,000 people employed.

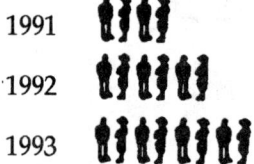

Figure 1.9
Employment in Metropolis from 1991–1993

In order to determine the number of people employed, multiply the number of "persons" by 10,000. Thus, the number employed in 1992 would be 6 times 10,000, or 60,000 people.

A pie chart takes its name from a pie, like Mom used to bake, that is then divided up by cutting it into pieces. A circle is drawn and divided up into pie pieces. The pieces are proportioned to the value of the variable. In order to illustrate the pie chart, we will use the components of national income, shown in Table 1.6.

Table 1.6
National Income Components (amounts in billions)

Compensation of Employees	2504.9
Proprietors' Income	289.8
Rental Income of Persons	16.7
Corporate Profits	284.4
Net Interest	326.1
National Income	3421.9

The first step in constructing a pie diagram from data is to convert the component values to percentages of the total. The results are presented in Table 1.7.

Table 1.7
National Income Components (in percentages)

Compensation of Employees	73.2%
Proprietors' Income	8.5%
Rental Income of Persons	.5%
Corporate Profits	8.3%
Net Interest	9.5%
National Income	100.0%

The component values are converted to percentages by dividing the value by the national income amount. For example, corporate profits divided by national income: 284.4/3421.9 = .083, or 8.3 percent.

The second step in constructing a pie chart is to convert the percentages to a portion of the circle. A circle is a diagram composed of 360 degrees. The first component, compensation of employees, accounted for 73.2 percent of national income; therefore, its share of a circle will be 73.2 percent of 360 degrees or 263 degrees. Table 1.8 presents the components in degrees.

Table 1.8
National Income Components

Compensation of Employees	263
Proprietors' Income	31
Rental Income of Persons	2
Corporate Profits	30
Net Interest	34
National Income	360 Degrees

The third step would be to actually construct the pie chart using the degrees for each component, as shown in Figure 1.10.

Functional relationships are either direct or inverse. A direct relationship means as the independent variable changes, the dependent variable changes in the same direction. In other words, as x increases, y increases; and as x decreases, y decreases. An inverse relationship means as the independent variable moves in one direction, the dependent variable moves in the opposite direction. As x increases, y decreases; and as x decreases, y increases. These movements are summarized in Figure 1.11.

The consumption function, $C = f(DI)$, is a direct relationship since consumption increases as disposable income increases. The demand function, $Q_D = f(P)$, is inverse since the quantity demanded of a good increases as the price of the item decreases.

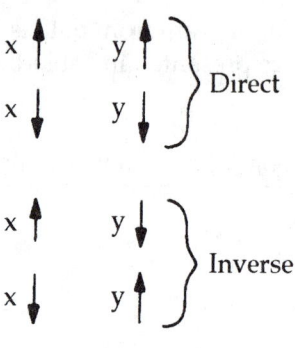

Figure 1.11
Functional Relationship

In addition to presenting functional relationships in mathematical form, $y = f(x)$, economists use graphs of the function. In the previous graphs presented in this chapter, a variable was plotted on either the horizontal or the vertical line, and time periods were plotted on the other. Thus, only one variable was involved. In a functional relationship, there are two variables: a dependent and an independent. Figure 1.12 presents the usual form this graph will be presented in.

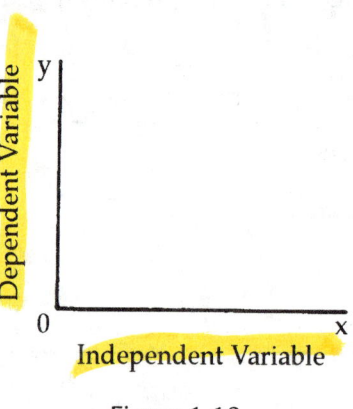

Figure 1.12
Graphing a Function

The dependent variable is placed on the vertical line and the independent variable on the horizontal line.

A graph of a functional relationship provides two main pieces of information:
1. that a functional relation exists, and
2. whether the relationship is direct or inverse.

In Figure 1.13 below, a functional relationship exists and it is direct. Notice that a direct relationship results in a line rising to the right.

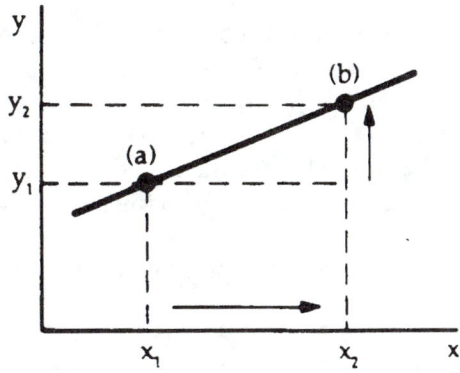

Figure 1.13
Direct Relationship

A function exists since as x changes from x_1 to x_2, y changes from y_1 to y_2. As x increases from x_1 to x_2, y increases from y_1 to y_2. Since both variables are increasing, the relationship is direct. If we draw a straight line through point (a), representing the values of x and y before the change in x, and point (b), representing the values of x and y after the change in x, we have a line which rises to the right. In mathematical terms, we could say the line, or graph, slopes upward.

In Figure 1.14 below, a functional relationship exists and it is inverse. Notice that an inverse relationship results in a line falling to the right.

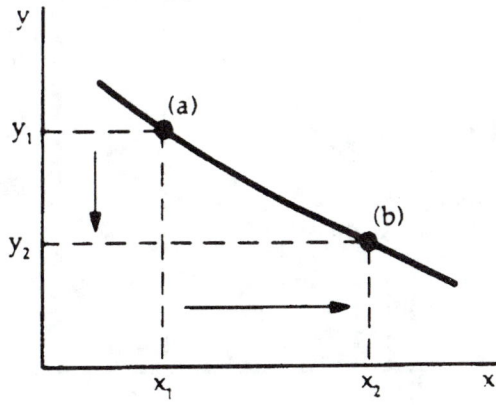

Figure 1.14
Inverse Relationship

A function exists since as x changes from x_1 to x_2, y changes from y_1 to y_2. As x increases from x_1 to x_2, y, however, decreases from y_1 to y_2. Since the variables move in opposite directions, the relationship is inverse. If we draw a straight line through point (a), representing the values of x and y before the change in x, and point (b), representing the values of x and y after the change in x, we have a line which falls to the right. In mathematical terms, we could say the line, or graph, slopes downward.

In mathematical terms, a slope upward is said to be positive, and a slope downward is said to be negative. Therefore, a direct function is a positive relationship and an inverse function is a negative relationship.

Since economists deal with hypotheses that are, in many cases, functional relationships, graphs are used extensively. As you read this book, you will notice this.

Slope

The slope of a line is an important concept in economics. The concept comes from the algebra of a linear function. A linear function is a statement in which two variables are related, and the rate of change in the variables is a constant. A linear function graphs as a straight line.

A function can be stated as: $y = f(x)$. This states that y is a function of x. For example, the amount of money people spend is a function of their income after taxes. If a functional relationship exists, as income changes there will be a change in the amount spent. Slope measures the rate of change in y as x changes.

The formula to measure slope between two points on a line is:

$$slope = \frac{Y_2 - Y_1}{X_2 - X_1}$$

The points are shown in Figure 1.15.

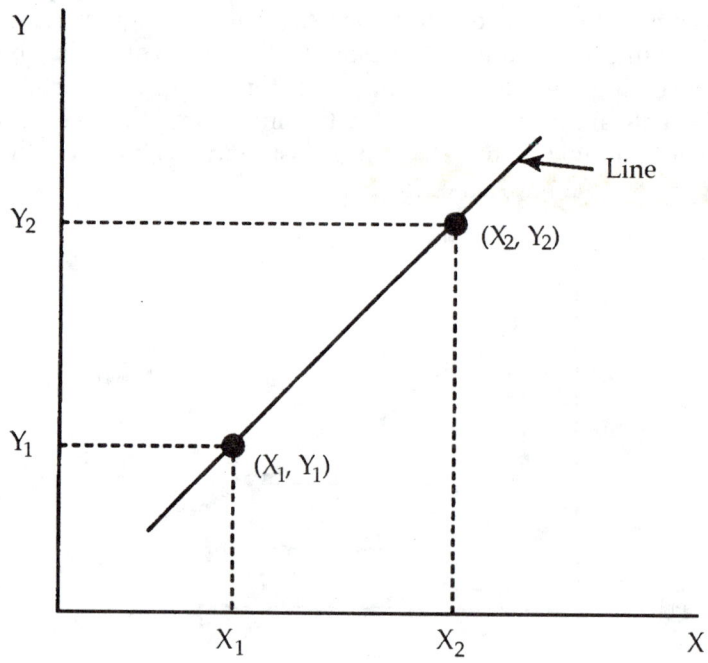

Figure 1.15
Slope

If the points on the line are (3,3) and (5,5) as shown in Figure 1.16, the slope will be:

$$slope = \frac{5-3}{5-3} = \frac{2}{2} = 1$$

Point 1 is (3,3), thus $X_1 = 3$, $Y_1 = 3$.

Point 2 is (5,5), thus $X_2 = 5$, $Y_2 = 5$.

A slope of 1 means that as X changes by 1, Y will change by 1.

A slope of 3 would mean that as X changes by 1, Y changes by 3. A slope of 2/3 would mean that as X changes by 3, Y changes by 2. A slope of .75 would be the same as 3/4 which would indicate that as X changes by 4, Y changes by 3.

A linear function graphs as a straight line. The slope on a straight line is the same at every point as shown in Figure 1.16.

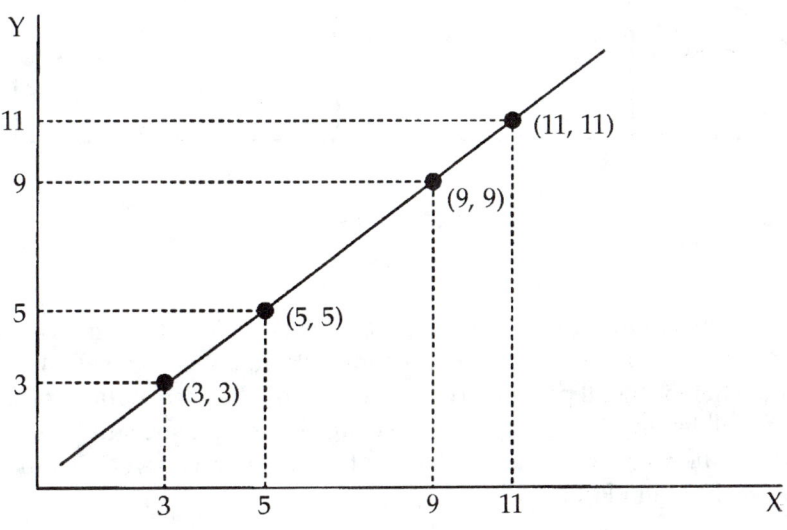

Figure 1.16
Slope

If the points on the line are (9,9) and (11,11), the slope would be:

$$\text{slope} = \frac{11-9}{11-9} = \frac{2}{2} = 1.$$

The slope is the same along a straight line. The slope between (3,3) and (5,5) is 1, and the slope between (9,9) and (11,11) is also 1.

Another way to express the concept of slope is:

$$\text{slope} = \frac{\text{change in Y}}{\text{change in X}} = \frac{\text{rise}}{\text{run}}.$$

Slope is the change in Y divided by the change in X. Slope is the rate of change in Y as X changes. Slope also is the number of units a line rises or falls vertically for each unit of horizontal change from left to right. In each of the examples in Figure 1.16 the run is 2 units. Each time X changed by 2, Y changed by two. The rise was 2 units. The change in Y (2 units) divided by the change in X (2 units) equals 1.

A slope can be either positive or negative. In the case of a negative slope the rise is negative. These slopes are shown in Figure 1.17.

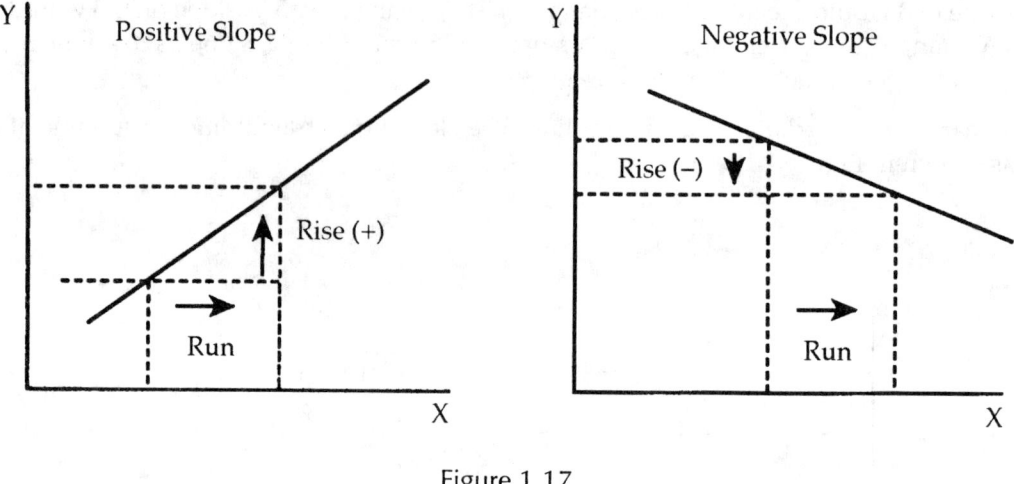

Figure 1.17
Slope

The concept of slope is important in many areas of economics. In macroeconomics the slope of the consumption line is called the marginal propensity to consume (MPC). The slope of the savings line is called the marginal propensity to save (MPS). The assumption is that the MPC and MPS is the same for all levels of income since these are slopes of a straight line.

On a straight line the slope is the same all along the line. For a curved line the slope is different along the line as shown in Figure 1.18.

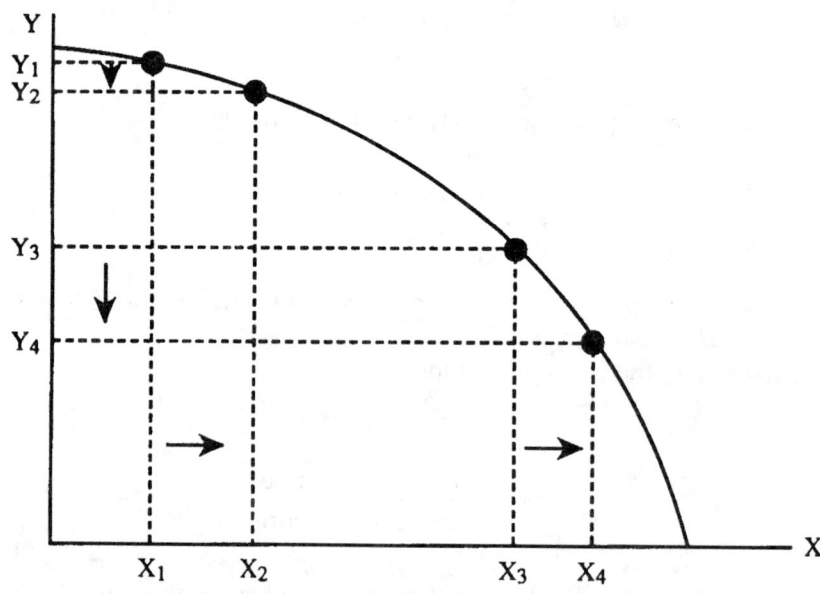

Figure 1.18
Slope

In a change from X_1 to X_2, Y drops from Y_1 to Y_2. When X changes from X_3 to X_4, the change in Y is from Y_3 to Y_4. The change in X in each case is the same amount. The change in Y, however, is greater when X changes from X_3 to X_4. The rates of change or the slopes are different.

In Figure 1.18 the slopes are different at each point on the curve. The slopes, however, are all negative. It is possible for a curve to have both positive and negative slopes as shown in Figure 1.19 and in Figure 1.20.

In Figure 1.19, the slopes are positive at first and then become negative. In Figure 1.20, the slopes are negative at first and then become positive.

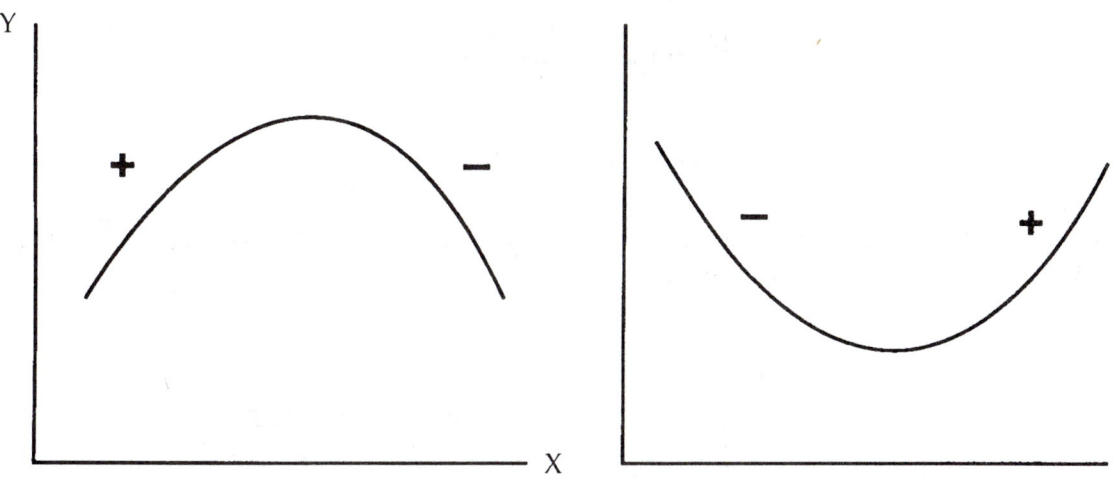

Figure 1.19 Slope   Figure 1.20 Slope

The concept of different slopes on a curved line will be covered in macroeconomics with the production possibilities curve and the marginal rate of transformation of one good for another good. In microeconomics the concepts of the production curve and the marginal physical product will be covered.

The concept of slope is very important in economics, and it is necessary for students to understand this concept to understand many economic principles.

45° Line

The 45 degree (45°) line is a special graph used in macroeconomics to show the relationship between income and consumption.

The lines on a graph form a 90 degree angle as shown in Figure 1.21. A 45 degree line cuts the 90 degree angle in half.

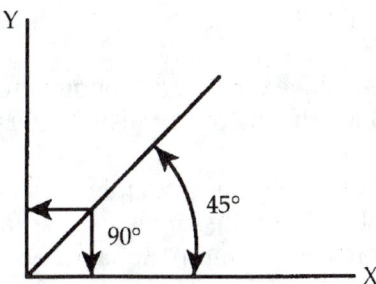

Figure 1.21 45° Line

The significance of the 45° line is that points on this line are the same distance from the x and y axes of the graph as shown in Figure 1.22. Point (a) has an x value of 20 and a y value of 20. Likewise point (b) has an x value of 50 and a y value of 50.

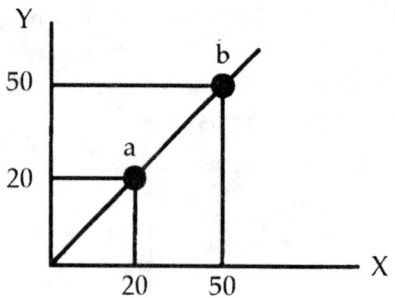

Figure 1.22 45° Line

In terms of income and consumption a person with an income of $25,000 after taxes would be spending exactly $25,000 as shown in Figure 1.23.

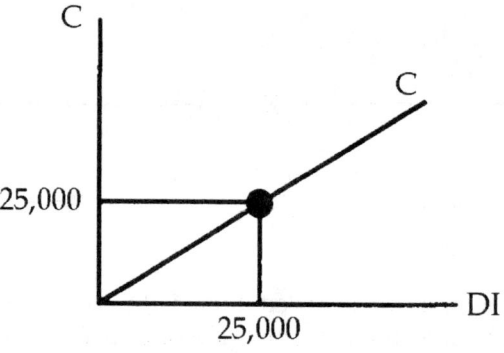

Figure 1.23 C-Line

Mastering Economics

An Overview of Economics

Economics is very much a part of everyday life. In many of the world's most pressing problems political, biological, social, cultural, and philosophical issues often predominate. But no matter how "noneconomic" a particular problem may seem, it will almost always have a significant economic dimension.

The crises that have led to wars have often had economic roots. Nations have fought for oil and rice and land to live on, although the rhetoric of their leaders has evoked God, Glory and the Fatherland.

For all students then, the study of economic principles will be a valuable asset to their understanding, as American citizens, of some of the problems that face the nation today: unemployment, inflation, taxes, money, interest rates, international trade, energy, etc.

The Fields of Economics

Economics covers many different fields of study and addresses many different issues. The following are the main fields.

- Theory

  This field covers the theories of behavior for individuals, businesses, government, and economies. It is separated into macroeconomics and microeconomics.

- Economic History

  This field follows the social, cultural, political, and economic forces that have led an economy to be at its current state.

- History of Economic Thought

  This field covers the contributions of the various writers whose ideas have become a part of economics. The first major writer was Adam Smith.

- Industrial Organization

  This field covers the structure and activities of industries in the economy.

- Public Economics

  This field covers the functions of government and its role in the economy.

- Urban Economics

  This field of economics covers the economic problems that especially apply to cities and specific regions of the country.

- Labor Economics

  This field covers the factors that determine wages, employment, and unemployment. It covers labor unions and their impact upon the economy. It covers the laws that deal with labor and collective bargaining.

- Money and Banking

  This field covers the history, definition, and uses of money. It also covers the commercial banking system and the Federal Reserve System and its role in the economy as regards monetary policy.

- Econometrics

  This field covers the uses of statistics, algebra, calculus, and models to discuss economic problems and solutions.

- Economic Development

  This field covers the less developed and the developed countries to determine the factors of growth and how economies can develop.

- Comparative Economic Systems

  This field covers the economic systems of capitalism, socialism, fascism, and communism. It covers the differences and the difficulties the systems have in handling the economic problems of the country.

- International Economics

  This field covers the economic trade and financial relations among countries. This field is increasing in importance each year as firms and countries are becoming global in their activities.

In a principles of economics course several of these fields are covered. For example, a macroeconomics course would include theory, economic development, money and banking, public economics, economic history, history of economic thought, and international economics. A microeconomics course would include theory, industrial organization, urban economics, labor economics, comparative economic systems, and international economics. An undergraduate student majoring in economics would take separate courses in each of these fields. A student pursuing a graduate degree, either the master's degree or the doctorate, would specialize in one of the fields.

Economics Statistics

There are many sources of statistics on the economy. The following are some of the sources that would be more relevant to courses in the principles of macroeconomics and microeconomics. These sources were used for statistical data in this text. These sources are available in most college and public libraries.

- *Demographic Yearbook.* (New York: United Nations)

  The book presents demographic characteristics of populations in over 200 countries. The information includes births, deaths, life expectancy, and other information.

- *Economic Indicators.* (Washington, DC: Council of Economic Advisors)

  This publication presents statistics on the current economic condition of the United States. The statistics include prices, wages, money, credit, gross domestic product, and others.

- *Economic Report of the President.* (Washington, DC: Government Printing Office)

  This is a review of the economic conditions in the United States. It is taken from the president's yearly address to Congress. It includes statistics about income, employment, and production. This information is from an annual report submitted by the Council of Economic Advisors to the President.

- *Federal Reserve Bulletin.* (Washington, DC: Board of Governors of the Federal Reserve System)

  This publication includes current financial and economic statistics including money, financial markets, banking institutions, and some international statistics.

- *Historical Statistics of the United States: Colonial Times to 1970.* (Washington, DC: U.S. Bureau of the Census)

  This book includes long-term historical trends for basic United States statistics.

- *Million Dollar Directory: Leading Public and Private Companies.* (Parsippany, NJ: Dun & Bradstreet Information Services)

  This directory presents brief facts about 160,000 leading U.S. public and private businesses. The directory lists officers, sales, employees, stock exchange, and other information about each business.

- *Monthly Labor Review.* (Washington, DC: U.S. Bureau of Labor Statistics)

  This publication includes information on various labor conditions: employment, unemployment, hours worked, compensation, collective bargaining, etc.

- *Statistical Abstract of the United States.* (Washington: DC: Bureau of the Census)

  This abstract includes statistical tables taken from government reports. It covers social, political, and economic statistical tables. It also references the source of each table.

- *Statistical Yearbook.* (New York: United Nations)

  This publication presents statistical data on each country which is a member of the United Nations. It includes information on population, employment, wages, finance, education, foreign trade, tourism, and other areas.

- *Statistics of Income.* (Washington, DC: Internal Revenue Service of the Treasury Department)

  This publication presents information on income based on individual and corporate tax returns.

- *Survey of Current Business.* (Washington, DC: U.S. Bureau of Economic Analysis)

  This publication is a major source of such current business statistics as: national income, gross domestic production, personal consumption expenditures, commodity prices, construction and real estate, labor earnings, domestic trade, foreign trade, business cycle indicators, and other business information.

- *The Fortune 500. (Fortune Magazine,* April issue)

  Fortune Magazine ranks the nation's largest companies by sales, assets, profits, and other variables.

- *Thomas Register of American Manufacturers.* (New York: Thomas Publishing Company)

  This publication lists over 145,000 companies by specific and brand name product. It is a good source to identify which company produces particular products.

- *U.S. Industrial Outlook.* (Washington, DC: International Trade Administration of the Department of Commerce)

  This publication discusses recent trends in about 350 specific manufacturing and service industries. It also discusses trends for the next five years in these industries.

Career Opportunities Available to an Economics Major

Once you master economics you may decide to pursue a career in this area. What are your opportunities as an economics major? What type of work might you actually do as an economist?

The trained economist is a valuable and respected member of many organizations—private businesses, public utilities, government agencies, colleges, and universities.

Depending on the amount of education you receive your future lies in one of these areas:

1. Working in one of a wide variety of positions in private business. These positions include the bank economist, the industrial economist, and the consultant.

2. Serving in a government agency at the local, state, or national level. Economic theories have increasingly influenced government decisions since the Depression of the 1930s occupied worldwide attention.

3. Teaching economics at the college and university level. Economics has been an academic subject for more than 150 years.

Employment Opportunities for Economists—1995 to 2005

Economists conduct research, collect and analyze data, follow economic trends, and forecast economic variables. Economists are usually interested in practical applications of economic policy. They advise business firms, insurance companies, banks, securities firms, industry and trade associations, labor unions, government agencies, and others.

According to the *Occupational Outlook Handbook* published by the U.S. Department of Labor–Bureau of Labor Statistics, people who graduate with a bachelor's degree in economics will encounter much competition in finding jobs through the year 2005. Those graduates who have strong backgrounds in mathematics, statistics, survey design, and computer science will have less difficulty in finding employment. A source of employment that is increasing is for secondary-school economics teachers, since economics is becoming a more popular course.

Employment opportunities are better for people graduating with the master's degree and the best for people graduating with the Ph.D. degree. Again those graduates who have strong computer and quantitative skills will have a better chance in finding employment.

Many graduates with degrees in economics seek employment in colleges and universities teaching economics. It is expected that there will be many teaching positions available since there is an expected wave of retirements among college faculties between 1995 and 2005. The opportunities will be best for those with doctorates. Those with the master's degree will be able to find some positions in junior and community colleges.

Economists also find jobs in related areas as financial managers, financial analysts, accountants, underwriters, actuaries, loan officers, credit analysts, marketing research analysts, urban and regional planners, and others.

In a survey conducted by the College Placement Council in 1993, graduates with the bachelor's degree received starting offers averaging about $25,200 a year. The median base salary for business economists was $65,000 in 1992, and the average for government economists was $53,500 a year in 1993. The lowest paid economists were those in teaching positions and those working for the government.

The conclusion from the data is that there are excellent paying jobs available for economists through the year 2005. However, the competition will be great for these positions because of the number of graduates. Those graduates who have computer and quantitative skills and excellent grades will have the best chance to acquire one of the higher paying positions.

SOLUTIONS

1. a. Production is a function of the amount of labor.

   b. The amount demanded for loans is a function of the interest rate.

   c. The amount of work is a function of the tax rates.

   d. The amount of oranges demanded is a function of the price of oranges.

2. Check with the instructor.

Chapter 2

The Basics of Scarcity

Learning Objectives

After reading this chapter, you should be able to:
1. Understand the concept of scarcity.
2. Identify the factors that limit an economy.
3. Understand the concept and consequences of choices.
4. Understand the production possibility analysis on a macro and micro scale.
5. Define and explain opportunity cost.
6. Read a graph of a production possibility analysis.
7. Understand the concept of efficiency as regards the production possibility analysis.
8. Understand the concept of increasing opportunity costs.
9. Understand and compute the marginal rate of transformation.
10. Know the sources of economic growth and understand how economic growth is indicated in the production possibility analysis.
11. Distinguish between the various economic systems.
12. Understand the mixed market structure.

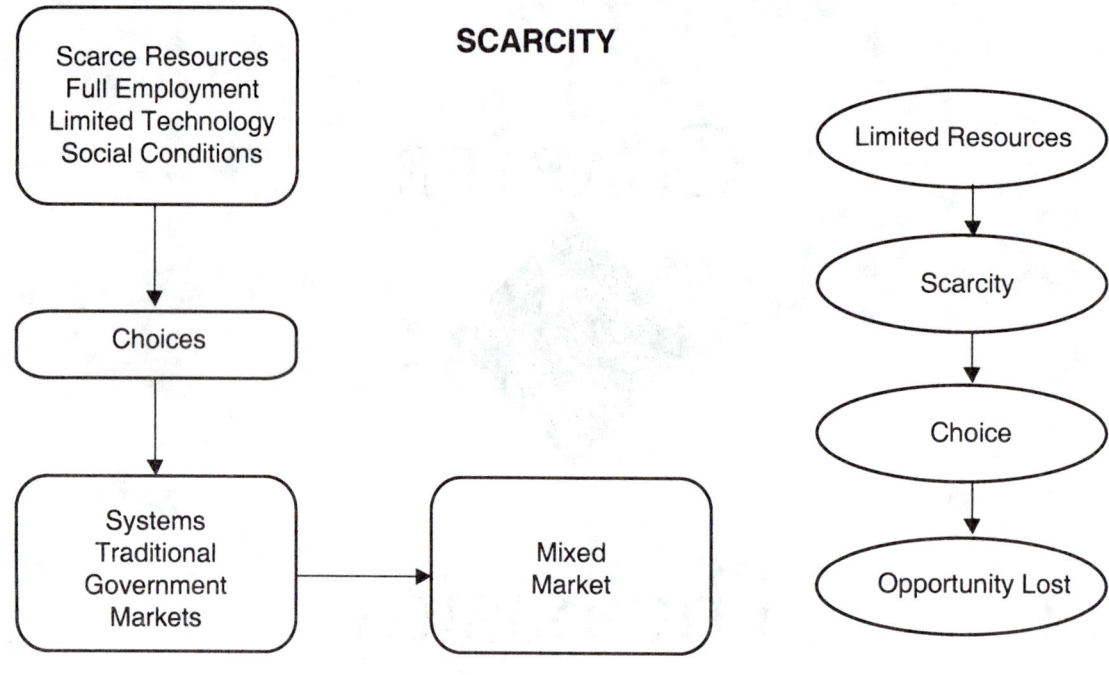

INTRODUCTION

Many economists have defined economics as "the study of the optimum allocation of scarce resources." This phrase can be translated into "the study of the best way to use scarce resources." Since there are many uses for resources which are scarce, choices have to be made. There are not enough resources for all of the uses. Scarcity, therefore, means choices have to be made. If choices are to be made and we want to find the best way to use the scarce resources, some system or set of principles is needed. This chapter will analyze the concepts of scarcity, choice, and systems.

Scarcity

Resources refer to natural items that are used to produce goods and services. Some examples are iron ore, tin, coal, and petroleum. These items are said to be scarce for, essentially, two reasons. The first reason is that the items exist in limited amounts. There is a certain amount of coal, for example, in the United States. It is not an item that can be manufactured. It is produced by natural forces and takes millions of years. In addition, not all deposits of natural resources have been found. Even after deposits are found, they may not be accessible because the technology is lacking to get at them. The Rocky Mountains, for example, contain shale oil. Shale oil is found in rock called shale. It is very expensive, at this time, to process the oil, however. As a result, even though the oil is there, we can't use it. Therefore, since resources exist in limited amounts, can't be manufactured, and are not easily accessible, they are said to be scarce.

The second reason that resources are said to be scarce is that there are so many uses for these items. Petroleum, in addition to being used to produce gasoline, is used to manufacture tires, plastics, synthetic fibers, and many other products. In addition to the resources existing in limited amounts, they are in great demand, thus making them scarce.

Coal and petroleum are called non-renewable resources since they can't be produced other than by natural forces. What about renewable resources, like timber, cotton, or soybeans? It is true that as timber is harvested, more trees can be planted. It takes years, however, for trees to mature. It takes cotton and soybeans a season to mature. If we are discussing today, these items do not yet exist. Today's amount is limited to what we can harvest now. Thus, even renewable resources are said to be scarce.

Chapter 2

The Basics of Scarcity

Learning Objectives

After reading this chapter, you should be able to:

1. Understand the concept of scarcity.
2. Identify the factors that limit an economy.
3. Understand the concept and consequences of choices.
4. Understand the production possibility analysis on a macro and micro scale.
5. Define and explain opportunity cost.
6. Read a graph of a production possibility analysis.
7. Understand the concept of efficiency as regards the production possibility analysis.
8. Understand the concept of increasing opportunity costs.
9. Understand and compute the marginal rate of transformation.
10. Know the sources of economic growth and understand how economic growth is indicated in the production possibility analysis.
11. Distinguish between the various economic systems.
12. Understand the mixed market structure.

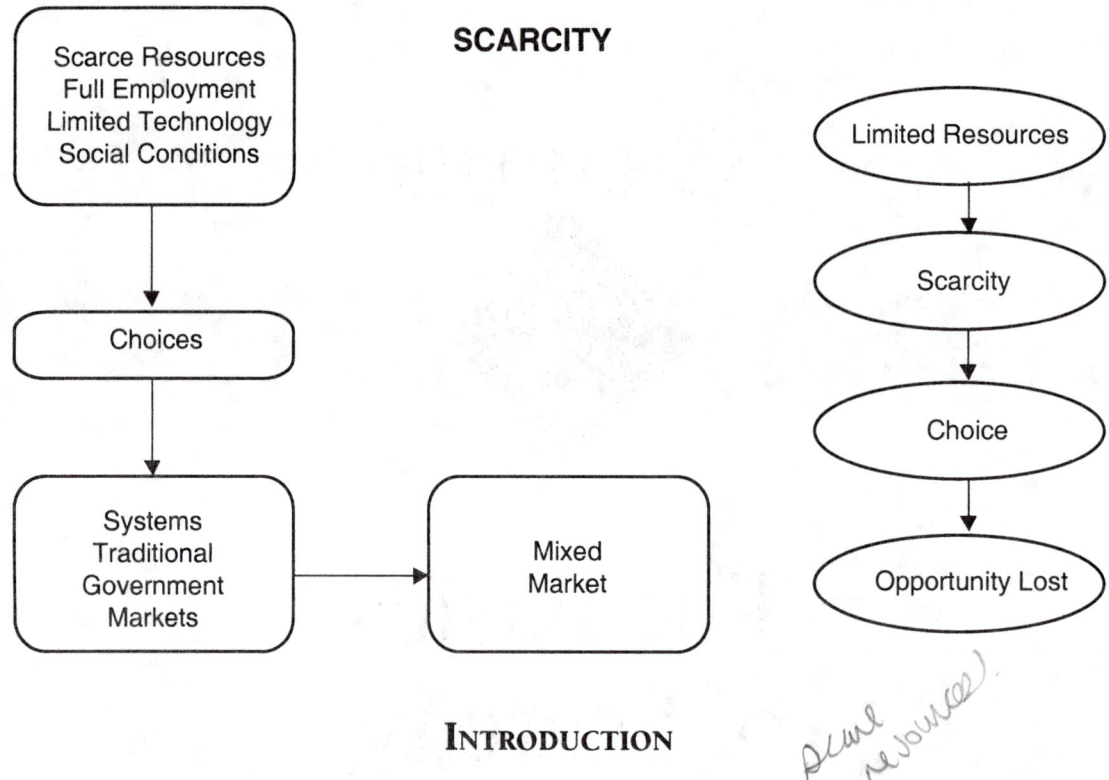

Introduction

Many economists have defined economics as "the study of the optimum allocation of scarce resources." This phrase can be translated into "the study of the best way to use scarce resources." Since there are many uses for resources which are scarce, choices have to be made. There are not enough resources for all of the uses. Scarcity, therefore, means choices have to be made. If choices are to be made and we want to find the best way to use the scarce resources, some system or set of principles is needed. This chapter will analyze the concepts of scarcity, choice, and systems.

Scarcity

Resources refer to natural items that are used to produce goods and services. Some examples are iron ore, tin, coal, and petroleum. These items are said to be scarce for, essentially, two reasons. The first reason is that the items exist in limited amounts. There is a certain amount of coal, for example, in the United States. It is not an item that can be manufactured. It is produced by natural forces and takes millions of years. In addition, not all deposits of natural resources have been found. Even after deposits are found, they may not be accessible because the technology is lacking to get at them. The Rocky Mountains, for example, contain shale oil. Shale oil is found in rock called shale. It is very expensive, at this time, to process the oil, however. As a result, even though the oil is there, we can't use it. Therefore, since resources exist in limited amounts, can't be manufactured, and are not easily accessible, they are said to be scarce.

The second reason that resources are said to be scarce is that there are so many uses for these items. Petroleum, in addition to being used to produce gasoline, is used to manufacture tires, plastics, synthetic fibers, and many other products. In addition to the resources existing in limited amounts, they are in great demand, thus making them scarce.

Coal and petroleum are called non-renewable resources since they can't be produced other than by natural forces. What about renewable resources, like timber, cotton, or soybeans? It is true that as timber is harvested, more trees can be planted. It takes years, however, for trees to mature. It takes cotton and soybeans a season to mature. If we are discussing today, these items do not yet exist. Today's amount is limited to what we can harvest now. Thus, even renewable resources are said to be scarce.

In addition to products of nature, we can classify as resources of a country its people, its technology, and its institutions. The population of a country is fixed at any point in time. If the population of the United States is 250 million people, it can't be 500 million the next day. We hear, today, how fast populations are growing, but they can't double overnight. It takes years.

If we are discussing the available labor force of a country, the size is even more limited. Children, senior citizens, the infirm, and those unwilling to work would have to be removed from consideration. If we want to consider teachers, the number of people who have the talent, desire, and credentials to do this type of work is limited still more.

At any point in time, there exists a certain level of technology or knowledge. Technology can grow, especially through research, but that is in the future. Today, we only have the technology and knowledge that has already been developed.

The institutions of a country can be considered a resource. Some examples would be the political structure, the social structure, the economic structure, the welfare structure, and the educational structure. These structures, at any point in time, are fixed. The political structure refers to how government operates its laws, regulations, and services. The laws of a country constitute a resource. Laws, however, are fixed. The procedure to change a law or add a new one is a long process in the United States. A law starts as a bill. It goes through committees in both parts of Congress. Then it goes to the full House of Representatives and the Senate. Finally, the President either signs or vetoes the bill. If he signs it, it is a law. If the Legislature does not override the veto, it does not become a law. The process may take days, months, or even years.

Popeye the Sailor is known for saying "I am what I am, and that's all I am." The same is true, here, for the government. At any point, the government can only be or do what has been delegated to it. The government is limited and, thus, governmental services are scarce. As an example, consider the role of the federal government in education. The Constitution of the United States makes no mention of education. Any involvement can only come about as a result of new legislation. Since government involvement would imply, mainly, the funneling of tax money to support education, and since, currently, this money is not available in unlimited amounts, government as a resource to support education is scarce.

In a macro sense, an economy faces scarcity. It is limited in what it is able to do by, essentially, four factors:

1. natural resources,
2. size and abilities of the population,
3. technology and knowledge, and
4. institutions.

If countries are at different levels of economic development, the reason for this will be that the countries have different levels of the four factors. The point of this section, however, is that even the countries that have vast resources, very able people, advanced technology, and flexible institutions are limited in what they can do.

In a micro sense, a business firm would be limited by the size of the company, the abilities of the employees, the technology the firm has available, and the firm's relation to the institutions of the country. A small company will have to pay higher prices for materials, be unable to hire very qualified workers, use older technology, and be unable to get defense contracts. A larger company will not have these disadvantages, but will still be limited in what it can do. Likewise, an individual is limited by factors such as income, education, social status, motivation, and other factors.

Resources are scarce. Scarcity places limits on what an economy is capable of accomplishing. It affects the operation and production of business firms. Finally, scarcity affects the lives of individuals directly by limiting incomes and the goods available to individuals. This results in a matter of concern because many individuals have what are called unlimited wants and needs.

Choices

Because of scarcity and limits of economies, governments, businesses, and individuals must make choices. There are unlimited wants and needs, but limited goods and services to satisfy them. Figure 2.1 presents a resource (petroleum) and four (4) possible uses for this resource.

In this example, petroleum is being used to produce synthetic fibers, tires, chemicals, and gasoline. The amounts produced of each are limited by the total amount of petroleum and the amounts being used for the other choices. Plastics are not being produced since there is no more available petroleum. Choices have been made.

Is it possible to change the choices? Yes, it is possible. Let us look at three different cases.

1. If we want to produce plastics, there is no problem if we have idle petroleum available. If, however, all the available petroleum is being used, there is a problem.

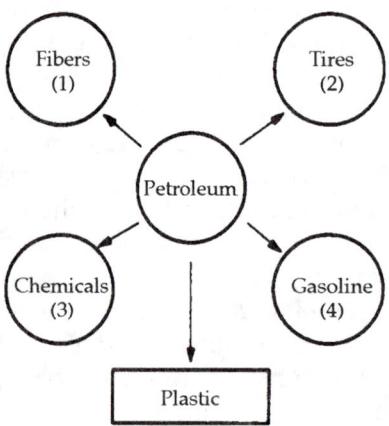

Figure 2.1
Uses of Petroleum

2. If all the available petroleum is being used, plastics could be produced by reducing the amounts of the other items being produced. We would have plastic, but less fibers, less tires, and less gasoline.

3. Since the problem seems to stem from there being limited available petroleum, the solution would be to find more petroleum. If this is possible, plastics can be produced without reducing the production of the other products.

Economists have developed a graphical model to explain the principles of scarcity and choices, called production possibilities. We will analyze production possibilities in both a macro and in a micro context.

PRODUCTION POSSIBILITIES—MACRO

This analysis assumes that a certain economy is producing only two possible products: bread and uniforms. In addition, we assume scarce resources are being used fully with no idle units. The level of technology and the institutions of the country remained fixed.

One possible choice would be to produce only bread. This is represented in Figure 2.2(a). Using all resources and employment for the production of bread, we could, perhaps, produce a maximum limit of 1,500 million loaves of bread a year. If instead of producing bread, we produced uniforms, 750 million uniforms could be manufactured as in Figure 2.2(b), again assuming full employment of resources and labor. In each case, there is a limit to the production of each item when only one is produced: 1,500 million loaves of bread or 750 million uniforms.

Assuming the economy is producing only bread (1,500 million loaves a year) what would be required to produce some uniforms (perhaps 75 million)? Figure 2.3 presents the answer.

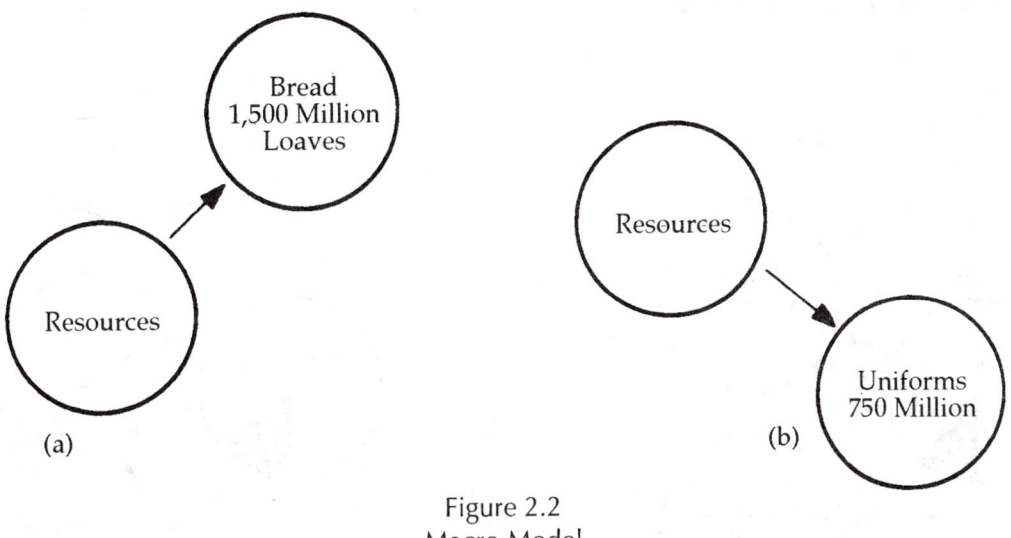

Figure 2.2
Macro Model

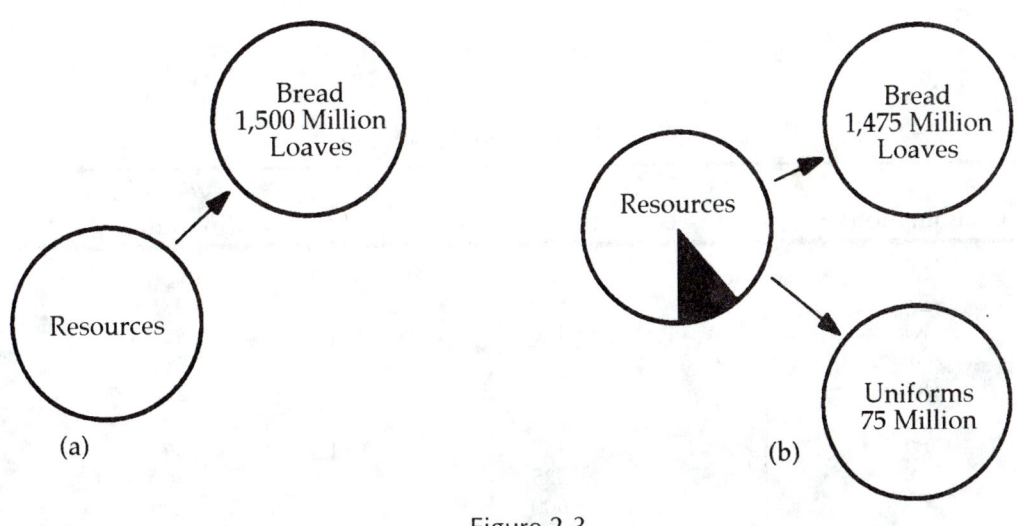

Figure 2.3
Macro Model

In order to produce uniforms, resources must be taken from the production of bread and used to produce uniforms. As a result, less bread can be produced: 1,475 million loaves, as shown in Figure 2.3(b). Here, the cost of producing the uniforms will include the resources used, the labor time involved, and the 25 million loaves of bread given up.

If the economy is producing 1,475 million loaves of bread and 75 million uniforms, what would enable us to produce even more uniforms, say 150 million? Figure 2.4 presents the answer.

Figure 2.4(b) indicates that more resources would have to be taken from the production of bread and funneled into the production of uniforms. As a result, 150 million uniforms could be produced at a cost of 50 million loaves of bread. Table 2.1 presents various combinations of bread and uniforms that could be chosen.

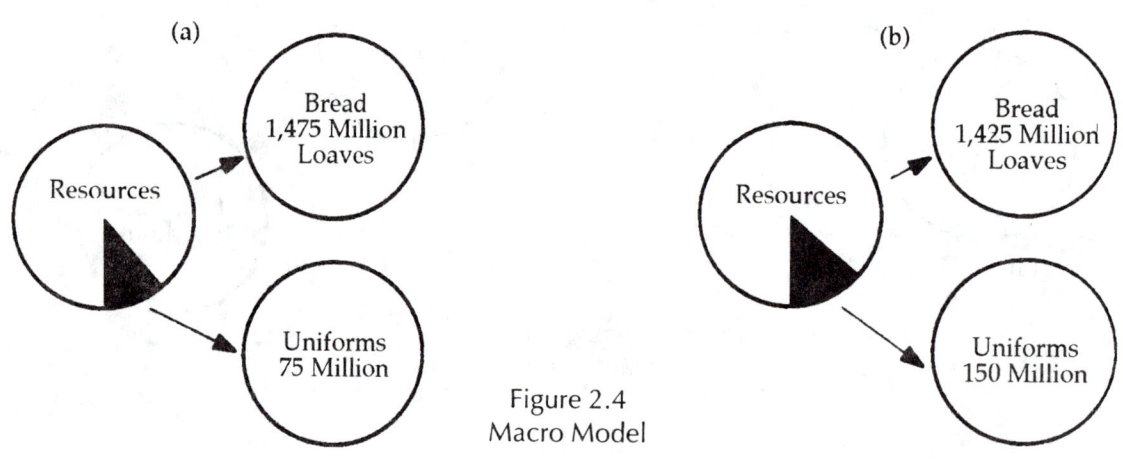

Figure 2.4
Macro Model

Table 2.1 Production Possibilities

Combination	Uniforms (in millions)	Loaves of bread (in millions)
(a)	0	1,500
(b)	75	1,475
(c)	150	1,425
(d)	225	1,350
(e)	300	1,250
(f)	375	1,125
(g)	450	975
(h)	525	800
(I)	600	600
(J)	675	375
(K)	750	0

There are three important conclusions to be drawn from the table. The first is that the economy can be at whichever combination it chooses. Secondly, in order to move from one combination to another, to increase the production of one good, the production of the other good must be reduced due to the fact that resources are scarce and fully employed. Thus, if the economy is at combination (g), producing 450 million uniforms and 975 million loaves of bread, but wishes 1,125 million loaves of bread, this is possible by producing 375 million uniforms, as shown in combination (f).

The third conclusion is concerned with several changes in combinations. If the economy is at combination (d), producing 225 million uniforms and 1,350 million loaves of bread, and chooses, instead, combination (e), producing 300 million uniforms and 1,250 million loaves of bread, the gain is 75 million uniforms, and the cost is 100 million loaves of bread. If the economy changes from combination (e) to (f), the number of uniforms increases from 300 million to 375 million. The gain is, again, 75 million uniforms. The number of loaves of bread, however, decreases from 1,250 million to 1,125 million, or a reduction of 125 million. This increase in the cost of additional uniforms will be explained by the principle of increasing opportunity costs. That is, a nation must sacrifice more and more of a product to produce each additional unit of another product.

Opportunity Costs

Opportunity costs refer to whatever is given up when a choice is made. If there are two choices, A and B, and B is chosen, A is the opportunity cost of B since A is given up. In Table 2.1, in order to have more uniforms, loaves of bread must be given up. Loaves of bread given up, thus, become the opportunity cost of acquiring uniforms. The total cost of uniforms would include the cost of the resources, the labor time, the machinery used, and the opportunity cost.

Another example of opportunity cost would be the cost of a college education. The student gives up money to pay for tuition fees, books, transportation, housing, food, and other expenses.

In addition, the student gives up doing other things, such as working, watching T.V., or sleeping. The student could be working and earning money, benefits, and experience. Thus, in computing the cost of acquiring a college education, the student should include the opportunity costs in addition to the money expenses.

Economists, however, restrict the value of the opportunity cost to the greatest value given up. Above all, we assume that by giving up work, the student gives up more than by giving up watching T.V. or sleeping. If we assume a college course requires 120 hours of a student's time, and the student could be working, earning 7 dollars an hour in wages and benefits, the opportunity cost would be 840 dollars.

In Table 2.1, we noticed the opportunity cost of acquiring uniforms increased as we moved down the table. This is referred to as the principle of increasing costs, and can be explained by the following.

When the decision was made at level (a) to produce uniforms, resources were removed from the production of loaves of bread and re-routed to a new industry: producing uniforms. The resources chosen were the ones best suited to the production of uniforms. Since uniforms may be made from cotton, land was chosen for its ability to grow cotton. Workers were chosen because they could produce uniforms. The land and workers were able to give a yield of 75 million uniforms.

In moving from level (b) to (c), second-best resources had to be used. Land and workers, not as well suited for cotton and uniform production, were chosen; and thus, the yield is not as great. If we want the same increase in uniforms as before, 75 million uniforms, additional resources would have to be taken from the production of loaves of bread. As we move down the table, the quality of the resources, as regards uniform production, decreases and, thus, an ever-increasing amount must be re-routed.

Opportunity Costs—Personal

Opportunity costs are the most informative way of considering costs, not just when studying economics, but always. Opportunity cost is the measure of what is given up when a person buys something or does something. Some examples are in order:

a. The important thing sacrificed when a person buys something is not just the money spent, but he next best thing that could have been purchased and enjoyed. Suppose a person buys a used $12,000 Chevrolet. The $12,000 could have been spent on many other items or could have been left in the bank to collect interest. Whatever is of the most value to the person is the opportunity cost for that person.

b. Opportunity cost applies to time as well. A student spends at least two hours outside of class for every hour in the class plus the class time. In addition to the tuition, the cost of the book, and the cost of the supplies and transportation, the hours given up to attend class would be included in the cost of the course. The most important activity to the student that the student could instead be doing during those hours is the opportunity cost. For each student the cost would be different, since what is more important to each student would be different. The student could be working and earning money, spending time with their children, watching television, working in their garden, or something else including sleeping.

c. Opportunity costs are useful for decision making. They represent the loss of benefit from choosing one alternative rather than the other.

Production Possibilities Graph

Figure 2.5 represents a graphical representation of the choices presented in Table 2.1.

Combinations (a) through (k) appear on a curved line. These combinations all represent full employment of resources. The curve, therefore, can represent a boundary or a limit as to what is possible in an economy. Combination (L), 600 million loaves of bread and 300 million uniforms, is a possible level of production; but since (L) lies below the production possibilities curve, it represents idle resources, operating at less than full employment. Combination (M), 1,000 million loaves of bread and 750 million uniforms, is not a possible level of production since (M) lies outside the production possibilities of the country. Possible production level combinations of loaves of bread and uniforms are any ones on or under the curve. Combinations on the line are, however, more desirable since they occur at full employment. Production possiblities curve analyze the process of resource allocation and production of goods and services.

The Basics of Scarcity

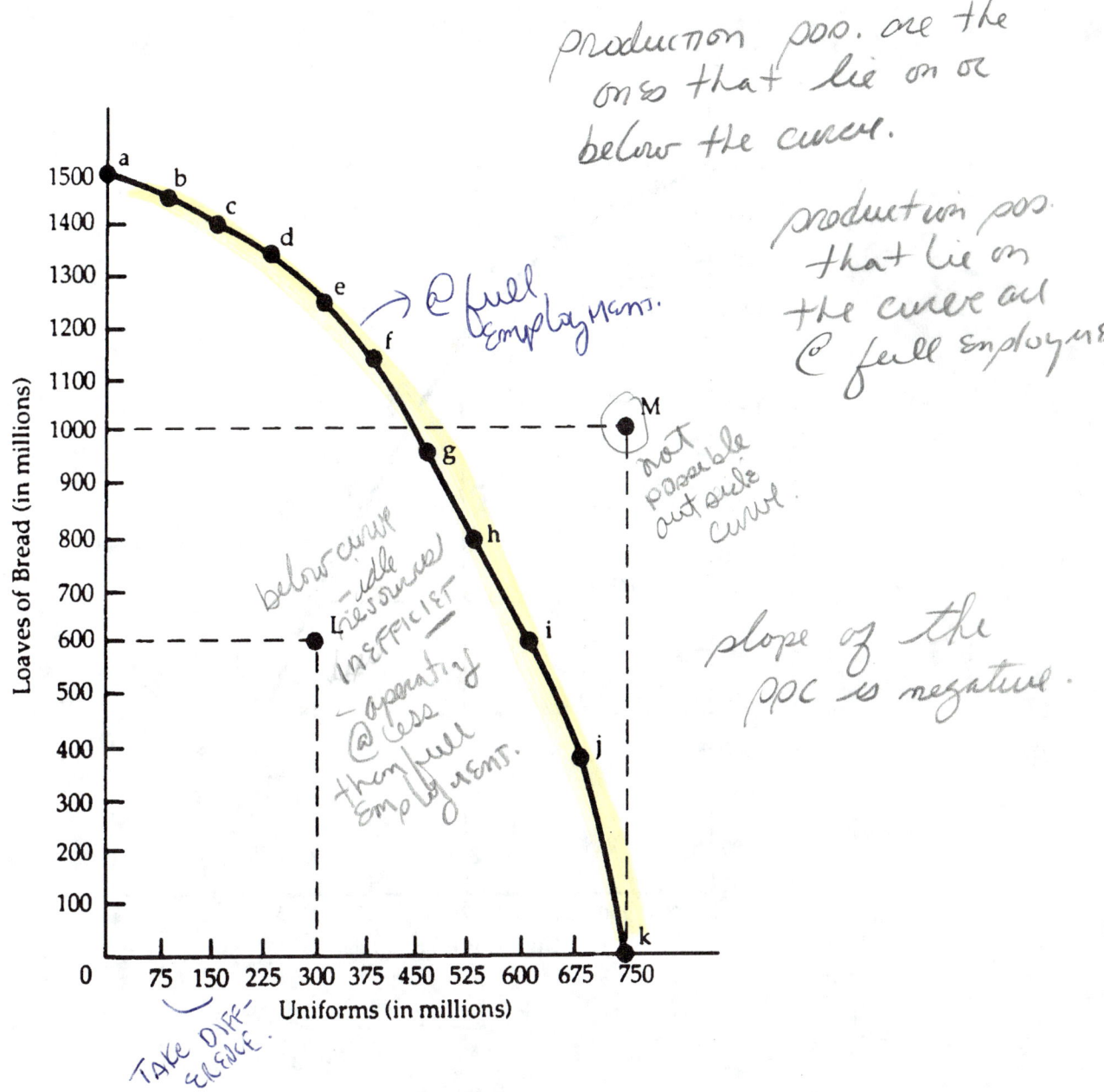

Figure 2.5
Production Possibilities Curve

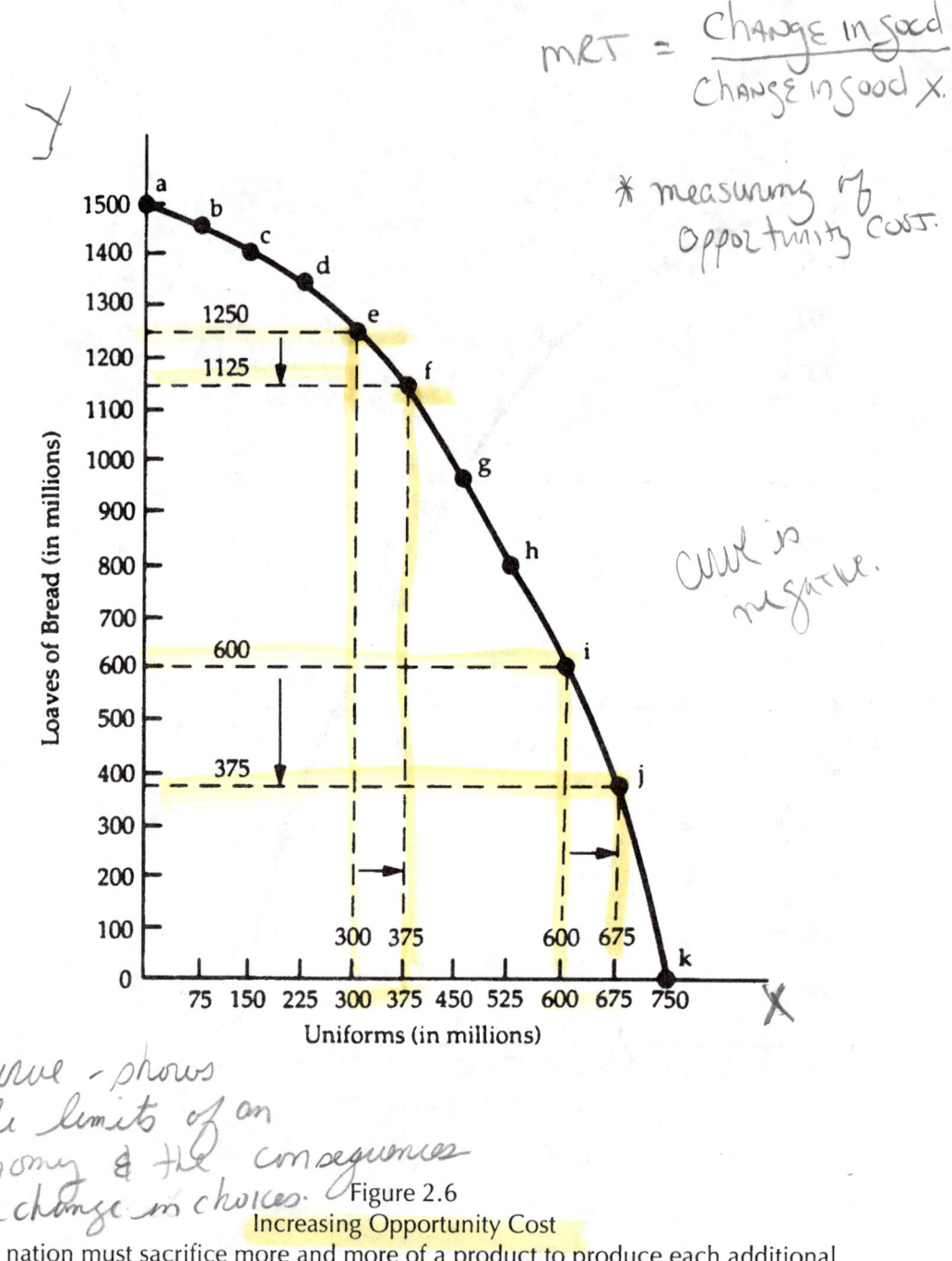

Figure 2.6
Increasing Opportunity Cost
(A nation must sacrifice more and more of a product to produce each additional unit of another product.)

Figure 2.6 shows the concept of opportunity cost and increasing opportunity cost. When the economy chooses combination (f) instead of (e), production of uniforms increases from 300 million to 375 million; whereas, production of loaves of bread decreases from 1,250 million to 1,125 million. However, when the economy chooses combination (j) instead of (i), the production of uniforms increases from 600 million to 675 million; but the production of loaves of bread decreases from 600 million to 375 million. In each case, the gain in uniforms was 75 million: but the decrease in loaves of bread, in the first case, was 125 million and, in the second, it was 225 million. The production possibilities curve, thus, is a useful tool in showing the limits of an economy and the consequences of a change in choices.

Marginal Rate of Transformation

The production possibilities curve shows that a country can be at only one point at a time. It is possible for the country to change its location on the curve, but there is a cost involved. The only way a country can have more of one good is to give up some of another good.

The slope of the production possibilities curve is negative. In order for Y to increase X must decrease. Likewise, for X to increase Y must decrease. In order to have more loaves of bread, the production of uniforms must be reduced. In order to have more uniforms, the production of bread must be reduced. The value of the slope of the production possibilities curve is called the marginal rate of transformation (MRT).

The formula for the slope or the marginal rate of transformation (MRT) is:

$$\text{MRT} = \frac{\text{Change in Good Y}}{\text{Change in Good X}}.$$

By moving from point (e) to point (f) in Figure 2.6, the economy gained 75 million uniforms and had to give up 125 million loaves of bread. The marginal rate of transformation (MRT) would be:

$$\text{MRT} = \frac{-125}{+75} = -1.67.$$

A marginal rate of transformation of –1.67 would indicate that the country had to give up 1.67 million loaves of bread (Y) to gain 1 million uniforms (X).

By moving from point (i) to point (j) in Figure 2.6, the economy gained 75 million uniforms and had to give up 225 million loaves of bread. The marginal rate of transformation (MRT) would be:

$$\text{MRT} = \frac{-225}{+75} = -3.$$

A marginal rate of transformation (MRT) of -3 would indicate that the country had to give up 3 million loaves of bread (Y) to gain 1 million uniforms (X).

The marginal rate of transformation (MRT) or the slope is higher for the move from points (i) to (j) than the move from points (e) to (f). Each move resulted in a gain of 75 million uniforms, but the cost of the uniforms increased. This is due to the production possibilities curve being a curved line instead of a straight line. The production possibilities curve is said to be convex to the origin. This means the curve bows outward from the origin.

The marginal rate of transformation (MRT) is a way of measuring the opportunity cost—the cost of acquiring more of one good in terms of what has to be given up of another good.

If the country moves from point (i) to point (f), the marginal rate of transformation or the opportunity cost would be:

$$\text{MRT} = \frac{+525}{-225} = -2.33 = \frac{+2.33}{-1}.$$

The marginal rate of transformation (MRT) would be –2.33. The opportunity cost here would be that the country would have to give up 1 million uniforms to acquire 2.33 million loaves of bread.

Economic Growth

Economic growth for an economy refers to increasing its production possibilities. This can be accomplished, for example, by finding new resources or substitutes. Instead of making tires out of petroleum, they could be made from sunflower seed oil. The productive abilities of the labor force could be increased by education and training. New technology could be developed. Figure 2.7 presents an example of the results of a technological change in the production of uniforms.

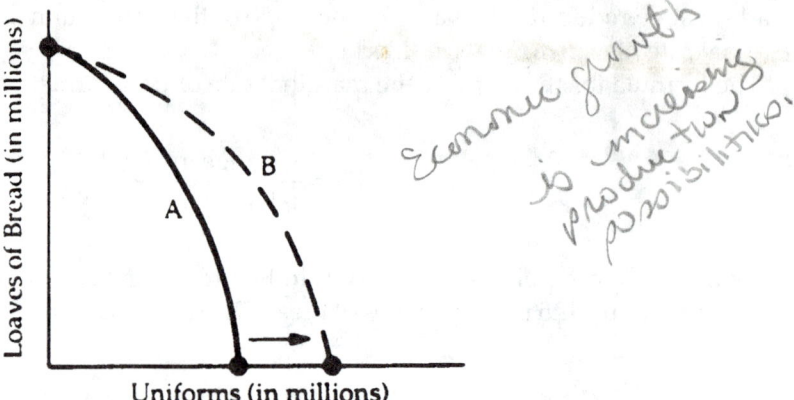

Figure 2.7
Increased Technology

As the result of a new process, there is less waste, and more uniforms can be produced using the same resources. The production possibilities curve moves to line B. No more loaves of bread can be produced than before, but more uniforms can be produced at each combination. Eventually, the technology may be applied to the production of bread, and the curve will look like the one in Figure 2.8.

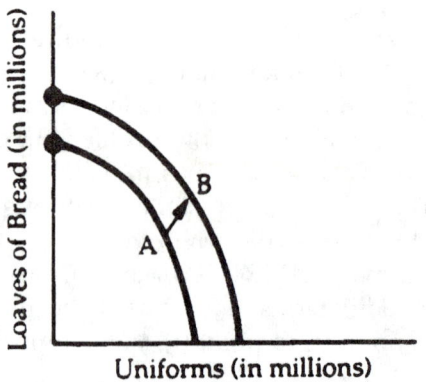

Figure 2.8
All Sector Growth

Economic growth, an increase in production possibilities, is brought about by:
1. increasing in resources or in finding better substitutes,
2. improving the skills of the labor force or increasing the size of the labor force,
3. improving technology, and
4. affecting the institutions to improve and act faster.

PRODUCTION POSSIBILITIES—MICRO

The production possibilities analysis can also be used on a micro scale. For example, the Stroh's Brewery Co. of Detroit, Michigan, used to produce both beer and ice cream. Figure 2.9 depicts a possible curve for Stroh's.

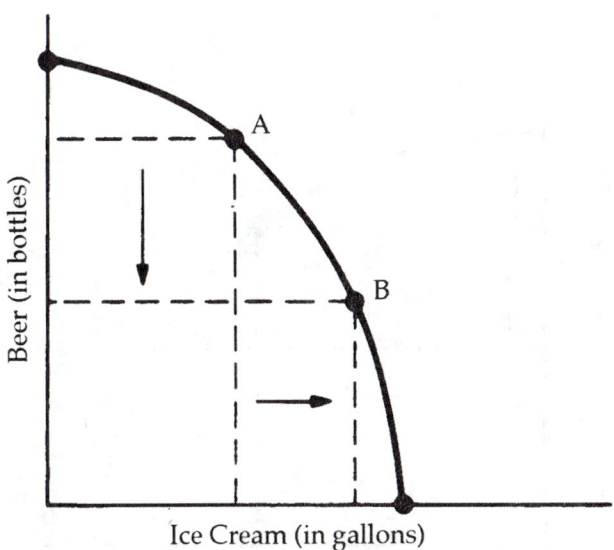

Figure 2.9
Micro Production Possibilities

Restricted by scarce resources, employment, technology, political and social institutions and, in addition, competition, there are limits to the most beer and ice cream that could be produced. If the company were producing at level A, but wanted to produce more ice cream, as at point B, this could only be done by reducing the amount of beer produced. In order to produce more of both goods, the company would have to add resources, add employment, add productive facilities, or improve the methods of production to be able to produce more with the current setup.

EFFICIENCY

Efficiency in economics means that resources, employment, and capital are being used to produce what the people want and that production is taking place at the least cost. Inefficiency means that resources, employment, and capital are not being used to produce what the people want or that production is not taking place at the least cost. Inefficiency also means that resources are being misallocated, meaning resources are being used for the wrong purposes.

Inefficiency can be shown in two forms on the production possibilities curve. The first form is when the economy is producing on the production possibilities curve but not the amounts the people want.

This form of inefficiency is shown in Figure 2.10. The economy is actually at point B, but the people want to be at point A. A possible situation could be that the government is engaged in military actions not popular with the people. Because of the military operations, military goods (Y) must be produced which means less consumer goods (X). The people, however, would prefer to get out of the military operations and live their lives in peace enjoying consumer goods.

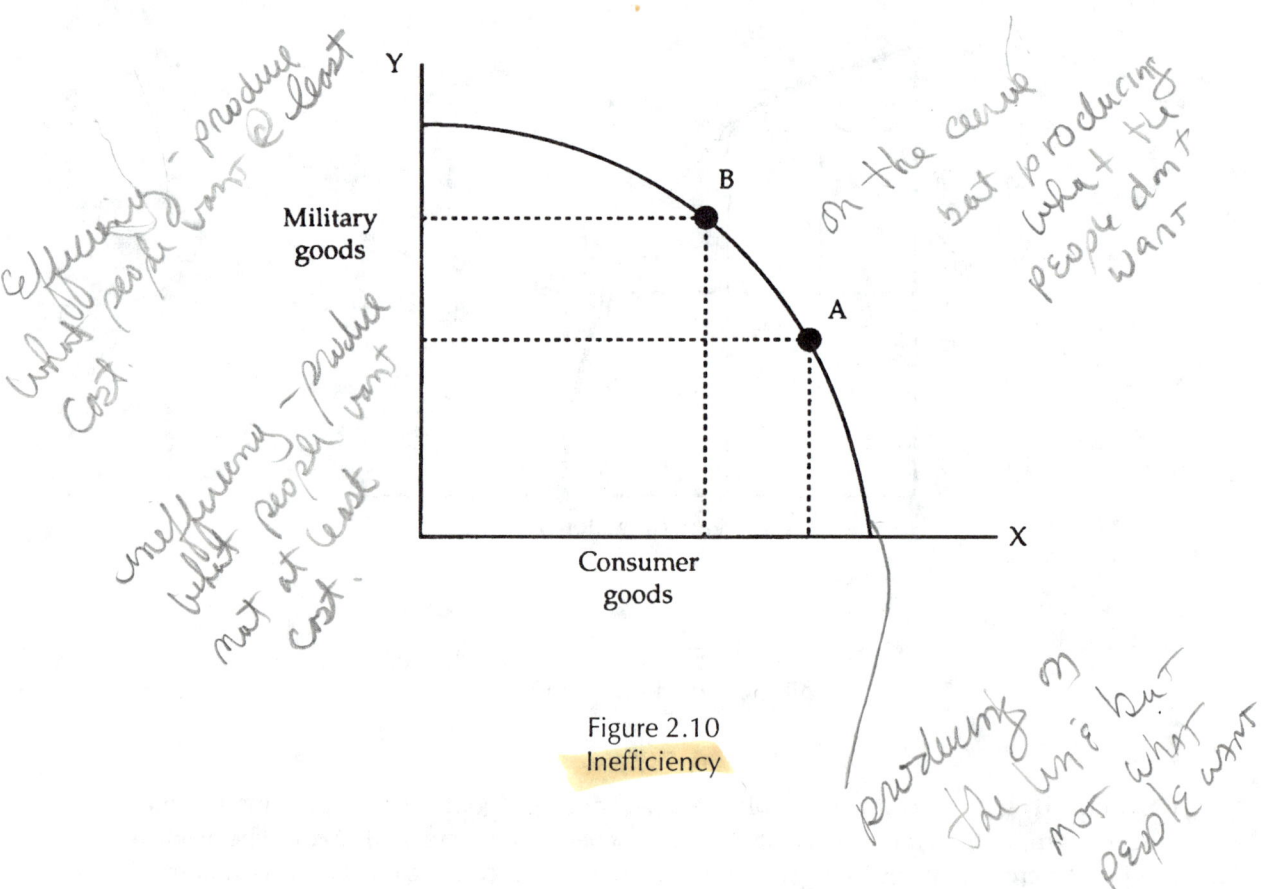

Figure 2.10
Inefficiency

The second form occurs when the production of the country is below the production possibilities curve as shown in Figure 2.11. Here the economy is not producing up to its potential.

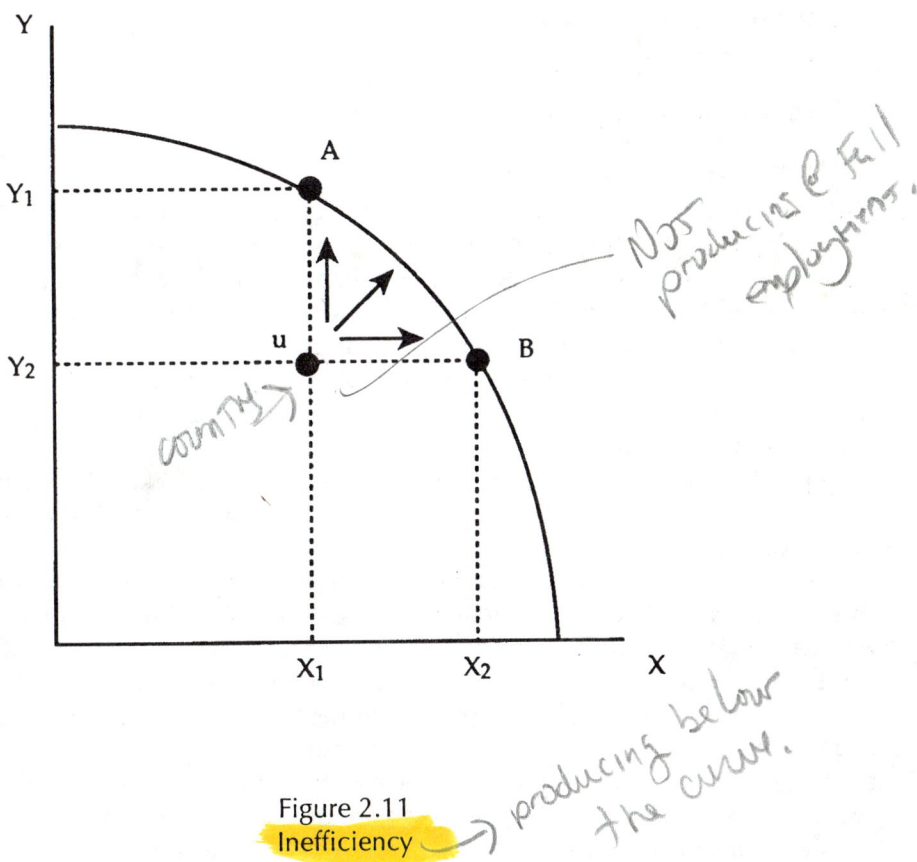

Figure 2.11
Inefficiency

The country is actually producing at point U. This level of production occurs because the economy is not using all of its resources, employment, and capital. Given the production of good X at X_1 the country could be producing at point A with a greater amount of good Y at Y_1. Likewise given the production of good Y at Y_2, the country could be producing at point B with a greater amount of good X at X_2. Since the country could be at a higher level on the production curve, anywhere between points A and B the country is said to be operating inefficiently. The economy is not producing at a full-employment level. The cost of producing at point U is the goods lost because the economy is not producing on the production possibilities curve. The economy is not producing the amount of good X at the least cost.

Economic efficiency, therefore, means that the economy is producing the goods the people want produced and that the production is taking place at full employment of resources, employment, and capital.

ECONOMIC SYSTEMS

Because of scarcity, choices must be made. The choices pertain to four (4) basic questions:
1. What should be produced?
2. How should the items be produced?
3. How many items should be produced?
4. For whom should the goods be produced?

In order to answer the questions, three types of economic systems have been developed: traditional, planned, and the market system. In a traditional system, all questions are answered by past practice. Consider a tribe of American Indians before the arrival of the Europeans. The men were hunters and protectors. The women and children were gatherers and farmers. Boys grew up to be men and to do men's work. Girls grew up to be women and to do women's work. There were rituals for all activities: hunting, fishing, farming, being born, and dying. Their lifestyle was the same for thousands of years. Their economy was basically a subsistence one, and the traditional system worked well.

In a planned system, a central authority, or government, makes all the decisions. The government decides who does what, what will be produced, how, and to whom the goods will be given. There may be a five- or seven-year plan in which every decision is made well in advance.

Since the government is making the decisions, the largest share of the scarce resources of the country will be allocated to government goods and services. Since national defense is a function of government, there will be a larger military sector in the economy. In addition, there will be government services in the areas of education, welfare, transportation, and communications. All factories and businesses will be run by government managers. The government will make decisions regarding careers and training. The motivation for the population to cooperate is two-fold. First, the government has the power to force cooperation through the military. Since, however, the government would prefer the people to volunteer cooperation, a system of rewards would be established. The goods and services are produced for those people who cooperate.

Tables 2.2 and 2.3 summarize two possible economies: one traditional, the other governmental.

Table 2.2 Traditional Precepts

1. Men hunt and protect.
2. Women gather and farm.
3. Children help the women.
4. Boys become men at age 12 and learn the methods of hunting.
5. Girls learn the tasks of women and become wives.
6. Goods which are necessary are produced, such as dwellings, utensils, weapons, food, and clothing.
7. Goods are shared as needed.
8. Rituals are followed to insure the desired results.
9. Those who do not follow the traditions are cast out.

Table 2.3 Governmental System

1. The government protects.
2. The government decides what careers individuals follow.
3. The government decides which goods are necessary and will be produced.
4. The government decides which methods will be used.
5. Goods are distributed as decided by the government.
6. Those who do not follow the dictates of the government lose their protection.

In a market system, the questions are answered by the economic forces of demand and supply. Sellers and buyers meet, and exchange takes place. What is produced depends upon what the buyers want. How it is produced is determined by the seller, so that a profit can be made. In a traditional economy, the motivation is tradition or the fear of being punished for not following it. In a planned economy, the motivation is force; the government requires cooperation. In a market system, the motivation is profit. The sellers profit if they provide goods in demand and at low cost. How many goods produced is, again, determined by demand. Finally, the goods are produced for those who want them and are able to buy them. The market system uses a price system to distribute the goods. A price is determined that is agreeable to the seller and to the buyer.

Everyone who has enough money to cover the price can buy the product. Table 2.4 summarizes the market system.

Table 2.4 Market System

1. A small government exists and protects.
2. Individuals choose their own careers based on abilities.
3. Goods are produced which buyers need or want.
4. Suppliers produce by methods to gain profit.
5. As many goods as are demanded are produced.
6. The price decides the quantity demanded and who receives the item.
7. The punishment for not following the system is a loss of goods or profits.

Arabic Tradition & Muslims: An Overview

Many economic policies of a country are influenced or dictated by religion or by tradition. In Arabic countries, where the religion of most of the people is Islam, many economic policies are dictated by the Koran, Islam's sacred book. Instead of taxes, Muslims pay "Zakah."

In Islam, the word "Zakah" is a duty enjoined by God and undertaken by Muslims in the interest of a society as a whole. The literal and simple meaning of "Zakah" is purity. The technical meaning of the word designates the annual amount in kind or coin which a Muslim with means must distribute among the rightful beneficiaries. When "Zakah" is payable, a certain percentage of the wealth should be distributed immediately in the right manner because the owner no longer has moral or legal possession of that percentage.

Every Muslim, male and female, who is in possession of approximately fifteen dollars or more in cash or kind at the end of the year must give "Zakah" at the minimum rate of two and one half percent. In the case of having the amount in cash, the computation is easy, simply multiply the amount by the percentage. When a person has wealth in business stocks or trade articles, he or she must evaluate the current value of the wealth at the end of every year and give "Zakah" at the same rate of two and one-half percent of the total value of the wealth.

If the wealth is investment in buildings and industries, the amount of "Zakah" would be based on the total net income from the investment and not on the value of the property. Hence, a person pays only on the net balance. All personal expenses, family allowances, necessary expenditures and all due debts are paid first. "Zakah" is a percentage of the net balance. "Zakah" is also obligatory on cattle and agricultural products. The computation of the amount, however, is more involved and varies from person to person.

The rate of two and one-half percent, however, is only a minimum. In times of emergency or arising needs, there is no rate limit. The more one gives, the better it is for everyone concerned.

The Koran classifies the due recipients of "Zakah" as follows:

1. The poor Muslims, to relieve their distress.

2. The needy Muslims, to supply them with the means whereby they can earn their livelihood.

3. The new Muslim converts, to enable them to settle down and meet their usual needs.

4. The Muslim prisoners of war, to liberate them by payment of ransom money.

5. The Muslims in debt, to free them from their liabilities incurred by pressing necessities.

6. The Muslim wayfarers, to pay their expenses to prevent them from being stranded in foreign lands.

7. The Muslim employees appointed by a governor to collect "Zakah," to pay their wages.

Islamic economies stress the interest or the welfare of society as a whole as opposed to the interest of the individual as is commonly stressed in capitalism. Islamic economic activities are associated more with spiritual and moral codes of life rather than with the pursuit of personal material goals like profit. The individual can accumulate wealth only as long as society as a whole is not threatened.

Islam and democracy are compatible and complementary. Both rest on accountability, consultation, open discussion, delegation and consensus. The opening words of the U.S. Declaration of Independence express deeply felt Islamic sentiments.

Muslims honor Judaic prophets, accord special esteem to Jesus and the Virgin Mary, and recognize as sacred the scriptures revealed to Moses and Jesus, namely the Torah and the Bible.

Muslims are united in Islam, literally, "submission." To them, submitting to God and doing good define piety. The Koran is the final divine revelation, providing a complete guide for human behavior. Its text was revealed directly to the Prophet Muhammad between 610 and 632 A.D. Though revered by Muslims as the last of God's prophets, Muhammad is not worshiped.

Muslim women, like men, have the right to obtain an education, own property and engage in business, professional and public life. Both women and men wear modest dress out of respect for public morality. If a society oppresses women or discriminates against them, it is in spite of Islam, not because of it.

The Muslim husband has the primary responsibility for family support, his wife for the household and children. Divorce is discouraged. Procedures vary by country, but either husband or wife may petition to dissolve a marriage. Polygamy is subject to restrictive conditions and is seldom practiced, never where it violates public law, as here in America.

Muslims assume personal responsibility for relatives and others in need. In Islam, a woman or an elderly person is almost never obliged to live alone.

Muslims are committed to rules. Sadly, some people who say they are Muslims—like some professed Christians or Jews—grossly violate these rules and the rights of others. In doing so, they do not act as Muslims. It is erroneous to call them fundamentalists, a term unknown in Islam and used mostly in false stereotyping.

Jihad has two meanings: one, non-violent struggling within oneself for a life of virtue; the other, fighting for justice, a supreme goal of Islamic teachings. Islam eulogizes moderation and abhors extremism, terrorism, fanaticism, oppression and subjugation.

Mixed Market Structure

Today, the economies of the world are a combination of the three types of systems. The United States' economy is the main topic of this course, so the emphasis will be placed on it. The United States' economy is called a mixed market structure. This means that, basically, the economy follows the above market system but there are many elements of tradition and government. The United States' economy is controlled by a Constitution and a system of laws that is over 200 years old. We follow a system of ethics which determines business practices of charging fair prices and using fair methods of selling and buying. There are restrictions against charging high interest on loans. Businesses have limited operations on Sunday. Women have been excluded from certain professions and high-paying jobs. These are some examples of how tradition is involved in the U.S. economy.

The U.S. government is also involved by taxing incomes, sales, and property. This tax money is then used to provide defense, welfare, and social services. State and local governments also tax and provide services, such as highways, police, fire departments, emergency services, and education. The government regulates businesses and individual conduct. It provides a system for retirement in the social security system.

The market system is controlled by buyers and sellers, each of whom exert a force. These forces are demand and supply. They will be examined in the next chapter.

Chapter Summary

1. Economics can be defined as "the study of the optimum allocation of scarce resources."

2. Resources tend to be scarce due to limited amounts and demand for them.

3. An economy is limited by natural resources, size and abilities of the population, technology and knowledge, and institutions.

4. Because of scarcity and limits, economies, governments, business, and individuals must make choices.

5. According to the production possibilities analysis:

    a. An economy can be at whatever combination of goods it chooses.

    b. In order to increase the production of one good, the production of another good must be reduced.

    c. As there are increases in the production of one good over time, the amount of resources taken increases each time. This is the principle of increasing opportunity costs.

6. Opportunity costs refers to whatever is given up when a choice is made.

7. Efficiency in economics means that resources, employment, and capital are being used to produce what people want and that production is taking place at the least cost.

8. Inefficiency means that a country is not producing what the people want or that the country is producing below the production possibilities curve.

9. The marginal rate of transformation is the slope of the production possibilities curve and measures the cost involved in gaining more of one good at the expense of another good.

10. Economic growth refers to increasing the production possibilities.

11. The choices a system must make are:

    a. What should be produced?

    b. How should the items be produced?

    c. How many items should be produced?

    d. For whom should the goods be produced?

12. Three types of systems have evolved: traditional, planned, and the market system.

Chapter 2
Key Concepts

1. **Choice**—People must select among alternative uses because of scarcity.
2. **Efficiency**—Resources, employment, and capital are being used to produce what the people want and that production is taking place at the least cost.
3. **Increasing Opportunity Cost**—More resources must be transferred each time they are transferred from one use to another.
4. **Inefficiency**—Resources, employment, and capital are not being used to produce what the people want or production is not taking place at the least cost.
5. **Marginal Rate of Substitution**—The slope of the production possibilities curve or the rate of change in the amount of one good as the amount of another good changes.
6. **Market System**—An economic system in which basic economic questions are answered by the economic forces of supply and demand.
7. **Mixed Market Structure**—An economic system in which the basic economic questions are answered by the forces of supply and demand, and also by government and tradition.
8. **Non-renewable Resources**—Resources that cannot be replaced when used.
9. **Opportunity Cost**—Whatever is given up when a choice is made.
10. **Planned System**—An economic system in which basic economic questions are answered by government decisions.
11. **Production Possibility**—A model which presents the maximum combination of goods and services that can be produced using available resources, labor, technology, and institutions.
12. **Production Possibilities Curve**—A curve which presents the largest combinations of two items that can be produced under existing conditions.
13. **Renewable Resources**—Resources that can be replaced when used.
14. **Resources**—Natural items that are used to produce goods and services.
15. **Scarcity**—Supplies of goods or services are less than the demand for them.
16. **Technology**—The use of more advanced machinery or newer methods of production to produce more with less, or the same, input.
17. **Traditional System**—An economic system in which basic economic questions are answered by past practice.

DISCUSSION QUESTIONS

1. Discuss how scarcity forces societies, government, businesses, and individuals to make choices.
2. Discuss the factors that restrict the production of goods and services in a country.
3. Explain opportunity cost and present some examples that you can think of.
4. Explain the concept of increasing opportunity cost and the effect it has on the production of a country.
5. Explain economic growth in terms of the production possibilities analysis.
6. Discuss the mixed market structure and how it includes traditional elements, some government involvement, and the market forces of supply and demand.
7. Distinguish between efficiency and inefficiency in economics.
8. Explain the concept of the marginal rate of transformation and its effect upon the production possibilities curve.
9. Distinguish among the three systems, traditional, planned, and market as to how the four basic questions are answered.

2.1 LEARNING PRACTICE

Consider the following table which shows the combinations of the production of two goods that are possible for a country.

Option	Good A	Good B
a.	0	10
b.	1	9
c.	2	7
d.	3	4
e.	4	0

(a) Draw the production possibilities curve.

(b) Compute the marginal rate of transformation for each combination.

(c) Develop another table which indicates:

    (1)   an increase in the technology of good A only.
    (2)   economic growth for the whole economy.

(d) Graph the tables developed in (c).

SOLUTIONS

(a)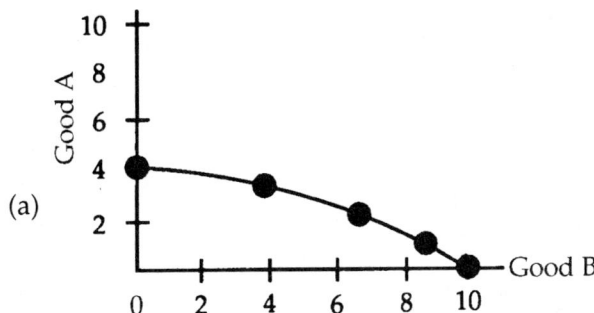

(b) a to b, MRT = 1
    b to c, MRT = 2
    c to d, MRT = 3
    d to e, MRT = 4

(c) (1)

Good A	Good B
0	10
2	9
4	7
6	4
8	0

or other higher numbers for A for points (b), (c), (d), (e).

(2)

Good A	Good B
0	12
2	11
4	9
6	6
8	0

(d)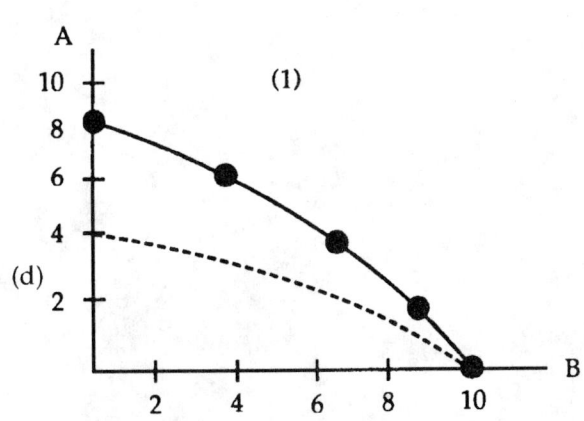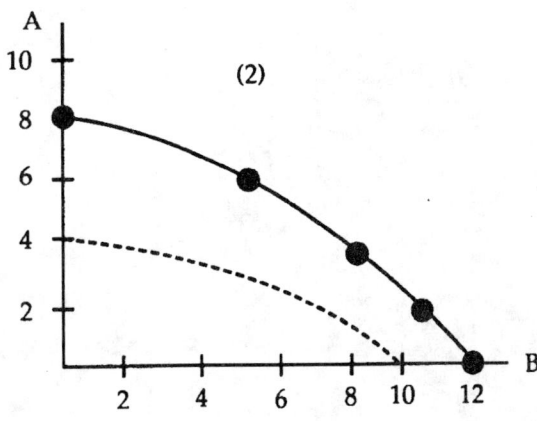

CHAPTER 3

The Market

LEARNING OBJECTIVES

After reading this chapter, you should be able to:
1. Define market and ideal market.
2. Distinguish between the concepts of quantity demanded and quantity supplied.
3. Explain demand schedules and demand curves which indicate the relationship between quantity demanded and price.
4. Explain supply schedules and supply curves which indicate the relationship between quantity supplied and price.
5. Graph demand and supply schedules.
6. Illustrate the shifts in the demand and supply curves.
7. Distinguish between individual demand and market demand.
8. Distinguish between individual supply and market supply.
9. Explain how a change in price reflects a change in the amount demanded or supplied.
10. Explain equilibrium price and quantity in the market.
11. Describe and explain price ceilings and price floors.
12. Explain the concept of minimum wage; interpret the direct result of minimum wage legislation.

An Introduction to the Market

What is the market? As a general definition, the market is a place where people gather together to trade or sell goods. But for the budding economist, the market is a little more than that. The economic market is an area or context where the economic activities of buyers and sellers are affected by the laws of supply and demand. These economic activities can be considered "transactions" made on a voluntary basis between different individuals. Today, these market activities range from the fast-paced buying and selling of stocks on the New York Stock Exchange to the selling of wheat and soybeans at a granary.

Markets throughout the world vary in size, with many appearing to be quite large. Transactions in markets occur by the millions every day, with buyers and sellers making voluntary choices of the quantities of goods to purchase, the quantity of goods to sell, and the prices at which to sell the goods. The voluntary aspect is important because sometimes market prices or market quantities are forced onto the buyers or sellers. On occasion, when a seller or buyer is able to control enough of an area of the market to determine prices or quantities, then a monopoly exists in this market. These monopolies deprive the economies of ideal markets.

The concept of the ideal market is that the market must be large enough so that no one individual or group can influence price or quantity (such as in a monopoly). The ideal market is sometimes referred to as a purely competitive market. If either buyer or seller can influence price, it is referred to as an imperfectly competitive market.

Demand and Supply

The principles of demand and supply are basic to understanding economics. As a matter of fact, it has been claimed that all questions in economics can be answered with the words demand and/or supply. In this section, the basics of individual and market demand and individual and market supply will be presented. The way that prices are determined in the market by demand and supply will also be presented.

Individual Demand

Under the concept of demand, we will present two approaches: individual demand and market demand. Individual demand can be defined as the quantities of a good that an individual is willing and able to buy at various possible prices. Let us pick an individual, Susan, and a good, oranges. The concept of demand states that Susan is willing to buy oranges, but different amounts at different prices.

For Susan, the amount of oranges she is willing to buy is determined by the price. As pointed out in Chapter 1, a functional relationship exists when one variable is determined by another. The dependent variable is the amount or quantity of oranges Susan is willing to buy. The quantity of oranges she is willing to buy can be termed the quantity demanded expressed as Q_D. The independent variable is the price of oranges. If we use P to represent price, the function can be expressed $Q_D = f(P)$. This can be further narrowed by using an additional sub notation (o) which will represent oranges. The functional relationship is now written as:

$$QD_O = f(P_O)$$

This is read as follows. The quantity demanded of oranges is a function of the price of oranges. There may be other independent variables involved, but, for now, these variables will not be included. When some variables are not included, economists add a Latin phrase "ceteris paribus." Literally, this means "other things being equal." Here, it is used to mean that only the price of oranges will be changing as we analyze the function. No other variables are allowed to change. In Chapter 1, it was mentioned that economists simplify their models to be able to analyze them more easily. That is what is being done here. We are assuming that only two variables are involved: the price of oranges and the amounts Susan is willing to buy at various prices. Table 3.1 presents all the assumptions we will use to develop Susan's demand for oranges.

Table 3.1 Susan's Demand for Oranges

1. Susan is willing to buy oranges.
2. The price of oranges changes from time to time.
3. Susan has five (5) dollars a week to spend on oranges.
4. There are substitutes for oranges, such as grapefruits, grapes, bananas, and others.
5. The price of grapefruits is 50 cents (.50).

Table 3.2 presents various possible prices for oranges at the supermarket where Susan regularly shops. In addition, we have presented the largest number of oranges Susan can buy at those prices with the five (5) dollars she has allocated a week for purchasing fruit. Susan, like many other people, has a limited (scarce) income and must make choices as to what to do with that income.

Table 3.2 What Susan is Able to Buy

Possible Price	Amount Able to be Purchased
$1.00	5
.50	10
.25	20
.20	25
.10	50
.05	100
.00	unlimited amount

If Susan has 5 dollars and an orange costs 1 dollar, Susan can buy 5 oranges (5/1). If an orange costs 20 cents (.20), Susan can buy 25 oranges (5/.20). If oranges cost 5 cents (.05), she can buy 100 oranges (5/.05). If oranges are free (.00), she can have as many as she can carry out of the store. Since it is highly unlikely that the price of oranges will be free (.00), this possibility will not be included in the remaining analysis. In Table 3.2, as the price changes, the quantity demanded changes: thus, we conclude a functional relationship exists. In addition, as the price drops, the quantity demanded increases; thus, we conclude an inverse functional relationship exists. The variables move in opposite directions, as summarized in Table 3.3.

Table 3.3 Inverse Relationship

Price of Oranges Ø	Quantity of Oranges Able to be Purchased ≠
Price of Oranges ≠	Quantity of Oranges Able to be Purchased Ø

Susan may decide, however, to buy different amounts than those she is able to buy. She may decide 1 dollar is a high price for an orange since she can buy a grapefruit for 50 cents. If she spends her weekly amount on grapefruit, she could have 10 grapefruits instead of only 5 oranges. She decides to buy 2 oranges (costing 2 dollars) and 6 grapefruits (costing 3 dollars). In this way, she gets more total fruit in her diet. To summarize, when the price of oranges is above the price of grapefruit, it is to her advantage to buy less oranges and more grapefruit. The reverse would also be true if the price of oranges is less than the price of grapefruit. For example, if the price of oranges is 25 cents (.25), she can buy more oranges (20) than grapefruit (10). She may decide to buy less oranges, however, since 20 a week means almost 3 oranges a day. Susan may not want that many oranges. The same would be even more true when the price of oranges is 5 cents (.05). She would be able to buy 100 oranges, which would be 14 a day. She would have to eat a little more than 1 orange every 2 hours.

Table 3.4 presents what Susan decides she would buy at various possible prices. Her decision is based on her fixed income, the fixed price of grapefruit, her willingness to substitute, and the changing price of oranges.

Table 3.4 Susan's Demand for Oranges

	Price	Quantity Demanded
(a)	1.00	2
(b)	.50	4
(c)	.25	8
(d)	.20	10
(e)	.10	12
(f)	.05	14

At this point, a distinction should be made between quantity demanded and demand. In Table 3.4, the quantity demanded refers to the amount Susan is willing to buy at a possible price. If the price is 25 cents (.25), the quantity Susan is willing to buy is 8 oranges. This could be stated: the quantity demanded at 25 cents (.25) is 8. Thus, the quantity demanded at 20 cents (.20) is 10, and at 10 cents (.10), the quantity demanded is 12. Susan's demand for oranges is represented by the entire table. An individual's demand for a product is defined as the quantities of a good that the individual is willing to buy at various possible prices.

Graphing Individual Demand

Figure 3.1 converts the information in Table 3.4 to a graph. Usually, the dependent variable is placed on the vertical line and the independent variable is placed on the horizontal. This is reversed, here, since this graph will be used for another analysis in which the actual price which will exist is determined. The actual price of oranges will be the dependent variable. This will be explained in the section on equilibrium.

Each dot represents a possible price for oranges and the quantity Susan would be willing to buy if that were the price. For example, at a price of 50 cents (.50), Susan would be willing to buy 4 oranges. If we connect all the dots with a line, the line slopes downward to the right, indicating an inverse relationship exists.

The Market 59

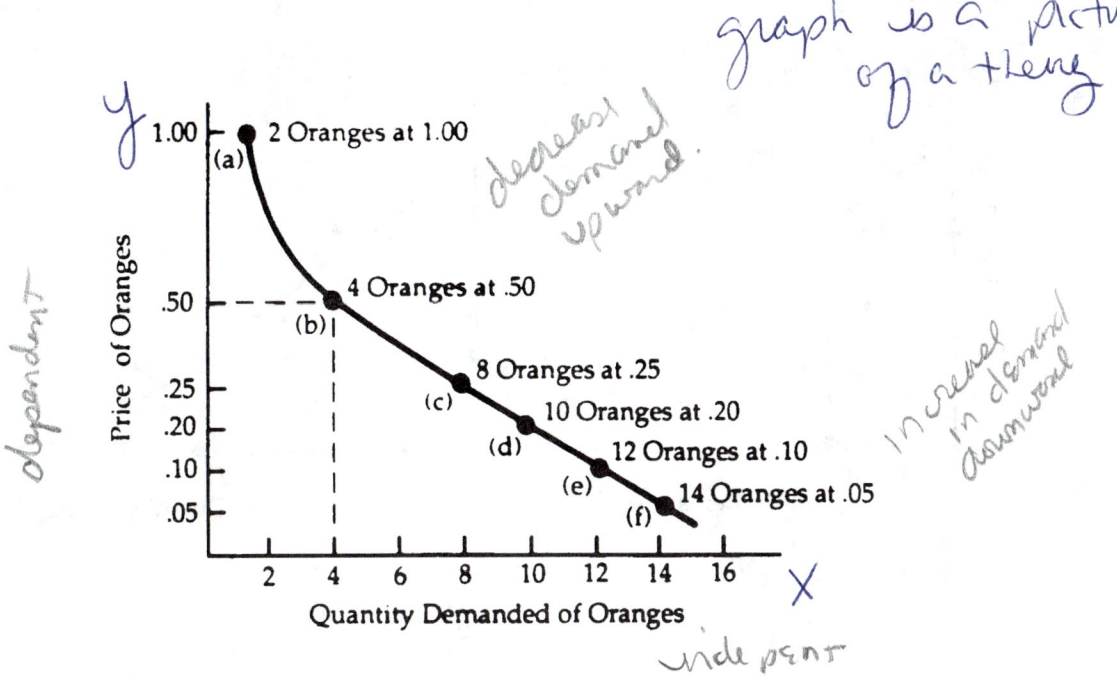

Figure 3.1
Graph of Susan's Demand for Oranges

The above graph can be redrawn using a straight line and general variable names, as indicated in Figure 3.2.

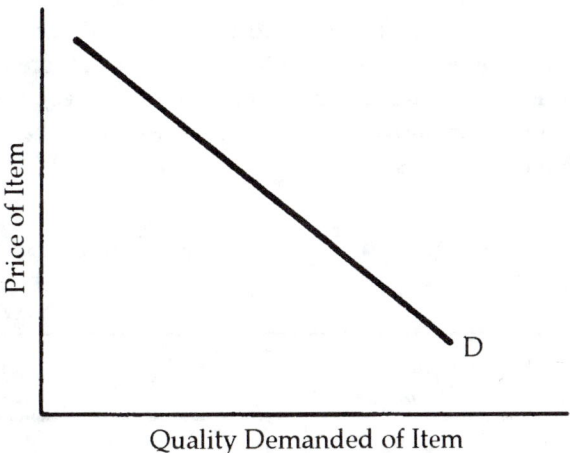

Figure 3.2
Generalized Individual Demand

Figure 3.2 presents a graph that depicts an individual's demand for a product. The line is titled demand (D), as it is a graphical representation of various possible prices and the quantities an individual would buy at those prices. The demand curve slopes downward, indicating an inverse relationship. Figure 3.3 depicts the inverse relationship.

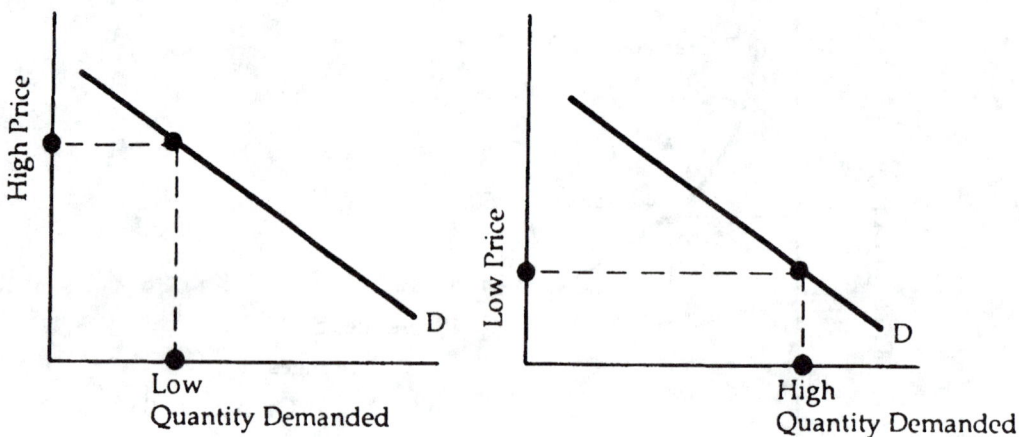

Figure 3.3
Inverse Relationship—Graphically

At high prices, the quantity an individual is willing to buy is low. At low prices, the quantity an individual is willing to buy is high. Since the dependent and independent variables move in opposite directions, the relationship is inverse.

Changes in Individual Demand

The prices of other items, an individual's income, an individual's tastes and preferences, fads, styles, and attitudes toward products may change. As a result, an individual's demand for a product may change. If Susan receives a raise and decides to allocate more of her budget for purchasing fruit, especially oranges, her demand for oranges will increase.

An increase in an individual's demand means that at every price, the individual is willing to buy more of the product. Table 3.5 shows Susan's old and new demand tables, and Figure 3.4 shows the old and new demand graphs.

Table 3.5 Increase in Individual Demand—Table Presentation

	(Old)			(New)	
	Price	Quantity Demanded		Price	Quantity Demanded
(a)	1.00	2	(g)	1.00	4
(b)	.50	4	(h)	.50	8
(c)	.25	8	(i)	.25	10
(d)	.20	10	(j)	.20	12
(e)	.10	12	(k)	.10	14
(f)	.05	14	(l)	.05	16

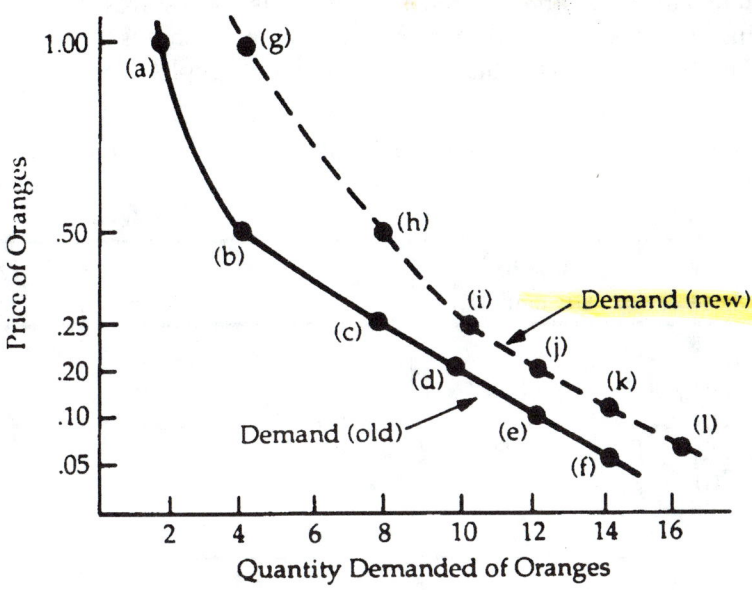

Figure 3.4
Increase in Individual Demand—Graphical Presentation

Table 3.5 indicates that, at every price, Susan is now willing to buy more oranges. Before, at a dollar, she was willing to buy 2 oranges. Now, with her higher income, she is willing to buy 4 oranges. Before, at 10 cents (.10), she was willing to buy 12 oranges. Now she is willing to buy 16.

In Figure 3.4, the demand with her new income is represented with the points (g) through (l). The broken line represents the graph of Susan's demand for oranges after the increase in her income. The increase in demand is depicted by a new line which is to the right of the old demand. This is summarized in Figure 3.5.

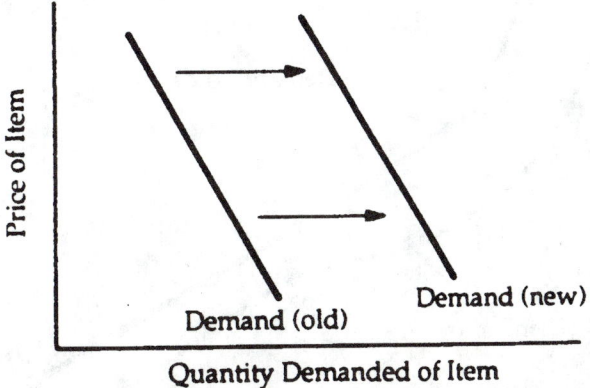

Figure 3.5
Increase in Individual Demand

A decrease in an individual's demand means that, at every price, the individual is not as willing to buy as much of the product as before. If Susan is laid off from work for a month, she may decide to reduce her weekly budget for oranges. Table 3.6 shows Susan's old and new demand tables, and Figure 3.6 shows the old and new demand graphs.

Table 3.6 Decrease in Individual Demand—Table Presentation

	(Old)			(New)	
	Price	Quantity Demanded		Price	Quantity Demanded
(a)	1.00	2	(m)	1.00	0
(b)	.50	4	(n)	.50	2
(c)	.25	8	(o)	.25	4
(d)	.20	10	(p)	.20	8
(e)	.10	12	(q)	.10	10
(f)	.05	14	(r)	.05	12

Table 3.6 indicates that, at every price, Susan is not willing to buy as many oranges as before. Now, at a dollar, she is not willing to buy any. Before, at 10 cents (.10), she was willing to buy 12 oranges. Now, since her income is less, she is willing to buy only 10 oranges. In Table 3.6, the demand with the lower income is represented with points (m) through (r). The broken line in Figure 3.6 represents the graph of Susan's demand for oranges after the decrease in her income. The decrease in demand is depicted by a new line, which is to the left of the old demand. This is summarized in Figure 3.7.

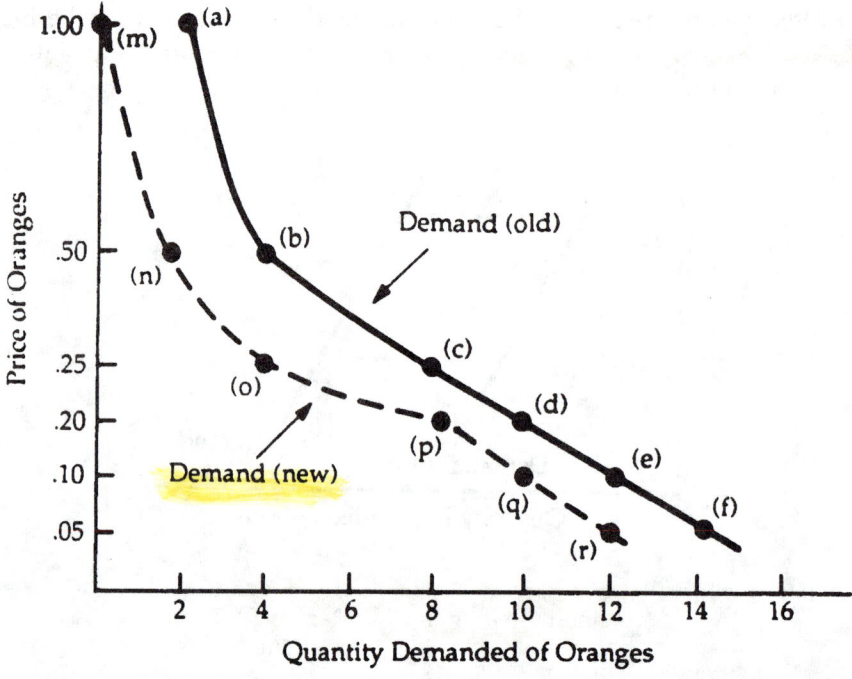

Figure 3.6
Decrease in Individual Demand—Graphical Presentation

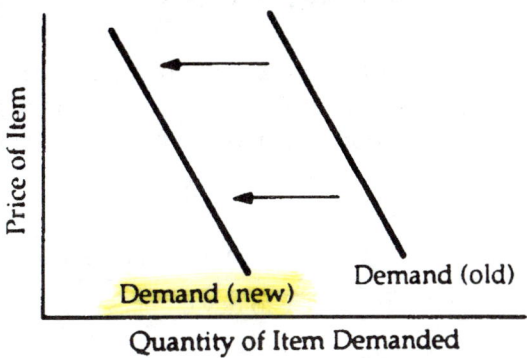

Figure 3.7
Decrease in Individual Demand

An increase in individual demand means that, at every price, the individual is willing to buy more of the item, and is depicted by the demand curve moving to the right. A decrease in individual demand means that, at every price, the individual is not as willing to buy as much as before, and is depicted by the demand curve moving to the left. A change in demand implies a new curve exists. A change in quantity demanded means there is a movement up or down an existing demand curve, as shown in Figure 3.8.

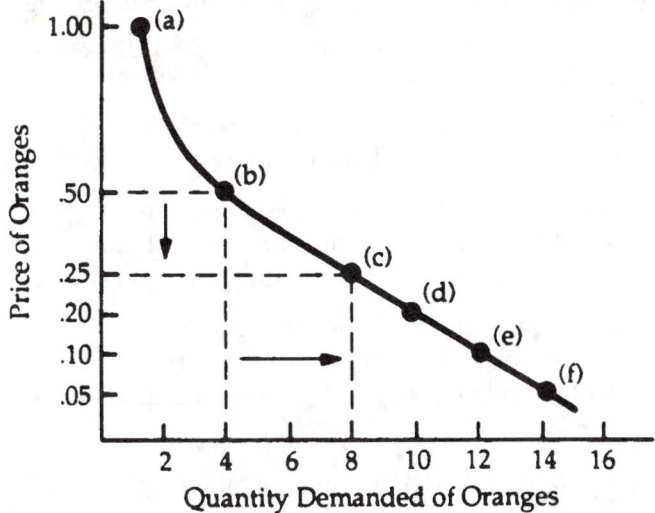

Figure 3.8
Changes in Quantity Demanded

If the price is 50 cents (.50), Susan is willing to buy 4 oranges. The quantity demanded is, therefore, 4 oranges at 50 cents. If the price drops to 25 cents (.25), Susan would be willing to buy 8 oranges. The quantity demanded would increase from 4 to 8 oranges. If the price rises from 50 cents (.50) to 1 dollar, Susan would be willing to buy only 2 oranges instead of 4. The quantity demanded would decrease from 4 to 2 oranges. A change in quantity demanded is caused by a change in the price of the item. The variables that can cause changes in demand will be covered at a later point in this chapter.

MARKET DEMAND

The market demand for a product is defined as the sum of all the individual demands. The market demand for oranges, therefore, is the sum of all the demands of the individuals who buy oranges. Table 3.7 presents the assumptions we make in order to develop an example of market demand.

Table 3.7 Market Demand Assumptions

1. There are 100 million people who are willing to buy oranges.
2. There are various possible prices in the market.
3. The market price changes from time to time.
4. Each person has a limited amount to spend on oranges.
5. There are substitutes for oranges.
6. Susan represents the typical or average person in the market.

Since Susan is assumed to be the average buyer, the market demand for oranges can be computed by multiplying the quantities she would be willing to buy at various possible prices by 100 million, the number of individuals, as shown in Table 3.8 and Figure 3.9.

The same conclusions that were made for individual demand apply here:

1. As the price of the product changes, the quantity demanded changes: thus, the market quantity demanded for a product is a function of the market price of the item.

2. The functional relationship is inverse. As the market price rises, the market quantity demanded falls. As the market price falls, the market quantity demanded rises.

3. An increase in market demand would refer to the market being willing to buy more oranges at every price. The market demand curve would move to the right, as shown in Figure 3.10, from line D to line D_1, representing an increase in demand.

4. A decrease in market demand would refer to the market not being willing to buy as many oranges at every price. The market demand curve would move to the left, as shown in Figure 3.10, from line D to line D_2, representing a decrease in demand.

Table 3.8 Market Demand for Oranges

	Market Price	Quantity Demanded (in millions)
(a)	1.00	200 (2 x 100)
(b)	.50	400 (4 x 100)
(c)	.25	800 (8 x 100)
(d)	.20	1,000 (10 x 100)
(e)	.10	1,200 (12 x 100)
(f)	.05	1,400 (14 x 100)

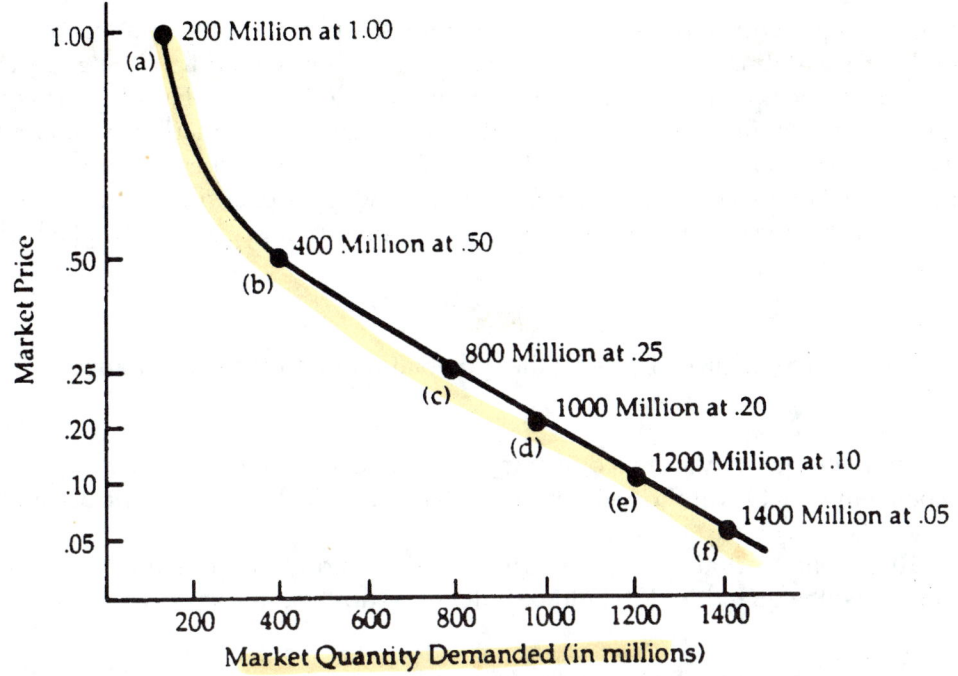

Figure 3.9
Market Demand for Oranges

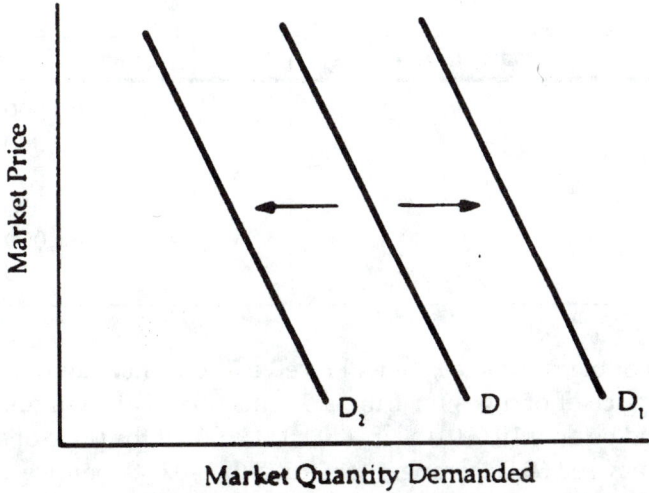

Figure 3.10
Changes in Market Demand

Firm's Supply

The concept of supply will be presented in two contexts: a firm's supply and market supply. A firm's supply can be defined as the quantities of a good a firm would be willing to put on the market at various prices. Otis owns an orange farm outside Orlando, Florida. The concept of supply states that Otis will put different quantities of oranges on the market at different prices. Oranges will refer to whole fruits to be sold to the public in various types of grocery stores.

A functional relationship is indicated. Price is the independent variable, and the quantity supplied of oranges is the dependent variable. Q_s will represent the quantity supplied. The function can, thus, be written:

$$Q_s = f(P).$$

This can be further narrowed by using the sub notation (o) to represent oranges.

$$QS_o = f(P_o)$$

This is read as the quantity supplied of oranges is a function of the price of oranges. Again, no other independent variables are to be allowed to change. Table 3.9 presents the assumptions of the firm's model.

Table 3.10 presents various prices for oranges Otis could get if he had oranges for sale in grocery stores, and the quantities he could be willing to supply at those prices.

Table 3.9 Otis' Supply of Oranges

1. Otis produces 200,000 oranges a year.
2. Otis can sell oranges to be used as fruit, or he can sell oranges to a company for juice.
3. If he sells the oranges for juice, he gets 7 cents (.07) a piece.

Table 3.10 Otis' Supply Table

	Market Price	Quantity Supplied
(a)	1.00	200,000
(b)	.50	180,000
(c)	.25	160,000
(d)	.20	120,000
(e)	.10	60,000
(f)	.05	0

If Otis sells all his oranges for juice, he will receive 7 cents (.07) an orange, or 14,000 dollars (200,000 x .07). If the price of oranges for fruit is 5 cents (.05), Otis will not sell any oranges for fruit. His income would be only 10,000 dollars (200,000 x .05). If the price of oranges for fruit rises to 10 cents (.10), Otis may sell 60,000 oranges for fruit and 140,000 for juice. His income would be (60,000 x .10) + (140,000 x .07), or 6,000 + 9,800, which equals 15,800 dollars. The higher price for oranges as fruit motivated him to sell more oranges for fruit and less for juice. Why didn't he sell all 200,000 as fruit? The increase in price was 3 cents (.03). When oranges are sold as fruit, they must be sorted, boxed, and handled differently. There is more work involved and the 3 cents (.03) difference is not enough to get Otis to process all the oranges as fruit.

If the price rises to 20 cents (.20). Otis may decide to supply 120,000 oranges as fruit and 80,000 as juice. This would raise his income to (120,000 x .20) + (80,000 x .07), or 24,000 + 5,600, which equals 29,600 dollars. As the price rises, Otis is willing to increase the quantity supplied since his income rises by doing so. If the price rises to 1 dollar an orange, he would sell all his oranges as fruit for an income of 200,000 dollars.

In Table 3.11, as the price changes, the quantity supplied changes: thus, we conclude a functional relationship exists. In addition, as the price rises, the quantity supplied rises; thus, we conclude a direct functional relationship exists. The variables move in the same direction, as summarized in Table 3.11.

Table 3.11 Direct Relationship

Price of Oranges ↓	Quantity Supplied as Fruit ↓
Price of Oranges ↑	Quantity Supplied as Fruit ↑

Quantity supplied refers to the amount of an item that will be put on the market at a price. The supply of an item refers to the quantities supplied at various possible prices. Figure 3.11 represents Otis' supply of oranges.

Graphing a Firm's Supply

Figure 3.11 converts the information in Table 3.10 to a graph.

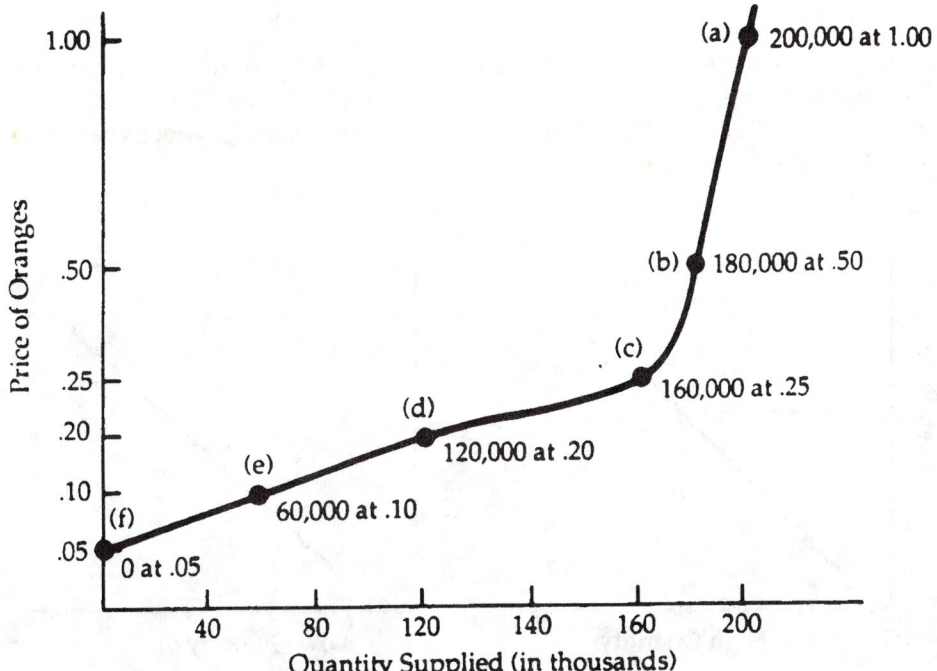

Figure 3.11
Graph of Otis' Supply of Oranges

Each dot represents a possible price for oranges as fruit and the quantity Otis would be willing to sell if that were the price. For example, at a price of 50 cents (.50), Otis would be willing to place 180,000 oranges on the market. If we connect all the dots with a line, the line slopes upward to the right, indicating a direct relationship exists. Figure 3.11 can be redrawn using a straight line and general variable names, as in Figure 3.12.

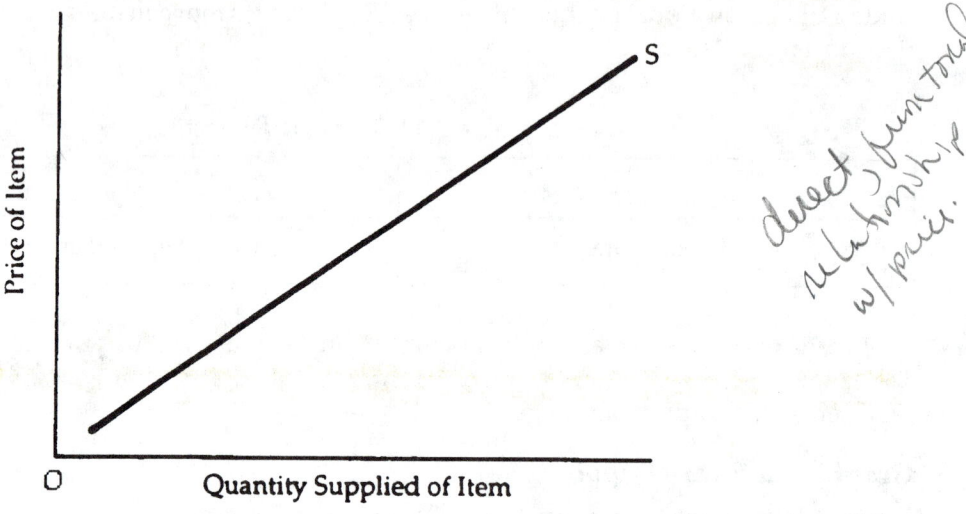

Figure 3.12
Generalized Supply of a Firm

Figure 3.12 presents a graph that depicts a firm's supply of a product. The line is titled supply (S), as it is a graphical representation of various prices and the quantities a firm will put on the market at those prices. The supply curve slopes upward, indicating a direct relationship. Figure 3.13 depicts the direct relationship.

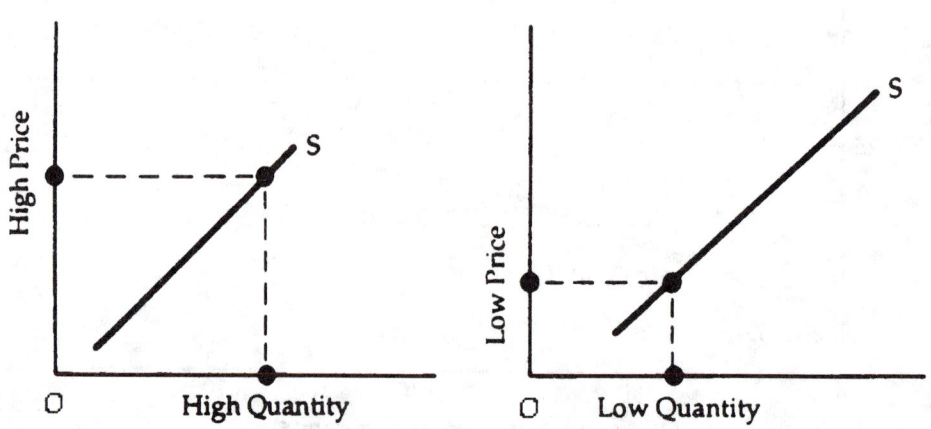

Figure 3.13
Direct Relationship—Graphically

At high prices, the quantities a firm is willing to supply are high. At low prices, the quantities a firm is willing to supply are low. Since the dependent and independent variables move in the same direction, the relationship is direct.

Changes in a Firm's Supply

Economic conditions, costs of production, the prices of other items, or other variables may change. As a result, a firm's supply of a product may change. If the price paid for oranges for juice drops from 7 cents (.07) to 4 cents (.04) because juice companies aren't selling juice, Otis' supply of oranges for fruit will increase.

An increase in a firm's supply of a product means that, at every price, the firm is willing to sell more of the product. Table 3.12 shows Otis' old and new supply tables, and Figure 3.14 shows the old and new supply graphs.

Table 3.12 Increase in Firm's Supply

	(Old)			(New)	
	Price	Quantity Supplied		Price	Quantity Supplied
(a)	1.00	200,000	(g)	1.00	210,000
(b)	.50	180,000	(h)	.50	200,000
(c)	.25	160,000	(i)	.25	180,000
(d)	.20	120,000	(j)	.20	160,000
(e)	.10	60,000	(k)	.10	120,000
(f)	.05	0	(l)	.05	60,000

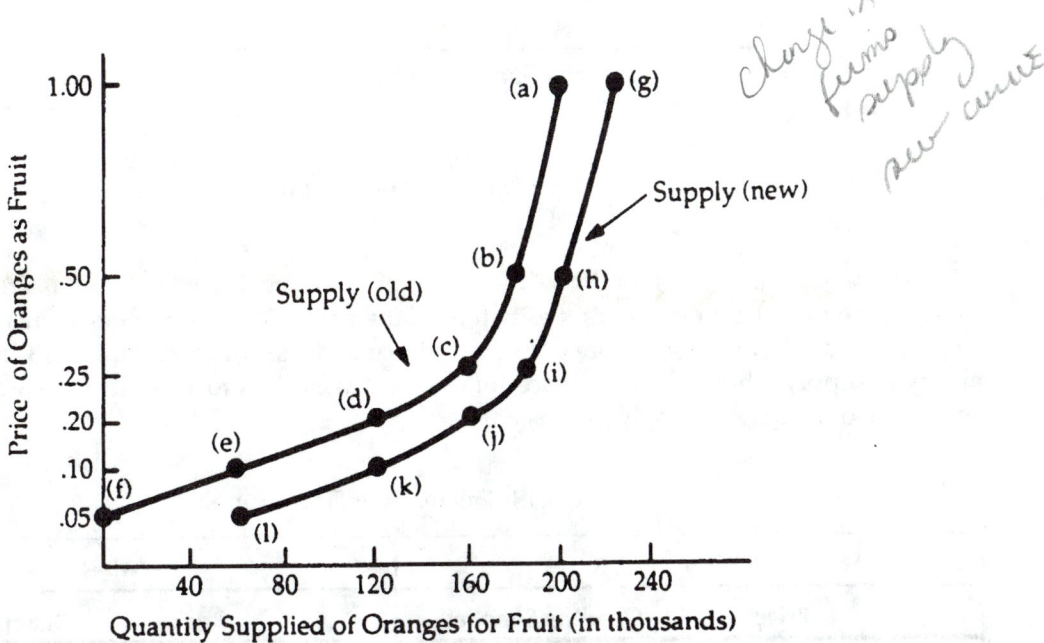

Figure 3.14
Increase in Firm's Supply

Table 3.12 indicates that, at every price, Otis is now willing to sell more oranges for fruit. Before, Otis would not supply any oranges at 5 cents (.05) because he would have given up 7 cents (.07). Now, he only gets 4 cents (.04) for juice oranges. The additional cent motivates him to supply more at 5 cents (.05) because he can increase his revenue. (200,000 x .04) = 8,000. (140,000 x .04) plus (60.000 x .05) = 5,600 + 3,000, which equals an income of 8,600. At the highest price of a dollar, Otis now decides the thing to do is produce oranges for fruit. He uses better fertilizer and priming methods and is able to increase his yield to 210,000 oranges.

In Figure 3.14, the increased supply is represented with the points (g) through (l). The broken line represents the graph of Otis' supply after the juice price dropped to 5 cents (.05) The increase in supply is, thus, depicted by a new line, which is to the right of the old supply line. This is summarized in Figure 3.15.

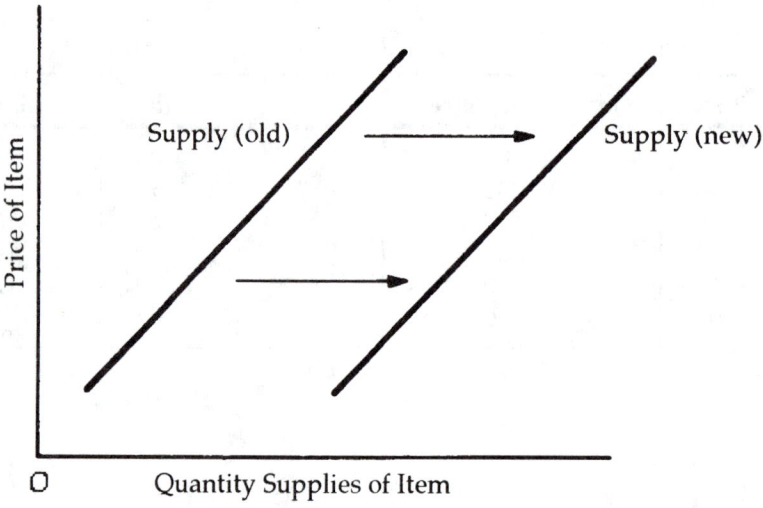

Figure 3.15
Increase in a Firm's Supply

A decrease in a firm's supply means that, at every price, the firm is not as willing to put as much of the product on the market as before. If the price for juice oranges increases to 12 cents (.12), Otis may decide to sell more oranges for juice and less for fruit. Table 3.13 shows Otis' old and new supply tables when the price for juice oranges rises to 12 cents (.12), and Figure 3.16 shows the old and new supply graphs.

Table 3.13 Decrease in Firm's Supply

	(Old)			(New)	
	Price	Quantity Supplied		Price	Quantity Supplied
(a)	1.00	200,000	(g)	1.00	180,000
(b)	.50	180,000	(h)	.50	160,000
(c)	.25	160,000	(i)	.25	120,000
(d)	.20	120,000	(j)	.20	60,000
(e)	.10	60,000	(k)	.10	0
(f)	.05	0	(l)	.05	0

Table 3.13 indicates that, at every price, Otis now supplies less oranges than before. Since the price for juice is 12 cents (.12), Otis will not put any oranges for fruit on the market at 5 cents (.05) or 10 cents (.10). In Figure 3.16, the broken line, points (l) through (g), represents the decrease in supply. The decrease in supply is depicted by a new line which is to the left of the old supply. This is summarized in Figure 3.17.

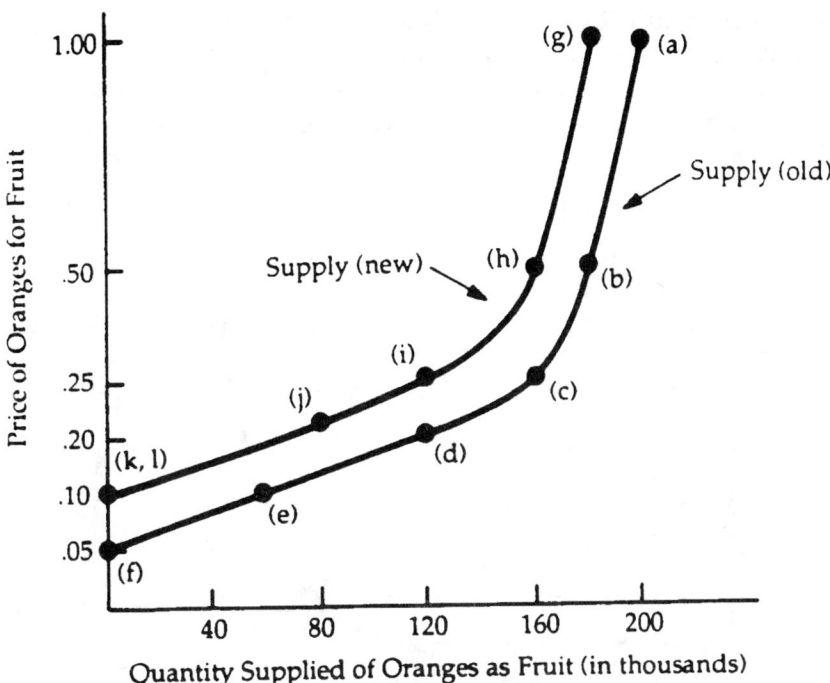

Figure 3.16
Decrease in Firm's Supply

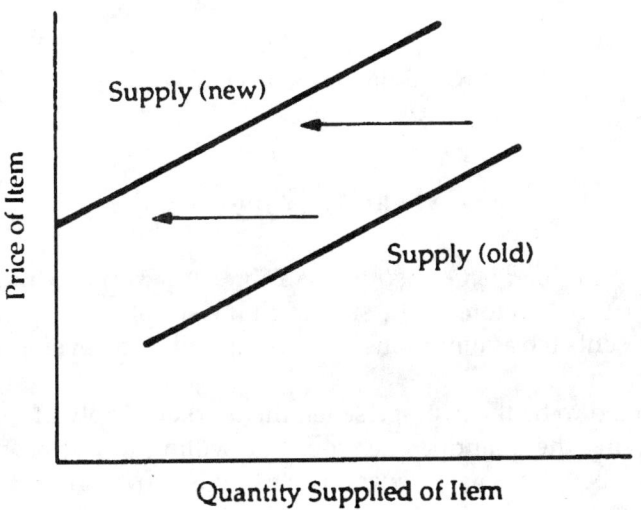

Figure 3.17
Decrease in a Firm's Supply

An increase in a firm's supply means that, at every price, the firm is willing to sell more of the product, and is depicted by the supply curve moving to the right. A decrease in a firm's supply means that, at every price, the firm is not as willing to put as much on the market as before, and is depicted by the supply curve moving to the left. A change in supply, thus, implies a new curve exists. A change in the quantity supplied means there is a movement up or down an existing supply curve, as shown in Figure 3.18.

If the price is 20 cents (.20), Otis is willing to put 120,000 oranges on the market for fruit. The quantity supplied at 20 cents (.20) is 120,000. If the price rises to 25 cents (.25), Otis would be willing to put 160,000 oranges on the market. The quantity supplied would, therefore, increase from 120,000 to 160,000. A change in the quantity supplied of an item is caused by a change in the price of the item. The variables that cause changes in the supply of a product will be covered in a later part in this chapter.

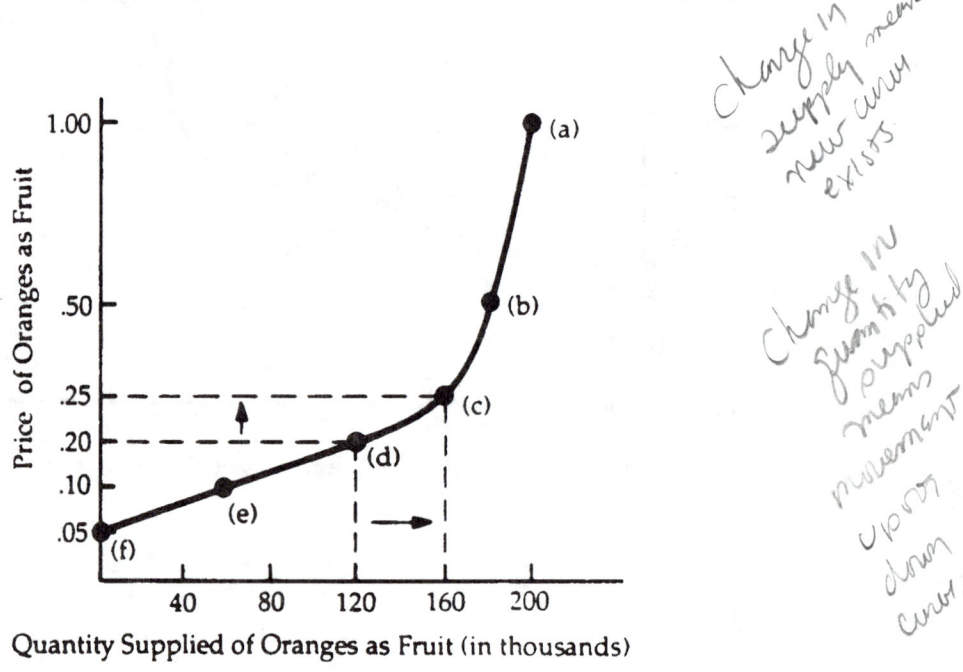

Figure 3.18
Changes in Quantity Supplied

MARKET SUPPLY

The market supply of a product is defined as the sum of the supplies of all firms. The market supply of oranges for fruit, therefore, is the sum of all the supplies of the firms that sell oranges for fruit. Table 3.14 presents the assumptions we make in order to develop an example of market supply.

Since Otis is assumed to be the average seller, the market supply of oranges as fruit will be computed by multiplying the quantities he would be willing to put on the market at various prices by 5,000, the number of orange growers. The result is shown in Table 3.15 and Figure 3.19.

Table 3.14 Market Supply Assumptions

1. There are 5,000 orange growers in the United States who provide oranges to be used as fruit.
2. An orange grower could sell oranges to be used for juice instead of for fruit.
3. There are various possible prices in the market.
4. The market price changes from time to time.
5. The price for oranges as juice is 7 cents (.07).
6. Otis represents a typical or average seller of oranges in the market.

Table 3.15 Market Supply of Oranges

	Market Price	Quantity Supplied (in millions)
(a)	1.00	1,000 (200,000 × 5,000)
(b)	.50	900 (180,000 × 5,000)
(c)	.25	800 (160,000 × 5,000)
(d)	.20	600 (120,000 × 5,000)
(e)	.10	300 (60,000 × 5,000)
(f)	.05	0 (0 × 5,000)

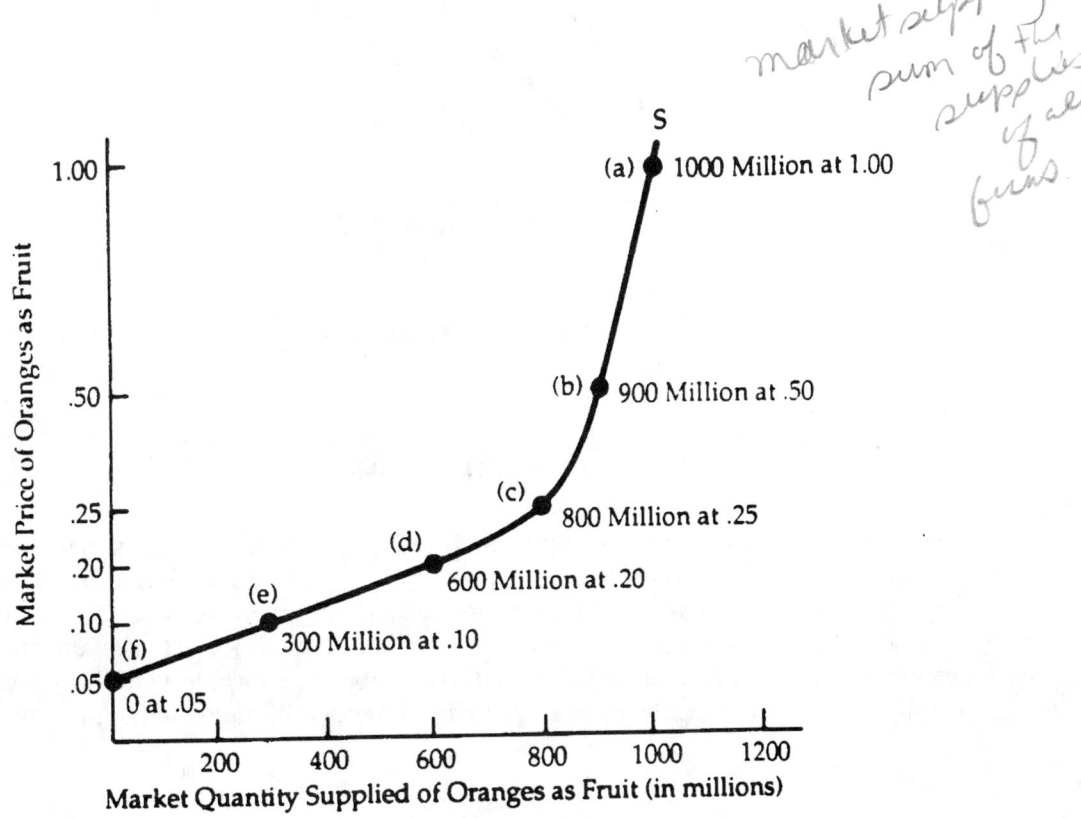

Figure 3.19
Market Supply of Oranges

The same conclusions that were made for a firm's supply apply for market supply.

1. As the price of the product changes, the quantity supplied changes thus, the market quantity supplied of a product is a function of the market price of the item. Supply is defined as the quantities of a good firms are willing to put on the market at various prices.

2. The functional relationship is direct. As the market price rises, the market quantity supplied rises. As the market price falls, the market quantity supplied falls.

3. An increase in market supply should refer to all the firms being willing to sell more oranges for fruit at every price. The market supply curve would move to the right, as shown in Figure 3.20, from Line S to line S_1, representing an increase in supply.

4. A decrease in market supply would refer to all the firms not being willing to sell as many oranges as fruit at every price as before. The market supply curve would move to the left, as shown in Figure 3.20, from line S to line S_2, representing a decrease in supply.

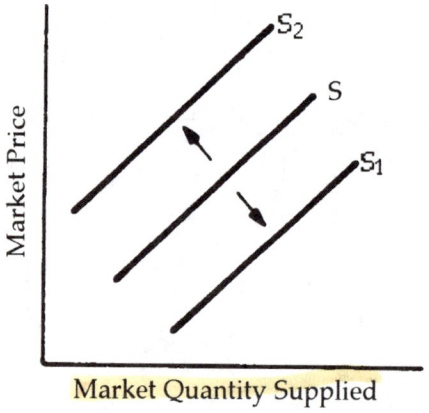

Figure 3.20
Changes in Market Supply

EQUILIBRIUM or market clearing price.

So far, we have stated that, at various prices, different quantities of a good will be put on the market and taken off the market. The next question is what will the market price be and what actual quantity of the item will be put on the market and taken off. This is answered by the concept of equilibrium. Table 3.16 combines the market demand for oranges and the supply of oranges used for fruit. This figure will be used to develop the concept of equilibrium.

We will take each price and indicate what would happen if that were the price of oranges.

Table 3.16 Demand and Supply of Oranges

	Price	Quantity Demanded	Quantity Supplied
(a)	1.00	200	1,000
(b)	.50	400	900
(c)	.25	800	800 ← Equilibrium price
(d)	.20	1,000	600
(e)	.10	1,200	300
(f)	.05	1,400	0

(a) At a price of 1 dollar an orange, the quantity demanded (Q_D) would be 200 million oranges: whereas, the quantity supplied (Q_S) would be 1,000 million oranges a year. The quantity demanded would be less than the quantity supplied. We could write this as:

$$Q_D < Q_S$$

There would be 800 million unsold oranges (1,000 – 200). This is called a surplus of oranges. In order to get rid of the surplus, sellers would reduce the price. The logic of how this would reduce the surplus is indicated in points (b) and (c).

(b) At a price of 50 cents (.50), the quantity demanded is 400 million oranges and the quantity supplied is 900 million. If the price is lowered to this level, the surplus will be reduced from 800 million to 500 million oranges (900–400). There is, however, still a surplus. 500 million oranges are unsold on the market. The price would be lowered still further.

(c) At a price of 25 cents (.25), the quantity demanded is 800 million oranges and the quantity supplied is 800 million. If the price is lowered to this level, the surplus is reduced from 500 million to 0 (800–800). There is no surplus. All the oranges supplied are demanded. The quantity demanded equals the quantity supplied.

$$Q_D = Q_S$$

To summarize, when the quantity demanded is less than the quantity supplied, a surplus exists. A surplus will lead to a reduction in price. The price will drop until there is no more surplus. One dollar (1) and 50 cents (.50) will not be the price of oranges since, at those prices, sellers would reduce the price to reduce the surplus.

(d) At a price of 5 cents (.05), the quantity demanded will be 1,400 million oranges, whereas, there will be no oranges available. The quantity demanded would be greater than the quantity supplied. This can written as:

$$Q_D > Q_S$$

A shortage of oranges would exist. People wanting to buy oranges would make offers of paying more for them, causing the price to rise.

(e) At a price of 10 cents (.10), the quantity demanded would be 1,200 million oranges and the quantity supplied would be 300 million. If the price rises from 5 cents (.05) to 10 cents (.10), the shortage would be reduced from 1,400 to 900 million oranges (1,200 – 300). People wanting oranges would offer more to make sure they get some. As a result, its price would rise.

(f) At a price of 20 cents (.20), the quantity demanded would be 1,000 million oranges and the quantity supplied would be 600 million. A shortage of 400 million oranges (1,000 – 600) would exist. People wanting oranges would bid the price up further.

(g) At a price of 25 cents (.25), the quantity demanded would be 800 million oranges and the quantity supplied would be 800 million. There would be no shortage, and prices would not rise.

To summarize, when the quantity demanded is greater than the quantity supplied, a shortage exists. A shortage will lead to an increase in the price of the item. The price will rise until there is no more shortage. The price will not be 5 cents (.05), 10 cents (.10), or 20 cents (.20) since, at those prices, buyers wanting the product would push the price up. Steps (a) through (g) are summarized in Table 3.17.

Table 3.17 Development of Market Price

Price of Item	Quantity Demanded	Quantity Supplied	Result	Consequence
1.00	200	1,000	Surplus 800	Price ↓
.50	400	900	Surplus 500	Price ↓
.25	800	800	—	Price →
.20	1,000	600	Shortage 400	Price ↑
.10	1,200	300	Shortage 900	Price ↑
.05	1,400	0	Shortage 1,400	Price ↑

At a price of 25 cents (.25), the quantity demanded equals 800 million oranges and the quantity supplied equals 800 million oranges. The quantity demanded equals the quantity supplied. There is no surplus, and there is no shortage. There is no pressure on prices to change. This price (25 cents) will be the market price for oranges. This price is called the equilibrium price. This is the price that balances the quantity demanded and the quantity supplied, as shown in Figure 3.21.

The price of 25 cents (.25) can be described by the following:

1. It is the price which balances the quantity demanded and the quantity supplied.
2. It is the price that clears the market. All items put on the market are purchased.
3. It is the price at which there is no shortage and no surplus.
4. It is the price that will not rise or fall.
5. It is the equilibrium price.
6. It is the actual market price.

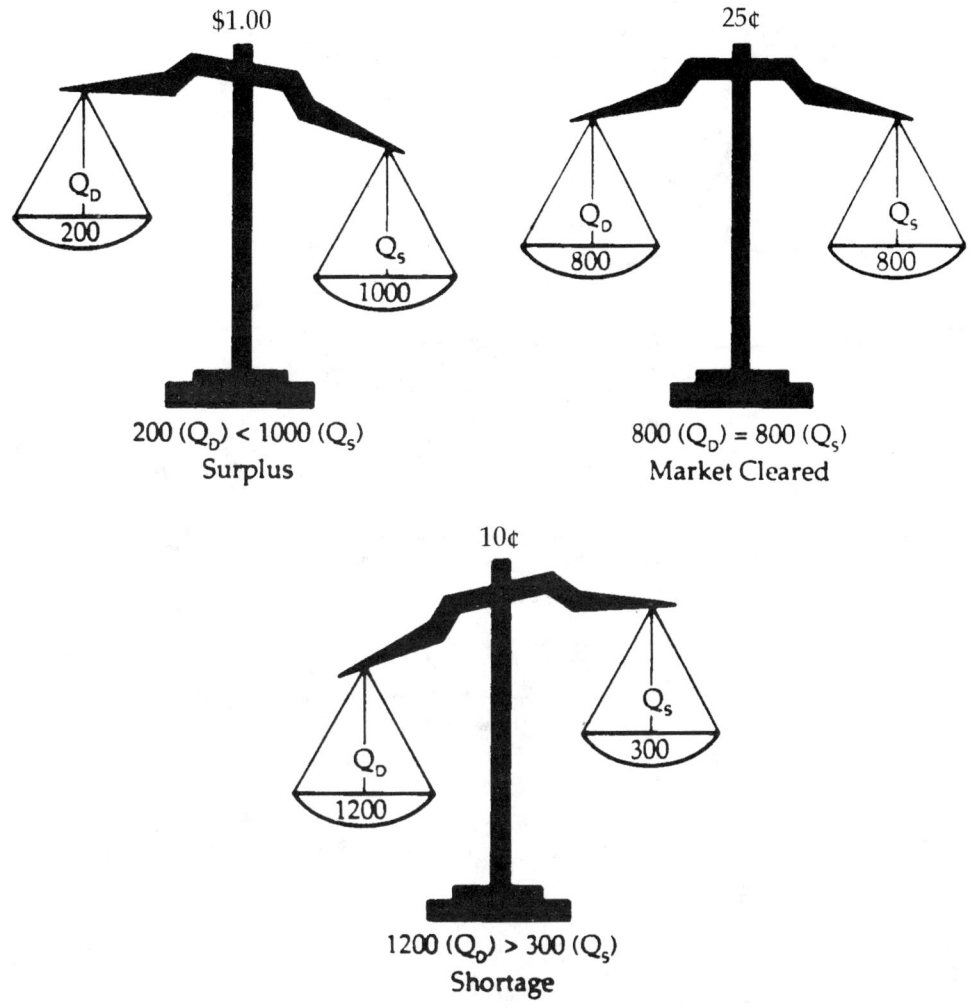

Figure 3.21
Equilibrium—A Balancing Price

There is only one price which will result in the quantity demanded (Q_D) equaling the quantity supplied (Q_S). This is the equilibrium price (P_E). At any higher price (P_H), the quantity demanded (Q_D) will be less than the quantity supplied (Q_S), resulting in a surplus. At any lower price (P_L), the quantity demanded (Q_D) will be greater than the quantity supplied (Q_S), resulting in a shortage. The equilibrium price occurs at the intersection of the demand and supply curves.

Figure 3.22 shows how this information would be presented graphically.

78   Principles of Microeconomics

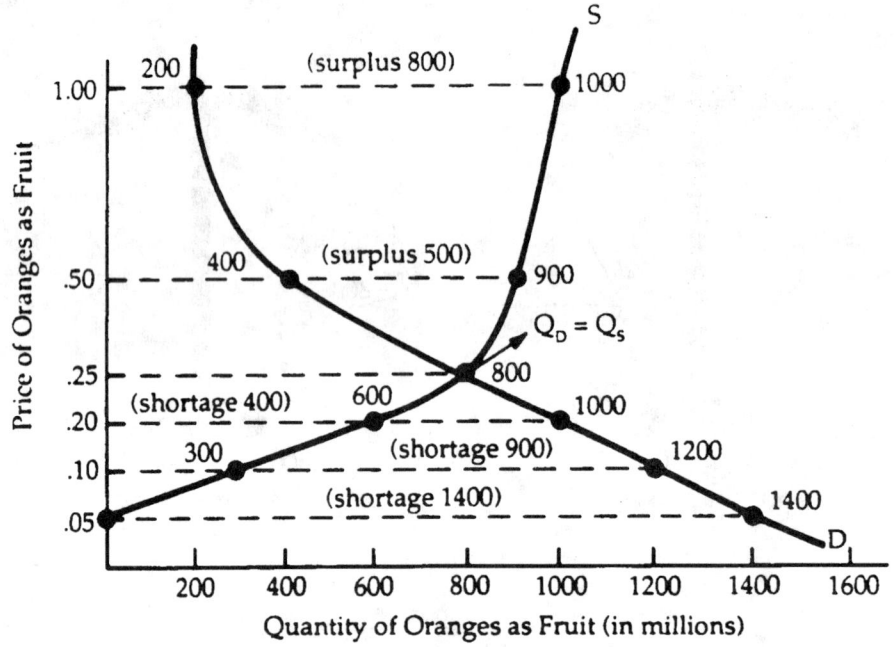

Figure 3.22
Equilibrium

Figure 3.23 presents the graphical presentation in a generalized form.

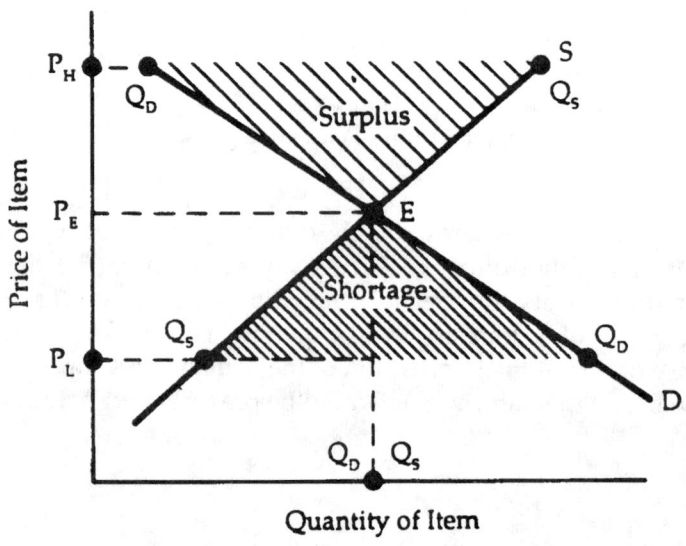

Figure 3.23
Equilibrium

CHANGES IN THE MARKET PRICE

The market price of oranges does change from time to time. This next section will present an analysis of a price change and of the factors that can cause such a change. We will start by considering four different possible cases.

1. **An Increase in Demand with No Change in Supply.** An increase in demand has been defined as the market being willing to buy more of a product than before at various possible prices. Graphically, it is shown by a movement to the right of the demand curve. Figure 3.24 presents such a situation, in generalized form.

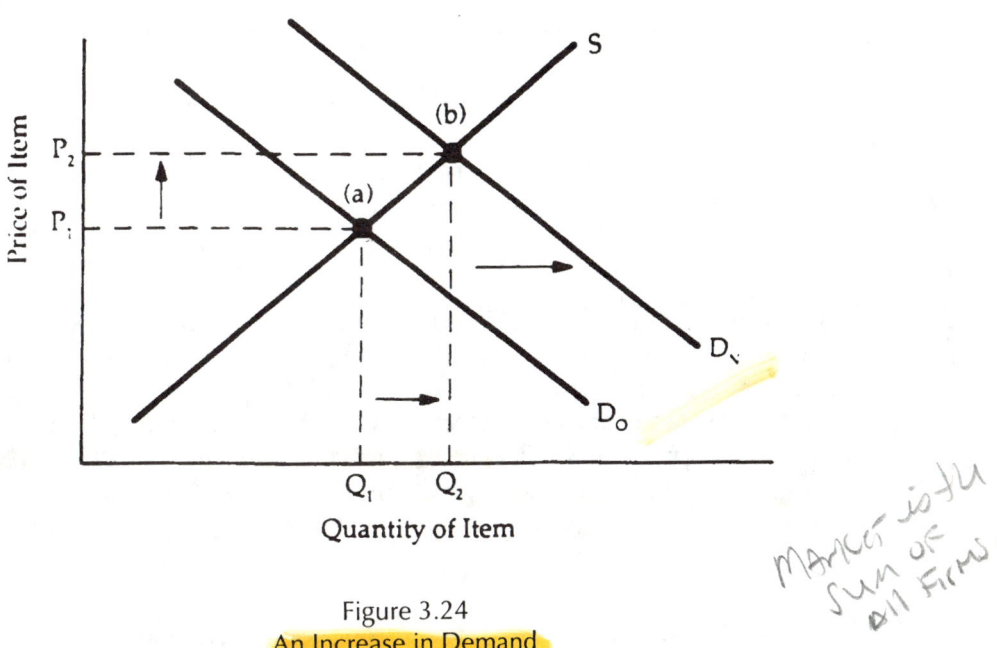

Figure 3.24
An Increase in Demand

An increase in demand is shown by a movement of the demand curve from D_O to D_N. The supply has not changed, thus, there is only one supply curve. Before the increase in the market, price is P_1, and the quantity demanded and supplied is Q_1. After the increase in demand, the market price is P_2, at the intersection of D_N and S, at point (b). The quantity demanded and supplied is Q_2. The consequence of an increase in demand has been an increase in the market price, the equilibrium price, from P_1 to P_2, and an increase in the market quantity demanded and supplied, from Q_1 to Q_2. This can be summarized as:

$$D\uparrow \ S \ P\uparrow \ Q_D\uparrow \ Q_S\uparrow$$

2. **A Decrease in Demand with No Change in Supply.** A decrease in demand has been defined as the market not being willing to buy as much of a product, at various prices, as before. Graphically, it is shown by a movement to the left of the demand curve. Figure 3.25 presents such a situation.

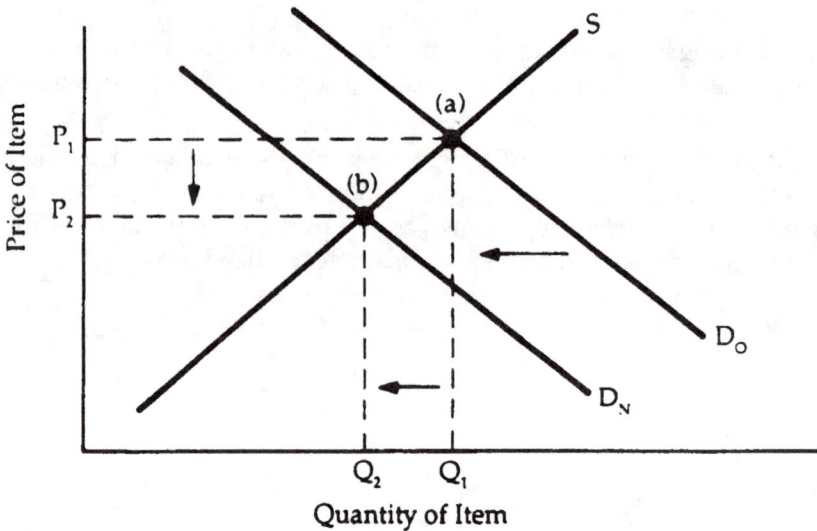

Figure 3.25
Decrease in Demand

A decrease in demand is shown by a movement of the demand curve from D_O to D_N. Again, the supply has not changed. Before the decrease in demand, the market price is P_1, and the quantity demanded and supplied is Q_1. After the decrease in demand the market price is P_2 at the intersection of D_N and S, at point (b). The quantity demanded and supplied is Q_2. The consequence of a decrease in demand has been a decrease in the market price, the equilibrium price, from P_1 to P_2, and a decrease in the market quantity demanded and supplied, from Q_1 to Q_2. This can be summarized as:

$$D\downarrow S P\downarrow Q_D\downarrow Q_S\downarrow$$

Table 3.18 summarizes the consequences of a change in demand.

Table 3.18 Changes in Demand

D ↑	S	P ↑	Q_D ↑	Q_S ↑
D ↓	S	P ↓	Q_D ↓	Q_S ↓

When the demand for a product increases and the supply does not change, shortages are created. The price rises. The quantity supplied increases due to the higher price. When the demand for a product decreases and the supply does not change, surpluses are created. The price falls. The quantity supplied falls due to the lower price.

3. **An Increase in Supply with No Change in Demand.** An increase in supply has been defined as sellers being willing to put more on the market, at various prices, than before. Graphically, it is shown by a movement to the right of the supply curve. Figure 3.26 presents this situation.

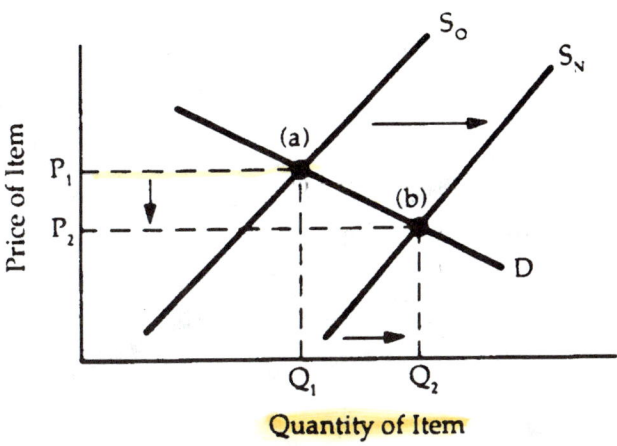

Figure 3.26
An Increase in Supply

An increase in supply is shown by a movement of the supply curve from S_O to S_N. The demand has not changed. Thus, there is only one demand curve. Before the increase in supply, the price is P_1 and the quantities supplied and demanded are Q_1. After the increase in supply, the market price is P_2, at the intersection of S_N and D, at point (b). The quantities demanded and supplied change from Q_1 to Q_2. The consequence of an increase in supply is a decrease in the price of the item and an increase in the quantity demanded and supplied. This can be summarized as:

$$S\uparrow \; D \; P\downarrow \; Q_D\uparrow \; Q_S\uparrow$$

4. **A decrease in supply with no change in demand.** A decrease in supply is defined as sellers putting less on the market, at various prices, than before. Graphically, it is shown by a movement to the left of the supply curve. Figure 3.27 presents this situation.

A decrease in supply is shown by a movement of the supply curve from S_O to S_N. The demand has not changed. Before the decrease in supply, the market price was P_1, and the quantities demanded and supplied were Q_1. After the decrease in supply, the price is P_2, at the intersection of S_N and D, at point (b). The quantities supplied and demanded are Q_2. The consequence of a decrease in supply has been an increase in the market price, the equilibrium price from P_1 to P_2, and a decrease in the quantities supplied and demanded from Q_1 to Q_2. This can be summarized as:

$$S\downarrow \; D \; P\uparrow \; Q_D\downarrow \; Q_S\downarrow$$

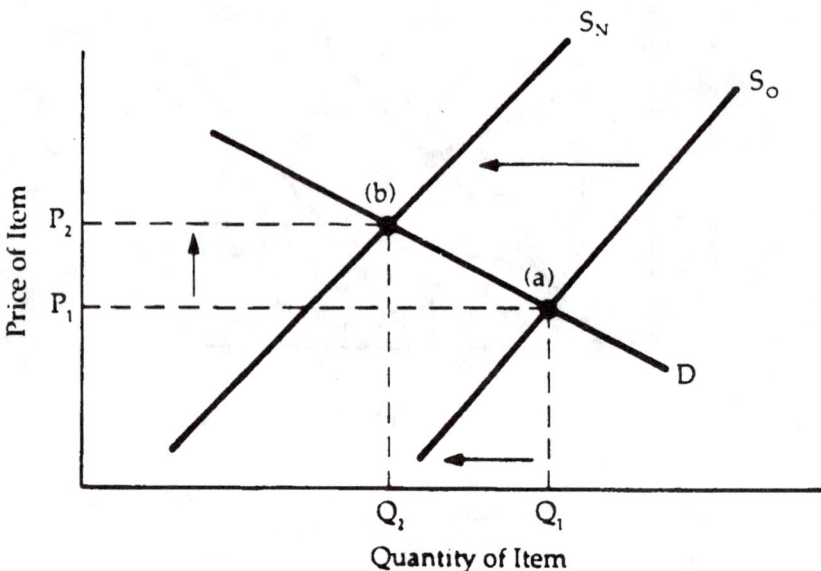

Figure 3.27
Decrease in Supply

Table 3.19 summarizes the consequences of a change in supply.

Table 3.19 Changes in Supply

S ↑	D	P ↓	Q_D ↑	Q_S ↑
S ↓	D	P ↑	Q_D ↓	Q_S ↓

When the supply of a product increases and the demand does not change, a surplus is created. The price falls. The quantity demanded will increase due to a lower price. When the supply of a product decreases and the demand does not change, a shortage is created. The price rises. The quantity demanded decreases due to the higher price.

The analysis is more complicated when both supply and demand change. Table 3.20 presents some possible cases and the result on price. The length of the arrow indicates the amount of change.

Table 3.20 Changes In Demand and Supply

(a)	D ↑	S ↑	P	Price Remains Same
(b)	D ↑	S ↑	P ↑	Price Rises Some
(c)	D ↑	S ↑	P ↓	Price Drops Some
(d)	D ↓	S ↑	P ↓	Price Drops A Lot
(e)	D ↑	S ↓	P ↑	Price Soars

In case (a), the increase in demand is matched by an equal increase in supply. The price will remain the same.

In case (b), an increase in demand is matched by a smaller increase in supply. The result is an increase in price. The increase in price is less than it would be, however, if supply did not increase.

In case (c), an increase in demand is matched by a larger increase in supply. As a result, the price will drop but not by as much if there had been no increase in demand.

In case (d), the demand drops and the supply increases. Both of these result in a large surplus, and the price drops a lot.

In case (e), the demand increases and the supply decreases. A very large shortage results, and the price soars.

There are other possibilities, and we encourage the student to devise some and figure out the results.

CAUSES OF CHANGES IN SUPPLY AND DEMAND

Changes in demand and/or supply can result in the equilibrium price of the product changing. The following tables summarize the variables which can cause changes in demand or supply.

Table 3.21 **Causes of Changes in Demand**

1. Changes in individuals' incomes.
2. Changes in tastes.
3. Changes in fads and styles.
4. Changes in prices. [of related items]
5. Changes in expectations.
6. Changes in institutions.
7. Changes in populations.

[VIOLATION OF C.P.]

Table 3.22 **Causes of Changes in Supply**

1. Changes in cost of production.
2. Changes in technology.
3. Changes in alternatives.
4. Changes in expectations.
5. Changes in institutions.
6. Changes in number of firms.

There are many factors that can cause a change in demand. As incomes change, people buy different amounts and different types of goods. Fads and styles change constantly. An increase in the price of bread can cause people to buy less bread and also less margarine. An individual's expectations regarding his future may change causing changes in demand. Congress may pass laws banning smoking in offices, leading many people to give up cigarettes. Each year there are more individuals.

Changes in supply could be the result of firms having lower costs and, thus, being willing to provide more items at lower prices. The lower costs could be due to better technology. An increase in the demand for low calorie beer may lead a brewery to produce less beer. Expectations regarding tax changes, regulations, and demand may lead a firm to change its supply. Laws banning smoking may lead cigarette companies to produce something else, like a soft drink. Each year, there are more firms or less firms in an industry, causing changes in market supply.

Quantity Demanded and Demand

A major source of confusion among students of principles of economics is the distinction between quantity demanded and demand. It is important that the student understand the difference between these two concepts.

Quantity demanded refers to the amount of a particular good that buyers are able and willing to buy at one specific point of time and at one given price. An example would be that Susan would be able and willing to buy two oranges if the price is a dollar and four oranges if the price is fifty cents. A different quantity demanded exists for every possible price of the good.

Demand refers to entire schedule of prices and the quantities demanded at those prices. It is a list of all the possible prices for the good and the quantities that buyers are able and willing to buy at those prices.

A change in the quantity demanded means that if the price changes from one dollar to fifty cents, Susan will be able and willing to buy a different quantity of oranges. A change in the quantity demanded is the result of a change in the price of the good. A change in demand means that the buyer is willing and able to buy a different quantity at every possible price. A change in demand is the result of a change in a variable other than the price of the good. An example would be a change in the income of the buyer.

On the graph a change in the quantity demanded refers to a movement from one point on the demand curve to another point on the same curve. A change in demand refers to a movement of the entire demand curve either to the right or to the left.

Quantity Supplied and Supply

Similar confusion also exists over the distinction between quantity supplied and supply. Quantity supplied refers to the amount of a good that sellers are able and willing to offer for sale at a point in time at a particular price. Otis is able and willing to offer for sale 200,000 oranges if the price is a dollar and is able and willing to offer for sale 180,000 oranges if the price is fifty cents. A different quantity supplied exists for each possible price of the good.

Supply refers to the entire schedule of possible prices and the quantities supplied at those prices. It is a list of all the possible prices for the good and the quantities that sellers are able and willing to offer for sale at those prices.

A change in the quantity supplied means that if the price changes from one dollar to fifty cents, Otis will be able and willing to offer a different quantity of oranges for sale. A change in the quantity supplied is the result of a change in the price of the good. A change in supply means that the seller is able and willing to offer for sale a different quantity for sale at each possible price. A change in supply is the result of a change in a variable other than the price of the good. An example would be a change in the cost of producing the good.

On the graph a change in the quantity supplied refers to a movement from one point on the supply curve to another point on the same curve. A change in supply refers to a movement of the entire Supply curve either to the right or to the left.

Changes in price cause movements up and down the existing demand and supply curves.

Price changes do not cause the demand and supply curves to move to a new location since each curve already contains one unique quantity demanded and one unique quantity supplied for each possible price.

PRICE CONTROLS

Without any intervention, the market will establish itself at a level of equilibrium, as shown in Figure 3.28. At this level, the market is cleared since the quantity supplied equals the quantity demanded.

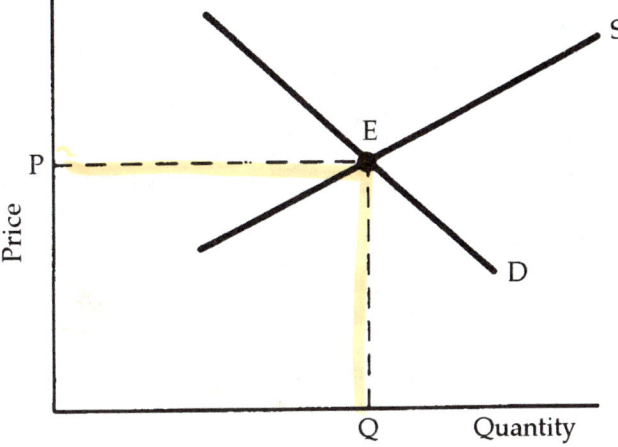

Figure 3.28
Equilibrium

There may be instances when it is decided that the equilibrium price is not the best price for society. We will analyze three different cases: (1) a price floor or a price minimum, (2) a price ceiling or a price maximum, and (3) a price freeze.

Price Floor

With a price floor, the price is set above the equilibrium price. The government may decide that the equilibrium price is not high enough and is causing social problems. Examples would be agricultural prices and wages.

Figure 3.29 presents the results of a price floor in which the price is raised above equilibrium and not allowed to drop. Since the price cannot drop, it would be considered a minimum price.

A consequence of establishing a price floor is that a surplus of the good is created. This occurs because at the higher price, the quantity demanded is less than the quantity supplied. Two instances in which the government has established price floors are minimum wages and agricultural prices.

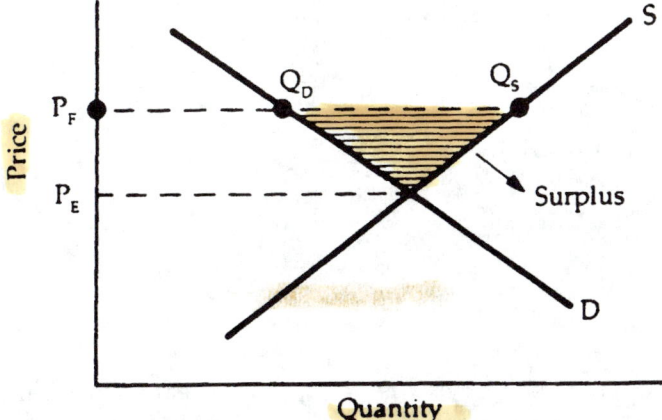

Figure 3.29
Price Floor

Minimum Wages

Minimum wages will be discussed further in later chapters. Here, the situation can be described, as in Figure 3.30.

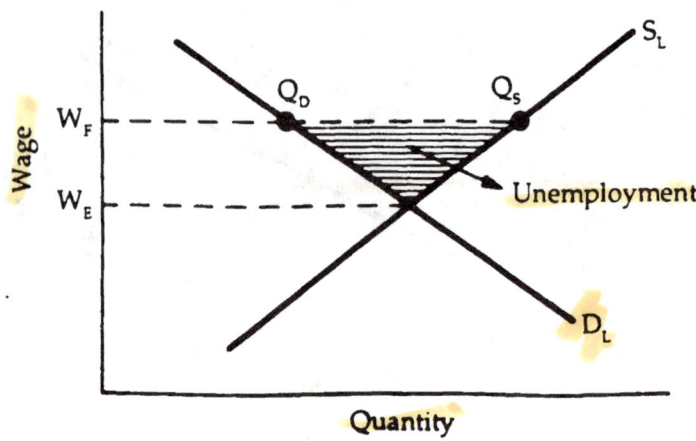

Figure 3.30
Minimum Wage

The demand for labor is an inverse function in that at higher wages, the demand for labor is low and at lower wages, the demand for labor is high. Thus, the demand for labor curve (D_L) slopes downward. The supply of labor is a direct function in that at higher wages, more people want to work and at lower wages, less people want to work. Thus, the supply of labor curve (S_L) slopes upward. The two curves intersect at W_E, which is the equilibrium wage. The government may decide to raise the wage to improve the incomes of workers to W_F. By law, this wage cannot be lower. Thus, it is a minimum. The result, however, is a surplus of labor due to the quantity supplied of labor exceeding the quantity demanded of labor. This means unemployment results.

Agricultural Prices

The American farmer, through technology and science, is a producer of large amounts of food products and other products. This has, however, not been to the farmer's advantage. When there is a large supply and not as much demand, the price drops. This has been the case with American farmers; large supplies, low demand, low prices. Low prices result in low incomes.

In order to offset this, the government has enacted price supports to raise the price of agricultural products. Essentially, how this works is as follows.

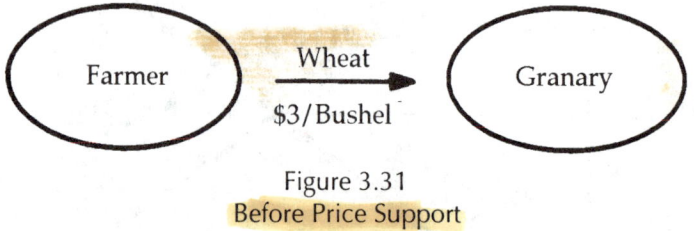

Figure 3.31
Before Price Support

Before the price support, the farmer was selling his wheat to the granary for 3 dollars per bushel. The government decides this price is too low, and the farmer may go bankrupt. The price is raised to 5 dollars. This is accomplished by the government being prepared to buy and sell all the wheat at 5 dollars.

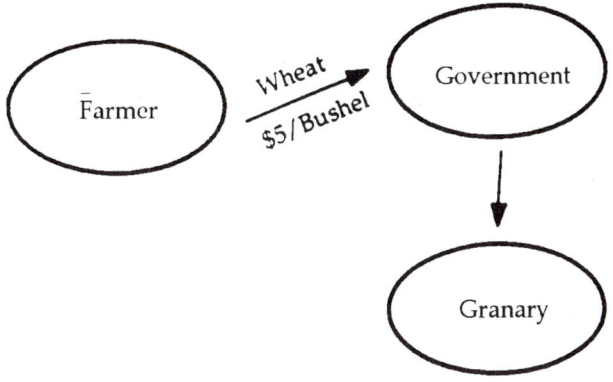

Figure 3.32
After Price Support

The farmer will now sell wheat to the government for 5 dollars per bushel. If the granary wishes to buy wheat, they have two choices: (a) buy from the government for 5 dollars, or (b) buy directly from the farmer for 5 dollars, as shown in Figure 3.32.

Since the price of wheat is above equilibrium, the quantity supplied by the farmers will increase, but the quantity demanded by the granary will decrease. The government will have a surplus of wheat to store.

Price Ceiling

A price ceiling is a price set below the equilibrium price and not allowed to rise. As such, it is a maximum price, as shown in Figure 3.33.

The price is set at P_C. The result is that the quantity demanded exceeds the quantity supplied, and a shortage is created.

This type of pricing could be used in wartime to restrict production of goods for consumers to insure enough goods are available for the war effort. An example would be price ceilings on gasoline for car consumption. Less gasoline would be produced for the consumer and more could be produced for the army.

A shortage is created which could cause a problem with consumer dissatisfaction. To counter this, the government could see that each consumer gets a share of the available gasoline. This is called rationing.

Price ceilings can cause secondary markets to develop, called black markets. In a black market people purchase goods at the legal price and resell at a new, illegal, higher price.

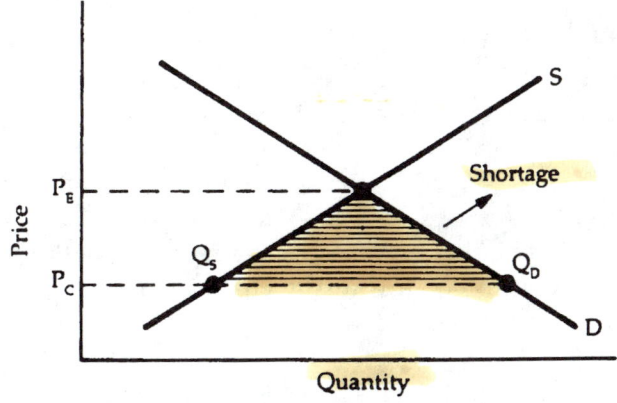

Figure 3.33
Price Ceiling

Price Freeze

In order to halt inflation the government has, in the past, imposed wage and price freezes. In this case, wages and prices are not set above or below equilibrium but, rather, are not allowed to increase from the existing level.

Take-A-Note

1. Price Floors and Price Ceilings

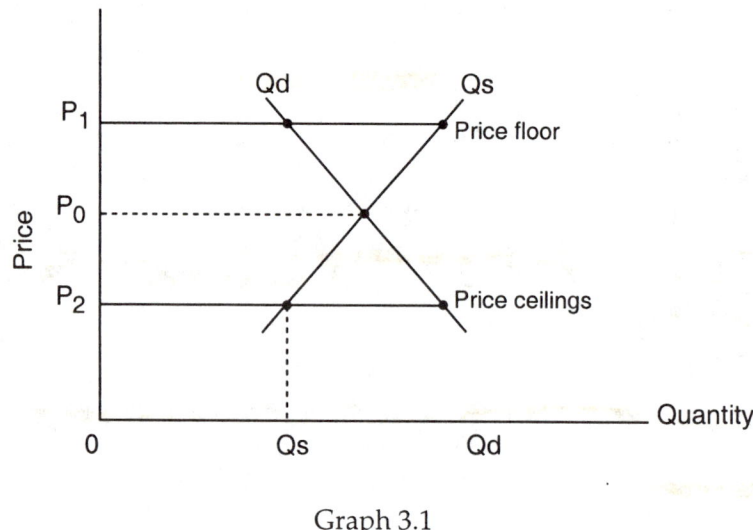

Graph 3.1

Equilibrium price at P_0 (there is neither a shortage nor a surplus of the good).

Price floors and price ceilings: legal prices set by government create disequilibrium in a product market because the legal price differs from the equilibrium market price.

A price floor (i.e., price support) is *minimum* price below which firms cannot legally sell a given product; price floor creates a surplus (Qs > Qd).

A price ceiling is a *maximum* price, above which firms cannot legally sell a given product, price ceilings create shortages (Qd > Qs).

2. The Law of Demand

Qd = f(P) ceteris paribus, a demand curve is downward sloping. Buyers are willing and able to buy at alternative prices during a given time period; buyers are willing to acquire more of a product at a lower price. Q & P are inversely related.

3. The Law of Supply

Qs = f(P) ceteris paribus, a market supply curve slopes upward. Producers can and will offer more of a product at a higher price. Qs & P are directly related.

4. Changes in Demand and Supply

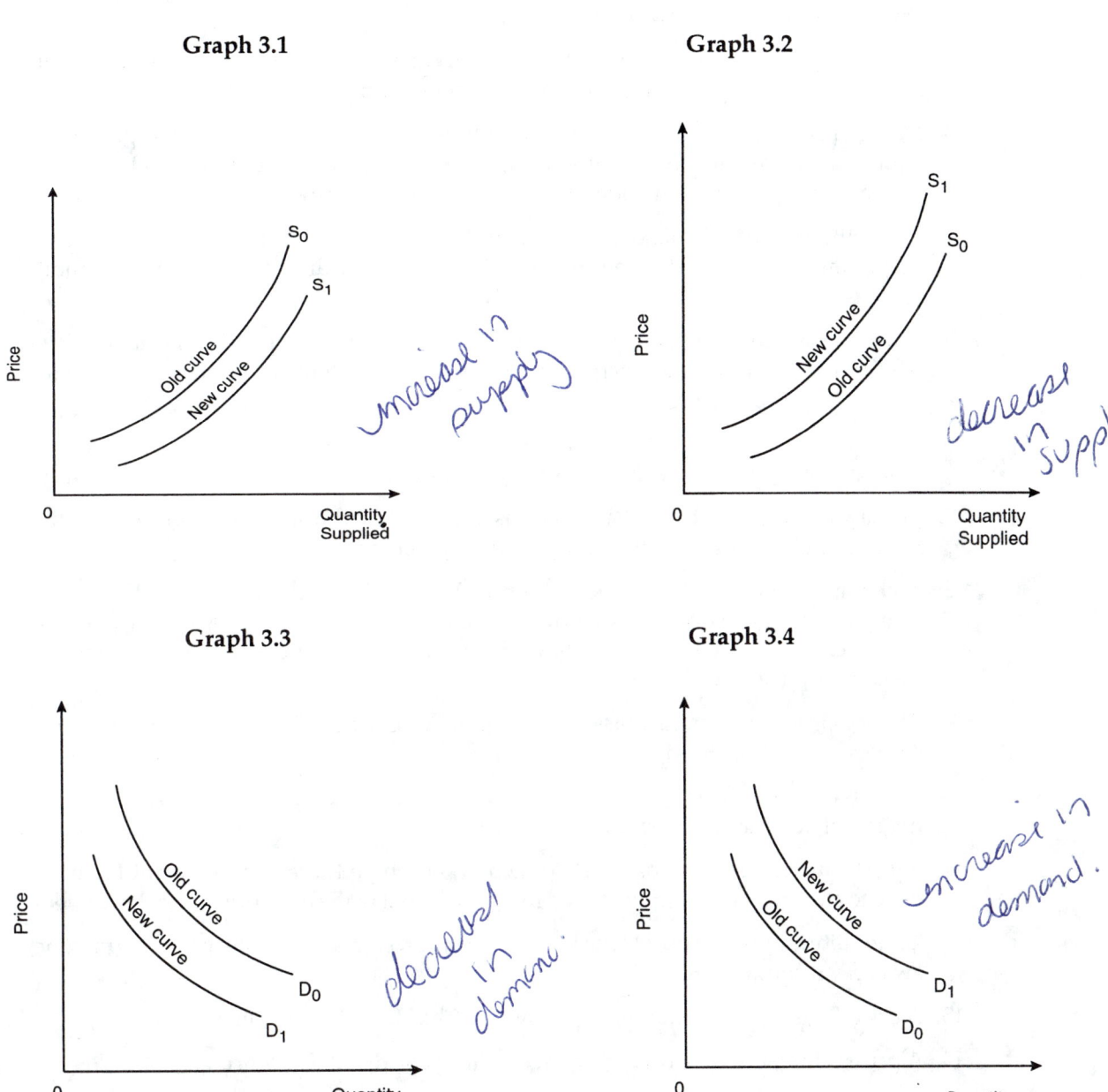

In graph 3.2, a decrease in supply, curve shifts to the left.
In graph 3.1, an increase in supply, curve shifts to the right.
In graph 3.4, an increase in demand, curve shifts to the right.
In graph 3.3, a decrease in demand, curve shifts to the left.

CHAPTER SUMMARY

1. The market is an area or context where the economic activities of the buyers and sellers are affected by the laws of demand and supply.

2. The concept of the ideal market is that the market must be large enough so that no one individual or group can influence the market (such as a monopoly).

3. Demand is a relationship between quantity of a good or service and the price consumers are willing to pay, ceteris paribus. The demand schedule shows a relationship between the quantity demanded for products and their prices.

4. When the quantity demanded is less than the quantity supplied, a surplus exists. A surplus will lead to reduction in price. The price will drop until there is no more surplus.

5. When the quantity demanded is greater than the quantity supplied, a shortage exists. A shortage will lead to an increase in the price of the item. The price will rise until there is no more shortage.

6. Changes in demand can be caused by changes in incomes, tastes, styles, prices of other goods, expectations, institutions, and populations.

7. The law of supply states that as prices rise, more of a product will be supplied by the firm. A firm's supply graph is an upward rising curve.

8. A change in the supply means the entire curve shifts to the right or to the left. A change in quantity supplied is a movement along the curve from one point to another. An increase in a firm's supply is shown by a shift in the curve to the right. A decrease is shown by a shift to the left.

9. Changes in supply can be caused by changes in cost of production, technology, alternatives, institutions, and numbers of firms.

10. There is only one price which will result in the quantity demanded equaling the quantity supplied. This is the equilibrium price.

11. Equilibrium is a state of balance in the market where there is no inherent force for price to change, and quantity offered for sale is equal to the quantity that is demanded.

12. Disequilibrium is any point where the market forces will cause the price to gravitate away from equilibrium.

13. A price floor is a minimum price set by law. The result is a surplus.

14. A price ceiling is a maximum price set by law. The result is a shortage.

15. Minimum wage laws are examples of price floors.

CHAPTER 3
KEY CONCEPTS

Black Market—People purchase a good at a price regulated by a price ceiling and resell it at a higher price.

Ceteris Paribus—A Latin phrase meaning other things being equal, which in economics means only certain independent variables are included in explaining changes in dependent variables. The phrase translates "all else equal."

Decrease in Demand—At every price buyers take less off the market.

Decrease in Supply—At every price firms are not as willing to put as much of a good on the market as before.

Economic Market—An area or context where the economic activities of buyers and sellers are affected by the laws of supply and demand.

Firm's Supply—The quantities of a good a firm would be willing to put on the market at various prices.

Ideal Market—A market in which no individual or group can influence price or quantity.

Increase in Demand—At every price buyers are willing to take more of the market.

Increase in Supply—At every price firms are willing to put more of a good on the market.

Individual Demand—The quantities of a good that an individual is willing to buy at various possible prices.

Market Clearing Price—The price at which the quantity supplied of a good equals the quantity demanded of the good so that all of it is sold—the market is cleared of the good.

Market Demand—The sum of all the individual demands—the quantities of a good that all individuals are willing to buy at various prices.

Market Equilibrium—The price at which the quantity demanded equals the quantity supplied.

Market Supply—The sum of the supplies of all firms—the quantities of a good that all firms are willing to put on the market at various prices.

Minimum Wage—The lowest wage employers may pay an individual.

Perfectly Elastic—There is no percentage change in price—there is only one price available to buyers.

Perfectly Inelastic—There is no percentage change in quantity demanded—there is only one quantity demanded.

Price Ceiling (Maximum)—The government sets the price of a good below the equilibrium price.

Price Control—The government fixes price usually above or below the equilibrium price.

Price Elasticity of Demand—A measure of the responsiveness of quantity demanded when price changes.

Price Floor (Minimum)—The government sets the price of a good above the equilibrium price.

Price Supports—The government sets the price of goods above the equilibrium price.

Pure Competition—An industry in which there is a very large number of firms all producing the same product with prices being determined in the market by supply and demand.

Quantity Demanded—The amount buyers will take off the market at a price.

Quantity Supplied—The amount of a good firms will put on the market at a price.

Shortage—A situation when the supply of a good is less than the demand for the good.

Slope—The rate of change in a function computed by change in Y divided by change in X.

Surplus—A situation when the supply of a good exceeds the demand for the good.

DISCUSSION QUESTIONS

1. It has been said that almost all questions in economics relate back to supply and demand. Based on the concepts of supply and demand that you have learned in this chapter discuss this statement.

2. Demand is called an inverse relationship. Explain what this means and why it is so.

3. What are some factors that will cause demand to either increase or decrease?

4. Supply is called a direct relationship. Explain what this means and why it is so.

5. What are some factors that could cause supply to either increase or decrease?

6. Explain how the equilibrium price is also called the market clearing price.

7. Equilibrium price has been defined as the price that balances supply and demand. Explain this in terms of surpluses and shortages.

8. Describe a market situation which will result in a price increase and one that will result in a price decrease.

9. Present an argument for the minimum wage and present an argument against it.

10. The United States supports the prices of some agricultural goods by price supports. Explain how the government could raise prices by altering the supply of or the demand for agricultural goods instead of by supports which cost tax money.

3.1 Learning Practice

(a) Given: Demand and Supply Schedule

P	Qd	Qs
1.00	200	1400
.50	400	1200
.25	600	1000
.20	800	800
.10	1000	400
.05	1200	200

(1) Construct the demand and supply curves.

(2) Determine the equilibrium price and quantity.

(3) Using the above table, explain the relationship between price and the quantity demanded.

(4) Using the above table, explain the relationship between price and the quantity supplied.

(b) Given: Surplus and Shortage

P	Qd	Qs
$1	30	0
2	24	3
3	18	5
4	12	12
5	6	15
6	5	18
7	2	20
8	0	21

(1) Determine the equilibrium price.

(2) Determine the equilibrium quantity.

(3) At the following prices, will there be a surplus or a shortage:

    a. $3
    b. $4
    c. $5
    d. $6

(4) At the following prices, will the price remain there, increase, or decrease:

    a. $2
    b. $4
    c. $6

Solutions

(a)

   (1)

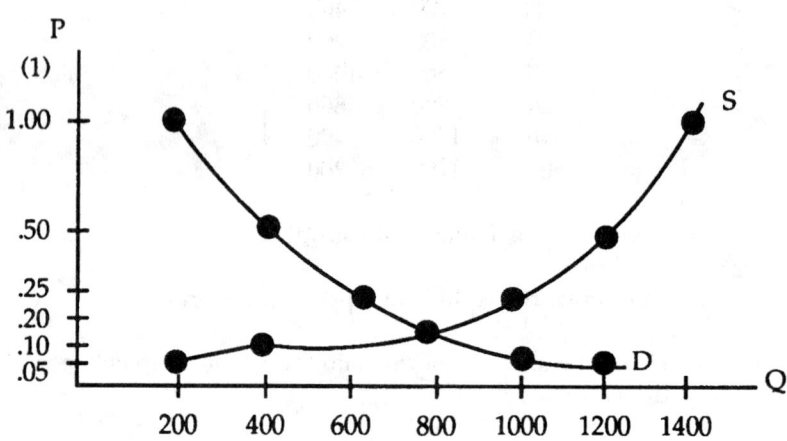

   (2)   price = .20
           quantity = 800
   (3)   inverse
   (4)   direct

(b)

   (1)   price = $4
   (2)   quantity = 12
   (3)   (a)   shortage
          (b)   no shortage, no surplus
          (c)   surplus
          (d)   surplus
   (4)   (a)   increase
          (b)   remain
          (c)   decrease

3.2 Learning Practice

Indicate the effects on the equilibrium price and quantity.

a. Change in Supply

Changes	No Change in Demand	The effects on the equilibrium price	The effects on the equilibrium quantity
Supply Increases			
Supply Decreases			

b. Change in Demand

Changes	No Change in Supply	The effects on the equilibrium price	The effects on the equilibrium quantity
Demand Increases			
Demand Decreases			

CHAPTER 4

Elasticity

LEARNING OBJECTIVES

After reading this chapter, you should be able to:
1. Define elasticity of demand, income elasticity, cross elasticity and elasticity of supply.
2. Distinguish among the types of elasticity of demand and supply: relatively elastic, relatively inelastic, perfectly elastic, perfectly inelastic and unitary elastic.
3. Compute the coefficient of elasticity of demand and explain the result.
4. Compute the coefficient of elasticity of supply and explain the result.
5. Compute the coefficient of income elasticity and explain the result.
6. Distinguish among normal, inferior and neutral goods.
7. Compute the coefficient of cross elasticity and explain the result.
8. Distinguish among complement, substitute and independent goods.
9. Distinguish between slope and elasticity.
10. Describe the graphs of demand and supply with different elasticities.

ELASTICITY

In the market, the price of goods and the quantities that will be demanded and supplied are determined by the concepts of demand and supply. The demand relationship states that the quantity demanded is a function of the price. The supply relationship states that the quantity supplied is also a function of the price of the goods. The demand for different kinds of goods could have different kinds of functional relationships. For example, the way the price of chicken and the quantity demanded of chicken are related is different from the way that the price of cigarettes and the quantity demanded of cigarettes are related.

Chapter 4 deals with a measurement tool that can describe these different functional relationships. The measurement is called elasticity. It can be used to measure the relationship between price and quantity demanded, income and quantity demanded, the price of one good and the quantity demanded of another good, and the price and quantity supplied.

PRICE ELASTICITY OF DEMAND

Elasticity is a way of measuring the responsiveness of one variable to a change in another variable. Price elasticity of demand is the absolute value of the percentage change in quantity demanded due to a percentage change in price.

A proposal has come before a state legislature to increase the tax on a pack of cigarettes by 5 cents (.05) in order to raise revenue to support a drug-prevention program in the public schools. Legislator Willis argues that by raising the tax, additional revenue will be raised. Legislator Brown, however, argues that by raising the tax, the price of cigarettes will rise to the consumer. Since the price is higher, consumers will buy less cigarettes and revenue will not increase. It may actually drop. The main concern, here, to the legislature, is whether revenue will increase because of the higher tax, or whether revenue will decrease because the higher price reduces sales of cigarettes.

The revenue for a chain of video stores has been sluggish for about six weeks. The managers of the stores, at a monthly meeting, are trying to find a way to increase the revenue to increase the return on their investment. The manager from Store No. 6 argues that the best way to increase revenue would be to reduce the rental charge for a videocassette. The lower charge, he argues, will generate more rentals and, thus, revenue will increase. The manager from Store No. 8 counters by saying rentals are already lower than any competitor, and the plan to lower the rental charge will simply result in lost revenue. He argues for allowing the customer to have the cassette for an additional day. The concern, here, to the managers, is whether reducing the price below its already low level will increase revenue or whether some other gimmick might be more appropriate.

In order to resolve the above questions, the legislators and managers should determine the price elasticity of demand for cigarettes and for videocassettes. Price elasticity is defined as a mathematical measure of how consumers respond when there is a change in the price of an item. It is determined by the use of the following formula:

$$E_p = \frac{\text{percentage change in quantity demanded}}{\text{percentage change in price}}$$

E_p represents elasticity. Since this is what we are trying to determine, it is placed to the left of the equal sign (=). How price elasticity is to be determined is placed to the right of the equal sign (=). Price elasticity is determined in three (3) steps:

1. The percentage change in quantity demanded is measured. In order to determine this percentage, the following formula is used:

$$\frac{Q_2-Q_1}{(Q_2+Q_1)/2}$$

Q_2 represents the quantity demanded after the price change.
Q_1 represents the quantity demanded before the price change.
Q_2-Q_1 represents the amount change in quantity demanded.
$(Q_2+Q_1)/2$ represents the average quantity.

$\dfrac{Q_2-Q_1}{(Q_2+Q_1)/2}$ represents the percentage change in quantity demanded.

2. The percentage change in the price of the item is determined. In order to determine this percentage, the following formula is used:

$$\frac{P_2-P_1}{(P_2+P_1)/2}$$

P_2 represents the new price.
P_1 represents the previous price.
P_2-P_1 represents the amount change in the price of the item.
$(P_2+P_1)/2$ represents the average price.

$\dfrac{P_2-P_1}{(P_2+P_1)/2}$ represents the percentage change in price.

3. The result from step 1 is divided by the result from step 2. The definitional formula from price elasticity, thus becomes:

$$E_P = \frac{\dfrac{Q_2-Q_1}{(Q_2+Q_1)/2}}{\dfrac{P_2-P_1}{(P_2+P_1)/2}}$$

Another way to express the formula would be to represent percentage change in quantity demanded by %Δ in Q_D, where the symbol % is used for percentage, the symbol Δ is used for change, and the symbol Q_D is used for quantity demanded. Percentage change in price would be represented by %Δ in P. P is used for price. The formula becomes:

$$E_P = \frac{\%\Delta \text{ in } Q_D}{\%\Delta \text{ in } P}$$

All price elasticity coefficients are negative and are preceded by a minus sign. Economists usually omit the minus sign. They use the absolute value.

Types of Elasticity

There are five types of elasticity:
1. Relatively elastic
2. Relatively inelastic.
3. Unitary elastic.
4. Perfectly elastic.
5. Perfectly inelastic.

Relatively Elastic

Relatively elastic demand is defined as the case where the %Δ in Q_D is greater than the %Δ in P. Thus, a change in the price of an item of 10 percent will cause the quantity to change by a greater percentage. A rise in the price of an item by 10 percent will cause the quantity demanded to drop by more than 10 percent. Table 4.1 presents an example.

Table 4.1
Relative Elastic Demand

Price	Quantity Demanded
(P_2) .88	160 (Q_2)
(P_1) .80	200 (Q_1)

Joan likes a bag of chips for lunch. In 1993, the price for a bag of chips was 80 cents (.80), and she purchased 200 bags that year. In 1994, the price went up to 88 cents (.88). She reduced her purchase to 160 bags.

Using the formula, we would have:

$$E_P = \frac{\frac{160-200}{(160+200)/2}}{\frac{.88-.80}{(.88+.80)/2}} = \frac{\frac{-40}{180}}{\frac{.08}{.84}} = \frac{-.22}{.10} = -2.2$$

The percentage change in price is 10 percent (.10 × 100), while the percentage change in quantity demanded is 22 percent (.22 × 100). The negative sign indicates the quantity demanded dropped by 22 percent.

If we divide –.22 by .10, the answer is –2.2. this is called the coefficient of elasticity of demand. The absolute value of the coefficient of elasticity will be greater than 1 if the demand is relatively elastic. In the formula:

$$E_P = \frac{\%\Delta \text{ in } Q_D}{\%\Delta \text{ in } P}$$

If the %Δ in Q_D is greater than %Δ in P, the answer is larger than 1 when divided. A larger number (.22) divided by a smaller number (.10) equals an answer greater than 1 (2.2).

A second way to determine the type of elasticity is to look at what happens to total revenue when price changes, as shown in Table 4.2.

Table 4.2
Elasticity—Revenue Approach

Price	Quantity Demanded	Total Revenue
(P_2) .88	(Q_2) 160	(R_2) $140.80 (160 x .88)
(P_1) .80	(Q_1) 200	(R_2) $160.00 (200 x .80)

When the demand is relatively elastic, the total revenue will decrease with a price increase, and increase with a price decrease. In Table 4.2, as the price rose from 80 cents to 88 cents, the total revenue dropped from 160 dollars to 140.80 dollars.

Because Joan decided to purchase less chips the total revenue of the chip company dropped. If all consumers react to the price increase as Joan did, the market demand for chips would be relatively elastic.

This can be shown graphically as in Figure 4.1.

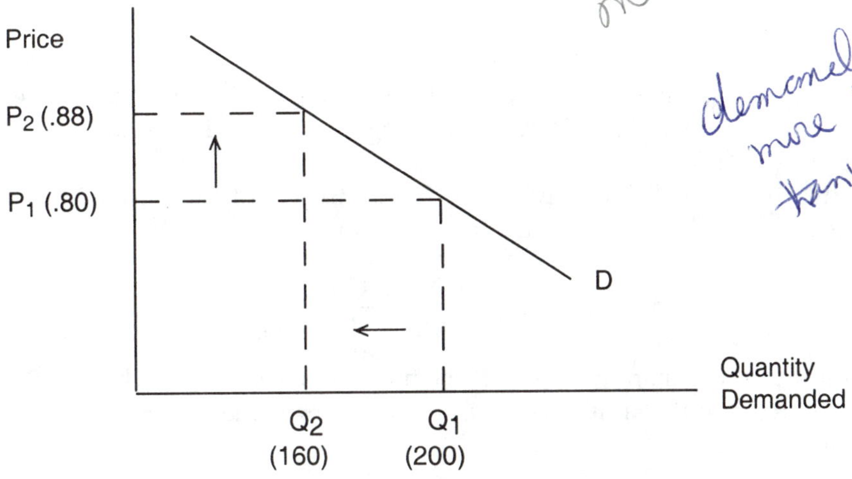

Figure 4.1
Relatively Elastic Demand

$$\%\Delta \text{ in } Q_D > \%\Delta \text{ in } P$$

The graph indicates that when the price rose from P_1 (.80) to P_2 (.88), the quantity demanded dropped from Q_1 (200) to Q_2 (160). The percentage change in the quantity demanded was greater than the percentage change in the price of the chips. Relatively elastic elasticity means that the demand curve has a gradual downward slope. The demand curve is closer to being horizontal than it is to being vertical.

Relatively Inelastic

Relatively inelastic demand refers to the case where the $\%\Delta$ in Q_D is less than the $\%\Delta$ in P. Thus, a change in the price of an item of 10 percent will cause the quantity demanded to change by less than 10 percent. Table 4.3 presents an example.

Mark likes to eat Three Musketeer Bars. When the price was 70 cents (.70) in 1993, he purchased 100 bars that year. When the price went up to 77 cents (.77) in 1994, he purchased only 95 bars. Table 4.3 presents Mark's demand for the candy bars.

Table 4.3
Relatively Inelastic Demand

Price	Quantity Demanded
(P_2) .77	95 (Q_2)
(P_1) .70	100 (Q_1)

Using the formula, we would have:

$$E_P = \frac{\frac{95-100}{(95+100)/2}}{\frac{.77-.70}{(.77+.70)/2}} = \frac{\frac{-5}{97.5}}{\frac{.07}{.735}} = \frac{-.05}{.10} = -.5$$

The percentage change in price is 10 percent (.10 x 100), while the percentage in the quantity demanded is only 5 percent (.05 x 100). Again, the negative sign indicates the quantity demanded dropped by 5 percent.

If we divide –.05 by .10, the answer is –.5. The coefficient of elasticity will be a number less than 1 if the demand is relatively inelastic. In the formula:

$$E_P = \frac{\%\Delta \text{ in } Q_D}{\%\Delta \text{ in } P}$$

If the %Δ in Q_D is less than the %Δ in P, the answer is less than 1 when divided. A smaller number (.05) divided by a larger number (.10) equals an answer less than 1 (.5). Table 4.4 presents the total revenue approach.

Table 4.4
Elasticity—Revenue Approach

Price	Quantity Demanded	Total Revenue
(P_2) .77	(Q_2) 95	(TR_2) $73.15 (95 x .77)
(P_1) .70	(Q_1) 100	(TR_1) $70.00 (100 x .70)

When the demand is relatively inelastic, the total revenue will increase with a price increase, and decrease with a price decrease. In Table 4.4, as the price rose from 70 cents to 77 cents, the total revenue rose from 70 dollars to 73.15 dollars.

Even though Mark purchased less candy bars, the higher price caused an increase in the revenue of the candy company. If all consumers react to the price change as Mark did, the total revenue of the company would increase. The market demand for Three Musketeer Bars would be relatively inelastic.

This can be shown graphically as in Figure 4.2.

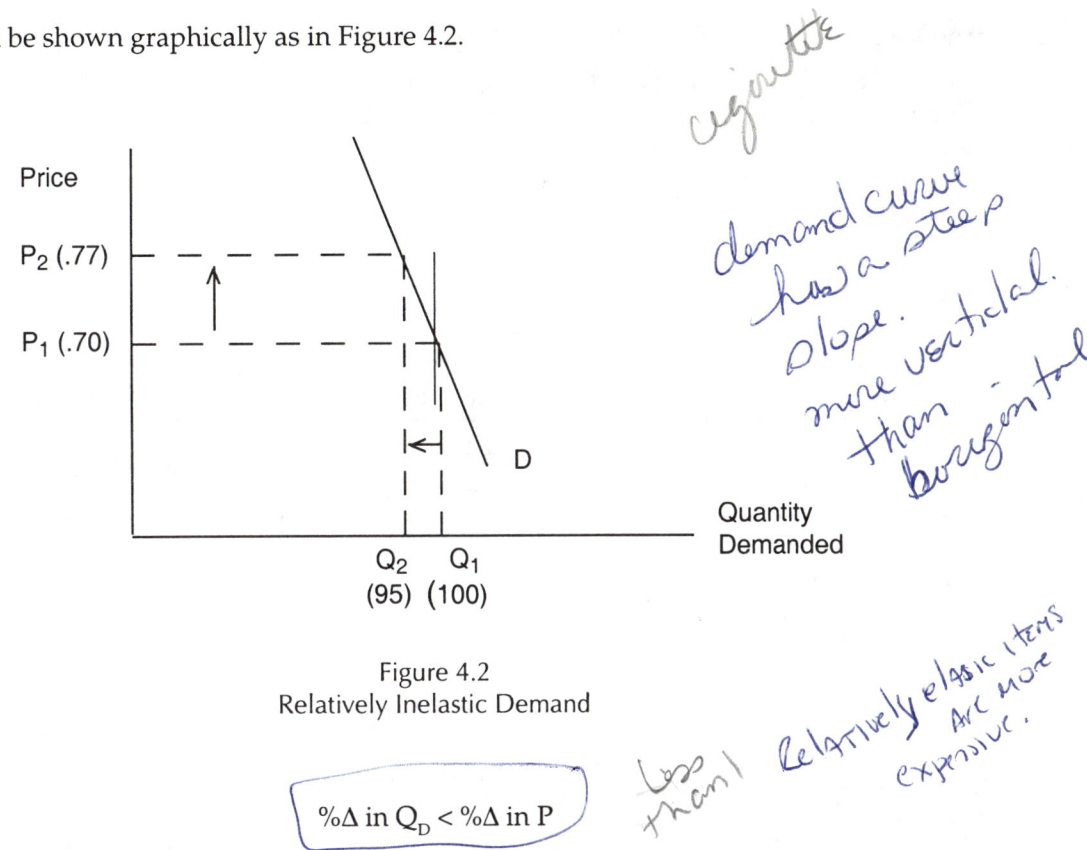

Figure 4.2
Relatively Inelastic Demand

$$\%\Delta \text{ in } Q_D < \%\Delta \text{ in } P$$

The graph indicates that as the price rose from P_1 (.70) to P_2 (.77), the quantity demanded dropped from Q_1 (100) to Q_2 (95). The percentage change in the quantity demanded was less than the percentage change in the price of the good. Relatively inelastic demand means that the demand curve has a steep slope. It is closer to being vertical than it is to being horizontal.

Characteristics

Most products tend to be of either relatively elastic or relatively inelastic demand. Relatively elastic products tend to be items that are relatively more expensive, take a larger share of the budget to purchase, have substitutes, have narrower definitions, and for which the consumer has more time to react to the price change. The last two traits need some explanation.

An item like cigarettes is broadly defined, whereas, an item like Benson & Hedges Ultra Lite 100s is narrowly defined. Cigarettes have few substitutes, whereas, Benson & Hedges Ultra Lite 100s have many.

Prices change, but the consumers may not react immediately. The price may rise on Monday, but the consumer doesn't shop until Saturday. As a result, on Monday the quantity demanded may change very little, indicating inelastic demand. As the week continues and more people shop, the quantity demanded may change greatly, indicating elastic demand.

At the beginning of this section, two cases were presented. The first dealt with a tax on cigarettes to raise revenue to support a drug-prevention program in public schools. The demand for cigarettes tends to be inelastic, thus, raising the price will not reduce the quantity demanded. Tax revenue will increase.

The demand for videocassettes would tend to be elastic. A good way to generate revenue, therefore, would be to lower prices. At lower prices, the quantity demanded will increase enough to increase revenue.

Unitary Elastic   %Δ in P = the %Δ in Q_D

Unitary elasticity occurs when the %Δ in P equals the %Δ in Q_D. The coefficient of elasticity is one (1). Total revenue does not change as a result of a price change.

Janet uses a lot of pens in her hobby of writing short stories. When the price of pens was $1.00 in 1993, she purchased 200 pens. In 1994, the price rose to $2.00. She purchased only 100 pens. Table 4.5 presents her demand for pens.

Table 4.5
Unitary Elasticity

Price	Quantity Demanded	Total Revenue
(P_2) $2.00 ($P_1$) $1.00	(Q_2) 100 (Q_1) 200	(TR_2) $200 ($2 x 100) (TR_1) $200 ($1 x 200)

The computations for the elasticity are:

$$E_P = \frac{\frac{100-200}{(100+200)/2}}{\frac{2.00-1.00}{(2.00+1.00)/2}}$$

$$E_P = \frac{\frac{-100}{150}}{\frac{1}{1.5}}$$

$$E_P = \frac{-.67}{.67}$$

$$E_P = -1.00$$

Since the percentage change in the quantity demanded equals the percentage change in the price, the coefficient of elasticity is 1.00. This is called unitary elasticity. The total revenue is the same before and after the price change. The total revenue before was $200 ($1.00 x 200). The revenue after was $200 ($2.00 x 100).

This can be shown graphically as in Figure 4.3.

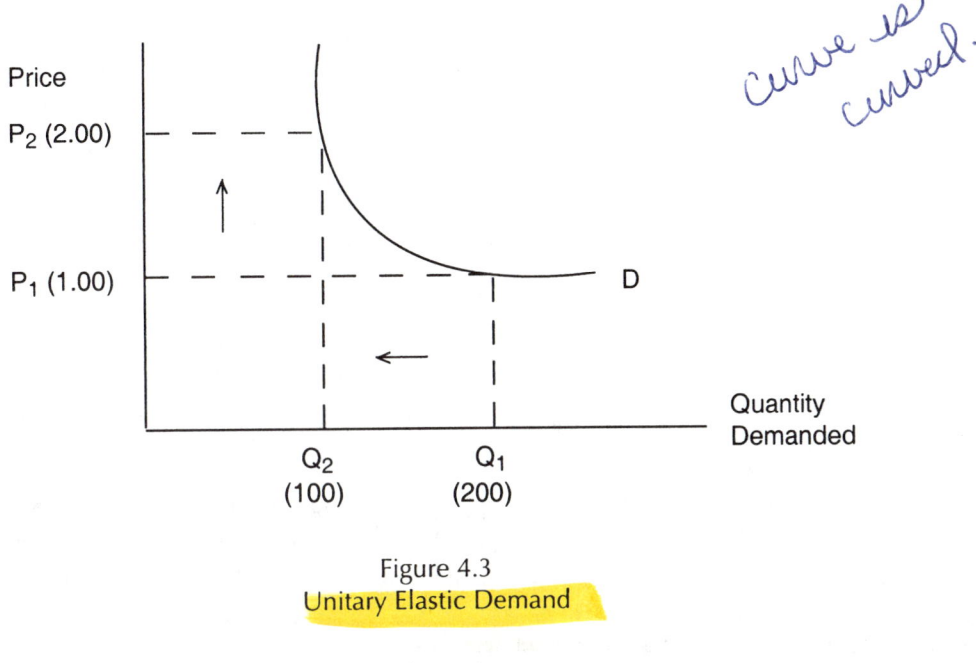

Figure 4.3
Unitary Elastic Demand

$$\%\Delta \text{ in } Q_D = \%\Delta \text{ in } P$$

The graph indicates that when the price rose from P_1 (1.00) to P_2 (2.00), the quantity demanded drops from Q_1 (200) to Q_2 (100). The percentage change in quantity demanded equaled the percentage change in the price. The unitary elastic demand curve is curved. If all consumers behave like Janet, the market demand for pens would be unitary elastic.

Perfectly Elastic Demand

Perfectly elastic demand refers to a situation in which there is only one price and any quantity that the consumer wants can be demanded. There is a market price for wheat, $3.50 per bushel. Farmer Dave wants to sell 1,000 bushels. The market will buy all 1,000 bushels at $3.50. Farmer Ken wants to sell 2,000 bushels. The market will buy all 2,000 bushels at $3.50 per bushel. There is one price set in the market, $3.50. The market will buy whatever is offered for sale. Table 4.6 presents the demand for wheat for the farmers.

Table 4.6
Perfectly Elastic Demand

Price		Quantity Demanded		Total Revenue
(P)	$3.50	(Q_2)	2,000	(TR_2) $7,000 (2000 x 3.50)
(P)	$3.50	(Q_1)	1,000	(TR_1) $3,500 (1000 x 3.50)

The computations for elasticity.

$$E_P = \frac{\frac{2{,}000 - 1{,}000}{(2{,}000 + 1{,}000)/2}}{\frac{3.50 - 3.50}{(3.50 + 3.50)/2}}$$

$$E_P = \frac{\frac{1{,}000}{1{,}500}}{\frac{0}{3.50}}$$

$$E_P = \frac{.67}{0}$$

$$E_P = ----$$

Since the percentage change in price in this case equals zero (0), the coefficient of elasticity is undefined. In arithmetic or in algebra, division by zero is undefined. If it were possible, the answer would be a very large number. We will leave it undefined. The total revenue is computed by price times quantity. Since the price does not change, total revenue increases if quantity increases. Total revenue decreases if quantity decreases.

This can be shown graphically as in Figure 4.4.

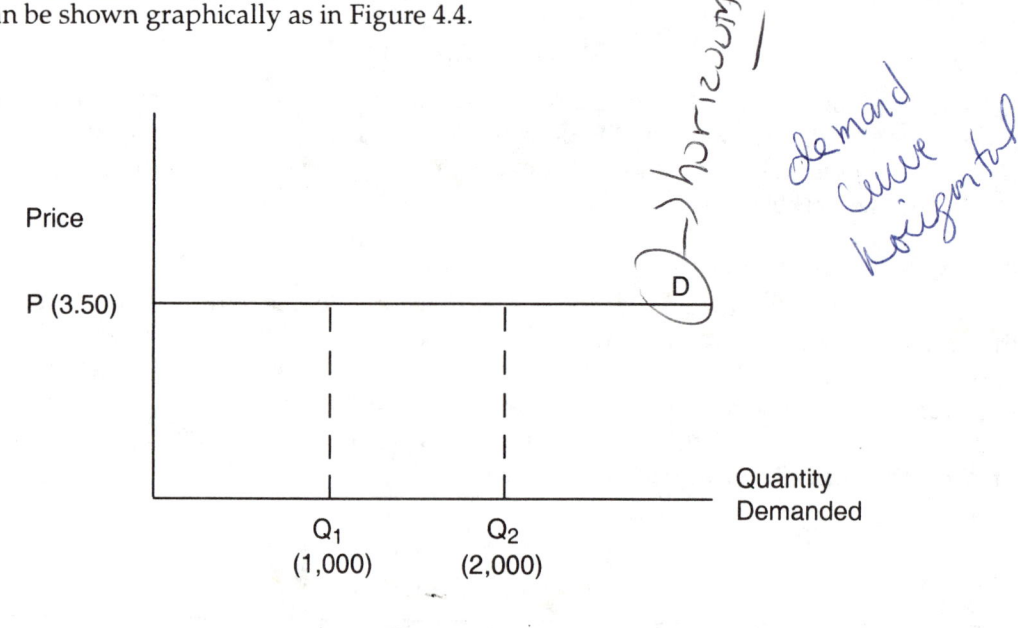

Figure 4.4
Perfectly Elastic Demand

There is no %Δ in P

The graph indicates that there is one price (P). At $3.50 the market will demand 1,000 bushels (Q_1) and will also demand 2,000 bushels (Q_2). The demand curve is horizontal.

Perfectly Inelastic Demand

Perfectly inelastic demand occurs when there is only one quantity demanded regardless of the price of the good. John needed a book for his macroeconomics class. He was able to buy one (Q_2) in his college bookstore for $50 ($P_2$). Samantha thought she could find the book cheaper somewhere else so she went to another college bookstore. She found the same book for $45 ($P_1$) at the other college bookstore. She bought one (Q_1). Don, the manager of the college bookstore, estimates the demand for macroeconomics books by finding out how many students have registered for the course and orders one for each student. Table 4.7 presents the demand for macroeconomics texts.

Table 4.7
Perfectly Inelastic Demand

	Price	Quantity Demanded	Total Revenue
(P_2)	50	(Q)$_2$ 1	(TR_2) $50 (1 x 50)
(P_1)	45	(Q)$_1$ 1	(TR_1) $45 (1 x 45)

Computations for the elasticity are:

$$E_P = \frac{\frac{1-1}{(1+1)/2}}{\frac{50-45}{(50+45)/2}}$$

$$E_P = \frac{\frac{0}{1}}{\frac{5}{47.5}}$$

$$E_P = \frac{0}{.11}$$

$$E_P = 0$$

Since the percentage change in quantity in this case equals zero (0), the coefficient of elasticity equals zero (0). Zero divided by any number equals zero. The total revenue is computed by price times quantity. Since there is one quantity, the total revenue increases when the price increases and decreases when the price decreases.

This can be shown graphically as in Figure 4.5.

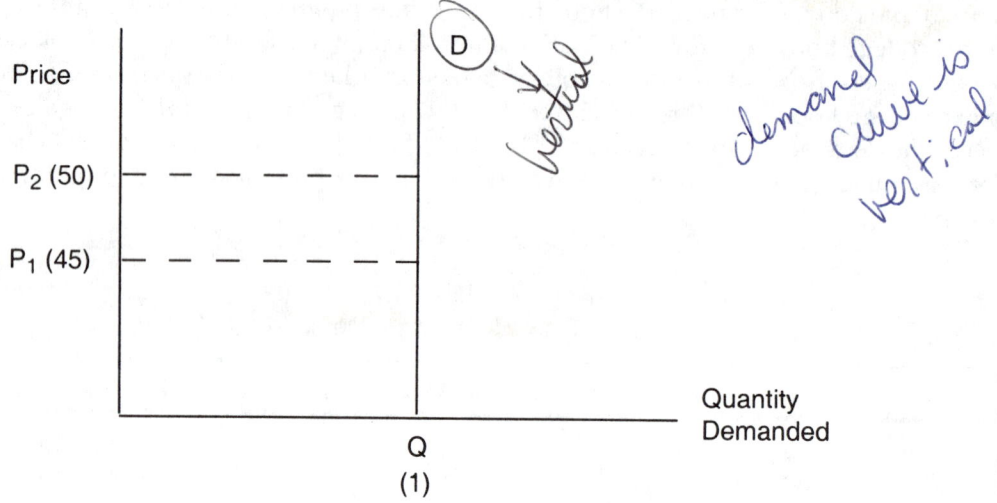

Figure 4.5
Perfectly Inelastic Demand

There is no % change in Q.

The graph indicates there is one quantity (Q). At a price of $50 ($P_2$) the quantity demanded is 1 (Q). At a price of $45 ($P_1$) the quantity demanded is 1 (Q). The demand curve is vertical.

Summary

Elasticity of demand is particularly important to producers. Together with the cost of production, it determines the prices firms can charge for their products. Thus a change in price (ΔP) can cause total revenue (TR) to increase, decrease, or remain the same, depending on the elasticity of demand.

Table 4.8 presents a summary of the analysis of elasticity.

Table 4.8 General relationship between percent of price change (%ΔP), percent quantity demand change (%ΔQ_D), elasticity and total revenue.

%ΔP	%ΔQ_D	Elasticity	Total Revenue	Type
↑ (10%)	↓ (15%)	Ed > 1	Decrease	
↓ (10%)	↑ (15%)	Ed > 1	Increase	Relatively Elastic
↑ (10%)	↓ (10%)	Ed = 1	Unchanged	
↓ (10%)	↑ (10%)	Ed = 1	Unchanged	Unitary
↑ (10%)	↓ (5%)	Ed < 1	Increase	
↓ (10%)	↑ (5%)	Ed < 1	Decrease	Relatively Inelastic

As indicated earlier in the chapter, elasticity of demand is always a negative number and economists usually omit the minus sign. Elasticity is measured in terms of whether it equals, is less than, or is greater than one (1). An elasticity of −2.2 would be considered greater than one (1), dropping the minus sign. Economists use the absolute value or the positive value. 2.2 would be greater than one (1), and would be relatively elastic.

Figure 4.6 shows demand curves of various elasticity.

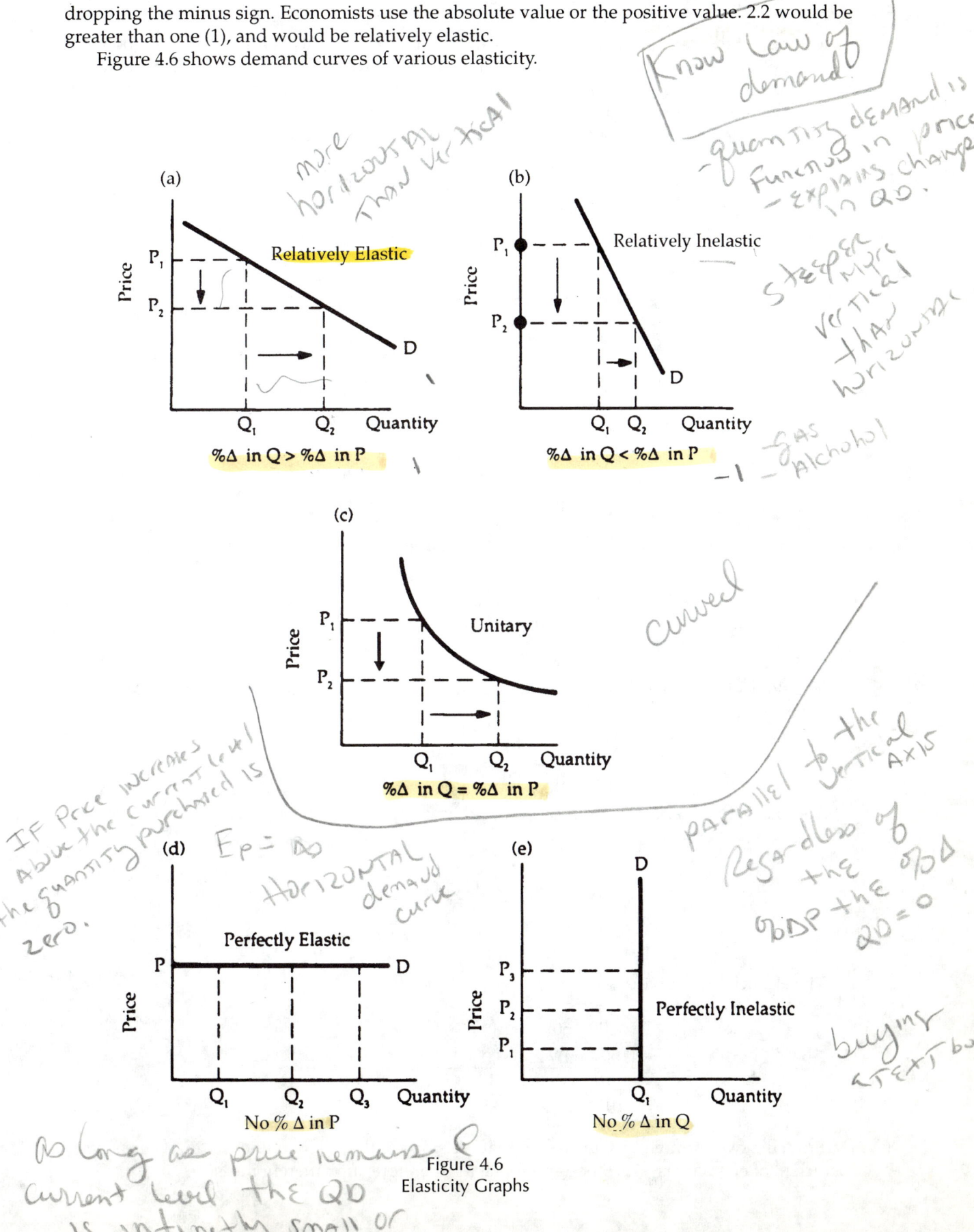

Figure 4.6
Elasticity Graphs

Slope

<mark>Elasticity is not the same as slope.</mark> Students often confuse the concept of elasticity of demand with the slope of the demand curve. The confusion is understandable. The slope of a demand curve does say something about consumer responsiveness: it shows how much the quantity consumed drops when the price rises by a given amount. Suppose that when the price rises from 10 dollars to 20 dollars, the quantity demanded decreases from 100 to 60, as shown in Figure 4.7.

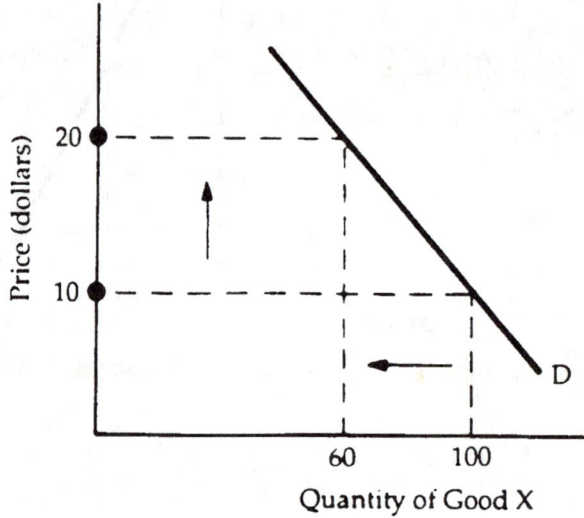

Figure 4.7
Slope of Demand Curve

The slope of the demand curve would be computed by the formula $\Delta Y/\Delta X$ or, here, $\Delta P/\Delta Q_D$. The slope would be:

$$\frac{\Delta Y}{\Delta X} = \frac{10-20}{100-60} = \frac{-10}{40} = \frac{-1}{4} = -.25$$

The elasticity of demand, in this case, would be computed by the formula:

$$E_P = \frac{\frac{Q_2 - Q_1}{(Q_2 + Q_1)/2}}{\frac{P_2 - P_1}{(P_2 + P_1)/2}}$$

The elasticity would be:

$$E_P = \frac{\frac{100-60}{(100+60)/2}}{\frac{10-20}{(10+20)/2}} = \frac{\frac{40}{80}}{\frac{-10}{15}} = \frac{\frac{1}{2}}{\frac{-2}{3}} = \frac{1}{2} \cdot \frac{-3}{2} = \frac{-3}{4} = -.75$$

From the two formulas, it can be seen that the slope of the demand line is $-.25$, whereas, the coefficient of elasticity is $-.75$. Slope and elasticity, therefore, are different measures.

INCOME ELASTICITY OF DEMAND

Income elasticity of demand measures the change in the quantity demanded of a good as the income of the buyer changes. The formula that is used to measure this elasticity is:

$$E_Y = \frac{\text{percent change in quantity demanded}}{\text{percent change in income}}$$

E_Y represents income elasticity. Since this is what we are trying to determine, it is placed to the left of the equal sign (=). How income elasticity is to be determined is placed to the right of the equal sign. Income elasticity is determined in three (3) steps.

1. The percentage change in quantity demanded is measured. In order to determine this percentage, the following formula is used:

$$\frac{Q_2 - Q_1}{(Q_2 + Q_1)/2}$$

Q_2 represents the quantity demanded after the income change.
Q_1 represents the quantity demanded before the income change.
$Q_2 - Q_1$ represents the amount change in quantity demanded.
$(Q_2 + Q_1)/2$ represents the average quantity.
$\frac{Q_2 - Q_1}{(Q_2 + Q_1)/2}$ represents the percentage change in quantity demanded.

2. The percentage change in income is determined. In order to determine this percentage, the following formula is used:

$$\frac{Y_2 - Y_1}{(Y_2 + Y_1)/2}$$

Y_2 represents the new income.
Y_1 represents the previous income.
$Y_2 - Y_1$ represents the amount change in income.
$(Y_2 + Y_1)/2$ represents the average income
$\frac{Y_2 - Y_1}{(Y_2 + Y_1)/2}$ represents the percentage change in income.

3. The result from step 1 is divided by the result from step 2. The definitional formula for income elasticity, thus, becomes:

$$E_Y = \frac{\frac{Q_2 - Q_1}{(Q_2 + Q_1)/2}}{\frac{Y_2 - Y_1}{(Y_2 + Y_1)/2}}$$

Another way to express the formula would be to represent percentage change in quantity demanded by %Δ in Q_D. The percentage change in income would be represented by %Δ in Y. The formula becomes:

$$E_Y = \frac{\%\Delta \text{ in } Q_D}{\%\Delta \text{ in } Y}$$

Income Elasticity

Maria recently received a raise. Her salary went from $25,000 in 1993 to $30,000 in 1994. In figuring her expenses for these two years, she noticed that her purchase of hamburger went from 20 pounds in 1993 to 10 pounds in 1994 and that her purchases of steak went from 8 pounds in 1993 to 12 pounds in 1994. This is shown in Table 4.9.

Table 4.9
Income Elasticity—Maria

Income	Quantity (Hamburger)	Quantity (Steak)
(Y_1) $25,000 ($Y_2$) $30,000	(Q_1) 20 (Q_2) 10	(Q_1) 8 (Q_2) 12

The income elasticity of demand for Maria is as follows:

1. Hamburger.

$$E_Y = \frac{\frac{10-20}{(10+20)/2}}{\frac{30,000-25,000}{(30,000+25,000)/2}}$$

$$E_Y = \frac{\frac{-10}{15}}{\frac{5,000}{27,500}}$$

$$E_Y = \frac{-.6667}{.1818}$$

$$E_Y = -3.67$$

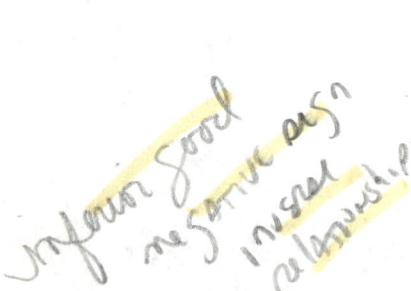

The sign of the income elasticity of hamburger for Maria is negative. This indicates that hamburger is an inferior good for Maria. A negative sign indicates that there is an inverse relationship. As income increases, the demand for hamburger decreases. As Maria's income increased, she purchased less hamburger. This indicates she prefers something else to the hamburger.

When the income elasticity of demand for a good is negative, this means the good is an inferior good for the buyer. This means that an increase in income will result in a reduction in the purchase of that good.

2. Steak.

$$E_Y = \frac{\frac{12-8}{(12+8)/2}}{\frac{30,000-25,000}{(30,000+25,000)/2}}$$

$$E_Y = \frac{\frac{4}{10}}{\frac{5,000}{27,500}}$$

$$E_Y = \frac{.40}{.1818}$$

$$E_Y = +2.20$$

The sign of the elasticity is positive. This indicates a direct relationship. This means that as income increases the demand for the good also increases. As Maria's income increased, she purchased more steak. If the income elasticity of a good is positive, it is called a normal good. Table 4.10 summarizes the types of goods.

Table 4.10
Type of Good, Income Elasticity

Sign	Type of good
positive	normal
negative	inferior

Normal Goods

The income elasticity of normal goods is positive. If the positive income elasticity is less than 1, the good is said to be income inelastic. This means that if a person's income increases, the demand for a particular good would increase by a smaller percentage. Recently George's income increased from $50,000 in 1993 to $60,000 in 1994. In 1993 he purchased 30 bottles of wine, in 1994 he purchased 34 bottles. The following computations measure George's income elasticity for wine.

Table 4.11
Income Elasticity—George

Income	Quantity—Wine
(Y_1) $50,000 ($Y_2$) $60,000	(Q_1) 30 (Q_2) 34

$$E_Y = \frac{\dfrac{34-30}{(34+30)/2}}{\dfrac{60,000-50,000}{(60,000+50,000)/2}}$$

$$E_Y = \frac{\dfrac{4}{32}}{\dfrac{10,000}{55,000}}$$

$$E_Y = \frac{.125}{.1818}$$

$$E_Y = .69$$

George's income increased by 18.18 percent and his purchase of wine increased by only 12.5 percent. The income elasticity of wine for George is inelastic. The percentage change in the quantity demanded is less than the percentage change in income.

If the positive income elasticity is greater than 1, the good is said to be income elastic. In Maria's example, the income elasticity for steak was positive and equaled 2.20. This indicates that as Maria's income increased by about 18 percent, her demand for steak increased by 40 percent. This indicates that for Maria steak is income elastic. The percentage change in the quantity demanded is greater than the percentage change in income. Table 4.12 summarizes this information.

Table 4.12
Normal Goods, Income Elasticity

Elasticity	Type of Elasticity	Percentage Change
< than 1	income inelastic	quantity changes less
> than 1	income elastic	quantity changes more

Luxury Items

If the income elasticity is positive and high, the good is said to be a luxury. If the income elasticity is positive, but low, the good is a necessity. Table 4.13 summarizes this information.

Table 4.13
Normal Goods: Necessity or Luxury

Elasticity	Type of Good
low positive	necessity
high positive	luxury

The definition for a necessity is a good that has a low positive income elasticity of demand. Food items would tend to have low positive income elasticities. A luxury item is a good for which the buyer has a high positive income elasticity of demand. Sports cars and ocean cruises would tend to have high positive income elasticities of demand.

Neutral Good

It is possible that the income elasticity of a good equals zero. This would mean that the quantity purchased does not change as the consumer's income changes. Sam's income increased from $21,000 in 1993 to $24,000 in 1994. In 1993 he purchased 30 cartons of cigarettes. In 1994 he also purchased 30 cartons of cigarettes. His income elasticity for cigarettes is:

Table 4.14
Income Elasticity—Sam

Income	Quantity—Cigarettes
(Y_1) $21,000	(Q_1) 30
(Y_2) $24,000	(Q_2) 30

$$E_Y = \frac{\frac{30-30}{(30+30)/2}}{\frac{24,000-21,000}{(24,000+21,000)/2}}$$

$$E_Y = \frac{\frac{0}{30}}{\frac{3,000}{22,500}}$$

$$E_Y = \frac{0}{.13}$$

$$E_Y = 0$$

Since he purchased the same amount of cigarettes in 1994 as he did in 1993, the percentage change in the quantity purchased was zero (0). There was a 13 percent increase in his income. Zero divided by any number equals zero. The income elasticity of cigarettes for Sam equals zero. Goods that have a zero income elasticity are called neutral goods.

CROSS ELASTICITY OF DEMAND

Cross elasticity of demand measures the effect a change in price of one good will have on the quantity demanded of another good. Cross elasticity of demand is the ratio of the percentage change in the quantity demanded of one good (Y) to the percentage change in the price of another good (X). The formula for cross elasticity of demand is:

$$E_C = \frac{\text{percentage change in the quantity demanded of y}}{\text{percentage change in the price of good x}}$$

E_c represents cross elasticity. Since this is what we are trying to determine, it is placed to the left of the equal sign (=). How cross elasticity is to be determined is placed to the right of the equal sign. Cross elasticity is determined in three (3) steps.

1. The percentage change in the quantity demanded of a good Y is determined. In order to determine this percentage, the following formula is used:

$$\frac{QY_2 - QY_1}{(QY_2 + QY_1)/2}$$

QY_2 represents the quantity demanded of good Y after the change in price of good X.
QY_1 represents the quantity demanded of good Y before the change in price of good X.
$QY_2 - QY_1$ represents the amount change in the quantity demanded of good Y.
$(QY_2 + QY_1)/2$ represents the average quantity demanded of good Y.
$\frac{QY_2 - QY_1}{(QY_2 + QY_1)/2}$ represents the percentage change in the quantity demanded of good Y.

2. The percentage change in the price of good X is determined. In order to determine this percentage the following formula is used:

$$\frac{PX_2 - PX_1}{(PX_1 + PX_2)/2}$$

PX_2 represents the new price of good X.
PX_1 represents the previous price of good X.
$PX_2 - PX_1$ represents the amount change in the price of good X.
$(PX_2 + PX_1)/2$ represents the average price of good X.
$\frac{PX_2 - PX_1}{(PX_1 + PX_2)/2}$ represents the percentage change in the price of good X.

3. The result from step 1 is divided by the result from step 2. The definitional formula for cross elasticity, thus, becomes:

$$E_C = \frac{\frac{QY_2 - QY_1}{(QY_2 + QY_1)/2}}{\frac{PX_2 - PX_1}{(PX_2 + PX_1)/2}}$$

Another way to express the formula would be to represent percentage change in the quantity demanded of good Y by %Δ in QY. The percentage change in the price of good Y would be represented by %Δ in PX. The formula becomes:

$$E_C = \frac{\%\Delta \text{ in } QY}{\%\Delta \text{ in } PX}$$

Cross elasticity can be positive, negative or equal to zero (0).

Complementary Good

Recently the price of peanut butter went from $2.50 per pound to $3.00. Mildred usually purchased 3 jars of jam a month to make sandwiches for her children. After the price increased for peanut butter, she reduced her purchases of jam to 2 jars per month. Mildred's measure of cross elasticity of demand is:

Table 4.12
Cross Elasticity—Mildred

Price of Peanut Butter	Quantity of Jam
(PX_1) $2.50 (PX_2) $3.00	(QY_1) 3 (QY_2) 2

$$E_C = \frac{\frac{2-3}{(2+3)/2}}{\frac{3.00-2.50}{(3.00+2.50)/2}}$$

$$E_C = \frac{\frac{-1}{2.5}}{\frac{.5}{2.75}}$$

$$E_C = \frac{-.40}{.18}$$

$$E_C = -2.22$$

The cross elasticity is negative. This indicates that, first, there is a relationship between the price of peanut butter and the quantity of jam that is purchased by Mildred and, second, that the relationship is inverse. This means that as the price of peanut butter goes up, the demand for jam goes down. The reason is that Mildred makes peanut butter and jam sandwiches for her children. Since the price of peanut butter has increased, she is buying less peanut butter. Since she is buying less peanut butter, she is buying less jam. She is making fewer peanut butter and jam sandwiches. Peanut butter and jam are called complementary goods.

Two goods are complementary goods if an increase in the price of one good causes the consumer to purchase less of the other good or a decrease in price of one good causes the buyer to purchase more of the other good.

The absolute value of the elasticity measure determines the magnitude of the change. For example if the elasticity is a small number, as .5, a change in the price of one good will cause a small change in the quantity demanded of the other. If the elasticity is a larger number, as 5, a change in the price of one good will cause a great change in the quantity demanded of the other.

Substitute Good

If the price of one good increases and the demand for another good increases, the goods are said to be substitutes. The price of strawberries was $2.00 a quart on Monday when Harry went to the store. He bought a quart. When he went back to the store on Friday, strawberries were $3.00 a quart. He bought a pound of grapes. Harry's measure of cross elasticity is:

Table 4.13
Cross Elasticity—Harry

Price of Strawberries	Quantity of Grapes
(PX$_1$) $2.00	(QY$_1$) 0
(PX$_2$) $3.00	(QY$_2$) 1

$$E_C = \frac{\frac{1-0}{(1+0)/2}}{\frac{3.00-2.00}{(3.00+2.00)/2}}$$

$$E_C = \frac{\frac{1}{.5}}{\frac{1.00}{2.50}}$$

$$E_C = \frac{2}{.4}$$

$$E_C = 5 \quad \text{positive}$$

The cross elasticity of demand is positive. This means that there is a relationship between the price of strawberries and the quantity demanded of grapes and that the relationship is direct. This means that as the price of strawberries increased the quantity demanded of grapes increased. This means that as the price of strawberries rose, Harry bought grapes instead of the strawberries. This means that grapes are a substitute for strawberries.

When the cross elasticity of demand is positive, the goods are substitutes for each other. An increase in the price of one good leads to a reduction in the quantity demanded of that good and an increase in the quantity demanded of another good.

Independent Good

If the change in the price of one good has no effect on the quantity demanded of another good, the goods are independent. If, for example, the price of ice cream were to increase, the quantity of paper demanded for use in a computer printer would not change. Likewise, if the price of dental floss were to drop, the quantity demanded of cat food would not change. For independent goods the measure of cross elasticity equals zero. In the formula the percentage change in the quantity of the good would be zero (0). Zero (0) divided by any number equals zero. Table 4.14 summarizes the kinds of cross elasticity.

Table 4.14
Cross Elasticity of Demand

Elasticity	Type of Good
Positive	Substitute
Negative	Complement
Zero	Independent

Price Elasticity of Supply

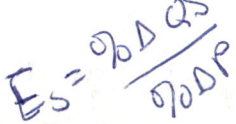

The price elasticity of supply measures the responsiveness of the quantity supplied to changes in the price of the item. The coefficient of price elasticity of supply (E_S) is calculated by the following formula:

$$E_S = \frac{\text{percentage change in the quantity supplied}}{\text{percentage change in price.}}$$

E_S represents price elasticity of supply. Since this is what we are trying to determine, it is placed to the left side of the equal sign (=). How the elasticity of supply is to be determined is placed to the right of the equal sign. The elasticity of supply is determined in three steps:

1. The percentage change in the quantity supplied is measured. In order to determine this percentage the following formula is used:

$$\frac{QS_2 - QS_1}{(QS_2 + QS_1)/2}$$

QS_2 represents the quantity supplied after the price change.
QS_1 represents the quantity supplied before the price change.
$QS_2 - QS_1$ represents the amount change in the quantity supplied.
$(QS_2 + QS_1)/2$ represents the average quantity supplied.
$\frac{QS_2 - QS_1}{(QS_2 + QS_1)/2}$ represents the percentage change in the quantity supplied.

2. The percentage change in the price of the item is determined. In order to determine this percentage, the following formula is used:

$$\frac{P_2 - P_1}{(P_2 + P_1)/2}$$

P_2 represents the new price.
P_1 represents the previous price.
$P_2 - P_1$ represents the amount change in the price.
$(P_2 + P_1)/2$ represents the average price.
$\frac{P_2 - P_1}{(P_2 + P_1)/2}$ represents the percentage change in price.

3. The result from step 1 is divided by the result from step 2. The formula for the price elasticity of supply, thus, becomes:

$$E_S = \frac{\dfrac{QS_2 - QS_1}{(QS_2 + QS_1)/2}}{\dfrac{P_2 - P_1}{(P_2 + P_1)/2}}$$

Another way to express the formula would be to represent percentage change in quantity supplied by %Δ in Q_S, where the symbol % is used for percentage, the symbol Δ is used for change, the symbol Q_s is used for quantity supplied. Percentage change in price would be represented by %Δ in P. P is used for price. The formula becomes:

$$E_S = \frac{\%\Delta \text{ in } Q_S}{\%\Delta \text{ in } P}$$

  All elasticity of supply coefficients are positive. There are five kinds of elasticity of supply:

1. Relatively Elastic
2. Relatively Inelastic
3. Perfectly Elastic
4. Perfectly Inelastic
5. Unitary Elastic

Relatively Elastic Supply

Relatively elastic supply means that the percentage change in the quantity supplied is greater than the percentage change in the price of the item. Acme Widget Co. produces widgets, a device used to scrape paint off of windows. In May the price for the widgets was $2.00, and the company produced or supplied 10,000 widgets. In July the price was raised to $2.50, and the company supplied 20,000 widgets. Table 4.15 summarizes this information.

Table 4.15
Acme Widget Co.—Elasticity of Supply

Price	Quantity Supplied	Percentage Change	E_S
(P_2) $2.50 ($P_1$) $2.00	(Q_2) 20,000 (Q_1) 10,000	67% in quantity 22% in price	3.05

The computations for the elasticity of supply are:

$$E_S = \frac{\dfrac{20{,}000 - 10{,}000}{(20{,}000 + 10{,}000)/2}}{\dfrac{2.50 - 2.00}{(2.50 + 2.00)/2}}$$

$$E_S = \frac{\dfrac{10{,}000}{15{,}000}}{\dfrac{.50}{2.25}}$$

$$E_S = \frac{.67}{.22}$$

$$E_S = 3.05.$$

The price elasticity of supply for the Acme Widget Co. is positive. All price elasticities of supply are positive since the relationship between price and quantity supplied is a direct relationship. As price increases, the quantity supplied increases. As price decreases, the quantity supplied decreases. Price and quantity supplied move in the same direction.

The price elasticity of supply for Acme Widget Co. is 3.05. The coefficient for relatively elastic supply is a number greater than 1. This means that the percentage change in the quantity supplied (67%) is greater than the percentage change in the price of the good (22%). This is referred to as the relatively elastic elasticity of supply.

Total Revenue Method

A method to determine the price elasticity of demand is to compare the total revenue before and after the price change. If the total revenue went up when the price went down the elasticity was relatively elastic. If the total revenue went down when the price went down, the elasticity was relatively inelastic. If total revenue moved in an opposite direction from price, the demand was relatively elastic. If total revenue moved in the same direction as price, the demand was relatively inelastic.

The supply relationship is direct. When the price increases, the quantity supplied and the total revenue increase. When the price decreases, the quantity supplied and total revenue decrease. Total revenue is not useful in determining the elasticity of supply at it always moves in the same direction as price.

Relatively elastic supply can be shown graphically as in Figure 4.8.

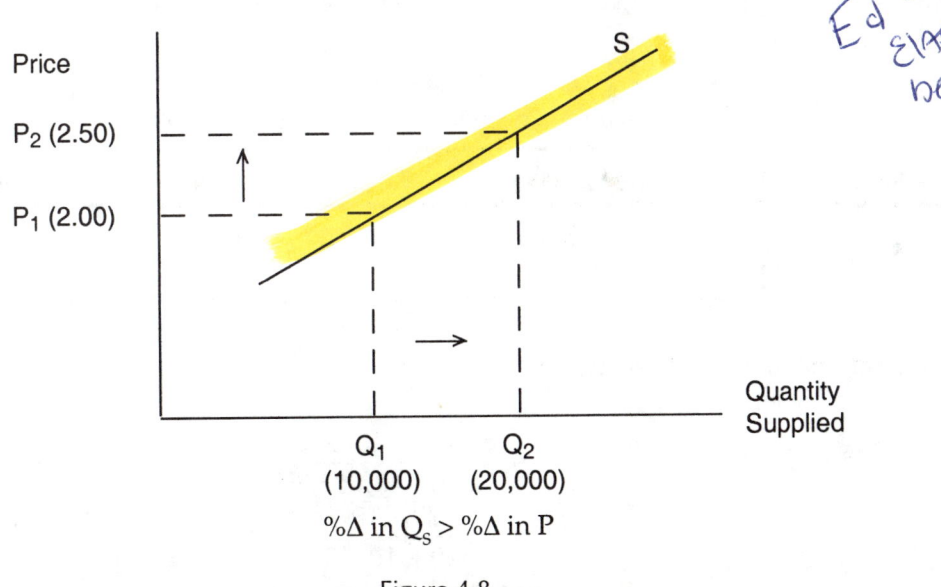

Figure 4.8
Relatively Elastic Supply

The graph shows that as the price rose from $2.00 ($P_1$) to $2.50 ($P_2$) the quantity supplied rose from 10,000 widgets (Q_1) to 20,000 widgets (Q_2). The percentage change in the quantity supplied (67%) was greater than the percentage change in the price (22%). Relatively elastic supply means that the supply curve has a more gradual slope. The curve is more horizontal than vertical.

Elasticity and Total Revenue

R. Elastic   %ΔQd > %ΔP
                 Ed > 1   TR↓ as P↑

Unitary   %ΔQ = %ΔP
                 Ed = 1   Total revenue constant as price increases

R. Inelastic   %ΔQ < %ΔP
                 Ed < 1   Total revenue ↑ as price increases

Perfectly   Horizontal demand curve
Elastic   Ed = infinity

Perfectly   Vertical demand curve
Inelastic   Ed = 0   TR↑ as P↑

Relatively Inelastic Supply

Relatively inelastic supply means that the percentage change in the quantity supplied is less than the percentage change in the price of the item. Bob's Ice-Cream Cone Co. supplied 40,000 cones when the price was .10 (10 cents) and supplied 50,000 cones when the price rose to .20 (20 cents) due to the higher price of sugar imposed by the Sugar Cartel. The data is summarized in Table 4.16

Table 4.16
Bob's Ice-Cream Cone Co.—Elasticity of Supply

Price	Quantity Supplied	Percentage Change	Elasticity
(P_2) .20 (P_1) .10	(Q_2) 50,000 (Q_1) 40,000	22% in quantity 50% in price	.33

The computations for elasticity are:

$$E_S = \frac{\frac{50,000 - 40,000}{(50,000 + 40,000)/2}}{\frac{.20 - .10}{(.20 + .10)/2}}$$

$$E_S = \frac{\frac{10,000}{45,000}}{\frac{.10}{.15}}$$

$$E_S = \frac{.22}{.50}$$

$$E_S = .33$$

The price elasticity of supply for ice-cream cones is .33. The coefficient is a number less than 1. This means that the percentage change in the quantity supplied is less than the percentage change in the price of the good. This is referred to as relatively inelastic elasticity of supply.

Relatively inelastic supply can be shown graphically as in Figure 4.9.

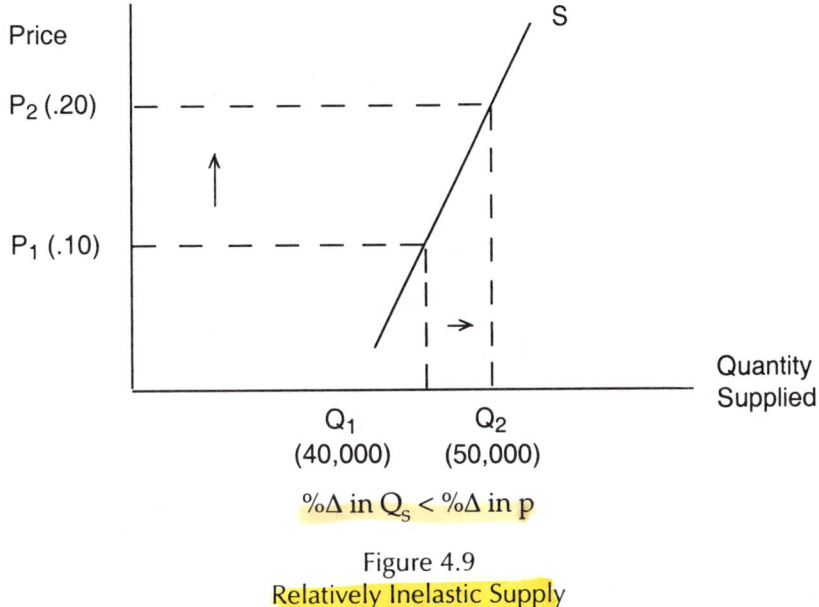

Figure 4.9
Relatively Inelastic Supply

The graph indicates that as the price rose from .10 (P_1) to .20 (P_2), the quantity supplied rose from 40,000 cones (Q_1) to 50,000 cones (Q_2). The percentage change in the quantity supplied is less than the percentage change in the price of the item. The graph is steeper. The graph is more vertical than it is horizontal.

Perfectly Elastic Supply

Perfectly elastic supply means that the percentage change in price equals zero (0). There is one price and firms will supply any quantity at that one price. Let's say that in 1994 Congress froze the price of lead pens at 50 cents (.50) to hold down business expenses and, thus, prices. The American Lead Pen Co. produces lead pens. Figure 4.17 indicates sales to two customers. Jane bought 300 pens (Q_1) in that year and Ken bought 500 pens (Q_2).

Table 4.17
American Lead Co.—Elasticity of Supply

Price	Quantity	% Change	Elasticity
(P_2) .50 (P_1) .50	(Q_2) 500 (Q_1) 200	86% in quantity 0% in price	undefined

The computations for elasticity are:

$$E_S = \frac{\frac{500-200}{(500+200)/2}}{\frac{.50-.50}{(.50+.50)/2}}$$

$$E_S = \frac{\frac{300}{350}}{\frac{0}{.50}}$$

$$E_S = \frac{.86}{0}$$

$$E_S = -----$$

Since the percentage change in price equals zero (0), the coefficient of elasticity of supply is undefined. If it were possible, it would be a very large number. The elasticity of supply is perfectly elastic.

Perfectly elastic supply can be shown graphically as in Figure 4.10.

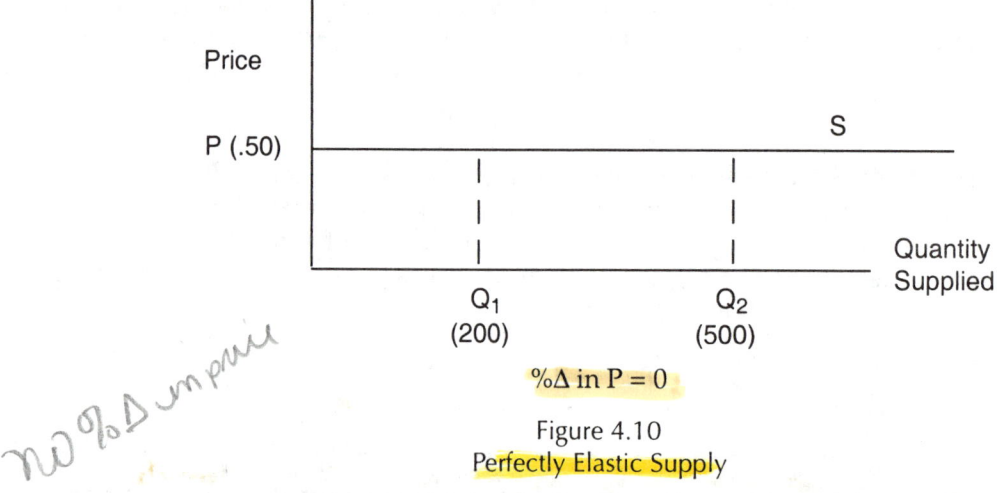

Figure 4.10
Perfectly Elastic Supply

The graph indicates that there is one price (P). At .50 the market will supply 300 pens (Q_1) and will supply 500 pens (Q_2). The supply curve is horizontal.

Perfectly Inelastic Supply

Perfectly inelastic supply occurs when there is only one quantity supplied regardless of the price of the good. Jonathan decided to sell his old car since he figured it needed some work. He placed an ad in the paper. Alicia phoned and offered $2,000 ($P_1$) for the car. About an hour later Matthew phoned and offered $2,700 ($P_2$). Jonathan, however, has only one car, and he sold it to Matthew. Table 4.18 presents Jonathan's supply of used cars.

Elasticity

Table 4.18
Jonathan's Car

Price	Quantity	% Change	Elasticity
(P_2) $2,700	(Q) 1	0% in quantity	zero (0)
(P_1) $2,000	(Q) 1	30% in price	

The computations for the elasticity are:

$$E_S = \frac{\frac{1-1}{(1+1)/2}}{\frac{2,700-2,000}{(2,700+2,000)/2}}$$

$$E_S = \frac{\frac{0}{1}}{\frac{700}{2,350}}$$

$$E_S = \frac{0}{.30}$$

$$E_S = 0$$

Since the percentage change in quantity in this case equals zero (0), the coefficient of elasticity of supply equals zero (0). When the coefficient of elasticity of supply equals zero (0), the elasticity is perfectly inelastic.

This can be shown graphically as in Figure 4.11.

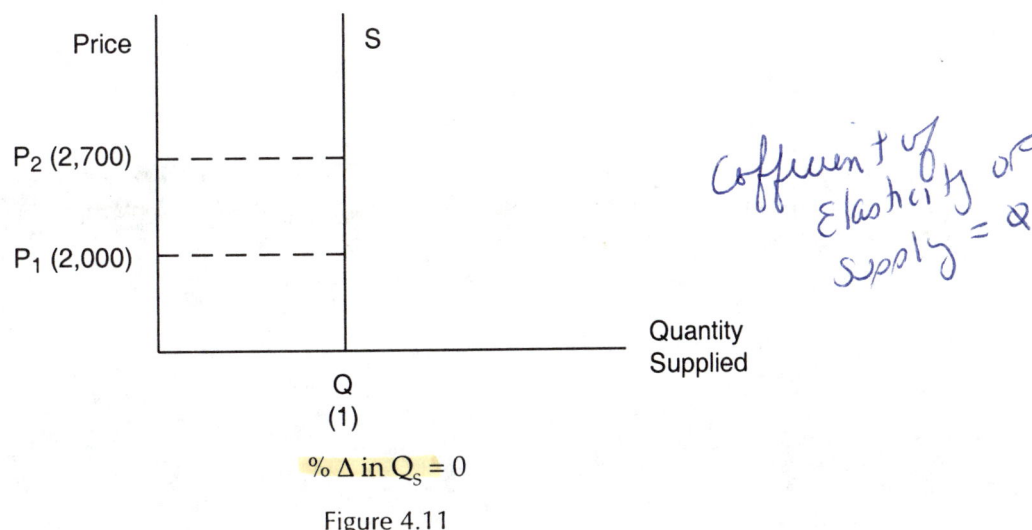

Figure 4.11
Perfectly Inelastic Supply

The graph indicates that there is one quantity supplied (Q). At a price of $2,000 ($P_1$) the quantity supplied is 1. At a price of $2,700 ($Q_2$) the quantity supplied is 1. The supply curve is vertical.

Unitary Elastic Supply   %∆P = %∆QS

Unitary elasticity occurs when the percentage change in price equals the percentage change in quantity supplied. The coefficient of elasticity equals one (1). Recently the Canary Company, a major supplier of cat food, raised the price of their product from $5.00 a bag to $6.00 a bag to cover increased costs. The company also increased the production from 25,000 bags (Q_1) to 30,000 bags (Q_2). Table 4.19 summarizes this information.

Table 4.19
Canary Company

Price	Quantity	% Change	Elasticity
(P_2) $6.00 ($P_1$) $5.00	(Q_2) 30,000 (Q_1) 25,000	18% in quantity 18% in price	1.00

The computations for the elasticity of supply are:

$$E_S = \frac{\frac{6.00 - 5.00}{(6.00 + 5.00)/2}}{\frac{30,000 - 25,000}{(30,000 + 25,000)/2}}$$

$$E_S = \frac{\frac{1.00}{5.50}}{\frac{5,000}{27,500}}$$

$$E_S = \frac{.18}{.18}$$

$$E_S = 1.00$$

The elasticity of supply for the cat food is 1. This means that the percentage change in the price (.18) and the percentage change in the quantity supplied (.18) are equal. When the elasticity is 1, the elasticity is called unitary.

This can be shown graphically as in Figure 4.12.

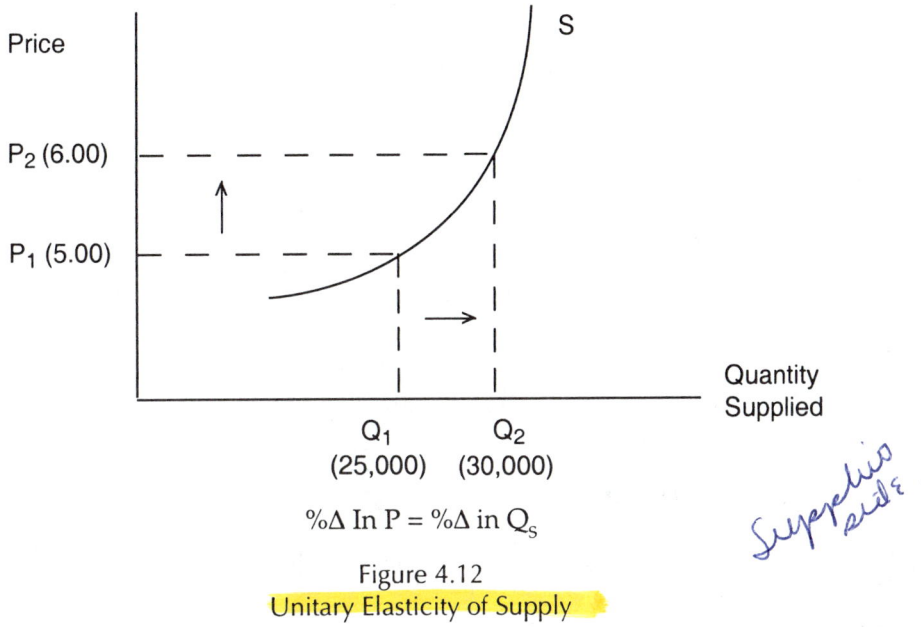

%Δ In P = %Δ in Q_S

Figure 4.12
Unitary Elasticity of Supply

The graph indicates that when the price rose from $5.00 per bag ($P_1$) to $6.00 per bag ($P_2$), the quantities supplied increased from 25,000 bags (Q_1) to 30,000 bags (Q_2). The graph is curved to show that the percentages are equal.

ELASTICITY ALONG THE DEMAND CURVE

Usually elasticity refers to describing the entire demand curve. The demand is said to be elastic or inelastic. The elasticity varies along the curve, however. Table 4.20 presents a demand relationship.

Table 4.20
Demand Schedule

Price	Quantity
$10	1
9	3
8	5
7	7
6	9
5	11
4	13
3	15
2	17
1	19

Case 1. If the price drops from $10 to $9, the quantity demanded rises from 1 to 3. The coefficient of elasticity is:

$$E_P = \frac{\frac{3-1}{(3+1)/2}}{\frac{9-10}{(9+10)/2}}$$

$$E_P = \frac{\frac{2}{2}}{\frac{-1}{9.5}}$$

$$E_P = \frac{1}{-.11}$$

$$E_P = -9.09$$

In the price range of $9 to $10, the elasticity of demand is relatively elastic. The coefficient is 9.09 which is greater than one.

Case 2. If the price drops from $3 to $2, the quantity demanded increases from 15 to 17. The coefficient of elasticity is:

$$E_P = \frac{\frac{17-15}{(17+15)/2}}{\frac{2-3}{(2+3)/2}}$$

$$E_P = \frac{\frac{2}{16}}{\frac{-1}{2.5}}$$

$$E_P = \frac{.125}{-.40}$$

$$E_P = -.31$$

In the price range of $2 to $3 the coefficient of elasticity equals .31, which indicates inelastic demand. The coefficient, .31, is less than one.

For price changes in the high price range, the elasticity tends to be elastic, and in the low price range the demand tends to be inelastic. Somewhere the demand would be unitary. Figure 4.13 indicates the ranges of elasticity along a demand line.

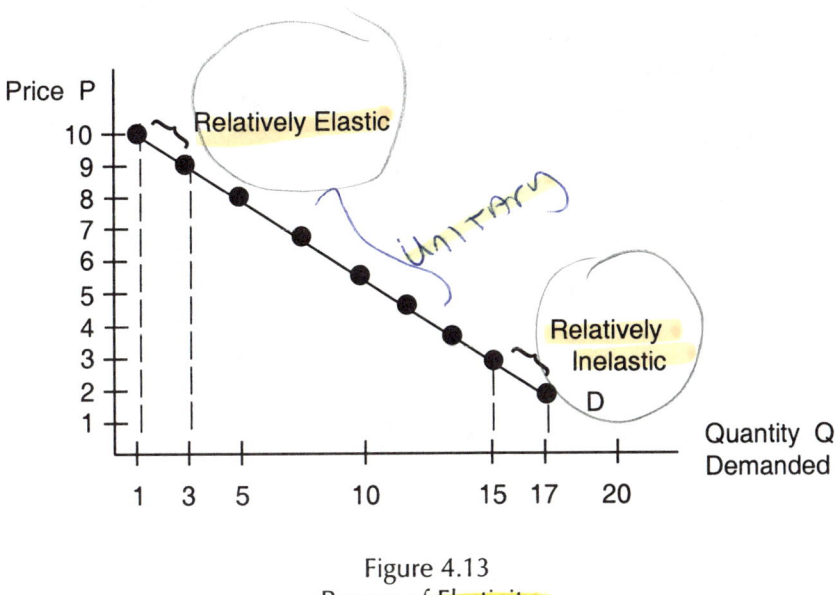

Figure 4.13
Ranges of Elasticity

The elasticity is relatively elastic for higher prices, unitary somewhere down the line, and inelastic for lower prices.

TAKE-A-NOTE
ELASTICITY

Elasticity is a fancy word for responsiveness. The price elasticity of the demand concept measures the degree of responsiveness of the QD of a product to a change in the price of a product. (The degree of consumer responiveness to price Δ.)

Elasticity of demand is particularly important to producers, change in price causes TR ↑, ↓ Or remain the same, depending on the elasticity of demand.

The price elasticity of demand is the ratio of % Δ in the QD to the percentage change in price.

Types of Elasticity

Relative Elastic   % Δ QD > % Δ P
TR ↑ as P ↓; coeff. > 1, TR decreases as the price increases.

(It has many substitutes, examples: automobiles, furniture, restaurant meals.)

Relatively Inelastic   Demand is inelastic if a rise in P induces an ↑ in TR.
% Δ QD < % Δ in P
TR ↑ as P ↑
Coefficient is less than one and > 0.
(There are no substitutes for the good, examples: gasoline, and the demand for cigarettes.) Consumers are relatively insensitive to a change in the QD.

Perfectly Elastic   No change in price, there is only on eP available to the buyers.
Coefficient is equal to infinity.
The demand curve is horizontal.
(Example: all of the farmer's wheat will be purchased by the market at the

Pefectly Inelastic:	No change in Q, only one QD at various prices. Coefficient is equal to 0. The demand curve is vertical. (Example: If Dr. Ruth gross revenue doubled when she doubled her surgical fees, the demand for her services within that price change would be perfectly inelastic. Despite an increase in price, consumers will purchase the same Q.) A rise in price has no effect on QD.
Unitary Elastic:	%ΔP > %ΔQD Coefficient is = to 1. TR does not change as a result of a price change. (A seller who continues to earn the same gross revenue from sales. Whether she raises or lowers her prices. Examples: private education, movies, TV receivers and carpet cleaning.)

Elasticity is an *invented concept*. Both economists and people managing business firms have a need to know what will happen if the price of a product is changed up or down. This is not just a theoretical question. The *strength of their response* of quantity demanded to changes in price **tells a firm's managers** *what will happen to total revenue* **should it be necessary or desirable to change price.**

The relationship between price elasticity of demand and *total revenue* **is of particular interest.** When demand is *elastic* (i.e., the coefficient of price elasticity is above 1.00), *price increases* cause total revenue *to decline* while price *decreases* cause total revenue *to increase*. Managers in such circumstances face even greater than normal incentives to develop measures that can cut costs and thus allow price to be reduced.

Conversely, when demand is *inelastic* (i.e., the coefficient of price elasticity is below 1.00), *price decreases* cause total revenue *to decline* while price *increases* cause total revenue *to increase*. In such circumstances, firms in the industry have an extra incentive to conspire and raise prices. **If output can be restricted, 1) cost will be reduced** *and* **2) total revenue will rise. This assures that successful output restriction will** *increase profits*. Note that one cannot always make a connection between the behavior of total revenue and profits, but in this case, the relationship is straightforward.

The Cross Elasticity of Demand

Substitute goods	Ed > 0
Complementary goods	Ed < 0
Independent goods	Ed = 0

Independent Goods:	Has a zero cross elasticity, as the P of a good changes, QD of other goods does not change.
Complementary Goods:	Have a negative cross elasticity, as P↑ QD↓.
Normal Goods:	A good whose demand ↑ when their income ↑. (Steak, airline travel and designer jeans) Normal goods have a positive income elasticity.
Inferior Goods:	Consumers purchase less when their income ↑. (Inferior goods have a negative income elasticity.)
Neutral Goods:	Have zero (0) income elasticity, as income changes, demand does not change. (Baby food and medicine)
Substitute Goods:	P↑ on tea-coffee is a substitute good, demand for coffee will ↑. Substitute goods have positive cross elasticity, as P↑ QD↑.

CHAPTER SUMMARY

1. Elasticity means responsiveness. Price elasticity measures consumer response to changes in price. The formula for elasticity of demand is:

$$E_P = \frac{\frac{Q_2 - Q_1}{(Q_2 + Q_1)/2}}{\frac{P_2 - P_1}{(P_2 + P_1)/2}}$$

2. Elasticity of demand is particularly important to producers. Together with the cost of production, it determines the prices firms can charge for their products. Thus, an increase in price or decrease in price causes total consumer expenditure to rise, fall or remain the same, depending on the elasticity of demand.

3. There are five types of elasticity: (1) perfectly elastic, (2) relatively elastic, (3) unitary elastic, (4) relatively inelastic, and (5) perfectly inelastic.

4. When the demand is relatively elastic, the total revenue will decrease with a price increase, and increase with a price decrease. The coefficient of elasticity is greater than one (1).

5. When the demand is relatively inelastic, the total revenue will increase with a price increase, and decrease with a price decrease. The coefficient of elasticity is less than one (1).

6. Unitary elasticity occurs when the percentage change in price equals the percentage change in quantity. The coefficient of elasticity is one (1).

7. When the demand is perfectly inelastic, any change in the price causes no response at all in the quantity demanded. The coefficient of elasticity is zero (0).

8. Perfect elasticity occurs when there is only one market price available to a firm or individual. The individual is able to buy whatever he wants at that price. The total revenue increases, by the amount of the price, every time an additional item is demanded.

9. The slope of a demand curve is different from the elasticity.

10. Income elasticity of demand measures the change in the quantity demanded of a good as the income of the buyer changes.

11. An inferior good is a good that has a negative income elasticity. As income increases, the demand for this good decreases.

12. A normal good is a good that has a positive income elasticity. As income increases, the demand for this good increases.

13. A neutral good has a zero income elasticity. As income changes, the demand for this good does not change.

14. Cross elasticity measures the effect a change in the price of one good has on the quantity demanded of another good.

15. A complementary good has a negative cross elasticity. As the price of a good increases, the quantity demanded of the complementary good decreases.

16. A substitute good has a positive cross elasticity. As the price of a good increases, the quantity demanded of a substitute good increases.

17. An independent good has a zero cross elasticity. As the price of a good changes, the quantity demanded of other goods does not change.

18. Price elasticity of supply measures the responsiveness of quantity supplied to changes in the price of an item.

19. Price elasticity of supply can be: relatively elastic, relatively inelastic, perfectly elastic, perfectly inelastic, unitary elastic.

20. Relatively elastic supply means that the percentage change in the quantity supplied is greater than the percentage change in the price of the item.

21. Relatively inelastic supply means that the percentage change in the quantity supplied is less than the percentage change in the price of the item.

22. Perfectly elastic supply means that there is one price and the firm will supply different quantities at one price. The percentage change in the price equals zero.

23. Perfectly inelastic supply means that there is one quantity that the firm will supply at different prices. The percentage change in the quantity supplied equals zero.

24. The elasticity along the demand curve is elastic for higher prices, inelastic for lower prices and unitary somewhere between.

Chapter 4
Key Concepts

Complementary Good—A good that has a negative cross elasticity of demand. As the price of one good increases, the quantity of another good decreases.

Cross Elasticity—A measure of the responsiveness of the quantity demanded to a change in the price of another good.

Elasticity—a measure of the responsiveness of one variable to another variable.

Income Elasticity—A measure of the responsiveness of the quantity demanded of a good to a change in income.

Independent Good—A good that has a zero cross elasticity. As the price of one good changes, the quantity demanded of another good does not change,

Inferior Good—A good that has a negative income elasticity. As income increases, the demand for the good decreases.

Neutral Good—A good that has a zero income elasticity. As income increases, the demand for the good does not change.

Normal Good—A good that has a positive income elasticity. As income increases, the demand for the good increases.

Perfectly Elastic Demand—A demand relationship in which there is only one price. Different quantities can be demanded at the one price. The elasticity is undefined.

Perfectly Elastic Supply—A supply relationship in which there is only one price. Different quantities can be supplied at the one price. The elasticity is undefined.

Perfectly Inelastic Demand—A demand relationship in which there is only one quantity demanded regardless of the price. The elasticity equals zero.

Perfectly Inelastic Supply—A supply relationship in which there is only one quantity supplied regardless of the price. The elasticity equals zero.

Price Elasticity of Demand—A measure of the responsiveness of the quantity demanded to a change in the price of the good.

Price Elasticity of Supply—A measure of the responsiveness of the quantity supplied to a change in the price of the good.

Relatively Elastic Demand—A demand relationship in which the percentage change in the quantity demanded is greater than the percentage change in the price of the good.

Relatively Elastic Supply—A supply relationship in which the percentage change in the quantity supplied is greater than the percentage change in the price of the good.

Relatively Inelastic Demand—A demand relationship in which the percentage change in the quantity demanded is less than the percentage change in the price of the good.

Relatively Inelastic Supply—A supply relationship in which the percentage change in the quantity supplied is less than the percentage change in the price of the good.

Slope—The change in Y divided by the change in X.

Substitute Good—A good that has a positive cross elasticity. As the price of one good increases, the quantity demanded of another good increases.

Unitary Elastic Demand—A demand relationship in which the percentage change in the quantity demanded equals the percentage change in the price of the good.

Unitary Elastic Supply—A supply relationship in which the percentage change in the quantity supplied equals the percentage change in the price of the good.

DISCUSSION QUESTIONS

1. Distinguish among price elasticity of demand, income elasticity and cross elasticity.
2. Distinguish between elastic and inelastic demand.
3. Distinguish among normal, inferior and neutral goods.
4. Distinguish among complement, substitute and independent goods.
5. If the government were to tax a good in order to raise revenue, explain why it would be better to tax a good for which the demand is inelastic.
6. Distinguish among relatively elastic, relatively inelastic, unitary elastic, perfectly elastic and perfectly inelastic demand using percentage changes in price and quantity.
7. Distinguish among relatively elastic, relatively inelastic, unitary elastic, perfectly elastic and perfectly inelastic demand using total revenue.
8. Distinguish among relatively elastic, relatively inelastic, unitary elastic, perfectly elastic, perfectly inelastic supply.
9. Discuss the factors that make demand for one good elastic and another good inelastic.
10. Distinguish between elasticity and slope.
11. Discuss how price changes of goods with various kinds of elasticity of supply can affect the revenues of companies.
12. Discuss whether a firm can increase revenue by raising price using both supply and demand concepts.

4.1 LEARNING PRACTICE

Compute the following price elasticities and describe the type of elasticity.

(a)

Price	Quantity Demanded
(P_2) $12 ($P_1$) $15	(Q_2) 1000 (Q_1) 400

(b)

Price	Quantity Demanded
(P_2) $20 ($P_1$) $10	(Q_2) 1000 (Q_1) 1100

Compute the following income elasticities and describe the type of good.

(c)

Income	Quantity Demanded
(I_2) $40,000 ($I_1$) $30,000	(Q_2) 400 (Q_1) 450

(d)

Income	Quantity Demanded
(I_2) $20,000 ($I_1$) $18,000	(Q_2) 300 (Q_1) 250

(e)

Income	Quantity Demanded
(I_2) $13,000 ($I_1$) $12,000	(Q_2) 200 (Q_1) 200

Compute the following cross elasticities and describe the type of good.

(f)

Price of good X	Quantity Demanded of Good Y
(P_2) $4.00 ($P_1$) $2.00	(Q_2) 125 (Q_1) 50

(g)

Price of Good X	Quantity Demanded of Good Y
(P_2) $1.00 ($P_1$) $ .50	(Q_2) 50 (Q_1) 75

(h)

Price of Good X	Quantity Demanded of Good Y
(P_2) $5.00 ($P_1$) $4.00	(Q_2) 40 (Q_1) 40

Compute the following supply of elasticity and describe the type of elasticity.

(i)

Price	Quantity Supplied
(P_2) $4.00 ($P_1$) $2.00	(Q_2) 350 (Q_1) 325

(j)

Price	Quantity Supplied
(P_2) $7.00 ($P_1$) $6.00	(Q_2) 490 (Q_1) 250

SOLUTIONS

(a) 22% change in price, 86% change in quantity demanded
E = –3.91, Relatively Elastic

(b) 67% change in price, 10% change in quantity demanded
E = –.15, Relatively Inelastic

(c) 29% increase in income, 12% decrease in quantity demanded
E = –.42, Inferior Good

(d) 11% increase in income, 18% increase in quantity demanded
E = +1.64, Normal Good

(e) 8% increase in income, 0% increase in quantity demanded
E = 0, Neutral

(f) 67% increase in the price of Good X, 86% increase in the quantity demanded of Good Y
E = 1.28, Substitutes

(g) 67% increase in the price of Good X, 40% decrease in the quantity demanded of Good Y
E = –.60, Complements

(h) 22% increase in the price of good X, 0% change in the quantity demanded of Good Y
E = 0, Independent

(i) 67% increase in price, 7% increase in the quantity supplied
E = .10, Relatively Inelastic

(j) 15% increase in price, 65% increase in quantity supplied
E = 4.33, Relatively Elastic

4.2 LEARNING PRACTICE

Based on the information provided below, whether the good or service is *relatively elastic, unitary elastic, inelastic* or *perfectly elastic*. Also determine what would happen to the TR for the sellers of the items given the indicated price change.

A. Medical care, salt, and gasoline

   $E_d = 0.1$
   P ↑ _____

B. $E_d = 1.2$ College tuition

   P ↓ _____

C. Silk shirts

   $E_d = 1.8$
   P ↑ _____

D. Cigarettes

   $E_d = 0.7$
   P ↓ _____

E. Carpet Cleaning

   $E_d = 1$
   P ↑ _____

4.3 LEARNING PRACTICE

a) Fill in the missing information:

Original P_1	New P_2	Original Q_1	New Q_2	Original Total Rev.	Coeff. of Ed.	Type of Elasticity
$2.00	$2.50	100	60	200		
$1.10	1.35	50	48	55		
$200.00	100.00	200	400	40000		

b) How might you determine if the demand for good X is relatively elastic, relatively inelastic, perfectly elastic, or unitary elastic between two prices?

Chapter 5

The Foundation of Consumer Choice

LEARNING OBJECTIVES

After reading this chapter, you should be able to:

1. State and explain the seven assumptions of utility analysis.
2. Discuss and solve the diamond-water paradox.
3. Define utility, total utility, and marginal utility.
4. Construct total utility schedules and curves which give information reflecting marginal utility.
5. Explain marginal utility schedules and curves.
6. Explain how a rational individual decides what to purchase, given necessary information about utility, income, and prices.
7. Discuss the importance of utility in explaining consumer choice.
8. Identify the various combinations of two goods that the consumer might buy on the basis of his or her budget constraint.
9. Derive an individual's demand curve for a particular good using an indifference map.
10. Graphically illustrate the slope of the budget line associated with a change in prices.
11. Graphically illustrate a budget line showing a shift caused by a change in income.
12. Construct total utility, marginal utility and disutility curves.
13. Calculate the marginal rate of substitution (MRS) and explain the tradeoff between units of two different goods.
14. Construct, identify, and explain the consumer maximization of utility.
15. State and explain (verbally and graphically) the tangency solution.
16. Explain the characteristics of indifference curves.
17. State and explain (verbally and mathematically) the concept of disutility.
18. Discuss the meaning of rational consumer.
19. Summarize the foundation of consumer choice (why consumers choose as they do).
20. Solve the learning practices as indicated at the end of the chapter.

Introduction

One of the key ideas in consumer choice in that people have only a limited amount of money to spend, so they look at the value of any purchase relative to other possible purchases—that is, they compare the marginal utility per dollar of different purchases and buy those goods and services with the highest marginal utility per dollar.

Hence, the idea that households and firms must make choices because of scarcity is the fundamental notion of economic analysis. Economists' views of consumer choice are based on seven assumptions.

1. Consumers must make choices because they have a limited income and are forced to choose which of their many wants to satisfy.
2. Prices are known (each commodity is not free and must be paid for).
3. The utility of each commodity is measurable.
4. The consumer is rational in his or her choice.
5. The consumers do not know, with certainty, all of the attributes of the goods they are choosing to consume.
6. As increasing amounts of particular goods are consumed, the additional satisfaction gained from each additional unit becomes smaller (principle of diminishing marginal utility).
7. Many goods have characteristics that make them satisfactory substitutes for other goods.

Within the framework of consumer consumption, there is a paradox. Conspicuous consumption occurs when goods are expensive and judged to be of better quality because of their high price. Diamonds demand a high price in view of their utility. They are desired and priced accordingly. However, water, which is a necessity of life and has a very high utility by comparison, is relatively inexpensive.

The Rational Consumer

A consumer who is assumed to be rational is one who seeks to obtain the greatest possible satisfaction from purchases. It is, therefore, rational to try to get the most out of one's income by selecting the mix of commodities that promises to offer the greatest amount of satisfaction. For example, if a consumer is faced with a choice of purchasing a dollar's worth of apples or a dollar's worth of plums, and the consumer prefers the plums, it would not be rational for him or her to purchase the apples. A rational consumer is consistent, wants to maximize satisfaction, prefers Good A over Good B because Good A gives more utility or satisfaction.

Total Utility and Marginal Utility

Total utility (TU) refers to the total satisfaction a person receives from consuming a commodity. Marginal utility (MU) refers to the change in satisfaction that a person receives from consuming more or less of a commodity. One can construct a utility function to better understand the concepts of total and marginal utility. A utility function is a preference function ordering a consumer's desire to consume differing amounts of a good.

Let's construct a utility function for a particular commodity, such as juice. First, select a convenient time period, an hour, for example. Then, for one unit (one can) of juice per hour, assign a number of utils, say 25 (you can choose any number at all: 1; 10,000; 1/20; 221/2. Ask yourself: "If I get 25 utils from one can, how many would I get if I consumed two cans of juice per hour rather than just one?" Suppose, after much reflection, you say 55. Ask yourself the same question about three cans of juice per hour, four, five, six, and so on.

Marginal utility is the amount of utility that an additional unit of consumption adds to total utility. The formula for marginal utility (MU) is:

$$MU = \frac{\Delta TU}{\Delta Q}$$

Marginal utility measures the additional satisfaction derived from one more or one less unit of consumption. In Table 5.1, the marginal utility is determined by the change in total utility due to an additional can of juice. For example, the first can of juice adds 25 utils to total utility. The second can of juice adds 30 utils to total utility. This number is calculated by subtracting the total utility of consuming one can of juice from the total utility of consuming two cans of juice (55-25=30).

Table 5.1
Utility Function for Juice

Can of Juice Per Hour	Total Utility (TU)	(MU) Marginal Utility
0	0	0
1	25	25
2	55	30
3	80	25
4	99	19
5	112	13
6	119	7
7	120	1
8	114	-6

Principle of Diminishing Marginal Utility (DMU)

The most important characteristic of the schedule shown in Table 5.1 is that the addition to total utility from each additional unit consumed becomes smaller. This characteristic is called diminishing marginal utility.

The principle of diminishing marginal utility states that marginal utility of a commodity will diminish over time as total consumption of the commodity increases. In other words, as you consume more units of a commodity, the additional units will increase total utility by an amount less than the preceding units. This principle is reflected in Table 5.1 and Figure 5.1. In Table 5.1 marginal utility declines further as the fourth can increases total utility by only 19 utils.

Figure 5.1 panel (b) shows the marginal utility curve that corresponds to the total utility curve in panel (a). Note that the total utility curve rises as the number of cans of juice consumed rises. The more cans of juice consumed each hour, the more satisfaction the consumer gets. But the curve begins to slope downward beyond a certain point, demonstrating the law of diminishing marginal utility: marginal utility declines as quantity consumed rises. At some point, there exists maximum consumption, after which additional units give no additional utility. Any additional units would actually reduce total utility. This is illustrated by the total utility curve. When the total utility curve reaches its maximum, marginal utility is zero. As marginal utility becomes negative, total utility must decline. In Table 5.1, total utility continues to increase from the first through the seventh can of juice consumed. Total utility increases because marginal utility is positive. The eighth can of juice yields a negative marginal utility of -6 and, consequently, total utility decreases from 120 to 114.

Total and Marginal Utility Graphically

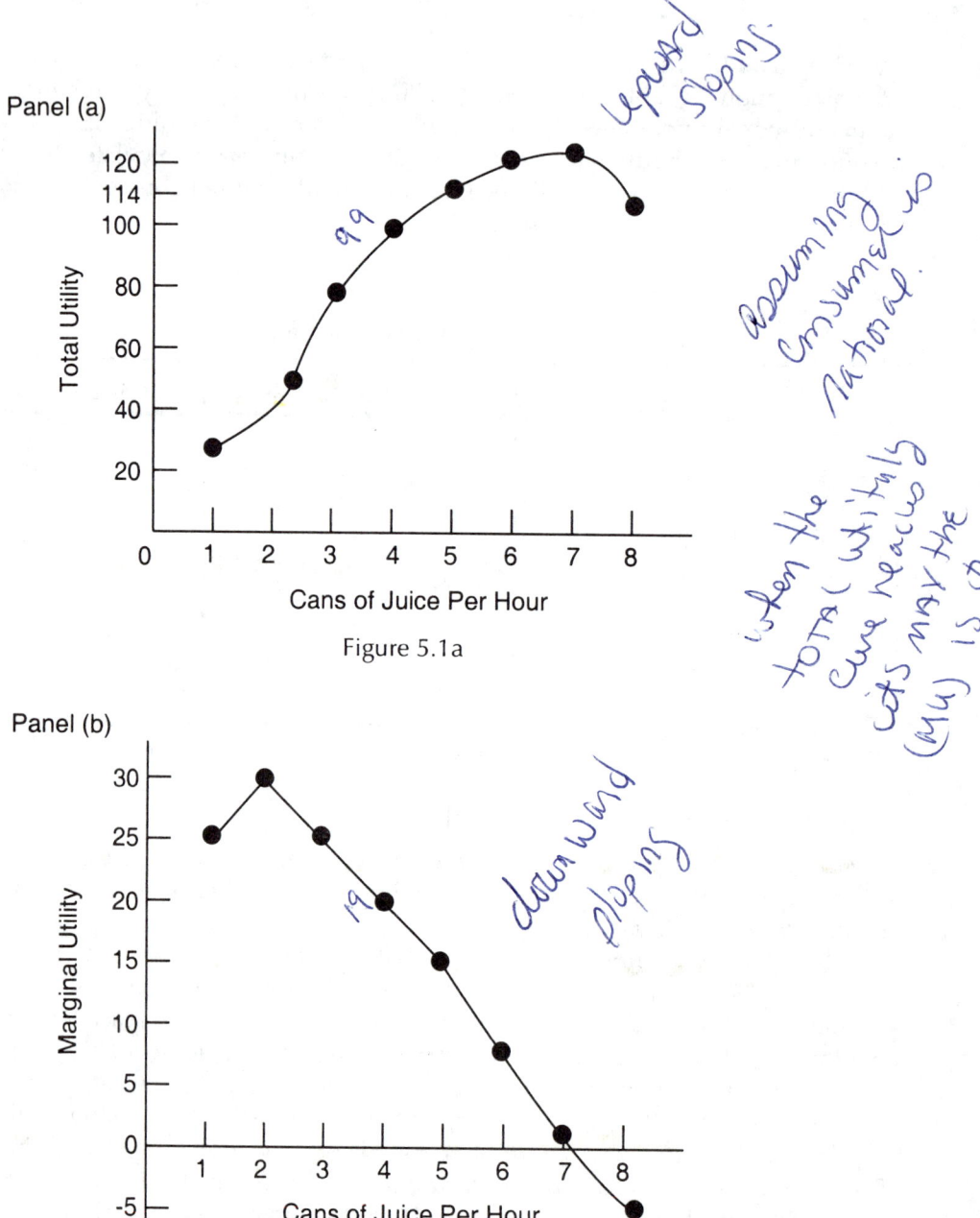

Figure 5.1a

Figure 5.1b

Utility Consumer Behavior

The concepts of utility and price now can be combined to show how consumers make choices in the marketplace. There is a variety of commodities in the marketplace and a variety of prices. If a consumer had an unlimited source of money, the price of the commodity would be irrelevant, and he or she would purchase the items which provide the greatest utility. However, most people don't have an unlimited source of money and therefore, price and income affect the choices made by the consumers. For instance, you may prefer caviar for a late night snack, but because of its high price and your limited income, you may purchase canned tuna instead. The reason for this behavior lies in price and utility and it's completely rational.

Let's examine further the effect of price and utility on consumer goods. Suppose, for example, you are considering purchasing a bottle of beer. Table 5.2 shows the choices that are available to you. The imported brand is your first choice because it yields the most utility. For the rational consumer, whose choices are affected by price and income, the more relevant question isn't which beer provides the most utility, but which beer has the most utility per dollar. In Table 5.2 the marginal utility per dollar is calculated by dividing price into marginal utility. The imported beer provides 14 additional utils to total utility and costs 1.75 dollars. Fourteen utils divided by 1.75 dollars (14/1.75) is equal to the marginal utility per dollar, eight, in this instance. Since the domestic beer has a calculated marginal utility per dollar of 10, it provides a better choice than either imported beer or generic beer (also a marginal utility of eight).

Table 5.2
Utility-Per-Dollar Comparisons

Choice	Marginal Utility (utils)	Price	MU Per Dollar
Imported Beer	14.0	$1.75	8
Domestic Beer	10.0	1.00	10
Generic Beer	4.0	.50	8

This choice implies that the extra satisfaction of the imported beer over the domestic beer is not worth 75 cents, but the extra satisfaction of the generic beer is worth the extra 50 cents it costs. Thus, in deciding how to spend money, consumers look at marginal utility per dollar rather than marginal utility alone. This is possible because money is the common denominator. Dollars can be used to buy any available good. So for the last dollar that you spend, you want to choose the item with the highest utility per dollar. In so doing, you economize by getting the most satisfaction per dollar. There are other things you can do with the extra 75 cents. The 75 cents spent on something other than in the domestic brand beer will yield more additional utils than the difference between the utility of the imported brand and the utility of the domestic brand. However, 50 cents spent on other goods will not yield more utils than spending it on domestic beer instead of generic beer.

Maximizing Total Utility

The self-interest hypothesis suggests that individuals will act to maximize their total utility (TU). Hence, the problem of choice is to find an item you can purchase with your income that offers the most satisfaction. That is, you maximize your satisfaction or total utility, subject to a budget constraint.

To see how marginal utility and price influence how a consumer maximizes total utility, consider an example with only two goods: beer and hamburgers. A unit of beer costs 50 cents and a unit of hamburger costs 1 dollar. The consumer has a limited amount of income, called a budget constraint. A budget constraint is a given level of income that determines the maximum amount of goods that may be purchased by an individual. Let's provide this consumer with 10 dollars' worth of purchasing power, and see how that income will be allocated between the two goods, so as to achieve maximum utility.

Table 5.3
Utility Schedule

	Beer			Hamburger			
Quantity Per Week (bottles)	MU	MU/P P=$.50	TU	Quantity Per Week	MU	MU/P P=$1.00	TU
1	25	50	25	1	52	52	52
2	24	48	49	2	50	50	102
3	23	46	72	3	48	48	150
4	22	44	94	4	46	46	196
5	20	40	114	5	44	44	240
6	18	36	132	6	40	40	280
7	15	30	147	7	36	36	316
8	11	22	158	8	32	32	348
9	8	16	166	9	27	27	375
10	5	10	171	10	22	22	397

The first dollar will be allocated to the hamburger because one hamburger yields 52 utils of satisfaction compared with 49 utils for a dollar's worth of beer. The next dollar spent also will be for a hamburger because it yields 50 utils, which is still greater than that of the alternative purchase. The third dollar is spent on beer because 49 utils of satisfaction gained from purchasing two beers are greater than the 48 utils that are yielded by a third hamburger. The process continues until the income of 10 dollars is spent. In maximizing total utility, the consumer will spend 3 dollars on six cans of beer and 7 dollars on seven hamburgers. This allocation produces 448 utils of satisfaction—the maximum total utility that can be purchased with 10 dollars of income. There is no expenditure pattern that will produce more satisfaction (try reducing beer consumption by two cans and increasing hamburger consumption by one, or vice versa).

The consumer's choices are based on a maximization rule that says that total utility is maximized when the last dollar spent on Good A yields the same utility as the last dollar spent on Good B. In algebraic from, the total utility is maximized where:

$$\frac{MUA}{PA} = \frac{MUB}{PB}$$

For example, the marginal utility of a bottle of beer, when six bottles per hour are consumed, is 18 utils, and the price of beer is 50 cents:

$$\frac{MU\ beer}{P\ beer} = \frac{18}{\$.50}$$

or, 36 utils per dollar. For hamburger, at the optimum consumption rate, the MU is 36 and the P is dollar:

$$\frac{\text{MU hamburger}}{\text{P hamburger}} = \frac{36 \text{ utils}}{\$1.00}$$

or 36 utils per dollar.

The above can be generalized to include all goods by saying an individual maximizes his or her satisfaction from a given amount of income when:

$$\frac{\text{MUA}}{\text{PA}} = \frac{\text{MUB}}{\text{PB}} = \frac{\text{MUC}}{\text{PC}} = ----- \frac{\text{MUN}}{\text{PN}}$$

Where the letters A-N represent all the goods an individual buys. Hence, once this condition is reached, consumer equilibrium is achieved. Thus, satisfaction cannot be improved by spending less on one good and more on another.

Disutility (DU)

Disutility refers to the marginal utility of an extra item being negative. This causes total utility to drop. For example, a third hamburger is too much and causes a person to become ill. That is, when the marginal utility is less than zero (MU < 0), then disutility occurs.

Table 5.1

Quantity per Week	TU Good A	MU Good A	TU Good B	MU Good B
0	0	0	0	0
1	30	30	40	40
2	55	25	75	35
3	75	20	105	30
4	90	15	130	25
5	100	10	150	20
6	105	5	165	15
7	105	0	165	0
8	103	−2	161	−4

Table 5.1 explains the following: Total utility is at a maximum value of 105 utils (Good A) when marginal utility equals zero (0). That is, at 7 units per week. The more units of goods we consume during a period of time, the less additional satisfaction. The marginal utility gained from consuming successive units of a good will decline as the amount consumed increases. At 2 units of consumption per week, diminishing marginal utility occurs for Good A and Good B. Total utility is at maximum value of 165 (Good B) when marginal utility equals zero (0). Disutility occurs for Good A and Good B at 8 units per week. That is, disutility occurs when marginal utility is less than zero (MU < 0).

However, to determine which of two goods is the better buy, a consumer should compare the products MU per dollar.

Example: A croissant costs $2.00 and has a MU of 30.
A muffin costs $1.00 and has a MU of 20.

Which should you buy?

The answer is the muffin, because it has a higher MU per dollar. The MU per dollar for the croissant is 30/2, or 15; whereas the MU per dollar for the muffin is 20/1, or 20.

The Diamond-Water Paradox

Early economists found it paradoxical that necessary commodities were often valued less by the market than luxury commodities. The debate was advanced by Adam Smith when he recognized that value could mean either value in use or value in exchange.

The diamond-water paradox illustrated that a commodity's value in use could not determine its value in exchange (price). To economists, it seemed reasonable that a commodity with a high use value, such as water, should have a high price value. Yet diamonds, while less useful, are more expensive than water. The diamond-water paradox is caused by the failure to separate total utility (TU) from marginal utility (MU).

TU determines value in use and MU determines value in exchange. The commodities that have the greatest value in use (TU) have little or no value in exchange (MU). Value in exchange, or marginal utility, is determined not by total satisfaction but rather, by what people are willing to pay for the last unit they buy.

The concept of utility is fundamental to demand theorists. Utility is the satisfaction an individual expects to receive from consuming a good or from a service. If a person wants to buy a commodity, it is said that the commodity has utility.

It is clear from this definition that utility is a subjective appraisal depending upon the individual concerned and the object considered. The utility for a particular good or service will vary from person to person. A glass of water, for instance, will have a great deal of utility to a Bedouin in the desert and relatively little to those of us who have access to water supplies.

It is important to note that utility measures the way a person feels about a good or service before buying it or consuming it. For example, you may want an expensive bottle of wine that is on display at a store. The wine has utility because you desire it. However, you may find the wine distasteful after purchasing it and receive no satisfaction from its consumption.

The lack of satisfaction from consuming the wine is irrelevant in economics. Utility is the satisfaction you expected to receive before buying the wine, not what you actually experienced after you consumed it. This distinction is important because utility is used to develop a demand curve. The demand curve shows that the amount of goods people will purchase is based on their anticipated satisfaction, and not the amounts that they would purchase based on their actual satisfaction from consuming that good.

Economists have created an arbitrary unit of measurement, called a util, to measure utility. Since utility is unique to each individual, a util is a satisfactory measuring device only as long as no attempt is made to compare the utils of different people.

To sum up, people will rarely pay a great deal per gallon to obtain water because they place a very low marginal value in water. Everyone would be willing to pay more for a gallon of diamonds than a gallon of water, because very few people are ever in danger of dying of thirst. Hence, what people are willing to pay is determined by the additional utility gained from the last unit they buy.

The diamond-water paradox illustrates that a commodity's value in use cannot determine its value in exchange (price). To economists, it seemed reasonable that a commodity with a high use value, such as water, would have a high price value. Yet diamonds, while less useful, are more expensive than water.

Indifference Curve Analysis

We have discussed the classical approach to consumer demand. That is, we have used the concept of measurable marginal utility to explain the factors which underlie the individual's demand curve. However, many economists disagree with this approach. They believe that this method is inherently flawed because utility cannot be measured. Remember that a util is a theoretical unit of measurement devised by economists to measure expected satisfaction. Opponents of the classical approach state that, at best, it can provide only theoretical insights into consumer demand. According to them, the classical method does not really have any practical application.

The Foundation of Consumer Choice

Another approach to explaining consumer demand is the indifference curve analysis. This method of viewing consumer behavior does not require the economist to measure utility, but simply to study the consumer's indifference to and preference for a variety of goods. Economists who espouse this theory believe that the concepts of indifference and preference can better approximate the way consumers actually make choices in the marketplace. In indifference analysis, a bundle of goods and services is offered to a consumer, and the consumer states his or her preference or indifference to that bundle of goods. By ranking goods from least desirable to most desirable, the proponents of indifference curve analysis feel that it better explains the foundations of consumer choice.

Let us examine the indifference curve approach further. Suppose Kathy is considering different combinations of chocolates and licorice sticks, as indicated in Table 5.5. Combination A contains 11 licorice sticks and two chocolates. When Kathy examines combination B, which contains 8 licorice sticks and 3 chocolates, she states that neither combination a nor combination B is preferred over the other. To Kathy, both combination a and combination B would provide the same amount of satisfaction. Therefore, she is said to be indifferent to the two combinations. When Kathy examines the other combinations, c, d, and e, she is indifferent to each of them as well. Since Kathy has indicated that all five combinations of licorice sticks and chocolates yield the same amount of satisfaction, we have created an indifference set for her.

Table 5.5
Kathy's Indifference Set

Combinations	Good y (Licorice Sticks)	Good x (Chocolates)
a	11	2
b	8	3
c	6	5
d	5	7
e	4	9

The indifference set can be geometrically represented by drawing an indifference curve corresponding to the indifference set in Table 5.5 as drawn in Figure 5.3. This indifference curve shows all combinations of the two commodities which give equal satisfaction and among which a consumer is indifferent. The slope of an indifferent curve indicates how much of one commodity the consumer is willing to give up in order to get an additional unit of the other commodity.

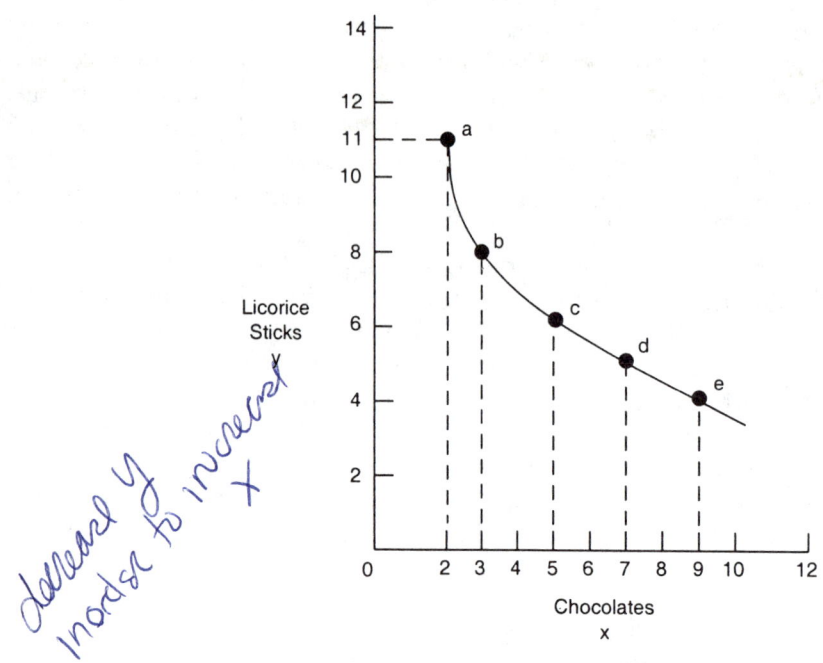

Figure 5.3
Indifference Curve
Indifference curves represent combinations of two goods that satisfy a consumer equally well. All combinations along the same indifference curve represent the same level of satisfaction.

Indifference curves are negatively sloped, or downward sloping to the right, because all points on the curve must represent equal amounts of satisfaction to the consumer. If each point on the curve provides equal satisfaction, the consumer is indifferent to all the combinations of goods represented by that curve. This means that if more than one good is added to a combination of goods, some of the other goods must be taken away to maintain the same level of satisfaction. Each combination represents a tradeoff in quantity while maintaining a constant level of satisfaction. In Kathy's case, if combination B presents more chocolates than combination A, it must also possess fewer licorice sticks since the combinations must yield the same level of satisfaction.

Consider the case where one combination of goods has more licorice sticks and more chocolates than any other combination. A consumer would obviously find this arrangement preferable and, thus would no longer be indifferent. This preferred combination of goods can no longer be represented by a point on the same indifference curve, but must be placed on a higher indifference curve. That higher indifference curve lies upward and to the right of the previous indifference curve. The indifference set represented by a higher indifference curve is preferred to that represented by a lower indifference curve. As Kathy moves from I to II to III to IV, in Figure 5.4 she receives more satisfaction. Such a series of indifference curves is called an indifference map. Every individual consumer has such a map, and movement to higher curves represents a gain in satisfaction.

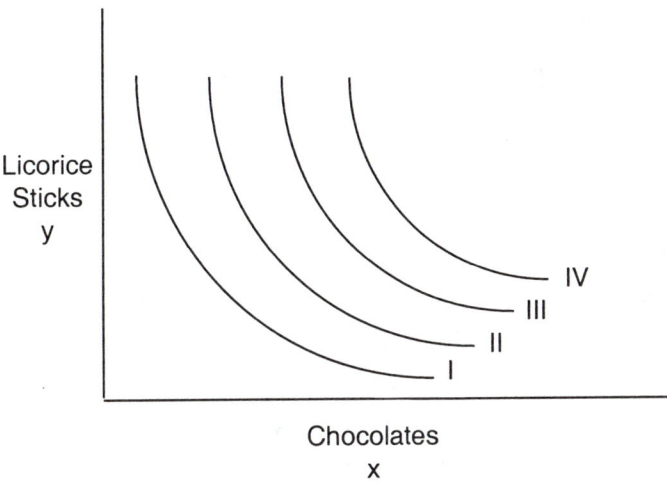

Figure 5.4
Indifference Map
Consists of a set of indifference curves. The higher curves represent higher levels of satisfaction.

The typical indifference curve for two goods will have two characteristics: curvature and convexity. The convexity feature means that as a consumer attains more units of one good and fewer units of another good, it takes more and more units of the more abundant good to compensate for the loss of one unit of the good that is becoming scarcer (see Figure 5.5).

At point A, the individual is consuming relatively large amounts of y and small amounts of x. To compensate for a reduction in consumption of one unit of y, the person would require three units of x to remain equally satisfied: but at point B, since less of y and more of x (eight units) to compensate for the loss of one unit of y. At point C, the individual now consumes a large amount of x and very little of y, so to give up one unit of y, 16 units of x would be needed to retain the same utility as before. Indifference curve analysis reflects the concept of diminishing marginal utility without assigning numerical values to utility.

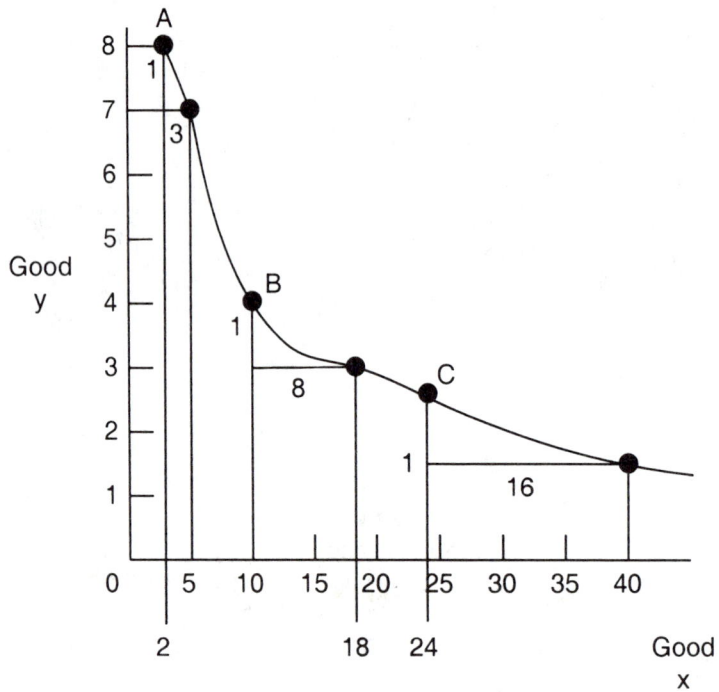

Figure 5.5
Convexity Feature of Indifference Curves
A typical indifference curve is convex to the origin.
This means that the more of a particular good that a consumer has,
the less important to him or her is an extra unit of this good.

Marginal Rates of Substitution (MRS)

The indifference curve represents different combinations of two goods which yield the same level of satisfaction to the consumer. The rate at which one good can be substituted for another along this curve is called the marginal rate of substitution. The marginal rate of substitution (MRS) of x for y, MRSxy, shows the willingness of the consumer to substitute between goods. That is:

$$\text{MRS} = \frac{\text{No. of units of y given up}}{\text{No. of units of x gained}}$$

In Figure 5.5 the MRSxy at point a is 1/3. That is, one unit of y must be sacrificed to gain 3 units of x. At point B, the MRSxy is 1/8, and at point C, it is 1/16. The declining value of MRSxy is a reflection of the principle of diminishing marginal rates of substitution, showing that as more of one good (x) is substituted for the other good (y), the value of Good x in terms of Good y declines.

In other words, the MRS is the amount of one good an individual is willing to give up to obtain an additional unit of another good while maintaining equal utility.

As Figure 5.6 shows the MRS of wheat to autos with less wheat and more autos, each additional auto becomes less valuable to the consumer. For each additional auto consumed, the consumer is willing to sacrifice smaller amounts of wheat. This means that the MRS of autos for wheat decreases as more autos are consumed.

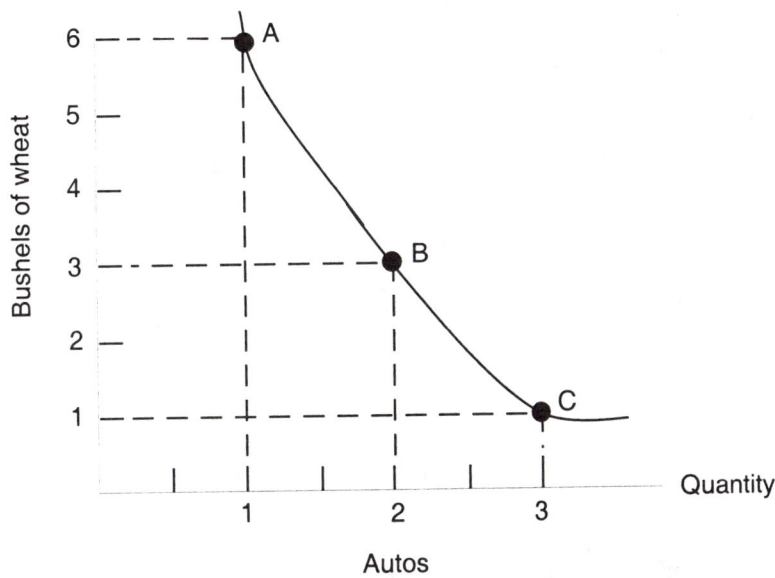

Figure 5.6 MRS of Wheat to Autos

Figure 5.6 shows all combination points are equally desirable along an indifference curve. Consumer is just as happy consuming, say 6 bushels of wheat and 1 auto at point A, 3 bushels of wheat and 2 autos at point B, and 1 bushel of wheat and 3 autos at point C.

Characteristics of Indifference Curves

Indifference curves have 3 properties:

    a. Downward slope

    b. Satisfaction is constant along an indifferent curve

    c. Indifferent curves do not cross each other

    d. Indifferent curves are down sloping from left to right as shown in Figure 5.7. That is, a negative slope is indicating only if both Good Y and Good X are compared (desirable). If you reduce the amount of one good, you will have to compensate the buyer by offering more of the other good so as to leave the buyer indifferent. Hence, your satisfaction increases when you buy more of either good.

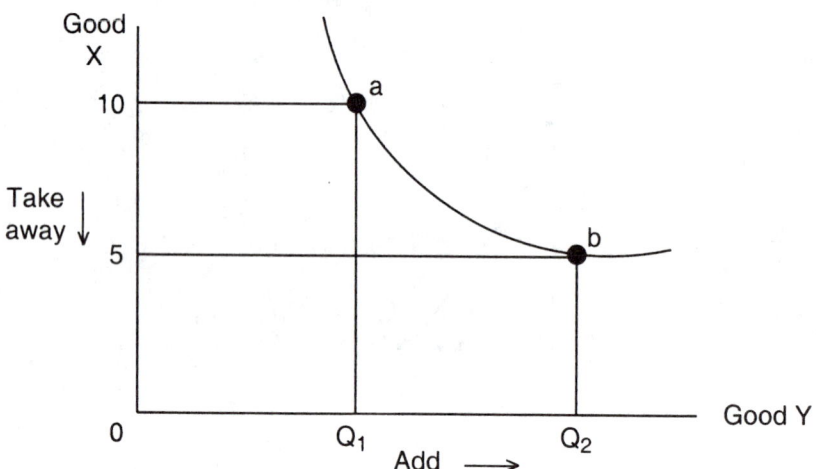

Figure 5.7
Indifference curve has a negative slope.

2. Satisfaction is constant along an indifference curve. If you are indifferent to all the bundles on an indifference curve, they must offer you the same satisfaction. For example, if you continue to reduce the amount of one good by an equal amount, you will have to compensate the household by offering increasingly large amounts of the other good, so as to leave the buyer indifferent. That is, take away 1 unit of Good X, add 1/4 unit of Good Y; take away 1 unit of Good X, add two units of Good Y.

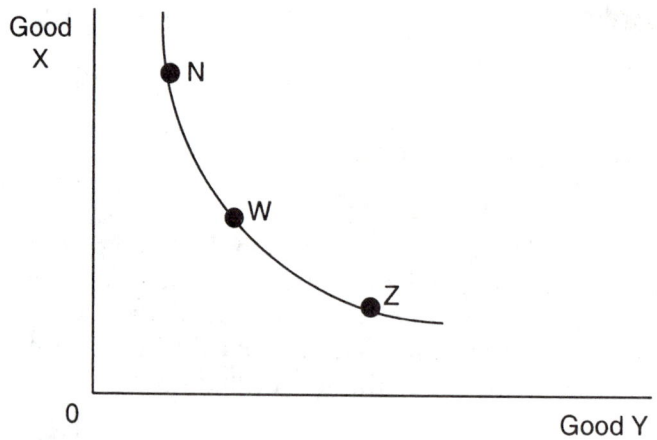

Figure 5.8

3. Indifference curves do not cross each other. If the buyer is rational, it would be impossible to have two indifferent curves cross on one household indifferent curve map as shown in Figure 5.9. You prefer bundle IC2 to bundle IC1; that is, bundle IC2 offers you more satisfaction than bundle IC1 and bundle IC3 offers you more than bundle IC2.

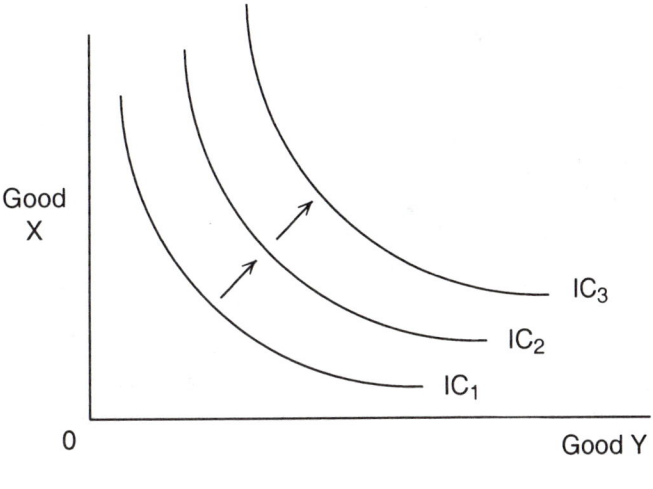

Figure 5.9

Thus all points on IC3 are preferred to all points on IC2 and IC1. (IC3 has more of both goods).

Suppose IC1 and IC2 cross each other as shown in figure 5.10. You will find the following relationships:

— On IC1, combination A = combination B
— On IC2, combination A = combination C.

Therefore, combination B = combination c. This conclusion is impossible since combination B has more of both goods and so it is preferred to combination C. Consequently, they cannot cross each other.

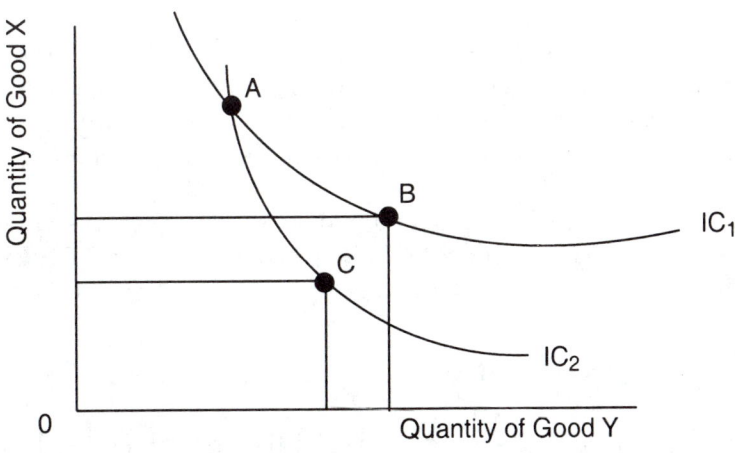

Figure 5.10

Figure 5.11 also shows that if indifference curves I and II crossed, then X=Y and Y=X. But since X is preferred to Z, the entire nexus becomes illogical.

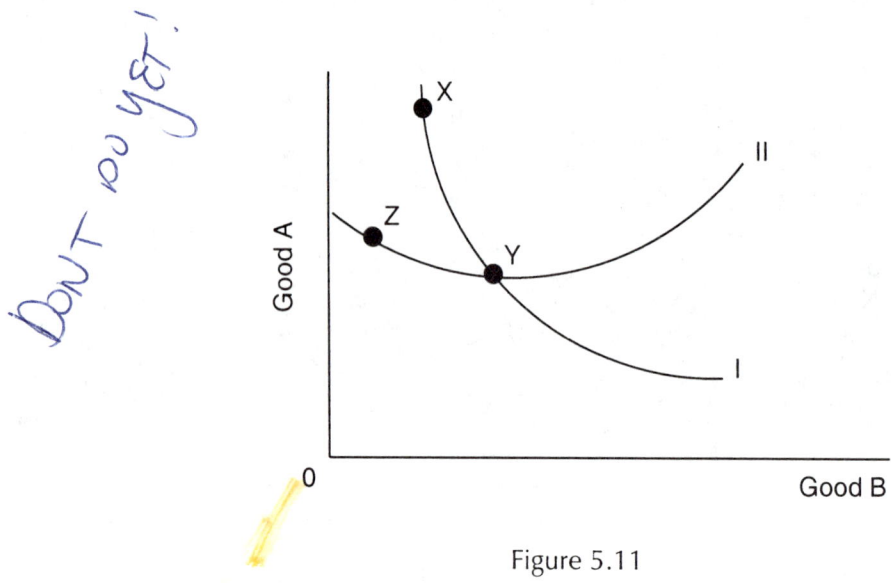

Figure 5.11

Budget Constraints

The budget constraint shows combinations of two goods that a buyer can purchase, given the price of each good and the buyer's income. The budget constraint places an upper limit on his or her purchases.

An indifferent map demonstrates a consumer's preferences. It makes it possible to compare points representing combinations of goods x and y to determine whether a consumer has a preference or is indifferent to each combination. All points on any single indifference curve are equivalent to each other in utility, even if utility cannot be measured. Points on indifference curves located above and to the right of other indifference curves represents combinations that are preferred.

The key question is which combinations of commodities are actually attainable by Kathy. That is, on which indifference curve on the indifference map can Kathy begin choosing combinations. The answer depends on the income available to her and the prices of the commodities.

Remember that commodity prices are determined by the markets, and Kathy cannot influence them. Kathy's limited income constrains her from buying all the commodities that she might desire. Her income is her budget constraint and, when drawn on the indifference map, is called the budget line.

To remain consistent with Table 5.5 assume that Kathy can consume either licorice sticks or chocolates. Suppose that she has a disposable income (D1) of 16 dollars. Licorice sticks and chocolates sell for two dollars and 1 dollar per unit, respectively. The construction of the budget line is illustrated in Figure 5.12.

If she spends the entire income (D1) on licorice sticks, she can buy 8 licorice sticks.

This number is determined by dividing income by the price of the good: $\frac{DI}{Py}$.

In this case $16/$2 = 8 licorice sticks. Thus, 8 is the y-intercept. The x-intercept is calculated in the same manner: $\frac{DI}{Px} = \frac{\$16}{\$1} = 16$ chocolates.

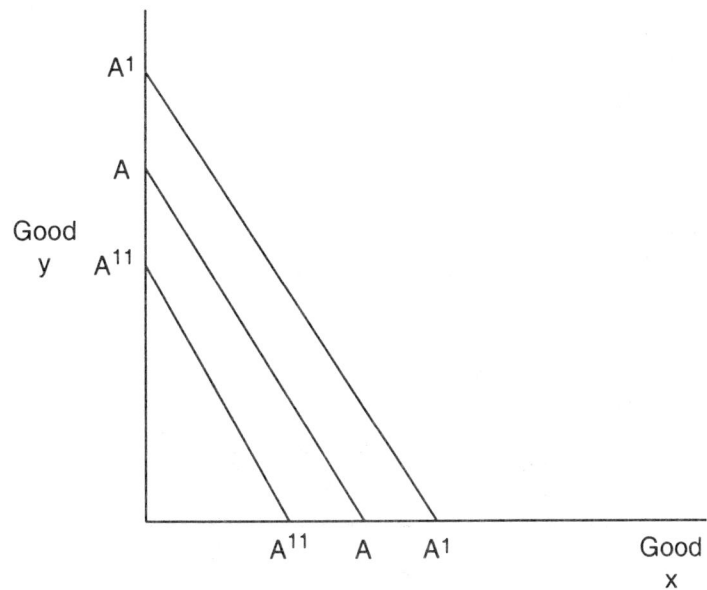

Figure 5.13
Effect of Income Changes on Budget Lines
Shifts in the budget line are caused by change in income. Increases in income shift the budget line outward (from AA to A¹A¹). While decreases in income shift the budget line inward (from AA to A¹¹A¹¹). In both cases, the slope of the budget line does not change.

Let's consider the effect of a change in prices on the budget line. A change in the price of one good affects only how much more of that good can be purchased, not the amount of the other good that can be purchased. For example, if the price of chocolates rises and Kathy spends all her income on licorice sticks, the price rise has no effect on the amount of licorice sticks purchased. However, if Kathy spends all her income on chocolates and the price of that commodity rises, Kathy will naturally purchase fewer chocolates. A price rise, then, will affect the budget line intercept of the good that has experienced the price rise.

The effect of a change in prices on the budget line is shown in Figure 5.14.

A price rise for Good x from P_{x1} to P_{x2} causes the budget line intercept to move closer to the origin, reflecting the fact that less x can now be purchased, assuming that income remains the same. A decrease in the price of Good x to P_{x3} means more x could be purchased, and the intercept moves away from the origin. This shows that the consumer can purchase more of Good x because it is cheaper.

Unlike a change in income, price changes cause the slope of the budget line to change. The slope of the budget line is the algebraic function $\Delta Y/\Delta X$. Notice that the slope is the negative of the ratio of the vertical intercept to the horizontal intercept.

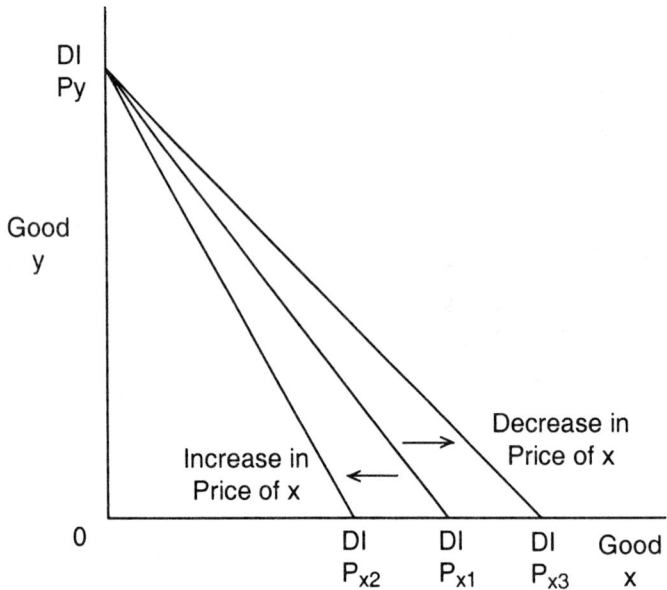

Figure 5.14
Effect of Price Changes on Budget Lines
P of a good will change the slope of a line. If P_x rises, the intercept of the budget line
at the horizontal axis will shift closer to the origin. If P_x drops,
this will shift the budget line away from the origin.

The slope of the budget line changes when the ratio of the price changes. A change in income, on the other hand, represented no change in relative prices and the slope of the budget line remains the same, as seen by parallel shifting of the budget line in Figure 5.13.

The Consumer's Maximization of Utility

We have now devised a means of measuring a consumer's preferences, using the indifference map, and have identified the ability of the consumer to attain those preferences, using the budget line. The next step is to show how the consumer actually maximizes his or her satisfaction.

Figure 5.15 combines a consumer's indifference map and budget line to show a point at which the consumer maximizes utility. Assuming no budget constraint, the consumer would want to choose any combination of goods on indifference curve I_3 because it is the highest indifference curve and the consumer would maximize his or her utility. In other words, any combination of goods on indifference curve I_3 is preferred to any combination on indifference curve I_2. Furthermore, any combination of goods on indifference curve I_1.

However, the consumer has a budget constraint and can only choose those combinations of goods that lie on the budget line. For example, the consumer could choose the combination of goods represented by points E, E^1, E^{11}, in Figure 5.8, because they lie on the budget line. The consumer could not choose a combination on indifferent curve I_3 because it lies above the budget line and is therefore, unattainable. The consumer could choose a combination of goods on indifference curve I_1 but would obtain less utility because the curve lies below indifference curves I_2 and I_3.

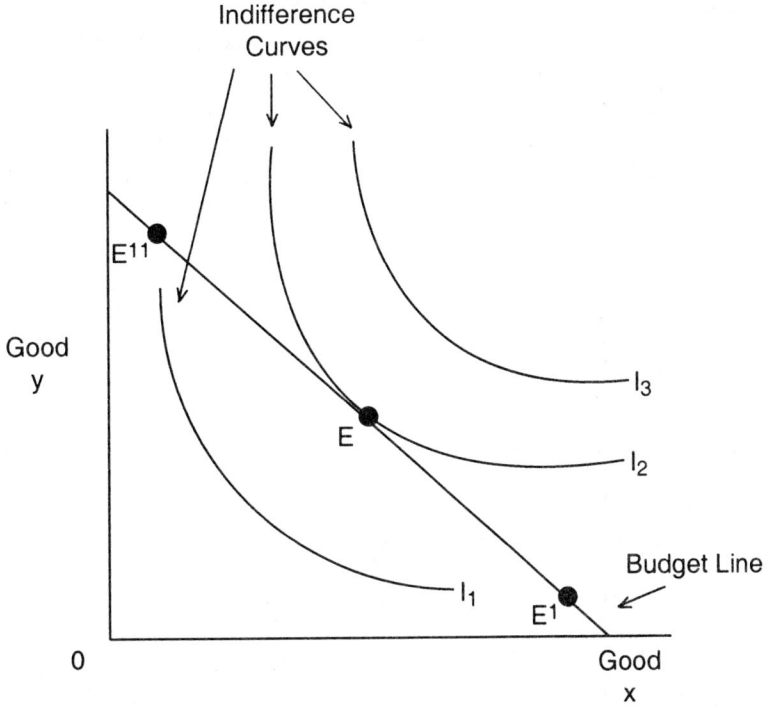

Figure 5.15
Consumer maximization of Utility
The consumer maximizes utility at point E, where the budget line is
tangent to the highest indifference curve.

To maximize utility, the consumer chooses a combination of goods represented by a point on the indifference curve which is tangent to the budget line. In this example, the consumer would select the combination of goods represented by point E because it lies both on the budget line and on indifference curve I_2. The consumer has selected a combination of goods which provides the greatest utility within his or her budget constraints.

Remember from geometry, that two curves that are tangent have equal slopes at the point of tangency. At the point of tangency between the indifference curve and the budget line, the marginal rate of substitution is equal to the ratio of the price of x to the price of y. That is:

$$MRSxy = \frac{Px}{Py}$$

This concept may seem highly abstract, but it simply means that the marginal rate of substitution expresses the willingness of the consumer to trade a certain amount of Good y; and the slope of the budget line reflects the market's willingness to trade a certain amount of Good x for a certain amount of Good y. In other words, market forces impose the relative price on the consumer, so the consumer adjusts consumption amounts in such a way that his or her trade-off is the same as that of the market. Figure 5.16 demonstrates this point.

Suppose you are consuming 30 units of Good y and 10 units of Good x (represented by point A). You would be willing to give up 10 units of Good y if you received 4 units of Good x. This means that you would be expected to consume more of Good x and less of Good y until your indifference curve shows that you will trade 1 unit of Good x for 1 unit of Good y, when the price of the two goods are the same.

Indifference curves that are within the budget constraint represent lower levels of utility than the highest attainable indifference curve. The consumer can increase his or her utility by moving in a direction where the higher indifference curves are tangent to the budget line.

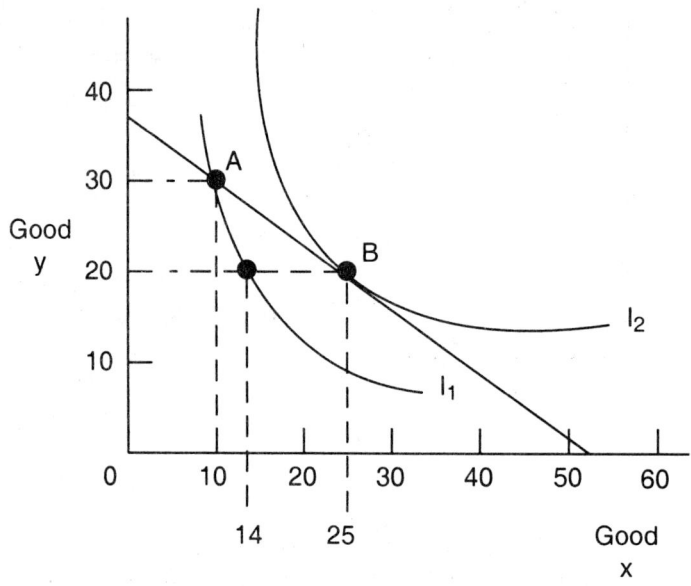

Figure 5.16
Tangency Solution

Derivation of the Demand Curve

In this area we will show the derivation of the demand curve using the indifference/budget line approach. If we assume a person has 20 dollars a week to spend on hamburgers and french fries, and that the price of a hamburger is $2.00 and an order of french fries is $1.00, a consumer can purchase 10 hamburgers or 20 orders of french fries or some combination in between. This is shown in figure 5.17 with budget line BL_1.

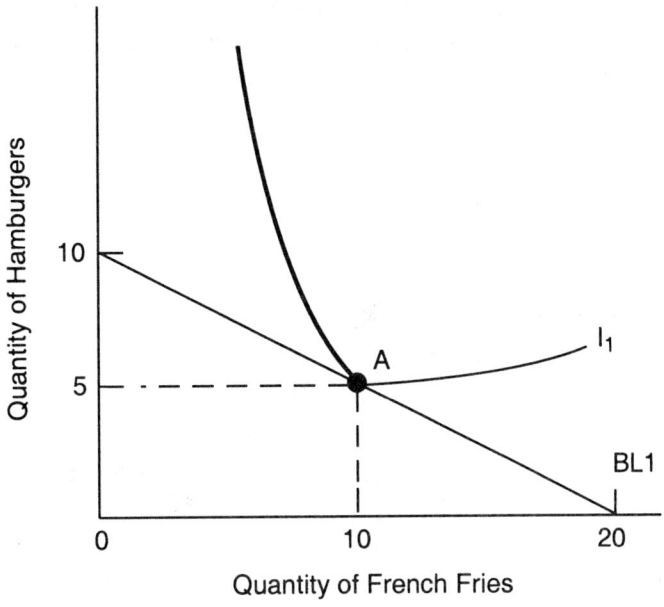

Figure 5.17
Derivation of the Demand Curve

To maximize utility the consumer will purchase 5 hamburgers and 10 orders of fries as shown at point A.

If the price of hamburgers drops to $1.00, the consumer can purchase 20 instead of ten, spending the whole $20, as shown in figure 5.18 with budget line BL_2.

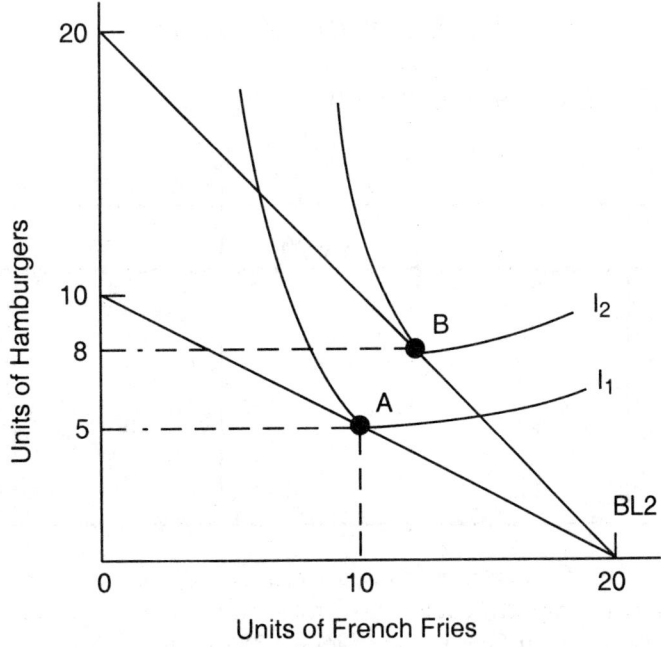

Figure 5.18
Derivation of Demand Curve

The consumer, to maximize utility, will move from point A to point B moving to a higher indifference curve and now will purchase 8 hamburgers.

This information can be shown by the traditional demand relationship as shown in Figure 5.19. At a lower price the consumer will purchase more of an item than at a higher price. We are now saying this is due to utility.

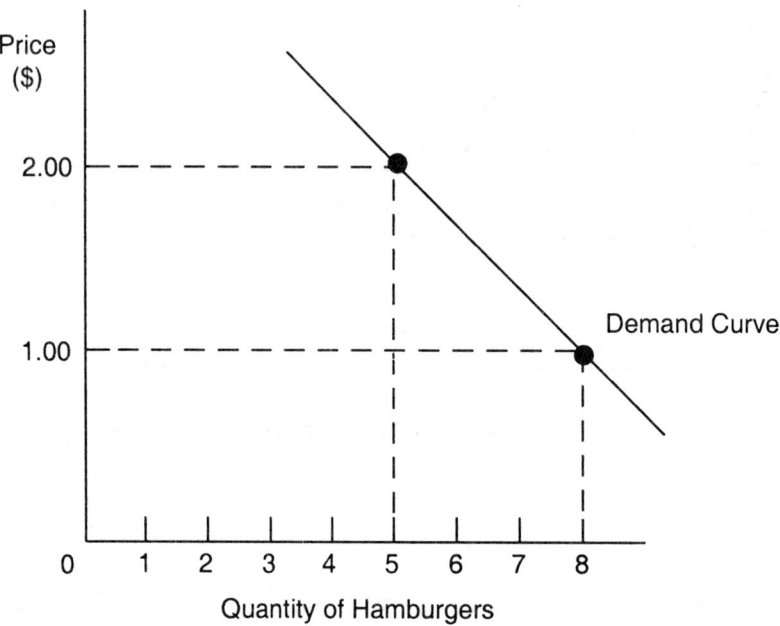

Figure 5.19
Derivation of Demand Curve

5.3 LEARNING PRACTICE

The following are hypothetical total utility (TU) schedules for product X and Y.

a. Compute the marginal utility (MU)

UNIT/WEEK	TU(X)	MU(X)	TU(Y)	MU(Y)
0	0		0	
1	30		20	
2	50		32	
3	60		40	
4	65		47	
5	65		50	
6	64		48	

b. At what amounts of consumption does diminishing MU occur for X and Y?
c. What rate of consumption would maximize utility of Good X? Explain.
d. Does disutility occur for Good X and Good Y? Explain.
e. Construct total utility, marginal utility and disutility curves.

SOLUTIONS

a. MU of X = 0, 30, 20, 10, 5, 0, –1

   MU of Y = 0, 20, 12, 8, 7, 3, –2

b. DMU occurs for Good X at 2 units per week; DMU occurs for Good Y at 2 units per week

c. Rate of consumption (5) would maximize satisfaction because MU = 0

d. Yes, because MU < 0 (negative)

5.4 LEARNING PRACTICE

$$\frac{MUA}{PA} = \frac{MUB}{PB}$$

The above shows consumer satisfaction maximization.

a. Explain this if

   MUA = 40 utils

   PA = $10

   MUB = 60 utils

   PB = $15

b. Explain this if

   MUA = 50 utils

   PA = $5

   MUB = 40 utils

   PB = $20

5.5 Learning Practice

Given the following graph, answer the questions.

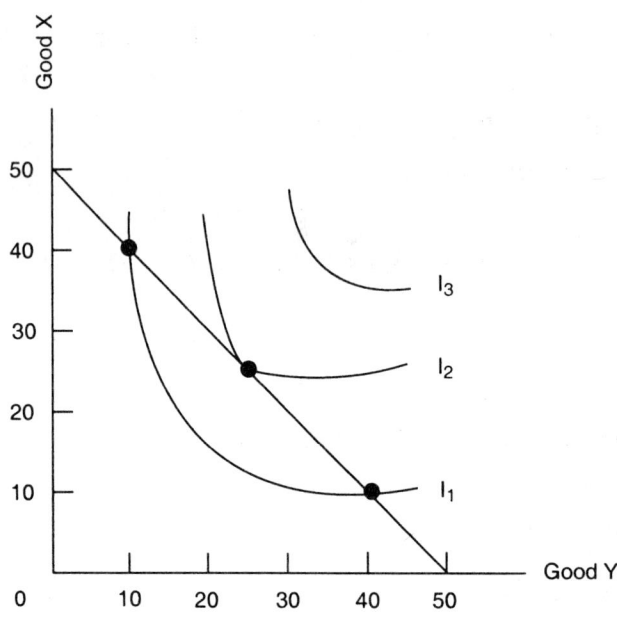

a. What combination of X and Y would yield the highest satisfaction and be purchased?

b. What combination yields the same satisfaction as A?

c. Show three ways the consumer could move curve I_3.

5.6 Learning Practice

Economics is unable to explain the value of goods in a sensible way. That is, a gallon of water is less expensive than a gallon of gasoline, yet is vital to our survival. How can gasoline be more valuable than water?

According to the text, is this statement true or false? Explain your answer.

5.7 Learning Practice

Combination	Q of Oranges	Q of Apples
A	4	6
B	3	6
C	3	8
D	2	11 1/2

Draw an indifference curve based on the above information, then label the combinations that are equally satisfactory to the individual.

5.8 Diminishing Marginal Utility (DMU)

Bring in a box of donut holes when discussing marginal utility (MU), and ask one student to eat the donuts during class period. As the class progresses, keep asking the student if he or she enjoys eating the last donut as much as the one before it. This can be a humorous and unforgettable way to demonstrate the law of diminishing marginal utility (DMU).

Dozen Donut Holes

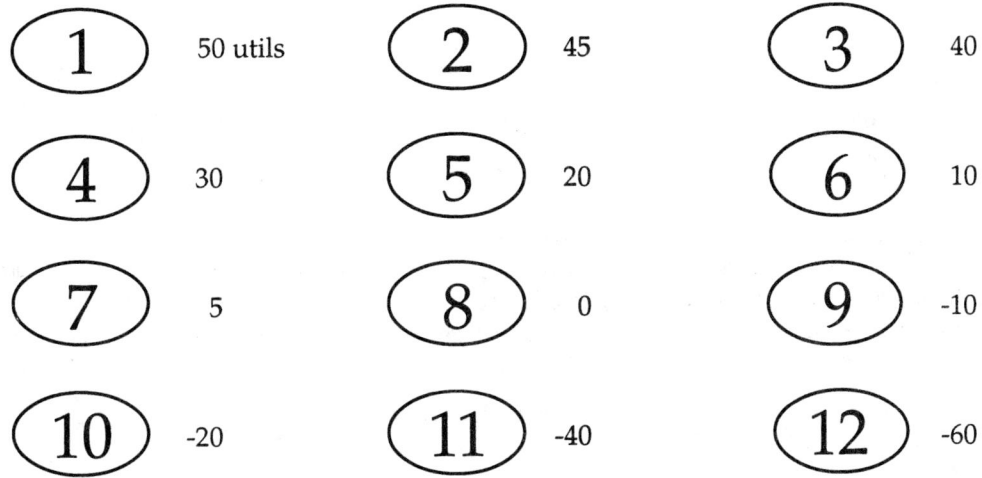

The principle which states that as more and more units of a variable resource are added to a set of fixed resources, the resulting additions to output eventually become increasingly smaller, is the principle of diminishing marginal returns.

At donut hole No. 8, TU is maximized because MU = 0. Disutility occurs at donut hole number 9. MU is negative. Furthermore, the satisfaction derived from consuming the sixth glass of water on a given day is typically less than the satisfaction derived from consuming the first glass of water. That is, as more and more units of a given product are consumed, beyond some point, the incremental gain in satisfaction from consuming one more unit declines.

5.9 Learning Practice

Table 5.6

Cans of Soda	Total Utility	Marginal Utility
1	14	--
2	--	12
3	36	--
4	44	--
5	--	6
6	54	--
7	56	--
8	56	--
9	54	--

Refer to Table 5.6. Answer the following:
a. What is the marginal utility of increasing from the second to the third can of soda?
b. What is the TU of the second can of soda?
c. What is the MU of increasing from the eight to the ninth can of soda?

Take-A-Note

Choosing Between Goods

1. If the MU of good X, relative to its P > MU of good Y relative to its P, we should buy more of good X and less of good Y. If we don't, then we are failing to maximize out TU, given our income. For example, if we are buying 10 donuts and 10 muffins each of which costs $1.00 but the last donut yields 20 utils of satisfaction, whereas the last muffin yields 15 utils, we could do better.

2. If MU donuts/P donuts > MU muffin/P muffin, then we should buy one less muffin and one more donut. In doing so, we will increase our TU. If this does not yet make MU donuts/P donuts = MU muffin/p muffin, then we should further redirect our spending until the two ratios are equal.

Diamond—Water Paradox

Some items essential to life cost less than luxuries, is best explained by the Diamond—Water Paradox (DWP). That is, additional units of a good provides less and less satisfaction, therefore, an abudant good such as water yields large Total Utility (TU), but Marginal Utility (MU) is small.

The commodity that has the greatest value in use (Total Utility), has little or no value in exchange, which is Marginal Utility.

Marginal Utility (MU) of Water is less than that of a Diamond.

Chapter Summary

1. Economists' views of consumer choice are based on the following assumptions:
   a. Consumers are rational.
   b. Utility can be measured.
   c. TU increases as consumption rises.
   d. MU diminishes as consumption goes up.
   e. Consumers' incomes are limited.
   f. Prices are known (each commodity is not free and must be paid for).
   g. Many goods have characteristics that make them satisfactory substitutes for other goods.

2. Utility is defined to mean satisfaction, which is measured in terms of util. It is vital to distinguish between total and marginal utilities because choices concerning a bit more or a bit less cannot be predicted from a knowledge of total utilities.

3. Consumers often pay far lower prices for commodities with a high use value, such as water, than they pay for goods and services considered less useful. This phenomenon is referred to as the "paradox of value." The paradox is resolved when one understands that the commodities that have the greatest value in use have little or no value in exchange. Thus, marginal utility is determined not by total satisfaction, but rather, by what people are willing to pay for the last unit they buy (MU).

4. The principle of diminishing marginal utility states that during some specified time period, a person's added satisfaction diminishes as he or she consumes additional units of the same commodity.

5. The basic tool of indifference curve analysis is the consumer's budget line. The budget line shows all combinations of commodities that are available to the consumers given their income, and the prices of the goods that they purchase if they spend all their income on them. The budget line is a straight line whose slope equals the ratio of the prices of the commodities. A change in price changes the slope of the budget line. A change in the consumer's income causes a parallel shift in the budget line.

6. Indifference curves normally have negative slopes. The slope of an indifference curve indicates how much of one commodity the consumer is willing to give up in order to get an additional unit of the other commodity.

7. The marginal rate of substitution (MRS) expresses the willingness of the consumer to trade a certain amount of Good X for a certain amount of Good Y.

8. To maximize utility, the consumer chooses a combination of goods represented by a point on the indifference curve which is a tangent to the budget line.

9. Indifference curves have specific shapes: downward sloping, convex to the origin, indifference curves cannot cross; indifference curves farther from the origin are preferred.

10. Disutility refers to the marginal utility of an extra item being negative. This causes total utility (TU) to drop. For example, a third hamburger is too much and causes the person to become ill.

11. If buyers are to get the most for their money, the last dollar ($) spent on Good Y must yield the same satisfaction as the last dollar spent on Good Z. Mathematically, this implies that the buyer's total satisfaction is at a maximum.

CHAPTER 5
KEY CONCEPTS

Budget Constraints—Combinations of two goods that a buyer can purchase, given the price of each good and the buyer's income. It places an upper limit on his or her purchases.

Budget Line—It shows the combination of quantities of two goods that the consumer can buy with a given level of income.

Consumer Maximization of Utility—Consumer chooses a combination of goods represented by a point on the indifferent curve which is tangent to the budget line.

Diamond-Water Paradox—Consumers often pay lower prices for commodities with a high use value, such as water, than they do for goods and services considered less useful. Total utility determines value in use and marginal utility determines value in exchange.

Diminishing Marginal Utility—Refers to the marginal utility of a commodity, which will diminish over time as total consumption of the commodity increases.

Indifference Curve—Combinations of two goods that satisfy a consumer equally well.

Indifference Map—Consists of a set of indifference curves. The higher curves represent higher levels of satisfaction.

Marginal Rate of Substitution (MRS)—Quantity of one good an individual is willing to give up to obtain an additional unit of another good while maintaining equal total utility.

Marginal Utility—Change in satisfaction that a person receives from consuming more or less of a commodity. In other words, it measures the additional satisfaction derived from one more or one less unit of consumption.

Rational Consumer—One who seeks to obtain the greatest possible satisfaction from purchases.

Utility—Satisfaction an individual expects to receive from consuming a good or from a service.

DISCUSSION QUESTIONS

1. Explain the seven assumptions of utility analysis.
2. Explain why diamonds can have a higher price than water, which is necessary for life.
3. Explain the concept of the rational consumer.
4. Explain the concept of marginal utility and the principle of diminishing marginal utility.
5. Explain how a consumer will maximize total utility.
6. Explain the concept of marginal rate of substitution on the indifference curve.
7. Using indifference analysis, explain how a consumer maximized utility.
8. Explain how an increase in income affects a consumer maximizing utility.
9. Given two goods in the indifference analysis, explain how an increase in the price of one good will affect a consumer maximizing utility.
10. Explain the tangency solution of budget lines and indifference curves.

Chapter 6

The Firm and Costs of Production

Learning Objectives

After reading this chapter you should be able to:
1. Summarize economic time periods that are open to the firm in production.
2. Distinguish the three types of business forms: sole proprietorship, partnership, and the corporation.
3. Explain the advantages of the corporation over the sole proprietorship and over the partnership.
4. Define, explain, and distinguish between implicit and explicit costs.
5. Explain the firm's inputs in the short run: fixed input and variable input.
6. Calculate and define average fixed cost (AFC), average variable cost (AVC), average total cost (ATC), and marginal cost (MC).
7. Identify production and costs in the long run.
8. Define, explain, and cite examples of economies of scale, diseconomies of scale and constant returns to scale.
9. Derive a long run average total cost (LRATC) curve with an unlimited number of short run average total cost (SRATC) curves.
10. Define total revenue and total costs.
11. Summarize corporate finance: stocks and bonds, and methods of raising finance capital.
12. Define the financial concerns of the firm: assets and liabilities.
13. Construct a total cost curve in the short run, showing TFC and TVC curves.
14. Calculate all various cost concepts.
15. Define, explain, and distinguish between normal profit, economic profit, economic loss and zero economic profit.
16. State the principle of diminishing returns and explain how it affects short-run average costs.
17. Determine when a firm should produce and when it should shut down.
18. Identify factors of production.
19. Define, explain, and cite examples of explicit costs, implicit costs and sunk costs.
20. Distinguish between economic profits and accounting profit and costs.
21. Solve the learning practices as indicated at the end of the chapter.

The Firm

A firm is an entity which is formed to produce goods or services. These are sold to make a profit. The firm hires workers, purchases capital and other resources, applies management skills, and takes risks to pursue its goals. Therefore, the firm requires resources that are necessary to produce goods. These resources are called Factors of Production. That is, labor, physical capital, land, material, and an entrepreneur.

Financial Concerns of the Firm

All business firms have a balance sheet, which presents a picture of the financial status of the firm, and which accounts for all the assets and liabilities of the firm.

    a. Assets—The left hand side of the balance sheet, lists the values of the firm, assets. Assets are things of value such as cash, equipment, buildings, and land, owned and controlled by an economic unit or a business entity. An entity is a thing in itself. Remember that a business entity is considered to be separate and distinct from the persons who supply the assets it uses. Property acquired by the business is an asset of the business. The owner is separate from the business and in fact has claims on it. If the business owes nothing against the assets, then the owner's right would be equal to the value of the assets. The owner's right, claim, or financial interest is expressed by the word equity, or investment in the business.

    b. Liabilities—The right hand side of the firm's balance sheet, lists the values of the firms liabilities. That is the debt of the firm. Hence, the net worth of the firm can be calculated as follows: assets–liabilities = net worth.

Types of Business Forms

There are three types of organizations that are common in American business. These are the sole proprietorship, the partnership, and the corporation.

Sole Proprietorship

Sole proprietorships are common among small retail stores, farms, service businesses, and professional practices.

    From a legal viewpoint, the business and the owner are not regarded as separate entities. The owner is personally liable for the debts of the business. If the business fails, creditors can force the owner to sell his or her personal assets to pay for the debts of the business. Also, the owner provides the funds for investment, and he/she manages the business; the owner makes the policy decisions, and all profit goes to the sole owner. The sole proprietorship is the most common form of business organization in the United States.

    The advantages of a sole proprietorship are that: a) it is easy to form, and b) there are high incentives to succeed. The disadvantages are that: a) the owner has unlimited liability, b) it is difficult for a person working independently to specialize in management functions, c) access to capital is limited, and d) it has limited life.

Partnership

A partnership is an unincorporated business that is jointly owned by two or more people. Partnerships are popular in the following professions: manufacturing, wholesaling, retail, trade, and businesses that emphasize personal service.

    A partnership is not a separate legal entity in itself, but merely a voluntary association of individuals. There is a legal agent for the partnership and it is bound by the acts of any other partner, as long as these acts are within the scope of normal operations. Each partner is personally responsible for all the debts of the firm. Partners share in policy making and management; decisions are made by majority vote of partners. The agreement between the partners is terminated automatically upon the death, retirement, or withdrawal of a partner; the bankruptcy or incapacity of a partner, or the completion of the project for which the partnership was formed. Characteristics of a partnership include; ease of formation, limited life, mutual agency, and unlimited liability.

The advantages of a partnership are that it has increased access to capital and it offers management more chances to specialize functions. The disadvantages are that its owners have unlimited liability, it has limited life, and its access to capital is less than that of a corporation.

Corporation

A corporation is a legal entity having an existence separate and distinct from that of its owners. Legally, a corporation is an artificial person having many of the rights and responsibilities of a real person. Corporations may own property, may sue and be sued in court, may sign contracts, and are responsible for their own debts and taxes.

Nearly all large businesses, and many small ones, are organized as corporations. The corporation is an ideal means of obtaining the capital necessary to finance large-scale operations. Corporations are the most common form of organization of large businesses because they obtain their equity capital from the issuance of shares of stock.

A charter establishing a corporation allows the corporation to sell shares of the ownership in order to raise money. These shares of ownership are called stock, and the people who buy them are stockholders. The stockholders are, therefore, the owners of the corporation. If the corporation were to fail, all stockholders would lose the money they invested in the stock. People buy stock as a form of personal investment. Stocks may yield dividends, which would be a source of income for the stockholder. In addition, the stockholder could sell the stock to someone else at a later date for a profit. Figure 6.1 shows the structure of American corporations.

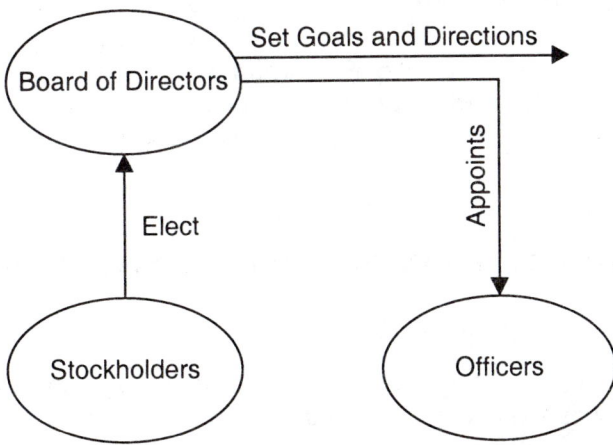

Figure 6.1

The owners of the corporation, the stockholders, elect the board of directors of the business through formal elections. The board of directors sets the direction or goals of the corporation and appoints the officers to run the business. If a stockholder could control a sizeable portion of the stock, this person could have a giant influence on the officers and direction of the corporation.

As compared to sole proprietorships and partnerships, corporations have five main advantages. These are:

    a. No personal liability for stockholders. Stockholder liability is limited to the amount of money invested in the corporation.

b. Ease of accumulating capital. As mentioned above, corporations raise capital by issuing shares of stock.

c. Ownership is easily transferable. Shares of stock may be sold from one investor to another without any disruption to the business.

d. Continuous existence. The continuing existence of a corporation is made possible by the issuance of transferable shares of stock. The continuity of the corporation is essential to most large-scale business activity.

e. Professional management. The stockholders own the corporation, but they do not operate it on a daily basis. To administer the affairs of the corporation, the stockholders elect a board of directors. The directors then hire a president and other corporate officers.

Corporations also have the following disadvantages:

a. A corporation has to pay taxes to both the state and federal governments (corporate income taxes, property taxes and so on). This leads to double taxation, which means that the corporation pays taxes on the gross income it earns, and distributes parts of the remaining income as dividends to stockholders; then the stockholders have to pay income taxes on the dividends, since this money constitutes personal income.

b. State and federal governments pass laws that restrict the behavior of corporations. These restrictions generally do not apply to sole proprietorships or partnerships.

c. The larger the corporation, the more ownership gets separated from control, and the greater the possibility of conflict of interest between managers and owners. Large corporations may have thousands of stockholders. Stockholders who hold only a few shares have neither the time nor the incentive to take an active part in controlling the corporation by their votes. Management may orient its policies first and foremost toward its own continued control of the corporation. In many large corporations, the stockholders may find it hard to control the management. If this occurs, the self-interest of these independent managers may conflict with the self-interest of the stockholders.

CORPORATE FINANCE: STOCKS AND BONDS

Bonds

Bonds are special kinds of promissory notes that are readily marketable for resale. Ordinarily, a bond will ensure periodic interest payments and the repayment of its principal when the bond matures. For example, a five year, nine percent, $2,000 bond would require annual interest payments of $180 plus the payment of $2,000 after five years.

Bondholders' income from the firm is much steadier than that of stockholders, but also more limited. Possible profit from a stock is limitless.

Bondholders have no direct voice whatsoever in corporate decisions. Their relationship with the firm is limited and indirect, while the stockholders' is less limited, and more direct.

Common and Preferred Stocks

The *common* stockholder provides "equity" capital. He shares in business decisions and profits, but must also share in losses. The common stockholder's income is not limited, as the bondholder's is, but it is less regular.

The *preferred* stockholder lies somewhere between the common stockholder and the bondholder. The preferred stockholder receives at most, a stated dividend, but does *not* get paid her dividend until after the bondholder has been paid *her* interest. Preferred stock has no "face value" like a bond; hence, holders of preferred stock are not repaid a lump sum at a maturity date, as a bondholder is.

In addition, stockholders are subject to the same fluctuations to which the firm is subject. While the return they may receive is potentially greater than that of bondholders, their potential losses are likewise greater. An important fact to note is the payment schedule. Stockholders are paid out of profits, which are calculated after bond payments are made. In the event of financial difficulties, bondholders have less risk of loss than stockholders.

Methods of Raising Financial Capital

- personal savings
- business savings (retained earnings)
- loans from banks and credit unions
- the sale of stocks and bonds

CHOICES OPEN TO THE FIRM IN PRODUCTION: ECONOMIC TIME PERIODS

The production function relates inputs to outputs. The inputs in the production function have prices and represent costs to the firm. In this section, we will examine economic time periods. To begin with, why suppliers would want to produce more items at a higher price; ceteris paribus, and what factors influence their ability to produce more goods and services. If we ask a supplier how many items should be sold at different prices, the answer would depend upon the economic time period involved. The following are considered as economic time periods.

(a) Very short run (VSR)

The very short run refers to a situation in which no inputs can be changed, thereby output cannot change either. That is, a firm cannot sell more than it has already produced even though the price is higher than originally expected. Hence, in this period a firm has no ability to change any of the following: labor, plant, equipment, technology and output.

(b) Short run (SR)

The short run period refers to a situation in which only labor vary and plant and machinery remain fixed. For example, if a firm needs labor, material, and equipment, it is said to be operating in the short period. That is, output can respond to changes in price in this period, but there is a limit to the amount that can be produced since some inputs are fixed. The SR is therefore, a long period in which the quantity of some input cannot be increased (i.e. plant, equipment, land, the services of management and labor).

(c) Long run (LR)

The long run is a productive period in which all resources are available. The LR is a time period in which all inputs may be varied but in which the basic technology of production cannot be changed. It may be helpful to think of the LR as a planning horizon. The LR corresponds to the situation facing the firm when it is planning to go into business, to expand the scale of its operations, to branch out into new products or new areas, or to change its method of production. In the long run, all costs are variable, and there are no fixed inputs.

(d) Very long run (VLR)

The very long economic period is a situation in which firm has ability to change labor, plant, equipment, technology and output. The very long economic period is generally used in discussion of macroeconomic consideration and economic growth and development.

The primary purpose of this part is to introduce the students to production and cost theory from the perspective of short-run and long-run analysis.

Business firms, regardless of their size, are concerned with costs and profits. Let us look at the following cost concepts.

Sunk Cost

A cost incurred in the past that cannot be changed by current decisions and cannot be recovered. Example: signs used by Kathy's Gourmet Burger generate sunk costs. These signs have zero resale value. That is, the investment made in signs is a sunk cost, it cannot be recovered. Therefore, sunk costs are completely lost, and are not affected by the manager's decision as to which alternative course of action to pursue.

Explicit Costs (Accounting Costs or Money Outlay)

Explicit costs are incurred by the firm in the purchase of inputs, including labor, raw materials, equipment, electricity, etc. These are out-of-pocket costs that are entered onto the firm's balance sheet. Explicit costs are ordinary expenses, such as wages and bills that accountants include in a firm's expenses. Business firms are assumed to want to maximize their profits and to minimize the costs of what they choose to produce. The cost structure of a firm shows how various measures of cost vary with the production level. In order to maximize profits and minimize costs, the firm must make decisions with regard to what and how much to produce. Firms must make decisions for two time spans; the short run and the long run. The distinction between the short run and the long run is that there are no fixed inputs and, therefore, no fixed costs in the long run. As a result, the costs are variable costs.

Implicit Costs

One of the most basic ideas in economics is that all costs arise from the need to choose among possible uses of scarce resources. In other words, all costs are opportunity costs. Implicit costs are the opportunity costs of resources owned by the firm. They are called implicit costs because they do not involve any contractual payments that are entered on the firm's balance sheet. The main implicit cost that is not entered on the firm's balance sheet is the opportunity cost of resources owned and used by the firm's owner. That is, cost measured by the value of alternatives given up. Unless implicit costs are considered, the firm cannot determine whether or not it is making an economic profit.

Opportunity Cost

Economists employ the opportunity cost concept when figuring a firm's cost. Therefore, total cost includes not only explicit payments for resources employed by the firm, but also the implicit costs associated with the use of productive resources owned by the firm.

TYPES OF PROFIT

In economics, both implicit and explicit costs are included in determining the type of profit that is achieved. There are three types: normal profit, economic profit, and an economic loss.

A normal profit is made when the firm is just covering the implicit costs in addition to the explicit costs. For example, a shoe firm instead of producing shoes could produce dog collars and leashes. If the firm did so, it could make $100,000. The $100,000 is the opportunity cost or implicit cost of the firm. It is what the firm gives up by producing shoes. A normal profit for the shoe firm would be to make $100,000. In this type of profit total revenue minus explicit and implicit costs equals zero. $100,000 – $100,000 = 0.

An economic profit occurs when the firm has a return over explicit and implicit costs. If the shoe firm made $150,000 after deducting explicit costs, the economic profit would be $50,000. $150,000 – $100,000 = $50,000.

An economic loss occurs when a firm receives a return that is less than the implicit cost. If the firm made $80,000 after deducting all explicit costs, it would actually incur an economic loss of $20,000. $80,000 – $100,000 = –$20,000.

Profits are an aid for business in decision making. If the firm is making a normal profit, it will continue as before. If the firm makes economic profits, the firm will be motivated to increase production. If the firm is incurring an economic loss, the firm will reduce output and seek another direction. In the above shoe firm example, the firm would be better off to produce dog collars and leashes. In all the above examples, the deciding factor as to what type of profit a firm makes is the implicit or opportunity costs.

Accounting Profit and Economic Profit, Marginal Revenue and Total Revenue

There are differences in definitions of profits used by economists and accountants.

Economic profit = Total Revenue (TR) minus Total Cost (TC) which includes opportunity cost • Accounting profit = sales revenue – expenses over one year.

(Accountants concentrate more on the funds that flow to and from a business firm, often neglecting to include some of the implicit costs that economists take into account.)

Accounting profit can be positive if the total revenue covers explicit costs but not opportunity costs.

Accounting profit cannot be negative if total revenue cannot even cover explicit, there is nothing left to cover opportunity costs.

Zero profits do not imply that a firm is about to go out of business. Companies with zero economic profits will be hampered in regards to growth and the development of new and better products. The industry will stop growing, because new firms will not enter an industry with zero economic profits.

Marginal Revenue (MR) is the change in the firm's total revenue per unit of output.
Mathematically:

$$\frac{\Delta TR}{\Delta Q}$$

Total revenue (TR) = P.Q. That is, the amount of money the firm will receive from the sale of its product or service.

SHORT RUN COSTS

In the short run a firm's total cost can be divided into the following seven cost concepts. The short run behavior of these costs is determined by the firm's production process. Hence, some of the firm's inputs are fixed and others are variables.

The data in Table 6.1 shows the cost schedules for an individual firm.

Total Fixed Costs

A fixed cost is the cost of a fixed input. In the short run, the fixed cost does not change as the firm's output level changes. Whether the firm produces more or less it will pay the same for such things as rent, insurance, and other costs that are independent of its output level. Even if the firm produces nothing (0), fixed cost is to shut down and go out of business, which is an event that can occur only in the long run. Therefore, fixed costs cannot be avoided in the short run. The total fixed cost (TFC) of a firm is the sum of all the individual fixed costs. TFC is the cost of the firm's fixed factors and is the same, no matter what the level of output. Therefore, the TFC is horizontal. TFC is shown in column 2 of Table 6.1.

Total Variable Costs

Variable costs are expenditures on inputs that can be varied in short run use. Variable costs are costs of production that change as the output level of the firm changes. When the firm increases the level of production, it uses more raw materials and might hire new workers. As a result, the firm's variable costs increase. Conversely, when the firm reduces the level of production it uses fewer raw materials and may lay workers off. This reduces the firm's variable costs. The total variable costs (TVC) of a firm is the sum of all of the expenditures on inputs for a given level of production. TVC is shown in column 3 of Table 6.1.

Table 6.1
Hypothetical cost schedules for an individual firm in the short run.

(1) Total Output (Q)	(2) Total Fixed Cost (TFC)	(3) Total Variable Cost (TVC)	(4) Total Cost (TC) TC = TFC +TVC	(5) Average Fixed Cost (AFC) TFC/Q	(6) Average Variable Cost (AVC) TVC/Q	(7) Average Total Cost (ATC) TC/Q	(8) Marginal Cost (MC) change in TC change in Q
0	$100	$0	$100				
1	100	90	190	$100.00	$90.00	$190.00	90
2	100	170	270	50.00	85.00	135.00	80
3	100	240	340	33.33	80.00	113.33	70
4	100	300	400	25.00	75.00	100.00	60
5	100	370	470	20.00	74.00	94.00	70
6	100	450	550	16.67	75.00	91.67	80
7	100	540	640	14.29	77.14	91.43	90
8	100	650	750	12.50	81.25	93.75	110
9	100	780	880	11.11	86.67	97.78	130
10	100	930	1030	10.00	93.00	103.00	150

Total cost (TC) is defined as the sum of total variable costs and the total fixed costs. The formula for this result is TC = TVC + TFC. Total costs are shown in column 4 of Table 6.1. A firm's total cost is $190.00 if it produces one unit, $270.00 if it produces two units, and $340.00 if it produces three units of output.

Marginal costs (MC) are important in determining a firm's ATC of output. In this context, MC exists because of variable costs. Hence, MC is the additional cost of producing one more unit of output. Let us figure out the MC of producing the eighth unit of output. MC is $110.00. How did we get it? We subtracted the TC of producing seven units of output ($750.00). Thus an airline can profit by offering "standby" customers a previously unsold seat at a substantial discount, just before takeoff because the marginal cost of additional passengers is very small.

We present MC for our example in column 8 of Table 6.1—Note that marginal cost is the difference between successive total cost amounts. This is because we are changing the output by (1) unit at each new row of Table 6.1.

Average fixed cost (AFC) is shown in column 5 of Table 6.1. An average is the total divided by the number of units of output. That is, AFC = TFC/Q. Average fixed cost is found by dividing column 2 by column 1.

Average variable cost (AVC)—We find AVC in our example in column 6 of Table 6.1. That is TVC/Q. Average variable cost can be found by dividing column 3 by column 1.

Average total cost (ATC)—We find ATC in our example in column 7 of Table 6.1. That is, TC/Q. Because Total Cost (TC) equals TVC + TFC or ATC = AVC + AFC. Average total cost is found by dividing total cost by quantity of output.

Terms, symbols, equation and definitions of costs in the short-run are shown in Table 6.2.

Table 6.2
Summary of Short-Run Costs

Term	Symbol	Equation	Definition
Total Cost	TC	TC = TFC+TVC	Total Cost (TC) is the total cost of producing any given level of output. TC is divided into two parts: Total fixed costs (TFC) and total variable costs (TVC).
Total Variable Cost	TVC	TVC=TC−TFC	Items of cost directly related to output (wages, raw materials, and some utility expenses).
Total Fixed Cost	TFC	TFC=TC−TVC	TFC is the cost of the firm's fixed factors. Even if the firm produces nothing (0), TFC will still have to be paid.
Average Total Cost	ATC	TC/Q or AFC + AVC	Average total cost is the total cost of producing any given output divided by that output.
Average Variable Cost	AVC	AVC=TVC/Q	Average variable cost may rise or fall as production increases (depending on whether output rises more rapidly or more slowly than total variable cost).
Average Fixed Cost	AFC	AFC=TFC/Q or AFC=ATC−AVC	A fixed cost does not vary with output. Average fixed cost per unit declines as output rises.
Marginal Cost	MC	MC=ΔTC/ΔQ	MC is the change in total cost per unit change in output.

SHORT-RUN COST CURVES

Short Run Cost Curves (TFC, TVC and TC curves)

The data provided in Table 6.3 can be used to show the shape of a typical firm's cost curves. We consider TFC, TVC and TC curves first. Then we show how marginal cost, AFC, AVC and ATC change with output.

In Figure 6.2 we have plotted the total fixed, total variable, and the total cost data shown in Table 6.1. Note that both the TVC and TC curves increase as output increases. That is, to increase output, the firm must increase its use of labor, which adds to both the TVC and the TC. The TFC curve, however, does not change as output increases.

Table 6.3
Hypothetical Cost Schedule

Output	TVC	TFC	TC	AFC	AVC	ATC	MC
0	0	$400	$400	0	0	0	0
1	100	400	500	400	100	500	100
2	150	400	550	200	75	275	50
3	175	400	575	133.33	58.33	191.67	25.10
4	190	400	590	100	47.50	147.50	15
5	200	400	600	80	40	120	10
6	230	400	630	66.87	38.33	105	30
7	270	400	670	57.14	38.57	95.71	40
8	350	400	750	50	43.75	93.75	80
9	440	400	840	44.44	48.88	93.33	90
10	550	400	950	40	55	95	110

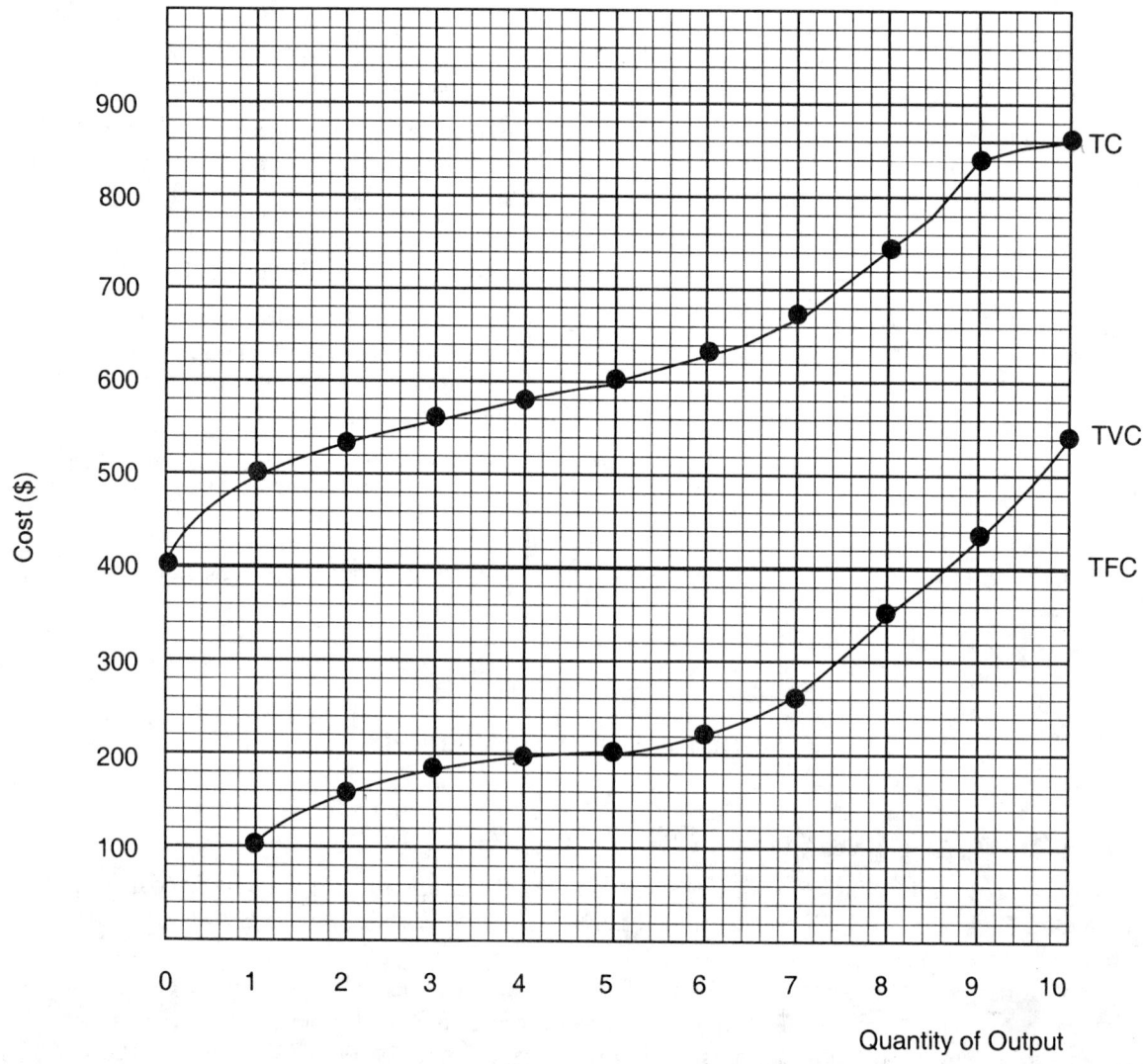

Figure 6.2
Total Fixed Cost, Total Variable Cost, and Total Cost Curves

Marginal Cost, Average Fixed Cost, Average Variable Cost, and Average Total Cost Curves

Figure 6.4 shows the graphical relationships between the marginal, average fixed, average variable, and average total cost curves using the data provided in Table 6.3. These curves are drawn to smoothly approximate the behavior of costs as output increases. The shape of TFC is horizontal. That is, TFC are $400 at all output levels, so as output increases, AFC declines. In contrast to the AFC curve, MC, AVC, and ATC curves are typically U shaped. Hence, the MC curve cuts the ATC curve and AVC curve at their lowest points. The ATC curve slopes downward as long as the MC curve is below it. AVC curve first decreases, then reaches a minimum, and then increases as output increases. The marginal cost and average variable cost are the same as the first unit of output. ATC curve assumes its shape from the vertical summation of the AFC curve and the AVC curve. Note the vertical distance between the ATC and AVC curves equals the AFC at a given output level. The total cost curves that emerge from Figure 6.4 can be drawn individually as shown in Figure 6.5.

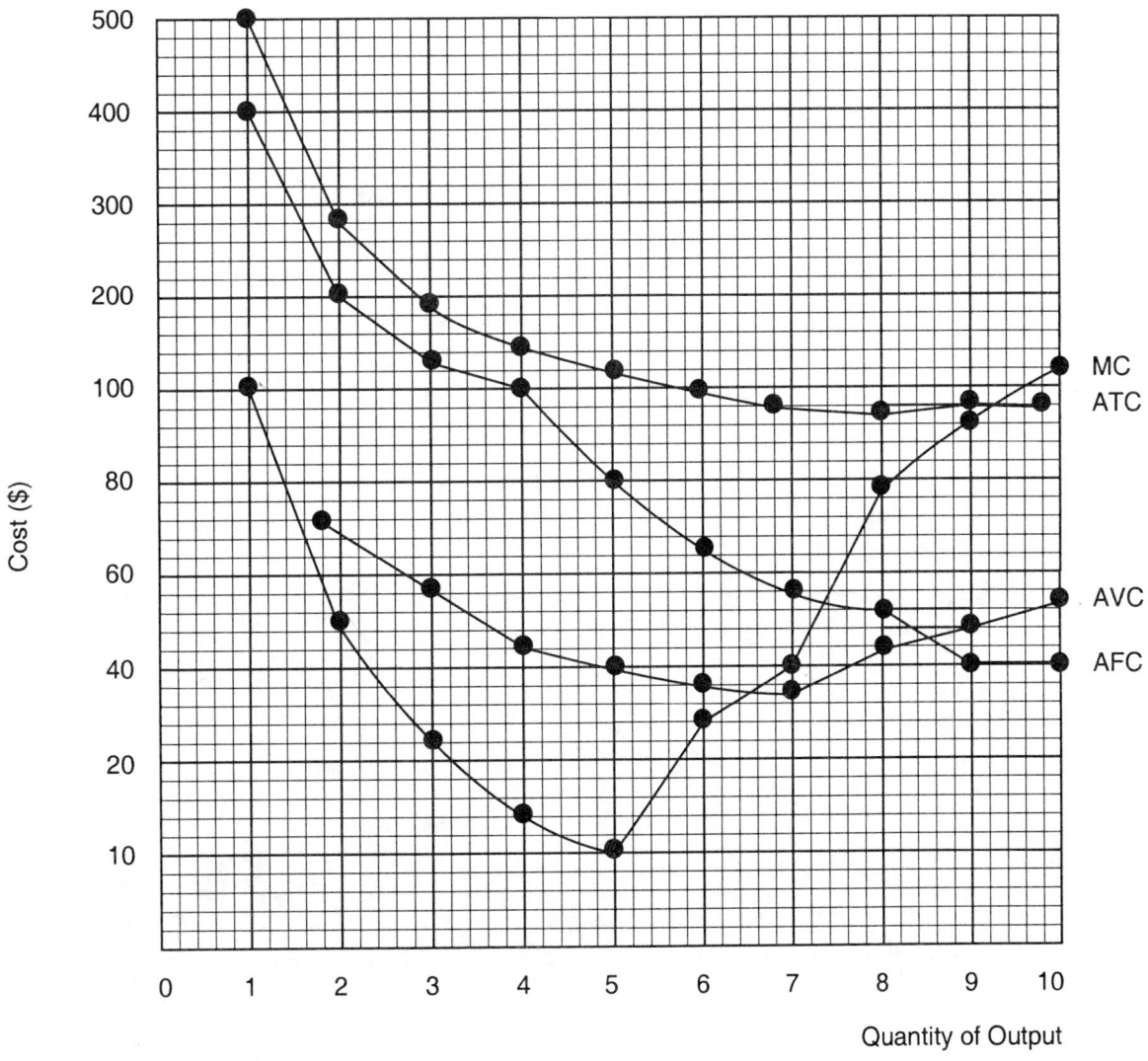

Figure 6.4
Short run cost curves, marginal cost, average fixed cost, average variable cost, and average total cost curves.

Shapes of Individual Cost Curves in the Short Run

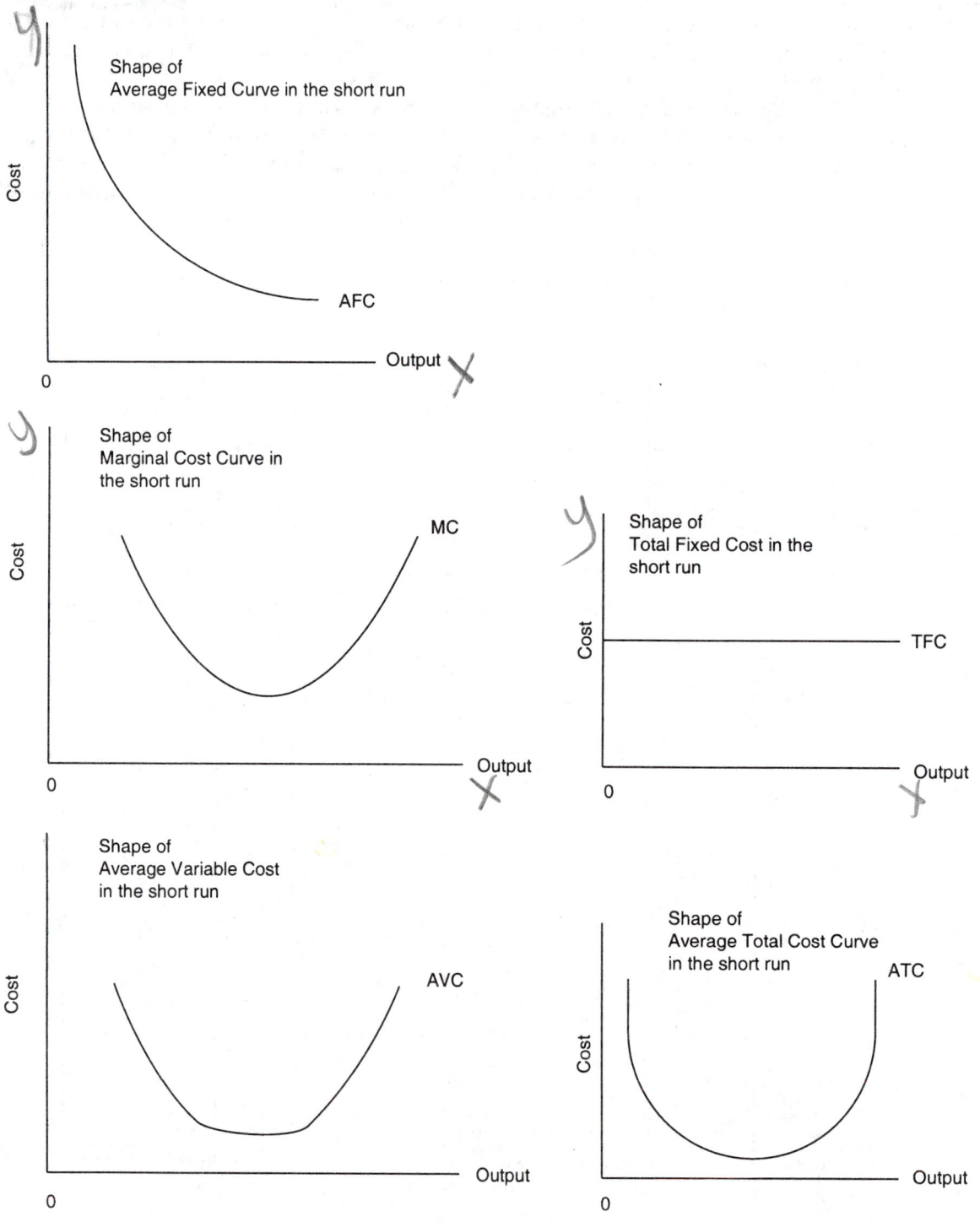

Figure 6.5

Relationships Between Cost Concepts in the Short Run

There is no relationship between marginal cost (MC) and average fixed cost (AFC), because AFC continually falls. Marginal cost (MC) equals average total cost (ATC) where ATC is at a minimum. As long as MC exceeds ATC, ATC rises; when MC is less than ATC, ATC falls. The relationship between MC and AVC is identical to that between MC and ATC.

Table 6.4 represents the AVC curve and the ATC curve getting closer to each other as output increases. That is, ATC = AVC + AFC. As output increases, AFC decreases. Therefore, as output expands most of what makes up ATC is the AVC.

Table 6.4

Output	TFC	AFC	TVC	AVC	TC	ATC	MC
0	$100	0	0	0	100	0	0
1	100	100.00	20	20.00	120	120.00	20
2	100	50.00	40	20.00	140	70.00	20
3	100	33.33	50	16.67	150	50.00	10
4	100	25.00	55	13.75	155	38.75	5
5	100	20.00	65	13.00	165	33.00	10

It follows that the ATC curve would get closer to each other as output increases, as shown in Figure 6.6.

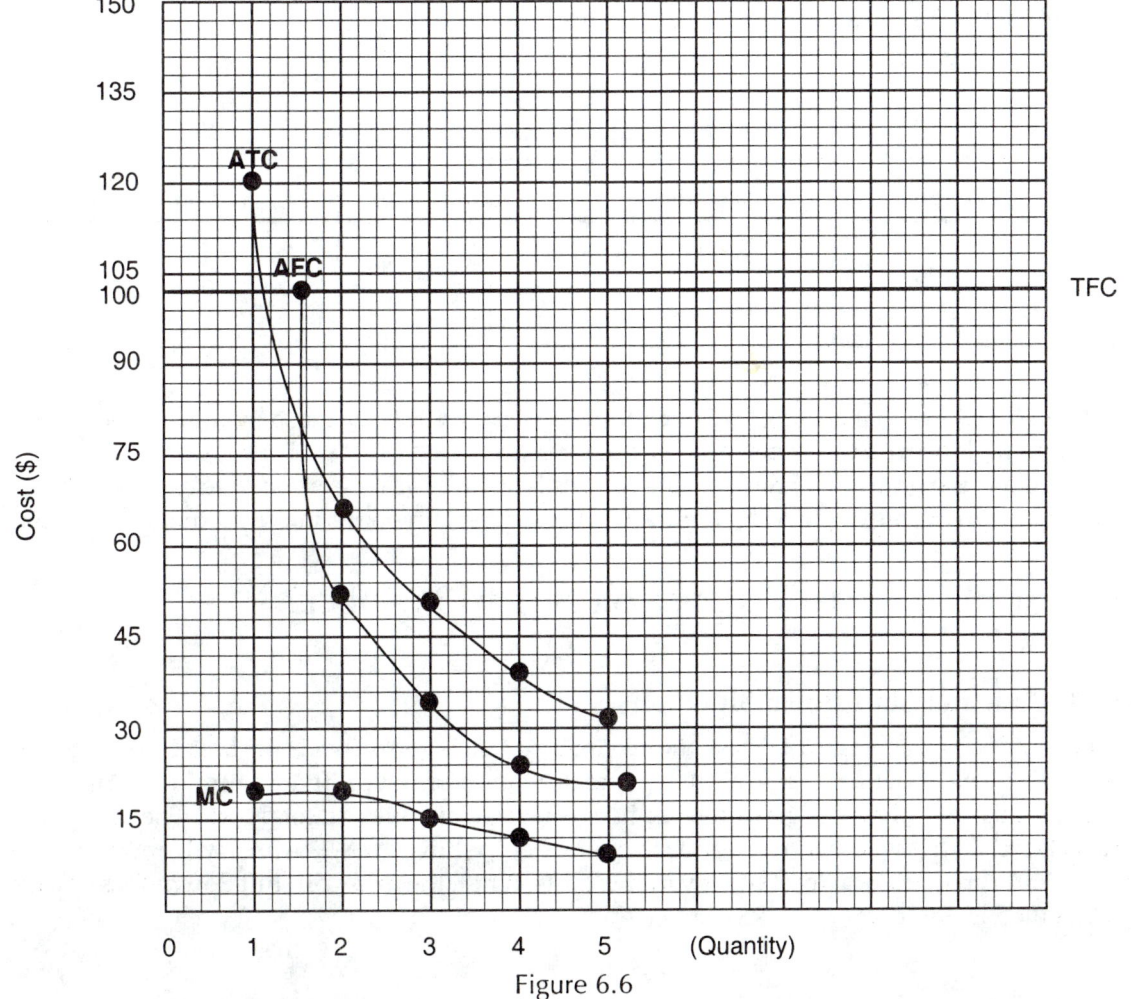

Figure 6.6

Remember, most output always costs more because of the added variable inputs that add to expenses. But just how rapidly those costs rise depends on the following:

- TVC increases at a constant rate if productivity remains unchanged as output (Q) increases.
- TVC increases at a decreasing rate if productivity rises as output increases.
- TVC increases at an increasing rate if productivity decreases as output rises.

Principle of Diminishing Returns

The principle of diminishing returns states that as more and more variable input is added to fixed input, the resulting additions to output will eventually become increasingly smaller.

Consider the following example: a worker with a sewing machine in a room producing dresses. The variable input is workers (labor) and sewing machines (capital), as they can be added or removed as needed. The room is the fixed input, as it is neither increased nor decreased in size. The output is dresses.

One worker with one machine is capable of producing a certain number of dresses, say four a day. If we add a second worker with a second machine, the total number of dresses would be at least eight a day. We will, however, add that the workers divide up the work. Each worker produces part of the dress, employing division of labor. The total is now 10 dresses instead of 8. This is an increase of 6 over the original 4. If we add a third worker and a third machine, let us assume output increases to fifteen. The increase is now only 5 due to too much division of labor or too small a room. The room cannot accommodate the number of workers. Example: If fertilizer is the only variable input, a 9% ↑ fertilizer per acre of soybeans cannot raise the soybean yield by 10% per acre. Table 6.5 shows the Principle of Diminshing Returns.

Table 6.5
Principle of Diminishing Returns

Workers	Machines	Output	Addition
1	1	4	4
2	2	10	6
3	3	15	5

Table 6.5 shows that adding variable input causes output to increase by more to begin with. After a point, however, the increase in output decreases.

Therefore, the principle of diminishing returns is an empirical assertion of real world example. It illustrates why firms stop adding inputs (workers) at certain points in the production process.

To Produce or Not to Produce?

Break Even and Shut Down Situations

When price equals average total cost, the economic profit is zero. That is the break even situation. Economic profit is defined as profit that is greater than normal profit and economic loss as less than normal profit. (Profit is the difference between total revenue and total cost.) The question the firm is faced with is whether to continue to operate or to shut down. The firm will operate at a *loss* in the short run if prices at least cover variable costs. If not, the firm will shut down. This situation is presented in Table 6.6.

Table 6.6
To Produce Or Not To Produce

Case	AFC	AVC	ATC	Price ($)	Loss ($)
1	10	14	24	16	8
2	10	14	24	12	12

In case 1 the price is $16 which is greater than the average variable cost. If the firm operates, the loss will be $8, ($16–24). If the firm shuts down, the loss due to covering fixed costs would be $10. The loss would be less if the firm operates.

In case 2 the price is $12, which is less than the average variable cost. If the firm operates, the loss would be $12 ($12–$24). If the firm shuts down, the fixed cost is only $10. The loss would be less if the firm shuts down.

The rationale of the rule is that the firm would be able to cover the variable cost and part of the fixed costs if price is greater than average variable cost. The firm would be unable to cover any of the fixed costs and only part of the average variable cost if the price is below the average variable cost. The loss would be less if the firm shuts down.

In conclusion, if market price falls to "cover" even variable costs, the firm would do better by shutting down than by continuing to produce. If the firm shuts down, it only has to pay off fixed costs. If the firm continues to produce, it will lose not only its fixed cost, but part of its variable costs as well. If price is sufficient to "cover" some variable costs, then the firm is better off producing than shutting down, since producing will provide it with the opportunity to cover part of its fixed costs.

CALCULATION OF BUSINESS PROFITS AND LOSSES

- Opportunity Costs: Opportunity cost is the sacrifice of the next best alternative when a choice is made.
- Explicit Costs: Costs incurred when an actual monetary payment is made.
- Implicit Costs: Represent the value of resources used in the production of a good for which no monetary payment is made.
- Sunk Costs: A cost incurred in the past that cannot be changed by current decisions and cannot be recovered.
- Accounting profit = Total revenue (TR) – Total Costs (TC). (based on explicit costs)
- Economic profit = Total revenue – (explicit + implicit costs). (deduct implicit costs)
- Normal Profit: A firm that is making zero economic profit is said to be making normal profit. That is, total revenue equals total cost.

COST ANALYSIS AND BEHAVIOR:
PRODUCTION AND COSTS IN THE LONG RUN

Long run average cost is made up of points from short run average cost curves, as shown in Figure 6.9. In other words, the LRAC falls when economies of scale prevail, remains constant with constant returns to scale, and rises with diseconomies of scale.

In the long run, all inputs are variable, including plant size. A firm owner can adjust all parts of the operation. The scale of a firm's operations can be adjusted to best fit the economic circumstances that prevail in the long run. The owner will seek the plant size that minimizes long run costs of producing the amount of output that maximizes profits. When all factors of production are variable, there is, of course, no longer a distinction between variable and fixed costs. In the long run, the only relevant average cost concept is the long run average total cost (LRATC), because when all factors are variable, so are all costs. The long run average total cost (LRATC) is made up of points from short run average cost curves, as shown in Figure 6.10. In particular, for any given output level, the firm is assumed to select the short run plant that enables production of that output at the lowest per unit costs.

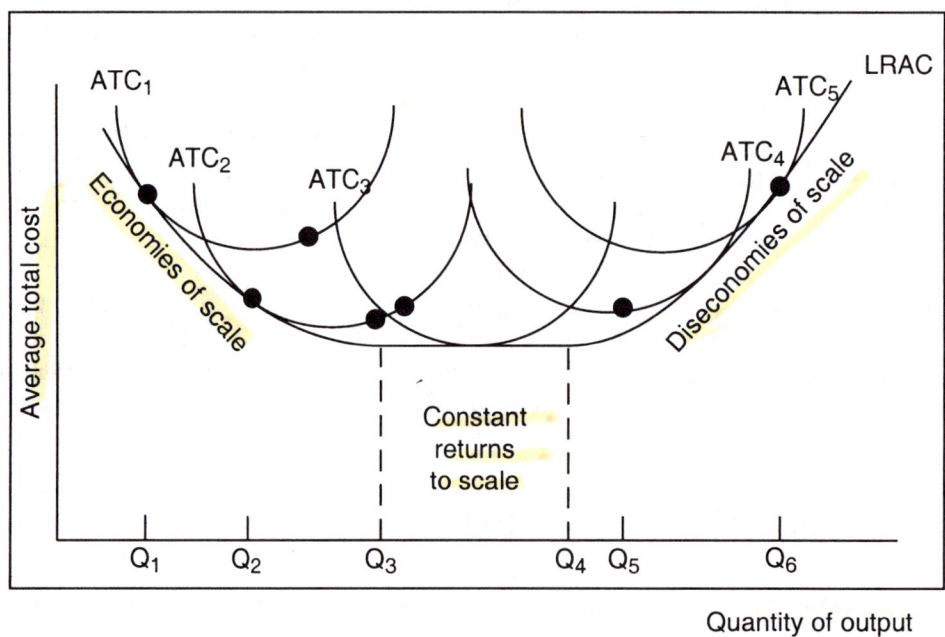

Figure 6.9
Cost curves with economies of scale, diseconomies of scale, and constant returns to scale.

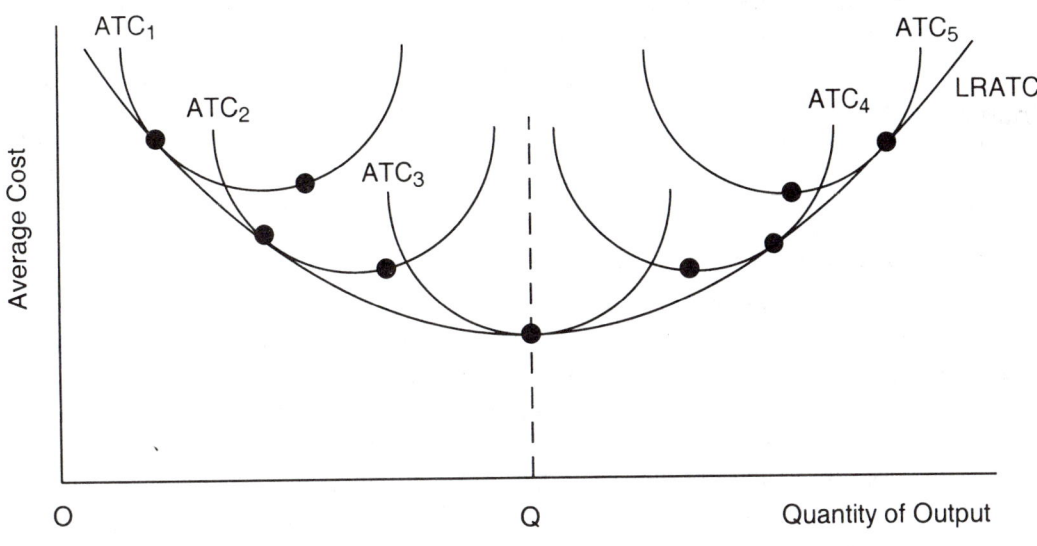

Figure 6.10
Long Run Average Total Cost Curve
Long run average total cost (LRATC) is made up of points from SRAC curves.

The LRATC curve is made up of all the points of tangency with the plots of an infinite number of short run average total cost (SRATC) curves. As output increases, the firm realizes economies of scale along the falling portion of the LRATC curve and diseconomies of scale along the rising portion of the LRATC curve.

ECONOMIES AND DISECONOMIES OF SCALE AND CONSTANT RETURNS TO SCALE

Economies of scale are the decreases in the LRATC of production that occur when the firm's plant size is increased, as represented by the falling portion of the LRATC curve. To a certain point, long run unit costs of production fall as output increases and the firm gets larger. There are several reasons why a larger firm might have lower unit costs. First, a larger operation means that more specialized processes are possible in the firm. Second, as the firm grows larger and produces more, valuable experience in production processes can cause lower costs. Third, large firms can take advantage of mass production techniques and reduce set up costs.

Economies of scale are simply a reduction of costs per unit of output resulting from an expansion in output and falling long run average total cost (LRATC) over a range of increasing output. For example, if output goes up by 10 percent, total cost goes up by less than 10 percent; thus, the average cost will fall. Economies of scale will often result from either specialization or technology.

Diseconomies of Scale

Diseconomies of scale are the opposite of economies of scale. It is a situation in which output increases less than proportionately to inputs as the scale of production increases. For example, a firm finds that doubling its input causes its output to less than double. The major diseconomies are a reduction of communication in a larger firm, increased management size, transportation and selling costs. In a larger company there may develop so many departments and sub-departments that no one knows what the other departments are doing. As a result there may be a duplication of effort and conflicts among departments may develop.

Larger companies require larger management sections. Managers usually earn higher salaries and thus increase costs. In addition, the problem of too many chiefs and too few subordinates may develop. Larger firms produce more and thus must sell more. In order to sell more additional costs such as advertising may be incurred. There may also be additional shipping costs. More trucks may have to be purchased and additional drivers hired.

Constant Returns to Scale

In Figure 6.9 between Q3 and Q4 are constant, so a given percentage increase in the output level, causes total cost to increase by the same percentage, which keeps LRATC constant. That is, the Long Run average cost curve first reaches its lowest level.

Figure (a) shows a long-run situation in which a firm at first encounters economies of scale as it increases production and adds plants. The long-run average cost curve drops. In the second phase of expansion, the firm experiences constant returns to scale. The long-run average cost curve levels out. In the third phase of expansion, the firm experiences diseconomies of scale as new plants are added. The long-run average cost curve rises.

Figure (b) indicates that as the firm increases production and adds plants, the long-run average cost curve drops due to economies of scale.

Figure (c) indicates that as the firm increases production and adds plants, the average cost curve is constant. Additional plants do not increase nor decrease the long-run average cost curve. This indicates constant returns to scale.

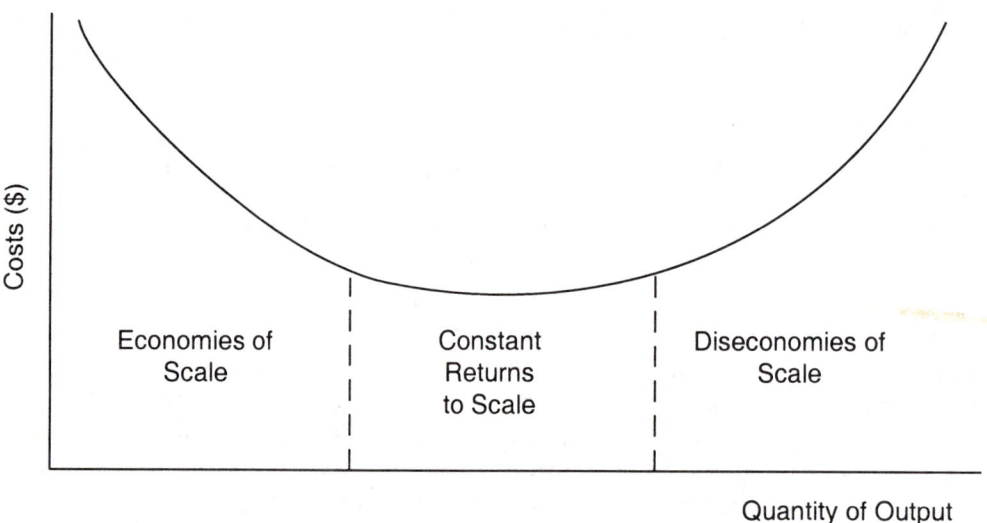

Figure (a)

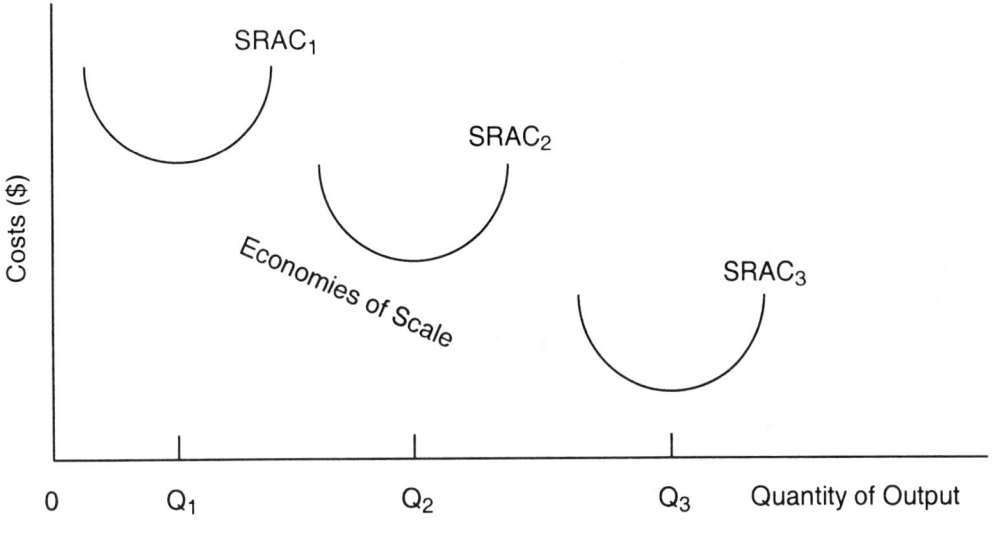

Figure (b)

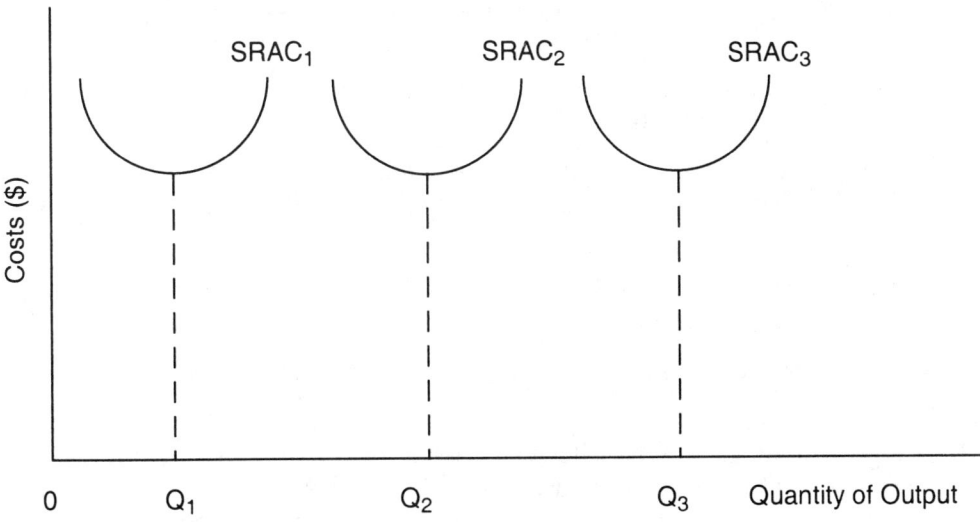

Figure (c)

Chapter Summary

1. Forms of organizations are: the sole proprietorship, the partnership, and the corporation.

2. Implicit costs are the opportunity costs of resources owned by the firm. The main implicit cost that is not entered into the firm's balance sheet is the revenue the firm could be earning doing something else.

3. Explicit costs are incurred by the firm in the purchase of inputs, including labor, raw materials, equipment, utilities, etc.

4. Total cost (TC) is the sum of total fixed cost (TFC) and total variable cost (TVC).

5. Average total cost (ATC) is equal to the sum of total fixed cost (TFC) and total variable cost (TVC) divided by output.

6. Marginal cost (MC) is the change in total cost (TC) associated with the production of an additional unit of output.

7. There are three types of profit a firm can make: a normal profit, an economic profit, and an economic loss.

8. Accounting Profit is the difference between explicit costs and total sales.

9. Normal profit is the opportunity cost of capital and enterprise. This is the level of profit that is necessary for a firm to remain in a competitive industry.

10. The short-run is defined as a period in which there are fixed factors. The long-run is defined as a period in which there are not fixed factors.

11. According to the principle of diminishing returns, as more and more variable input is added to fixed input, output will initially increase, but after a point, the increase will begin to decrease.

12. According to the shut-down rule, a firm should shut down if the price of their product is less than the average variable cost.

13. The marginal cost curve above the shut-down point equals the supply curve of the firm.

14. The long-run average total cost (LRATC) curve is made up of points from short-run average cost (SRATC) curves of various plant sizes. For any given output level, the firm is assumed to select the short-run plant size that enables production of that output at lowest per unit cost.

15. Economies of scale exist whenever cost per unit decreases as output expands. Economies of scale most often result from either specialization or technology.

16. The shape of the short run average total cost is determined by the principle of diminishing returns.

17. Constant returns to scale is a given percentage increase in all inputs, produces the same percentage increase in output. Economists believe that constant returns to scale is present in most industries.

18. Diseconomies of scale are the opposite of economies of scale. An increase in wage rates, raw material prices, interest rates or other prices causes a firm's cost to rise.

Hence, it is a situation in which output increases less than proportionately to inputs as the scale of production increases. For example, a firm finds that doubling its input causes its output to rise less than double.

19. A firm might want to produce its good even after diminishing marginal returns have set in and marginal cost is on the rise. The reason is that as long as P > MC, a firm will increase its total profits by increasing its output. So, even if MC begins to increase, producers will likely continue to produce until MC = P.

20. In the short-run, the firm operates only if its revenue exceeds its variable cost (VC). This is the same as saying that the firm operates only if the market price exceeds its AVC.

21. If there is no output for which P > ATC but there is a range of output for which P > AVC and TR > TVC, then the firm will minimize its losses by producing the output at which P = MC.

6.13 Learning Practice

Table 6.13 gives the short-run total cost of Bob's gourmet burger stand for different amounts of output per unit.

a. What is Bob's total fixed cost?

b. Fill in the columns in the table (6.13).

c. Draw TC, TFC, ATC, AVC, AFC, and MC curves.

Table 6.13
Bob's Gourmet Burger Stand

Burgers	TC	TFC	TVC	AFC	AVC	ATC	MC
0	$6.50	$____	$____				
1	9.50	____	____	$____	$____	$____	$____
2	10.50	____	____	____	____	____	____
3	11.50	____	____	____	____	____	____
4	12.50	____	____	____	____	____	____
5	13.50	____	____	____	____	____	____
6	14.50	____	____	____	____	____	____
7	18.00	____	____	____	____	____	____
8	20.50	____	____	____	____	____	____
9	24.00	____	____	____	____	____	____
10	29.00	____	____	____	____	____	____

6.14 Learning Practice

The students are to use the following table:

Units per Month	TC per Month	TFC per Month	TVC per Month	ATC per Month	AFC per Month	AVC per Month	MC per Month
0	$30,000	30,000	0	0	0	0	0
1	$50,000						
2	$70,000						
3	$90,000						
4	$110,000						
5	$132,000						
6	$158,000						
7	$188,000						
8	$222,000						
9	$260,000						
10	$305,000						

Bob Doorman owns a construction firm, Bob's Grand-Garages Company, Inc., that specializes in the construction of garages. Bob's cost schedule is presented in the table.

a. Fill in the missing cost information for: TFC, TVC, ATC, AFC, AVC, and MC.

b. The current market price for garages of the quality produced by Bob's Company is $30,000. Assume Bob wants to maximize profits. Determine:

1. How many garages he should produce per month.
2. What his profit or loss would be.

c. Suppose there is population growth in the area, causing the demand for garages to expand. The market price of the garages rises to $34,000. Determine:

1. How many garages he should produce per month.
2. What his profit or loss would be.

d. Suppose that a new company owned by Ron Windowman, Ron's Extra-Special Garage Company, Inc. causes Bob to lower is price to $26,000. Determine:

1. How many garages he should produce per month.
2. What his profit or loss would be.

Examples

Using Figure 6.15, reveals the following:

a. Curves 1,3 and 4 represent AFC, ATC and MC.

b. At output Qo, the AFC is measured by the vertical distance represented by DE.

c. Curve #2 represent AVC.

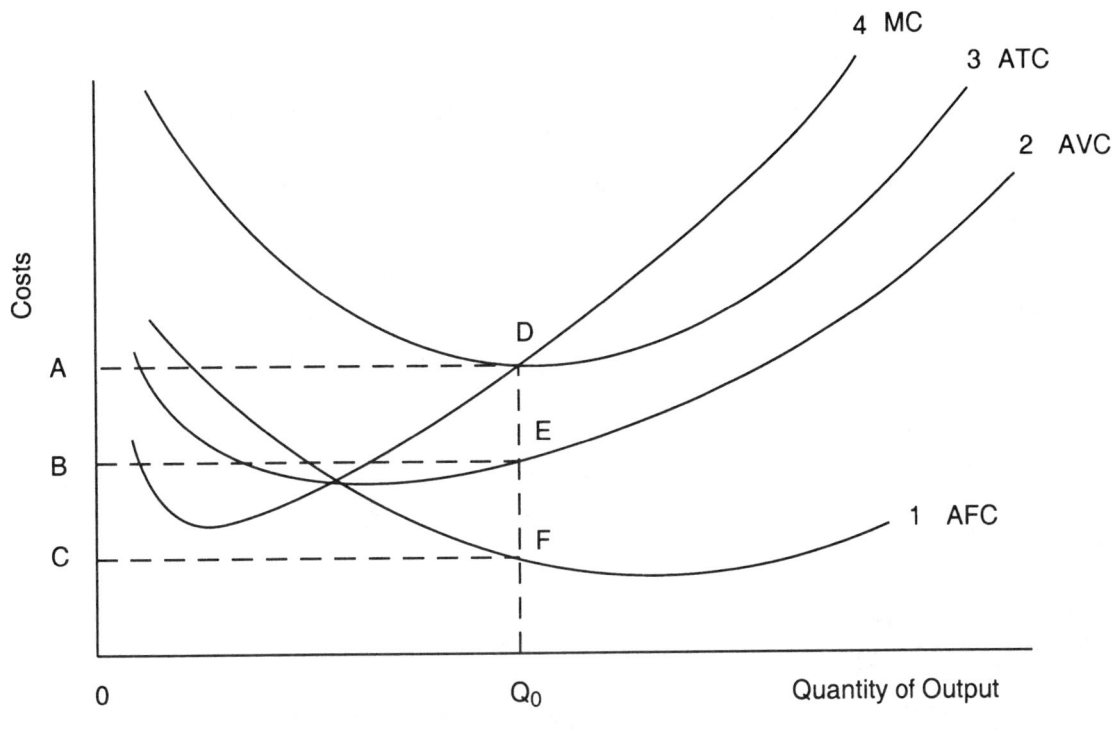

Figure 6.15

6.16 Learning Practice: Distinguishing Opportunity Costs and Sunk Costs

In order to find the opportunity of an action, first specify the next best alternative. This is what would be done if the action in question were not chosen. Then calculate the total cost for the action and its alternative; calculate the opportunity cost; subtract the cost for the alternative from the cost for the action. (This difference is the opportunity cost of the action.)

Calculate the sunk costs (any costs that are the same for both the chosen action and its alternative). A cost incurred in the past that cannot be changed by current decisions and cannot be recovered is a sunk cost. Sunk costs are completely lost.

BCR Airline is studying the question of when to cancel flights for its Port Huron to Detroit route. Flying nearly empty seats looks like bad business. The company wants to know the opportunity cost of going ahead with a scheduled round-trip flight. There are two scheduled flights each day.

The following cost data are to be used in this case:

Salary of crew	$1,100 per day
Fuel	375 per round trip
Mortgage on plane	125 per day
Landing fees	100 in Port Huron
	150 in Detroit
Soft drink and snack costs	125 per round trip

a. Calculate the opportunity cost to BCR Airlines of each round trip.

b. Calculate the sunk costs.

6.17 Learning Practice and Solutions

Given the following information, state whether the firm should shut down or continue to operate in the short run.

a. Output 100 units

Price = $10

AFC = $3.00	ATC = $7.00
AVC = $4.00	Price > AVC

Continue to operate

b. Output = 70 units

Price = $5.00

AFC = $2.00	ATC = $9.00
AVC = $7.00	

Shut down

P < AVC

c. Output = 150 units

Price = $7.00

AFC = $5.00	ATC = $11.00
AVC = $6.00	

Continue to operate with a loss. AVC < P

TAKE-A-NOTE

The Average-Marginal Relationship

When the marginal is greater than the average, it pulls the average up. When the marginal is equal to the average, the average does not change. When the marginal is less than the average, it pulls the average down.

A *sunk* cost is a cost that was paid in the past and will not change regardless of the present decision. We ignore sunk costs because they are not part of the opportunity cost of the action we are considering.

However, the publisher of the study guide has paid a number of costs to put this book in your hands. One of these costs was management's salaries. If Pearson Education sells out the entire first printing, and is considering whether to print another 10,000 copies, these costs are sunk costs and have no relevance to the decision.

A Firm's Cost

The following are an example of implicit and explicit costs for a firm.

Explicit Costs	Implicit Costs
Cost of raw materials	Owner's time (labor income)
Rend paid out	Owner's money (investment income forgone)
Manager's salaries	Opportunity cost of owner's land (rent forgone)
Interest on loans	
Hourly worker's wages, Insurance premium	

6.18 LEARNING PRACTICE

Hypothetical Cost Schedules for an Individual Firm in the Short Run

(1) Total Output (Q)	(2) Total Fixed (TFC)	(3) Total Variable (TVC)	(4) Total Cost (TC)	(5) Average Fixed (AFC)	(6) Average Variable (AVC)	(7) Average Total (ATC)	(8) Marginal Cost (MC)	Profit or Loss
0	$100	$0						
1	$100	$90						
2	$100	$170						
3	$100	$240						
4	$100	$300						
5	$100	$370						
6	$100	$450						
7	$100	$540						
8	$100	$650						
9	$100	$780						
10	$100	$930						

Price = $110.00

a. Compare the profit/loss at each level
b. Calculate TC, AFC, AVC, ATC and MC

6.19 Learning Practice

(Average and Marginal Test Scores)

Number of Test Taken	Total Score	Marginal Score	Average Score
0	0		--
1	80		
2	150		
3	240		
4	328		

a. Fill in the missing information.
b. What is the relationship between the marginal and the average scores?

6.20 Learning Practice

Determine whether each of the following cost items would most likely to be a Fixed Cost (FC) or a (VC) item or category by placing a check in the appropriate column.

Cost Item	Variable Cost (VC)	Fixed Cost (FC)
Hourly worker's wages		
Manager's salaries		
Raw material		
Rent for building and land		√
Advertising		
Sales commissions		
Shipping costs to retail outlets		
Fire and theft insurance		√

6.21 Learning Practice

Fill in the missing information.

A purely competitive firm.

Output	Price $	Total Revenue	Total Cost	Average Revenue	MR	MC	Amount of Profits/Loss
0	$20		$30				
1	20		35				
2	20		40				
3	20		45				
4	20		50				
5	20		55				
6	20		60				

Key Concepts

Average Fixed Cost—Total fixed cost divided by quantity.

Average Total Cost (ATC)—Equal to the sum of average fixed cost and average variable cost divided by output.

Average Variable Cost—Total variable cost divided by quantity.

Break-Even Point—Price equals average cost and there is a normal profit.

Constant Return to Scale—The scale at which long-run average cost curve first reaches its lowest level. That is, a given percentage increase in all inputs produces the same percent increase in output.

Corporation—Legal entity having an existence separate and distinct from that of the owners. Corporations are the most common form of organization for large businesses because they obtain their equity capital from the issuance of shares of stocks.

Diseconomies of Scale—A situation in which output increases less than proportionately to input as the scale of production increases.

Economic Loss—A return which is less than implicit cost.

Economic Profit—Total revenue minus implicit and explicit cost equals an amount greater than zero.

Economies of Scale—A reduction of costs per unit of output resulting from an expansion in output and failing long-run average total cost over a range of increasing output.

Explicit Costs—Ordinary expenses, such as wages and bills that accountants include in a firm's expenses.

Firm—The type of business structure.

Fixed Input—A factor of production that does not vary as production increases or decreases.

Implicit Costs—Refers to the opportunity costs of resources owned by the firm. They do not involve contractual payments that are entered on the firm's balance sheet.

Long Run—A period in which there are no fixed factors.

Long Run Average Cost (LRAC)—A curve is made up of all the points of tangency with the plots of an infinite number of short-run average cost curves. The shape of a firm's long-run average cost curve depends on how average costs change as production is expanded.

Marginal Cost (MC)—Additional cost of producing one more unit of output.

Marginal Revenue (MR)—the change in the firm's total revenue per unit of output.

Normal Profit—Total revenue minus implicit and explicit costs equals zero.

Partnership—An unincorporated business that is jointly owned by two or more people. A partnership is not a separate legal entity in itself, but merely a voluntary association of individuals.

Principle of Diminishing Returns—As more and more variable input is added to fixed input, output will initially increase, but after a point, the increase will begin to decrease.

Proprietorship—A business owned by one individual.

Short Run—A period in which there are fixed factors of production.

Shut-Down Rule—If the price is below the average variable costs the firm should shut down because the cost of shutting down is less than that of producing.

Total Cost (TC)—The sum of the firm's total fixed cost and its total variable cost at any given level of output.

Total Fixed Cost (TFC)—Does not vary with the level of output. It will be the same whether output is one unit or a hundred units. This cost is also referred to as unavoidable cost.

Total Revenue—Price an item sells for multiplied by the number of units sold (p.q.).

Total Variable Cost (TVC)—The cost of the firm's variable factors.

Variable Costs (VC)—Costs of production that change as the output level of the firm changes.

Variable Input—A factor of production that increases or decreases as production increases or decreases.

Discussion Questions

1. Distinguish among the three types of business firms: proprietorship, partnership, and corporation.
2. Discuss the advantages of the corporation over the other types.
3. Distinguish between explicit and implicit costs.
4. Distinguish between fixed and variable costs.
5. Explain average total cost in the short-run.
6. Define marginal cost.
7. Discuss economies and diseconomies of scale and how they impact on average total cost in the long-run.
8. Explain why average total costs both in the short-run and in the long-run at first decline as production increases but then begin to increase.
9. Discuss the three kinds of economic profit.
10. Distinguish between the short run and the long run.
11. Explain the principle of diminishing returns and how it affects short-run costs.
12. Explain the shut-down rule.
13. Explain the derivation of the long-run average total cost curve.
14. Discuss constant returns to scale.
15. Distinguish between opportunity costs and sunk costs.
16. Draw cost curves with economies of scale, diseconomies of scale and constant returns to scale.

Chapter 7

How Markets Function: Pure Competition

LEARNING OBJECTIVES

After reading this chapter, you should be able to:
1. Summarize the term market structure and the assumption of pure competition.
2. Identify the four types of sellers' market structures.
3. Define and explain the characteristics of pure competition.
4. Explain the demand curve facing a purely competitive firm.
5. Determine and identify graphically the short run supply curve for a purely competitive market.
6. Define, calculate, and graphically show each of the following for a purely competitive firm: total revenue, average revenue, and marginal revenue.
7. Identify graphically and calculate the profits and losses for pure competition.
8. Illustrate graphically a purely competitive firm in the long run equilibrium.
9. Briefly evaluate pure competition, indicating both the advantages and disadvantages.
10. Explain how agriculture fits the purely competitive model.
11. Illustrate graphically a loss in pure competition with shut-down.
12. Identify pure competitive firm at different price levels.
13. Explain the profit maximization principle.
14. Solve the learning practices as indicated at the end of the chapter.

MARKET STRUCTURES

Market structure is a model of the way business firms behave, based on several characteristics of the firms involved, and implying that firms will pursue particular strategies in the market place.

The term market structures refers to the features of a market that may affect the behavior and performance of the firms in the market. The differences are great enough that we are able to identify four distinct types of sellers' market structures: Pure Competition (PC), Monopoly, Monopolistic Competition (MC), and oligopoly. Furthermore, the characteristics of market structures are: the number of firms, the ease of entry of new firms into the market; and product differentiation.

This section tries to answer certain questions about the firm. These are: what output will the firm produce, what price will it charge, what will be the profit received by the firm, and what will be the relationship between price and average cost, and between price and marginal cost.

Appendix 7.1 summarizes the similarities and differences among the above market structures, and the features of each market structure.

CHARACTERISTICS OF PURE COMPETITION

The teaching of economic analysis in United States begins with the assumption of "pure competition." This assumption reflects the philosophical structure of the American market. In everyday use, the word competition refers only to competitive behavior of individual firms and in a quite distinct concept, competitive market structure.

Let us focus our attention upon pure competition, beginning with an elaboration of our definition. Pure competition is an ideal model and there are no industries that are purely competitive, though the two that probably come closest are the sale of standardized agricultural products and the purchase and sale of financial securities (common stocks) by private individuals. Pure competition represents the simplest, most idealistic, and thus, the most unrealistic market structure. A market is said to operate under pure competition when the following five conditions are satisfied:

1. **Large Number of Sellers of the Same Product.** A basic feature of a purely competitive market is the presence of a large number of independently active sellers, usually offering their products in a highly organized market. Farm commodities and purchase and sale of common stocks are illustrative.

2. **Price Taker.** The individual competitive producer is a price taker; he or she cannot adjust the market price, but can only adjust to it (no single seller has any control over price). Each firm produces such a small fraction of total output that increasing or decreasing its output will have no effect on product price. If one firm decides to stop producing output, the market is not affected. To illustrate, assume that there are 20,000 competing firms, each of which is currently producing 200 units of output; total supply is 4,000,000. If one of these 20,000 firms cuts its output to 100 units, will this affect price? No, and the reason is that a reduction of output by a single firm has almost no impact on total supply. Specifically, the total quantity supplied declined from 4,000,000 to 3,999,900. This clearly accounts for only a small fraction of total output.

Hence, if there are 2,000 different sellers of a particular good, and they are all charging exactly the same price, this is powerful evidence that sellers are price takers. Furthermore, the firm can sell any output at the market price, so there is never any reason for the competitive firm to sell for less.

One of the main reasons that economists like the price-taker model is that there is no problem deciding what price the seller should ask. He can sell all that he wants to at the market equilibrium price. He simply "takes" his selling price from the market.

3. Identical Products (Homogeneous). All firms in a purely competitive market sell the same product. Given price, the consumer is indifferent as to the seller from which the product is purchased. In the agricultural industry, for example, a buyer cannot determine if the milk that was purchased came from Farmer A or Farmer B, nor does it really matter since the milk is the same.

    In other words, all firms produce a homogeneous product, one that is so standardized that the consumer cannot differentiate the output of various producers.

    Due to the identical nature of each of the products, having an edge over a competitor is not possible on the basis of quality. Promotion through the use of advertising is not possible either, because the features of the products are all the same.

4. Easy Entry and Exit to and from the Industry. Purely competitive firms are free to enter and leave the industry at will, unimpeded by government restrictions or other barriers. In particular, no significant obstacles, such as legal, technological, financial, or other, exist to prevent new firms from coming into being and selling their outputs. This leaves the entrepreneur an open door to the establishment of a profitable corporation.

5. Perfect Information. Each firm and each customer is well informed about the available products and their prices. They know whether one supplier is selling at a price lower than another.

The structural characteristics of pure competition are shown in Table 7.1.

Table 7.1
Structural Characteristics of the Purely Competitive Market Model

Characteristics	**Description**
Number of Firms	A very large number of sellers, all small.
Price Taker	The firm has no control over price. Instead, the firm accepts the price set by supply and demand in the market.
Type of Product	Identical or homogeneous.
Conditions of Entry	Free entry and exit.
Perfect Information	Each firm and each customer is well informed about the available products and their prices.
Examples in U.S. Economy	Agriculture; purchase and sale of common stocks by private individuals.
Demand Curve	Faces horizontal demand curve where MR = MC = P.
Type of Profits	Normal profit in the long run and guaranteed.

Demand, Cost, Revenue, and the Profit Maximization Output

In pure competition a distinction is made between the firm and the industry. The industry is the sum of all the firms producing the same type of product. This means that the demand and supply curves of the industry are the same as those of the market. The demand curves for pure competition are shown in Figure 7.1. In the pure competition model, the industry or the market is represented on the left side of the figure, and the firm is represented on the right side. This presentation is based on the characteristic that the firm takes the price from the market.

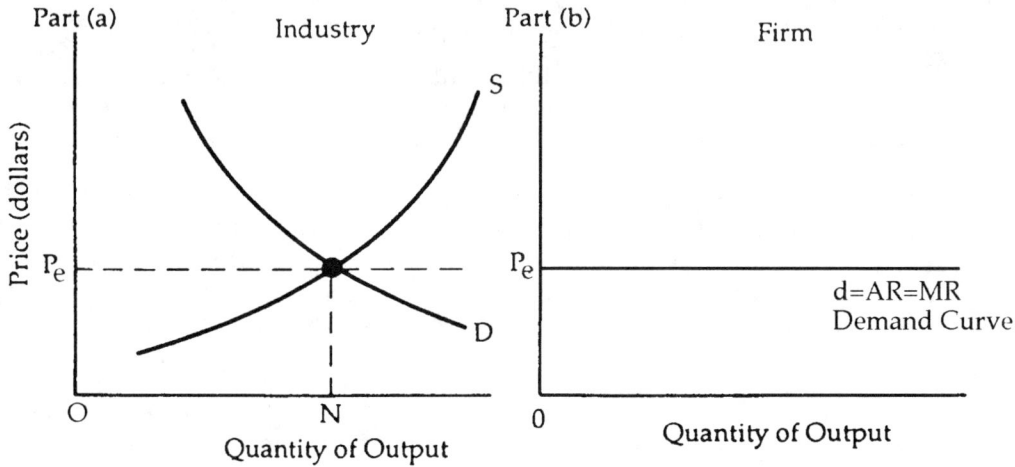

Figure 7.1
Demand Curves for Pure Competition

The equilibrium price of the product (Pe) and the output (ON) will be set at the intersection of the supply and demand curves. The industry demand and supply curves for the entire competitive market are shown in Figure 7.1 part (a).

The firm's demand curve is perfectly elastic (horizontal line) for two reasons. First, if the firm were to raise its price above Pe, it would sell nothing since buyers can get the identical product at the price Pe from other firms. Second, since the individual firm's output capacity is but a drop in the bucket compared to that of the entire industry, the firm can effectively sell all it can produce at the market equilibrium price Pe. A horizontal demand curve means that the firm can sell any amount of output without affecting the price. Because the demand curve is horizontal, the competitive firm's marginal revenue (MR) is a horizontal straight line that coincides with its demand curve, hence, MR = P. Therefore, for the firms in pure competition, P = AR = MR. This equation is illustrated in Table 7.2.

Table 7.2
Price, Average Revenue, Total Revenue, and Marginal Revenue
in a Purely Competitive Market.

Qd (output)	Price ($)	TR (P x Q)	AR (TR/Q)	MR (ΔTR/ΔQ)
0	5	0	0	0
1	5	5	5	5
2	5	10	5	5
3	5	15	5	5
4	5	20	5	5
5	5	25	5	5

Total revenue is equal to price times quantity. Since the price is equal to $5 regardless of how much is sold, total revenue increases at a constant rate of $5.

Average revenue is equal to total revenue divided by the quantity. Average revenue is equal to the price. Marginal revenue is equal to the change in total revenue divided by the change in quantity. In pure competition, marginal revenue is equal to average revenue and to the price of the item. Since this is the case, the demand curve, the average revenue, and the marginal revenue curves are the same as shown in Figure 7.2.

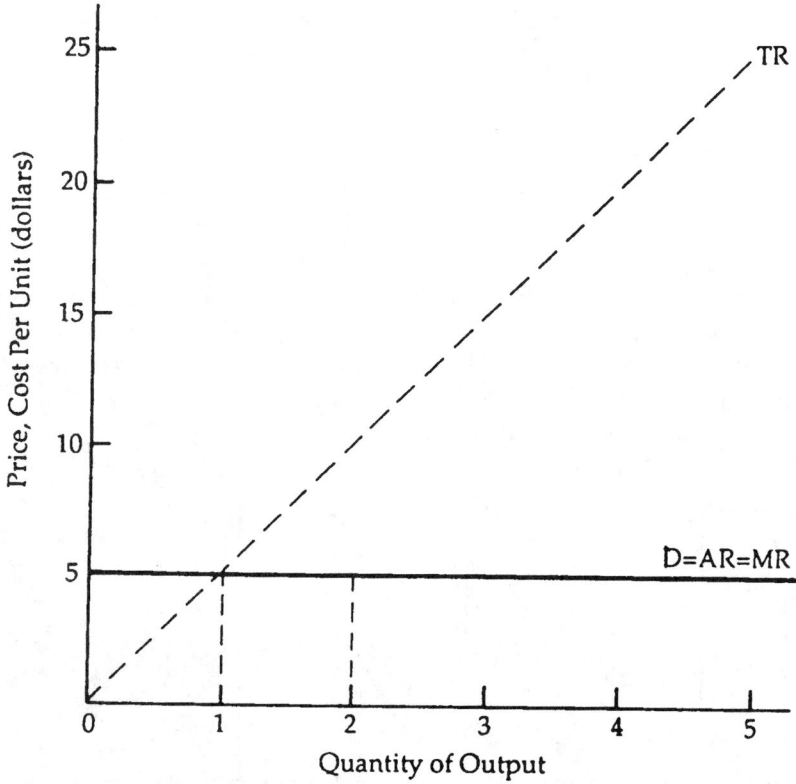

Figure 7.2
Total Revenue and Marginal Revenue for Pure Competition

The Competitive Firm's Short Run Supply Curve

The firm's supply curve is the portion of its marginal cost curve above AVC. At prices below the minimum possible AVC, the quantity supplied will be zero because the firm would cease operations. To determine the quantity at any price greater than the minimum possible AVC, trace a horizontal line to the MC curve. Dropping a vertical line to the horizontal axis gives the quantity supplied at the price in Figure 7.3.

At a price of P_1 the quantity supplied is 100 units. At price P_2 the quantity supplied is 200 units. If the price were to drop below P_0, the firm would not supply any units of the product. The smallest amount supplied, therefore, would be 50 units at a price of P_0.

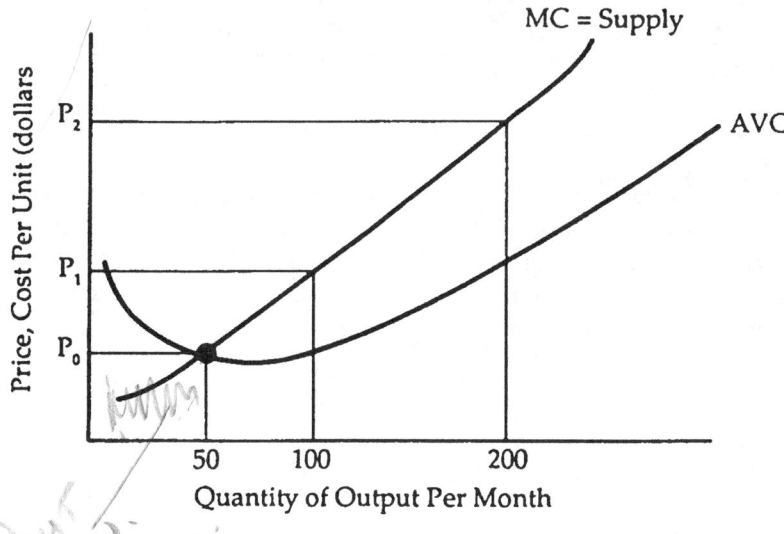

Figure 7.3
Competitive Firm's Short Run Supply Curve

Industry Supply Curve

The industry supply for a product is defined as the sum of all the individual firms' supplies. Figure 7.4 illustrates how supply curves for Firm A, Firm B, and Firm C can be added to show the industry supply curve. For each firm we will assume that no output will be supplied below P_1. At a price of P_1, 5 units will be supplied for an industry supply of 15 units. At a price of P_2, 10 units will be supplied for an industry supply of 30 units.

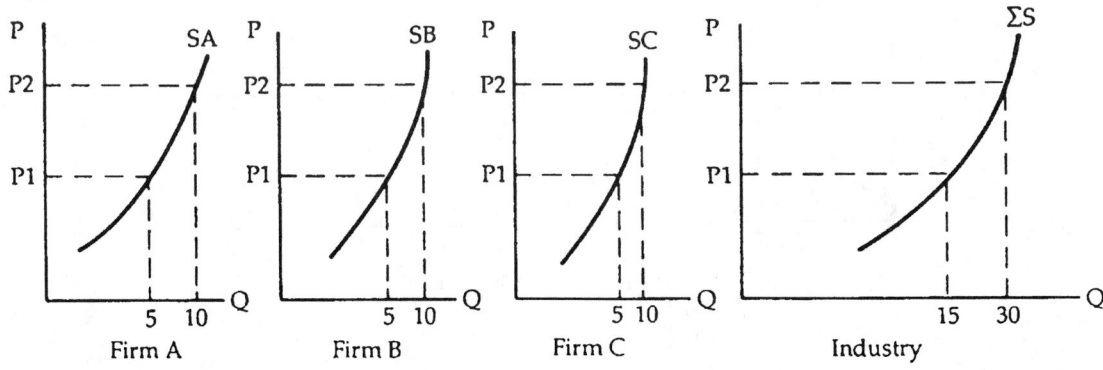

Figure 7.4
Industry Supply Curve

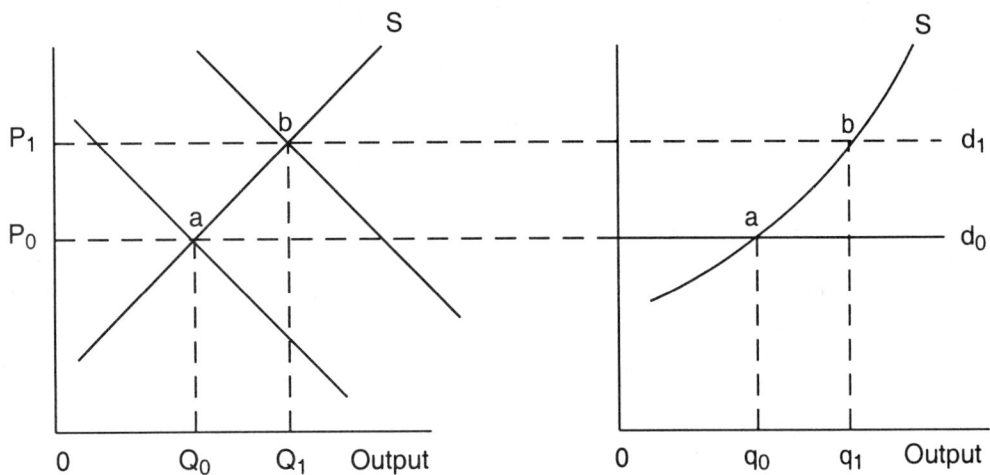

Figure 7.5
Change in Demand: Purely Competitive Industry and the Firm.

Looking at Figure 7.5 reveals the following: An increase in the demand for an industry output raises the equilibrium price to P_1; and the firm output to Q_1.

Profit Maximization Principle: Unit Cost Minus Unit Revenue

Marginal Revenue is the change in the firm's total revenue per unit of output. Mathematically

$$\text{Marginal Revenue (MR)} = \frac{\Delta \text{ Total Revenue (TR)}}{\Delta \text{ Output (Q)}}$$

Since the MR coincides with demand curve, and the purely competitive firm sells all units at the same price, MR will be equal to the market price.

A firm always maximizes its total profit at the output rate where the marginal profit on the last unit sold equals zero. If the production and sale of one more unit of output will add more to a firm's total revenue than to its total costs, the sale of the unit must necessarily add something to the firm's total profits.

If, however, the extra cost of producing and selling one more unit is greater than the extra revenues the firm gains, the firm's total profits will be reduced by selling that unit. Marginal revenue is defined as the addition to total revenue attributable to the sale of one more unit of output, whereas marginal cost is defined as the addition to total cost resulting from the production and sale of one more unit of output. Hence, to maximize profits the firm must be cognizant of the marginal revenue and the marginal cost of each successive unit of output.

Short Run Profit Maximization Under Pure Competition

The data below show the profit-maximizing level of output chosen by a purely competitive firm, Hamatramek, Inc., given a market price of 600 dollars per unit. The output can be found by comparing total cost and total revenue, as shown in Table 7.3.

It can also be found by comparing marginal cost and marginal revenue. (Because the firm is a price taker, marginal revenue is equal to price.) Regardless of the approach used, the profit-maximizing output is 8 units per day and the maximum profit per day is 1,275 dollars.

Table 7.3
Profit Maximization Using Total Revenue and Total Cost and Marginal Revenue and Marginal Cost.

Quantity of Output	Total Revenue	Total Cost	Total Profit	Marginal Cost	Marginal Revenue
0	$0	$1000	−$1000	—	—
1	600	1300	−700	$300	$600
2	1,200	1550	−350	250	600
3	1,800	1775	25	225	600
4	2,400	1975	425	200	600
5	3,000	2225	775	250	600
6	3,600	2525	1075	300	600
7	4,200	2925	1275	400	600
8	4,800	3525	1275	600	600
9	5,400	4425	975	900	600
10	6,000	5725	275	1300	600
11	6,600	7525	−975	1800	600

Profit Rule

In order to maximize revenue, the firm should produce where MR = MC, as shown in Figure 7.6.

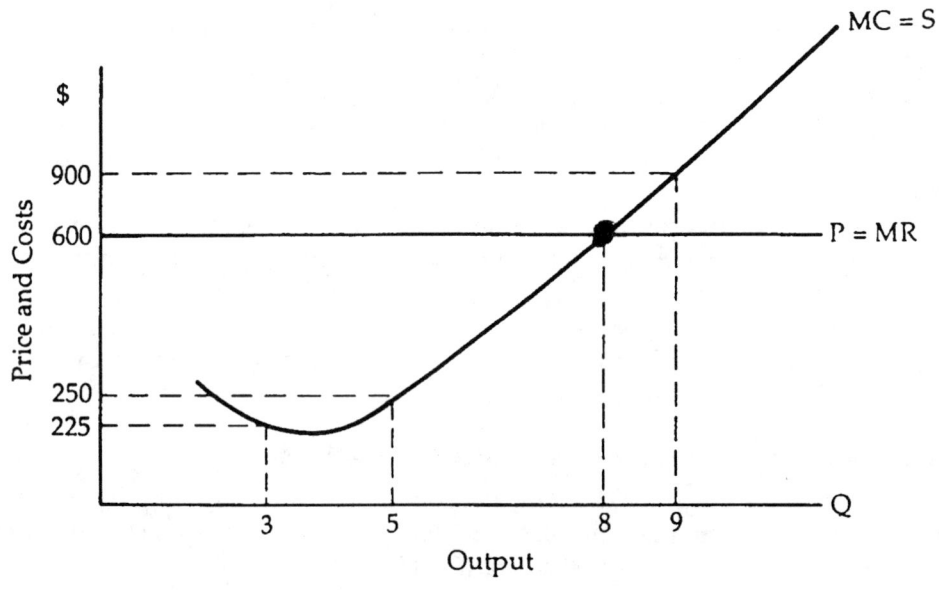

Figure 7.6
Profit Rule

To produce the third item costs an additional $225, whereas the item can be sold for $600. Additional profit can be made by producing the third item. To produce the fifth item costs an additional $250, whereas the item can be sold for $600. Additional profit can be made by producing the fifth item. To produce the ninth item costs an additional $900, whereas the item can only be sold for $600. The ninth item should not be produced. The firm should stop at the eighth item since the additional cost of producing the item just equals the price or marginal revenue. At this quantity the item earns the greatest profit, which is $1275, as shown in Table 7.3.

Short Run Equilibrium of the Competitive Firm

In the short run, there are three profit possibilities: economic profit, normal profit, and an economic loss. Figure 7.7 illustrates the example of an economic profit.

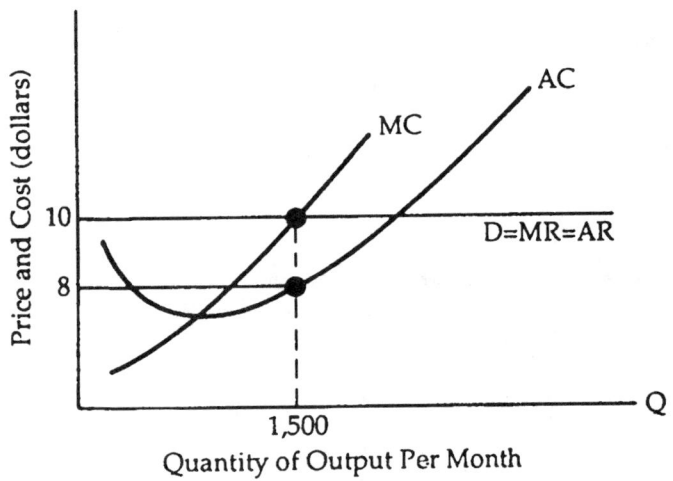

Figure 7.7
Economic Profit in Pure Competition.

Following the profit rule, the firm will produce where the marginal revenue equals marginal cost. This occurs at 1500 units per month at a price of $10. The total revenue is $15,000. The total cost of producing 1500 units is 1500 x $8 which equals $12,000.

Since the total cost is less than the total revenue, the firm is making an economic profit of $3,000 ($15,000–$12,000). Figure 7.8 illustrates the example of a normal profit. In this example the firm will produce 1000 units at a price of $12. The total revenue is equal to $12,000 (1000 x $12). The total cost also equals $12,000 (1000 x $12). Since total revenue equals total cost, the firm is said to be making a normal profit.

Figure 7.9 illustrates the example in which a firm is incurring a loss and decides to continue production. Figure 7.9 illustrates the example in which the firm is incurring a loss but decides to cease production and shut down.

In Figure 7.9, total revenue equals $9,600 (800 x $12); total cost equals $11,200 (800 x $14); variable cost equals $5,600 (800 x $7); fixed costs equals $5,600 (800 x (14 – 7)).

In this example, the firm should continue to produce, since the loss involved with shutting down is the fixed cost of $5,600, whereas the cost involved with continuing is $1,600 ($9,600–$11,200).

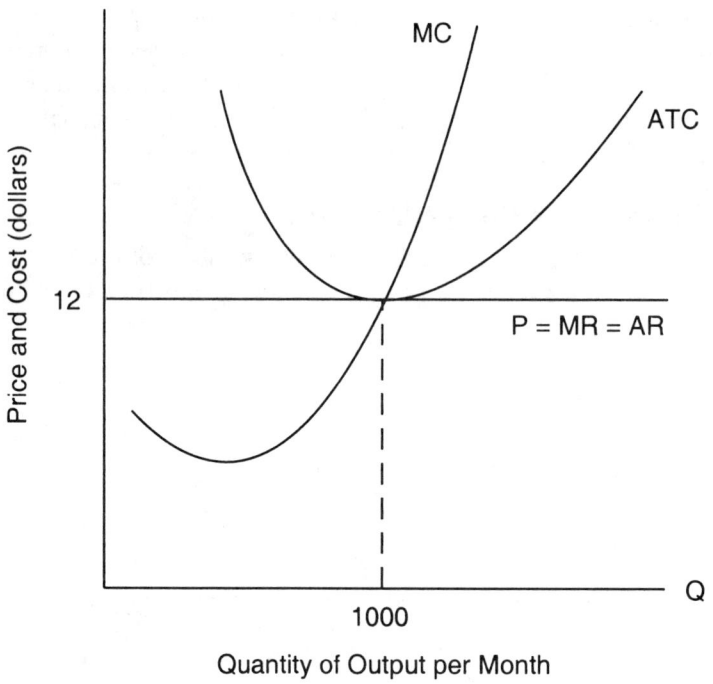

Figure 7.8
Normal Profit in Pure Competition (ATC = P)

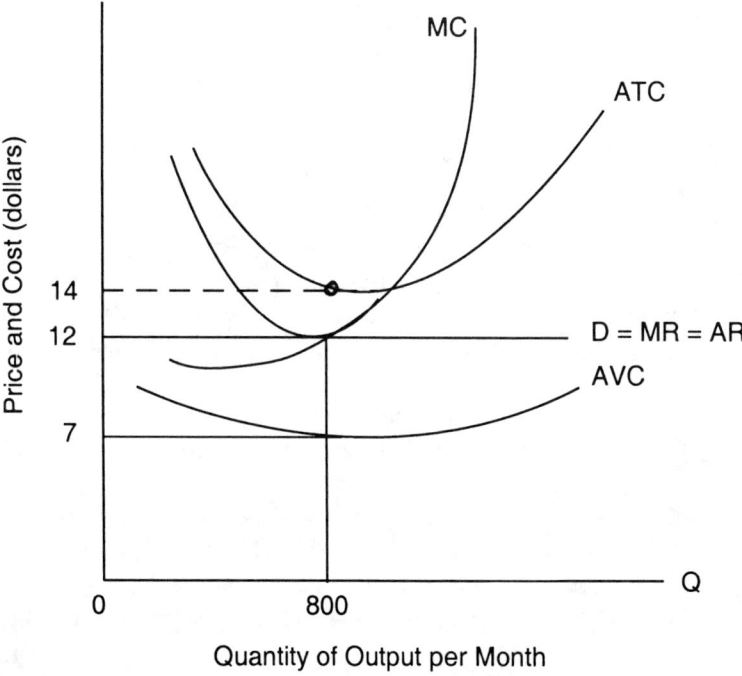

Figure 7.9
A Loss in Pure Competition (ATC > P)

When price is less than average variable cost, the firm incurs a loss. In Figure 7.10, the price is $5 but the AVC is $7. The total revenue is $3,000; (600 x $5); the total cost is $11,400 (600 x $19); total variable cost equals $4,200 (600 x $7); and total fixed cost equals $7,200 (600 x $12).

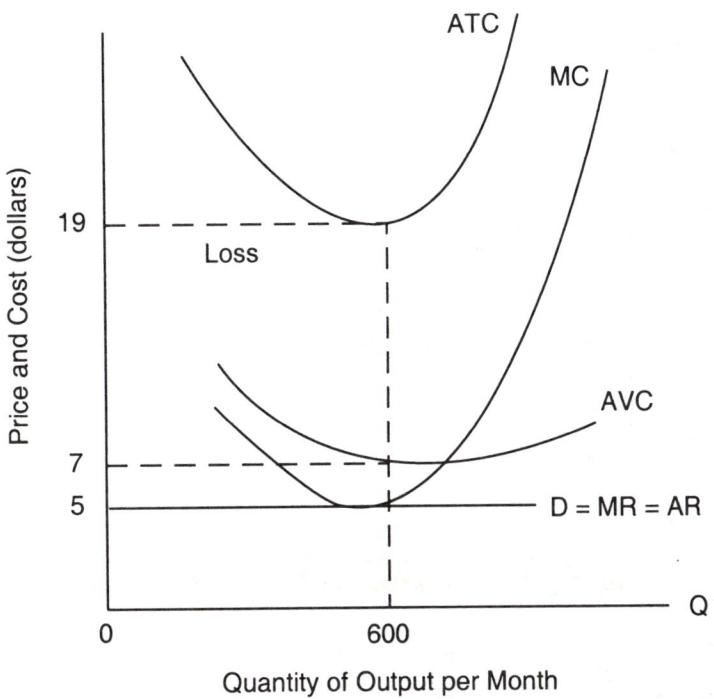

Figure 7.10
Loss in Pure Competition With Shut Down (AVC > P)

As long as the firm in purely competitive industry is able to cover its variable costs and a portion of its fixed cost, it will produce rather than shut down. If VC of operating > revenue generated at all levels of output, the firm by operation, would suffer a loss equal to its FC plus the uncovered portion of its VC.

The total loss in this example is $3,000 − $11,400 = $8,400. The firm would be better off not to produce and lose only the $7,200 in fixed costs.

The firm in a purely competitive market will attempt to maximize its profits by maintaining a level of output at which P = MC.

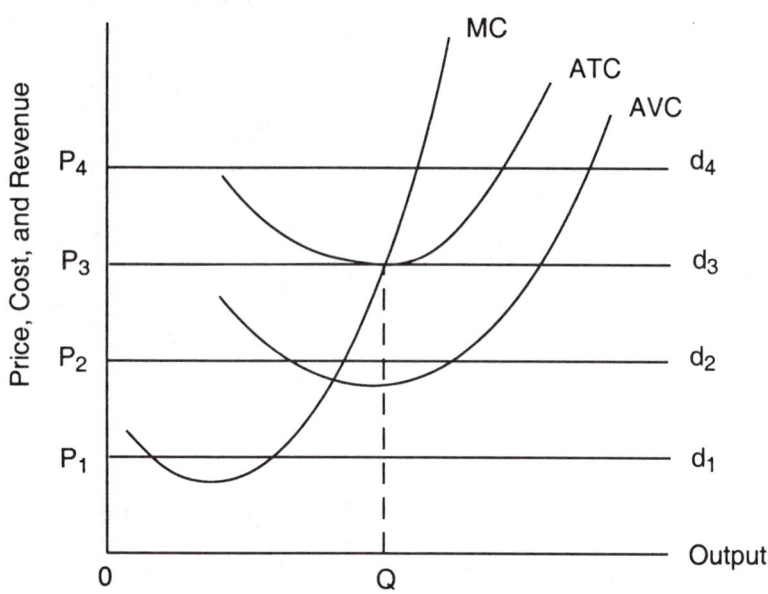

Figure 7.11
Purely Competitive Firm at Different Price Level

Example: Using Figure 7.11 indicates the following:
- The firm incurs losses at P2 but should remain in operation.
- If a firm is losing money but total revenue is sufficient to cover variable costs of production, it should remain in operation to minimize short run losses.
- The firm incurs losses and should shut down at P1.
- If a firm's losses are greater than its fixed cost, it should shut down to minimize short run losses.
- At P3, the firm is earning normal profit. That is the minimum payment for the use of owner's capital needed to keep the enterprise in business over the long run.
- At P4, the purely competitive firm is making an economic profit.
- If there is no output for which price exceeds average total cost (ATC), but there is a range of output for which P > AVC and TR > TVC, then the firm will minimize its losses by producing the output at which P = MC.

Purely Competitive Firm in the Long Run Equilibrium

The long-run equilibrium situation of a purely competitive firm is a normal profit (zero economic profits). If there are economic profits in the short run, new firms will be attracted into the industry. The additional firms will cause the market supply curve to increase or move to the right. As a result of the increased supply, the price of the product will decline. As the price drops but costs do not, economic profits will be eliminated.

If there are losses in the short run, some firms will leave the industry. The reduced number of firms will cause the supply curve to decrease or move to the left. As a result of the decreased supply, the price of the product will rise. As the price rises but costs do not, losses are eliminated.

The result is that a normal profit is achieved in the long run due to the freedom of entry and exit of firms in this model. A normal profit is shown in Figure 7.12.

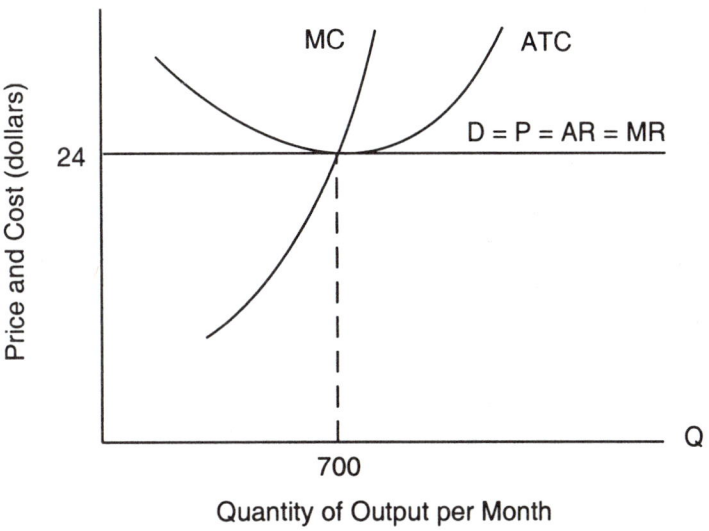

Figure 7.12
Purely Competitive Firm in Long Run Equilibrium

The total revenue for the firm in Figure 7.12 is $16,800 (700 x $24). The total cost is also $16,800 (700 x $24). When total revenue equals total cost, the firm achieves a normal profit (0).

Profits in a Competitive Industry:
How Much Profit Is Earned in a Competitive Industry?

In the long-run equilibrium, the surprising answer is zero (0). This is a strange result: Why? The answer is because of freedom of entry and exit. As firms enter a purely competitive industry attracted by positive economic profits, the market supply of the product will increase causing prices and profits to drop. This process would continue until profits had fallen to zero. However, zero economic profits means that the average total cost (ATC) equals price (P). Firms with zero economic profits will be hampered in regards to growth and to the development of new and better products.

Economics of Agriculture

The industry that most closely fits the model of pure competition is agriculture. We can identify six main characteristics of agriculture in the United States:

1. A purely competitive structure:

   American agriculture is characterized by a very large number of firms or farms. The firms are producing a homogeneous product, for example wheat or milk. It is not possible to distinguish one farmer's wheat from another farmer's after the wheat is put into the bin. In one gallon of milk purchased at the supermarket could be milk from several or many farmers. In addition, there are few barriers to entry into farming and to exit from farming. Farm prices are determined in the market, and the farmer takes the price.

identical output of the purely competitive industry may be less than ideal. Consumers would have relatively few product choices because products would all be homogeneous: all shirts would look alike, and so, too, would pants, shoes, bicycles, houses, etc.

Finally, in an economic system made up of purely competitive markets and homogeneous goods, there would be little need for advertising. This, however, can be termed either an advantage or a disadvantage, depending on one's point of view. Though pure competition is often considered the ideal, it is unlikely that most would advocate an economy composed entirely of purely competitive markets.

CHAPTER SUMMARY

1. Pure competition is a market structure characterized by a large number of sellers of the same product and a price taker. Since firms sell identical units, a firm that attempts to raise its prices will find that it sells nothing. This means that the demand curve facing any individual firm is horizontal at the market price. Also, for the purely competitive firm, there are no restrictions and no barriers to entry. Each firm and each customer is well-informed about the available products and their prices.

2. In a purely competitive industry, all firms produce a homogeneous product, one that is so standardized that the consumer cannot differentiate between the output of various producers.

3. A purely competitive market is very efficient because it produces where P = MC, and the MC of production is the same for all producers.

4. Under pure competition, the firm's demand curve is infinitely elastic, horizontal at the market-determined price. The firm's demand curve is the same as its average revenue curve.

5. The industry supply for a product is defined as the sum of all the individual firm's supplies.

6. The profit maximizing rule for a purely competitive firm is to produce where MC = MR.

7. The purely competitive firm will make an economic profit if total revenue is greater than total cost.

8. The purely competitive firm will make a normal profit if total revenue equals total cost.

9. The purely competitive firm is incurring a loss if total revenue is less than total cost.

10. The firm should not shut down in the short run if TR exceeds total variable cost (TVC).

11. The purely competitive firm should go out of business immediately if the market price is less than the firm's AVC and the situation is not expected to improve in the future.

12. A competitive firm will tend to expand its output as long as the market price is greater than MC.

13. The long-run equilibrium situation of a purely competitive firm is a normal profit.

14. In the long run, the purely competitive firm produces where P = AR = MR = MR = MC = ATC. This is termed productive efficiency.

15. The closest industry to pure competition is agriculture, which has five characteristics: a purely competitive structure, price and income inelasticity, rapid technological changes, resource immobility, and decline.

16. Among the programs to assist the farmer are: price supports, crop restrictions, increasing demand, direct payments, and relocation programs.

CHAPTER 7
KEY CONCEPTS

Homogeneous Product—A product that is so standardized that the consumer cannot differentiate the output of various producers.

Industry—All the firms producing the same or similar products.

Marginal Revenue—Is the change in the firm's total revenue per unit of output.

Market Structure—Refers to all aspects of a market, such as the number of firms and the types of products sold.

Perfect Information—Each firm and customer is well-informed about the available products and their prices.

Price Taker—Each firm produces such a small fraction of total output that increasing or decreasing its output will have no effect on product price.

Productive Efficiency—The firm is producing where marginal cost equals marginal revenue at the lowest average total cost.

Profit Maximizing Rule—The firm should produce where MR = MC.

Pure Competition—An industry in which there are a very large number of firms all producing the same product, with prices being determined in the market by supply and demand.

TAKE-A-NOTE
WHAT IS PURE COMPETITION?

- Perfect knowledge of market price and quantity
- No discrimination
- Perfect mobility of resources
- Homogeneous commodity
- Large number of buyers and sellers
- MC = P   Added cost of the resource equals its value to the consumer
- MR = MC   Profit maximization rule
- MC = ATC = LRATC (optimum output with optimum plant and hence optimum resource use)
- MR = AR(P)   Purely competitive market
- ATC = AR   Normal profit

- MC = ATC (The most efficient combination of variable and fixed resources)
- The equilibrium conditions are as follows:
  MC = P = MR = AR = ATC = LRATC

DISCUSSION QUESTIONS

1. Explain the concept of market structures.
2. Present the five characteristics of pure competition.
3. Explain why the demand curve of a purely competitive firm is infinitely elastic.
4. Explain why a purely competitive market is considered to be very efficient.
5. Explain what enables a purely competitive firm to make short-run economic profit.
6. What is the rule for profit maximization for a purely competitive firm?
7. Under what cost conditions should a purely competitive firm shut down?
8. Explain the long-run equilibrium situation in pure competition.
9. What are the advantages and disadvantages under pure competition?
10. Indicate how agriculture fits the purely competitive model.
11. Discuss the major problems in agriculture.
12. Select a solution to the agricultural problem you feel is the best and indicate your logic.
13. How much profit is earned in a competitive industry?
14. A purely competitive firm will shut down if price is below AVC.
15. In pure competition resources are allocated in a very inefficient manner.
16. Pure competition promotes innovation and research.
17. In pure competition, there is a great need for advertising.
18. A firm can always be better off by producing instead of shutting down.
19. The industry is the sum of all the firms producing the same product.
20. In pure competition, price exceeds average revenue.
21. If total revenue exceeds total cost, the firm is producing an economic profit in the long run.
22. If total cost equals total revenue, the firm is making a normal profit.
23. If the price of a product is below the AVC, the firm should shut down.
24. In pure competition, in the long run, P = AR = MR = ATC = MC.
25. The demand for farm goods is highly elastic.
26. The income elasticity for farm goods is inelastic, which means as incomes increase, a greater percentage is spent on them.
27. American farmers tend to be very immobile regarding their ability to seek other employment.

28. American agriculture is characterized by over production.

29. The farmer is able to raise his price whenever costs increase.

30. A price support is a price set below equilibrium to improve the income of American farmers.

31. Under a direct payment plan to improve incomes, the government pays an amount which is the difference between the market price and a certain target price.

7.13 Learning Practice and Solutions

Profit Maximizing For a Competitive Firm

Output (Q)	TR	TC	MR	MC	Profit TR–TC
0	$0.00	$25.00	$0.00	$0.00	$–25.00
1	5.00	29.80	5.00	4.80	–24.80
3	15.00	37.25	5.00	3.50	–22.25
6	30.00	44.75	5.00	2.00	–14.75
10	50.00	50.25	5.00	1.00	–0.25
15	75.00	64.00	5.00	4.75	11.00
21	105.00	125.00	5.00	17.00	–20.00

The firm confronts a market price of $5.00 per unit, its MR is $5.00. TR increases by $5.00 per additional unit that is produced and sold. The firm maximizes its profit at an output of 15 units. For small output less than 11, the firm would actually experience losses. At 15 units of output, an $11.00 is earned (The difference between total revenue and total cost). Also, at 21 units of output the firm would experience a loss of $20.00 (TC > TR).

7.14 Learning Practice

A. Given the following graph, answer the questions.

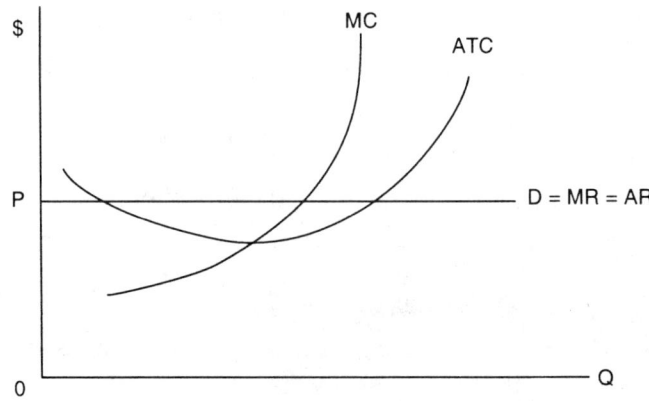

Indicate on a graph:
    The level of production
    The type of profit.

B. Given the following graph, answer the questions.

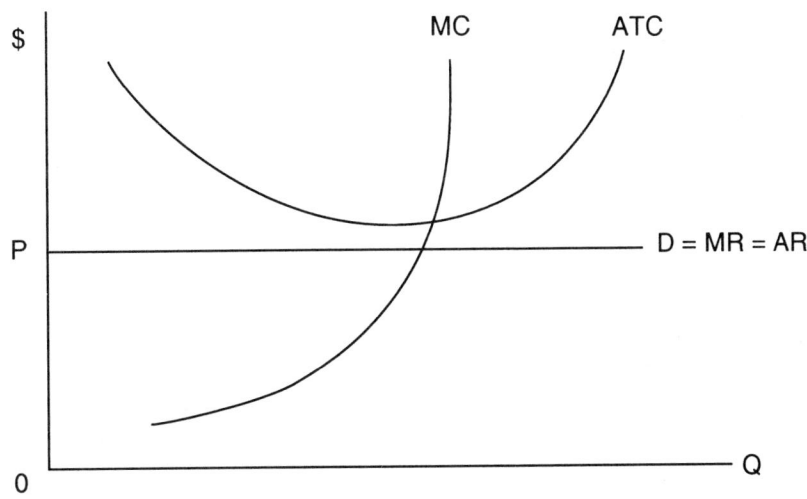

Indicate on a graph:
   The level of production
   The type of profit.

C. Construct the following conditions in a purely competitive market.

Normal profit

Profit Rule in the short run

Economic profits in the short run

Economic losses in the short run

Economic losses with shut-down

CHAPTER 8

Pure Monopoly

LEARNING OBJECTIVES

After you have studied this chapter in the text, and attended class lectures regularly, you will be able to:

1. Define and cite examples of pure monopolies.
2. Indicate the major characteristics which differentiate a pure monopoly from other market models.
3. Identify and graphically construct the demand and marginal revenue curves for the pure monopolist.
4. Explain verbally and graphically the relationship between output, price, and marginal and total revenue.
5. Identify elastic, inelastic, and unitary elastic regions on a negatively sloped demand curve.
6. Graphically indicate the profit or loss associated with a short run equilibrium for a monopolist under conditions of economic profit and economic loss.
7. Verbally and graphically describe the long run equilibrium under pure monopoly.
8. Discuss factors that give rise to monopoly and misallocation of resources.
9. Briefly describe the three types of price discrimination associated with monopoly.
10. Understand the characteristics of the monopoly market model.
11. Summarize the deadweight loss of monopoly.
12. Explain the meaning of market power.
13. Solve the learning practices as indicated at the end of the chapter.

Introduction

Monopoly

At the opposite end of the competitive spectrum from pure competition is monopoly. A pure monopoly is an industry in which there is only one supplier of a product, for which there are no close substitutes, and in which it is very hard or impossible for another firm to coexist.

Monopolies tend to be rare in the real world, and those that do exist are usually natural monopolies.

Some examples of natural monopolies are public utilities, such as gas, electricity, local telephone service company, water, sewage, trash collection, and cable television. These operations are given an exclusive right to operate by the government. The government has control over each of these operations, through regulation, to prevent them from abusing their monopoly power.

Regulation of natural monopolies is based on the theory that they are protected by formidable barriers to entry. Some firms, notably the public utilities, have been granted monopolies and are protected by law from competition.

When granted monopoly, a firm is typically required to submit to regulation of its profits. Profit regulation is thought to be necessary because it is believed that the monopoly firms would charge exorbitant prices since no price-cutting competitors exist.

Characteristics

The following characteristics differentiate a pure monopoly from other market models: (a) a single seller, (b) no close substitutes, (c) price control, (d) entry into the industry by other firms is blocked.

a. A single seller. This means that a single firm produces or supplies that product or service. Monopoly has neither rivals nor direct competitors because entry into the industry is effectively barred. The pure monopoly and the industry are one and the same.

b. No close substitutes. Pure monopoly refers to the only seller of a good that has no significant substitutes. Products produced by the monopolist are characterized as unique. This uniqueness contributes to the monopolist's power over the consumer, because the consumer is faced with no alternative choices.

c. Price control. This means the firm exercises considerable control over the price. The firm faces a downward sloping demand curve.

d. Entry into the industry by other firms is blocked. Government gives one firm the right to operate a public utility.

Certain monopolies arise because of economies of scale: these are called natural monopolies. In a natural monopoly, the average cost of production declines throughout the relevant range of production. Therefore, a given level of output can be produced at the least cost when there is only one producer in the industry. This is illustrated in Figure 8.1. A single firm can produce 100 units at an average cost of 10 dollars leading to a total cost of 1,000 dollars. With two firms each producing 50 units, total cost rises to 1,500 dollars. With four firms producing 25 units apiece, total cost climbs to 2,000 dollars. Other options are similarly inferior to monopoly. If output is to be produced with the fewest resources, there can be only one firm in the industry.

Although costs are minimized with one producer, restricting output to a single firm has an ambiguous effect on price. To remain in business, a company must charge a price that covers costs. If the industry were comprised of two or more smaller firms, they would have higher average costs than the monopolist and therefore require a higher price to stay in business. In other words, the monopolist's lower costs permit it to charge a lower price. On the other hand, there is no guarantee that the monopolist will actually charge less—at least voluntarily. This is why governments often regulate natural monopolies. The government may attempt to take advantage of economies of scale by allowing only one producer while, at the same time, trying to protect the public by restricting the ability of the monopolist to raise price.

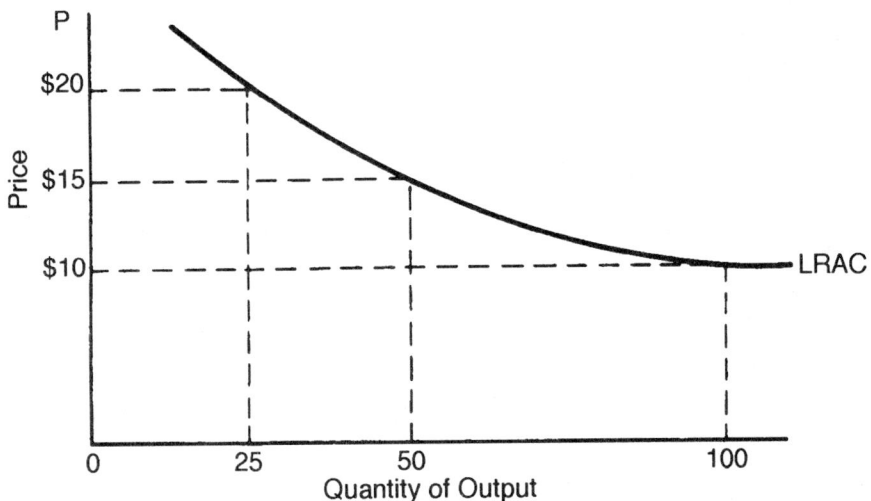

Figure 8.1
Long Run Average Cost—Monopoly

Table 8.1
Quantity, Price, Total Revenue, Marginal Revenue Under Monopoly

(A) Quantity	(B) Price ($)	(C) Total Revenue (TR)	(D) Marginal Revenue $\frac{\Delta TR}{\Delta Q}$
0	$9.00	$ 0	$
1	9.00	9.00	9.00
2	8.40	16.80	7.80
3	7.80	23.40	6.60
4	7.20	28.80	5.40
5	6.60	33.00	4.20
6	6.00	36.00	3.00
7	5.40	37.80	1.80
8	4.80	38.40	.60
9	4.20	37.80	−.60
10	3.60	36.00	−1.80
11	3.00	33.00	−3.00
12	2.40	28.80	−4.20

Price, Output, Marginal Revenue, and Total Revenue under Monopoly

Table 8.1 illustrates the relationships among price, output, and total revenue under monopoly. Columns (A) and (B) in the table give data on the demand for the product of a pure monopolist. AS the table makes clear, the greater the output, the lower the price at which buyers will be willing to purchase. For any output, total revenue equals price times quantity (TR = P x Q). Thus, as output increases, total revenue (TR) first rises, then reaches a maximum at about eight units of output, and then falls.

Demand-Marginal Revenue Curve Under a Monopolist

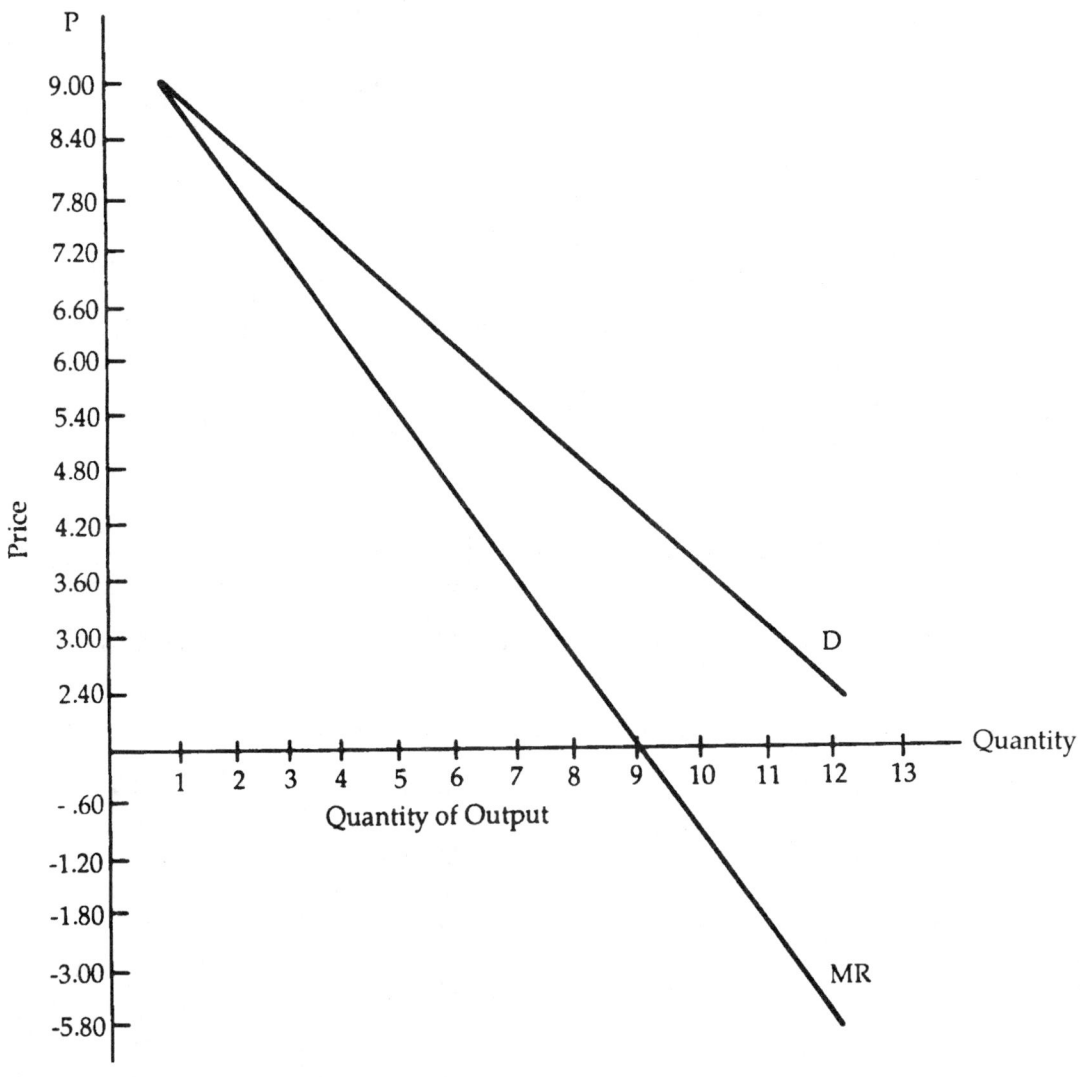

Figure 8.2
Demand Curve and Marginal Revenue Curve Under Monopoly

A monopolist firm faces the market demand curve for the industry. This occurs because the monopolist is a single seller; in other words, is the industry. All market demand curves have negative slopes. Since the demand (D) curve facing a monopolist has a negative slope, the marginal revenue (MR) curve is going to lie below the demand curve. Because the demand curve is negatively sloped, the monopolist must lower its price in order to sell more units of output, as shown in Figure 8.2.

The demand curve for a monopolist is downward sloping. This means the monopolist must lower price in order to sell additional units of the product. The marginal revenue curve is a separate curve that lies beneath the demand curve. Thus, with an increase in sales, marginal revenue, in turn, becomes less than the price. This is illustrated in Figure 8.3.

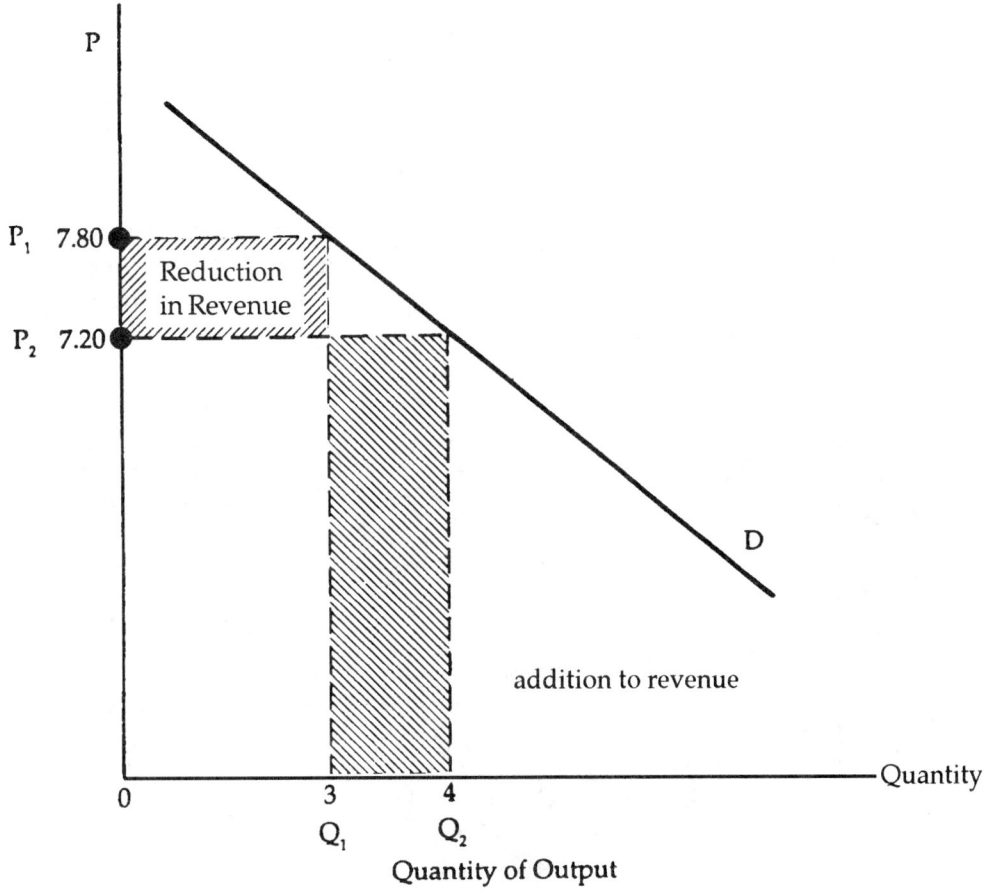

Figure 8.3
Marginal Revenue Under Demand Curve

A downward sloping demand curve means that in order for the firm to sell more, the firm has to charge a lower price, P_2, not just for the last unit sold, but for all units that could have been sold at the higher price, P_1. Revenue is lost when the price drops from P_1 to P_2. In Figure 8.3 this is shown as a drop from \$7.80 to \$7.20. The drop in revenue is equal to \$7.80 − \$7.20 x 3 = \$1.80. Revenue is gained by the sale of additional units from Q_1 to Q_2. This is shown in Figure 8.3 as an increase from 3 to 4 units. The additional revenue is \$7.20 x 1 = \$7.20. The net gain is \$7.20 − \$1.80 = \$5.40 which is the marginal revenue for the fourth item in Table 8.1.

Demand Curves for a Monopolist and Pure Competitive Firms Compared

The purely competitive firm faces a horizontal demand curve. Thus, it can increase or decrease its output without affecting the prices, as shown in Figure 8.4.

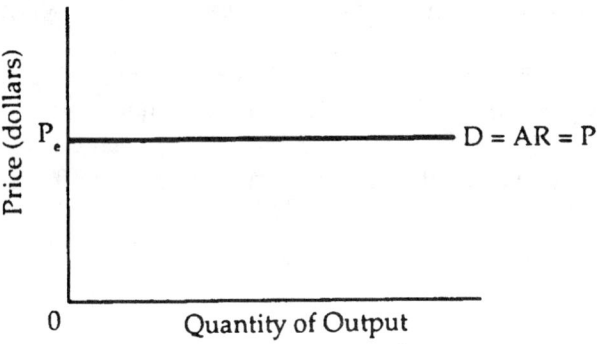

Figure 8.4
Demand Curve—Purely Competitive Firm

In Figure 8.5, the demand curve facing a monopoly is negatively sloped. The monopolist must decrease its prices in order to sell additional units of output, as shown in Figure 8.3. The basic difference in the slopes of the demand curves causes fundamental differences in production by monopoly and pure competition.

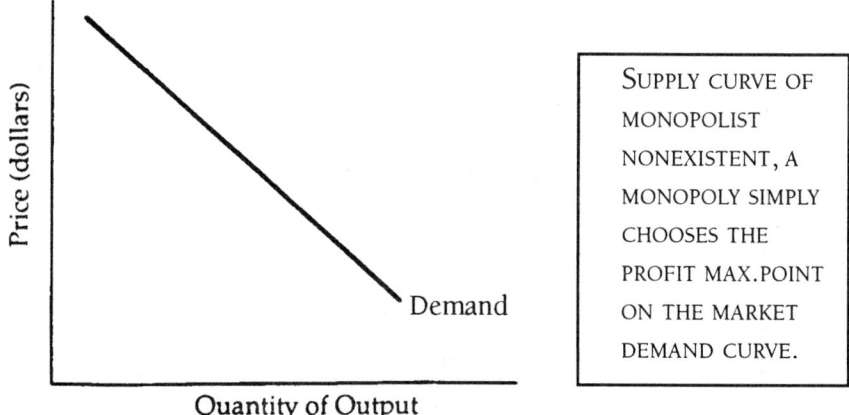

Figure 8.5
Demand Curve—Monopoly

Supply Curve of the Monopolist

Supply curve of monopolist *nonexistent,* a monopoly simply chooses the profit-maximization point on the market demand curve. Since monopoly is a price maker, there is no need to ask how much the monopoly would produce at any price. The monopoly sets the price at the same time it chooses output. That is, the supply decision is based on the consumer's demand rather than on price.

Monopoly and Price Elasticity of Demand

A common misconception about monopoly behavior is that monopolies can earn more profit when the demand for the product they sell is inelastic. It is thought that when the demand for a monopolist's product is inelastic, the monopoly is freer to raise price without losing its customers.

The overall demand for most products is either relatively elastic or relatively inelastic. Along each demand curve are regions of different elasticity: relatively elastic, unitary elastic, and relatively inelastic. Figure 8.6 illustrates the demand curve for a monopoly with the different regions of elasticity identified.

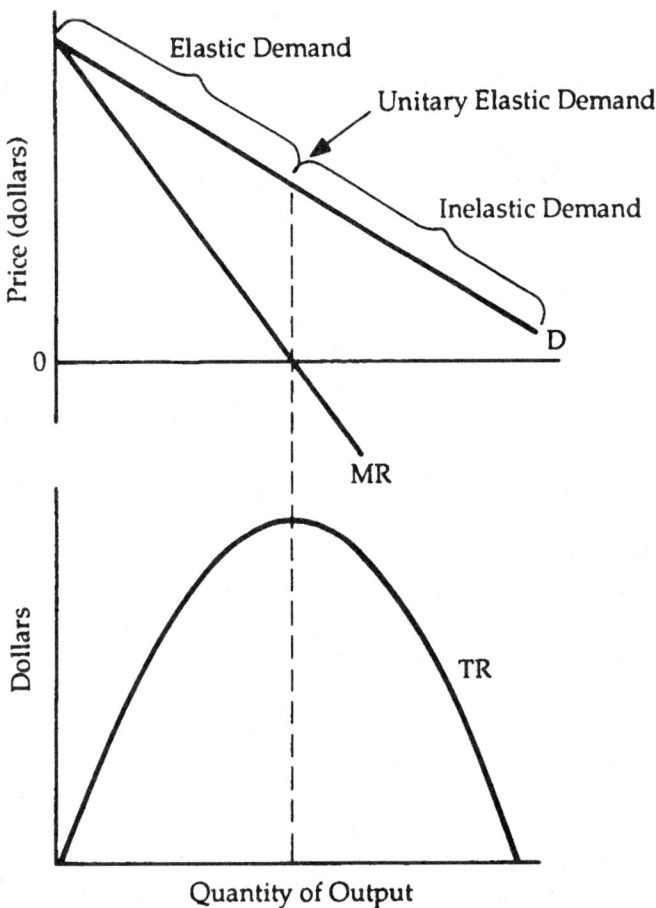

Figure 8.6
Elasticity—Demand Curve for a Monopoly

When marginal revenue (MR) is greater than zero, total revenue is increasing. In this range, as price drops, total revenue increases. As prices rise, total revenue decreases. This is characteristic of elastic demand. This is shown in Table 8.1 for prices $9.00 to $4.80. When marginal revenue equals 0, total revenue has reached its highest level. At this level there would be unitary elasticity. When marginal revenue is less than zero, total revenue is decreasing. In this range, as price drops, total revenue drops. As price rises, total revenue rises. This is characteristic of inelastic demand. This is shown in Table 8.1 for prices $4.20 to $2.40. Figure 8.6, therefore, illustrates that a monopoly can only increase revenue by raising prices in the lower price range. In this range, the demand is inelastic. If prices are already high, raising them will result in losing customers and revenue dropping.

Price Searcher

The monopolist is called a price searcher. The monopolist searches for the profit maximizing price at which to sell the product. The monopolist is a price maker with the power to make its selected price the market price.

Non-Price Competition

The monopoly is the only firm in the industry. Thus there is no competition and no need to compete. Instead, the monopoly will become involved with public relations to convince the public the monopoly is not such a bad firm. The monopolist will promote the idea the firm is providing a valuable service and that the rates are regulated.

Short Run Output—Marginal Revenue and Marginal Cost

The approach to determining the monopolist's profit-maximizing level of output is based on marginal revenue and marginal cost. In many cases, the marginal approach provides additional insight into the output decision because, while we might be able to determine the quantity of output using the total curves, we cannot easily see the price charged by the monopolist.

Figure 8.7 depicts a standard set of production cost curves and the demand and marginal revenue curves for the monopolist. If the demand curve is downward sloping, the marginal revenue curve lies below it. Therefore, at every quantity of output, price is greater than marginal revenue.

The problem facing the monopolist in Figure 8.7 is to determine the quantity of output that provides the highest level of economic profit. If production is increased from Q_1, how is economic profit affected by the changes in output, based on marginal cost and marginal revenue? As output increases from Q_1, the marginal cost of production is relatively low, as shown by the marginal cost survey, but marginal revenue is relatively high, and profit is increasing. Thus, an extra unit of output adds more to revenue than it adds to cost.

As long as marginal revenue is greater than marginal cost, it is profitable to increase production. Only when the monopolist reaches Q_e, the additional cost becomes greater than the additional revenue, the marginal cost curve lies above the marginal revenue curve, and the level of profit is reduced. The profit-maximizing level of output, Q_e, occurs when marginal cost equals marginal revenue.

Note the similarity between perfect competition and monopoly. The monopoly maximizes profit by equating marginal cost to marginal revenue. Likewise, for the perfectly competitive firm, profit is maximized at the quantity at which marginal cost is equal to marginal revenue, but price is also equal to marginal revenue.

But price is not equal to marginal revenue for the monopolist. What price does the monopolist charge for Q_e? Once the monopolist determines the profit-maximizing level of output, the price is given by the demand curve. For Q_e output, the market is willing to pay P_e for each unit. Note that since marginal revenue is less than price, and the monopolist equates marginal revenue to marginal cost, marginal cost is also less than price. This is the case for any firm that faces a downward-sloping demand curve and seeks to maximize profit.

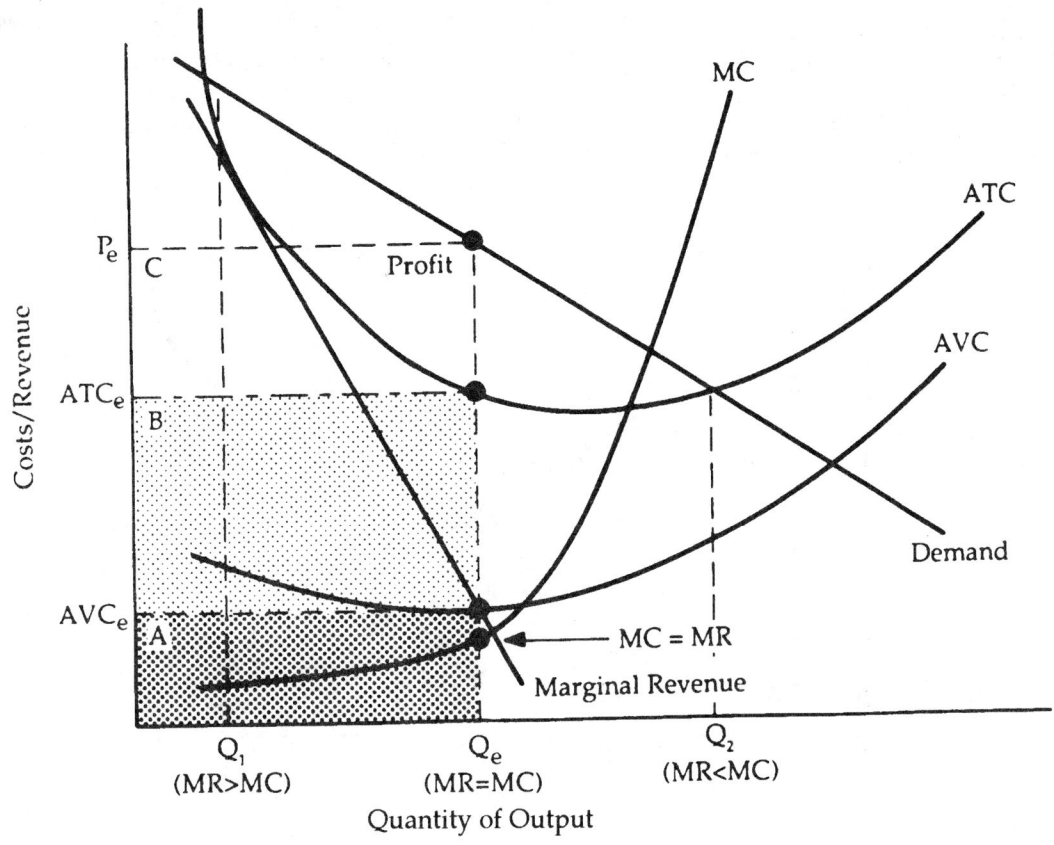

Figure 8.7
Short Run Output—Marginal Revenue and Marginal Cost

The MR = MC rule will tell the monopolist where to find its profit-maximizing output level. The same outcome can be determined by comparing total revenue and total costs incurred at each level of production. Figure 8.7 also reveals that the monopolist, in this case makes a positive economic profit. At Q Short Run Output—Marginal Revenue and Marginal Cost

The MR = MC rule will tell the monopolist where to find its profit-maximizing output level. The same outcome can be determined by comparing total revenue and total costs incurred at each level of production. Figure 8.7 also reveals the monopolist, in this case makes a positive economic profit. At Q_e, average variable cost is AVC_e, and total variable cost is area A. Average total cost is ATC_e, and total cost is area A + B, with B being total fixed cost. Therefore, total revenue received by the monopolist is the area A + B + C, which is equal to P_e times Q_e. The difference between total revenue and total cost is area C, economic profit.

Monopoly Profits and Loss and Breaking Even

A pure monopolist, like any other firm, may have a normal profit, an economic profit, or an economic loss in the short run. Figure 8.8 illustrates a normal profit.

An Example of a Monopolist Breaking Even and Making a Profit

The monopoly will produce Q_1 where MR equals MC. At that level of output the price is P_1 and the average total cost is ATC_1. Since price equals average total cost, total revenue equals total cost, which is defined as a normal profit. Figure 8.9 illustrates the case of an economic profit.

The monopolist firm will earn economic profits as long as its price exceeds average total cost. The monopoly firm in Figure 8.9 will produce at Q_1 in order to make the most profit. At that quantity, Q_1, the price P_1 exceeds the average total price, ATC_1, illustrating an economic profit.

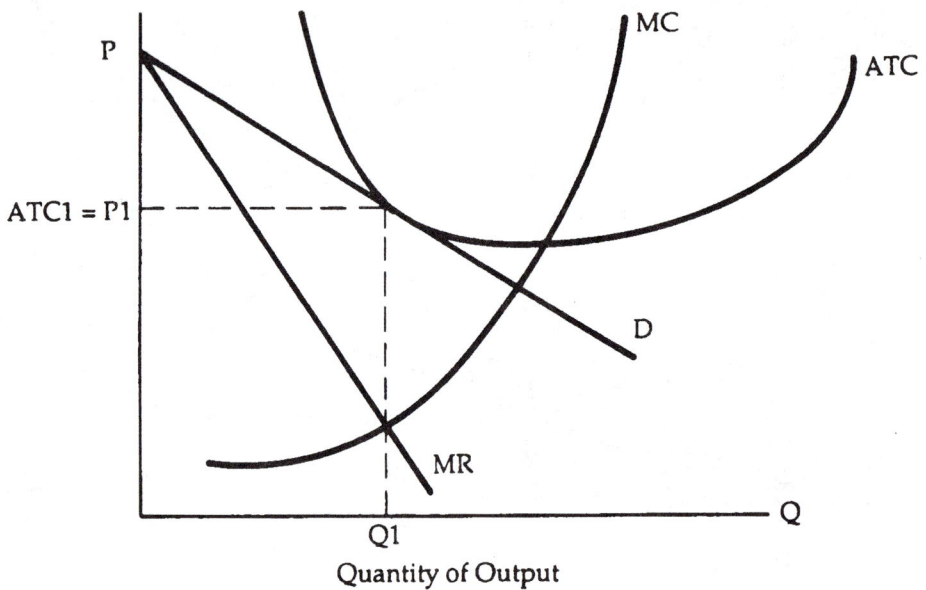

Figure 8.8
Normal Profit (ATC = P)

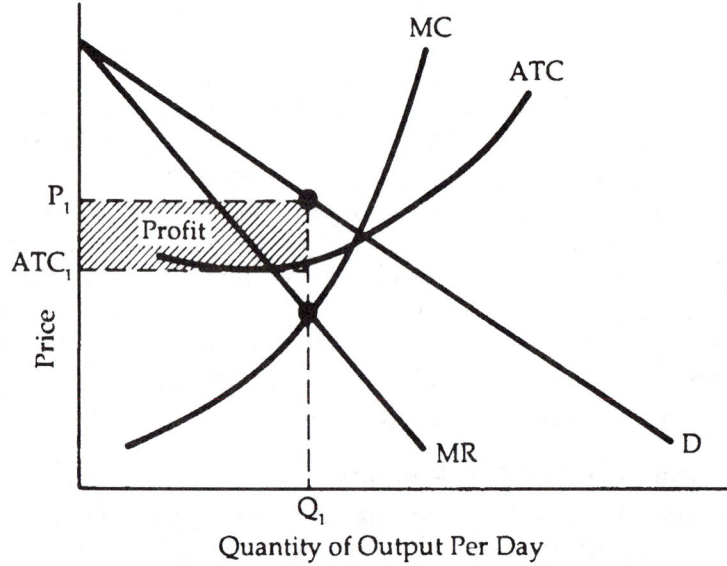

Figure 8.9
Economic Profit (P > ATC)

A monopolist's profit is determined by the difference between ATC and price, as shown in Figure 8.9.

An Example of a Monopolist Making a Loss

A monopolist could experience losses in the short-run if average total cost (ATC) exceeded price (P).

Figure 8.10 illustrates the case of an economic loss. The monopolist firm will incur an economic loss if its price is less than the average total cost. The monopoly firm in Figure 8.10 will produce at Q_1 in order to incur the least loss. At that quantity, Q_1, the price P_1, is less than the average total cost, ATC_1, illustrating an economic loss. In this example the firm will continue to operate since the price is above the AVC. If the price is below the AVC the monopoly firm will go out of business.

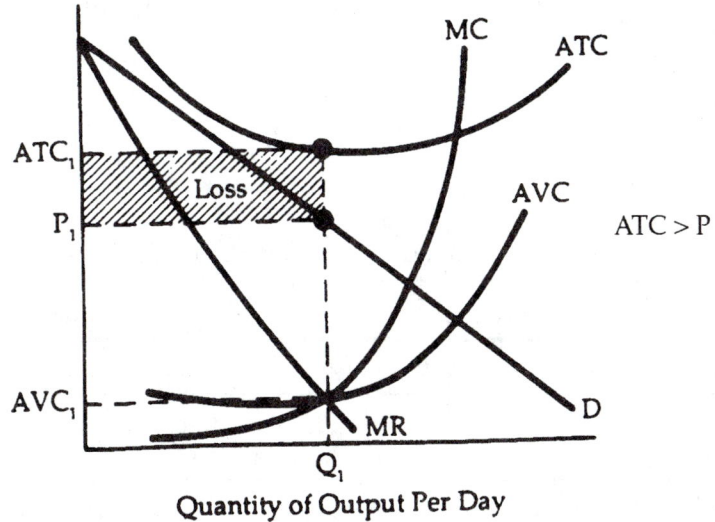

Figure 8.10
Economic Loss (ATC > P)

Long Run Equilibrium of Monopoly

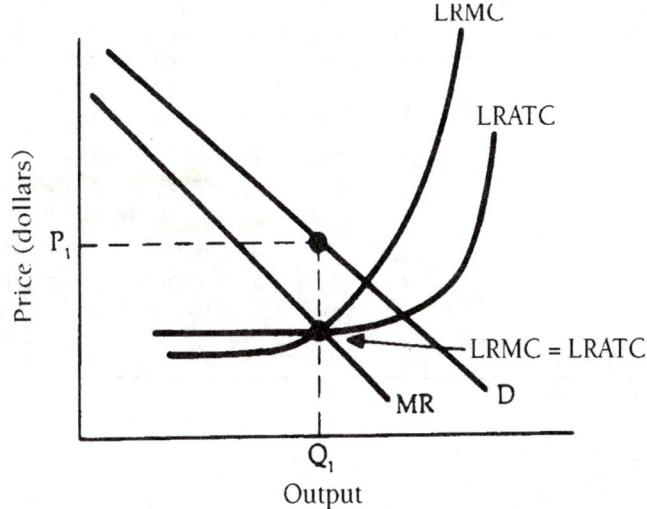

Figure 8.11
Long Run-Monopoly (LRATC = LRMC)

The price a monopolist charges is higher than that of a competitive market due to the restriction of output; a monopolist can make a profit in the long run.

Monopoly profits will be protected in the long run by barriers to entry. That is, barriers to entry prevent new firms from entering the industry and sharing in the profit. In the long run, a profit-maximizing monopoly expands its operations until the output corresponding to MR = LRMC is produced. If the monopolist can earn economic profits at that price, it must be presumed that free entry by any other seller into the market is impossible. If this were not the case, entry of new firms would increase supply and, eventually, push the price down to a level that would permit only normal profits. Maintenance of a monopoly, over the long run, would be impossible if free entry prevails in the market.

However, a monopolist is not guaranteed an economic profit. If price is less than average total cost, but greater than average variable cost, the monopolist continues to produce output at a loss. If price falls below average variable cost, the monopolist shuts down production. This is exactly the same as for pure competition.

Characteristics of Monopoly

Table 8.2 lists the characteristics of the monopoly model.

Table 8.2
Characteristics of Monopoly Market Model: Summary

Characteristics	Description
Number of firms	One.
Type of product	No close substitutes (there are no substitutes for water, sewage disposal, or trash collection).
Conditions of entry	Impossible. Complete protection from entry of rivals.
Control of price	Considerable.
Non-price competition advertising	Mostly public relations.
Type of profits	Normal and/or economic profit in the long run.
Where to find in the U.S. economy	Public utility services, including electricity, natural gas, local telephone, water, sewage disposal, trash collection, and cable television.
Miscellaneous	P > MR and P > MC. The marginal revenue curve is below and steeper than the demand curve. The demand curve facing a monopoly is negatively sloped. The monopolist must decrease its prices in order to sell additional units of output. Pure monopoly is difficult to find because a modern corporation produces several products and the firm is unlikely to have a monopoly in all its product line.

Price Discrimination

Price discrimination occurs when the same commodity is sold at more than one price. Price discrimination can occur even when the commodities being sold are not the same. In this case, the discrimination occurs because the ratios of prices to marginal costs are different for products which are similar.

There are three types of price discrimination which are in practice today. In first degree price discrimination, the monopolist is aware of the maximum amount that each consumer will pay for each amount of the commodity.

First degree price discrimination is not a common occurrence because it is rare that a monopolist would know each individual consumer's demand curve. In Figure 8.12, the monopolist practicing first degree price discrimination will set a price of P_2, since this is the highest price that a particular consumer is willing to pay, even though normal practice dictates the price at Q_1 should be P_1.

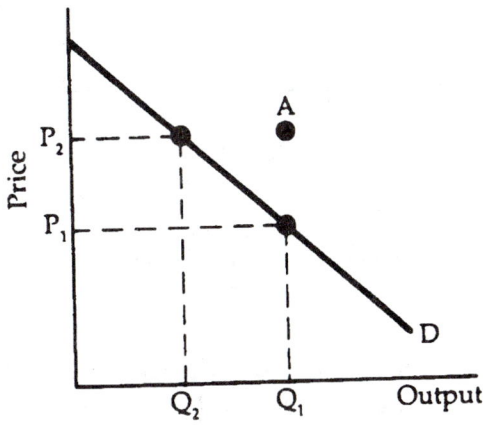

Figure 8.12
First Degree Price Discrimination

Another type of price discrimination occurs when a monopolist charges based on the amount purchased. In this case, the monopolist charges a specific price based on the amount of the good or the service that the consumer purchases. Second degree price discrimination is widespread today in many of our public utilities. For example, the telephone company charges a higher amount per minute for the first three minutes used during a phone call, but after the first three minutes, the amount charged per minute decreases. This type of price discrimination is a useful ploy in attempting to lure the consumer into buying more of a particular product or service (see Figure 8.13).

In second degree price discrimination, the monopolist charges a different price per unit, based on the quantity the consumer purchases.

The final type of price discrimination occurs when buyers fall into classes with considerable differences in the price elasticity for the product. This is known as third degree price discrimination. These differences in the price elasticities for a particular product are a result of differences in income, tastes, or availability of substitutes between the classes of those consumers purchasing the product. In order for third degree price discrimination to occur, buyers must be unable to transfer the commodity easily from one class to another.

Whether price discrimination is good or bad, from the consumer's standpoint, depends on whether this discrimination has positive or negative consequences to the individual. For example, at a local nightclub, persons who identify themselves as students will be given a discount on the amount they pay to enter. Obviously, students will agree with this sort of price discrimination, because they are the ones who are benefiting from it.

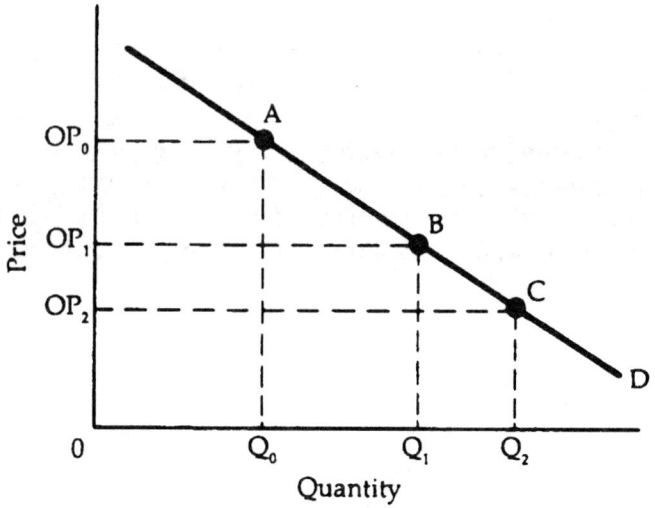

Figure 8.13
Second Degree Price Discrimination

Dumping

Dumping refers to selling the same product in different markets at different prices. Domestic demand tends to be more inelastic than the demand abroad due to foreign buyers having more alternative sources from which to purchase the product. The demand for a monopolist's product in a foreign country tends to be more elastic. Figure 8.14 illustrates the example of price discrimination referred to as dumping. The monopolist will produce and sell Qt of the product since at that quantity MR ($MR_d + MR_f$) equals ($MC_d + MC_f$).

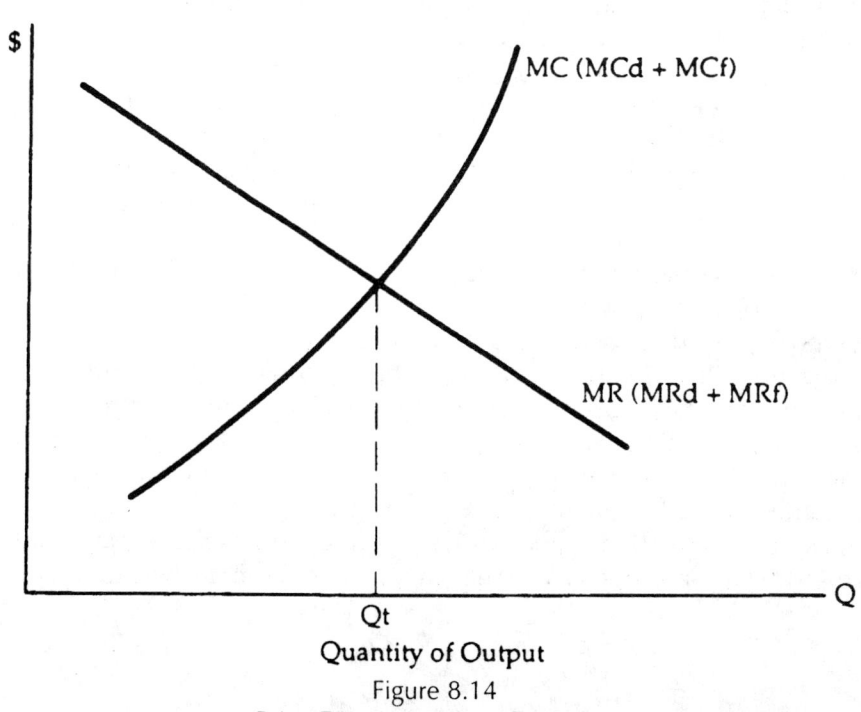

Figure 8.14
Price Discrimination—Dumping

The price charged in the foreign market will be Pf which is lower than the domestic price.

The monopolist will divide production into part for the domestic market and part for the foreign market. The quantity produced for the domestic market will be Q_d since at that quantity MR_d equals MC_d in the domestic market as shown in Figure 8.15. The price charged in the domestic market will be P_d. The quantity produced for the foreign market will be Q_f since at that quantity MR_f equals MC_f in the foreign market as shown in Figure 8.16.

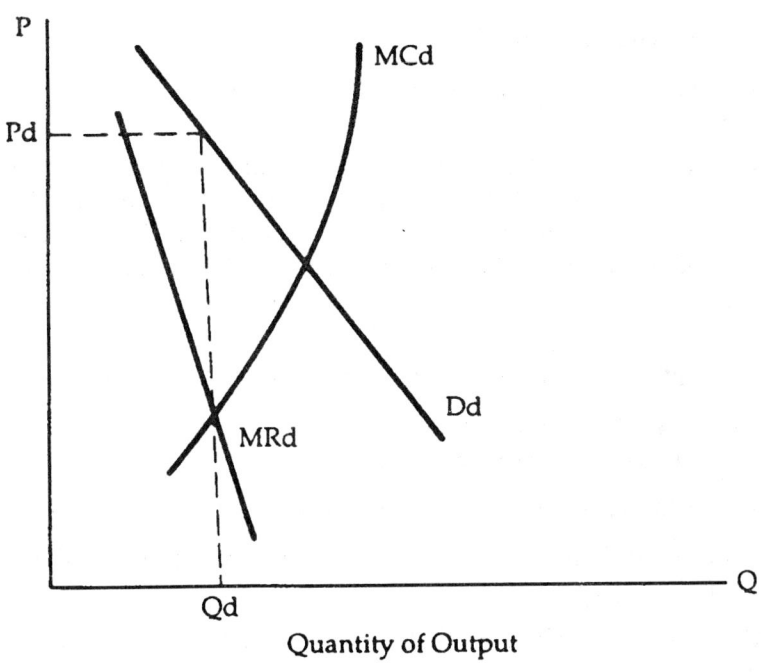

Figure 8.15
Price Discrimination—Domestic Market

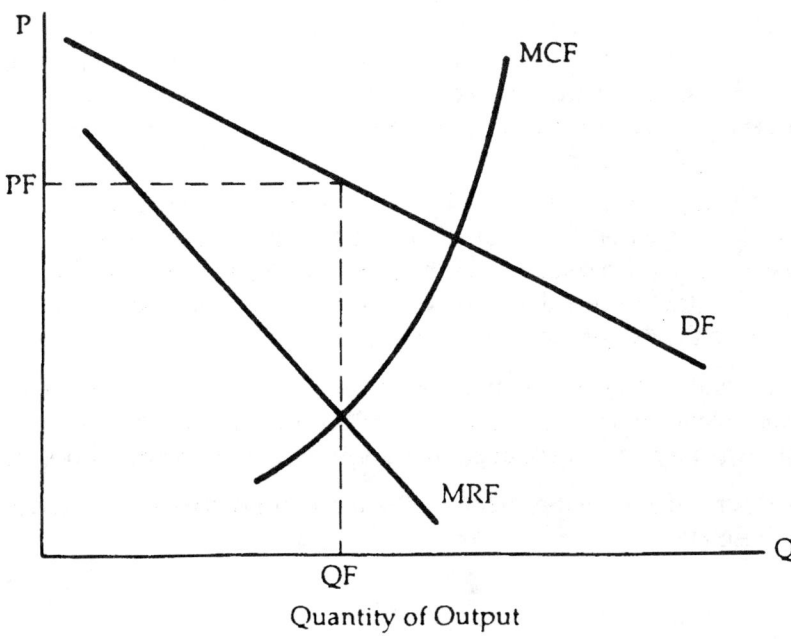

Figure 8.16
Price Discrimination—Foreign

Market Power

Market power is the term economists use to describe the ability to hold control over prices and profits. The most widely held theory assumes that the extent of a firm's market power depends on certain characteristics existing in the market where it operates. The following characteristics are believed to be especially important:

- The share of an industry's sales held by its leading firms.
- The ease with which new firms can enter an industry.
- The extent to which the products of a seller are differentiated from those of other sellers of similar products.

The monopoly is a price maker. The firm controls output and prices but is not free of market forces, since the combination of output and price that can be sold depends on demand. However, Pure Competitive firm faces no temptation to price discrimination. This is because the firm can sell any output at the market price, so there is never a reason for the firm to sell for less.

There are a number of ways price discrimination could be implemented into the subway system:

- They could charge higher prices for cars in the front or rear of the train.
- They could charge different rates for different travel times, namely day or night; weekday (prime time) or weekend (leisure).
- They could also charge for standing room seats to maximize space per dollar.
- The frequent travelers could be given a discount rate and the sporadic user could be charged a premium price.
- They could make one car a luxury/first class type car for frequent business travelers and charge a premium price; also adding extra security.

Can a firm charge different prices to its customers? Examples of price discrimination are: a) owners of stadiums and theaters have had practical price discrimination for many years. Different seats are sold for different prices; b) airlines charge different prices for different "classes" of passengers; c) Bell Telephone charges different rates for long-distance calls at different times of the day and on different days; d) quantity discounts are given to some buyers of electricity if the amount used exceeds a certain value; e) people who buy individual tickets for the subway pay more for the same service than do monthly pass-holders, and most passengers pay more per ride than do students and senior citizens.

- How much is a patient willing to pay for an open heart surgery? Physicians have access to information on the incomes of their patients (customers). The reasonable expectation is that a rich patient will be charged more. On the other hand, physicians charge poor customers less than they charge rich ones because their concern for the sick outweighs their desire to maximize profits.
- Many restaurants offer a lower price at a salad bar to those who order an entree; ice cream shops usually charge less for a second scoop than for a first. (Taking the order, opening the cash register—neither has to be repeated for the second scoop of ice cream).
- For price discrimination to be effective, the original purchaser of a product must not be able to resell it.

How Is Monopoly Created?

The main characteristic of a pure monopoly is the set of barriers to entry, which prevent other firms from entering the market. Obviously, if there were no barriers to entry, the monopoly would cease to exist. Some of the important barriers to entry which exist include the following:

a. Control of inputs. A single firm may control the entire supply of basic input that is required in the manufacturing process. This would effectively freeze out any potential entrants until technological advancement allows for the production of the product or service without that particular input.

b. A second barrier to entry exists when a situation occurs which is known as a natural monopoly. Natural monopolies can prevail for such products as local provision of electric power, gas, and telephone services. Natural monopoly is an industry in which advantages of large-scale production make it possible for a single firm to produce the entire output of the market at lower average cost than a number of firms each producing a smaller quantity.

c. A third barrier to entry occurs when the government awards a market to a particular firm. Consequently, the government will influence the actions of the firm in the form of regulations. These regulations generally take the form of output restrictions and price limitations.

d. The government can impose legal barriers as ways of excluding competitors, such as patents, copyrights, registered trademarks and operating licenses. A patent grants to the inventor of an invention the exclusive right to the invention for 17 years. Copyrights are similar to patents but differ in that they are grants of legal property for designs and written documents. Copyrights also include computer software. Trademarks refer to protected names of products or companies. Patents, copyrights, and trademarks are examples of the government assigning private property rights. Licensing refers to a firm being required to obtain the permission of the government before it can operate in an industry. Local governments may license doctors, lawyers, real estate agents, barbers, etc. These licenses are to control the quality of the services provided but they also have the tendency to reduce the number of firms.

e. Capital: a firm will not be able to enter the market because large amounts of capital outlay would be necessary to form a business.

f. If economies of scale exist, society can often benefit when a natural monopolist is government regulated.

g. Declining cost of production—a single firm may be able to supply the entire market for a good at a profitable price. As the firm produces more, the production costs decline. Since one firm can supply the entire market, it would be difficult for a new firm to compete for a share of the market. This type of situation is called a natural monopoly. By forcing competition, resources would not be utilized to capacity, creating a misallocation of resources. The public may insist on governmental regulation for natural monopolies. Government regulation is intended to decrease, but not eliminate, a monopolist's profit.

Although there are reasons for creating monopolies, there are many reasons for opposition:

a. People believe monopolies restrict supply, which creates higher prices.

b. Monopolies misallocate resources, which creates a burden on society.

c. A monopoly has less incentive to control costs since it has no direct competition.

d. Without competition, monopolies may not quickly adopt technological advances.

Resource Allocations

Because the monopolist produces at an output where P > MC, the monopolist is said to use resources inefficiently.

Under a monopolist, output occurs at a point where P > MC, which is an inefficient use of resources. The monopolist should produce more output so that P = MC. Thus, pure competitive firms (PC) operate at P = MC.

A monopolist produces too little output and charges a higher price, as shown in Figure 8.17. Because of its low output, a monopolist is not allocating society's resources efficiently.

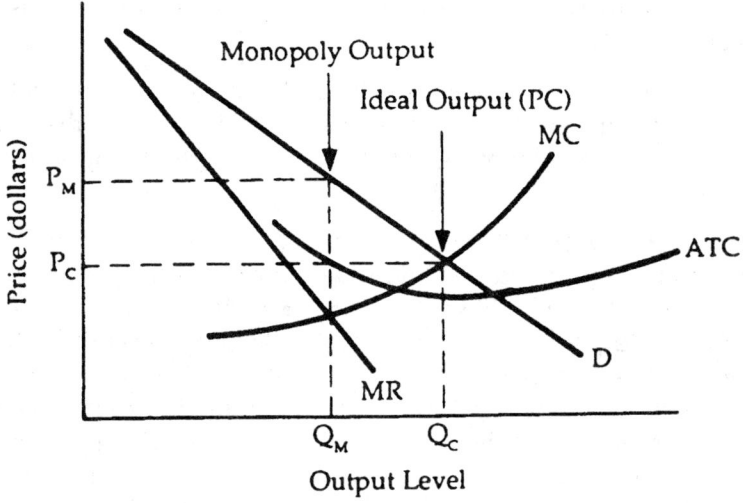

Figure 8.17
Resource Allocation

A monopolist refuses to increase output because to do so would decrease price, and this could cut into the firm's economic profits. Because of these conditions, it is easy to see that a monopolist inefficiently allocates its resources.

The negative aspects of a monopoly are numerous. Monopolists keep the market's output below the necessary level for proper resource allocation. They set prices that are above the natural price and, therefore, raise their profit above the correct rate.

For all these reasons, the monopolist is not a beneficial market structure to the consumer. Another drawback of a monopoly is that this type of market structure does not give the consumer alternative choices of products. If the consumer does not buy the monopolist's product, he or she must do without. This allows the monopolist to produce products and services which may be substandardized, from the standpoint of the consumer. However, changes necessary to improve the performance of the monopoly may not be made because there are no competitive firms to push the monopoly into improving its product and services.

Another negative aspect of a monopoly is that barriers to entry do not enable firms to enter and exit from the industry.

Deadweight Loss of Monopoly

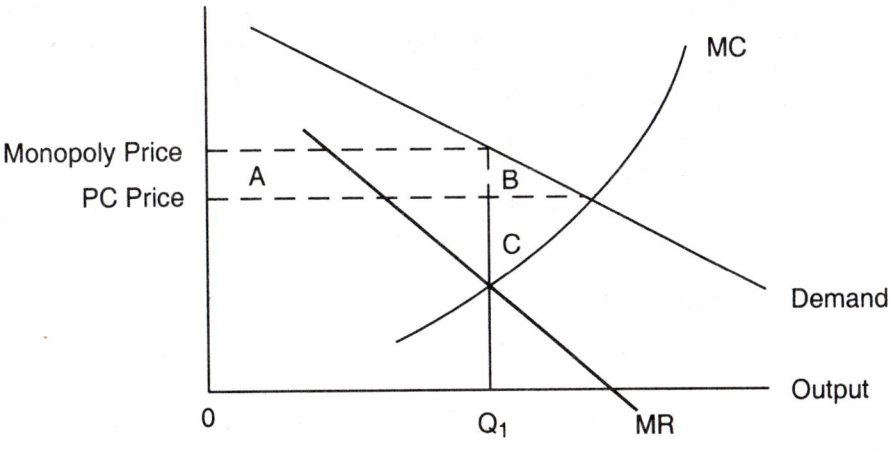

Figure 8.18
Deadweight loss of monopoly

Looking at Figure 8.18, a competitive industry operates at a point where P = MC, where as a monopolized industry operates where P > MC. For this reason, the consumer will be worse off in an industry organized as monopoly than in one organized competitively. We sum up, the distance between the demand curve and the MC curve to generate the value of the lost output due to monopoly behavior. The total area between the two curves from the monopoly output to the competitive output is the deadweight loss. The loss due to the monopoly is given by area B + C in Figure 8.18. The area provides a measure of how much worse off people are paying the monopoly price than paying the competitive price. The area B + C measures the value that the consumers and the producers place on the extra output that has been produced.

Facts About Monopoly

Price, Marginal Revenue, Marginal Cost and Profit

The monopolist is the industry, and therefore is faced by a normal downward sloping industry demand. Being the entire industry, the monopolist's supply is large enough to effect prices. That is, when it decreases the quantity it produces price rises; and increasing output will drive it down.

In these situations, Marginal Revenue is always less than price. For the monopolist to sell more it must lower the price on all units, including those it could have sold at the higher price had it not put more on the market. The monopolist's selling price is on the demand curve, *vertically above the point of intersection of marginal revenue and marginal cost.*

In monopoly, price exceeds marginal cost. This means that society values the last item produced more than its cost. Hence, society is willing to pay more than the opportunity cost of the last item's production.

The profit equation is Q(P – ATC). Significantly, it is not (P – ATC). For example, if the monopolist sells one unit for $50 when average total cost is $30, then its profit per unit and total profit is $20 (=$50 – 30). If the same monopolist can sell 200 units for $20 when ATC is $19, then, though its per unit profit is $1 (=$20 – $19), its total profit is $200 [200 ($20 – 19)]. And this is much better than $20.

Detroit Edison

Detroit Edison is the electric company for Southeastern Michigan. It serves about 1,905,000 customers or about 5 million people. The customers consist of both urban and rural communities. The area covers only about 7,600 square miles, but it contains about half the population of the State of Michigan. Its sales of electricity are 33% to residential customers, 36% to industrial customers, 26% to commercial customers, and 5% to municipalities. In addition, Detroit Edison produces steam heat for businesses in downtown Detroit, producing steam for about 470 customers. Detroit Edison is an example of a natural monopoly. It is believed that the public would be better served if this company is allowed to operate as a monopoly, but that the rates it charges should be controlled by a regulatory agency.

Regulating a Natural Monopoly

There are three ways that the rates or prices charged by monopolies can be set by a regulatory agency.

1. Allow the monopoly to produce and charge the price where MR = MC. This, however, results in high prices and a misallocation of resources.

2. Allow the monopoly to charge a rate or price equal to the marginal cost of producing the service. The problem with this method is that is difficult to actually determine the marginal cost of producing an item.

3. Allow the monopoly to charge a rate or price equal to the average cost of production which can be easily determined from the company's accounting records. Charging a rate equal to the average cost of production allows the monopoly to make a normal profit.

That is, regulating of natural monopolies is usually based on fair rate of return pricing concepts. The formula is the price should equal ATC plus a fair rate of return. Governments commonly regulate natural monopolies like utilities.

Public Ownership of Monopoly: The Post Office

Economists generally prefer private ownership if at all possible because firms seeking profit tend to be more efficient. In some cases, however, the government decides to run the monopoly. When the government does a bad job, the cost is to the taxpayer and consumer.

Chapter Summary

1. The most accurate description of a monopoly is a firm that is the sole producer of a product of which there are no good substitutes.

2. The demand curve of a monopolist is downward sloping and above the monopolist's marginal revenue curve, illustrating that marginal revenue decreases and is less than prices, as additional units are sold beyond the first.

3. The most important difference between monopoly and pure competition is the downward sloping curve facing the monopolist, as opposed to the horizontal demand curve of pure competition.

4. For a monopoly, P > MC, and the value of the last unit produced is greater than the value of goods not produced. Because the monopoly is the only producer of a product, its MC curve is the market supply curve.

5. A monopolist maximizes profits in the short run by producing where marginal revenue (MR) equals marginal cost (MC), but maximizes profits in the long run by producing where MR equals long run marginal cost (LRMC).

6. A monopoly can earn economic profits in the long run (LR) because of barriers to entry that prevent potential competitors from entering the market.

7. A monopolist maximizes profits by producing the amount of output for which MC = MR.

8. In the short run, a monopolist firm will earn profits as long as P > ATC.

9. Some of the important barriers to entry which exist include the following:

    a. A single firm may control the entire supply of a basic input.

    b. A natural monopoly is an industry in which one firm is able to produce the product at a lower average cost than a number of firms each producing a smaller quantity.

    c. The government awards a market to a particular firm.

    d. The government grants patents, copyrights, trademarks, and licenses.

10. Monopolies are bad for society because the monopolist charges too high a price and produces too little output. This is a result of an inefficient use of resources.

11. A pure monopolist may engage in price discrimination in order to increase profit.

12. When a seller charges different prices to different consumers of the same product or service, this is called price discrimination. There are three types of price discrimination:

    a. First degree price discrimination.
    b. Second degree price discrimination.
    c. Third degree price discrimination.

    However, in order to carry out effective price discrimination, a seller must be able to prevent consumers from reselling the product to other consumers.

13. Market power is the term economists use to describe the ability to hold control over prices and profits.

14. The distance between the demand curve and the MC curve to generate the value of the last output due to monopoly behavior is called deadweight loss. This distance

provides a measure of how much worse off people are paying the monopoly prices than paying the competitive price.

15. Alternative prices are not considered by a monopolist so a supply curve does not exist in a monopoly, the demand curve of the monopolist is down-sloping because the monopolist is the industry.

16. Pure monopoly is difficult to find because a modern corporation produces several products and the firm is unlikely to have a monopoly in all its product line.

Take-A-Note

The word monopoly comes from two Greek words meaning one seller. Supply curve of monopolist nonexistent, a monopoly simply chooses the profit-maximization point on the market demand curve. Price > MR except the first unit sold, the reason is that monopoly must lower prices of all units in order to sell more.

Five defining characteristics of pure monopoly: (1) In a pure monopoly, there is only one firm in the industry. (2) The pure monopolist produces a unique product with no close substitute. (3) The firm is a price maker, in that it searches along its industry demand curve for the profit maximizing output and price point, and the price it chooses becomes the market price. The firm's pure monopoly power is revealed by its ability to set the market price. (4) The firm may engage in goodwill advertising as a form of nonprice competition to improve its public image. (5) Barriers to entry are so expensive that entry into the industry is blocked.

Why Monopolies Arise?

- A key resource is owned by a single firm.
- The government gives a single firm the exclusive right to produce some good.
- The costs of production make a single producer more efficient than a large number of producers.

Questions and Answers

A. Can you give examples of price discrimination?
- Quantity discounts (buy two get the third half-price)
- Financial Aid (Universities charge high tuition and then offer Financial Aid to those who aren't willing to pay the higher tuition)
- Movie Tickets (children and senior citizens pay less)
- Airline Fares (round trip tickets between two cities when stay over weekends are less expensive to the consumer)

B. Why a monopoly doesn't have a supply curve?

Since monopoly is a price maker, there is no need to ask how much the monopoly would produce at any price. The monopoly sets the price at the same time it chooses output. That is, the supply decision is based on the consumer's demand rather than on price.

C. Do you believe that monopolies pose a problem socially? If so, what can the government do in this matter?

- Monopolies fail to allocate resources
- Monopoly charge prices above marginal cost
- Monopoly produce less than the socially desirable quantity of output

Government can respond to the problem of monopoly in the following: Regulate the behavior of monopolies; turning private monopolies into public ownership; make monopolized industries more competitive.

CHAPTER 8
KEY CONCEPTS

Barrier to Entry—Factors that prevent other firms from entering an industry.

Copyright—Exclusive rights to written documents including computer software.

Deadweight Loss—The consumer will be worse off in industry in monopoly than in one organized competitively.

Dumping—Charging a lower price in a foreign market.

Fair-Rate-of-Return Pricing Concepts—The formula is that price that should equal ATC plus a fair rate of return.

First Degree Price Discrimination—The monopolist charges the highest price a consumer will pay for each amount of the commodity.

Market Power—Is the term economists use to describe the ability to hold control over prices and profits.

Monopolist Demand Curve—The demand curve of the firm is the demand curve of the market.

Natural Monopoly—The given level of production that can be produced at the least cost if there is only one firm in the industry.

Patent—Exclusive rights to an invention for 17 years.

Price Control—The firm exerts considerable control over the price of the item.

Price Discrimination—This occurs when a seller charges different prices to different consumers of the same product or service.

Pure Monopoly—An industry in which there is only one supplier of a product, for which there are no close substitutes.

Second Degree Discrimination—The price is based on the amount that the consumer purchases.

Single Seller—A single firm produces or supplies a product or service.

Third Degree Price Discrimination—The price is based on different elasticities.

Trademark—Exclusive rights to the name of a company or product.

Discussion Questions

1. What are the characteristics of a pure monopoly?
2. Define natural monopoly.
3. Explain the profit maximizing rule for a monopoly.
4. Explain how the demand curves of a monopoly differ from that of a purely competitive firm.
5. What enables a monopoly to make profits?
6. When would a monopoly incur losses?
7. Explain the long-run condition in a monopoly.
8. Discuss some barriers to entry which lead to monopoly power.
9. Explain why a monopolist uses resources inefficiently.
10. Distinguish among first-degree, second-degree, and third-degree discrimination.
11. Explain the concept of dumping.
12. Explain why allowing a monopoly to charge a price equal to the average total cost is a good approach for regulation.
13. Briefly explain the deadweight loss of monopoly.
14. What is meant by a barrier to entry? What kinds of such barriers are there?
15. What does the demand curve for a monopoly firm look like and why?
16. How do the predictions of the models of pure competition and monopoly differ?
17. Demonstrate graphically the profit-maximizing positions for a monopolist.
18. How does a monopolist choose the quantity of output to produce and the price to charge?

8.19 LEARNING PRACTICE:
MONOPOLISTIC FIRM: SHORT RUN POSITION

Using Figure 8.19, answer the following:
   a. Find the price level for this monopolistic firm.
   b. What type of profit or loss is shown?
   c. Indicate the amount of the profit/loss.
   d. At what level does the firm produce?

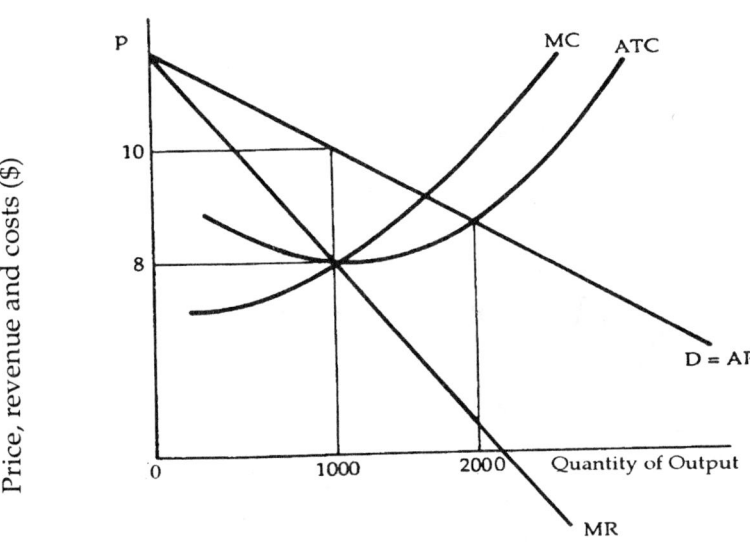

Figure 8.19

8.20 LEARNING PRACTICE AND SOLUTIONS:
MONOPOLY PRICE, OUTPUT AND SUPPLY CURVE

We will use the word monopoly in reference to any firm that faces a downward-sloping demand curve for its output. For monopoly, MR lies below the demand curve illustrating that as additional units are sold, MR decreases and it will be less than P except for the first unit sold. For monopoly, P > MC and the value of the last unit produced > the value of goods not produced. Because the monopolist is the sole producer of a product, its demand curve is the industry demand curve. Price exceeds Marginal Revenue (MR), because the monopolist must lower the price to increase sales.

Table 8.3

Output	Price	Total Revenue	Marginal Revenue
0	$6.00	0	0
1	6.00	6.00	6.00
3	5.00	15.00	4.50
6	4.00	24.00	3.00
10	3.00	30.00	1.50
15	2.40	36.00	1.20
21	2.00	42.00	1.00

Looking at Table 8.3 reveals the following:

Marginal Revenue derived from the third unit is $15 - 6 = 9/2 = \$4.50$ (ΔTR), Marginal Revenue is less than the demand price of $5.00. Moreover, price must be reduced on all units sold to sell more units. Marginal Revenue (MR) is less than the price, because to sell more output the price must be lowered as shown in Table 8.3. Hence, monopoly has no supply curve.

Moreover, price will exceed marginal revenue because the monopolist must lower price to boost sales. The added revenue will be the price of the last unit less the sum of the price cuts which must be taken on all prior units of output.

8.21 Learning Practice

Use the following data for a pure monopoly to calculate the firm's:

(a) total revenue;

(b) marginal revenue;

(c) marginal cost;

(d) average total cost;

(e) draw total revenue and marginal revenue curves.

Q	(P = AR)	TR	MR	TC	MC	ATC
0	$0			$60		
1	58			$100		
2	57			136		
3	56			168		
4	55			200		
5	54			235		
6	53			276		
7	52			322		
8	51			375		

CHAPTER 9

Monopolistic Competition

LEARNING OBJECTIVES

After you have studied this chapter in the text, and attended class lectures regularly, you will be able to:

1. Define monopolistic competition.
2. List the key characteristics of the market structure.
3. Explain the meaning of product differentiation.
4. Explain the meaning of non-price competition in a monopolistically competitive market.
5. Explain the meaning of freedom of entry and exit in monopolistic competition.
6. Provide and recognize real-world examples of the monopolistically competitive model.
7. Identify and explain the major issues in advertising.
8. Identify and explain the demand, price, and output determination for monopolistic competition.
9. Explain and graphically represent the long run conditions facing a monopolistic competitor.
10. Determine and graphically represent the level of short run profit for a monopolistic competitor.
11. Determine and graphically represent the level of short run losses for a monopolistic competitor.
12. Evaluate monopolistic competition in comparison to a pure monopoly.
13. Solve the learning practices as indicated at the end of the chapter.

Monopolistic Competition

Pure competition and pure monopoly are the exception, not the rule in American capitalism. MC is a market structure that falls between the extremes.

The search for a model that has the composition of elements of both pure competition and monopoly led to the theory of monopolistic competition (MC), developed by Chamberline and Robinson.

In this chapter, we study market structures that have the characteristics of pure competition and pure monopoly. The case of monopolistic competition is one in which firms have some market power but are limited in their exercise of this power by the freedom of entry and exit, as well as the close substitutes. The lack of homogeneous product affects the behavior of monopolistically competitive firms. Let us discuss the characteristics of a monopolistically competitive market.

Product Differentiation

The major characteristic of monopolistic competition in the types of products offered is product differentiation. Although there are high degrees of similarity among the products, each product has its own unique characteristic. This may include the packaging of the product, the type of warranty offered, or advertising. The end result is that markets that produce the same general types of products often have their own special features which attract consumers to their products.

An example that is applicable to monopolistic competition would be the horse on Polo shirts. With many clothing manufacturers producing the same types of apparel, having this horse not only gives the product a distinguishing feature, but may represent status in the eyes of the consumer. In other words, product differentiation means that basically similar products are changed in a way that creates some difference. It does not matter what, as long as the difference is important to the purchaser and, therefore, influences consumer preference. The products of monopolistically competitive firms are close, but not perfect, substitutes for each other. The firms attempt to advertise their products in order to increase profits. This activity gives rise to non-price competition among the firms.

Products may be differentiated by several factors: location, design, service, quality, reputation, packaging, and advertising. Since the products are somewhat different from those of rivals, the firm has some monopoly power to raise price without losing all sales.

The demand curve for a monopolistically competitive firm will be relatively elastic or relatively inelastic depending upon how differentiated the product is from those of rival firms. The more differentiated the product, the more inelastic the demand will be due to fewer substitutes. The less differentiated the product, the more elastic the demand will be, due to there being more substitutes. The demand curve will be relatively elastic or relatively inelastic, which means the demand curve will be downward sloping. The firm will be a price searcher.

Numerous Rivals

In monopolistic competition there are a large number of firms, so that, as a result, each has only a small share of the total market. This results in the relative independence of the firms. This relative independence of monopolistic competitors means that they don't have to worry about retaliatory responses to every price or output change. Therefore, modest changes in the output or price of any single firm will have no perceptible influence on the sales of any other firm. A monopolistic competitor can raise its own price without losing all of its customers to rival firms.

Freedom of Entry and Exit

Entering into a monopolistically competitive market is relatively easy, but may be somewhat complicated due to product differentiation. When a new business wants to enter into the market, it must not only raise enough capital to begin operations, but also to attract customers away from businesses already in operation.

In short, monopolistic competition refers to industries comprised of a relatively large number of firms operating non-collusively in the production of differentiated products. Ease of entry makes for competition by new firms in the long run.

Non-Price Competition

Competing on the basis of price among monopolistic competitors is not a very effective way to increase market share or sales. Price reductions are not a very effective way to increase sales or market share in monopolistic competition. Then, if monopolistic competitors don't compete on the basis of price, how do they really compete?

A prominent form of non-price competition is advertising. It is a tool that is used to enhance a firm's product image, thereby increasing the size of its captive market. There is sharp disagreement as to the economic benefits of advertising. There are those who argue that advertising expenditures are socially desirable on the ground that they:

a. increase the information to consumers.

b. support newspapers, magazines, radio, and television.

c. promote the development of new products.

d. lead to greater competition.

e. result in lower costs, and

f. induce a higher level of spending, which results in greater total employment.

The critics of advertising argue:

a. that most advertising is persuasive, but not informative.

b. that advertising wastes resources.

c. that it entails significant external costs which are not paid by advertisers.

d. that it does not lower costs.

e. that it leads to more monopoly in the economy.

f. that it does not really increase spending, and

g. that advertising expenditures are a significant barrier to entry.

Nonprice competition is significant. That is, product differentiation means that there is a wide range of choice to consumers, but critics argue that there is too large a range of choice. Also, with so many choices, consumers may use price as a judge of quality, assuming that price means high quality.

On the other hand, the MC firm frequently prefers nonprice competition to price competition, because the latter can lead to the firm producing where price equals average total cost thus making no economic profit. Nonprice competition may result in monopoly power; the firm's product has become more differentiated from now fewer competitors in the industry. This increase in monopoly power allows the firm to raise its price, demand and marginal revenue. This results in a larger output, and more economic profits.

Lastly, since product differentiation exists in fact or in the mind of the consumer, MC firms have some limited control over price, for they have built up some loyalty to their brand.

Consequences of Advertising

The consequences of advertising depend upon the ability of the monopolistically competitive firm to increase its sales above the level without advertising. Figure 9.1 illustrates the situation in which the firm is unable to increase sales and the result is a higher average total cost (ATC_2), which would tend to reduce profits.

Figure 9.2 illustrates the situation in which a firm is able to increase sales as a result of advertising. The result is increased sales and a lower average total cost (ATC_2) due to economies of larger production, even though there is a higher average total cost curve, ATC, with advertising.

In addition to advertising, firms can attempt to win customers by using differences in style, quality, service, warranties, and names of products. For example, a Big Mac is available only at McDonald's and a Whopper is available only at Burger King. Some store may have extended hours, such as some convenience stores, which are open 24 hours a day. Other stores may give bonuses, such as free car washes with a fill up of gas. A favorite in the past was the use of stamps that could be exchanged for premiums. The use of stamps is still popular in some parts of the country. Any policy designed to increase sales that does not involve lowering price is termed nonprice competition.

Moreover, advertising is often used to increase the individual firm's demand, as a form of nonprice competition and to create a barrier to entry. Advertising can have two effects: It increases a firm's output and increases unit costs.

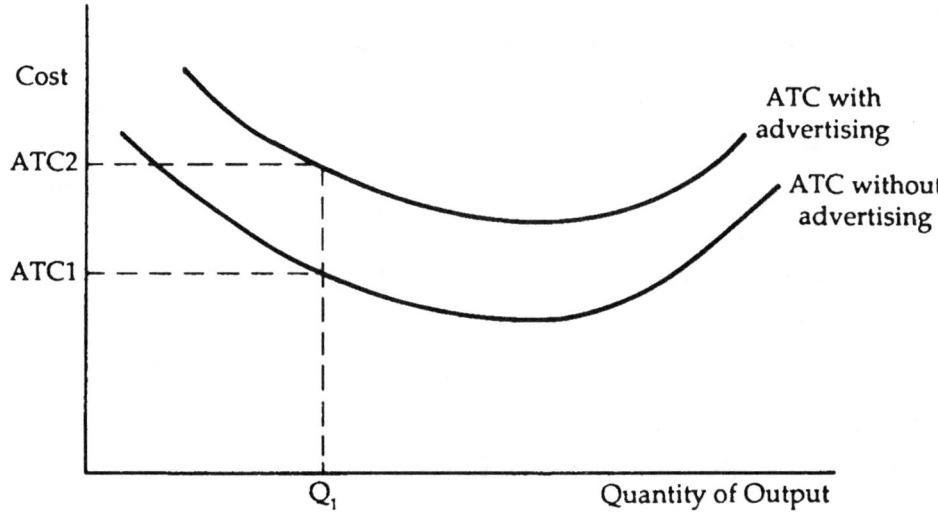

Figure 9.1
Advertising With No Increase In Sales

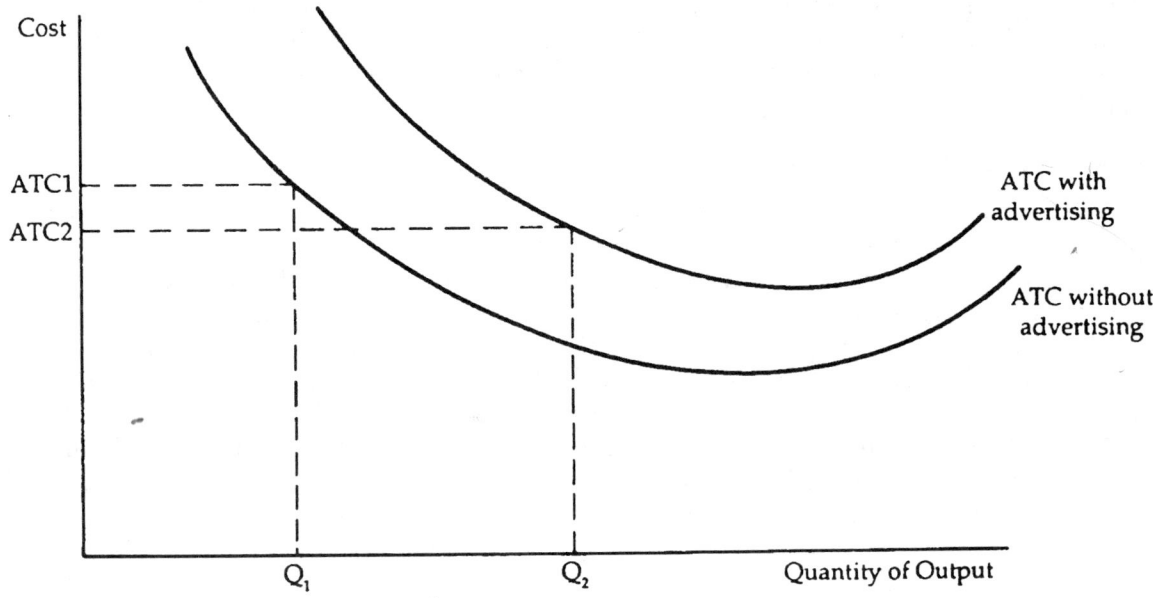

Figure 9.2
Advertising With Increase in Sales

Supply Curve

In monopolistic competition, a firm will follow the profit maximizing rule of producing where marginal revenue equals marginal cost. The demand curve is downward sloping and marginal revenue falls faster than price. As a result, price does not equal marginal revenue.

The profit rule does not equate MC = AR = P. As a result, the marginal cost curve is not the supply curve of the monopolistically competitive firm. A firm faced with a downward sloping demand curve has no supply curve. This is because there is no single price at which the firm will supply a given quantity, as illustrated in Figure 9.3.

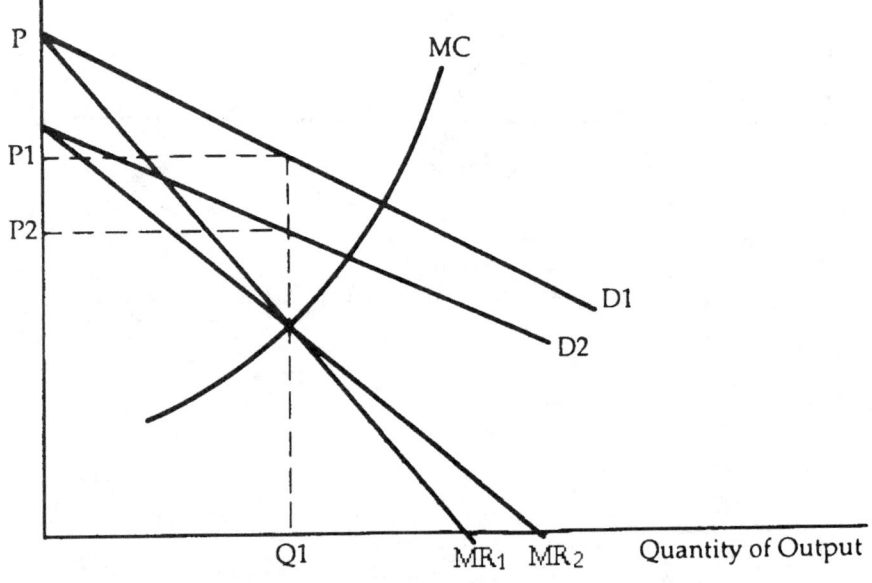

Figure 9.3
Single Output at Different Prices

Depending upon the demand for the product the price will be at different levels. If the demand is D_1, the price of the product will be P_1. If the demand for the product is D_2, the price of the product will be P_2. Thus the same quantity will be provided at two different prices, depending upon the demand.

Short-Run Conditions: Profits and Loss

In the short run, the firm in monopolistic competition can earn a normal profit, an economic profit, or incur a loss. An example of each is shown in Figures 9.4 and 9.5.

In Figure 9.4, the firm will produce Q_1, since marginal revenue equals marginal cost at that quantity. At that quantity, price equals average total cost. Thus a normal profit is illustrated.

In Figure 9.5, showing short run equilibrium in monopolistic competition, the demand curve will be more elastic than that facing a monopolist, and less elastic than that facing a pure competitor. The elasticity of this demand curve will depend upon the number of rivals the firm has, and the degree of product differentiation. A monopolistically competitive firm equates marginal revenue and marginal cost (point G). It sells output at a price (point F) which is above marginal cost. Total profits in the short run are the KPFG area.

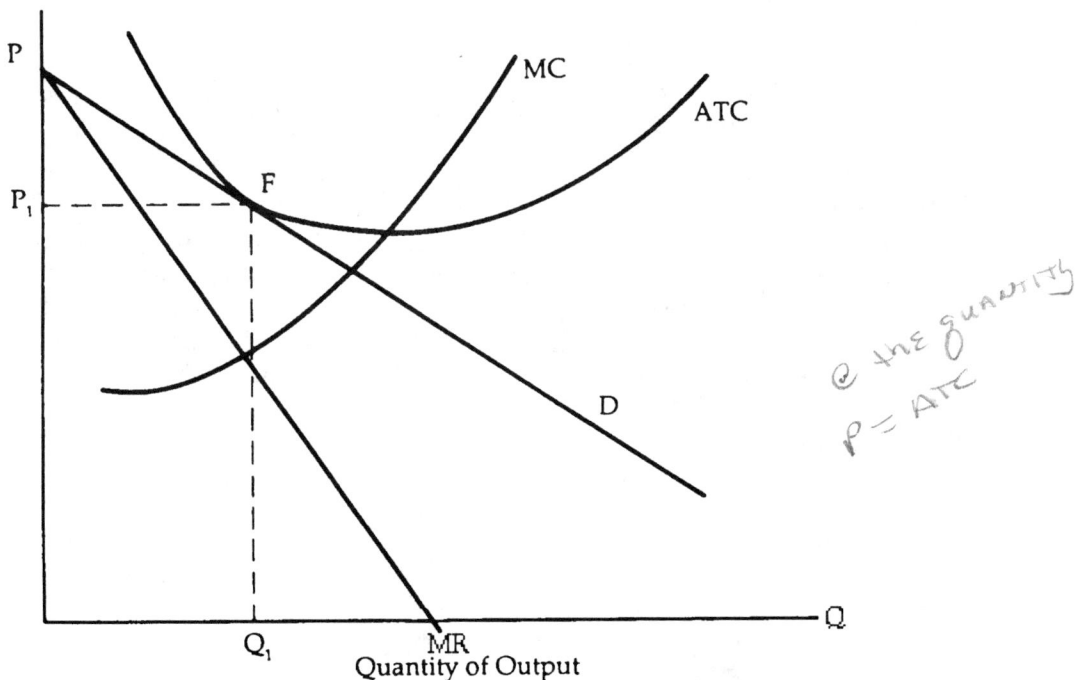

Figure 9.4
Short Run Normal Profit (P = ATC)

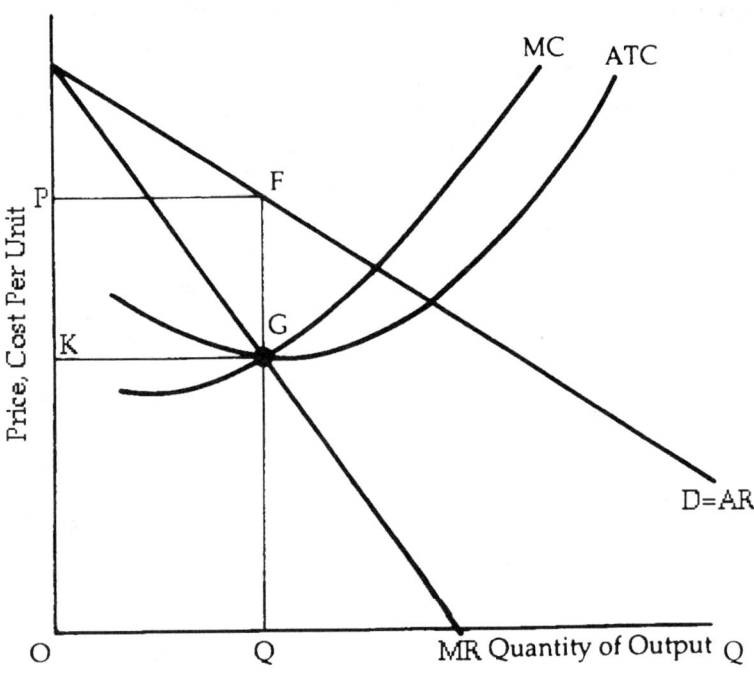

Figure 9.5
A Short Run Profit (P > ATC)

Monopolistically competitive firms may earn economic profits or incur losses in the short run. The firm will maximize its profits in the short run by producing the output designated by the intersection of MC and MR, for reasons with which we are now familiar. The representative firm in Figure 9.6 has a less favorable cost and demand situation, putting the monopolistic firm in the position of real losses in the short run. Losses in the short run is the shaded area.

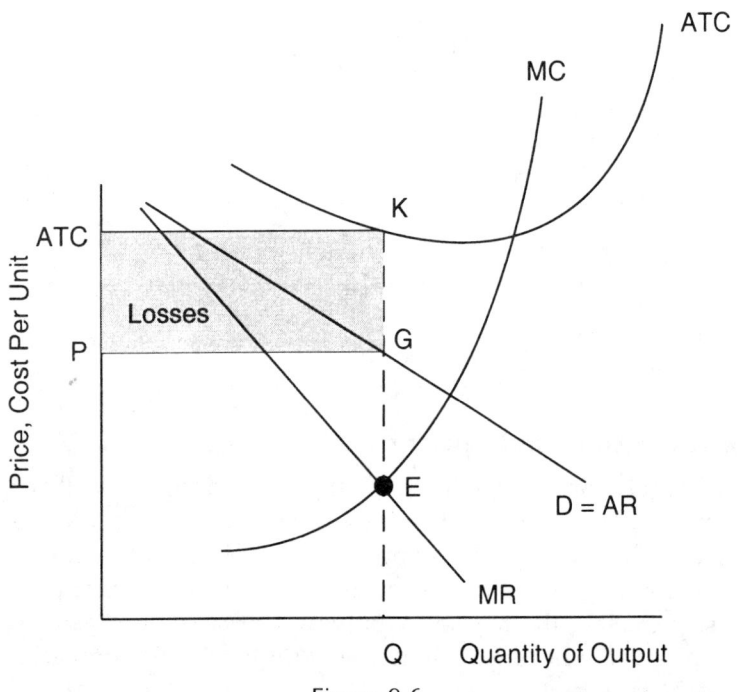

Figure 9.6
Short Run Losses (ATC > P)

Long Run Equilibrium Condition in the Monopolistic Competition

If there are economic profits in the short run, new firms will be attracted into the industry. As new firms enter the industry, the demand curves of the original firms will shift to the left, indicating a decrease in the demand for their products. As the demand curve shifts to the left, the price of the product will drop, reducing the amount of economic profit. In the long run, new firms will be attracted into the industry as long as there are economic profits to be made. The result is that all economic profits will be eliminated.

If firms incur losses, and if the price is below the average variable cost, they will leave the industry. As firms leave the industry, the demand curves of the other firms shift to the right, indicating an increase in the demand for their products. As the demand curve shifts to the right, the price of the product will rise, reducing losses for those firms incurring losses.

The final effect in the long run is a tendency toward a normal profit due to the freedom of entry and exit of firms. This is illustrated in Figure 9.7. The firm will produce Q_1 where MR = MC. The price will be indicated at point K, P_1. Since P_1 equals average total cost, the firm is making a normal profit (zero profit).

However, a monopolistic competitor differs from a monopolist in that a monopolist competitor makes zero economic profit in the long-run equilibrium.

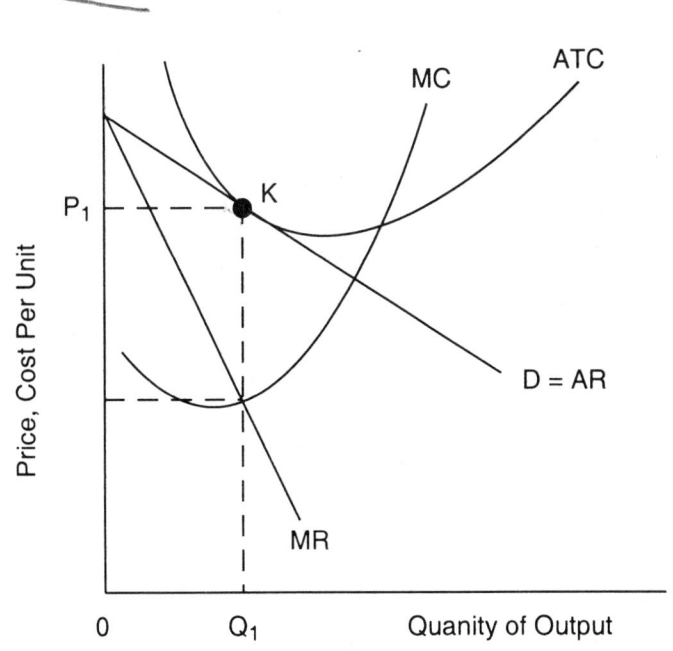

Figure 9.7
A Long Run Equilibrium in Monopolistic Competition (LRATC = P)

The Meaning of Zero Profits in Industry

In the long run, in a purely competitive industry and in a monopolistically competitive industry, economic profits will tend to be equal to zero because of freedom of entry and exit. As firms enter a purely competitive industry attracted by positive economic profits, the market supply of the product will increase causing prices and profits to drop. If firms are incurring losses, those firms will exit the industry causing the market supply and prices to decrease. As a result negative profits will be eliminated. The net effect, therefore, is for the purely competitive firm to have zero economic profits in the long run.

If a monopolistically competitive firm is earning positive economic profits in the short run, new firms will be attracted into the industry. The demand curve for the firm will decrease resulting in lower prices and profits. If firms are incurring negative profits in the short run, they will exit the industry. As those firms exit, the demand curves of the remaining firms will increase causing higher prices and profits. The net effect is for a monopolistically competitive firm to have zero economic profits in the long run.

Zero economic profits means that the firm is just making the amount of money that could be made doing something else with the money invested in the company. For example, if Treasury bills are paying 6% and the company represents an investment of $10,000,000, the company could make $600,000 by purchasing Treasury Bills. If the firm has accounting profits of $600,000, economists would say the firm has zero economic profit. In other words the firm's accounting profit just equals the opportunity cost of the money invested in the firm.

Companies with zero economic profits will be hampered in regards to growth and to the development of new and better products. The industry will stop growing as new firms will not enter an industry with zero economic profits.

MONOPOLISTIC COMPETITION AND MONOPOLY COMPARED

The distinction between monopolistic competition and monopoly is that a monopolist is the single producer of a product, for which there are no good substitutes, that operates in a market with high entry barriers. Monopolistic competitors provide closer substitutes, and face a more elastic demand curve than the monopolist who supplies remote substitutes, and faces steeper demand curves.

Because the monopolist is the only firm producing the product, the firm's demand curve is the industry demand curve, which is negatively sloped. The supply curve cannot be uniquely determined, as the monopolist can choose any price and output combination that maximizes profits. The monopolist cannot differentiate his product as the monopolistic competitor does.

Blockage to entry protects the monopolist, while the monopolistic competitor has no entry barriers and has freedom of entry or exit. The stronger the barriers, the easier it is to protect the monopoly position. Some industries, by their very nature, tend to foster monopoly.

The monopolist has no rivals, while the monopolistic competitor confronts many sellers offering differentiated products. The monopolist practices price discrimination and controls the price of the product. The monopolistic competitor has some control over the price, but encourages non-price competition instead of price competition.

Table 9.1
Characteristics of Monopolistic Competition Market Model

Characteristics	Description
Number of firms	Large number of sellers.
Type of product	Differentiated. Product differentiation means that basically similar products are changed in some way to create some differences in the eyes of the customers.
Conditions of entry	Freedom of entry and exit.
Non-price competition	Considerable emphasis on advertising, brand names, trade markets, etc. Through product development and advertising outlays, a firm may strive to increase the demand for its product more than non-price competition increases its costs. Each firm believes that the other firms in the market will ignore its actions.
Type of profits	Normal profit in the long run.
Where to find in the U.S. economy	Restaurants, shoe stores, gas stations, clothing stores, newsstands, bakeries, barber shops, dry cleaners, grocery stores, book publishing companies, and countless others.
Miscellaneous	P > MR and P > MC. Demand curve for firm downward sloping and highly elastic. There is no supply curve for a monopolistically competitive firm.

Evaluating Monopolistic Competition

Monopolistic competition falls short of the purely competitive model, yet few economists are alarmed by this. In fact, in some industries, the advantages of monopolistic competition may outweigh the disadvantages. At issue are the costs and benefits of product differentiation.

Resources are not allocated efficiently under monopolistic competition. As illustrated in Figure 9.8, price exceeds marginal cost—the value to consumers of another unit of output is greater than the marginal cost of producing it. Long run equilibrium for the firm occurs where demand is tangent to the long run average cost curve. Because the firm's demand curve is downward sloping, this tangency can occur only on the declining segment of the average cost curve, not where average cost is at a minimum. This is illustrated in Figure 9.9.

The firm produces Q_1 at an average cost of $LRAC_0$. Had the firm produced Q_2 output instead, the average cost would have been only $LRAC_1$.

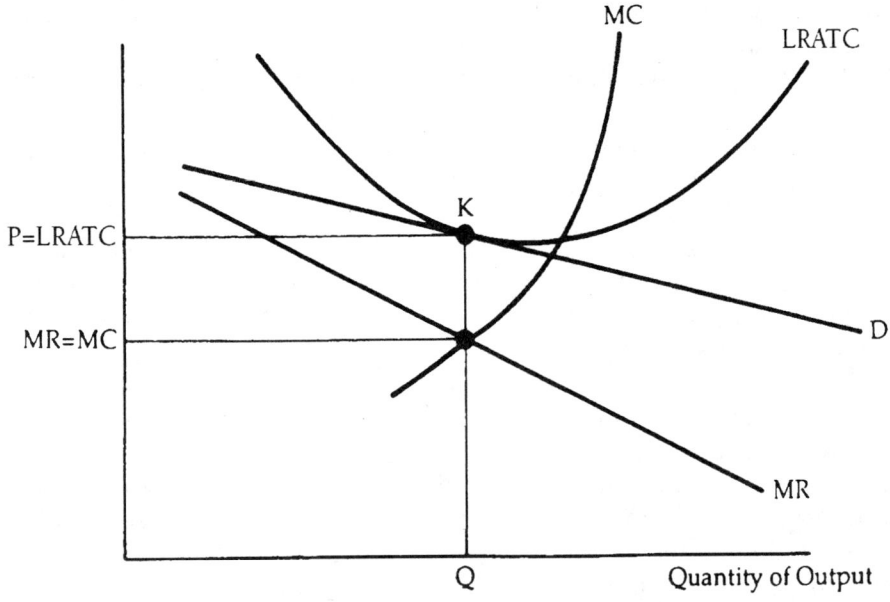

Figure 9.8
Long Run Equilibrium (LTRATC = P)

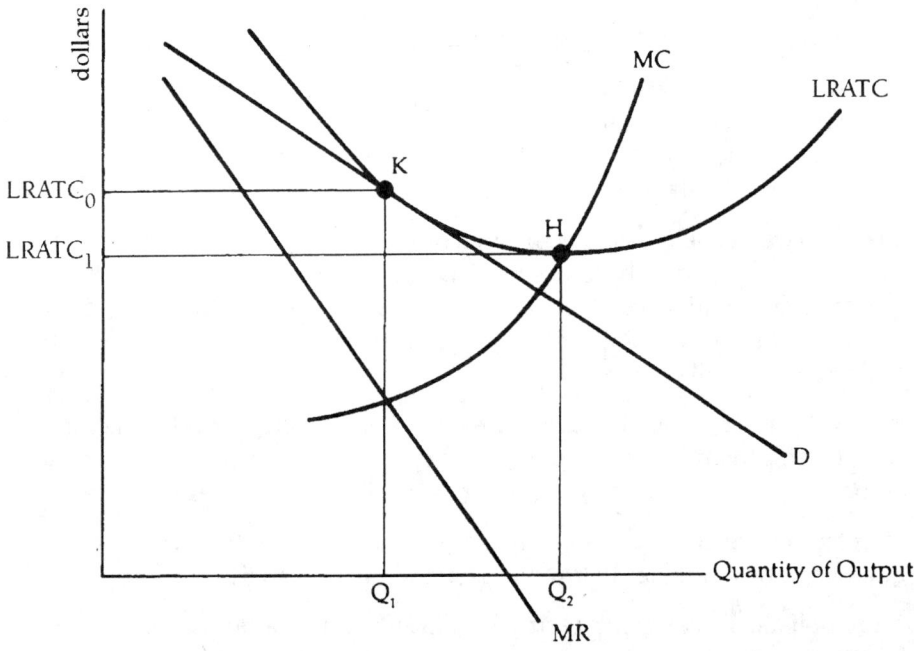

Figure 9.9
The Higher Costs of Monopolistic Competition

Restaurants

The restaurant industry is an example of the monopolistic competition model. In this section we will describe five restaurants in the Detroit Metropolitan Area.

El Zocalo: This Mexican restaurant located in an area called Mexican Town specializes in saucy and spicy dishes from Mexico at reasonable prices.

Backstage: The menu is basic, with burgers, omelets, and deli type food. The food is upstaged by the spectacle of the customers, who are members of the punk and the local fun-seeking communities in the Six-mile/Woodward area.

The Whitney: The restaurant is in the Whitney Mansion on Woodward Avenue and is one of the highest priced restaurants in the Detroit area. It is a favorite place for late dinners for the entertainers appearing at the Fox Theater. The third floor has a piano bar and rooms for customers wishing to just order dessert.

The Lark: This five star restaurant is located in West Bloomfield. The decor is like a Portuguese country inn. The specialty of the Lark is rack of lamb Ghengis Khan, each order of which comes with its own numbered tag.

Les Auteurs: This four star restaurant is located in Royal Oak. It is called an American Bistro, with specialties such as black bean cake studded with smoked turkey, grilled chicken breast with mushroom-cheese tortellini, and gourmet pizza.

There are perhaps several hundred restaurants in the Detroit area, as in any large city. They offer a great variety of menus and prices. In addition to the actual food they serve, they are also providing an atmosphere to make dining more enjoyable. The restaurant industry fits the monopolistic competition model perfectly.

CHAPTER SUMMARY

1. The monopolistic competition model is the major form of imperfect competition.

2. Under monopolistic competition, there are many small buyers and sellers. Each of these sellers produces a product that is somewhat different from every other seller's product: that is, each firm has a partial monopoly of some product characteristics. There is freedom of entry and exit and non-price competition.

3. The major characteristic of monopolistic competition is product differentiation. The products of monopolistically competitive firms are close, but not perfect, substitutes. The product differentiation is related to the controversial subject of advertising. A firm in monopolistic competition will try to attract customers by differentiating its product from that of its rivals.

4. There is a sharp disagreement as to the economic benefits of advertising. Through product development and advertising outlays, a firm may strive to increase the demand for its product more than non-price competition increases its costs.

5. The demand curve confronted by a monopolistic competitor is highly elastic. The marginal revenue curve lies below the demand curve, as with a monopoly.

6. The monopolistically competitive firm faces a substantial amount of competition from rival firms. Typically, the demand is more elastic the larger the number of competitors and the smaller the degree of product differentiation.

7. As with a monopoly, there is no supply curve for a monopolistically competitive firm. Whenever a firm faces a negatively sloped demand curve, the firm has no supply curve.

8. A monopolistically competitive firm can earn an economic profit or incur a loss in the short run as can a monopolist or a purely competitive firm, but may earn only a normal profit in the long run.

9. In the long run, equilibrium exists under monopolistic competition. Free entry eliminates economic profits by forcing the firm's demand curve into a position of tangency with its average cost curve.

10. Each firm under monopolistic competition is so small that none is significantly affected by, or pays much attention to, what other firms in the market do.

11. Monopolistically competitive firms can compete through nonprice competition such as advertising. By shifting the demand curve, advertising can increase a firm's profits.

Key Concepts

Monopolistic Competition—Major form of imperfect competition. The major characteristic of monopolistic competition is product differentiation.

Non-Price Competition—Competing with other firms on a basis other than charging a different price. An example would be the use of advertising.

Product Differentiation—Basically similar products are changed in some way to create some differences in the eyes of customers.

Discussion Questions

1. Explain product differentiation.
2. What are the advantages of advertising?
3. Describe the long run situation in monopolistic competition.
4. How does a monopolistically competitive firm maximize profits?
5. Describe the characteristics of monopolistic competition.
6. How do pure competition and monopolistic competition differ?
7. How do monopoly and monopolistic competition differ?
8. Explain why an MC will only realize a normal profit in the long-run.
9. Are advertising expenditures wasteful?

PRACTICE QUESTIONS AND PROBLEMS

Suppose that the graph drawn in Figure 9.0 represents a monopolistic competitive firm (long-run position).

    a. Indicate the quantity the monopolistic competitive would produce.

    b. What is the amount of profit/loss?

    c. Does the graph in Figure 9.0 show a profit max. equilibrium point? Why or why not?

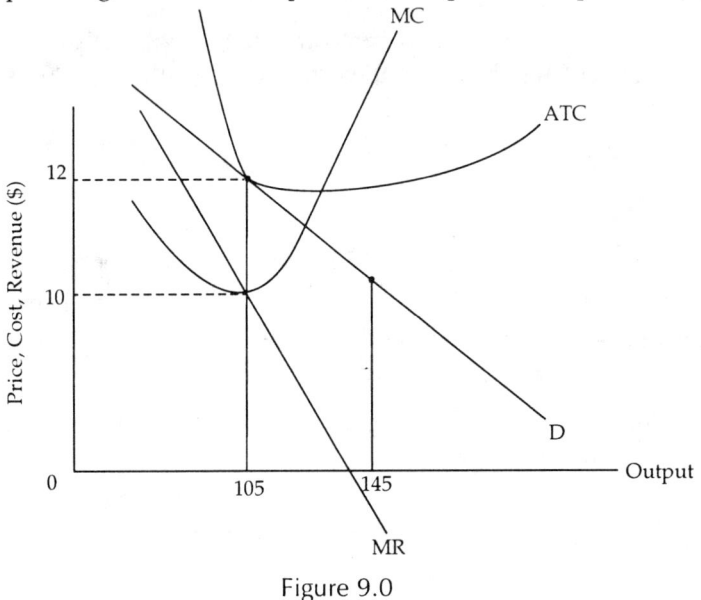

Figure 9.0

9.1 LEARNING PRACTICE

Suppose that the graph drawn in Figure 9.1 represents a monopolistically competitive firm.

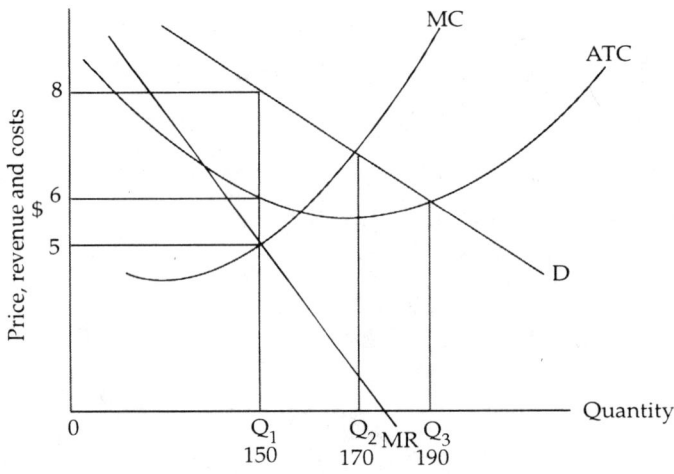

Figure 9.1

    a. Where would the profit maximization monopolistically competitive firm produce?

    b. What is the amount of profit/loss?

    c. Determine the type of profit or loss is indicated?

9.2 Learning Practice

Monopolistic competitor firm: short run position

Using Figure 9.2, answer the following questions:
   a. Find the price level for this MC firm.
   b. What type of profit or loss is shown?
   c. Indicate the amount of profit/loss.
   d. At what level does the firm produce?

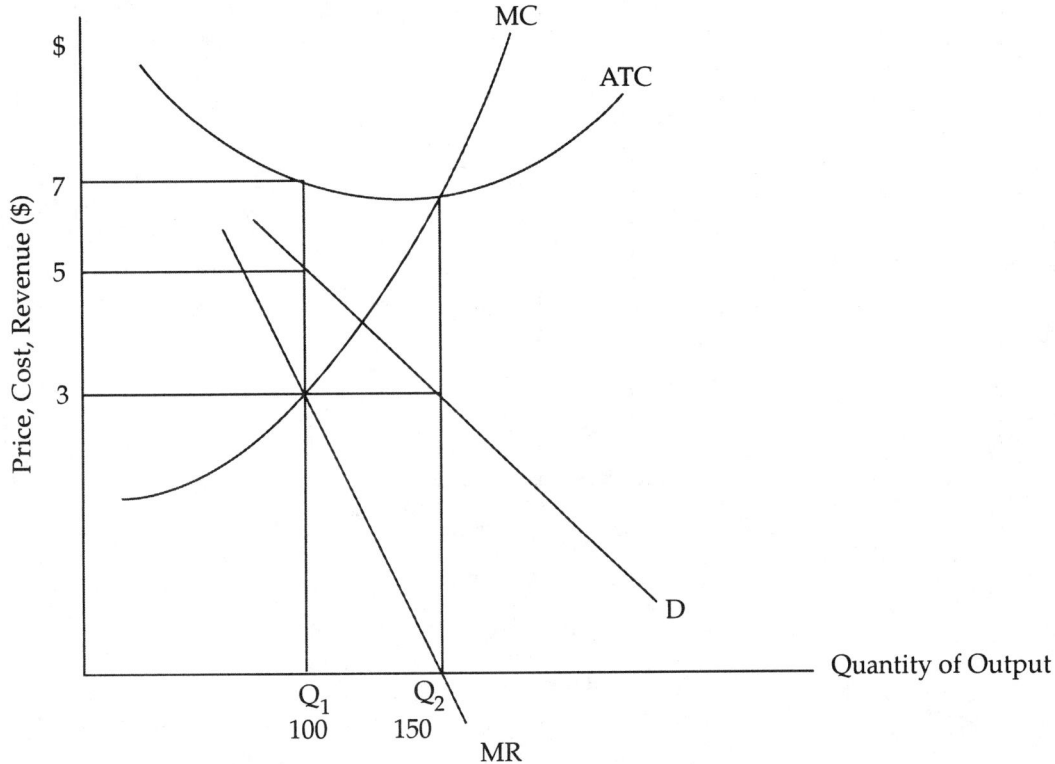

Figure 9.2

9.3 Learning Practice

Monopolistic competitor (MC): long run position

Given Figure 9.3, answer these questions:

a. What type of profit is indicated?

b. What is the amount of profit?

c. At what level will the firm produce?

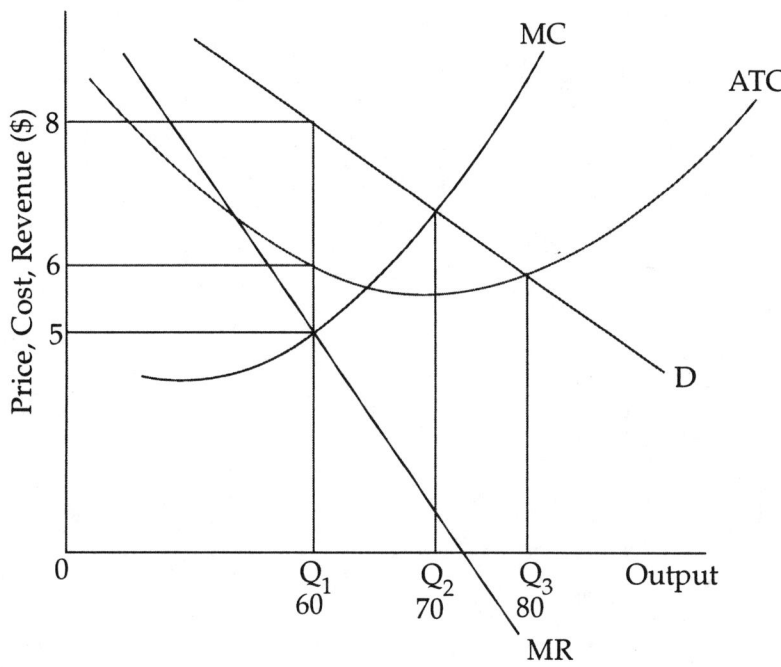

Figure 9.3

CHAPTER 10

Oligopoly

LEARNING OBJECTIVES

After reading this chapter you should be able to:

1. Explain the general characteristics of oligopolistic industries.

2. Identify an oligopoly by the product they produce.

3. Understand the critical characteristics of an oligopoly, which is the concept of interdependence.

4. Discuss the price rigidity in the oligopolistic model.

5. Briefly evaluate mergers, collusion, and cartels.

6. Identify and explain the three types of mergers.

7. Define, calculate, and graphically explain oligopoly in long run equilibrium.

8. Understand the meaning of potential entry and barriers to entry to discourage competition.

9. Construct and explain the kinked demand curve model.

10. Briefly evaluate game theory and the Cournot model.

11. Recognize and provide an example of an oligopoly in the U.S. economy.

12. Explain the pricing policies in a differentiated oligopoly.

13. Discuss the difficulties to enter an oligopolistic industry.

14. Solve the learning practices as indicated at the end of the chapter.

Introduction

Throughout the economic history of the United States, there can be found only a few examples of monopolies of important products. A more accurate description of the market structure of the American economy can be found in the definition of oligopoly. Without having the market control enjoyed by a single seller, a firm, or a small group of independent sellers, can obtain a significant portion of total sales of a good or service and therefore, effectively control market prices. Thus, most real world businesses approximate either monopolistic competition or oligopolistic market structures. The most identifiable tendencies of oligopolies are:

1. Few firms.
2. Interdependence.
3. Price rigidity.
4. Mergers and collusion.

The word oligopoly means few sellers. Oligopoly is an industry in which a few firms dominate the market. Each firm has a certain degree of monopolistic power. Most of the sellers have a large enough market share to influence the market price. Pepsico and Coca-Cola, for example are the two major firms in the soda pop industry, with a number of smaller firms competing. The combined market share of Pepsico and Coca-Cola is somewhere around 70 percent. That statistic also qualifies the soda pop industry as an oligopolistic market. Some other examples of oligopolistic industries are the telephone and telegraph, motor vehicle, cigarette, electric lamp, sewing machine, and breakfast cereal industries, to name a few. Thus, the number of firms in each case is sufficiently small that any one firm's actions can affect market conditions.

Interdependence

Oligopoly is a market structure with a few firms producing similar or differentiated products that dominate a market.

The critical characteristic of an oligopoly is the concept of interdependence. Oligopolists plan their strategies based on a rival firm's actions. An example of this can be easily observed in the auto industry. Assume there are three competing firms, and one decides to lower its price, and therefore increase its market share. You can immediately see either a matching price by the other two firms, or a retaliation by setting prices below the new price. This proves that no firm in an oligopolistic industry will consider price-cutting without looking at the consequences it may face.

Interdependence among oligopolists is expressed in how they make important decisions. An oligopolist would not change the price of its product, the quantity of its product, or its advertising outlay without at least taking into consideration what the response of its rivals might be.

Setting prices in an oligopolistic market is normally done by individual firms. As the market conditions change, or competitors introduce new prices, firms generally change their prices accordingly. When products are homogeneous, the adjustment process and response occurs with speed and accuracy. By contrast, when the products are differentiated, oligopolists are less sensitive to a competitor's change in price. Any response by rivals may be very slow and weak. Oligopolies usually charge a higher price and produce a smaller output than monopolistic competitors. This is due to the fact that there is not a lot of incentive to reduce costs, and that oligopolies sometimes respond to a reduced demand by raising prices to overcome fixed costs. In addition, oligopolies set prices higher than their marginal costs. Significantly, each firm forecasts or expects a certain response from its rivals to any price or output decision that it might take. There is no general oligopoly theory.

Price Rigidity

One major difference between oligopolists and firms in the other three market structures is that oligopolists are much slower to change their prices. This occurs because one of the firms in a particular industry is seen as the leader by its rivals. Many times this is the firm that is the largest or most dominant. The dominant firm then sets the price, based on its prediction that the industry will follow. The dominant firm allows the smaller firms to produce all that they can at that price, and then supplies the rest. The tendency among rival firms is to follow a price decrease, but ignore a price increase. Oligopolists use this method of pricing to avoid price wars. They fear a price war will eventually lead to underselling and a loss of profits. Some economists have labeled this as a tacit collusion, meaning that firms communicate price decisions through a leader.

Non-price competition in oligopolistic markets definitely exists, especially when the product is differentiated. The primary promotional methods used in non-price competition are advertising and product quality.

Advertising is very strong in markets that produce differentiated products. In the automobile manufacturing industry, millions of dollars annually are spent on advertising in order to convince consumers about the quality and superiority of its product. On the other hand, producers of homogeneous products such as steel, copper, and zinc have no reason to advertise their products because the buyers are often skilled and able to detect differences.

Some economists claim that oligopolies spend too much money on misleading advertising and drive up costs by spending a disproportionate amount of money on superficial product differentiation. Oligopolies also tend to have higher prices and lower output than in pure competition. This is because an oligopoly, generally, has a steady market share, thus reducing incentives to cut costs. It can also control the market price, thereby reducing output while maintaining a profitable operation.

Oligopolies are categorized by the products they produce.

   a. *Pure Oligopoly (PO)*. An oligopolistic industry that produces a homogeneous or standardized product such as steel and aluminum. Also, a single price charged for the output of all the firms.

   b. *Differentiated Oligopoly (DO)*. An industry that produces products that are different. As its name implies, this involves producing a product that differs significantly from the output of other rivals. Hence, products are close substitutes and cannot be priced very differently from the other without a substantial loss of market share. The range of prices in this industry will depend on the amount of product differentiation.

MERGERS, COLLUSION, AND CARTEL

Oligopolies also engage in mergers, collusion, and cartels. A merger is when two or more firms legally combine to form a larger firm. Collusion is the act of joining with other producers in an effort to limit competition and increase joint profits. Collusion occurs when such agreements are implicit. A cartel is a group of firms that get together and make joint price and output decisions. The principal purpose of their anti-competitive efforts is to raise their prices and profits above equilibrium.

Mergers

Firms may merge for any number of reasons. Some of these reasons are summarized below.

   a. To take advantage of awareness that a company is undervalued.

   b. To achieve growth more rapidly than by internal growth.

   c. To avoid risks of internal startups or expansions.

d. To reduce dependence on a single product or service.
   e. To increase earnings per share.
   f. To enhance the power of the owner or management.
   g. To eliminate competition. By merging, the firm adds to its market share with a greater overall market percentage.
   h. To avoid the expense of complying with government regulations.
   i. To offset seasonal or cyclical fluctuations.
   j. To respond to a change in structure due to death, retirement, or taxes.

In addition to the advantages mentioned above, there exist some additional reasons why companies might consider a merger:

   a. Straight Market Power. Mergers can raise market power well above the power previously held. Separately, the firms lose, but by combining, they can move to the forefront. This results in higher profitability, which is the basic goal of the firm.
   b. Technical Economies. A merger may achieve economies of scale if the two firms were previously smaller than minimum efficient scale.
   c. Cheaper Inputs. Mergers may make it possible for the firm to buy its inputs more cheaply. These pecuniary gains may affect the input used by the firm. Raw materials or advertising space may be acquired more cheaply by the merged firms.
   d. Easier Market Entry. Entry into a new market is usually easier by merger than by starting anew.

Mergers are of three different types: vertical, horizontal, and conglomerate. A vertical merger is the joining of two or more firms that perform different stages of the product process into a single firm. (Automobile companies merge with steel mills; petroleum extraction firms merge with refineries.) Vertical mergers do not necessarily limit competition in an industry.

A horizontal merger is a merger between two firms in the same market (for example, two car companies, or two oil refining companies) into a single firm. Horizontal mergers have the greatest potential for limiting competition, because as the number of firms in the market declines, the remaining firms have greater market power. Mergers between oligopolistic firms in the same industry tend to reduce competition and increase the market power of the resulting firm.

A conglomerate merger occurs between two firms in unrelated industries. For example, the merging of a restaurant chain and a steel company. Pure conglomerate mergers present the most difficult problems for antitrust laws. Much of the recent trend in mergers has been of the pure conglomerate form because the courts have not been able to pass a ruling on whether a purely conglomerate merger can have anti-competitive effects.

Anti-competitive mergers can take several forms. The only requirements are that the effects be substantial and that they take place within the relevant product and geographic markets. Horizontal mergers always involve the removal of a competitor from the market. Vertical mergers often involve barriers to entry to competitors such as access to supplies or markets.

Collusion

Oligopolistic interdependence may result in collusion. Collusion is inconsistent with pure competition and monopolistic competition models. In oligopoly, there is a tendency for the firms in an industry to maximize their joint profit and to divide that profit in some prearranged way. Collusion includes price-fixing, market-sharing, profit-pooling, and other devices. However, there are both natural and legal reasons why collusion does not usually take place. Obstacles to collusion are: differing demand and cost conditions among firms in the industry; the temptation to cheat; potential entry of new firms if prices are too high; and antitrust laws which prohibit collusion.

Cartel

A cartel is a group of suppliers of a commodity that agrees to restrict output with the aim of maximizing or increasing the total profit of the group. When their members are governments or firms located in different nations, it is an international cartel.

OPEC or the Organization of Petroleum Exporting Countries is a group of 13 oil-producing nations that sells petroleum on the world market. Members are all the Arab oil-producing nations and Iran, Venezuela, Indonesia, Nigeria, and Gabon.

OPEC was able to capture control of petroleum pricing in 1973-74, when the price of oil rose from $3 to $13 per barrel. By agreeing to restrict competition and to exploit their joint market power, the oil-exporting countries found they could exercise considerable control over world oil prices, as seen in the 1970s. In December 1980, the price of oil averaged almost $36 per barrel. Oil prices fell during the 1980s to $11 per barrel in 1986. Oil prices increased to almost $40 per barrel during the Gulf War.

Cartels generally require outright collusion among other firms (a secret agreement for fraudulent or illegal purposes). However, if the industry is concentrated, tacit collusion is possible. Collusion price-fixing agreements, for most manufactured products, are illegal in the United States, but are legal in many international markets. All well known cartels operate in international markets. International cartels control most of the sales in markets for basic resources such as tin, diamonds, chrome, phosphate, and petroleum.

The main purpose of a cartel is to coordinate the output and pricing of its members to maximize industry profits. A cartel, if not legally regulated by a government, carries the seed of its own destruction because there are substantial gains to cheating if others do not cheat. If one cheats and everyone cheats, they are likely to be worse off.

The most important requirement for the effective maintenance of any cartel, over time, is that its members have control over the bulk of production. Cartels have trouble maintaining high prices if numerous competitors are not members. The greater the number of participants in the cartel, the less likely cheating will be detected. A restriction of output below the competitive level leads to allocative inefficiency, can lead to profits in the short run, and is the goal of joint profit maximizers, such as cartels.

The following reasons exist for the "success" of the OPEC cartel from 1971 to 1985.

a. World demand for oil was relatively inelastic in the short run.

b. Other oil-producing countries could not quickly increase their oil outputs in response to the price increases.

c. The member countries provided a large part of the world supply of oil.

On the other hand, there are problems in maintaining the price of OPEC's oil because of the following:

a. increasing efforts to conserve oil,

b. increasing levels of non-OPEC oil production,

c. rigid OPEC production quotas, and

d. increasing competition from other fuels.

If resources are truly mobile, and a cartel restricts output to raise prices and profits, then other firms will enter the market and underprice the cartel, causing the cartel members to follow suit with price reduction.

A cartel can succeed only if it can meet four conditions or solve four problems.
A cartel can succeed only if the following problems are overcome:

Dominance: Enough firms must participate that they can control the market. When the cartel controls supply, the price so established must become the market clearing price. Nonmembers must form a small enough percentage of the market to be a nonfactor.

Agreement: Cartel members must agree on limited quotas and prices.

Cheating: Due to the incentive of increased profits, cheaters, those who offer special, secret discounts to preferred buyers, must be detected. (Even though there is no effective punishment.)

Entry: Cartel members must decide on the correct balance of profit versus restricting entry that there pricing dictates. Higher profits attract more new investment, increased capacity, and a weaker, shorter lived cartel if new market participants take enough market share. (Weaker profits of new entrants join the cartel.) Lower profits make the cartel a less attractive investment, discouraging new entrants and prolonging the cartel, but this is done by sacrificing profits, which are the main objective of the cartel to begin with.

Oligopoly in the Long Run Equilibrium

Economic profits can exist in oligopolistic industries in the long run because of barriers to entry, barriers created by existing firms, and barriers created by government policy, as shown in Figure 10.1. If 500 units per month are produced and sold at 20 dollars per unit, and the ATC = 17 dollars, the oligopoly will earn an economic profit of 3 dollars per unit, or 1,500 dollars per week. The profit-maximizing oligopolist charges a price ($20) which is greater than the MC ($12). The results are resource misallocation and a loss of welfare to society.

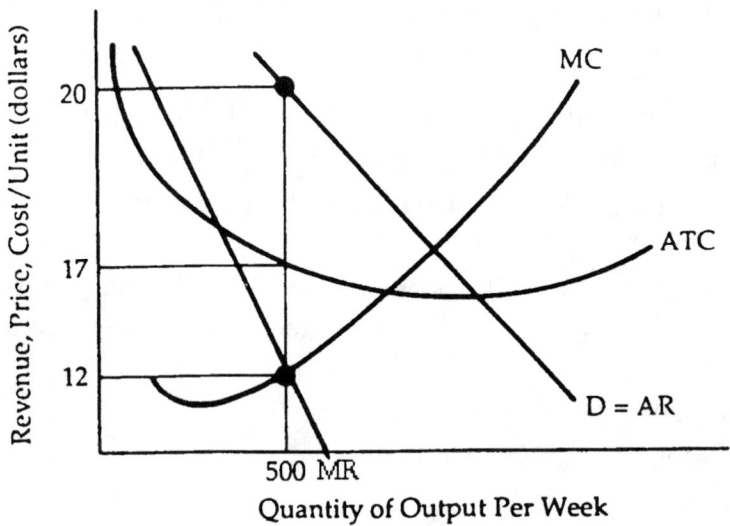

Figure 10.1
Economic Profit in the Long Run (P > ATC)

Potential Entry to an Oligopolistic Industry

Conditions to entry refers to the potential reasons why a firm might choose to enter an industry dominated by oligopolies. The major reason is the potential for larger economic profits when entering the industry. Industries with low marginal costs are particularly attractive. In addition, if there is a large market where a major portion is untapped, there is a real potential for entry into the industry. Finally, a technological breakthrough by a small firm can increase that firm's potential for becoming an oligopoly.

Although there is potential for entry, the barriers for entry are what many oligopolistic firms count on to discourage competition. The major barrier to entry is the size of the market. If the market is defined and the big firms have a large portion of it, there may not be enough market share left to make it profitable for a new firm to enter. The potential for economies of scale is reduced because the new firms will not be able to produce and sell enough to offset the large fixed and startup costs. In addition, oligopolies can think in the long run, in terms of cost. This allows them to spread fixed costs over a larger base. But the new firm has to think in the short run in order to overcome startup costs.

The best example of this is the auto industry in America. The "Big Three" have over 50 percent of the market share in a market that has not significantly grown in the past few years. Because of the enormous cost of an auto assembly plant, not many new firms have been able to successfully enter the marketplace. Only established foreign auto-makers or government backed enterprises have experienced some degree of success. Also, a new firm has to convince a large number of dealerships to handle its product. Even if a "new" auto-maker did that, why would anyone go out of his/her way to buy the new product? He/She would not (probably)—at least not until the new firm had established a name for itself.

OLIGOPOLY MODELS

Oligopoly behavior is difficult to analyze. The main reason is the lack of an adequate model to best represent an oligopoly. In addition, none of the current models agree.

Kinked Demand Curve Model

The kinked demand curve model is a model of oligopolistic behavior which describes two interrelated characteristics of oligopolistic pricing. This model was introduced by Paul Sweezy in 1939. This theory is designed to describe the inflexibility, or so-called "stickiness of pricing."

This theory makes the following assumptions:

1. Management fears the worst when making decisions to increase or decrease prices. When prices do change, firms tend to change their prices together.

2. Prices of oligopoly markets will see a more elastic demand for higher prices than for lower prices, as shown in Figure 10.2. That is, a demand above existing price signifies relatively elastic demand; and demand below the existing price signifies relatively inelastic demand.

3. The kinked demand model assumes a noncollusive oligopoly.

For a price increase from 8 dollars to 10 dollars, there is a sharp decrease in output from Q_0 to Q_1, which signifies that the demand is very elastic in this part of the demand curve. This means that if a firm decides to raise its price, it is unlikely that the competing firms will follow. However, a corresponding price decrease from 8 dollars to 6 dollars will only marginally increase output, from Q_0 to Q_2, signifying that the demand is inelastic. However, there are criticisms of the kinked demand model.

1. There is no explanation of why $8.00 is the original price.

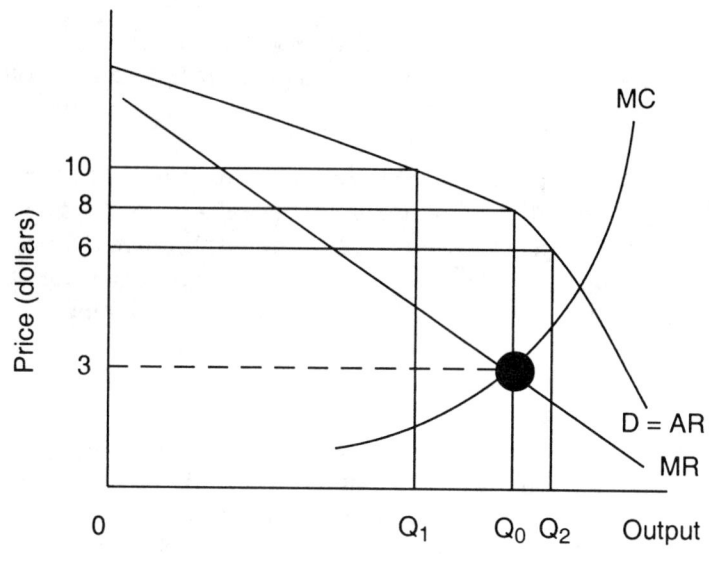

Figure 10.2
Kinked Demand Curve Model

2. In the real world, oligopoly prices are often not rigid.

The disadvantage of the kinked demand curve is that it does not explain how price is determined. In practice, however, price increases usually follow external forces such as increases in taxes or wages. Linking price increases to external forces has the effect of shielding the oligopolies from public criticism.

An interesting aspect of the kinked demand curve is that a firm's price is likely to be "sticky." The demand curve each firm faces depends on how competitors respond to price changes. Therefore, strategic behavior occurs when what is best for firm A depends on what firm B does, and vice versa. The kinked demand curve describes strategic behavior. If firm A raises prices, firm B will not, and firm A will lose sales; if firm A lowers prices, firm B *also* will, and *neither* will gain sales. Thus the consequences of firm A's changing of prices depends on the reaction of firm B. According to the kinked demand curve model, rivals will not follow a price increase; rivals will follow a price decrease.

PRICING POLICIES

Although there is no model to determine how a firm sets its price, the kinked demand curve illustrates the effect of oligopolies on market prices. In short, if I raise my price, the others will not follow me; if I lower my price, they will match me dollar for dollar. Therefore, the kinked demand curve is one explanation of oligopolistic behavior. While it explains price rigidity, it does not explain how the price is determined in the first place. The price will tend to be higher than the competitive price but lower then monopoly price, while output is greater than monopoly output but less than competitive output.

The pricing policies are not completely clear because price decisions are interdependent.

1. The price charged by one firm will significantly affect another firm's sales.

2. Each firm is uncertain as to how the other firms will react to price changes.

3. One firm will act as a price leader either because it has the lowest costs of production, or because it dominates the industry's sales. All other firms will follow by charging the same price.

Why Do Oligopolistic Firms Exist?

Oligopoly is a market structure in which a few firms produce either a standardized or differentiated product, and entry is difficult. An oligopoly exists because of the following factors: Innovation, large economies of scale, few firms controlling essential resources, and successful differentiation. This makes entry difficult, but not impossible. The high degree of capital investment required, substantial advertising budgets and traditional brand loyalty.

The Dominant-Firm Industry

A dominant-firm industry is an industry that contains a large firm with a group of smaller rivals producing homogeneous or very similar products, and is characterized by easy entry into the industry. A firm can become dominant through various paths—monopolization, merger, or development of a superior product. U.S. Steel became the dominant firm in the steel industry by its attempts to monopolize the industry. General Motors became the dominant firm in the automobile industry through merger. IBM became the dominant firm in the computer industry through the development of a new product.

The dominant firm acts as a price searcher and produces to maximize profits. The other smaller firms accept the price of the dominant firm and will make a profit if price exceeds average total cost, as shown in Figure 10.3.

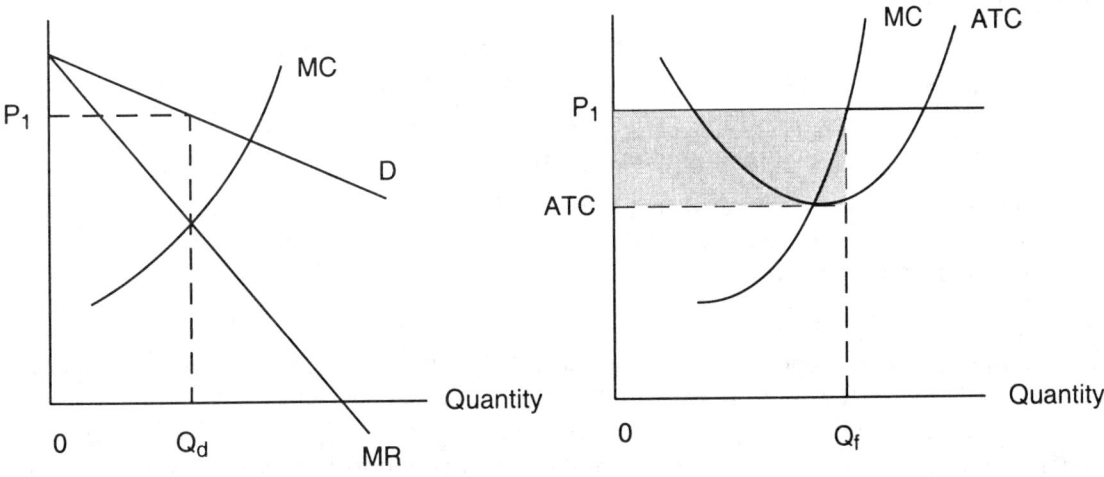

Figure 10.3
Dominant Firm Model

The dominant firm will produce Q_d and charge P_1 in order to maximize profit. The smaller firm will accept the price of P_1 and will produce Q_f since at that quantity price equals marginal cost. In the illustration in Figure 10.3, the firm is making an economic profit as a result.

General Motors

The automobile industry is an example of an oligopoly. Domestic production is from three companies: Ford, Chrysler, and General Motors. General Motors is the world's largest industrial company, and it produces, assembles, and sells mainly automobiles, trucks, buses, and related parts and accessories. GM Hughes Electronics Corp. is the leading supplier of electronic systems for the U.S. military. The company provides radar, weapons control systems, guided missile systems, and defense satellites. The subsidiary Electronic Data Systems provides computer services.

General Motors was founded in 1908 by William Durant and originally included Buick, Oldsmobile, Pontiac, and Cadillac. Over the years, the company followed a three pronged policy:

1. To produce a variety of cars to satisfy a variety of tastes.

2. To develop as widely as possible in automobile engineering.

3. To integrate backwards into the manufacture of components.

As a result of this policy, General Motors is a leader in the automobile industry, with about half of domestic car sales in the United States. General Motors is considered the dominant firm.

Game Theory

Game theory is another model of oligopolistic behavior. This is a way to analyze how rational decisions are made by competitors in uncertain conditions. The theory was developed by Von Neumann and Morgenstern. This model assumes that each firm has a strategy based on the rival firm's strategy. If your rival can gain an advantage by knowing that you will respond rationally, it may be beneficial for you to establish a reputation for being occasionally irrational. The behavior involves threats that must be believable by rivals, or they are worthless. Game theory is excellent for understanding interdependence of firms, and it even allows for pricing models. However, it is difficult sometimes to know exactly what the rival firm will do, and thus the decision-making of the firm is still based on guesswork.

Cournot Model

The Cournot model was established in 1838, and contains the following:

1. Existence of duopoly (two sellers) and non-cooperation between them. If these two sellers could agree to collude instead of competing, they could set a different level of output and share the higher monopoly profit.

2. Output level is the decision variable, and each firm maximizes output. (The Cournot equilibrium is the collection of output of the firms at their output level, corresponding to the maximization of profit.)

3. Homogeneous product.

Oligopoly can be approached from either of two directions: cooperative or non-cooperative. The former is based on the assumption that the oligopolists will collude and that they will be able to make legally binding agreements. Under the non-cooperative approach, the oligopolists act independently of one another in the sense that they do not collude; however, they do choose their policies taking into account the behavior they expect from their fellow oligopolists.

The negative aspects of Cournot's model are that firms do not produce homogeneous products; in fact, they generally differentiate. Also, the Cournot model does not accept market dynamics, such as the number of firms, the determination of price, or the potential for collusion. In the Cournot model, firms take their rival's output as given, and end up producing more than in the monopoly quantity but less than in the competitive industry.

Table 10.1
Characteristics of Oligopolistic Market Model

Characteristics	Description
Number of Firms	Few producers, each with limited market power due to intense rivalry.
Type of Product	Products may be standardized or differentiated. (Diff. products: detergents, greeting cards, automobiles.)
Conditions of Entry	Potential entry, varying degrees of difficulty.
Control of Price	Price leadership usually by the largest firm. No firms in an oligopolistic industry will consider price-cutting without looking at the consequences they may face. The existing producers view their price and production actions as interdependent.
Non-Price Competition	Typically, a great deal, particularly with product differentiation, style, and service. Advertising very strong in markets that produce differentiated products.
Type of Profits	Normal and economic profits in the long run.
Where to find in the U.S. economy	Carbonated soft drinks, aircraft manufacturing, cement, autos, steel, cereals, textile, beer, oil refining industries, toothpaste, aluminum, computers, and many household appliances. (Steel, cement, zinc, copper and oil refining industries are examples of standardized oligopolies.)

Prisoner's Dilemma

Suppose that Kathy & Charles are arrested for robbing a convenience store. The DA meets separately with each one saying "we have a lot of evidence indicating you robbed the convenience store, so you better confess. If you do, I'll give you a break. If you alone confess, I'll see to it you get only six months in jail. If you both confess, I'll see to it that you get 10 years. But if you don't confess, and your partner does, I'll see to it you get 20 years." Both Kathy & Charles are sure that, if neither confesses, they will get 2 years.

A. In this situation, what is the payoff matrix?

B. What strategy will each choose, given that each tries to get the most lenient sentence possible?

The payoff matrix is as follows:

Possible strategies for Charles	Kathy's payoff Possible strategies for Kathy		Charles's payoff Possible strategies for Charles	
	Confess	Not Confess	Confess	Not Confess
Confess	10	20	10	1/2
Not confess	1/2	2	20	2

The payoff matrix shows that, if Charles confesses, Kathy is better off to confess than not to confess. If he does not confess, she is also better off to confess than not to confess. Thus, her dominant strategy is to confess. Similarly, the payoff matrix shows that Charles is better off to confess if Kathy confesses and that he is also better off to confess if she does not confess. Thus, his dominant strategy too is to confess. A game of this sort is called the Prisoner's Dilemma. Note that in this situation each will do better by being altruistic than by selfishly trying to minimize his or her own stay in jail.

Miscellaneous

In oligopoly, P > MR and P > MC. Facing downward sloping demand curve. Oligopolists restrict output and are less than inviting to firms that might like to enter the industry. The results are misallocation and a loss of welfare to society.

Many people associate monopoly with "big business," but in the developed economies Oligopoly is not monopoly characterizes big business. Oligopoly may take on many forms. It may consist of a group of giant firms that dominate the industry, or it may consist of one dominant firm coexisting with many smaller firms. An Oligopoly may result from innovations, cost conditions, control of essential resources, legal restrictions, differentiations, large fixed costs, or mergers. Each firm in an oligopolistic industry must closely watch the actions of the other firms because the action of one can dramatically affect the others. Because of this interdependence, it is under Oligopoly that rivalry among firms takes its most active and aggressive form. An Oligopoly has elements of both perfect competition and monopoly. There are a few firms in an Oligopoly, not an infinite number or just one. Mergers in an Oligopoly can be horizontal, vertical, or conglomerate. The major criticism of Oligopoly is that if oligopolists collude successfully the result is similar to monopoly.

CHAPTER SUMMARY

1. Oligopoly is the most frequently encountered market structure in large sectors of the U.S. economy. Oligopoly products may be standardized or differentiated. Hence, oligopoly is important because there are so many real world examples of it. The word oligopoly means few sellers.

2. Oligopolies have the following characteristics of behavior: Few firms, interdependence, price rigidity, mergers, and collusion.

3. An oligopoly is a market dominated by a few sellers, at least several of which are large enough to be able to influence market price.

4. The kinked demand curve is one explanation of oligopolistic behavior. The model predicts that the seller will not tend to change prices, hence, price rigidity. It does not explain how the present price was reached. If a firm raises its prices, revenue falls, and that demand above the existing price signifies relatively elastic demand, and demand below the existing price signifies relatively inelastic demand.

5. Predicting the behavior of oligopolies is especially difficult, primarily because of their interdependence. Each firm is uncertain as to how the other firms will react to price change. One firm will act as a price leader either because it has the lowest costs or production, or because it dominates the industry sale. The price leader produces where MC = MR, and charges the highest prices the demand for its product allows.

6. Oligopolistic interdependence may result in collusion. However, there are legal reasons why collusion does not actually take place.

7. Oligopolists restrict output and are less than inviting to firms that might like to enter the industry. The results are misallocation and a loss of welfare to society.

8. Economic profits can exist in an oligopolistic industry in the long run because of natural barriers to entry, barriers created by existing firms, and barriers created by governmental policy.

9. Oligopoly models are: the kinked demand curve, game theory, and the Cournot model.

10. Non-price competition in oligopolistic markets exists, especially when the product is differentiated. Advertising is very strong in a market that produces differentiated products, such as automobiles.

11. Oligopolists behaving as monopolists produce where MR = MC, and charge the highest possible price for their products, given demand.

12. Oligopolies engage in mergers, collusion, and cartels.

13. Mergers between oligopolistic firms in the same industry tend to reduce competition and increase the market power of the resulting firm.

14. Pure oligopoly is an industry that produces a homogeneous or standardized product such as steel and aluminum.

15. Differentiated oligopoly—an industry that produces a product that differs significantly from the output of the other producers.

16. Game theory assumes that each firm has a strategy based on the rival firm's strategy, and it's difficult to know what the rival firm will do. Oligopoly behavior is similar to a game of strategy, such as poker, chess, or bridge. Each player's action is interdependent with other players' actions.

17. The Cournot model applies to an oligopoly with a fixed number of firms, and does not accept market dynamics such as the determination of price and the potential for collusion.

18. An oligopoly exists because of large economies of scale, innovation, few firms controlling essential resources and successful differentiation.

19. Oligopolists are often reluctant to lower the price of a good that they sell because they can never be quite sure how rivals will interpret such an action. Fearing a price war, they may instead resort to non-price competition such as advertising more.

20. The degree of rivalry among the firms in an oligopoly industry helps to determine whether the firms produce on their lowest available curves because the greater the competition among them, the more they will be pushed to be efficient.

21. An oligopoly exists because of the following factors: innovation, large economies of scale, few firms controlling essential resources, and successful product differentiation. This makes entry difficult but not impossible.

22. Cartel is a collusive arrangement that is open and formal. An arrangement that allows the participating firms to earn monopoly profits. The main purpose of a cartel is to coordinate the output and pricing of its members to maximize industry profits. There are many obstacles to collusion.

Chapter 10
Key Concepts

Cartel—Group of firms that get together and make joint price and output decisions (fix output and prices).

Collusion—Act of joining with other producers in an effort to limit competition and increase joint profits.

Conglomerate Merger—A merger between two firms in different and unrelated industries.

Cournot Model—Established in 1838. Has few assumptions about oligopoly.

Dominant Firm Industry—An industry that contains a large firm with a group of smaller firms producing similar products.

Game Theory—Assumes that each firm has a strategy based on the rival firm's strategy.

Horizontal Merger—A merger between companies in the same market.

Interdependence—Interdependence among oligopolists is expressed in how they make important decisions.

Kinked Demand Curve—Model of oligopolistic behavior which describes two interrelated characteristics of oligopolistic pricing.

Merger—Where two or more firms legally combine to form a larger firm.

Oligopoly—Market dominated by a few sellers, at least several of which are large enough in the total market to be able to influence market prices. Oligopoly products may be standardized or differentiated.

Price Rigidity—Oligopolists are much slower to change their prices than firms in the other three market structures.

Vertical Merger—A firm acquires another firm that is either in a buyer or a seller relationship to it.

DISCUSSION QUESTIONS

1. Describe the characteristics of an oligopoly.
2. Explain interdependence and the pricing policies of an oligopolistic firm.
3. Explain price rigidity.
4. Discuss carefully how price is determined in a differentiated oligopoly.
5. Present the reasons firms merge.
6. What is the distinction between horizontal, vertical, and conglomerate mergers?
7. Explain collusion.
8. What is a cartel and what are its advantages?
9. What is the long-run situation in oligopoly?
10. Compare the four market structures.
11. Explain the Cournot model; apply to oligopoly.
12. Discuss the game theory in oligopolistic industry.
13. Describe the dominant firm industry.
14. Briefly discuss why do oligopolies exist.
15. Kinked demand curve model: What's wrong with it?
16. Why does the upper portion of the kinked demand curve signify relatively elastic demand, and the lower portion signify relatively inelastic demand?

10.1 Learning Practice

Suppose that the graph drawn in Figure 10.4 represents an oligopolistic firm. Answer the following:
Total Revenue (TR) = $
Total Cost (TC) = $
Amount of profit/loss = $
Type of profit/loss = $
Show profit/loss on the above graph.

Solutions

TR = $30,000 (P.Q)
TC = $24,000 (ATC.Q)
Amount of profits = $6,000 (TR–TC)
Type of profit = Economic profit
Profit = Shaded area

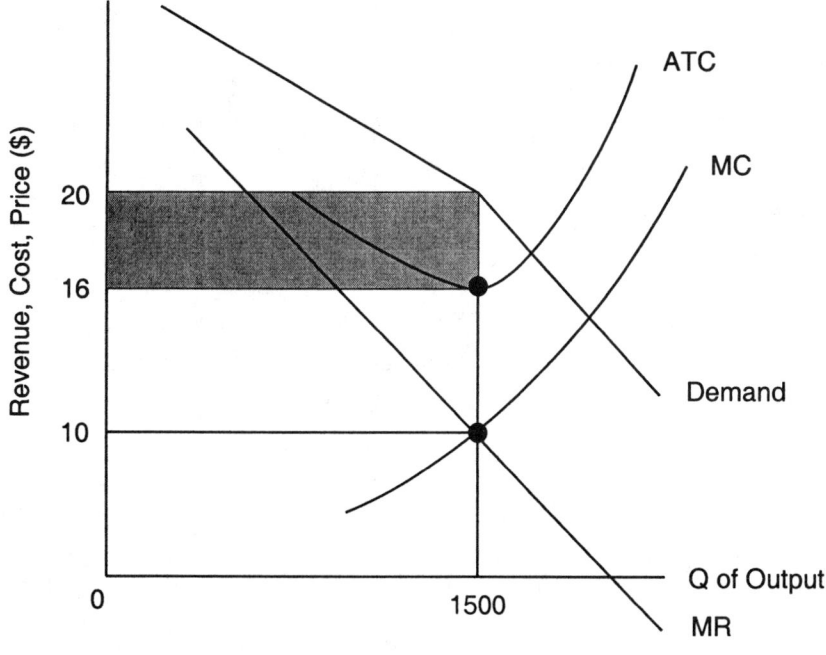

Figure 10.4

10.2 Learning Practice and Solutions

According to the kinked demand curve model, if a firm raises its prices, revenue falls, and that demand above the existing price signifies relatively elastic demand; and demand below the existing price signifies relatively inelastic demand. Therefore, the kinked demand curve is highly elastic for a price increase but inelastic for a price reduction. The differing elasticities are based on the assumption that rival firms will match a price reduction but not a price increase.

Oligopoly

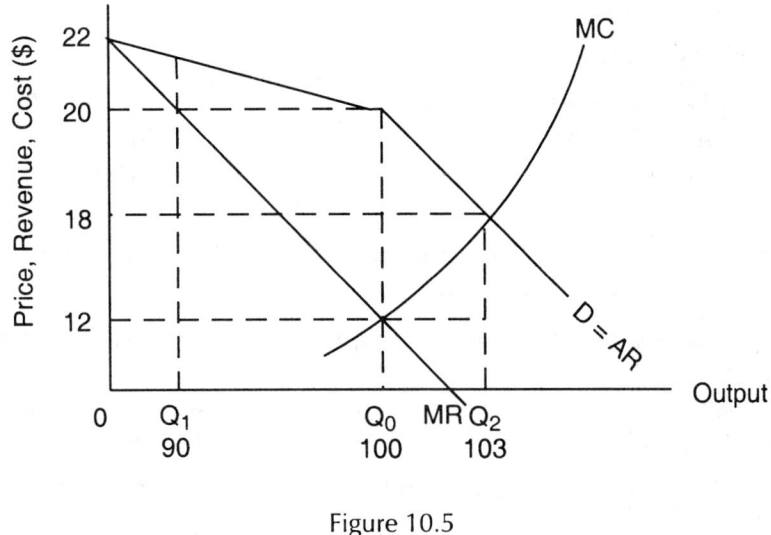

Figure 10.5

Figure 10.5 represents an oligopolistic firm. The existing price is $20.00.

Answer the following:
  a. What will happen to total revenue as the price increases from $20 to $22.00?
  b. Demonstrate that demand above the existing price signifies relatively elastic demand.
  c. Demonstrate that demand below $20.00 signifies relatively inelastic demand.

- The individual firm believe that rivals will match any price cuts. That is, each firm views its demand as relatively inelastic for price cuts, which means they will be selling at lower prices. Hence, each firm's total revenue will be lower.

    That is demand is relatively inelastic if P ↓, total revenue ↓

- With regard to raising prices, there is no reason to believe that rivals will try to take away some of the customers from the price-increasing firm. Thus, any firm which "gets greedy" will lose many sales. That is, raising prices when demand is relatively elastic will decrease revenue.

    P ↑ demand is relatively elastic, total revenue ↓

10.3 Learning Practice

Graphs of all market models

Match the following descriptions to the correct graph below. Indicate on each graph the area of economic profit or loss, and state if the firm is just making normal profits.

a. A purely competitive firm is earning economic profits in the short run. Graph no. _____.

b. A purely competitive firm in long-run equilibrium is shown in graph no. _____.

c. A natural monopoly is shown in graph no. _____.

d. A monopolistically competitive firm earning economic profits in the short run is shown. Graph no. _____.

e. A monopolistically competitive firm experiencing economic losses in the short run is shown in graph no. _____.

f. A monopolistically competitive firm in long run equilibrium is shown in graph no. _____.

g. An oligopolistic firm earning economic profits in the long run is shown in graph no. _____.

h. A monopolistic firm experiencing an economic loss, and that firm should discontinue operating is shown in graph no. _____.

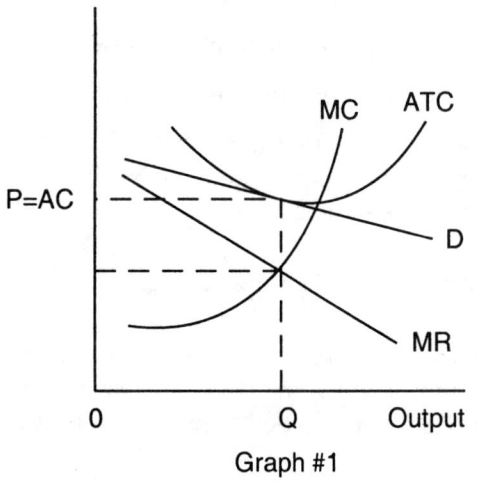

Graph #1

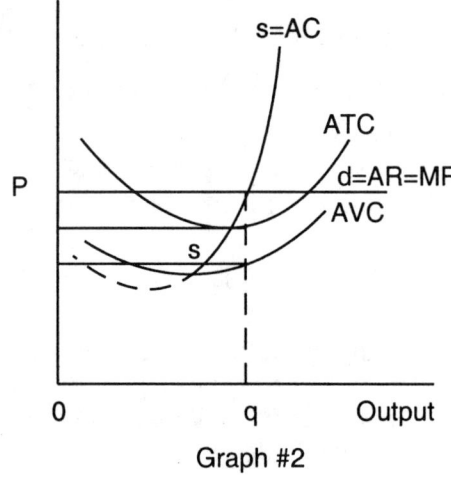

Graph #2

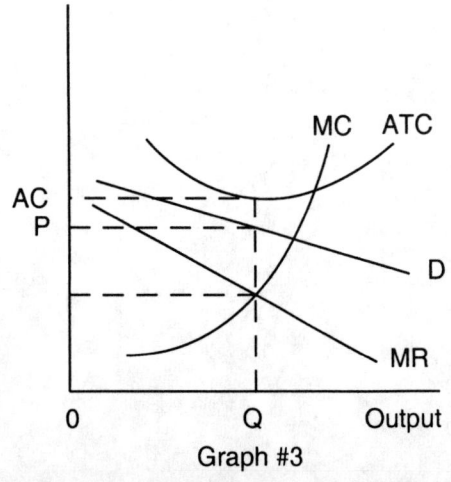

Graph #3

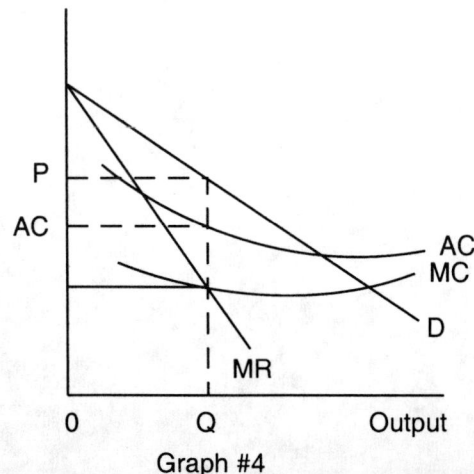

Graph #4

Oligopoly

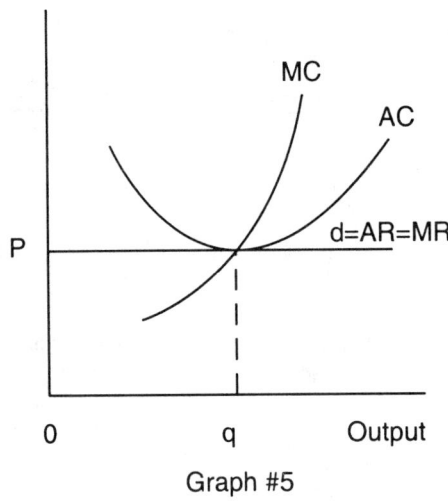

Graph #5

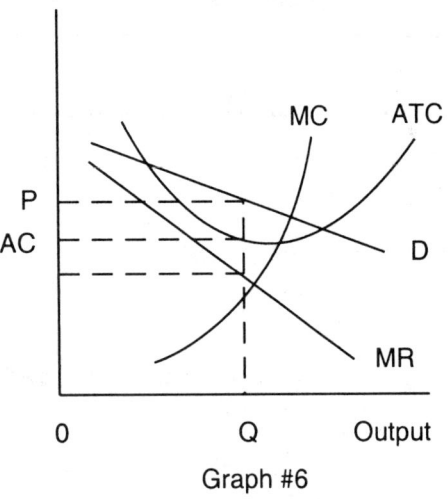

Graph #6

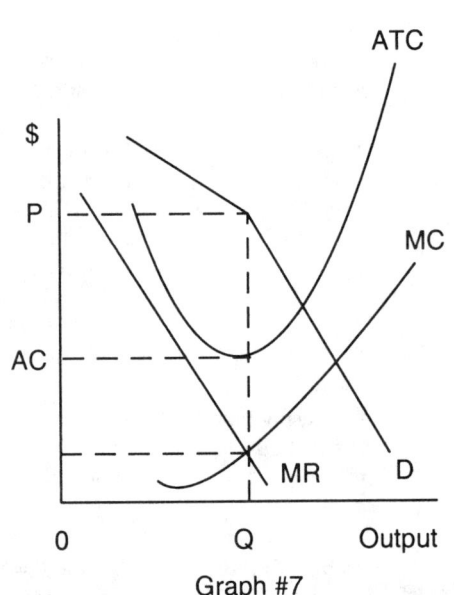

Graph #7

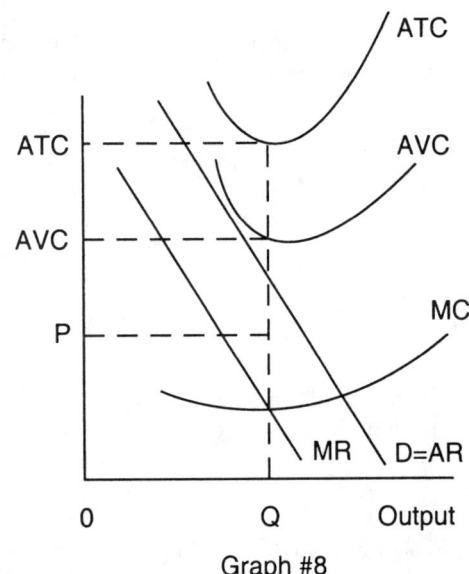

Graph #8

SOLUTIONS

a. #2   c. #6   e. #3   g. #7
b. #5   d. #4   f. #1   h. #8

A Comparison of Various Market Structures

	Characters	Perfect (pure) Competition	Monopoly	Monopolistic Competition	Oligopoly
1	Number of firms	Many	One	Many	
2	Entry & Exit	No entry or exit barriers	Substantial & effective barriers	No entry or exit barriers	Major barriers to entry
3	Type of product	Standard (Homogeneous product)	Unique (no close substitutes for products)	Differentiated products	Standardized or Differentiated
4	Demand curve	The market's demand is negative sloped. The firm's demand is horizontally (P=D=AR=MR)	Downward sloping	Downward sloping	Downward sloping
5	Marginal Revenue Curve	Coincides with demand curve	Lies below demand curve	Lies below demand curve	Lies below demand curve
6	Control of price & market power	None. Each firm ignores actions of others.	Considerable market power and control overprice.	Diffused market power and little control over price.	Price leadership usually by the largest firm. Shared market power and control over price. Decision-making is mutually inter-dependent.
7	Non-price Competition	Price taker	Price maker	Advertising brand names, trade markets	Each firm is concerned about actions of other firms.
8	Types of profits in the short-run	Normal (P=ATC) Economic (P>ATC) Loss (P<ATC)	Normal (P=ATC) Economic (P>ATC) Loss (P<ATC)	Normal (P=ATC) Economic (P>ATC) Loss (P<ATC)	Normal (P=ATC) Economic (P>ATC) Loss (P<ATC)
9	Types of profits in the long run	Normal P=MR=MC	Potential long-run Economic profit (P>(MR=MC)	Normal P>(MR=MC) LR equilibrium occurs where dmand is tangent to the LRAC at the declining point which means LRAR=LRAC	Normal and Economic profit P>(MR=MC) P+LRAC+P>LRAC
10	Profit rule in the Short-Run	At Level of Output where MR=MC	At Level of Output where MR=MC	At Level of Output where MR=MC	At Level of Output where MR=MC
11	Where to find the US Economy	Agricultural products gold mining, industries, taxicab services & cleaners	Local cable, TV, water, gas & electric company, the only store in town	Retail stores, retaurants, etc.	Automobiles, steel co., cigarettes, beer & soft drink

CHAPTER

Labor Markets, Wages & Unions

LEARNING OBJECTIVES

After you have studied this chapter in the text, and attended class lectures regularly, you will be able to:

1. Explain equilibrium in the purely competitive labor market.
2. Discuss the rule of hiring where MRP equals MFC.
3. Explain equilibrium in the monopsony labor market.
4. Briefly trace the historical development of labor unions in the United States.
5. Understand the following legislation dealing with labor unions: Norris-LaGuardia Act, Wagner Act, Taft-Hartley Act, and Landrum-Griffin Act.
6. Provide and recognize examples of different types of labor unions in this country.
7. Identify the purposes of labor unions.
8. Determine the equilibrium wage and quantity in a purely competitive labor market, given demand and supply conditions.
9. Verbally and graphically explain how a union raises the wage rate of its workers when the labor market is purely competitive.
10. Compare the results, in terms of employment, of a union that raises wages by restricting supply to one that raises wages by increasing demand.
11. Identify and discuss the major factors that give rise to wage differentials.
12. Understand monopsony in the market for nurses.
13. Discuss the determinants of income.
14. Understand the concept of Marginal Revenue Product of Labor (MRPL).
15. Evaluate discrimination, concerns and benefits from immigrants.
16. Solve the learning practices as indicated at the end of the chapter.

INTRODUCTION

The two markets of the economy are the *goods market* and the *factor markets*.

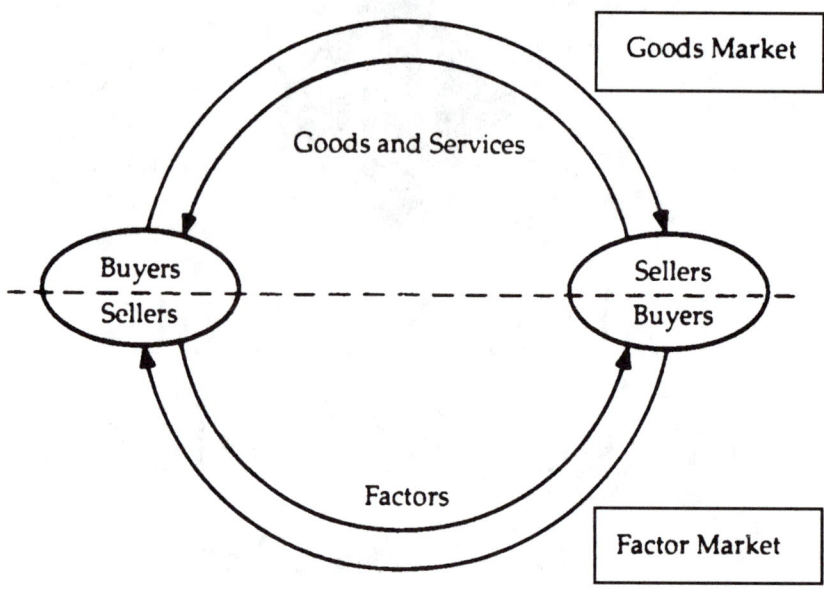

Figure 11.1
Goods and Factor Markets

In Figure 11.1, the two markets of the economy are shown: the goods market and the factor market. In the goods market, goods and services are provided by sellers and purchased by buyers. The market types are: pure competition, monopoly, monopolistic competition, and oligopoly. In the bottom half of Figure 11.1, we show that sellers of goods and services are buyers of the factors of production to produce the goods. The factors are resources, labor, capital, and managerial services. The sellers of goods are buyers of the factors. The buyers of goods and services are sellers of the factors. The payment for the use of the factors constitutes income to the sellers of the factors. In this chapter we will discuss the factor of labor in pure competition and monopsony. We will also discuss unions and their impact on wages.

Competitive Labor Market

A firm's willingness to pay for labor, or its demand for labor, will be based on the value of the output produced by labor. The demand is based on the marginal revenue product of labor (MRPL). The marginal revenue product of any worker is the marginal physical product of that worker times the price of the output sold. That is, the marginal contribution to the firm's revenue.

The marginal revenue product of labor tells us how much each worker is worth to the firm. It tells us how much revenue a particular worker will generate for the firm. Thus, an increase in the price of the product produced or in the marginal product of the worker will increase the demand for labor. Table 11.1 illustrates the computation of marginal revenue product (MRP).

Figure 11.2 illustrates the marginal revenue product curve, which also represents the demand curve for labor of the firm. The demand for labor curve is downward sloping because of the law of diminishing returns. It shows the quantity of labor (or labor hours) that would be employed at each of the various possible wage rates. Alternatively, it shows the value of the marginal product of labor of the last worker employed out of each of the various quantities of labor that could be employed.

Table 11.1
Marginal Revenue Product

(1) Number of Workers	(2) Marginal Physical Product of Each Workers (per hour)	(3) Price per unit of output	(4) Marginal Revenue Product of Labor (MRPL)*
1	5	$2.50	$12.50
2	4.5	$2.50	$11.25
3	4.0	$2.50	$10.00
4	3.5	$2.50	$8.75
5	3.0	$2.50	$7.50

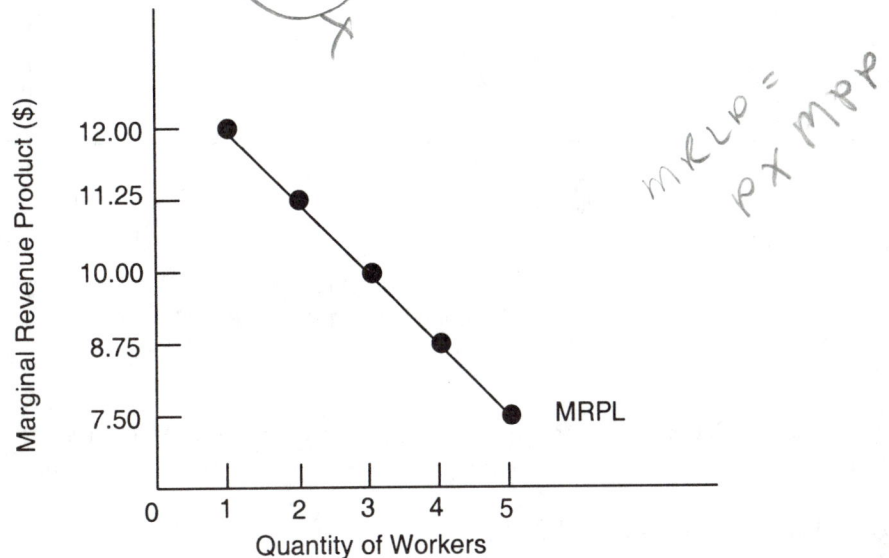

Figure 11.2
Marginal Revenue Product Curve

The demand for labor or any resource will always slope downward—that is, there will exist an inverse relationship between its price and the quantity demanded. The MRPL is simply the price multiplied by the marginal physical product, which is Column (2) times Column (3). Because of diminishing returns, which states that as variable input is added to fixed input, eventually the additions to output will decrease, the marginal physical product of each worker falls steadily as additional units of input are employed. Since price is multiplied by a number which decreases as more labor is hired, the marginal revenue product decreases as more labor is hired.

Figure 11.3 illustrates the purely competitive factor market. The wage is determined in the market by the demand for, and the supply of, labor. In this example, the wage is $10 per hour. The firm can hire all the workers it wishes at the wage of $10. There is no need to pay more, and workers would work elsewhere at $10 if the firm offered less. The wage represents the marginal factor cost (MFC), which is the increase in total costs incurred when a firm hires an additional worker. For the purely competitive firm the MFC curve represents the supply curve of labor, and it is perfectly elastic.

---

*MRPL, it tells us how much each worker is worth to the firm (Marginal contribution to the firm's revenue). Firms will hire additional workers as long as MRPL is greater than the MFC.)

In order to maximize profits, the firm should hire workers as long as the MRP of the worker is greater than or equal to the MFC. In Figure 11.3, this occurs at 3 workers. For any worker beyond this point, the MFC will exceed the MRPL. It will cost more to hire a worker than the worker will generate for the firm.

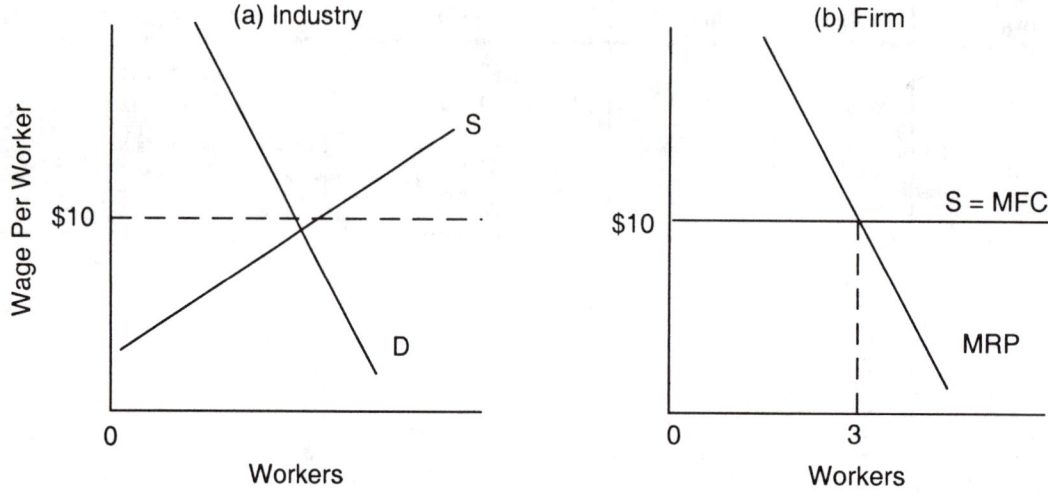

Figure 11.3
Equilibrium Labor Market

THE AVERAGE, MARGINAL AND TOTAL PRODUCTS OF LABOR

Average Product of Labor (APL)

APL is defined as the quantity of output divided by the quantity of labor employed. In Table 11.2, if the firm hires (3) workers to produce (15) units of output, then the average product of labor is 15/3 = 5 units of output per worker. If it hires (5) workers to produce 24 units of output, then the APL is 4.8 units of output per worker.

$$APL = \frac{Q \text{ of output}}{Q \text{ of labor employed}}$$

Total Product of Labor (TPL)

TPL is the quantity of output that the firm can produce and depends only on the quantity of labor it employs. That is, the quantity of output that can be produced with a given input.

Column (1) and Column (2) of Table 11.2 shows a typical relationship between labor and total product.

Marginal Product of Labor (MPL)

MPL is defined as the additional output produced due to the last unit of labor employed. That is, when the quantity of labor increased from 4 units to 5 units, the total product increases from 20 to 24.

$$\frac{\Delta Q \text{ of output}}{\Delta Q \text{ of labor employed}}$$

MPL associated with various quantity of labor are shown in Column (3) of Table 11.2.

Table 11.2
Average, Marginal and Total Products

(1) Quantity of Labor	(2) Total Product	(3) Marginal Physical Product of Labor (MPPL)	(4) Average Product of Labor (APL)
1	4	4	4
2	9	5	4.5
3	15	6	5.0
4	20	5	5.0
5	24	4	4.8
6	27	3	4.5

Equilibrium Quantity of Labor—Monopsony

Suppose there is only one firm which is the major buyer of labor, as may be the case in a small town with only one industry, or in a community or neighborhood. There may be one school district which hires teachers, one hospital which hires nurses, one governmental unit which hires staff for parks and recreation. A single buyer of a factor of production is referred to as a monopsony.

Since the firm would constitute the industry, the firm faces an upward rising supply curve. This means that in order to hire additional workers the firm has to pay a higher wage. This is shown in Table 11.3.

Table 11.3
Labor Market for Monopsony

Quantity	Wage	Total Wage	Marginal Factor Cost
1	5	5	5
2	5.50	11	6
3	6	18	7
4	6.50	26	8
5	7	35	9
6	7.50	45	10
7	8	56	11
8	8.50	68	12
9	9	81	13
10	9.50	95	14

In the purely competitive model, the MFC just equaled the wage. In the case of the monopsonist, it equals the cost of hiring one more worker, which includes the additional worker's wage and the additions to the wages of all the workers already employed. To attract more workers the monopsonist must offer a higher wage to both the new worker and to the previously hired workers who will not work for less than the new employees just hired. As a result, marginal factor cost is always greater than wage. To hire the second worker will cost 6 dollars. This is the result of a wage of $5.50 for the second worker and a $.50 increase for worker no. 1. Both worker no. 1 and no. 2 will be earning $5.50 in wage. To hire the third worker will cost 7 dollars. This is the result of a $6 wage for the third worker and a $.50 increase for worker no. 1 and no. 2. All three will be receiving $6 per hour. To hire the fourth worker will cost 8 dollars. This is the result of a wage of $6.50 for the fourth worker and a $.50 increase for the previously hired workers.

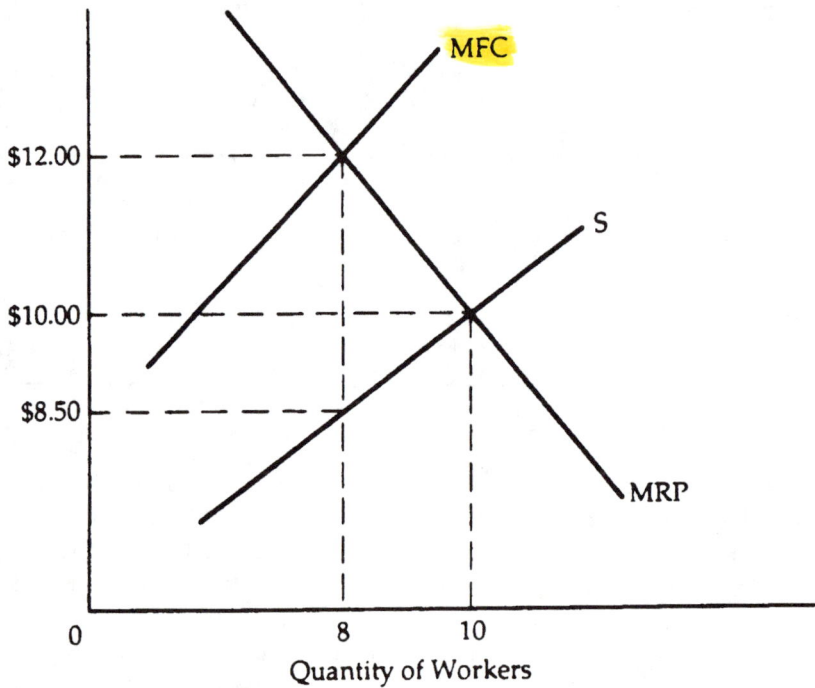

Figure 11.4
Monopsony Equilibrium

The quantity of labor a monopsonist will hire is determined where the MFC of an additional worker and the MRP of that worker are equal, as shown in Figure 11.4. As illustrated, the firm will hire 8 workers. The MFC will be $12, and each worker will be paid a wage of $8.50. If the market were purely competitive, the firm would hire where the supply curve intersects the MRP curve (10 workers at $10). That is, the monopsonist hires fewer workers and also pays less. Additionally, the MFC curve lies above the supply curve of labor because it has to pay a higher wage rate in order to attract additional workers, and this higher wage rate must then be paid to all of its workers.

Characteristics of Monopsony

W < MRPL

a. A monopsonist pays a wage rate that is less than the marginal revenue product of labor (MRPL).

b. The wage rate it must pay workers varies directly with the number of workers it employs.

c. The type of labor is relatively immobile.

d. The firm's employment is a large portion of the total employment of the type of labor.

e. The difference between the MRPL and the wage rate is referred to as monopsonistic exploitation.

f. Hiring rule where MRP = MFC.

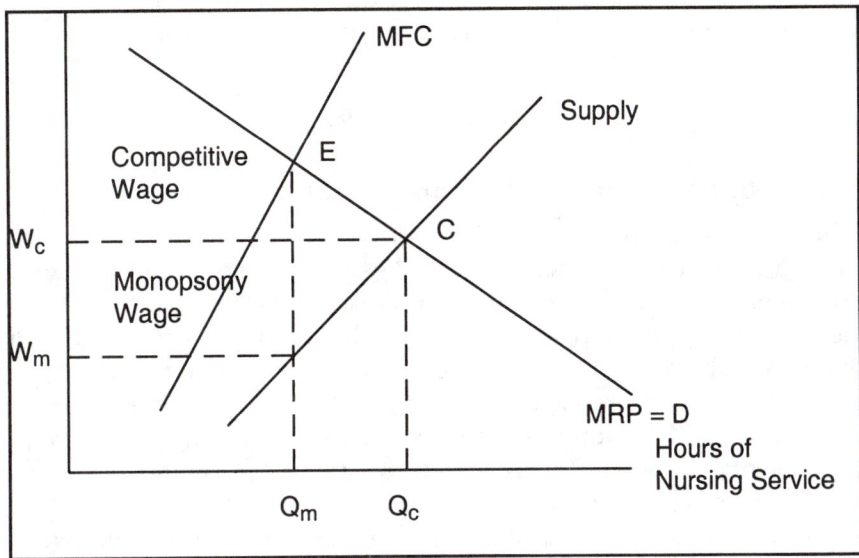

Figure 11.5

Monopsony in the Market for Nurses

A monopsonist, as the single buyer of labor, faces the entire upward-sloping supply curve. A monopsonist will hire workers up to the point where the MFC equals MRP, point E in the graph. As this point, the firm hires quantity Q_m workers and pays only W_m in wages. In a competitive situation, equilibrium would occur at point C, and Q_c workers would be hired at wage W_c.

A monopsony market consists of a single buyer and many sellers—a buyer's monopoly. As the only buyer, the monopsonist faces the market supply curve of labor (Figure 11.5).

For the monopsonist to hire one more worker, it must pay more than it paid for the last worker hired. But if an employer cannot pay more than its other workers, it must raise the wages of all its employees. The marginal factor cost (MFC)—the cost of hiring an additional worker—is equal to the additional employee's wage rate plus the additional wages that must be paid to all other employees. The MFC curve lies above the supply curve—also the average factor cost curve—for the monopsonist.

- A monopsonist will hire workers up to the point where MFC equals marginal revenue product (MRP), point E in the graph. At this point, the firm hires quantity Q_m workers and pays only W_m in wages, the minimum necessary to attract those employees. In a competitive situation, equilibrium would occur at point C, and Q_c workers would be hired at wage W_c.

- The graph shows that monopsonists pay workers less than the value of their MRP. The difference between the MRP and the wage is referred to as monopsonistic exploitation. The degree of exploitation depends in part on the elasticity of supply. In a perfectly competitive market, each employer faces a perfectly elastic supply curve for labor—a horizontal line at the market wage. An employer with monopsony power faces an upward-sloping supply curve, which is less elastic.

In the short run, hospitals have a substantial amount of monopsony power so that if a hospital lowered wages, not all of its employees would leave immediately, which indicates monopsony power. The hospital can pay below the Marginal Revenue Product (MRP).

One factor affecting hospitals' monopsony power is the fact that nurses regard different hospitals as very imperfect substitutes. Each hospital has a different patient mix, location and work rules. Nurses gain benefits from seniority and face search costs to find alternative employment.

In the short run, these factors contribute to the inelasticity of supply for nurses. In the long run, the effect of these factors is not as strong. Also, nurses are now finding greater employment opportunities outside of hospitals, which increases the elasticity of supply.

Labor Unions

Evolution of the Labor Movement in the United States

Let us look at the development of unionism in America.

Over a hundred years ago, President Grover Cleveland signed a bill making Labor Day a national holiday. Ironically, earlier that same year, President Grover Cleveland ordered federal troops to control the Pullman strike. The evolution of labor unions has changed the lives of many Americans. There are both positive and negative implications of labor unions.

The American labor movement started in 1792 when Philadelphia shoemakers organized the first local. The evolution of labor unions thereafter proved to become a bloody battle as businesses fought the inevitable. After 1830, the unions became reform-minded and tried to change the economic and social system instead of bargaining with employers. Many of the craftsmen in the unions were not fully used to the idea of being wage earners. They still thought of themselves as being self-employed. The rise and growth of large industry was a threat to these craftsmen. The leaders or intellectual reformers sought to direct the workers along anticapitalist and antiindustrial lines. The Knights of Labor, which became popular in 1869 and 1886, marked the establishment and then rapid decline of this type of reformism in the American labor movement.

During the Industrial Revolution and the post-Civil War period, the Knights of Labor gave way to the emerging craft unions. This was marked by the American Federation of Labor (AFL) formed in 1886 under Samuel Gompers which became the symbol of the new unionism. The American Federation of Labor unionists accepted the fact that industrial capitalism was going to stay around along with the wage system. The focus of the unions had to be on the improvement of the workers through collective bargaining. From this time on many of the craft unions flourished.

During the great depression that began in 1929, trade unions began to falter. Franklin D. Roosevelt's New Deal (1933) changed their fortunes. The New Deal allowed government to intervene in the economy strengthening the unions and the workers. Part of the New Deal was the development of the National Labor Relations Act of 1935 also known as the Wagner Act. The Wagner Act strengthened the unions' right to organize and bargain.

In the mid 1930s labor was also a key contributor in creating Social Security. Although this step was considered a step towards socialism, it is now widely accepted by both the Republican as well as the Democratic parties. During the "Great Depression," unions pressured the government to instigate unemployment insurance. During the 1930s labor also pushed the idea of minimum wages through the U.S. Congress. In addition, union membership grew from three million in 1933 to more than eight million in 1938. In 1945, membership grew to fourteen million. Union membership as a percentage of the U.S. labor force has been declining over the past decades. The decrease can be attributed to the decline in blue-collar industries, where union organizing has traditionally been strongest; to the increased benefits now enjoyed by nonunion workers.

Today, we are witnessing the evolution of another form of labor organization—the employee associations which are representing members in collective bargaining for the first time. Unlike the craft and industrial unions, the employee association did not originate as a labor organization designed for collective bargaining, but as a professional society or a state civil service employees lobby. Only lately has it taken on the responsibility of employee representation and collective bargaining that lead us to regard it as a labor organization.

Recent activities of professional employees in private, nonprofit institutions such as hospitals and private colleges and universities suggest that they may prefer professional associations to unions, and that they are ready to turn to collective bargaining.

The greatest accomplishment of the labor movement may be considered the application of an eight-hour workday/five days a week. In 1909 it was common to see children working in textile plants. Child labor laws however, abolished those practices.

Unions also pushed workers' compensation laws through congress and state legislatures. Although these laws were often abused, they were able to eliminate two major archaic doctrines: a) assumption of risk by workers when hired, b) contributory negligence by injured workers.

In the 1970s the Occupational Safety and Health Administration was crafted by Congress due to the lobbying by labor. Many have felt this to be an unnecessary intrusion into America's factories while others have seen the benefits due to an increasingly safer workplace.

The operation of the labor market touches most of us directly. Over 75 percent of personal income is derived from labor markets. An employer who treats workers poorly will likely experience higher turnover, especially of its best employees, and lower productivity. Thus, when management acts as if it is free to manipulate its work force, it is more likely to find a movement toward unionization.

Unions are a major force in the United States and are often supported on the basis of equity, because of the argument that workers, in the absence of unions, would not receive a fair wage. The average wage in unionized industries is from 15 to 20 percent higher than the average wage in non-unionized industries. Many people hold strong opinions about unions: they either hate them or love them.

Pre-Civil War

Labor unions and, notably, the craft unions, are similar in many respects to the guilds of the Middle Ages. But there are actually more differences than similarities between the two types of organizations. Unions, as we know them today, are a result of the industrialization of the United States during the early 19th century. The workers of the period were often brutally exploited by the capitalists and were helpless to fight against the sweatshops and child labor practices of the industrial despots. Although these practices have ended in the United States, workers still feel that unions are needed to offset the great power of giant corporations.

The first union in the United States was probably formed in Philadelphia by shoemakers in 1792. In 1794, New York printers formed a Typographical Society. Other early craft unions of carpenters, painters, and mechanics were also formed, but were ineffective during this era. In 1834, a National Trades Union was founded, but was short lived. It wasn't until 1842 that the United States Supreme Court recognized the legal right of workers to join unions.

Perhaps the most important contribution of these early unions was their introduction of political action. During the mid-1800s, American labor experimented with several forms of unionism: Marxism, Utopianism, and reformism, to name a few. These philosophical excursions quickly floundered because of their failure to produce short-term gains for workers.

Post-Civil War

National union movements began in the U.S. after the Civil War, to boom in the 1930s, 1940s, and early 1950s.

Here, we outline a few of the major steps in the evolution of the U.S. organized labor movement. Union activity increased following the Civil War. This period, known as the repression phase in union history, saw a significant increase of industrialization with northern carpetbaggers and the West being opened up by the construction of the railroad. By 1870, there were 32 major craft unions with a total membership of about 200,000. The Knights of Labor, founded in 1869, was a national union set up somewhat along industrial union lines. This organization fought for political, as well as economic, reform. The power of the Knights of Labor declined after the Chicago Haymarket bombing in 1886.

American Federation of Labor

In 1881, several trade unions combined to form the Federation of Organized Trades and Labor Unions of the United States and Canada. The union was never very effective and by 1886, was in decline. In December of 1886, delegates from the union, as well as from the Knights of Labor, met for the purpose of establishing an effective and more enduring trade union than ever known before. They formed the American Federation of Labor (AFL) and elected Samuel Gompers as its first leader. Gompers headed the AFL for more than 30 years and did more to shape the American labor movement than any other person. The AFL's initial membership stood at approximately 316,000 workers grouped in 25 national unions.

The new AFL sought to avoid the mistakes that led to the decline of the Knights of Labor and other early unions. It has been successful, largely, due to three features of the organization and to its philosophy:

1. The AFL represents a form of business—unionism—a labor philosophy that emphasizes the basic issues of pay and working conditions, rather than seeking the overthrow of private property rights or the establishment of socialism.

2. The AFL concentrated on organizing skilled workers, rather than unskilled laborers that could easily be displaced during periods of economic depression, or during strikes. This was based upon the principle of craft unionism and resulted in the AFL serving as an umbrella organization of national craft unions.

3. The AFL disassociated itself from any type of political party or movement. Instead, the AFL set a policy of membership support of candidates, friendly to the labor movement regardless of political affiliation. Gompers believed that excessive political involvement would ultimately lead to internal disruption and weaken the economic goals of the union.

The AFL's most significant accomplishment, in its early history, was the gain of an 8-hour work day. Despite this, however, the union was slow to grow until the beginning of the 20th century. By 1904, it had approximately 1.7 million members, which accounted for 80 percent of all union membership. Although most industries were bitterly opposed to the unions, some, including construction, publishing, glass, ceramics, coal, and railroads, began to accept collective bargaining with unions as normal. Its membership peaked at about 5 million in 1920, but declined to around 3 million in 1930. The Great Depression of the 1930s was a time of economic chaos for most Americans, resulting in tremendous unemployment and a corresponding decline in union membership.

Congress of Industrial Organization (CIO)

One of the causes of the decline of the AFL was its philosophy of not organizing the unskilled workers. With the advent of the assembly line, the numbers of unskilled workers employed in mass production industries increased, which led to a conflict over the question of proper union structure. The move to organize the mass production industries (steel, automobiles, rubber, and electrical equipment) was opposed by craft union advocates, who insisted that the only way to operate the AFL was under their jurisdiction. In 1936, eight industrial unions, under the leadership of John L. Lewis, withdrew from the AFL and formed the Congress of Industrial Organization.

The CIO was very successful during the 1920s, mostly in the unionization of the steel industry. Many other industries were also successfully unionized during this period, and by the end of 1938, membership exceeded 4 million. The success of the CIO proved that craft unionism was not the only method for successful labor organization.

AFL-CIO Merger

After World War II, the political and legislative climate began to turn against the unions. Attempts at unionization of the South, expected to produce millions of new members, were relatively unsuccessful. At the same time, the leadership of the two unions changed. The new leaders had not been directly involved in the bitter dispute that led to the split between the two unions. The distinction between craft and industrial unions became less important, as each had clearly established its place. As a result, the two labor federations signed an agreement to join in December, 1955.

UNIONS AND LEGISLATIONS

Public Policy of the 19th Century

The development of craft unions was a natural response to the industrialization of the United States. Craftsmen often banded together to further their interests in the form of "working-man's societies." Their goal was to obtain increased wages, shorten working hours, establish and maintain a closed shop, and to control the conditions of apprenticeship. These early societies frequently did not last more than a few years. As their objectives either succeeded or failed, which happened more often than not, they disappeared. There were two major factors which directly influenced the longevity of these early unions. First was the cyclical nature of the economy of the early 1800s. The second was the hostility of the early courts toward union activity.

Union membership rose and fell with the economy. During prosperous periods, membership would rise only to decline during periods of economic depression. Workers would often band together to attempt to prevent falling wages during the economic depressions. In response, the employers would hire non-union workers and frequently band together, themselves, to thwart the union effort and break the strike.

Under English common law, societies of workers were considered illegal conspiracies in restraint of trade. Conservative judges contended that union actions employed to obtain their objectives were generally held to be illegal; e.g., in a landmark case decided in Massachusetts in 1842, the court declared that unions were not necessarily illegal in themselves, but restricted the aims unions could pursue and the means they could use to achieve them. Throughout the 1800s, the courts employed both antitrust laws and injunctions to effectively impede the labor movement.

The Sherman Act of 1890 was passed by Congress for the purpose of preventing the growth of business monopolies. The courts, however, interpreted the ambiguous wording of the Act to include labor unions as conspiracies in restraint of trade. In a series of cases from 1908 through the 1920s, the courts used the conspiracy doctrine, the Sherman Act, and injunctions to inhibit the growth of unionism.

Clayton Act

The Clayton Act stated that unions in competing companies could join forces in order to raise wages without violating the antitrust provisions of the Sherman Act.

Norris-LaGuardia Act

During the 1930s, the attitude of the federal government changed from one of indifference to one of encouragement. The Democratic administration believed that strong unions, through collective bargaining, could achieve higher wages and increase total spending, and thus, help relieve the Great Depression. In 1932, the Norris-LaGuardia Act limited the powers of federal courts to issue injunctions in labor disputes and made "yellow-dog" contracts unenforceable in federal courts. A yellow-dog contract was an agreement signed by an employee stating that he would not join a union. It was one of the main weapons used by employers in the 19th century to prevent union organization. The Norris-LaGuardia Act essentially stated that the courts were still responsible for protecting property and preventing the use of violence. As long as the unions remained non-violent, they had the right to strike, picket, and assemble.

Wagner Act

In 1935, the government furthered its support of union growth. The Wagner Act (officially the National Labor Relations Act) guaranteed the rights of self-organization and the right to bargain collectively with employers. The Act established its own enforcement agency, the National Labor Relations Board (NLRB). The three member board was responsible for overseeing enforcement of the Act, arranging for representatives' elections, and hearing complaints on violations of the Act. The Act also listed several "unfair labor practices" on the part of management. Employers could not interfere with the rights of workers to form unions, outlaw unions, or engage in blacklisting or spying. Employers were required to bargain in good faith with any union representing their employees. Under the Wagner Act, unions soon became strong and powerful. Towards the end of World War II, and after a series of strikes which threatened the national welfare, a Republican Congress passed legislation which amended the Wagner Act.

Taft-Hartley Act

The Taft-Hartley Act of 1947, which was passed over President Harry S. Truman's veto, attempted to adjust the government's position toward neutrality in labor relations. Thus, the right of individual workers to join or not join a union was established and supported by law. Additionally, the Act modified the structure and the power of the NLRB to prosecute. It retained a list of unfair employer labor practices, but also placed certain restrictions on unions. The Act prohibited a union from restraining or coercing workers: placing certain limitations on secondary boycotts (action taken by a union against a company doing business with an employer whose workers are on strike), and "featherbedding" (forcing an employer to pay for services not performed). The Act also required unions to bargain collectively with employers, outlawed the closed shop, required a 60-day "cooling-off" period before a strike could be called, and provided for federal intervention in strikes that threatened to create a national emergency.

Landrum-Griffin Act

Passed in the fall of 1950, this Act was the last major piece of legislation defining government policy towards unions. It required reporting and disclosure of certain financial transactions and administrative practices of labor unions, guaranteed free speech and free assembly for union members in connection with union affairs, provided for secret ballots at union elections, and banned former communists and convicted felons from serving as union officers for five years after leaving the party or being released from prison. This legislation was an attempt to protect union members from corrupt leaders.

This Act also amended the Taft-Hartley Act by strengthening its provisions against secondary boycotts, placing limitations on picketing for purposes of gaining recognition as a union, and permitting state agencies and courts to take jurisdiction of cases that the NLRB refused to accept. Under the Act, the Secretary of Labor was given broad powers in investigating violations of the Act.

The most important development in the U.S. labor movement in the 1960s was the sharp growth in public employee unions with the right to strike for better wages and working conditions. The biggest obstacle most public employee unions face is the legal prohibition of such strikes by local, state, and federal law.

Civil Rights Act

The Civil Rights Act of 1964 prohibits discrimination in hiring, promotion, or termination of employment on the basis of race, color, religion, national origin, and sex. While this act does not directly refer to increasing or decreasing the power of organized labor, it does provide protection against discrimination for the workers. The government established the Equal Employment Opportunity Commission (EEOC) to police the provision of the Act.

The following labor laws associated with the labor movement were some of the integral laws that are responsible for making labor unions what they are today:

Table 11.4
Selected Legislation Concerning Labor Unions

Name of Legislation	Year of Adoption	Major Features
Civil Rights Act	1964	Established the Equal Employment Opportunity Commission (EEOC). The Act prohibits discrimination in hiring, promotion, or termination of employment on the basis of the following: race, color, religion, national origin and sex.
Landrum-Griffin Act	1959	This legislation was an attempt to protect union members from their corrupt leaders; it banned former convicted felons from serving as union officers for five years after being released from prison, and required employers to file reports on any payment they make to union officers. Guarantees free speech and free assembly for union members in connection with union affairs.
Taft-Hartley Act	1947	Prohibits a union from restraining or coercing workers. It required unions to bargain with employers; outlawed the closed shop; required a 60-day "cooling-off" period before strike. The act gives the President of the U.S. the power to order a "cooling-off" period during which workers cannot strike. Federal intervention in strikes that threatened a national emergency; example: air traffic controllers, railroad and postal workers.

Wagner Act	1935	Guarantees workers the rights of self-organizing, prohibits management from engaging in unfair labor practices such as discrimination against union members. Employers were required to bargain in good faith with any union representing their workers.
Norris-LaGuardia Act	1932	The Norris-LaGuardia Act limited the powers of federal courts to issue injunctions in labor disputes and made "yellow-dog" contracts unenforceable in Federal courts. The court is responsible for protecting property and preventing the use of violence.
Clayton Act	1914	Exempts labor organizations from antitrust law, unions in competing companies can combine to raise wages.

Types of Labor Unions

a. Trade (craft) union—A union whose membership is made up of individuals who practice the same craft or trade, such as the plumbers' or musicians' unions.

b. Industrial unions—A union such as United Automobile Workers of America (UAW) and United Mine Workers (UMW), whose membership is made up of all workers in the same industry.

c. Public employee union—A union whose membership is made up of local, state, or federal government employees.

d. Employee association—An organization whose members belong to a particular profession and band together to promote that profession, such as the American Bar Association or the American Medical Association (AMA).

Laborers and Wages: Approaches to Increase Wages

Labor unions are collective organizations whose primary goals are to improve the wages and working conditions of their memberships. It was difficult for them to become established in the U.S. At first, many people resented them and considered them a threat to the American free enterprise system. However, they became powerful during the 19th and 20th centuries through strikes, boycotts, or by forcing a closed shop.

Collective Bargaining and Wage Rates

From its earliest days through the 1930s and continuing today, unionism has had two faces. On the one hand, unions can be seen as organizations that attempt to exercise monopoly power in order to raise their members' wages. On the other hand, they can be regarded as the collective voice of workers, bargaining for safety, democracy, and dignity in the work place as well as wages and benefits; and striving to serve the diverse interests of more and less skilled members, older and younger workers, and union leadership, as well as rank and file.

Some labor markets are affected by strong unions. In a purely competitive labor market, there are three major approaches that the union may take to raise the wage rates of its members. First, unions may restrict the supply of labor. This could be accomplished by threatening an employer with a strike. This would create a shortage of labor and effectively raise the wage rate.

The labor union can restrict the supply of labor and charge a wage rate above the competitive equilibrium, thus decreasing the market supply of labor by pressuring employers for shorter work weeks, early retirement, and longer vacation. This effect is illustrated in Figure 11.6. If a union threatens to strike if it does not receive a particular wage rate, then it is effectively limiting the supply of U.S. labor services.

Second, unions might try to raise the wage rate of its members by restricting the number of people who can join the union. Decreasing the supply of labor results in a higher wage rate from 80 dollars to a 100 dollars per day, but a lower level of employment (from 800,000 workers to 700,000 workers).

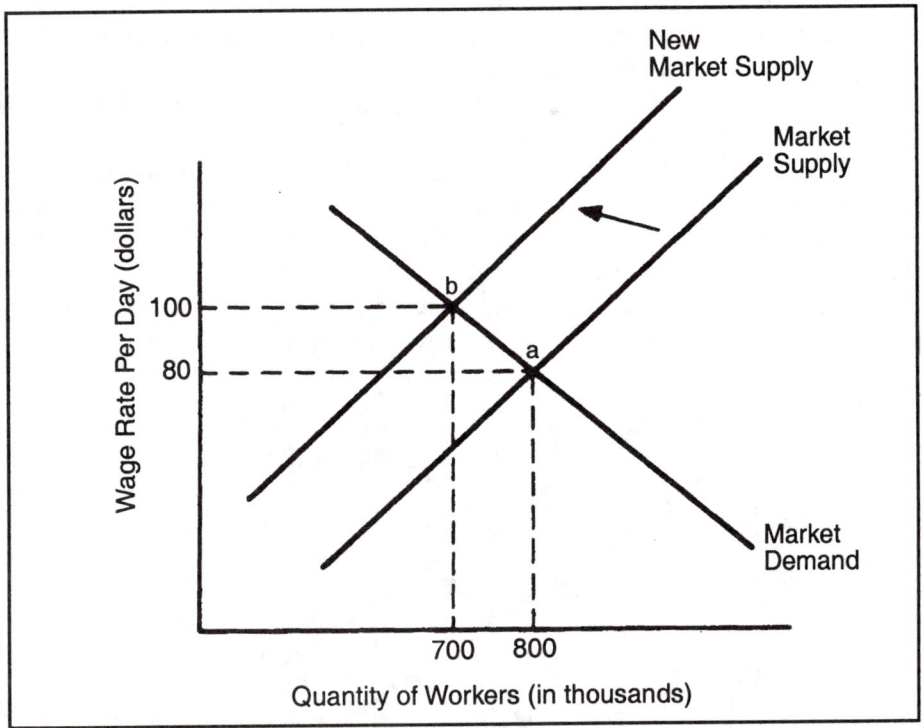

Figure 11.6
Raising Wages by Restricting Supply

Third, industrial unions which organize all available or potential workers, including skilled, unskilled, and even highly skilled labor, may exercise exclusive control of the labor market. The union will be able to place great pressures on the firms to obtain a wage rate above the equilibrium wage rate. Rather than face a strike, the firms will meet the unions' demands for higher wages. Employers, however, will eventually reduce their employment, which constitutes an effective restraint on the unions' demands for higher wages.

EQUILIBRIUM IN A COMPETITIVE LABOR MARKET

In any real-life economy, the smooth functioning of factor supply and demand curves is seldom accomplished in all aspects. Many imperfections exist; laborers may not generally know about jobs in other localities or occupations; there may be discrimination by gender or minority group status; there may be general unemployment in the economy as a whole; the individual laborer faced with the necessity of having a job may be at the mercy of a locally monopsonistic employer, and so on.

Supply and demand conditions in a purely competitive labor market are similar to supply and demand conditions in a purely competitive market. Significantly, the supply of labor is difficult because supplying labor involves two decisions: whether to work or not, and once the decision to work is made, how many hours should be worked. In addition, if they decide to work they may increase their market wage by postponing work and acquiring human capital skills through education.

As we see in Figure 11.7, equilibrium in a competitive labor market will be established at the wage rate that equates the quantity supplied with the quantity demanded. In this example, equilibrium is at point E, where the demand curve crosses the supply curve. The equilibrium wage is 80 dollars per day and the equilibrium employment is 800,000 workers.

The union might try to raise the wage rate of its members by increasing the demand for workers.* The results are that the number of workers increases from 800,000 to 900,000 workers and the wage rate increases from 80 dollars to 100 dollars per day.

The increased demand results in increased wages as employers seek additional labor to fill their production needs. The higher wages will be attractive to workers receiving less, and they will migrate from lower paying jobs to the higher paying jobs. Hence, increasing the demand for labor by increasing the demand for products produced by the union workers, by increasing the productivity of these workers, and by increasing the prices of resources which substitute for the labor provided by the members of the union.

Figure 11.7 shows that an increase in the demand for labor in a purely competitive labor market will result in a higher wage rate and employment level.

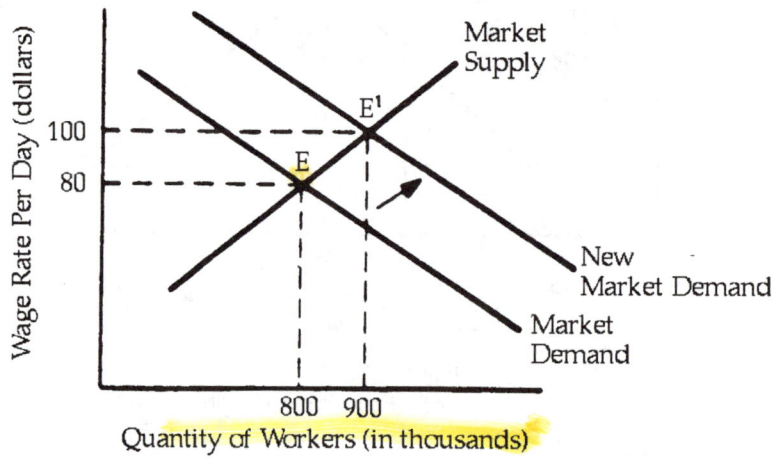

Figure 11.7
Raising Wages by Increasing Demand

Economists offer two views of whether or not unions are successful in raising wages. First, when union and non-union wages are compared, it can be stated that organized workers have probably achieved wage rates 10 to 15 percent higher than would otherwise be the case. It can be concluded from this that unions are subject to the same prevailing market forces which dominate the market place. Higher wages tend to mean fewer jobs, and this inverse relationship places an important restraint on the ability of the union to raise wages.

- Unions prefer to raise wages by increasing the demand for labor.
- Unions may try to increase the demand for their products through a) advertising, b) political lobbying to protect their jobs in various ways, c) forcing retention of obsolete jobs for their members.
- Unions sometimes increase productivity through the following: a) training, b) job security, c) better job morale, etc.

The second view of a union's effect on wages includes the overall wages of both organized and unorganized labor. Here, it seems that the level of real wages has not been influenced significantly by the activities of the unions. While union members may receive higher wages, non-union members receive about 5 percent less. Higher wages in the organized sector of the market will result in some unemployment. The unemployed union member will seek employment in the unorganized sector. The increase in the labor supply in the organized sector will depress real wages in that section. The effect is that of unions achieving higher wages at the expense of the unorganized labor force. The overall effect on wages of the total labor market is insignificant.

Effect of a Single Union on Wage Rates and Employment

Labor unions are aware that actions taken by them to increase wage rates may also increase the unemployment of their members and may, therefore, limit their demands for higher wages; but the unemployment effect of higher wages is lessened by increases in, and a relatively inelastic demand for, labor.

The basic analysis is presented in Figure 11.8. W_1 is the wage that would be obtained if there were no external intervention in the labor market. The union's objective is to raise the wage to W_2. If it succeeds—and everything else remains constant (ceteris paribus)—then, when the wage rate is raised to W_2, business firms will cut employment from E_1 to E_2.

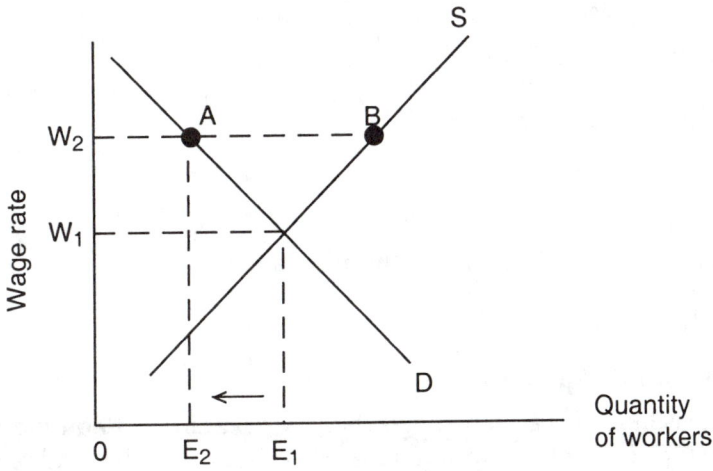

Figure 11.8

Wage Differentials

There are considerable wage differentials that cannot be explained by the usual factors. Most of the unexplained differentials in wages are attributable to natural ability, motivation, and differences in chance.

The general level of wages is dependent upon the role of supply and demand for labor in a specific market situation. Wage differences exist within these markets and require explanation.

Wage differentials arise from several different factors. The qualifications of workers result in higher wages being paid to the workers possessing highly developed skills. An example of this is the difference in skills between a laborer and a violinist. They are not competing in the same labor market and the skill levels are significantly different. There would be fewer violinists in the market than laborers, and therefore, a shortage of marketable skills exists. The wages of highly skilled violinists create a wage differential.

Another example concerns the desirability of a particular job. Some jobs may be more or less desirable than others. Sanitation workers are well paid and perform a necessary service for society, yet their wages are commensurate with highly paid assembly line workers. These wage differentials are called equalizing differences because they must be paid to compensate the non-monetary differences in different jobs.

Other sources of wage differentials arise from imperfection in the market. Geographic immobility of work force results from potential labor that is unwilling to relocate to a new area to seek employment. Labor market institutions (government, unions, and monopolistic employers) also create wage differentials by creating restrictions in membership or qualifications. Finally, wage differentials may result from discrimination against racial, ethnic, or other minorities including women.

In sum, not all labor receives the same wage. Wage differentials exist because of the following: (a) the labor force consists of non-competing groups; (b) jobs vary in difficulty and attractiveness; and (c) laborers are not perfectly mobile because of geographic, institutional, and sociological situations. Some economists have argued that differences in the earnings of workers are to a large extent the result of differences in the amounts invested in human capital.

Summary of Wage Differentials

Wage Differentials exist because of the following:

a. the labor force consists of non-competing groups;

b. jobs vary in difficulty and attractiveness;

c. laborers are not completely mobile;

d. job desirability;

e. qualifications;

f. differences in the amount invested in human capital;

g. discrimination.

German Workers vs. Ethiopians

A worker in Ethiopia is likely to earn much less than a worker in the Republic of Germany. Workers in Germany produce goods that are, as a rule, in much greater demand on the world market than those goods produced by workers in Ethiopia. As a consequence, the demand for labor will be higher in Germany, driving up wages.

German workers are considered more productive, owing largely to superior training, better tools, and better production techniques. Thus, marginal physical product is higher, which raises the marginal revenue product, which should also result in higher wages.

Actions to Decrease Wage Differentials in the U.S.

What actions can the government take to decrease wage differentials?

a. better enforcement of anti-discrimination legislation.

b. more complex coverage of minimum wage legislation.

c. a greater availability of funds for scholarships to students who could otherwise not afford to attend a college or university.

d. better dissemination of information concerning the availability of jobs.

e. incentives to work.

f. investment in human capital.

DETERMINANTS OF INCOME

The important determinants of income include endowments, work intensity, human capital, compensating wage differential, risk taking, discrimination, and age. In addition to these factors, inherited wealth and luck play roles in the determination of income. Listed below you will find a description of each of the determinants of income.

Endowments: The more natural skills or intelligence an individual has or the more natural resources a nation has, the greater is the income, other things being equal.

Work Intensity: Those who work longer hours or put more effort into each hour of work tend to earn higher incomes than others, other things being equal.

Human Capital: The greater the training or education and the higher the marginal product, the higher are rates of pay.

Compensating Wage Differential: Pay rates differ according to the nature of a job. Difficult or hazardous jobs pay higher rates than easy or risk free jobs, other things being equal.

Luck: There is an element of luck in income receipts. Winning the lottery has nothing to do with one's productivity. Entering an occupation at a time when the population's interest in the occupation is increasing can significantly increase income.

Risk Taking: Entrepreneurship involves the willingness to take a risk. Risk and reward sometimes go hand-in-hand.

Age: Income tends to rise as age increases until retirement or near-retirement. Older workers tend to earn more than younger workers.

Inherited Wealth: Some people are born into wealth. Fewer than half of the 400 richest people in the United States built their fortunes on their own.

Discrimination: Limited access to education and training and to certain jobs can limit income.

LEGISLATIONS CONCERNING LABOR

1917—Smith-Hughes Act extended federal, technical and financial aid to local communities for vocational education programs that would be controlled by local school authorities. This helped create industrial educational programs and technical high schools.

1926—Railway Labor Act established that employees shall have the right to organize and bargain collectively through representatives of their own choosing. It also took steps to insure the effectiveness of this right in practice by prohibiting employers from interfering in any way with the organization of its employees and by requiring them to bargain with the unions selected.

1932—Norris-LaGuardia Act placed elaborate restrictions on the use of injunctions in labor disputes with the objective of taking the disputes out of the hands of the Federal courts, for all practical purposes, and leaving them to be settled by the parties themselves.

1933—National Industrial Recovery Act (NIRA) provided for the establishment of industry associations throughout the economy with authority to coordinate company policies on prices, wages, and market shares.

1935—National Labor Relations Act (commonly known as the Wagner Act) entitled workers to bargain collectively over wages, hours and other terms and conditions of work and also led to the rule that each work site would have just one union in order to prevent company-dominated unions from dividing the work force, thus effectively throwing together skilled craftsmen and production workers. It afforded industrial workers and unions a new method or organizing—the secret-ballot election. Also, it established the National Labor Relations Board (NLRB) to enforce and administer the law, to listen to charges of unfair labor practices and to decide on them, and to administer the secret-ballot elections.

1935—Social Security Act provided compensation for those without income from work: unemployment insurance, old-age pensions, aid to families with dependent children, disability and blindness benefits, and general relief. The pension policy encouraged older workers to retire and open jobs to younger people and redistribute income through progressive taxes.

1937—*Fitzgerald Apprenticeship Act* provided for federal support for skilled development programs established through collective bargaining. Apprenticeship regulated the labor supply and helped preserve the crafts' bargaining power and their authority in the plant.

1938—*Fair Labor Standards Act* established terms of minimum wages and maximum hours, to mandate specific agreements. Equal Pay Act governs sex wage discrimination.

1946—*Employment Act* qualified the goal of national policy to "maximum" employment consistent with free enterprise, deleted the full employment budget and plan and substituted an annual Economic Report of the President, and prevented the planning function from being centralized in the Budget Bureau under presidential control by creating a three-person Council of Economic Advisors appointed by the president with Senate concurrence.

1947—*Taft-Hartley Act* extended the area of government regulation from the process of collective bargaining to the terms of the collective bargaining agreement. It provided additional facilities for mediation of labor disputes affecting commerce, and equalized legal responsibilities of labor organizations and employers. It was said to be a way to restore the balance of power between labor and management. It also contained amendments to Wagner Act such as: new regulations in employee elections, damage suits against unions, requirement of financial and constitutional reports from unions and non-Communist affidavits from their officers.

1958—*Welfare and Pension Plans Disclosure Act* which dealt with union administration and mismanagement of union pension funds.

1959—*Landrum-Griffin Act* (also known as the Labor Reform Act) extensively regulated the internal affairs of unions. According to the law, national unions must hold a periodic election at least every five years. The law consisted of a bill of rights for union members to insure certain standards of democracy within unions and guarantee individual due process in his role as a union member.

1961—*Area Redevelopment Act* (ARA) passed. Originally it was sought by Senator Ralph Flanders and the Committee for National Trade Policy, an influential group of liberal businessmen who sought to reinforce labor support for free trade by support for programs to compensate those hurt by broadening competitive pressures.

1962—*Trade Expansion Act* provided for compensation (trade adjustment assistance) for workers who lost their jobs as a result of free trade.

1962—*Manpower Development and Training Act (MDTA)* passed to respond to problems created by dislocations in the economy arising from automation or other technological developments to fill the need for improved planning to assure that men, women and young people would be trained and available to meet shifting employment needs. The Act funded skill and occupational programs for workers already employed or in the labor force.

1964—*Civil Rights Act* passed which gave freedom of an individual for admission into a union on a nondiscriminatory basis. Prohibits discrimination because of race, color, national origin, religion, sex, etc., in any term, condition or privilege of employment.

1976—*Humphrey-Hawkins Full Employment and Balanced Growth Act* combined two bills: the Balanced National Growth and Economic Planning Bill which developed sectorial optional plans, adopted a multiyear focus, and took a broader view than the federal budget; and the Equal Opportunity and Full Employment Bill which sought to make full employment (3% unemployment) a legally enforceable right. The government would be the employer of last resort and prevailing wages would be paid.

1986—*Immigration Reform and Control Act* Employers must verify the employment authorization of all individuals hired after the passage of the Act. Two types of documentation are required: documentation of right to work and documentation of identity. With limited exceptions, I-9 forms must be completed at the time of hire. Cannot discriminate because of national origin or citizenship status.

1988—*Truck and Bus Safety Regulatory Reform Act.* In part provides for pre and periodic post employment, reasonable cause and post-accident testing. Random and certain post-accident drug testing.

1992—*Americans with Disabilities Act.* Federal law prohibiting discrimination against disabled employees or applicants. Passed in 1990, took effect in 1992.

1993—*Family and Medical Leave Act (FMLA).* The FMLA provides up to 12 weeks of unpaid leave for a child's birth, adoption, or foster care arrival. In addition, leaves may be taken to care for spouse, parent, or child with a severe health problem. The FMLA applies to all companies that have (50) or more employees. The firm must provide health benefits while the employee is on leave and must give the returning employee their prior or equivalent job back.

DISCRIMINATION AND IMMIGRATION

Discrimination

The definition of discrimination: when factors unrelated to worker's Marginal Physical Product (MPP) acquire a negative or positive value on the labor market, discrimination exists. Discrimination has always been present in the labor market. There are several forms of economic discrimination. Most experts would agree that the greater incidence of poverty among few segments of society is partly the result of discrimination.

Economic discrimination occurs when female or minority workers, who have the same abilities, education, training and experience as white male workers, are accorded treatment with respect to hiring, promotion, and wage rate.

Wage discrimination occurs when minority workers are paid less than whites for doing the same work. This practice violates Federal law.

Employment discrimination means that unemployment is concentrated among minorities—Hispanics, women and blacks may be the last hired and the first fired.

Human-Capital discrimination occurs when investments in education and training are less than whites.

Racial discrimination—(1993) African Americans' family income inequality is at its highest level since 1967.

Racial Discrimination

According to the Census Bureau data (1993) African Americans' family income inequality was at its highest level since 1967. Since the 1960s, economists tracking black economic status have concluded that there has been little progress made toward achieving economic parity.

In a free enterprise economy, economic forces flow from ownership of human and other resources. That is, lack of ownership means lack of income earning, resources and organized enterprises to create jobs. It is worth noting that any group not owning business and financial capital becomes dependent on others. The aggregate of ownership gaps are tremendous. The gap appears because of segregation and discrimination. Society can close the ownership gaps to equalize the opportunities for ownership. If we do not close the ownership gaps, the racial economic equality will be in the U.S. for a long time. The costs of racial discrimination are difficult to estimate.

Immigration

There has been a great debate on the immigration issues in the U.S. The immigration of workers into the U.S. is a controversial issue because this international movement of labor has economic effects on the American economy.

How does immigration relate to migration? Immigration is simply migration that occurs between countries. That is, people cross national boundaries when they move. More specifically, we talk about immigration as migration into a country and, using a related term, say that "emigration is migration out of a country." These are two sides of the same action. Immigration into one country is nothing more than emigration out of another. Hence, any country that's doing better than its neighbors is likely to see immigrants knocking on the door asking for a slice of the economic pie. Immigrants tend to move from poorer, less developed countries to wealthier, more developed ones.

Concerns and Benefits from Immigrants

Concerns expressed by natives when immigrants hit town:

a. Immigrants will take away jobs from the natives and cause wages to drop.

b. Immigrants are likely to need more public services such as health care and welfare than natives. (If you are a middle class suburban consumer, then your taxes might go up for the public services used by immigrants).

c. Cultural infringement; when immigrants move into a country, they bring with them their own culture, beliefs, and social values. However, if they try to impose their beliefs on natives, then, resentment fills the air.

Immigrants are not all bad; it is a source of growth and prosperity.

a. Labor: a significant amount of growth in the U.S. economy during the 1800s can be traced directly to the immigrants who came from Europe and Asian countries.

b. Most immigrants are willing to work for lower wages, the cost of producing goods also is low, profits high. It is also good for consumers who pay lower prices.

c. Lower wages: Immigrants are willing to do work that natives won't, such as house keeping, migrant farm work, and gardening.

Immigration enthusiasts (among whom I count myself, albeit with some important reservations) like to point out that Americans have never been eager to accept new arrivals, for all our rhetoric about being an "immigrant nation." As Rita Simon of the American University law school noted recently, "We view immigrants with rose colored glasses, turned backward." Perhaps, then, there is nothing much new in the worries so many people express about whether this generation of immigrants will indeed assimilate to American norms. Nevertheless, immigrants in 1994 made up 12 percent of the supplemental security income rolls as compared with only 4 percent in the mid 1980s.

Factors Affecting the Demand for Labor

There are many technical issues that determine how the demand for products is translated through firms into a demand for labor (and other factors of production). Four general principles that affect the firm's demand for labor are:

a. Changes in the demand for a firm's product will be reflected in changes in its demand for labor.

b. The structure of a firm plays an important role in determining its demand for labor.

c. A change in the other factors of production that a firm uses will change its demand for labor.

d. A change in technology will change its demand for labor.

CHAPTER SUMMARY

1. Sellers of goods and services are buyers of the factors of production. As always, in the market economy, equilibrium is reached where the relevant supply and demand curves intersect.

2. The marginal factor cost is the cost of hiring a worker. In pure competition, it equals the wage of the worker. In monopsony, it equals the wage plus the increases to the previously hired workers.

3. The firm should hire where MRP = MFC to maximize profits in both pure competition and in monopsony.

4. The marginal revenue product of labor is the additional product of the worker times the price of the output sold.

5. Average Product of Labor is the quantity of output divided by the quantity of labor employed.

6. Total Product of Labor is the quantity of output that the firm can produce which depends only on the quantity of labor it employs.

7. Marginal Product of Labor is the additional output produced due to the last unit of labor employed.

8. The monopsonist hires fewer workers and pays them less than the purely competitive firm.

9. Unions are monopolistic sellers of labor.

10. The major goal of labor unions is to improve the wages and working conditions of their members. By exercising their strength, unions influence wages, benefits, and other working conditions.

11. Unions engage in collective bargaining in order to improve conditions of employment and to secure a more desirable relationship between union and management.

12. The earliest successful labor organization in this country was the Knights of Labor. The power of this organization declined after the Chicago Haymarket bombing in 1886.

13. The American Federation of Labor (AFL) was founded in 1881, and was led by Samuel Gompers from 1886 until 1924. Now merged with the CIO, the AFL maintains a pre-eminent position among unions today.

14. The Congress of Industrial Organization (CIO) was the first union to organize semi-skilled workers in the mass production industries. After more than two decades of independence, it merged with the AFL in 1955.

15. Throughout most of their early history, unions were generally unpopular, and they did not receive support in the courts until the passage of the Norris-LaGuardia Act of 1932.

16. The Wagner Act provided unions with the opportunity to organize unskilled as well as skilled workers. Given this, the ability to organize and, if necessary, strike, gave industrial unions real clout.

17. The Taft-Hartley Act gives the President of the U.S. the power to order a "cooling-off" period during which workers cannot strike.

18. The Landrum-Griffin Act, passed in 1959, was the last major piece of legislation defining government policy toward unions. This legislation was an attempt to protect union

members from their corrupt leaders. Under the Act, the Secretary of Labor is given broad power in investigating violations of the Act.

19. Types of labor unions are:
    (a) Trade (craft) such as plumbers' and musicians' unions,
    (b) Industrial unions, such as the UAW and United Mine Workers (UMW),
    (c) Public employees unions, and
    (d) Employee associations, such as the American Bar Association and the American Medical Association (AMA).

20. Equilibrium in a purely competitive labor market occurs where the quantity of labor supplied equals the quantity of labor demanded.

21. Reasons for wage differentials between workers include:
    (a) social discrimination,
    (b) differences in demand for different types of workers (qualifications),
    (c) desirability of a particular job, and
    (d) differences of productivity of workers. Government can take several actions to decrease wage differentials.

22. Determinants of income include endowments, work intensity, human capital, compensating wage differential, risk taking, discrimination, and age.

23. In order to increase the demand for union workers, a union may attempt to increase the productivity of union members, increase the demand for union-made products and decrease the competition for non-union made goods.

24. Increasing demand for labor in a competitive labor market results in a higher wage rate and employment level, whereas decreasing the supply of labor results in higher wage rate but a lower level of employment.

25. In labor markets in which labor unions represent workers, the unions attempt to raise wage rates by reducing the supply of labor, or imposing upon employers wage rates in excess of the equilibrium wage rate which would prevail in a purely competitive market. That is, unions can raise their members' wage rate by restricting the supply of labor in a given market through control of union membership, by negotiating for higher wage rates through strikes or threats of strikes, and by increasing the demand for union-made products.

26. Discrimination exists when factors unrelated to worker's marginal physical product acquire a negative or positive value on the labor market.

27. Immigration is simply migration that occurs between countries.

28. The immigration of workers into the U.S. is a controversial issue because this international movement of labor has economic effects on the American economy. Immigrants tend to move from poorer, less developed countries to wealthier, more developed ones.

29. Immigration is not all bad; it is a source of growth and prosperity: most immigrants are willing to work for lower wages; they are willing to do things that natives won't such as housekeeping, farm work and gardening.

30. Concerns expressed by natives when immigrants hit town: immigrants will accept lower wages and are likely to need more public services, then taxes might increase because of the services used by them.

CHAPTER 11
KEY CONCEPTS

American Federation of Labor—Several trade unions combined to form the federation of organized trade and labor unions of the U.S. and Canada.

Civil Rights Act—Prohibits discrimination in hiring, promotion, or termination of employment on the basis of color, religion, national origin, and sex.

Clayton Act—Exempts labor organizations from antitrust law. It made the strike a legal right for workers.

Collective Bargaining—Workers and management negotiate a contract specifying wages and working conditions.

Congress of Industrial Organization (CIO)—The first union to organize semi-skilled workers in the mass production industries.

Discrimination—When factors unrelated to the worker's marginal physical product acquire a negative or positive value on the labor market, discrimination exists.

Employee Association—An organization whose members belong to a certain profession band together to promote that profession.

Equilibrium in a Competitive Labor Market—Established a wage rate that equates the quantity supplied with the quantity demanded.

Fair Labor Standard Act—Sets standards for minimum wages, maximum work hours, and child labor practices.

Immigration—Migration that occurs between countries.

Industrial Union—A union which includes all workers in an industry.

Landrum-Griffin Act—Major piece of legislation defining government policy toward unions; an attempt to protect union members from their corrupt leaders.

Marginal Factor Cost—The increase in total costs incurred when a firm hires an additional worker.

Marginal Product of Labor—The additional output produced due to the last unit of labor employed.

Marginal Revenue Product—The marginal product of a worker multiplied by the price of the output sold.

Monopsony—There is only one firm which is the major buyer of labor in a market.

Norris-LaGuardia Act—Limited the powers of federal courts to issue injunctions in labor disputes.

Public Employee Union—A union whose membership is made up of local, state, or federal government employees.

Taft-Hartley Act—The Act modified the structure and the power of the NLRB to prosecute. The Act required unions to bargain collectively with employers. (Required a 60-day "cooling-off" period before a strike could be called, and provided for federal intervention in strikes.)

Total Product of Labor—The quantity of output that the firm can produce depends only on the quantity of labor it employs.

Trade Union—A union whose membership is made up of individuals who practice the same craft or trade.

Wagner Act—Guaranteed the rights of self-organization and the right to bargain collectively with employers.

Wage Differentials—Wage differentials exist among workers, with some workers earning higher wages than others.

Work Intensity—Those who work longer hours or put more effort into each hour of work.

DISCUSSION QUESTIONS

1. Explain how a purely competitive firm decides how many workers to hire.
2. Explain the hiring rule of MRP = MFC.
3. Explain how a monopsony decides how many workers to hire.
4. What are the major provisions of the following legislation?
   a. Norris-LaGuardia
   b. Wagner Act
   c. Taft-Hartley
   d. Landrum-Griffin
5. Distinguish the 4 types of labor unions.
6. Discuss how collective bargaining and unions impact on wages.
7. Explain why wage differentials exist. How does the government try to reduce wage differentials?
8. What are the determinants of income?
9. Are unions too powerful?
10. Air traffic controllers lost their jobs in the early 1980s. Former President Ronald Reagan fired air traffic controllers because they had violated the Taft-Hartley Act. Why? or Why not?
11. What is the difference between immigration and immigrants.
12. Explain why natives express their concerns when immigrants hit town.
13. Do you agree that immigration is not all bad, it is a source of growth and prosperity?
14. How do unions increase wages?
15. Beauty plays a role in the career of people in ordinary jobs. Do you agree? Why or why not?

11.1 LEARNING PRACTICE AND SOLUTIONS

An approach to expand employment and higher wage. Unions may try to increase the demand for their products through advertising, political lobbying to protect their jobs, forcing retention of obsolete jobs for their members, increase productivity through training, more job security and better job morale.

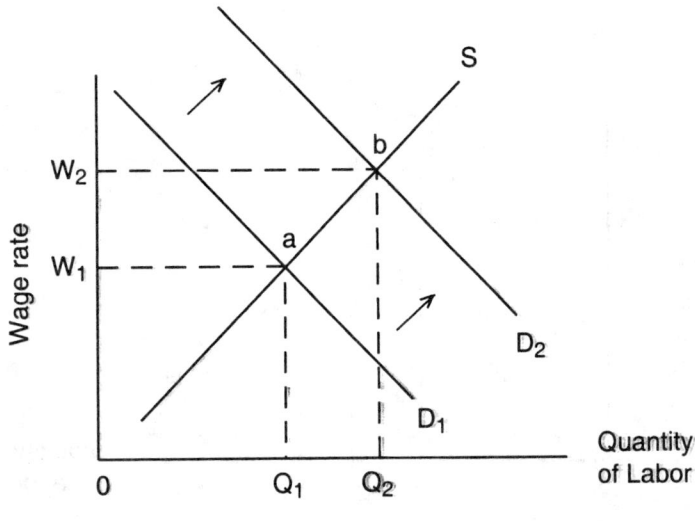

Figure 11.9

Given the equilibrium condition in a purely competitive labor market, a union may try to raise the wage rates of its members by raising the demand for labor. That is, an increase in the demand for labor union from D_1 to D_2 can result in expanded employment opportunities (from Q_1 to Q_2) and higher wages from union members (W_1 to W_2).11.2

11.2 LEARNING PRACTICE

Use Table 11.5 to answer the following questions:
   a. Determine the value of marginal product of labor for each worker a firm could possibly employ.
   b. What does the value of the marginal product of any worker tell us?
   c. Graph the marginal revenue product of labor (MRPL) for these workers. Does the curve slope downward or upward? Why?

Table 11.5

Number of Workers	Marginal Physical Product of Each Worker (per hour)	Price Per Unit of Output	Marginal Revenue Product of Labor (MRPL)
1	7	$1.50	—
2	6	$1.50	—
3	5	$1.50	—
4	4	$1.50	—
5	3	$1.50	—

11.3 LEARNING PRACTICE AND SOLUTIONS

How may the Competitive Labor Market restrict the Supply of Labor to raise wages? This is an approach that a union may take to raise the wage rates of its members.

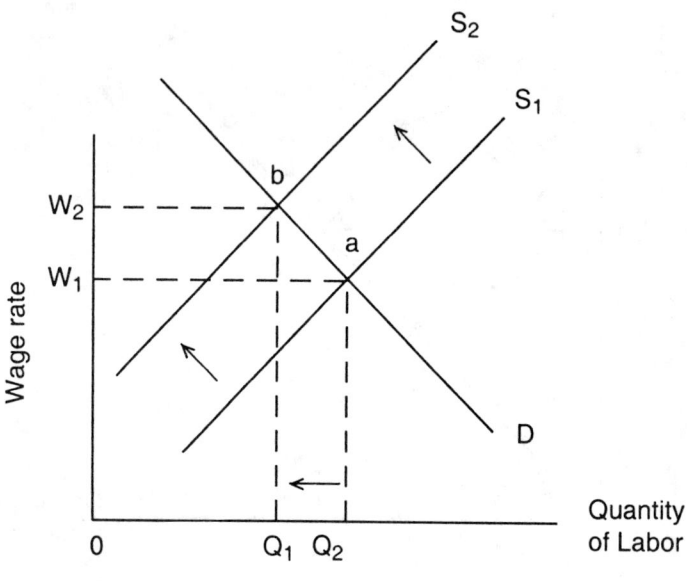

Figure 11.10

Using Figure 11.10, a union's control over the allocation of jobs to its membership effectively gives the union the power to restrict the supply of labor and raises the wage rates of union members (W_1 to W_2). The power of unions to negotiate above competitive wage rate (at W_2) is a power to reduce the employment level (Q_2 to Q_1). Hence, an important restriction on the wage rate that is negotiated is the incentive unions have to maintain employment for their members and dues coming from their members.

11.3 LEARNING PRACTICE
PURELY COMPETITIVE LABOR MARKET

No. of Workers	Total Product of labor	Average Product of labor	Marginal Physical Product of labor	Price unit	MRPL
1	6			$2.00	
2	11			$200	
3	15			$2.00	
4	18			$2.00	
5	20			$2.00	

a. Fill in the missing information.

b. Assume the hourly wage per worker is $5.15. How many workers should the firm hire?

c. What is the hiring rule in a purely competitive labor market?

d. Construct marginal revenue product of labor (MRPL) based on the above data.

e. Explain the meaning of marginal revenue of labor.

Hint: In order to decide how many workers to hire, the firm needs only to compare what the workers add to the revenue.

Chapter 12

Regulation and Antitrust Policy

LEARNING OBJECTIVES

After you have studied this chapter in the text, and attended class lectures regularly, you will be able to:

1. Briefly describe the regulatory process: the government's role in terms of competition and market regulation.
2. Explain the purpose of antitrust policy.
3. Trace the history of the major legislation prohibiting the restriction of competition.
4. Provide and recognize examples of major regulatory bodies.
5. Identify and discuss the basic antitrust laws.
6. Understand the following legislation: Sherman Act, Clayton Act, Robinson-Patman Act, and Federal Trade Commission Act.
7. List and recognize the exemptions from antitrust laws.
8. Discuss health and safety regulations.
9. Understand the significance of regulation and antitrust policy in terms of specific business practices and market monopolization.
10. Understand a fair-rate-of-return pricing concept.
11. Discuss the effectiveness of the antitrust laws.
12. Understand the consequences of bringing professions under antitrust laws.

INTRODUCTION

We are all aware that the capitalistic system rests upon the free market concept. But how freely do our markets really operate? Regulation, rules, and "red tape" are a fact of life in the everyday business world. From the merger of multi-national corporations to the diameter of a ladder rung used in a factory, it is probably safe to say that all business activities are regulated to some extent. As society became more complex through industrialization, regulatory agencies were created to recognize and resolve the problems of a changing nation. In this chapter, we will discuss government regulations which have a profound impact on private industry and the public.

Regulation is carried out by Local, State, and Federal government. Regulation often used to regulate the rate of natural monopolies, usually based on fair-rate-of return pricing concepts. The regulatory pricing formula is that price should equal ATC plus a fair-rate-of return. Also, regulation often takes the form of minimum quality standards. That is, preventing goods and services below a prescribed minimum quality from reaching the market.

Throughout U.S. history, governmental agencies have been created when the public realized abuse had occurred in an industry. These agencies include the Civil Aeronautics Board (CAB), which governed the economic regulation of the airline industry. The CAB was "directed to do everything in its power to further the progress of commercial aviation." In the late 1960s the CAB allowed airlines to keep air fares high and increase their number of flights to certain cities. At the same time airlines began flying larger planes with a greater passenger capacity. This resulted in flights which were less than half full. The airlines appealed to the CAB for fare increases. Laws enacted in the 1970s deregulated the airline industry and eliminated the spiraling cost of airline tickets.

Airlines were not the only public transportation industry regulated by the U.S. government. The railroads were regulated to be protected from other modes of transportation. Governmental agencies have also been created to monitor the health and safety of our environment and work force.

THE REGULATORY PROCESS

Administrative and regulatory agencies are created by Congress for a number of reasons. First, it may be possible for Congress to provide adequate detail when passing legislation. Second, Congress may create expert agencies to develop laws and policies reflecting sound judgment and knowledge. An example of an expert agency is the Nuclear Regulatory Commission. Finally, and perhaps most important, Congress will form regulatory agencies to protect the public. The failure of private business to be self-regulating can result in consequences contrary to the public interest.

Regulatory agencies are unique in that they possess powers of all three branches of government. Problems facing the regulatory agencies revolve around their work force, extreme costs, and contrived procedures. Personnel problems stem from the hierarchical structure of the agencies and the type of employees they attract. Pay is relatively low at high levels, when compared with similar positions in private business. This makes it difficult to attract and retain the best people. At lower levels, employees have civil service protection, making it difficult to fire them for substandard performance. They may feel their jobs are secure, regardless of their performance level. Because a level of expertise is necessary in many agencies, key personnel are often recruited from the industry being regulated. As a result, conflicts of interest are often prevalent in the regulatory agencies. Often the interests of the industry are promoted rather than the interests of the public.

Regulation is extremely costly and is often cited as a prime source of inflation. The public absorbs the costs of regulation as taxpayers and as consumers. Laws which decrease competition also pass on costs to consumers, indirectly, because decreased competition allows for higher prices than would prevail in an openly competitive market. A primary cause of the high cost of regulation is the processing of all paper work required by the agency. The red tape involved in dealing with these agencies, as well as the backlog of cases, causes delays in decision-making. Cases may pend for years, by which time the dispute may no longer be an issue. Recent calls for regulatory reforms were promoted by the cost and procedural problems of the agencies.

Analysis of Regulation

Regulations are widespread and affect all Americans as producers or consumers. Industries such as the railroad are regulated in virtually all of their activities. Other firms however are subject to product safety requirements but few of the other regulations. Regulations are imposed by both the state and federal authorities.

Why do we need regulations? One reason is to regulate natural monopolies, that is, natural monopolies have the ability to present all of the opportunities for abuse of monopoly position if there were no regulations. Without regulations, natural monopolies could potentially decrease their supply while increasing their price substantially. Excessive competition may be another reason for regulations. Institutions such as banks must be protected from failure due to their impact on the community. There is a fine line between the usefulness of regulations and their use to cloak industry protection in the guise of public protection. Regulations also reduce transaction costs by trying to ensure the assumption that buyers are continuously observing all other buyers and sellers and that they find the right combination of price and quality with little or no effort. It also allows the allocation of scarce resources and allocation of power and wealth without exclusive reliance on market mechanisms.

How do regulations negatively impact businesses? Regulations can become very costly. It has been proposed many times that regulatory schemes should undergo a regular cost-benefit analysis. Many conservatives would argue that regulations diminish freedom and make the economy less efficient. Regulations also suppress competition by restricting entry or setting a mandatory floor under prices. Regulations kept air fares up, supporting above market salaries for large numbers of airline personnel. Due to many of these complaints, ever since the mid 1970s the trend has been towards deregulation.

What would happen if all governmental regulations were abolished? Individual firms could operate in a more efficient manner, because most health and safety regulations are costly. Regulation causes costs to increase, supply to decrease, and prices to increase. Regulation creates scarcity. If industries were deregulated, costs would decrease, supply would increase, and prices would decrease.

Rationale for Regulation

Proponents of these policies usually base their support on limiting the likelihood of injury to the public. For example:

a. Federal officials require cars to have seat belts to save lives.

b. Local building codes require plumbers to obtain licenses so that homeowners aren't cheated by incompetents.

c. The FDA requires extensive testing so that drugs with harmful side effects aren't used.

d. Rent Control (rent below the market rate to create lower affordable rents).

e. Airlines have been subject to safety regulations, a form of social regulation, since their inception, and this form of regulation has been essentially unaffected by economic deregulation.

f. The original philosophy of public utility regulation was to grant a monopoly where necessary to achieve the advantages of large-scale production but to prevent the monopolist from restricting output and raising prices.

Rent Control in a Large City: Is This a Good Idea?

Rent controls are a good illustration of price ceilings. Students, as citizens, should be aware of long-term consequences of rent controls, whose short-run appeal is so strong.

Because of the introduction of a price ceiling below equilibrium, a shortage of houses at the legislated rent has resulted. Now, more people can afford houses; the quantity supplied should be reduced at the lower rent. As a result, some builders will build structures other than houses, and fewer houses will be rented.

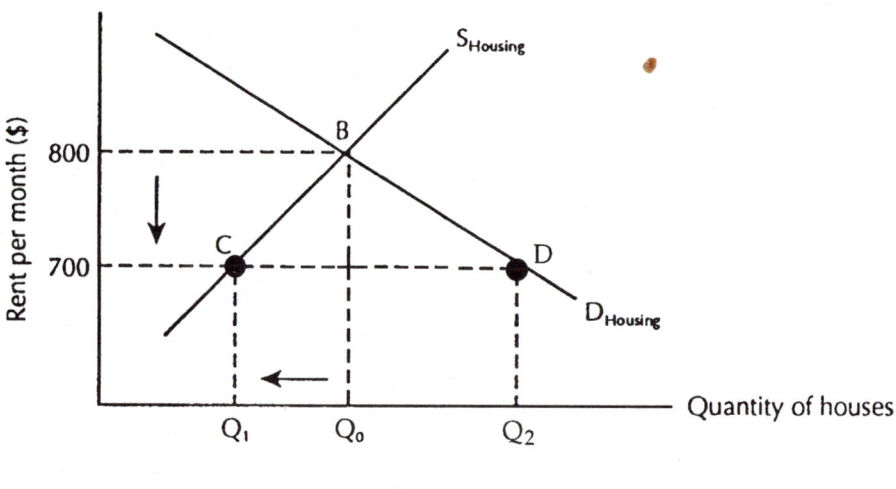

Figure 12.1

Price Controls: Agricultural Price Support

An agriculture price support is a minimum price government determines farmers will receive for their product. Thus not all agricultural products have price supports.

In Figure 12.2, at a price of $7 per bushel (as compared to the $5 per bushel equilibrium price), consumers of wheat pay higher prices. A surplus of wheat results, fewer bushels of wheat are bought by private citizens, and government buys and stores the surplus of wheat (which taxpayers pay for).

The effects of agricultural prices supports are (a) a surplus, (b) fewer exchanges (less wheat bought by private citizens), (c) higher prices paid by consumers of wheat, and (d) government purchase and storage of the surplus wheat (for which taxpayers end up paying).

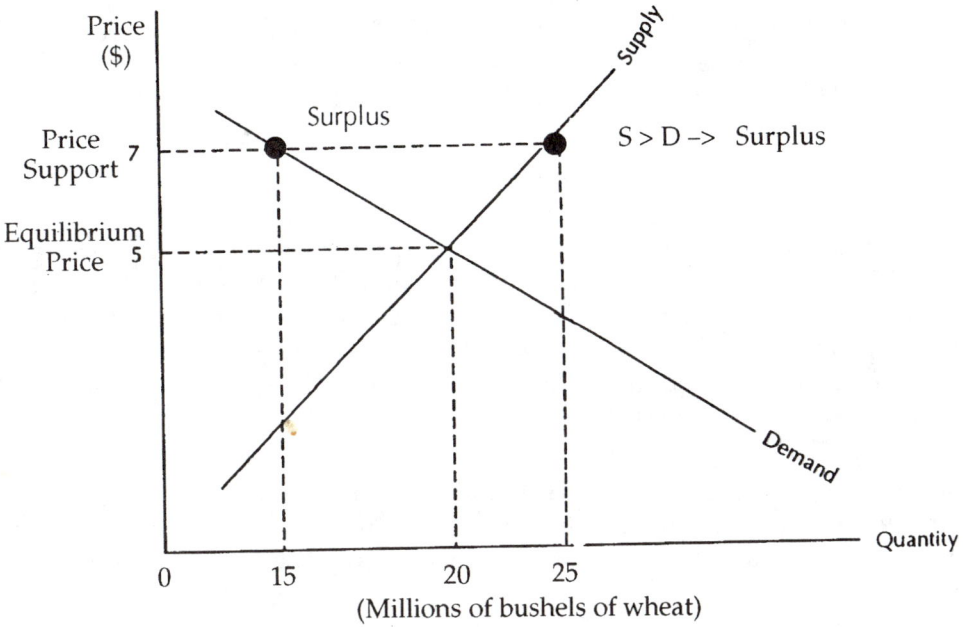

Figure 12.2

If the government imposes a price floor on whole milk and buys the resulting samples, can it later sell what it has bought and recoup its expenditure? What else can the government do with the milk surplus?

The government will have a difficult time recouping its expenditure by selling the milk it purchased. This is because the sale of the milk will result in an increase in the supply of milk on the market and will force the price down. The government will necessarily have to buy it at one price and sell it at another. By forcing the price down in order to rid itself of its own surplus, the government will be reducing the price received by farmers. The government has three options. First, it can give milk away to those people who would not have otherwise been in the milk market. Second, it can store the milk. Third, it can destroy the milk. At various times the government has used all three policy options.

However, proponents of price controls make the following arguments: (a) Government control of prices is necessary to prevent erosion of citizens' purchasing power—especially among people living on fixed incomes. (b) Price increases have little effect on the quantity of goods produced. Therefore, government should control prices to prevent firms from earning windfall profits. (c) Large corporations control the market, not vice versa. Therefore, government intervention is necessary to check their power. (d) When price controls are imposed on monopolistic firms, they can actually expand production.

Opponents of price controls make the following major arguments: (a) Competition lends sufficient control to the market; government intrusion is unnecessary. (b) Government control is an affront to individual freedom.

Minimum Wage Controversy

The minimum wage contains the following criticisms:

    a. The minimum wage forces employers to pay a higher than equilibrium wage.

    b. Most minimum wage workers are teens from affluent families who do not need protection from poverty.

The case for the minimum wage argues that incomes rise when minimum wages are raised; increasing minimum wage may increase productivity. Hence, workers will be more productive if they have more motivation, and higher wages could also improve their health. Significantly, minimum wage laws increase wages with minimum effects on employment. Studies suggest that an increase of 10 percent in minimum wage might cause 1 to 3 percent in unemployment.

DEREGULATION

The original purpose of government regulation was to prevent monopoly and to foster competition. However, regulation has resulted in restricting competition rather than promoting it. The trucking and airline industries are examples of industries which were regulated in such a way as to prevent competition. The dissatisfaction with the results of regulation has let to widespread deregulation in recent years. The Airline Deregulation Act of 1978 allowed the airlines to select their routes and to set prices for the first time in four decades. Let us consider the following effects of deregulation.

- Deregulation introduced competitive pricing into the industry, which generally has led to lower prices. That is, the primary economic motivation for deregulation in telecommunications, air travel and interstate trucking is that deregulation will drive prices in the market down.

- Regulated industries opposed deregulation because regulation protects them from new entrants and competition.

- The increased competition following deregulation has forced airlines to be very cost conscious and to pay no more for salaries than is necessary to recruit the right numbers of qualified people.

- Profits of the older firms in airlines and trucking fell sharply and in many cases turned into losses. On the other hand, new entrants often had substantial cost advantages over the older firm, i.e., the entrants often entered the industry using non-union labor and paying lower wages.

- Many union members were forced to take pay cuts. Others lost their jobs due to cost cutting reorganization by the firms. Deregulation has badly hurt unions such as the Teamsters and the Airline Pilots' Association.

- The basic argument for deregulation is that deregulation will result in more efficient operation and lower consumer prices. One argument against deregulation is that after deregulation markets that are not very profitable may not be served at all.

- Economic deregulation during the 1980s was part of a more general increase in reliance on the marketplace and a reduction in reliance on government. The 1980s witnessed considerable privatization of activities that previously were provided by governments, especially at the state and local level.

- Deregulations have caused temporary instability within some industries such as the airline industry. Deregulations have also caused the transportation services to become less predictable and have caused the collapse of the savings and loan industry, thus weakening the banking sector. Deregulation has pushed average prices down, forced improvements in efficiency, and promoted innovation in the affected industries.

Arguments for deregulation include:
1. Deregulation is less costly to the public which has absorbed the high cost of regulation, both in taxes and as consumers who wind up paying higher prices for the products of regulated industries.

2. Deregulation allows industries to set their own prices which leads to competitive pricing, which in turn leads to lower prices to the consumer.

3. Deregulation opens the market to new industry and new competition which could have the effect of causing older firms to reevaluate themselves, their product and their prices.

4. Under deregulation new firms could enter the industry at a much lower cost due to use of non-union workers, thus paying lower wages.

Arguments against deregulation include:

1. Without some form of government regulation, industry is left to regulate themselves. If industry is unwilling or fails in this, the public suffers.

2. Deregulation has caused some long-standing airline and trucking firms to incur heavy losses.

3. Deregulation has badly hurt some unions because many union members were forced to take pay cuts, while others lost their jobs because of cost cutting reorganization of firms.

ANTITRUST PHILOSOPHY

We are all aware that the capitalistic system rests on the free market concept. But how freely do our markets really operate? Regulation, rules, and "red tape" are a fact of life in the everyday business world. From the merger of multi-national corporations to the diameter of a ladder rung used in a factory, it is probably safe to say that all business activities are regulated to some extent. As society became more complex through industrialization, regulatory agencies were created to recognize and resolve the problems of a changing nation.

Antitrust is the American name for laws, agencies, and actions to protect and promote competition. Antitrust laws were first developed in the late 1800s to put an end to the growing abuse of the trust. A trust is a group of firms that act as a monopoly to restrict output and raise prices. A group of businesses in the same industry would use a trust to eliminate competition by setting prices and production levels and dividing the market. Although technically the businesses were distinct, they were controlled by a group of shareholders. Antitrust laws are discussed in detail.

Trusts, mergers, and monopolies are attractive to companies because they result in excess profit. The element of competition is eliminated, allowing firms to charge higher prices than they could in a competitive market. A merger can decrease competition by uniting two firms engaged in the same line of business, known as a horizontal merger. A recent example of a horizontal merger is that between Chrysler and American Motors. Antitrust laws are applicable to this type of merger, as they tend to lessen competition in the industry. Vertical mergers join two firms, one of which supplies a component of the other's product, i.e., if General Motors were to acquire Firestone Tire. This last type of merger is least likely to be opposed by the government because the firms are not in direct competition.

There are many reasons companies undertake mergers. Mergers are a low cost way to grow because they achieve technical economies of scale. An entry into a new market is usually easier by merger than by starting fresh because firms can avoid the mistakes and costs of a newcomer to an industry. Through mergers, managers gain corporate power and the firm raises its market power or even gains monopoly control. Mergers are also used as defensive strategies. Companies may use them to avoid being acquired by another firm or to avoid compliance with government regulations pertaining to new production facilities. Mergers can be used as a way to arrange a sale brought about by special circumstances, such as the death or retirement of high-ranking officials in the firm, or changes in the tax laws. Finally, a merger can allow a company to take advantage of an offer too good to pass up.

There is a fine line between competitive efforts at monopolizing and collusive efforts at monopolizing. After all, isn't it the goal of most businesses to be at the top of their industry in sales and to produce the maximum profit possible? Aren't efforts at product differentiation, cost cutting, and research and development aimed at monopolization? All businesses try to differentiate their product so that, in the eyes of the consumers, there are no close substitutes. In addition, all contracts providing for purchase arrangements, are, technically, in restraint of trade! Yet, these contracts are a necessary element in everyday business transactions.

Collusion among firms to fix prices, supply, and market is detrimental to consumer welfare and generally elicits an antitrust response from consumers and the government. Excess profit earned by a firm is a sign of the inefficient allocation of resources; that is, consumers pay more for a smaller amount of a product than they would have in a competitive environment. Antitrust attempts to distinguish between profit-making through the creation of efficient markets and profit-making through manipulation of output and prices to the detriment of consumers.

Basic Antitrust Laws

To combat the rampant abuse of power by the trusts in the late 1800s, the states first started to enact antitrust laws. These proved to be largely ineffective, and were rarely enforced because the states lacked the resources and incentives to prosecute companies who provided many jobs and tax dollars to their states. In addition, trusts were really a national problem, beyond the scope of state legislation.

The federal government's first action in the antitrust arena was the enactment of the Interstate Commerce Act (ICA), in 1887, to control the railroads where the first trust problems arose.

Sherman Act

Congress created the Sherman Act, which is considered the foundation for all antitrust legislation. The Sherman Act of 1890 prohibits any "contract, combination, or conspiracy in restraint of trade" and any "monopolization, or conspiracy or combination to monopolize." The courts do not interpret the Sherman Act as prohibiting every restraint of trade, but only unreasonable restraint of trade. Two individuals who would like to engage in a partnership may in some sense restrain trade, but not unreasonably and therefore not unlawful. However, arrangements among competitors to fix prices, divide markets, and engage in boycotts directly aimed at excluding or limiting competition can be viewed as an illegal act.

Section One states:

> **Every contract, combination in the form of trust or otherwise, or conspiracy, in restraint of trade or commerce among the several States, or with foreign nations, is declared to be illegal . . .**

Section Two of the Act provides that:

> **Every person who shall monopolize, or attempt to monopolize, or combine, or conspire with any other person or persons, to monopolize any part of the trade or commerce among the several States, or with foreign nations, shall be deemed guilty of a felony . . .**

This section is directed at monopolies and the intentional attempt to acquire monopoly power over a market. Initially, the Sherman Act was ineffective due to the vagueness of the language, the abundance of possible cases, and the lack of additional funding for investigations by the Justice Department. As a result, trusts continued to form and profit until President Theodore Roosevelt's Administration at the turn of the century. Growing public concern prompted Roosevelt's "trust-buster" era. Some of the landmark trusts defeated by the Sherman Act included: the Northern Securities trust and the Standard Oil trust. During the Standard Oil case, the rule of reason was developed to further define violations of the Act. It held that violations must constitute undue or unreasonable restraints of trade or monopolization attempts.

There are four separate penalties which can apply to the violations of the Sherman Act. A crime under the Sherman Act is now a felony, punishable by fine or imprisonment. The courts are empowered to issue injunctions to prevent continued violations of the Act, or they can even force a divestiture in a monopoly situation. Injured parties are allowed to seek damages of up to three times their actual loss by initiating a civil suit. Finally, property acquired through violation of the Act, which is subsequently transported across state lines, is subject to forfeiture. Enforcement of the Sherman Act, as well as investigation of possible violations, is the responsibility of the Antitrust Division of the U.S. Department of Justice.

Section 3:

This section states that *"every contract, combination in form of trust or otherwise, or conspiracy, in restraint of trade or commerce in any Territory of the United States or of the District of Columbia, or in restraint of trade or commerce between any such Territory and another, or between any such Territory or Territories and any State or States or the District of Columbia, or with foreign nations, or between the District of Columbia and any State or States or foreign nations, is declared illegal."*

Section 4:

Gives district courts in the United States jurisdiction to prevent and restrain violations of the Sherman Act. It also gives the court the right to restraining orders as necessary.

Section 5:

This gives the courts the right to summon and subpoena parties before the court even if they do not reside in the district in which the court is held.

Section 6:

Any parties involved in allegations of violations under the Sherman Act who try to move from state to state or to a foreign nation may be subjected to the court forfeiting their property to the United States.

Section 7:

This section describes the term "person" or "persons" throughout the act. These terms include corporations and associations existing under U.S. or foreign laws.

Clayton Act

The Clayton Act of 1914 is a supplement to the Sherman Act. It prohibits certain practices that were not included in the Sherman Act. Some of the violations are: mergers and acquisitions involving actual or potential competitors, or buyers or sellers if their effect is to lessen competition or create a monopoly in a given industry. Also, sale terms that force buyers to deal with a competitor of the seller, where such restrictions may substantially lessen competition or may create a monopoly in the given industry.

Section 1:

Defines the term "Antitrust laws" as "an Act to protect trade and commerce against unlawful restraints and monopolies" approved on July 2, 1890. It also defines the term "Commerce" as trade or commerce amount the several states have with foreign nations, or between the District of Columbia or any Territory of the United States or the District of Columbia or any foreign nation. However, no part of this act pertains to the Philippine Islands. The term "person" or "persons" is defined identically to the Sherman Act—Section 7.

Section 2:

Section 2 was added due to the Robinson-Patman Act amendments to the Clayton Act. Under Section 2, it is unlawful to discriminate in price between different purchasers of commodities of like grade and quality where the effect of the discrimination may substantially lessen competition or tend to create a monopoly in any line of commerce, or to injure, destroy, or prevent competition with any person who either grants or knowingly receives the benefit of such discrimination.

In any hearing under this section the burden of proof lies on the person charged with the violation of this section. The seller must prove that his lower price or service was made in good faith to meet an equally low price of a competitor, or the services furnished by a competitor.

It is unlawful for a person engaged in commerce, to pay or grant, or to receive anything of value as a compensation except for services rendered in connection with the sale or purchase of goods, wares, or merchandise.

Section 3:

This section states that "it is unlawful for any person to engage in commerce, to lease or make a sale or contract for the sale of commodities whether patented or unpatented, for use, or consumption, or resale within the United States or fix a price charged, or discount from, or rebate upon a price of a competitor where the effect of such a contract or agreement may be to substantially lessen competition or tend to create a monopoly in any line of commerce."

Section 4:

Any person who is injured in his business or property by reason of anything forbidden in the antitrust laws may sue and recover threefold the damages he sustained and the cost of the suit, including a reasonable fee of an attorney.

Section 6:

This section states that the labor of a human being is not a commodity or article of commerce. Nothing that is contained in the antitrust laws can be construed to forbid the existence and operation of labor, agricultural, or horticultural organizations.

Section 7:

This section states that "no person engaged in commerce or in any activity affecting commerce can acquire, directly or indirectly, any part of the stock or other share capital or any assets of another person engaged also in commerce or in any activity affecting commerce that may result in substantially lessening competition or would tend to create a monopoly."

Section 8:

This section sets the boundaries of an individual serving as a director or officer in any corporation that is engaged in whole or in part in commerce and by virtue of their business and location of operation are competitors to avoid violation of the antitrust law due to the possibility of eliminating competition by agreement between the corporations.

Section 11:

> This section depicts the procedures and authorities involved in enforcing compliance with sections 2, 3, 7 and 8.

Section 12:

> This section states that any suit, or proceeding under the antitrust laws against a corporation may be brought not only in the judicial district where it is located but also in any district where the corporation does business.

Section 13:

> This section specifies the guideline for witnesses and subpoenas in judicial districts.

Section 14:

> This section describes the punishment enacted on individual directors, officers, or agents of a corporation who have authorized, ordered, or done any acts constituting a violation of the antitrust laws.

Section 15:

> Gives district courts in the United States jurisdiction to prevent and restrain violations of the Clayton Act. It also gives the court the right to restraining orders as necessary.

Section 16:

> This section gives any person, firm, corporation, or association the right to sue for and have injunctive relief, in any court against threatened loss or damage by violation of the antitrust laws.

The Robinson-Patman Act

The Robinson-Patman Act of 1936 is an amendment of the Clayton Act. It prohibits certain discriminatory prices, services, and allowances in dealing between merchants. Given the circumstance, the Act prohibits a seller from granting lower prices to favored buyers. If, however, the discounts are made to meet competitors' lower prices, the discount is not considered illegal. The plaintiff must prove that the discrimination may substantially lessen competition or tend to create a monopoly. A private plaintiff may also need to prove actual harm to his business from the challenged pricing.

Section 3:

> This section of the Robinson-Patman Act is not part of the Clayton Act. This act states that "it is unlawful for any person engaged in commerce to be part of or assist in a transaction of sale or contract to sell which may discriminate to their knowledge against competitors of the purchasers, in that, any discount, rebate, allowance, or advertising service charge is granted to the purchaser over and above any discount, rebate, allowance, or advertising service charge available at the time of such transaction to said competitors in respect of a sale of goods of like grade, quality, and quantity; to sell, or contract to sell, goods in any way part of the United States at prices lower than those exacted by said person elsewhere in the United States for the purpose of destroying competition or to sell at such an unreasonably low price to destroy a competitor.

The Federal Trade Commission Act

The Federal Trade Commission Act of 1914 prohibits "unfair method of competition" and "unfair or deceptive acts or practices." If an individual violates the Sherman Act, they also violate the FTCA. The FTCA is used to prevent violations of both the specific antitrust laws and the public policy expressed in those laws.

Federal Trade Commission Act (38 Stat 717, 1914, as amended)

5. (a)(1) Unfair methods of competition . . . and unfair or deceptive acts or practices in or affecting commerce, are hereby declared unlawful.

(6) The Commission is hereby empowered and directed to prevent . . . using unfair methods . . . or deceptive acts or practices in commerce.

5. (1) Any person . . . who violates an order of the Commission to cease and desist . . . shall pay a civil penalty of not more than $10,000 for each violation . . . each day of continuance . . . shall be deemed a separate offense.

Ironically, in the midst of antitrust law development was the institution of rent control in New York City. Some form of rent control has existed there since 1920, amid much controversy. The social reforms of the time brought attention to the shortage of affordable housing. Rent control was, and still is, a proposed answer to this problem. Since 1950, Los Angeles, San Francisco, Washington, D.C., and several other large communities have instituted rent controls, and many other cities are now considering them.

Although a popular policy with the public, rent control is one subject agreed upon by most economists. Based on the simple supply and demand model, a price suppressed below its natural level creates a shortage in the market. Consumers are unable to satisfy their demand for housing at that price, and suppliers are unwilling to build more housing at an unprofitable price level. Uncontrolled rents settle at the level where quantity demanded equals quantity supplied, as in any other market.

The only implied advantage to rent control—lower affordable rents—is heavily outweighed by all the disadvantages. Indeed, rent control seems to compound, rather than solve, the housing problem in this country by making investment in rental housing an unprofitable venture. New units are not built and existing buildings are not maintained, as evidenced by New York's dilapidated rent-controlled areas. In addition, the shortage created allows landlords to discriminate against "unsuitable" applicants and to charge outrageous "key" money (moving in fees) and "parking fees" to compensate for the difference between controlled rent and the fair market value rent. Nevertheless, rent control remains a politically popular policy, much to the dismay of economists.

EXEMPTIONS FROM ANTITRUST LAWS

Common carriers (ship, rail, and motor) are regulated by Interstate Commerce Commission (ICC). Agricultural and fishing cooperatives are regulated by the Capper-Volstead Act. These mergers may be challenged through specific procedures—Export Trade Association exempted by the Webb-Pomfence Act.

Anti-Monopoly Legislation

Table 12.1 summarizes the major legislation that pertains to the prevention of monopoly in the United States. The Sherman Act declared monopoly to be illegal. The Clayton Act spelled out certain practices that would be considered monopolizing, such as: tying contracts and stock purchases if the effect lessens competition. The Robinson-Patman Act outlawed predatory price cutting. The Celler-Kefauver Act regulated mergers in the form of a company purchasing the assets of a competing company. The Hart-Scott-Rodino Act requires firms to report mergers or acquisitions to the Federal Trade Commission and to the Department of Justice before they take place.

New-Wave Regulation

New-wave regulation refers to the legislation passed in the 1960s and 1970s on consumer protection, the environment, and energy. Examples are: The Environmental Protection Agency (EPA), passed in 1964 to regulate pollution of the environment, the Consumer Product Safety Commission (CPSC), to regulate the safety of products, the National Highway Traffic Safety Commission (NHTSC), passed in 1970, to regulate motor vehicles. These agencies specify rules and regulations and set fines for violations.

The argument in favor of these commissions is that they provide information about products that consumers would not otherwise have and that consumers can make more rational decisions about their purchase. The argument against the commissions is that they constitute an intrusion into the market where decisions are best made by firms and individuals acting independent of the government.

Table 12.1
Selected Legislation and Government Regulatory Agencies

Legislation	Year of Adoption	Major Provision(s)
The Sherman Act	1890	The first antitrust law. Section 1 of the act declared every contract, combination, or conspiracy in the restraint of trade to be illegal. Section 2 made it illegal to monopolize or attempt to monopolize.
The Clayton Act	1914	Prohibits tying contracts, exclusive dealing, interlocking directorates and the acquisition of the stock of a competing company if such acquisition would substantially lessen competition.
The Robinson-Patman Act	1936	This Act made predatory pricing illegal. This is the practice of selling below cost to destroy a competitor.
Celler-Kefauver Anti-Merger Act	1950	It is Illegal in certain circumstances for a firm to merge with another by purchasing its assets.
Hart-Scott-Rodino Act	1970	Antitrust Improvement Act. The act amending the FTC Act to require firms to report mergers or acquisitions to the FTC and Department of Justice before their consummation.

HEALTH AND SAFETY REGULATION

The last area of regulation to be examined in this chapter is health and safety regulation. Although a large amount of government resources is devoted to consumer health and safety issues, that area is beyond the scope of our discussion. We will discuss the work environment.

Regulation in the work place became a necessity during the industrialization of the U.S. The advent of large factories changed employment relationships that were relatively simple up to that time. To force corporations to provide a safe and healthy work environment, Congress and state legislatures have developed legislation defining minimum labor and safety standards required in the work place. The first type of employee protection law passed by the state involved workers' compensation.

In response to evidence of safety neglect in corporations, the Fair Labor Standards Act was adopted by Congress in 1938. The FLSA also served as an attempt to stimulate and stabilize the economy after the effects of the Depression. The Act set standards for minimum wages, maximum work hours, and child labor practices.

No major new legislation was passed by Congress until 1970, when the Occupational Safety and Health Act was adopted. Prior to OSHA, the enforcement of health and safety standards was the responsibility of individual states. In the wake of 10,000 annual on-the-job fatalities, 2,000,000 disabling injuries, and 400,000 cases of occupational diseases, Congress created OSHA to protect over sixty million workers.

The Act gives employers a duty to provide a work place free from "recognized hazards causing or likely to cause death or serious physical harm to employees." Compliance with OSHA health and safety standards is mandatory for both the employer and the employee.

To facilitate the development of health and safety standards in the wide rage of industries, the OSHA adopted standards under existing federal law, as well as consensus standards, within each industry. The enforcement and administration of the Act is the responsibility of the Secretary of Labor. Penalties for violation of OSHA statutes are based on a schedule of fines classified from non-serious to serious. OSHA officials are authorized to inspect work sites without notice. Employee representatives are allowed to accompany the inspector, and they have a right to be informed of the findings. OSHA forbids disciplinary action or discrimination against an employee who files a complaint or exercises his or her rights under the Act.

While organized labor was originally one of OSHA's biggest supporters, it has since become one of its biggest critics. Both labor and management feel they are burdened with petty regulations which have no effect on safety.

The cost-benefit issue in health and safety regulation is highly emotional and controversial.

How Are the Antitrust Statutes Interpreted and Enforced?

There are three laws that currently define the government's antitrust policy: the Sherman Antitrust Act (1890), the Clayton Antitrust Act (1914), and the Federal Trade Commission Act (1914).

Until about 1914, the courts used the rule of reason to judge the actions of companies. Under the Sherman Act, being a monopoly or attempting to monopolize was not illegal. To be illegal, a company's action had to be unreasonable in a competitive sense, and anticompetitive effects had to be demonstrated.

In 1914, the Clayton Act and the Federal Trade Commission Act was passed and the courts used the *per se* rule to judge the actions of companies. Actions that were *potentially* monopolizing tactics were illegal.

Since the 1980s, the courts have returned to the looser rule-of-reason-standard. The only tactic currently deemed intrinsically illegal is collusion, or price fixing. This most recent phase began without support from the majority of economists and with the support of only a small minority of the legal profession.

Actions against violations of the antitrust statutes may be initiated by the U.S. Department of Justice, by the Federal Trade Commission, and by private plaintiffs.

The Justice Department concentrates on collusion restraints, monopolization, and mergers under the Sherman Antitrust Act. Its suits are filed in federal district courts and enforce violations with fines, jail sentences, and divestitures.

The Federal Trade Commission is headed by five commissioners appointed by the president. The Commission enforces the Clayton and Federal Trade Commission Acts. Complaints are handled through administrative hearings and enforcement against offenders is through fines and divestitures.

Private plaintiffs (consumers or business) may file suit in court against offenders. They may sue under the Sherman or Clayton Antitrust Acts. Private parties can be awarded treble damages, amounts totaling three times the proven damages, if they win.

The Effectiveness of the Antitrust Laws

The effectiveness of the antitrust laws in preventing monopoly and maintaining competition has depended on the zeal with which the Federal government has enforced the laws, and on the interpretation of these laws by the Federal Courts. Two major issues have arisen in the interpretation of the antitrust laws.

1. Whether an industry can be judged on the basis of its monopolistic *structure* or on the basis of monopolistic *behavior*.

2. Whether to define the market in which firms sell their products narrowly or broadly.

The actual practice of antitrust law in the United States has sometimes penalized business firms just for being efficient or innovative! Advocates of repealing the antitrust laws argue that the legal expense cause by antitrust laws are expensive, the growth in international trade has increased competition, monopolies are often the result of superior innovation, and modern technology has created substitutes for the products of monopolies.

Bringing Professions Under Antitrust Laws: Good or Bad Idea?

Professionals and professions should be reviewed for anticompetitive behavior, but only within reasonable guidelines. In some instances, a behavior that appears on the surface to be anticompetitive in actuality is not that at all. Many small towns, because of the size of their populations, can support only one person practicing a particular profession. For example, several doctors in a town of 500 people could not survive, because of diseconomies of scale. Several doctors would create competition and lower the fees that would be charged, but because of the small number of people who would patronize each physician, the physician would not be able to earn a sufficient income to support her- or himself and his or her family. This reduction in income could also lead to a reduction in the quality and quantity of services that could be offered as well. One doctor could probably serve the demands of the town's population, but competition will have been eliminated, and the doctor could therefore raise his or her fees.

Most professions such as attorneys and doctors have a code of ethics, and many argue that these codes take the place of enforced government regulation. This is not necessarily true. Some codes of ethics also attempt to set minimum fees that can be charged by members, and this is, in fact, anticompetitive in nature and harmful to the public welfare! Codes of ethics may have a positive effect on an industry, but at the same time, they may be harmful to the public. Ethical codes can regulate activities only within a profession or trade, and can have little impact on the relations of the industry to other industries, or to the society as a whole. It is one thing to regulate the activities of lawyers or stockbrokers that adversely affect individuals within those industries. It is a totally different problem to adopt and enforce ethical codes to subordinate the entire business of law or investment advice to the interests of the whole society or economy. Codes of ethics are very limited in their ability to replace government regulation as a form of control.

Social Regulation

Social regulation is concerned with the conditions under which goods and services are produced and the impact of these goods on the public. The following government agencies are concerned with social regulation:

- The Occupational Safety and Health Administration (OSHA), which is concerned with protecting workers against injuries and illnesses associated with their jobs.

- The Consumer Product Safety Commission (CPSCP), which specifies minimum standards for safety of products.

- The Food and Drug Administration (FDA), which is concerned with the safety and effectiveness of food, drugs and cosmetics.

- The Equal Employment Opportunity Commission (EEOC), which focuses on the hiring, promotion, and discharge of workers.

- The Environmental Protection Agency (EPA), which is concerned with air, water, and noise pollution.

Chapter Summary

1. Regulation in business has grown at a pace equivalent to that of the business world in the last 100 years. Although there is controversy regarding the effectiveness of the regulatory agencies discussed here, their primary goal remains the preservation of a competitive market and the protection of consumers and workers. Toward that end, antitrust laws were developed to regulate business practices and prevent abuse of power through market monopolization.

2. Regulation is carried out by local, state and Federal government. Regulation is often used to regulate the rates of natural monopolies, usually based on a fair-rate-of-return pricing concepts. The regulatory pricing formula is price should equal ATC plus a fair rate of return (8% estimates).

3. The first major antitrust regulation was the Sherman Act, passed in 1890. It was directed at collusive practices resulting in monopoly situations. Because the Sherman Act was largely ineffective due to its vagueness, the Clayton Act was adopted to outlaw or regulate specific business practices, including price-fixing, restraint of trade, contracts, mergers and acquisitions, and interlocking directorates. The Federal Trade Commission was created in 1914 to investigate violations of the Sherman and Clayton Acts. Its main responsibility, however, is to guard consumers against unfair and deceptive business practices.

4. Rent control is another example of government regulation in private industry. Although its purpose contradicts the price-fixing clause of the Clayton Act, rent control is considered by some social reformers to be the answer to the shortage of affordable housing. However, economists have been virtually unanimous in their criticism of rent control. They feel rent control has compounded, rather than solved, the housing problem by making real estate investment less profitable than other investment opportunities.

5. Government regulation in occupational health and safety was examined. OSHA (1970) was created to provide nationally uniform standards of health and safety. The state regulations that existed prior to this time ranged from extremely rigid to virtually nonexistent. Since its inception, OSHA has been criticized by both labor and management for over regulation in some areas and under regulation in others. The cost-benefit factor is becoming an increasingly important consideration in the passage of new legislation. The FTC, OSHA, and many other regulatory agencies are now pursuing cost-effective legislation in an endeavor to achieve a balance between necessary regulations and the costs they impose on society.

6. Private markets may fail to allocate resources efficiently. In such cases, government regulation can increase the well-being of society. Even the harshest critics of regulation acknowledge the legitimate role of government. At issue is not the need for government regulation but its scope.

7. Those seeking to reduce government's role attack regulations on two grounds: (a) regulations are sometimes extended to markets that would operate more efficiently unregulated, and (b) in markets where intervention is appropriate, regulation is often excessive. Regulations impose costs on society. These consist of both the administrative costs of regulatory agencies, including staff salaries and overhead, and the costs of complying with regulations. In addition to the extra paperwork, regulations force firms to add product features they would not otherwise provide (e.g., catalytic converters on automobiles) and to alter production processes.

8. Before deregulation, the ICC forced trucks to return empty on long hauls rather than pick up additional cargo. Moreover, by equalizing fares across competing tracks and railroads, the ICC removed the incentive to use the most efficient mode. For example, trucks are often more efficient than trains for transporting goods short distances while trains are more efficient for long hauls. Ideally, these cost differences would be reflected in rate schedules, so that shippers would choose the least costly mode of transportation. The ICC, however, frequently equalized rates to guarantee each industry that a share of both long-distance and short-distance travel would be used for long hauls.

9. From an economic perspective, the costs of regulation should be compared with the benefits. Further regulation is advantageous to society when the benefits from additional regulation exceed the costs of additional regulation. But when the additional benefits fall short of the additional costs, then regulation is excessive.

10. Students, as citizens, should be aware of the long-term consequences of rent controls, whose short-term appeal is so strong. A shortage of houses at the legislated rent has resulted, and some builders will build structures other than houses.

TAKE-A-NOTE

Federal Trade Commision (FTC) 1914

- Oversee and promote free and fair competition in the interest of others.
- Violations not defined under Sherman Act or Clayton Act are reviewed on a case-by-case basis to determine if practices are "unfair or deceptive."

The Clayton Act (1914)

- The act served to correct the errors from misinterpreting the Sherman Act.
- Unions in competing companies are permitted to join forces to raise wages. This is no longer defined as a restraint of trade.
- Prohibit tying contracts, exclusive dealings, and acquisition of stock of a competitor if acquisition would substantially reduce competition.
- Outlaw anti-competitive practices not defined under the "contracts, conspiracies, and combinations" section of the Sherman Anti-Trust Act.

The Robinson-Patman Act (1936)

- The legislation created to permit the freedom to change prices when there is no threat it will lead to unfair practices.

- Permitted price differences if they are justified by offsetting cost differences, or if prices are lowered to meet the prices of a competitor. Prices below marginal cost are declared illegal.

Chapter 12
Key Concepts

Anti-Trust Philosophy—Refers to the American name for laws, agencies, and actions to protect and promote competition.

Celler-Kefauver Act—This Act regulates a firm merging with a competitor by purchasing the assets of the firm.

Clayton Act—Outlaws anti-competitive practices which did not fall under the "contracts, conspiracies, or combinations" clause of the Sherman Act.

Common Carriers—Ship, rail, and motor are regulated by the Interstate Commerce Commission.

Deregulation—The policy of removing government regulations from industry and allowing the market to operate.

Exclusive Dealing—An agreement to sell the products of only a certain producer.

Federal Trade Commission—Responsible for fostering an environment conducive to free and fair competition in the interest of consumers.

Hart-Scott-Rodino Act—This Act requires firms to give prior notice of a merger or acquisition of the Department of Justice.

New-Wave Regulation—Legislation from the 1960s and 1970s on consumer protection, the environment, and energy.

Occupational Safety and Health Act (OSHA)—Congress created OSHA to protect American workers.

Regulatory Agencies—Refers to agencies which were created to recognize and resolve the problems of a changing nation. Regulatory agencies are unique in that they possess powers of all three branches of government.

Rent Control—The government regulates rent below the market rate to create lower affordable rents.

Robinson-Patman Act—Allows price differences if they can be justified by offsetting cost differences or if the new price is adopted to meet the lower price of a competitor.

Sherman Anti-Trust Act of 1890—The Foundation of all antitrust legislation dealing with restraint of trade, and monopolizing.

Social Regulation—Concerned with the conditions under which goods and services are produced and the impact of these goods on the public.

Total Requirement Arrangement—An agreement to purchase all the requirements of a product from the seller of a product.

Tying Contract—A buyer agrees to buy additional products in order to purchase product.

DISCUSSION QUESTIONS

1. Discuss the pros and cons of government regulation of business.

2. Present the major features of the following legislation:
   a. Sherman Act
   b. Clayton Act
   c. Robinson-Patman Act
   d. Federal Trade Commission Act
   e. Fair Labor Standards Act
   f. Occupational Safety and Health Act

3. Present the rationale for regulation.

4. Discuss the effectiveness of the antitrust laws in preventing monopoly and maintaining competition.

5. What would happen if all government regulations were abolished?

6. If the government imposes a price ceiling on gasoline, what will be the result?

7. Bringing professions under Antitrust laws: Good or Bad idea?

8. What is the best way to deal with monopoly power? In your opinion, what is the best approach? Do you advocate antitrust laws, or regulations, or something else we didn't discuss? Give reasons for your answer.

9. What does it mean when we say that the airline industry has been deregulated? What have been the impacts of deregulation on fares, service, safety and industry?

Chapter

Externalities

Learning Objectives

After you have studied this chapter in the text, and attended class lectures regularly, you will be able to:

1. Define the term positive and negative externalities.
2. Distinguish between private costs and social costs.
3. Distinguish between private benefits and social benefits.
4. Explain the concept of the misallocation of resources.
5. Discuss the various types of pollution and their causes.
6. Present various solutions for pollution.
7. Explain the meaning of "Free Rider."
8. Define market failure and market success.
9. Discuss the concept of internalizing.
10. Discuss the importance of property rights.

Introduction

For economists to advocate a particular government policy, they must believe that the government will do good and implement the people's desires. If the government structure precludes that, almost all economists become supporters of government nonintervention, or Laissez-faire. Hence, when there are externalities, the private price no longer necessarily reflects the social price, and therefore the market may not work properly.

Market Success

In the competitive market, supply and demand are brought together, thereby determining prices and the quantities to be produced. This is shown in Figure 13.1.

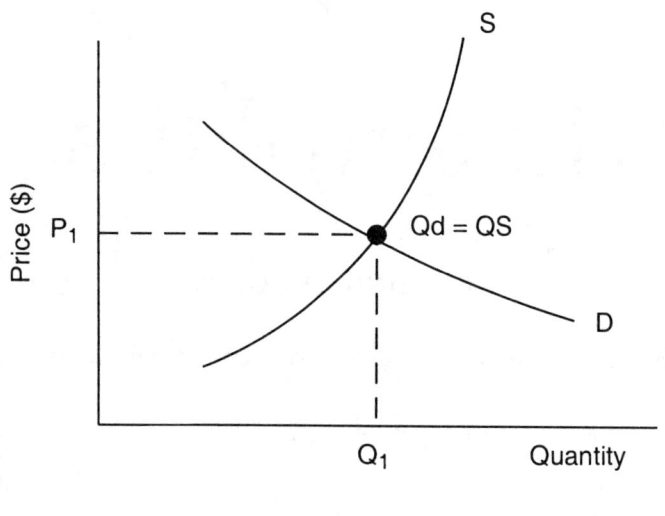

Figure 13.1
Equilibrium

At the price of P1, the quantity demanded (QD) is equal in the quantity supplied (QS), with the actual quantity being produced at Q1.

Marginal Cost

Supply is determined by the marginal cost structure of the firm, as indicated in Figure 13.2. According to the shutdown rule, the firm should produce as long as the price received is greater than the average variable cost, since the amount received is greater than the additional costs incurred. At higher prices, the firm will produce more, as indicated in Figure 13.3.

At a price of P1, the firm will supply Q1, based on the level of marginal cost at that point. At a higher price, P2, the quantity supplied will be Q2, a higher level.

Externalities

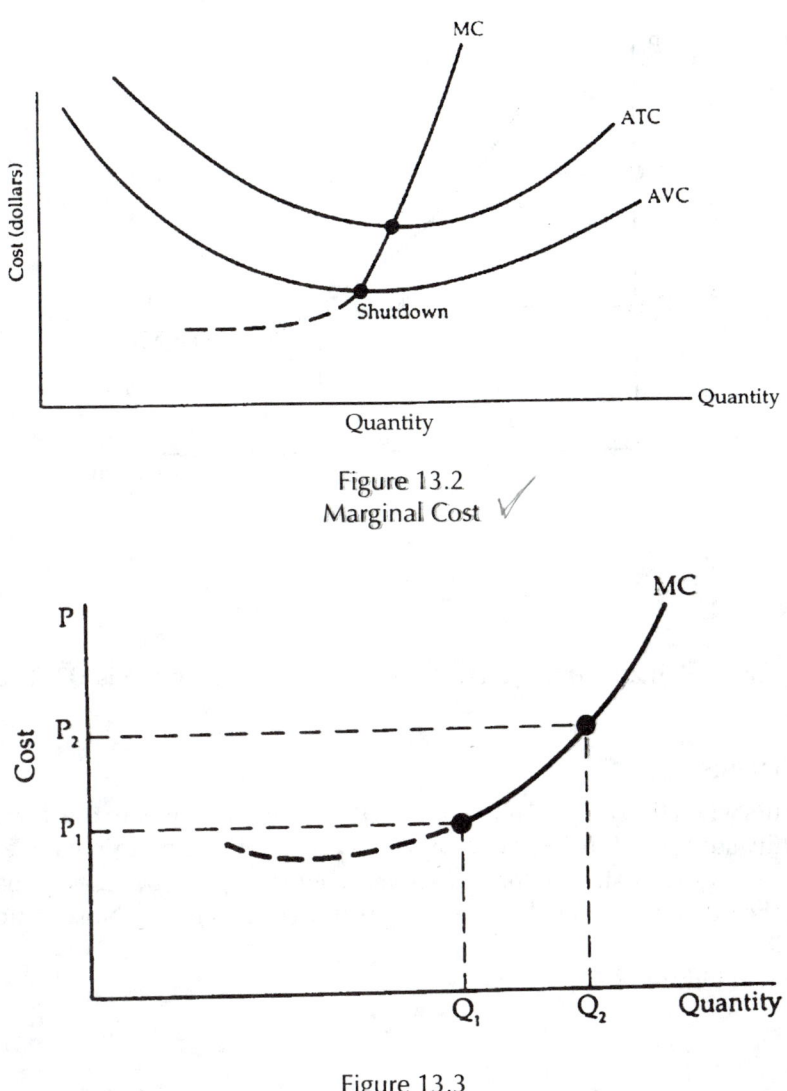

Figure 13.2
Marginal Cost

Figure 13.3
Firm's Supply Curve

To reverse the analysis: In order for the firm to produce Q1, a price of P1 is needed. To produce a greater quantity, Q2, a higher price is needed, P2. The marginal cost function thus becomes the supply function of the firm. Likewise, the market supply function would be the result of the sum of all the firm's cost functions.

Marginal Benefit (MB)

Demand is related to marginal benefit, which refers to the additional benefit gained from additional consumption. This is shown in Figure 13.4.

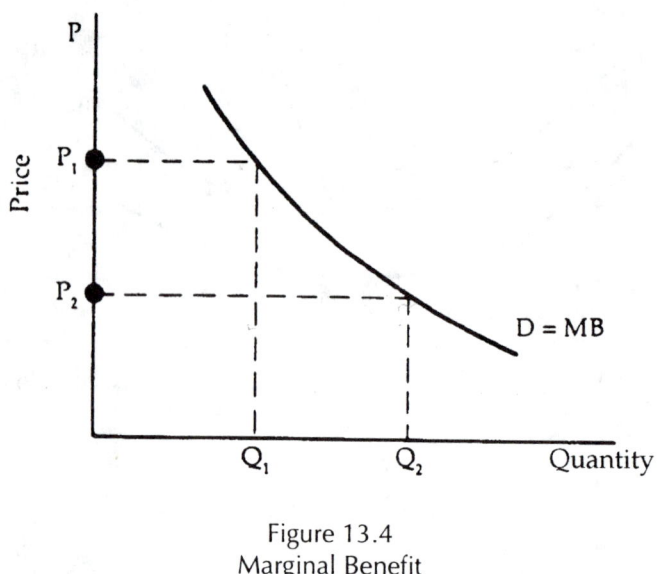

Figure 13.4
Marginal Benefit

At P1, the quantity demanded is Q1. At P2, the quantity demanded is Q2. The marginal benefit is also greater.

Economic Efficiency

Equilibrium occurs when the demand and supply curves intersect, where the quantity demanded equals the quantity supplied. Since the demand curve also reflects marginal benefit and the supply curve reflects marginal cost, equilibrium occurs where marginal benefit equals marginal cost. At equilibrium, the market is said to be allocating resources efficiently. No additional gains from trade are possible.

This is shown in Figure 13.5.

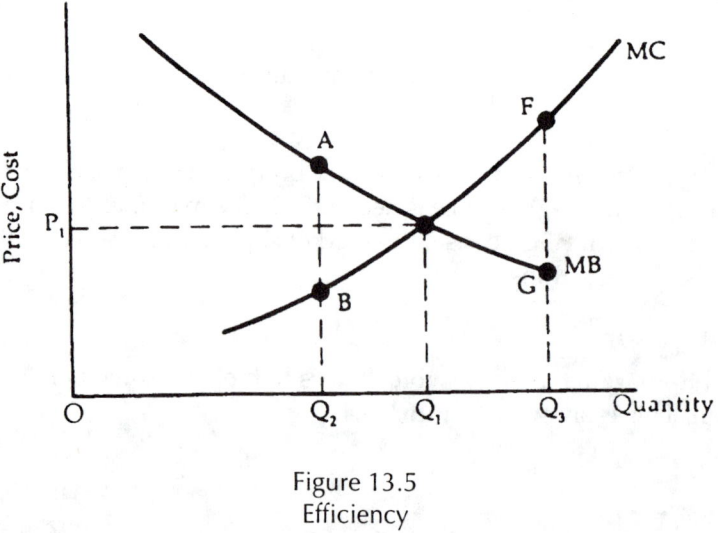

Figure 13.5
Efficiency

In the above figure, if production is not at the equilibrium level (Q1), but rather at Q2, the marginal benefit (A) will be greater than the marginal cost (B). There will be an incentive to increase production. Resources will be allocated to this use. If production is at Q3, the marginal benefit (G) will be less than the marginal cost (F). Production will be cut back. Resources will be taken from this use and allocated to another.

At equilibrium, there are no pressures to increase or decrease production. Welfare is at its best, and economic efficiency is achieved. Economic efficiency or success refers to an efficient use of resources. This occurs at that level where the quantity demanded equals the quantity supplied, or where marginal benefit equals marginal cost. There is no pressure to increase production at this level, thus allocating resources from other uses to this use. Likewise, there is no pressure to decrease production at this level, thus, allocating resources from this use to other uses.

Market Failure

There are many circumstances in the working of the free enterprise system that do not result in the most desirable outcomes. When this happens, we say that free markets have failed. That is, market failure does not mean that nothing good has happened. Market failure is defined in this context as the inefficient use of resources resulting from externalities. As a result, marginal cost does not equal marginal benefit. A market failure can result from broad types of reasons: poorly defined property right such as the environment, from a public good, free riding and from monopoly.

Environmental Quality

The Criminal Justice System, the Interstate Highway System, the National Parks, the Public Schools, National Defense, and Air Traffic Control are all examples of goods and services that are provided by governments in the U.S.

EXTERNALITIES: POSITIVE AND NEGATIVE

This chapter will present externalities—Costs and Benefits outside the production and consumption process. The topic of pollution will also be presented.

Externalities refer to either benefits or costs to individuals not directly involved in the production or consumption of an item. Benefits are considered to be positive externalities, sometimes referred to as external benefits. Costs are considered to be negative externalities, sometimes referred to as external costs (spillover costs).

Two distinctions are made in discussing externalities. They can accompany acts of either production or consumption, and they can be either positive or negative (costs).

From these two distinction, we describe four basic types of externalities:

Positive production externalities: anyone who has walked past a bakery and smelled the fresh bread has experienced this concept. Here, the consumer (or society) has received a benefit without paying for it.

An example of a positive externality would be the following: a neighbor decides to put new siding and windows on his house, thus making it more attractive. As a result, the neighborhood is more attractive, and house prices go up. The remodeling has resulted in benefits to third parties at no cost to them. Another example: A citizen who becomes well-informed about community issues.

Positive externalities tend to create free rider problems because positive externalities are benefits that spillover to people who don't pay for them. The problem of *"free riders"* arises in a society when goods can't be provided exclusively to those who pay for them. Examples: Library books, Police protection, an Interstate highway, and Postal Service. That is, a free rider in economic theory is someone who does not contribute toward covering the cost of goods which he desires because he knows his paying or not-paying will make no difference in their availability to him.

Negative production externalities: walking past a polluting factory. Positive consumption externalities exist when one family grows beautiful flowers in its garden and the whole neighborhood benefits. Negative consumption externalities exist when a moviegoer chews his popcorn so loudly that no one else can watch the movie.

An example of a negative externality would be the following: A farmer uses a new chemical fertilizer to increase the production of soybeans and to cut down the growth of weeds. As a result, however, the chemical eventually drains into a nearby river and kills thousands of fish and vegetation. The river is a major fishing spot for many people. The use of the chemical has resulted in a cost to third parties, at no cost to the farmer.

Negative externalities are costly.* Cigarette smoke in a crowded restaurant, acid rain, the use of highways by additional vehicles, Kathy's neighbor blasting her out of of bed with his new stereo at 4:00am. Externalities are not always negative. If you are vaccinated against measles as a child, you provide a positive externality to your school playmates because you will not spread this disease.

Externalities indicate the failure of the market structure to properly allocate scarce resources. There are too many resources being directed to the production of goods possessing negative externalities (costs), and not enough resources being directed to the production of goods possessing positive externalities (benefits).

To illustrate the externality problem, consider the case of increasing the production of good X. If more of good X is produced, resources shift from other goods, and the output of the other goods will fall. As we know, this reduced output is the opportunity cost of producing additional quantities of good X. It may be called the social cost of producing more of X. Now suppose the extra output of X causes a pollution problem. Society must somehow shift additional resources to correct the problem (or let the people bear the extra cost in terms of reduced health status). Thus the social cost of producing more of X is the last output of other goods as expected, plus further reduced output because even more resources are needed to clean up the mess.

The firm producing good X may be unconcerned about the pollution it causes, and as a result the social cost will exceed the private cost, because the firm does not have to pay for the pollution.

Collective Consumption of Goods as a Source of Inefficiency

Collective Consumption goods are called Public Goods. These public goods are consumed jointly. Examples of public goods are police protection, and fire departments. In these goods no one should be excluded from the consumption of public goods. The nature of public goods causes a conflict between self-interest and the public interest of economic efficiency. However, there is a type of good that itself provides externalities. A good usually has these characteristics:

If more of it is consumed, then less will be available for others, and if one person obtains the service of the good, then someone else must lose the benefit. Such goods are called private goods. In constrast, some goods do not have these characteristics. Such goods are called public goods. A public good has one or both of the following characteristics: (1) it is not reduced in supply if consumption of it increases; and (2) if it is provided to one individual, then it will be equally available to all. A public good is one which is non-exhaustible or non-exclusive in consumption. One of the most often cited examples of a public good in national defense. Once one person is provided with the service of an army, then others in the country receive the benefit as well. In addition, the service is available to everyone equally—roads, parks, and television and radio signals are other examples of public goods. While the public wants these items, the free market would not generate them on its own. Government intervention is a requirement.

With these limitations stated, it is important to recognize that the market mechanism is an effective allocator of scarce resources. Left on its own, it can perform best in most cases. However, microeconomics is only one aspect of the economic system. Fiscal and Monetary policy play a big role. These subject areas belong to macroeconomics.

---

*Society has to make some changes to ensure that divorce will be an expensive one (Negative externality).

Marginal Private Benefits (MPB) Vs. Marginal Social Benefits (MSB)

In the market model, where production and pricing decisions are based on supply and demand, it is assumed there will be optimum (best) allocation of scarce resources. Given consumer demand and production costs, resources are allocated to the production of certain goods and services to achieve the greatest private and social benefit.

We now consider the situation where private and social benefits may be different, and a misallocation of scarce resources can occur. Marginal private benefit refers to the additional benefit an individual receives from the consumption of a product. Marginal social benefit refers to the benefit society gains when an additional item of a good is produced or consumed. Because of external costs, the marginal social benefit tends to be less than the marginal private benefit. This is shown in Figure 13.6.

There are private benefits to the farmer for using fertilizer as increased revenue due to increased production. Since, however, the fertilizer causes pollution and death to fish, the marginal social benefit is less.

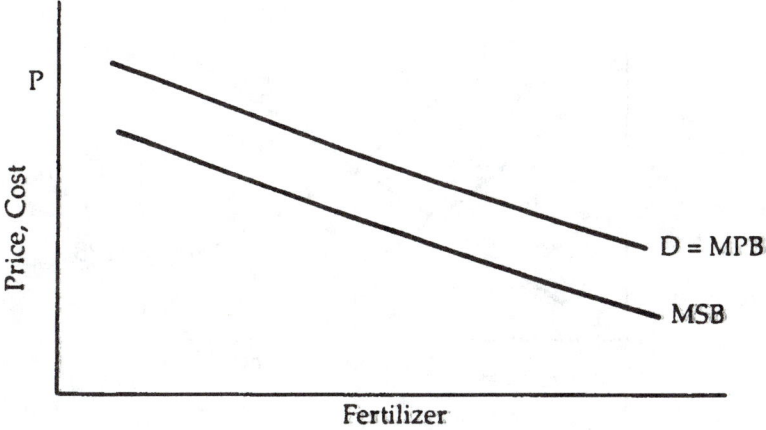

Figure 13.6
Marginal Social Benefits

Marginal Private Costs (MPC) Vs. Marginal Social Costs (MSC)

Marginal private cost refers to the additional cost to a firm to produce an additional item. Marginal social cost refers to the additional cost to society resulting from the increased production or consumption of an item. Because of externalities, the marginal social cost tends to be higher than the marginal private cost. This is shown in Figure 13.7.

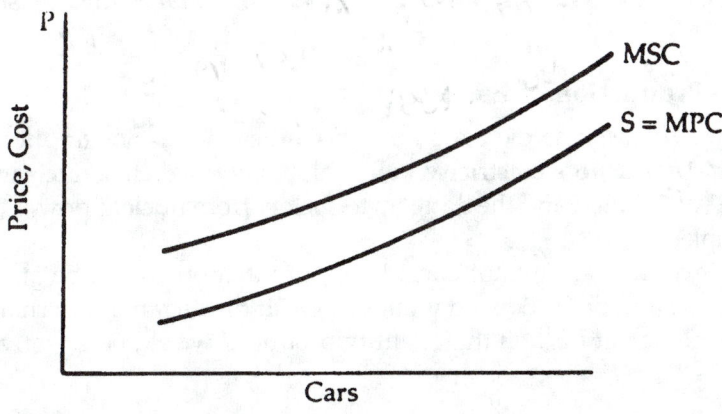

Figure 13.7
Marginal Social Costs

There are private benefits in the consumption of a car, but there also many social costs, such as increased pollution, traffic congestion, highway repair and construction, accidents, etc. As a result, the marginal social cost is greater than the marginal private cost. This is reflected in a higher curve for the marginal social cost.

Cost-Benefit Analysis

In this section, we will use cost-benefit analysis to indicate how externalities result in market failure, namely, the misallocation of scarce resources.

Example 1—The Consumption of Fertilizer

We will assume that the production of fertilizer does not result in either positive or negative externalities. Thus, the marginal private cost (MPC) equals the marginal social cost (MSC). Because of pollution and the killing of fish, the marginal social benefits are less than the marginal private benefits. This is shown in Figure 13.8.

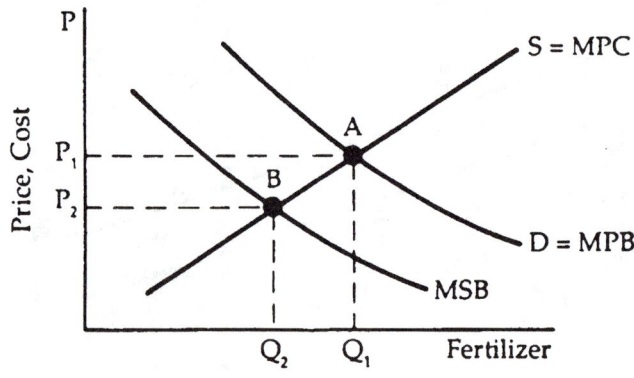

Figure 13.8
Example 1—Fertilizer

By not including the negative externalities, production will be at level Q1. If the negative externalities are included, the marginal social benefit line is below the marginal private benefit line. Equilibrium occurs where the MPB and MPC lines intersect. The addition of the MSB line changes equilibrium from point A to point B. The level of production drops from Q1 to Q2.

At point A, the market fails because there is overproduction of fertilizer, since negative externalities are not included. Too many resources are allocated for the production of fertilizer, since the price is higher. The price is at P1, rather than at P2, which takes into consideration negative externalities.

Example 2—The Production of Electricity

For this example, we will assume there are no externalities in the consumption of electricity, but that there are for the production. Electricity, here, will be produced in a nuclear power plant. The negative costs will be pollution and the dangers to society from nuclear power plants. Figure 13.9 presents this example.

If the negative externalities are not considered, production would be at point A. The price would be at P1 and the amount produced would be Q1. If the negative externalities are included, the price would be higher, at P2, and the quantity produced would be lower, at Q2, as shown at point B. Not including these social costs would result in its misallocation of resources, since more electricity would be produced. Again, the market fails to properly allocate resources.

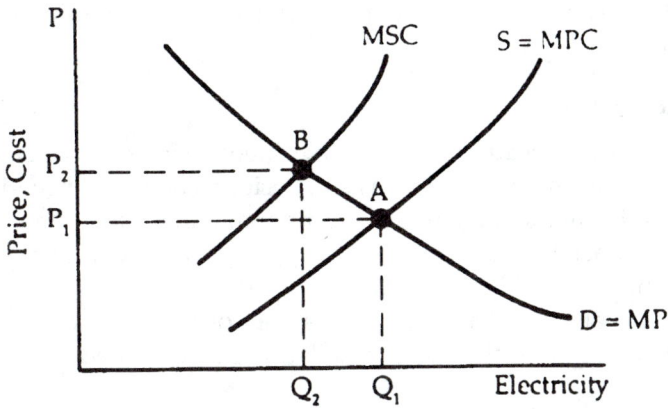

Figure 13.9
Example 2—The Production of Electricity

Example 3—The Production and Consumption of Automobiles

In this example, we will assume there are negative externalities in both the production and consumption of automobiles. The production of automobiles results in the pollution of air and water. Noise is generated, and the plants are sometimes ugly and take up much land that could be used for other purposes. The consumption of automobiles results in air pollution, traffic congestion, accidents, deaths, and the need for highways. Figure 13.10 presents this example.

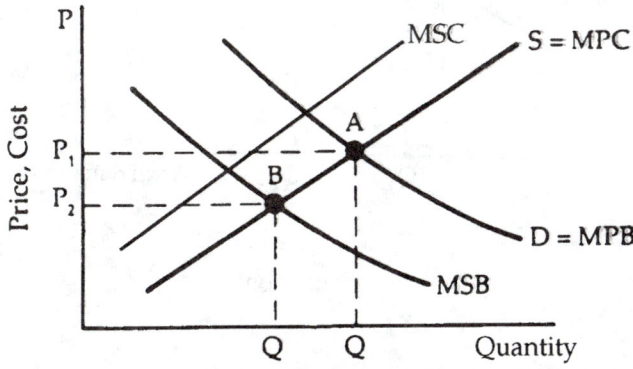

Figure 13.10
Example 3—Production-Consumption Automobiles

Not including externalities puts the firm at point A. The price would be P1, and the quantity of cars produced would be Q1. Including externalities presents a lower benefit curve for society and a higher cost curve for society. The level would be at point B. The price would be now lower, at P2, and the quantity produced would also be lower, at Q2. Resources would be misallocated, and the production of cars would be too high if externalities are not included.

The three previous examples all indicate that when negative externalities are not included, a misallocation of resources occurs.

In the next example, we show the case where there are positive externalities which are not included.

There are private benefits to the farmer for using fertilizer, such as increased revenue caused by increased production. However, because the fertilizer causes pollution and the death of fish, the marginal social benefit is less.

Example 4—Sex Education

This example deals with sex education programs in schools. There would be a cost involved and, we assume, no negative externality raising costs to society. The initial benefit would be that students gain important information on sex. The additional benefit to society could be fewer sex-related diseases and less need for abortions, both of which can cost taxpayers money. This example is shown in Figure 13.11a.

Production would be at point A if externalities are not included, and at point B, if they are included. If positive benefits are included, there would be more sex education programs, but at a higher price.

In this example, a misallocation of resources also occurs, but it is that not enough resources are being directed into sex education. As a result, society is receiving less much-needed sex education. Much-needed means, here, that there are many benefits to be gained.

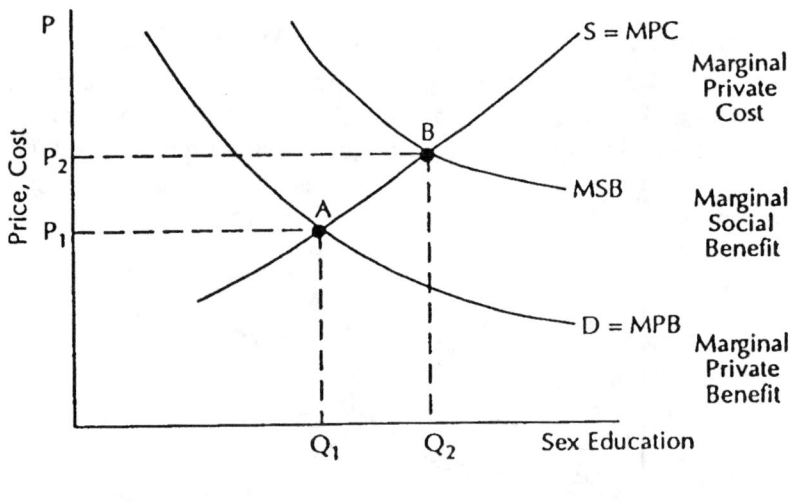

Figure 13.11a
Sex Education

In conclusion, when there is a positive externality, the marginal social cost is below the marginal private cost, as shown in Figure 13.11b. The price for the good, P1, is too high and the quantity, Q1, too low compared to the ideal price and quantity of Po, Qo.

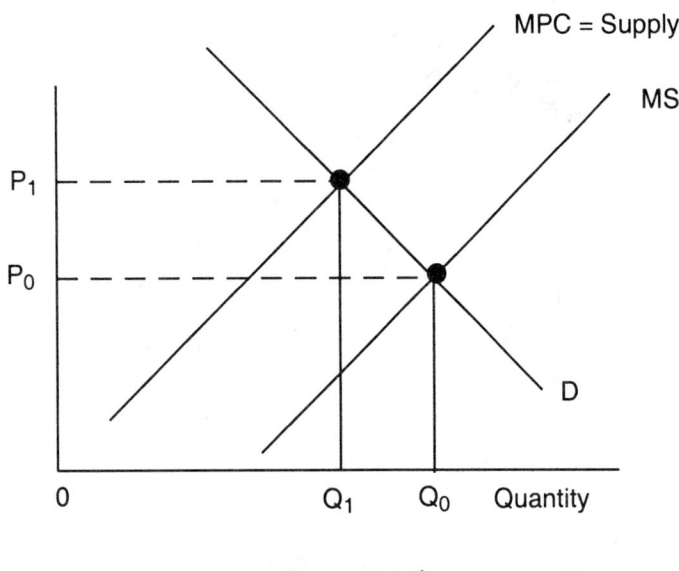

Figure 13.11b

In the next section, we will present a major negative externality that plagues society today: Pollution.

POLLUTION: THE PROBLEM

Since the 1970s, pollution has been gaining attention as a serious problem. Pollution refers to the contamination of soil, water, or the atmosphere by the discharge of harmful substances.

Air and water have usually been considered to be free goods. This essentially means that they exist in unlimited quantities, and there is no price charged for their use. There are no costs associated with their use, and, therefore, people and firms tend to misuse both. There is no penalty for contaminating the air or water.

Air and water are used in the production process in many firms. There is no charge for the use of air, but there may be some charge for the use of water. Air and water are discharged after the production process in a damaged or polluted state. This creates additional problems called social costs, such as diseases from inhaling the pollutants and the resources required to clear the air and water of pollutants. These costs are borne by segments outside the production process, not by the firms. These costs are called negative externalities.

Prices

In a competitive market, prices reflect the real cost of production. Based on these prices, resources are allocated, and the well-being of society is maximized.

If all costs are not included, the firm's marginal cost structure will be lower than it should be. As a result, the firm's price will be lower. Resources will flow to this firm, and overproduction will result. Profits will be higher. This is shown in Figure 13.12.

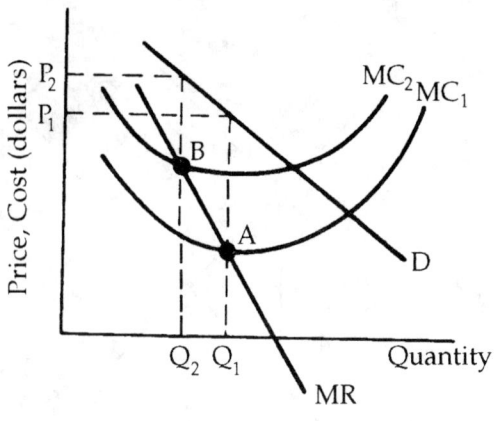

Figure 13.12
Prices with Pollution

If the costs of air and water are not included, the marginal cost is at MC1. Following the profit rule, the firm will produce, guided by point A, at which MC = MR. The price charged will be P1, and the quantity produced will be Q1.

If, however, the costs of air and water are included, the marginal cost is at MC2. The firm will now be guided by point B. The price charged will be P2, and the quantity produced will be Q2. Including the costs of air and water results in a higher price and a lower quantity produced.

Resources

Resources are said to be misallocated when prices do not include all costs and tend to be lower. This results in overproduction due to higher demand for the products. Resources are being taken from other uses to produce the lower priced items. Consumers have to give up the other items no longer being produced. This is shown in Figure 13.13.

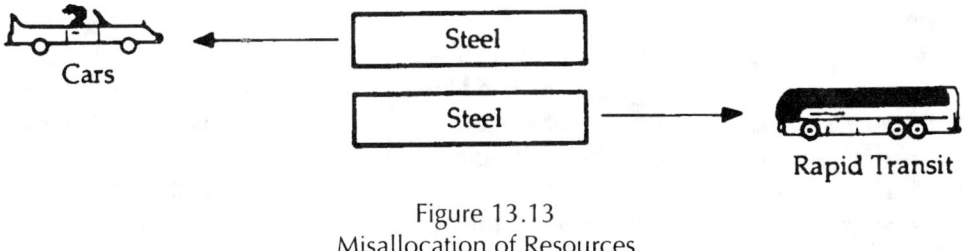

Figure 13.13
Misallocation of Resources

In Figure 13.13, steel is directed into the production of cars. This is the result of lower prices and greater demand. As a consequence, there is little steel directed to the production of rapid transit systems. A cost to the consumer and society, resulting from these lower prices, is less rapid transit.

Sources of Pollution

Environmental pollution is any discharge of material or energy into water, land, or air that causes or may cause acute (short-term) or chronic (long-term) detriment to the Earth's ecological balance or that lowers the quality of life. Unitil relatively recently in humanity's history, where pollution has existed, it has been primarily a local problem. The industrialization of society, the introduction of motorized vehicles, and the explosion of the human population, however, have caused an exponential growth in the production of goods and services. Coupled with this growth has been a tremendous increase in waste by-products. The indiscriminate discharge of untreated industrial and domestic wastes into waterways, the spewing of thousands of tons of particulates and airborne gases into the atmosphere has caused a big effect. Technology has begun to solve some pollution problems, and public awareness of the extent of pollution will eventually force governments to undertake more effective environmental planning and adopt more effective anti-pollution measures.

Water pollution is the introduction into fresh or ocean waters of chemical, physical, or biological material that degrades the quality of the water and affects the organisms living in it. This process ranges from simple addition of dissolved or suspended solids to discharge of the most insidious and persistent toxic pollutants (such as heavy metals, and nondegradable).

Indeed, air pollution, the second source of the pollution, is the accumulation in the atmosphere of substances that, in sufficient concentrations, endanger human health or produce other measured effects on living matter and other materials. Among the major sources of pollution are power and heat generation, the burning of solid wastes, industrial processes, and especially, transportation. Therefore, air pollution on a regional scale is in part the result of local air pollution—including that produced by individual sources, such as automobiles—that has spread out to encompass areas of many thousands of square kilometers. Meteorological conditions and landforms can greatly influence air pollution concentrations at any given place, especially locally and regionally.

Summary of Major Sources of Pollution

(a) Air

The major air pollutants, by source, are:
  Total suspended particulate (TSP)
  Sulfur dioxide (SO_2)
  Carbon monoxide (CO)
  Nitrogen oxide (NO)
  Volatile organic compound (VOC)
  Lead (PB)

The internal combustion engine of the automobile is the major source of carbon monoxide and lead emissions. Sulfur dioxide results from the use of coil and oil to produce electricity. Iron and steel mills, refineries, chemical plants, smelters, and lumber and rubber manufacturers are among the major industrial sources of pollutants. Solid waste is also a cause of air pollution.

(b) Water

The major sources of water pollution are agriculture, industries, and cities. In agriculture, the use of irrigation and fertilization is a cause of pollution. Irrigation leads to increased salinization. The use of pesticides and herbicides causes increased nitrates in water. This occurs as water from rain or irrigation enters the soil and drains off into the drainage systems and the streams and rivers.

Industries dump waste and polluted water back into the water system. The major harmful elements discharged are cadmium and mercury. These and other contaminants lower the oxygen level of the water, threatening fish.

Municipal sewage systems account for another major source of water pollution. The major harmful elements would be phosphates and nitrates not removed in the treatment facilities.

(c) Noise

A third type of pollution is noise. Noise is defined as any loud, discordant, or disagreeable sound. Noise results in nervousness, stress, discomfort, and can lead to reduced hearing.

Noise results from the manufacturing process in which machinery is used. On the assembly line, drills and hammers create loud noises. In the office, typewriters and other equipment emit sounds. Cars, buses, trains, and airplanes all create excessive sounds.

HEALTH AND SAFETY

Pollution is considered to be a threat to the health and safety of people. Air pollution increases the incidence of emphysema, bronchitis, heart disease, and cancer. Smog causes low visibility for drivers, and that low visibility could lead to accidents.

Water pollution causes unsafe drinking water and increased costs in purifying it. Sea life becomes contaminated and dangerous as a food source. People are unable to swim in certain waters due to the dangerous contaminants.

Noise pollution leads to hearing discomfort, stress, and loss of hearing.

LONG TERM EFFECTS OF AIR POLLUTION

The long term effects of air pollution include: an increased incidence of certain diseases, the erosion of buildings and other items built from stone, and the development of either the greenhouse effect or the ice-age effect.

In the greenhouse effect, there is the absorption of solar radiation by the earth. The result is a gradual rise in the temperature of the atmosphere as the radiation is unable to dissipate into space. The result is reduced food production and the loss of animal and, eventually, human life.

In the ice-age effect, the increased pollution in the air causes increased precipitation and lower temperatures. As a result, there is more snow and the accumulation increases. As in the greenhouse effect, the result is reduced food production and the loss of animal and human life.

SOLUTIONS

In this section, two major approaches to correcting pollution will be presented. These are: internalizing the externality and direct regulation.

Internalizing

Internalizing is the process of equating marginal social cost and marginal private cost, or equating marginal social benefit with marginal private benefit. Figure 13.14 presents an illustration of this.

Internalizing, in this situation, would refer to the farmer having to pay a higher price or a tax for the use of fertilizer. The difference in price or tax would equal in value the amount needed to correct the destruction or misuse of resources, such as the death of fish in rivers polluted by the fertilizer. Because of the higher price, less resources would flow to fertilizer and production would be less at Q2.

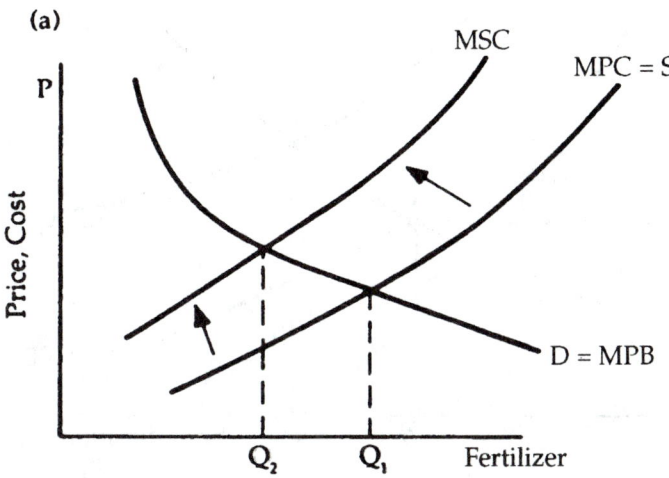

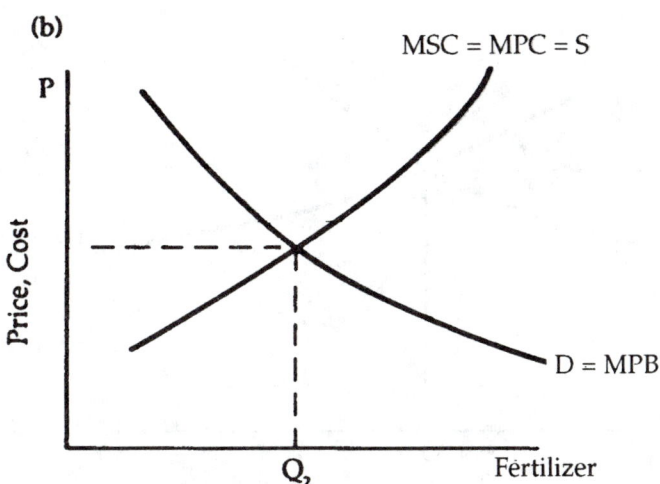

Figure 13.14
Example 1—The Consumption of Fertilizer

In Figure 13.15 the benefits to society are greater than to the individual. By increasing the price, these benefits are paid for by the consumer and more sex education is provided at Q2.

Instead of asking the consumer to pay the increase, the government could provide a subsidy, as shown in Figure 13.16

If the desired level of sex education is at Q1, in order to equate MSC with MSB, the consumer would pay P1, and the government could subsidize to raise the price, to P2.

Internalizing essentially refers to including all costs involved in the production and a consumption of an item. Doing so results in the equating of marginal social and private benefits and, likewise, equating marginal social and private costs. Resources are, accordingly, properly allocated.

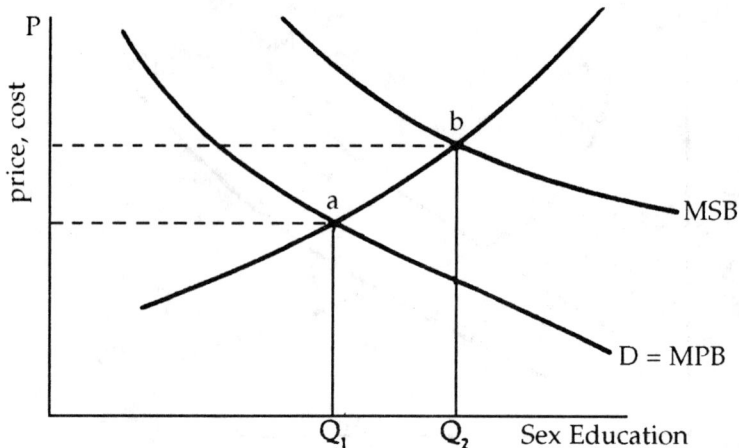

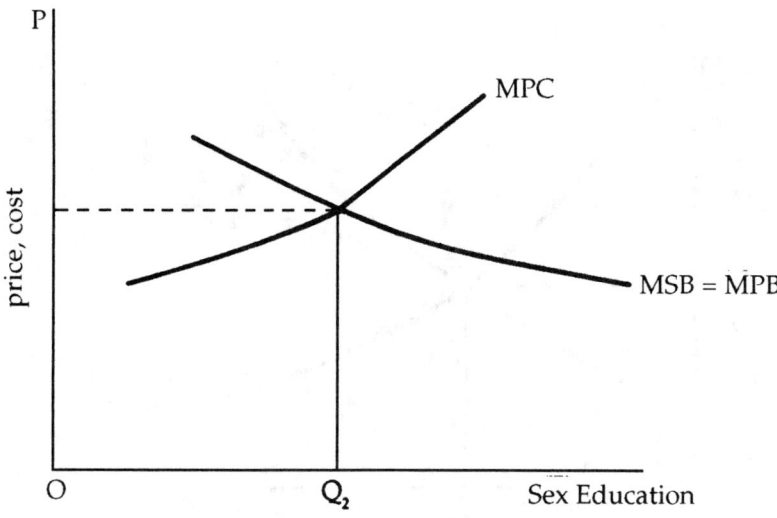

Figure 13.15
Example 2—Sex Education

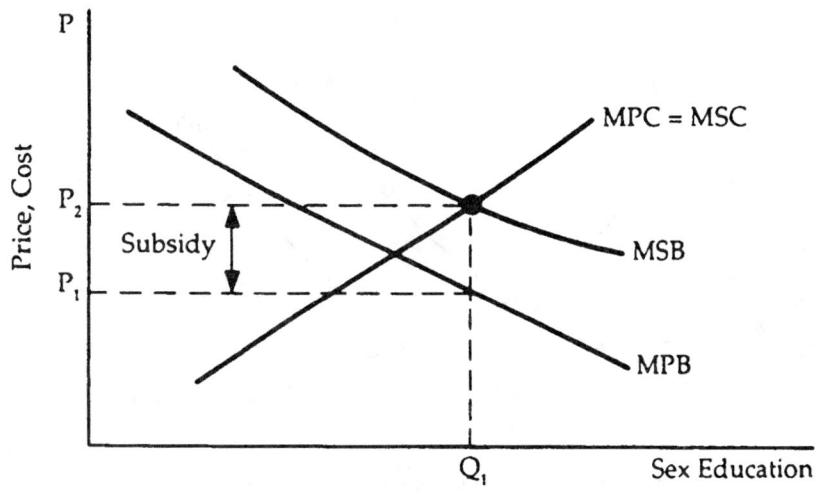

Figure 13.16
Government Subsidy

Direct Regulation

The government could directly regulate business and impose pollution standards that must be met. An example would be the Clean Air Act Amendment of 1970, which mandated a 90 percent reduction in automobile hydrocarbon and carbon monoxide emissions. The problems with direct regulation are the delays that industry can cause. The above standards were actually delayed until 1980.

Assignment of Property Rights

Property rights are defined in terms of rights to use, dispose of, and/or benefit from the objects generated from the property in question.

In the example of the farmer's fertilizer which kills fish, the people who fish the river could be assigned the property rights of the river. Since the fertilizer would kill some of the fish and make others unsafe, the fishermen would have to be compensated for their loss.

The compensation would increase the marginal private costs of the farmer to equal the marginal social costs. Because of the higher cost, the farmer would reduce production and the use of fertilizer to the efficient level, as shown in Figure 13.17.

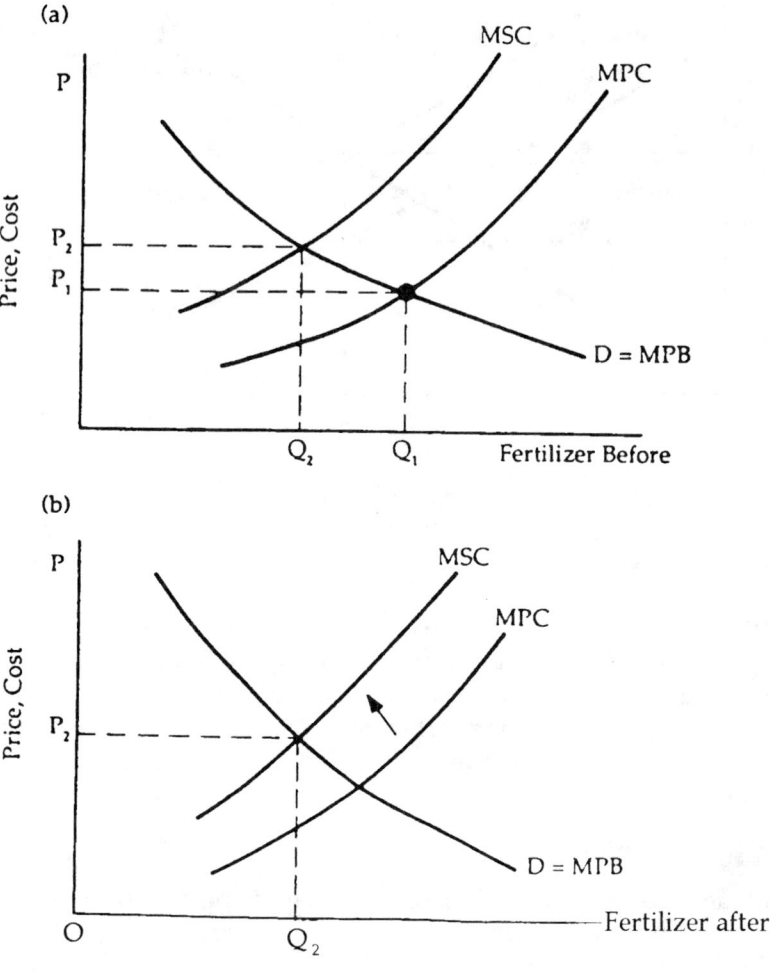

Figure 13.17
Assigning Property Rights

By assigning property rights to the fishermen, the cost to the farmer rises so that the MPC = MSC. As a result, the price rises to P2 and the quantity produced drops to Q2. Resources are channeled away from farming, and there is less pollution. Assigning property rights appears to be an efficient method of reducing pollution.

The government can attempt to reduce pollution by direct regulation, in which laws are passed mandating certain standards, assigning property rights, taxing the pollution or the product, and subsidizing firms to help cover the costs of reducing levels.

One method of achieving reduction in pollution is the use of standards and regulations. Because this approach works outside the market, it is unlikely to achieve goods results. Firms may choose to violate the standards, legislators may postpone implementation of standards, and more expensive methods of cleaning emissions than are necessary may be imposed.

Economists prefer the assignment of property rights, the use of corrective taxes, and the selling of pollution permits.

Finally, consider the negative externality of pollution in your hometown. Where might be the consequences of having the government intervene to reduce pollution? What would happen if the government passed a law saying there could be no pollution?

The following implications of federal laws enacted to eliminate pollution: awareness programs are essential, massive restriction of manufacturing, an increase in the price of goods, unemployment will rise, greater demand for substitutes, an increase in imports; and if the industry is forced to pay for the clean up, the cost will rise, supply will decrease, prices will rise, etc.

Take-A-Note

Externalties: Positive and Negative

Whenever some economic transaction between two parities affects a third party, an externality exists. An economic transaction is any economic activity, such as the production, distribution, and/or consumption of some product. A third party is any individual market participant or group of market participants who did not intend to engage in the transaction but is affected by it. A negative externality (e.g., pollution) is one that imposes a cost on the third party. A positive externality (e.g., education) is one that provides a benefit to the third party. Positive and negative externalities are sometimes called spillover benefits and costs, respectively. Products that exhibit negative externalities are overproduced by the private market, because the producers' marginal cost is less than the marginal social cost of production (MC < MSC). Products that exhibit positive externalities are underproduced by the private market, because the producers' marginal revenue is less than the marginal social benefit (MR < MSB). One of the laissez-faire roles of government is to reduce externalities, by forcing firms to internalize them. Historically, government has usually taxed products that exhibit negative externalities to increase the producers' marginal cost and reduce production. The government has usually subsidized products that exhibit positive externalities to increase producers' marginal revenue and increase production. Efficiency requires that (MC = MSC), (MR = MSB), and (MSC = MSB) for both producers and society at the level of output firms choose to produce for society.

Chapter Summary

1. Externalities refer to either benefits or costs affecting parties not directly involved in the production or consumption process.

2. External benefits are called positive externalities.

3. External costs are called negative externalities.

4. Private benefits are benefits to an individual or firm from the production or consumption of a good.

5. Private costs are costs to an individual or a firm from the production of a good.

6. Social benefits are benefits received by society from its production or consumption of the good, in addition to the good itself.

7. Social costs are costs borne by society, in addition to the costs borne by the firm.

8. A result of not including social benefits and costs is the misallocation of scarce resources.

9. If social costs are not included, prices tend to be lower and too many resources are allocated to this good.

10. If social benefits are not included, prices tend to be higher and not enough resources are allocated.

11. A major external cost to society is pollution.

12. The major types of pollution are air, water, and noise.

13. There are both short term and long term effects to pollution.

14. The suggested solutions to pollution are: internalizing social costs, direct government regulations, and the assignment of property rights. Economists prefer the assignment of property rights, the use of corrective taxes, and the selling of pollution permits.

Chapter 13
Key Concepts

Cost-Benefit Analysis—Comparing costs with benefits.

Economic Efficiency—An efficient use of resources. This occurs at the level where the marginal benefit equals marginal cost.

Externalities—Refers to either benefits or costs to individuals not directly involved in the production or consumption of an item.

Free Rider—is someone who does not contribute toward covering the cost of goods which he desires because he knows his paying or not-paying will make no difference in their availability to him.

Internalizing—Process of equating marginal social cost and marginal private cost or equating marginal social benefit with marginal private benefit.

Marginal Benefit—The additional benefit gained from additional consumption.

Marginal Private Benefit (MPB)—Refers to the additional benefit an individual receives from the consumption of a product.

Marginal Private Cost—The additional cost to a firm to produce a product.

Marginal Social Benefit (MSB)—Refers to the benefit society gains when an additional item of a good is produced or consumed.

Marginal Social Cost—The additional cost to society from the production of an additional item.

Market Failure—Defined as the inefficient use of resources resulting from externalities. As a result, marginal cost does not equal marginal benefits.

Market Success—Equilibrium at which the quantity demanded equals the quantity supplied.

Pollution—Refers to the contamination of soil, water, or the atmosphere by the discharge of harmful substances.

Property Rights—Stating that the air, water, etc. are private property and should be paid for if abused.

DISCUSSION QUESTIONS

1. Explain how the supply curve is derived from the AVC analysis.
2. Explain the concept of marginal benefit.
3. Explain economic efficiency.
4. Explain market failure.
5. Define the concept of externalities.
6. Distinguish between marginal social and marginal private benefits.
7. Distinguish between marginal social and marginal private costs.
8. Develop an example to show a situation in which negative externalities exist.
9. Develop an example to show a situation in which positive externalities exist.
10. Explain the concept of the misallocation of resources. — *is not including social benefits & costs is the*
11. Explain how the market system results in pollution.
12. Explain the concept of internalizing.
13. Discuss which would be better: internalizing all costs or direct regulation.
14. How would assigning property rights solve the pollution problem?
15. What are the long-term effects of pollution?
16. How much of a public good should the government provide? → *The good should be provided to everyone or all equal counts.*
17. Is it possible to eliminate the free-rider problem?
18. What would happen if the government passed a law saying that there could be no pollution?

Chapter 14

Global Perspectives: International Trade and Protectionism

Learning Objectives

After you have studied this chapter in the text, and attended class lectures regularly, you will be able to:

1. Explain the concept of terms of trade.
2. Discuss the major reasons for trade: cost advantages, variety of goods, greater choice, expansion of markets, and political reasons.
3. Discuss the free-trade theory based on absolute and comparative advantage.
4. Discuss the protectionist theory and the forms of protectionism: tariffs, quotas, orderly marketing agreements, local content laws, anti-dumping provisions, and others.
5. Present the arguments for protectionism: the infant industry argument, national defense argument, protect jobs argument, high wages argument, diversity argument, and retaliation argument.
6. Discuss the consequences of tariffs.
7. Distinguish between flexible and fixed exchange rates.
8. Identify the sources of political risk in foreign investment in less developed countries.
9. Discuss the problems of local ownership as a national objective in less developed countries.
10. Discuss the factors that contribute to the precarious situation of foreign capital in LDCs.
11. Discuss the objectives of the Overseas Private Investment Corporation and the Foreign Assistance Acts of 1969.
12. Discuss the need for two-way communication for successful importing and exporting.
13. Identify the problems associated with a weak distribution infrastructure.
14. Present recommendations to achieve successful training of people in the host country by American firms.
15. Discuss the Foreign Corrupt Practices Act, which prohibits bribes.
16. List the reasons why less developed countries are poor.

SCOPE OF INTERNATIONAL TRADE

International trade is of varying importance to different countries, as indicated In Table 14.0.

Table 14.0
International Trade in Selected Countries

Country	Percent of GNP
Canada	28
Japan	15
Netherlands	64
United Kingdom	26
United States	10

Source: Bureau of Commerce (1995)

For nations such as the Netherlands, foreign trade is extremely important, as it constitutes about 64 percent of the gross national product of the country. For Japan, the percent of gross national product is only 15 percent, and for the United States even lower than 10 percent of gross national product.

U.S. Trading Partners (1995)

Country	Exports (percentage)	Imports
Western Europe	40	10
Canada	31	31
Japan	16	28
Australia, New Zealand and South Africa	4	2
OPEC	7	10
Eastern Europe	2	1

Canada is the U.S., most important trading partner with 31 percent of the American exports and providing nearly 31 percent of our imports. The U.S. exports capital goods, industrial supply, automobiles and agriculture. The major areas of the world to which the U.S. exports are Asia, Western Europe, and North America.

The major imports of the United States include: machinery, transport equipment, mineral fuels, manufactured goods, clothing, and food and live animals. The major imports of the United States are presented in Table 14.1.

Table 14.1
Imports of the United States, (General)

Item of Imports to the U.S.

Food and Live Animals
Beverages and Tobacco
Crude Materials
Mineral Fuels
Chemicals
Manufactured Goods
Machinery
Transport Equipment
Clothing
Footwear

Terms of Trade

The gains a country receives from foreign trade is measured by the terms of trade. The terms of trade measures the relationship between the prices a country gets for its exports and the prices it pays for imports over a period of time. It is calculated by dividing the country's export price index by the country's import price index and multiplying by 100 to express it as a percentage as shown below.

$$\text{Terms of Trade} = \frac{\text{Export price index}}{\text{Import price index}} \times 100$$

Example: If the terms of trade equal 107, this means that to purchase a given quantity of goods, the country had to give up 7% fewer exports.

INTERNATIONAL TRADE: FREE-TRADE THEORY

This chapter provides analysis of international trade and protectionism. First, it reviews important facts about the reasons for trade and the consequences of trade. Second, it examines how international specialization based on comparative and absolute advantage can mutually benefit trading partners. Third, we will stress the types of trade barriers and arguments in favor of protectionist barriers. Fourth, countries can be classified into three types: Most Developed Countries (MDC) or first world countries, second world countries, and Third World countries.

The most significant business developments in the last 45 years have been both the rapid growth of international business and the increase in the number of firms involved. International trade has been growing faster than the growth of world output.

The free-trade theory refers to the idea that it is in the best interests of all that trade among nations be free from artificial barriers, such as taxes, quotas, or other restrictions. The theory can be summarized by Figure 14.0.

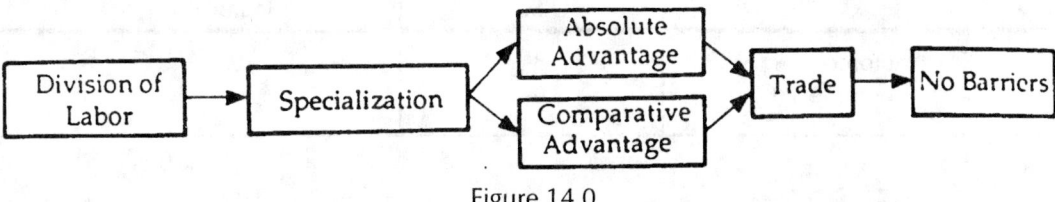

Figure 14.0

The pure theory of international trade deals with the basis for trade and the gains from trade; i.e., why do countries trade and what do they gain from trade?

Some of the underlying assumptions commonly made to simplify the pure theory of international trade are: a world of two countries; two goods; two factors: laborers are mobile domestically but immobile internationally; zero trade barriers and transportation costs; perfect competition prevails.

The concept of mercantilism inspired Adam Smith, a Scottish economic philosopher, in 1776 to write *An Inquiry into the Nature and Causes of the Wealth of Nations*, more commonly referred to as *The Wealth of Nations*. He believed that economic, political and religious liberties were so closely related that a threat to one endangered the others. It was his contention that the rules of the science of economics he founded would promote liberty and the wealth of nations. "Market forces, not government controls, should determine the direction, volume and composition of international trade." His theory laid the groundwork for modern theories of trade.

In my own classes, I have used the example of an automobile. Let us say one worker had to make a whole car from scratch. The worker had to mine the iron, smelt the steel, mine the bauxite, smelt the aluminum, drill the oil, make the plastics, make all the parts, and put them all together and drive it off the assembly line. How many cars do you think we would have produced in a year?

I don't think we would produce very many. The point, here, is that we don't do it that way. We divide up the work, and have people specialize in areas. As a result, we produce millions of cars a year.

In which areas should a person specialize? In the area in which they have some skill, some knowledge, some expertise, and some liking. In other words, in some area in which the person has an advantage.

The concept of specialization can also be applied to nations. Countries have advantages in certain products due to climate, soil, location, labor skills, and management skills. For example, Costa Rica has the conditions for bananas, Columbia for coffee, Japan for automobiles, and the United States for agricultural products. This refers to absolute advantage. Absolute advantage refers to a country being able to produce more of a particular product from the input used. Since the main element of input is labor, we could state: absolute advantage refers to being able to produce more per unit of labor. This can be summarized as follows.

a. Absolute Advantage

Adam Smith advocated that with free trade each nation should specialize in producing the items that it would produce more efficiently, in which it has an *Absolute Advantage*.

A country is considered to have an absolute advantage if it can produce a product at a lower cost than any other nation, or if it is the only nation that can provide it. "If all nations followed this principle, each would specialize in producing the good or goods in which it enjoys an absolute advantage." Each country would import all other products it wished to have and both trading countries would benefit.

Example of absolute advantage:

Output per Unit of Input

	U.S.	Japan
Automobiles (A)	8	9
Computers (C)	16	12

In the U.S., 8 automobiles can be produced per unit of input as can 16 computers. In Japan, 9 automobiles can be produced per unit of input as can 12 computers. In this example, the U.S. has an absolute advantage in the production of computers while Japan has an absolute advantage in the production of automobiles. The ratio of superiority in computers is 16C to 12C. The ratio of superiority in automobiles for Japan is 9A to 8A. Therefore, the nation is said to have an absolute advantage if a good can be produced less expensively there than elsewhere.

b. Comparative Advantage

The most important proposition in the theory of the gains from trade is that trade allows all countries to obtain the goods in which they do not have a comparative advantage at a lower opportunity cost than they would face if they were to produce all commodities for themselves. This allows all countries to have more of all commodities than they could have if they tried to be self-sufficient.

The fundamental concept of comparative advantage arises from countries having different opportunity costs of producing particular goods. This creates the opportunity for all nations to gain from trade.

In 1817, Ricardo introduced the *Comparative Advantage* principle that recommended if a nation were less efficient in the production of 2 products it could still gain from international trade if it were not equally less efficient in the production of both goods. Based on the belief that although one nation has an absolute disadvantage compared to a second nation in the production of two commodities, its absolute disadvantage is less in one of the commodities. A country should specialize in producing the commodities for which it has the greatest comparative advantage or the least comparative disadvantage in relation to other countries.

The product that a country will produce depends on many factors, including the presence of natural resources, the cost of labor and capital, and its location in relation to other markets. If a country has a comparative advantage in one commodity, it must have a disadvantage in another commodity. As long as the opportunity cost of doing the same job differs from different people or different countries, each will have a comparative advantage.

Example 1:

> Linda, the district director of a government agency can type faster than her secretary Carol. She therefore has an absolute advantage over Carol in typing ability. Should the district director spend her valuable time typing or should she attend to her director duties which she is much more qualified at performing than Carol?
>
> It would be a wiser decision to let Linda perform her director duties in which she is more qualified than Carol. Linda may be making "good" use of her time typing, but not making the "best" use of that time.

Example 2:

Output per Unit of Input

	U.S.	Japan
Automobiles (A)	8	2
Computers (C)	16	12

The U.S. has an absolute advantage in the production of both commodities. However, the superiority of the U.S. in automobiles (8A to 2A) is greater than its degrees of superiority in computers (16C to 12C). The U.S. has a comparative advantage in the production of automobiles and a comparative disadvantage in the production of computers (8A/2A > 16C/12C).

Japan has a comparative advantage in computers and a comparative disadvantage in automobiles (12C/16C > 2A/8A). Therefore, the inequality 8A/2A > 16C/12C is equivalent to the inequality of 12C/16C > 2A/8A.

The comparative advantage theory is assumed to depend on relative factor proportions or availabilities, under the assumption that all countries have access to the same production technology and differ only in their endowments of factors of production.

Example 3:

Comparative and Absolute Advantage
Output per Worker/Day

	Tons of Steel	VCRs
South Korea	80	40
Japan	20	20

Looking at the above data, the following points can be drawn:
—The opportunity cost of one VCR in Japan is 1 ton of steel.
—The opportunity cost of one VCR in South Korea is two tons of steel.
—With international trade, the maximum number of VCRs that Japan would be willing to export to South Korea in exchange for each ton of steel is 1 VCR.
—With international trade, the maximum amount of steel that South Korea would be willing to export to Japan in exchange for each VCR is 2 tons of steel.
—According to the principle of comparative advantage, South Korea should export steel; for Japan, there is no basis for gainful trade.
—South Korea has the absolute advantage in the production of both steel and VCR.

Advantages to a Country that Engages in International Trade

Advantages to a country that engages in international trade are as follows:

a. The nation specializes in the production of certain goods.

b. The nation reaches a higher indifference curve, thus a higher level of satisfaction.

c. The nation gains by greater consumption of *two* goods.

d. The nation has become part of the global community.

REASONS FOR TRADE

International trade is beneficial to all nations that participate. Individuals within nations do not necessarily gain. Those who are able to export more, gain because the demand for their product increases. The price of the product rises, and profits rise. Workers benefit, because the demand for their service rises, as do their incomes.

In this section, we will look at several reasons why foreign trade is desirable. These reasons include: cost advantages, more variety of products, greater choice, expansion of markets for domestic goods, and political reasons.

a. Cost Advantage

Industries in certain countries have cost advantages due to conditions in the country, such as soil, climate, resources, and labor costs. As a consequence, these industries are able to produce a product cheaper than industries in other countries. Adam Smith in *The Wealth of Nations*, advised that one should not try to make at home what one could buy cheaper from a foreign country.

b. Variety of Goods

Foreign trade enables consumers to purchase goods from all over the world. Many of these goods would be totally unavailable otherwise. Our college has a student center with automated machines dispensing food and drink. One of the more popular machines is the coffee machine. From this machine, students get coffee, tea, and hot chocolate. All three of these items are imports. We also import petroleum, tin, cobalt and other minerals, bananas, diamonds, shoes, clothes, T.Vs., video recorders, compact disc players, spices, automobiles, and many others. Our lives would be quite different without imports.

c. Greater Choice

Greater choice refers to two different meanings. (1) Since there are more types of goods available, there are more choices. If there were only strawberries, a person would have to put strawberries on their cereal. There are, however, bananas. A person now can make a choice and have a variety of fruit with their cereal. (2) There are now more choices for each product, such as automobiles. Without trade, a person must choose among General Motors, Ford, and Chrysler. With trade, there are more choices: Datsun, Mazda, Toyota, V.W., and others.

The greater choice benefits the consumer in several ways: greater variety and lower prices, and better quality of goods due to the increased competition.

d. Expansion of Markets for Domestic Goods

By purchasing imports, consumers increase the revenue of foreign producers. In turn, these revenues will increase the incomes of the workers of these producers. Additional income is generated, which creates a market for goods and services. Domestic producers can then sell the goods produced, but not sold in the home country, in this new market.

An example would be an industry producing bottle openers. After many people in the home country have purchased one, the industry would be seeking ways to increase sales. One way would be to somehow increase the market. A way to do this would be by foreign sales in countries which lack bottle openers.

e. Political Reasons

Foreign trade can be used for political reasons. To indicate that a country wishes to be friends with another country, it will pursue trade with that country. Trade is a form of friendship, a form of sharing. If, on the other hand, a country wishes to indicate it does not approve of the policies of another country, it can withhold trade. The United States does not allow trade with Cuba, for example. This is due to the problem of Cuban activists in Latin America and Africa promoting communism. By not allowing trade, the United States gets a message across and also prevents Cuba from getting goods and materials to make the lives of their people better. In addition, Cuba has fewer goods and materials to use to promote its political philosophy.

Protectionism Theory

Because foreign competition hurts some businesses and workers, they have an incentive to seek government protection. If they are successful, then government will impose either a tariff or a quota on imported goods. Protectionism is the oldest issue in economics and one gaining much attention today. Therefore, international business must face the reality that this is a world of tariffs, quotas, and non-tariff barriers designed to protect a country's market from intrusion by foreign companies.

Tariffs can be *ad valorem* or *specific*. An ad valorem tariff is a trade tax equal to a given percentage of a selling price. In other worlds, it is a fixed percentage of the value of an imported product as it enters the country. A tax of 15 percent per imported item would be an example of an ad valorem. Tariffs may be used as revenue-generating taxes or to discourage the importation of goods, or for both reasons. In addition, tariffs are arbitrary, discriminatory, and require constant administration and supervision. A quota sets a maximum on the quantity of a good that may be imported during a given period of time. There is a limit on television sets in the U.K., there are Italian restrictions on Japanese motorcycles, and there are U.S. quotas on sugar, textiles, and peanuts. There are three important differences between tariffs and quotas. First, quotas firmly restrict importation. Tariffs do not. Second, quotas invite more government enforcement because each imported foreign item is limited to a specific amount. Tariffs place no such restriction on foreign producers. Third, tariffs encourage foreign firms to decrease their prices to offset these taxes.

Imports are restricted in a variety of ways other than tariffs. These nontariff barriers (NTB) are:

Boycott

A government boycott is an absolute restriction against the purchase and importation of certain goods from other countries.

- Export Subsidies are payments by government to an industry to encourage exports or discourage imports.

- Voluntary Export Restraints (VER): A VER is an agreement between an importing country and an exporting country for a restriction on the volume of exports. A VER is similar to a quota. Japan has a VER on automobiles to the U.S.; that is, Japan has agreed to export a *fixed number* of automobiles annually.

- Orderly Marketing Agreements (OMA) refer to a negotiated agreement among nations to institute voluntary export quotas. OMA's serve several purposes: (1) they inform an exporting nation of the concern that exists in the importing nation; (2) they reduce the need for more severe trade restrictions; (3) they cut down or limit the exports to a nation; and (4) since they are voluntary, the exporting country is seen in a better light by the importing nation.

- Local Content Requirement refers to a certain percentage of a product's total value that has to produced domestically. For example, Brazil may have an 85 percent requirement for cars. This means that 85 percent of the value of cars sold in Brazil would have to be produced in Brazil. Local content requirements serve two purposes: (1) they encourage domestic production of items; and (2) they discourage the practice of importing cheaper foreign parts, as in the automobile industry.

- Anti-dumping policies against other countries and agreements to stop them. Dumping refers to a producer's selling its products in a foreign country at a price that is below the price charged in the home country, or at a price that is below the cost of production. Domestic producers would be upset by this because they would be forced to compete with lower prices, thus, losing profits.

Specific Limitations on Trade

include import licensing requirements, embargoes, minimum import price limits, and local content requirements.

Government Participation in Trade

includes government procurement policies, includes countervailing duties (CVD), and domestic assistance programs.

Customs and Administrative Entry Producers

include valuation systems, antidumping practices, tariff classifications, documentation requirements; and fees.

Charges on Imports

include border taxes, import credit discriminations, variable levies, special supplementary duties, administrative fees, and prior import deposit requirements.

Standards

may include packaging, labeling, marking standards, intergovernmental acceptances of testing methods and standards.

WHY DO NATIONS RESTRICT TRADE?

Countless reasons are espoused by protectionists to maintain government restrictions on trade, but essentially all arguments can be classified as follows:

a. Protection of an infant industry

b. National defense

c. Maintenance of employment and reduction of unemployment

d. Retaliation and bargaining

e. Maintenance of the standard of living and high wages

While the benefits of free trade include a greater variety of goods, the economics of scale, an expansion of domestic markets, cost advantages, and greater choice, many people support trade restrictions. The following are some of the arguments to support their views:

Workers are paid less in foreign countries, and U.S. industries are therefore unable to compete.

Some argue that the United States loses money when it flows overseas in payment for imports.

It is often argued that foreigners impose tariffs and quotas on U.S. output, so we must retaliate or lose sales in both domestic and foreign markets. Hence, foreigners need American dollars to buy from the U.S. To get those dollars, we must buy from foreigners. So foreign tariffs on U.S. exports ultimately hurt the foreign nation that imposed them as well as America. If the U.S. retaliates, trade is reduced even further. The harm is compounded, not negated. However, the threat of a retaliatory tariff may act as a bargaining chip in international trade conferences.

It is argued that tariffs increase workers' employment opportunities. This may be effective in the short run, but in the long run, reduced imports will result in reduced exports, which will *increase* unemployment.

It is also argued that new industries deserve protection (the "infant industry" argument). The infant industry for an LDC can be protected through an import tariff, until its costs are low enough for it to stand competition.

Consequences of a Tariff

In the following section, we will present the effects of foreign trade and tariffs. Figure 14.1 presents a beginning situation with no trade.

In the following demand and supply functions, the price of the goods will be P_0 and the equilibrium quantity will be Q_0. All demand is satisfied by domestic supply.

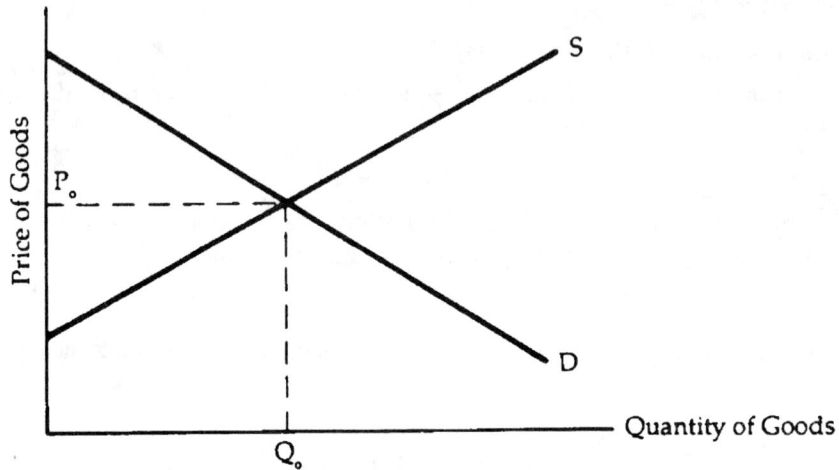

Figure 14.1
Demand & Supply (No Trade)

If we assume that the price of these goods from foreign suppliers is lower, and that the goods can be imported at the lower price, we have the following supply curve (S'), as shown in Figure 14.2. P_1 represents the foreign price.

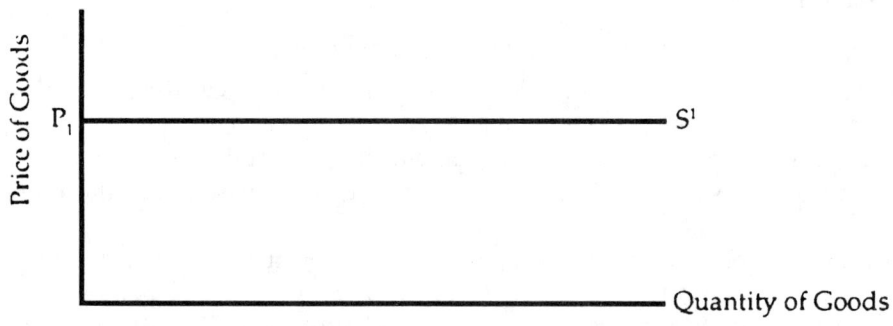

Figure 14.2
Supply of Foreign Goods

The supply curve (S') is horizontal, which indicates that different quantities can be imported at price (P1). To show the effects of foreign trade, we will put the two graphs together in Figure 14.3.

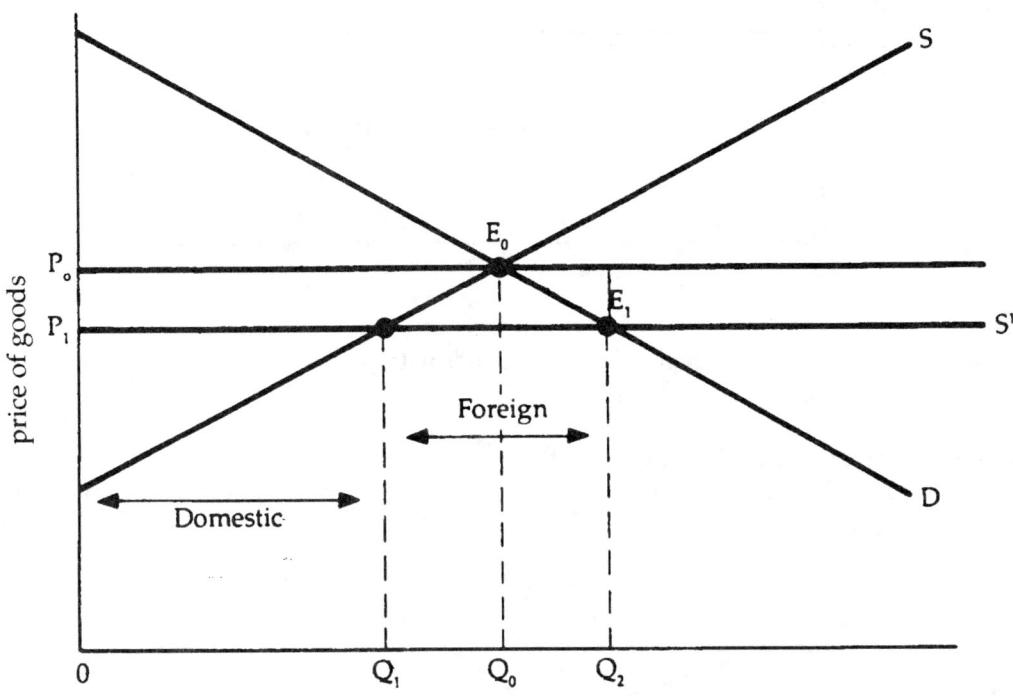

Figure 14.3
Demand & Supply (Foreign Trade)

Without trade, the price of the product is P_0, and the quantity supplied by market domestic producers is Q_0. This is the equilibrium level denoted at E_0. Because the foreign market has been added, and we assume that any amount is available at price (P_1), the new supply curve is S'. Equilibrium now occurs at the intersection of the demand curve (D) and the new supply curve (S') at E_1. The total supply on the market is now Q_2. The effects are the following:

a. There is an increase in the amount of the product available to the consumers, from Q_0 to Q_2.

b. The market price of the product is lower than before. It dropped from P_0 to P_1.

c. The domestic level of production has dropped from Q_0 to Q_1. In Figure 13.11, domestic production is indicted by 0 to Q_1, and foreign production is indicated by Q_1 to Q_2. This will lead to unemployment.

d. The revenues of domestic producers have thus been affected by: (1) lower prices, and (2) lower quantities. As a result, there would be a greater loss of revenue for these producers under these conditions.

In order to offset the negative effects, let us assume it is decided to impose a tariff upon foreign goods and analyze the effects. In Figure 14.4 we show the tariff by the line S''.

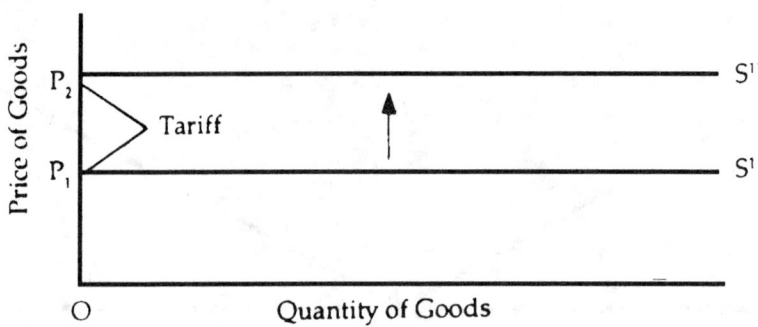

Figure 14.4
Supply of Foreign Goods with Tariff

The original price was P_1. P_2 represents the price after the imposition of the tariff. $P_2 - P_1$, therefore, represents the tariff. Figure 14.5 shows the effects of adding a tariff, as shown by the new supply line at price P_2.

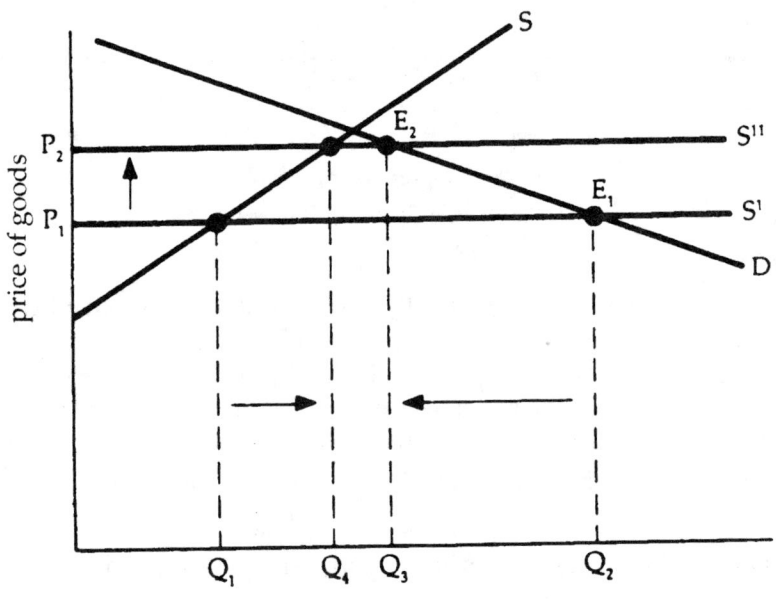

Figure 14.5
Demand & Supply (After Tariff)

The effects of imposing a tariff are the following:

a. There is a decrease in the amount of the product available to the consumer from Q_4 to Q_3.

b. The market price of the product is higher than before by the amount of the tariff. The price has risen from P_1 to P_2.

c. The domestic level of production has risen from Q_1 to Q_2. The foreign share of the market is now Q_2 to Q_3.

d. The revenues of domestic producers will increase because their share of the market is greater.

e. The government revenue has increased due to the tariff, which is a tax. Taxes are the property of government.

Thus, the losers in a tariff are the consumers who now have higher prices and fewer goods and the foreign suppliers, who have a lower level of sales. The winners are domestic producers, with greater sales, and the government, with additional revenues.

FOREIGN EXCHANGE MARKETS

In this section, we will examine one aspect of international finance. It deals with the rate which currencies exchange with each other.

Trade between two countries differs from domestic trade because the countries use different monies, but this problem is resolved by the existence of foreign-exchange markets in which the money used by one country can be purchased and paid for with the money of other countries.

The United States uses the dollar, Mexico the Peso, France the Franc, Germany the Mark, and Japan the Yen. Canada also uses a dollar, but it is not the same as a U.S. dollar. Hence, the foreign exchange market refers to the organizational setting within which firms, individuals, and banks buy and sell foreign currencies. (The two major foreign exchange markets are in London and New York.) The foreign exchange market actually involves the use of such intermediaries as bankers, currency traders, and brokers. This is a market in which currencies of different countries are bought and sold. Most foreign exchange transactions are made over the telephone or with electronic equipment. Written contracts are rare. The honor system, although unusual in most forms of international business, is necessary because exchange rates change so frequently.

There are actually two major types of foreign exchange transactions. One type of transaction involves the intermediate exchange of currencies in the *spot* market. The other promises to make an exchange of currencies in the future and is known as the *forward* market.

a. The Spot Market

The spot rate is the exchange rate between the two countries for their immediate trade for delivery within two days.

The spot rate is used when a firm wants to change one currency for another. For example, a banker can either handle the transaction for the firm or have it handled by another bank. Within a short period of time, the firm knows exactly how many units of one currency are to be received or paid for a certain number of units of another currency.

Let's suppose, for example, that a U.S. company wants to buy 2,000 books from a British publisher. However, the publisher wants four thousand British pounds (£4,000) for the books so the American company needs to change some of its dollars into pounds to pay for the books. If the British pound is currently being exchanged for U.S. $1.65, then £4,000 equals $6,600. The U.S. company pays $6,600 to its bank and the bank exchanges the dollars for £4,000 to pay the British publisher. In recent years, the spot price of the British pound has been about U.S. $1.5000 or about £0.6667 to $U.S.

In the U.S. however, the conversion price is quoted in two different ways: (a) how many British Pound (£) are needed to buy 1 U.S. $, and (b) how many U.S. $ are required to buy 1£.

b. The Forward Market

Forward market is an obligation to buy or sell at a set exchange rate. A forward contract guarantees which currencies are to be traded, when the exchange is to occur, how much of each currency is involved, and which side of the contract each party is on (each party's beginning and ending currencies). By entering into a forward contract, a firm eliminates one uncertainty—the exchange rate risk of not knowing what it will receive or pay in the future. However, note that any possible gains in exchange rate changes are also eliminated and the contract may cost more than it turns out to be worth. Hence, business people generally dislike uncertainties. This is a major reason for the existence of the forward market. Therefore, forward rates are today's cost for a commitment by one party to deliver to or take from another party an agreed amount of currency at a fixed future date, 30, 60, 90, or 180 days.

Forward exchange rates allow individuals to lock into an exchange rate now for a future transaction. By contracting now to buy or sell currency in the future, individuals are insulated from costly currency depreciations (or profitable currency appreciations). In other words, the risks of holding foreign exchange assets and liabilities can be balanced, or hedged.

If a currency's forward exchange rate is greater than the spot rate, it is said to sell at a premium. If the forward rate is less than the spot rate, it is said to sell at a discount.

FOREIGN EXCHANGE AND FOREIGN EXCHANGE RATES

Foreign exchange is the currency of other nations. This money can be of one foreign currency or many. American firms owning German Marks, therefore, have foreign exchange. German firms holding U.S. dollars count these dollars as at least part of their exchange holdings.

The *foreign exchange rate* is the price at which one currency might be converted to another. In other words, it is the *rate* at which a firm might *exchange* one currency for another.

Changes in Demand and Supply of Currency

The equilibrium exchange rate in Figure 14.6 occurs when the quantity demanded of a foreign currency equals the quantity of that currency supplied to the foreign country. In the flexible Exchange Rate System, the exchange rate can change if either the supply or demand changes, or both change. To explore this change, we will assume for now that there are two countries, the U.S. and the U.K.

The most common reason for exchange of dollars for British Pounds is to buy goods produced in the U.K.; U.S. importers must pay with British pounds (£). When the exchange rates are allowed to float, they are determined by the forces of supply and demand. Hence, an excess demand for British pounds will cause the pound to appreciate against the dollar. When the price of British pounds rises, the British can obtain more dollars for each pound. This means that U.S. goods and services appear less expensive to British buyers. On the supply side of the market, the situation is reversed.

One of these currencies is *foreign*, it is called the *foreign exchange rate*. Foreign exchange and foreign exchange rates are usually unavoidable aspects of international business. Since one part usually has either to pay or receive a foreign currency, people must be able to convert currencies. This conversion takes place in what is known as the *foreign exchange market*.

The foreign exchange market can be portrayed using supply and demand curves. Suppose, for example, that the U.S. and Japan are the only countries in the world, and all reserves are held in foreign exchange. In the dollar market, the supply of dollars results from U.S. purchase of Japanese goods or financial assets. The demand for dollars comes from the Japanese demand for U.S. goods or financial assets. At the equilibrium price (the exchange rate), the demand and supply of U.S. dollars are equal.

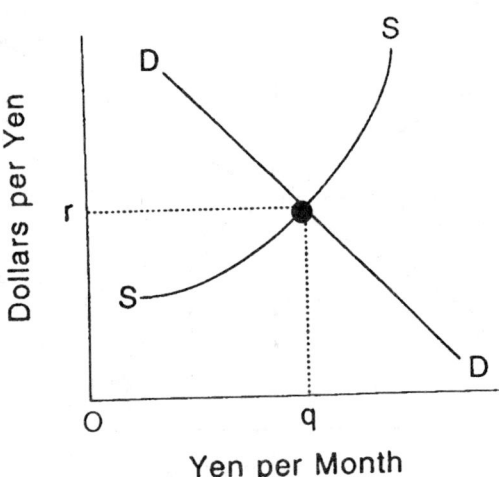

Figure 14.6
U.S. Demand, Supply, and Exchange Rate for Japanese Yen
Demand for Japanese Yen is represented by DD and supply is SS. The equilibrium exchange rate is r dollars per Yen and the equilibrium quantity of Yen is q.

If the price of a dollar is 5 francs, than a condominium priced at 250,000 dollars will cost 1,250,000 francs (250,000 x 5 = 1,250,000). The Frenchman will exchange his 1,250,000 francs for 250,000 dollars and purchase the condo.

This system is called flexible because the exchange rate can change if either the supply or demand change, or both change. Figures 14.7 and 14.8 indicate the consequence of changes in supply. In Figure 14.7, an increase in supply is indicated by a movement from curve S to curve S_1. This is the result of more dollars entering the foreign exchange market by owners of dollars buying other currencies. The consequence is that the exchange rate will drop to ER_2. People in France can now buy dollars more cheaply.

In Figure 14.8, a decrease in supply is indicated by a movement from curve S to curve S_1. This is the result of fewer dollars being available in the foreign exchange market because of their being purchased rather than other currencies. The consequence is that the exchange rate will rise to ER_2. The price of dollars will be higher in France.

Exchange rates can also change because of changes in demand, as indicated in Figures 14.9 and 14.10.

In Figure 14.9, an increase in demand is indicated in a movement from D to D_1. This is the result of an increase in purchase of American goods by foreigners needing dollars for payment. The consequence is an increase in the exchange rate from FER_1 to FER_2. Because of an increased demand for American goods, the price of the American dollar has increased.

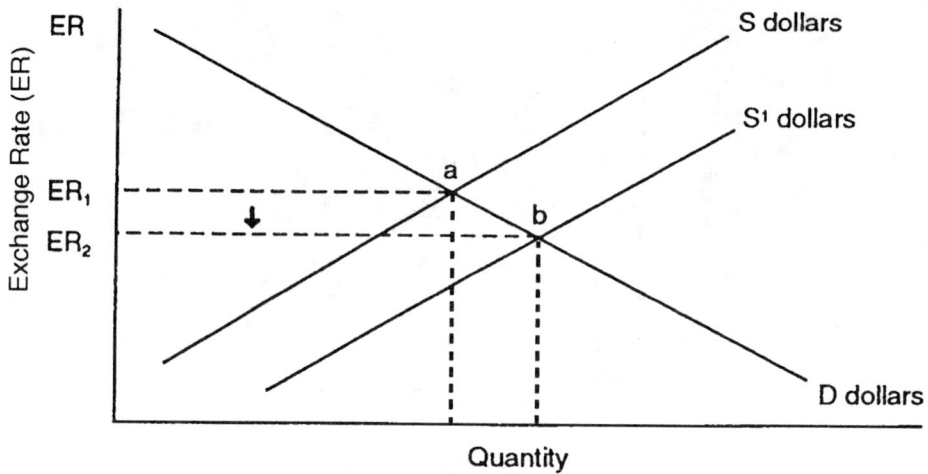

Figure 14.7
Increase in Supply of Dollars

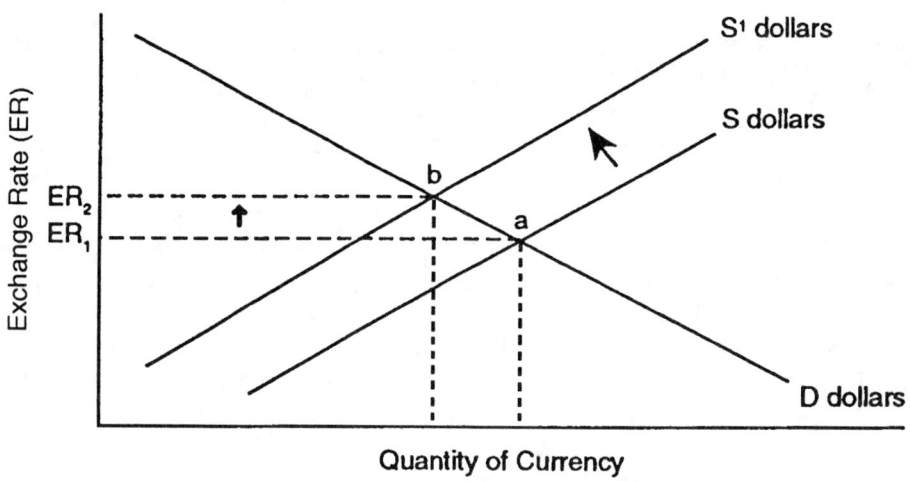

Figure 14.8
Decrease in Supply of Dollars

In Figure 14.10, a decrease in demand is indicated in a movement from D to D_1. This is the result of fewer purchases of American goods by foreigners. There is less of a need for American dollars. The consequence is a decrease in the exchange rate of ER_1 to ER_2. Because of a lower demand for American goods, the price of the American dollar has decreased.

Therefore, increases in an exchange rate are caused by either decreases in the supply of a currency or by increases in the demand for a currency. Decreases in an exchange rate are caused by either increases in the supply of a currency or by decreases in the demand for a currency.

American exports create a demand for dollars and generate a supply of foreign currency in the foreign exchange markets. They increase the money supply in the U.S. and decrease foreign money supplies. And they earn monies that can be used to pay for American imports. Also, American imports create a supply of dollars and generate a demand for foreign money in foreign exchange markets. They also decrease the money supply (MS) in the U.S. and increase foreign money supplies. And they use up monies obtained by exporting.

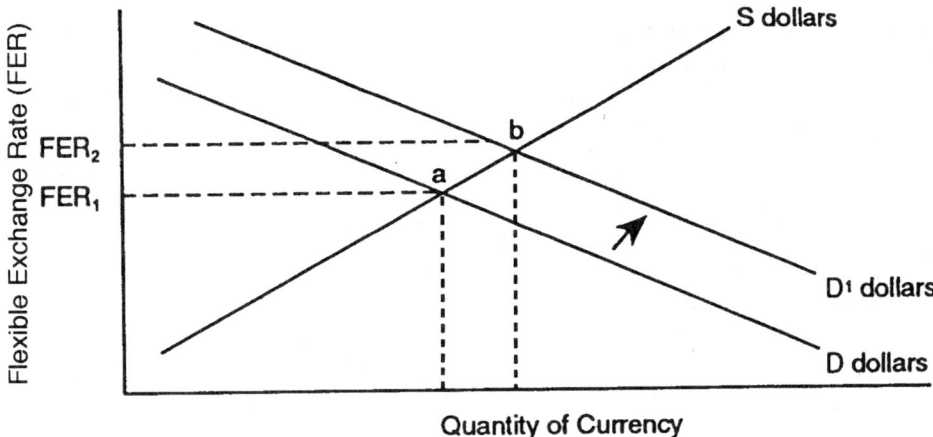

Figure 14.9
Increase in Demand for Dollars

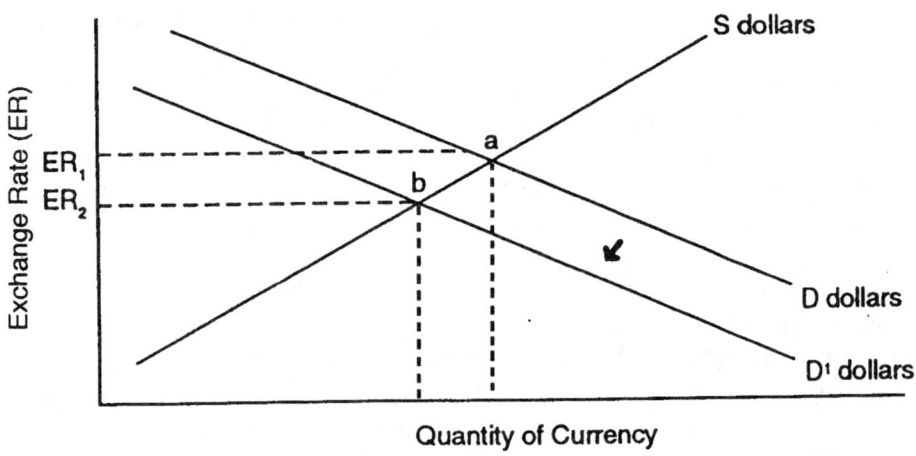

Figure 14.10
Decrease in Demand for Dollars

THE GOLD STANDARD

In ancient times, ensuring the convertibility of paper money into gold was meant to maintain confidence in the country's value at home and abroad. Economists typically date the beginning of the gold standard to the period between 1880 and 1914. The gold standard is a system whereby national currencies are fixed in terms of their value in gold, thus creating fixed exchange rates between currencies. Hence, each currency has a mint parity price, fixed exchange rates prevail, and all currencies are linked to each other through their prices in gold. Therefore, the gold standard fixes the price of gold in terms of currencies. For example, suppose that the price of an ounce of gold is 100 Francs in Cameroon and $400 in the United States. The Cameroon franc is worth four times the value of the U.S. dollar.

Bretton Woods System

Bretton Woods is the site in New Hampshire where a group of experts from 44 countries met in 1944 and agreed on an international monetary system of fixed exchange rates. The focal point was the U.S. dollar. Under the Bretton Woods System agreement, if a country is experiencing a fundamental disequilibrium,* it should devalue its currency. The above system required countries to actively buy and sell dollars to maintain fixed exchange rates when the fixed rate differed from the free market equilibrium rate. The Bretton Woods system stipulated that all countries should peg their currencies against the dollar, which was in turn pegged to gold. The currencies of these nations are therefore bound to fluctuate in gold value along with the U.S. dollar. The system officially dissolved between 1965–1975, especially from the 1971 Smithsonian agreement to 1973.

In sum, the Bretton Woods system created the International Monetary Fund and the World Bank; it was a gold exchange standard; it used the U.S. dollar as a reserve currency, and it tried to maintain exchange rates through foreign exchange market intervention (the buying or selling of currencies by a government or central bank to achieve a specified exchange rate).

Exchange Rates

a. Fixed Exchange Rate (FER)

Fixed exchange rates are used in developing countries. FERs are set by central banks, affecting the supply of, or demand for, currency or by backing currency with a set amount of gold. Fixed exchange rates put pressure on a nation to manage its macroeconomic policy in concert with other nations. FER prevailed in the world for most of the post-World War II era, and can be maintained over time only between countries with similar economic policies and underlying economic conditions. Under that system, governments must intervene in the foreign exchange market in order to maintain the exchange rate. Therefore, when an exchange rate is fixed at other than equilibrium rate, either excess demand or excess supply will persist.

Arguments For and Against the Fixed Exchange Rate System

The case for the fixed exchange rate system is based primarily on the security it affords people who engage in international trade. Traders do not have to worry about changes in the exchange rate affecting the profitability of their deals. To the extent that the fixed exchange rate system reduces the fixed cost of international trade, it should stimulate international trade. The case against the fixed exchange rate system is founded largely on the argument that many economic forces are constantly coming to bear on international currency markets. Countries will find it extraordinarily difficult to keep their exchange rate fixed, primarily because of their limited reserves. Persistent deficits can give rise to speculation in international currencies, which can destabilize international currency markets. The sudden and dramatic increases in exchange rates can add to the risk of doing international business. Fixed exchange rates impose discipline and add certainty to international deals. Flexible rates are favored by some for their adjustments.

b. Flexible Exchange vs. Managed Floating Exchange Rates

In 1971, the U.S. and most other countries decided to abandon the fixed exchange rate system in favor of managed float rates. The managed floating of exchange rates relies on foreign exchange markets to establish equilibrium exchange rates, but permits central banks to buy and sell foreign

---

*Temporary imbalances in the foreign exchange market (or in the balance of payments) are to be financed with the help of the International Monentary Fund.

currencies to manage short-term changes in the exchange rate. In other words, Managed Floating Rate (MFR) occurs when governments intervene. They may be trying to support their weak currency or to prevent it from appreciating too fast. (MFR are in use in the G-8 nations: U.S., Germany, Japan, U.K., France, Canada, Italy, and Russia.)

Flexible Exchange Rate (FER) or float is the condition in which market forces operate without government intervention. That is, the exchange rate responds to the forces of supply and demand, and the currency values in terms of other currencies are not fixed by agreements between governments, but instead are permitted to fall or rise in value according to market forces. Flexible exchange rates are in use in most of the world today.

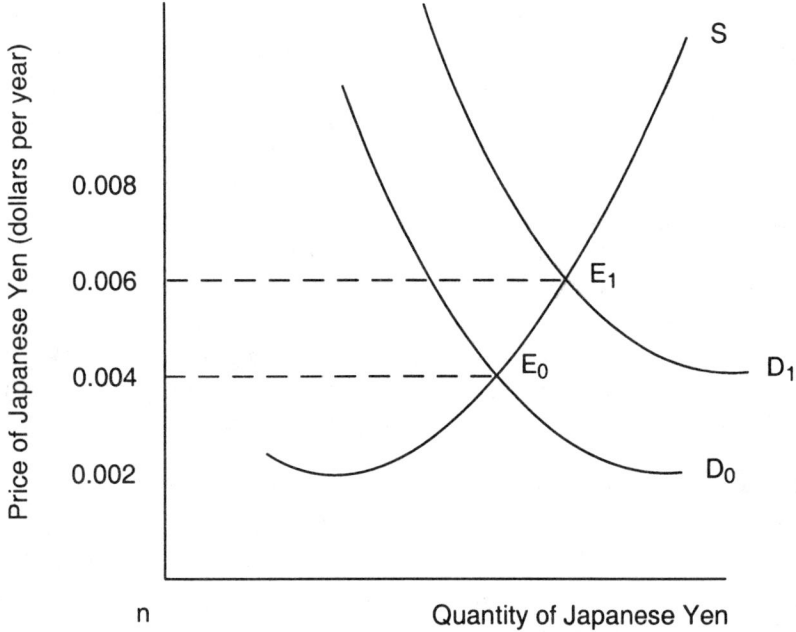

Figure 14.11
An Exchange Rate—Determined on a Free Market

The equilibrium exchange rate is at point Eo on the foreign exchange market. That is, one Yen costs four-tenths of a cent, or 1 dollar buys 250 Yen. If the demand for Yen rises to D1, the equilibrium exchange rate will change to Yen, 0.006 per dollar; that is, the Yen appreciates in value and the dollar depreciates.

The supply curve of Yen is positively sloped because as the price of Yen increases, Japan is willing to exchange more Yen for dollars. For example, suppose that wheat sells for 4 dollars per bushel in the United States. If the price of Yen is 0.004 dollar, then a bushel of wheat costs 1,000 Yen.

If the price of foreign currency rises, then the price of imports rises, and the demand for foreign currency falls. An increase in the exchange rate increases the supply of foreign currency for the U.S. dollars.

The demand for dollars arises from American exports of goods and services: capital flows into the United States, and the desire of firms, foreign banks, and governments to use American dollars as an international medium of exchange.

The supply of dollars to purchase foreign currencies arises from American exports of goods and services: capital flows from the U.S. and the desire of holders of dollars to increase the size of their holdings.

Currently, international exchange rates are labeled as being flexible (floating). The flexible exchange system determines exchange rates by supply and demand for the currency in question without government intervention in the foreign exchange markets.

By examining the supply and demand curves, one can observe that an over-supply of a currency without an increase in demand will cause a drop in the price of that currency (the price being the exchange rate between the countries surveyed). On the same note, an increase in demand for a currency without an increase in supply will lead to a price increase of the currency.

Net exports (exports-imports) are a measure of the international trading status of a country. A nation that imports more than it exports is said to have a negative balance of trade. A country that exports more than it imports has a positive balance of trade—it is forced to convert more of its currency into a foreign currency than other importing countries are having to convert into that country's currency. This imbalance will cause an over-supply of that nation's currency on the foreign exchange market and will lead to a drop in the price of that currency.

The power of the floating exchange system is that it allows countries to recover from the over-supply of currency. As the price of the currency drops, the attractiveness of that nations' products improve because they are cheaper to the nations with higher priced currency. This will cause an increase in demand for that nation's products and an increase in demand for that nation's currency. The result is that the price of that nation's currency increases.

Determination of Exchange Rate

Other factors which determine the exchange rate of a nation under the floating exchange rate system include:

   a. The Nation's Interest Rates. Interest rate is the price paid for money. To borrow money, one must pay an interest rate to use the money for the period of time agreed to by the people involved. The purpose of the interest rate is to reward the lender for taking the risk of lending his capital over the given length of time. A country that offers high interest rates to nations, or its own citizens, will create a high demand for its currency. This high demand for currency will cause an increase in the price of the currency. Warning: offering high interest rates is not as easy a solution as it seems for countries in need of capital.

   b. The Nation's Economic Strength or Performance. The floating exchange rate is a direct reflection of a nations' economic performance on the international market. As discussed earlier, a nation with a negative trade balance is importing more than it exports. The question that must be answered is why? Is the nation a poor third-world country that depends heavily on other nations to support its economy: or is it a poorly managed nation that is constantly being overthrown by different factions of its own nation? These are examples of situations that can shape a nation's exchange rate. Accounting with an unstable government is considered by many nations as a high-risk nation in terms of trading, goods, services, and capital. This high risk will be reflected in its exchange rate.

   c. Purchasing Power Parity (PPP). This is a theory that predicts exchange rate adjustments so that equivalent goods are equivalently priced throughout the world. The purchasing power parity also forecasts that the exchange rates will adjust to eliminate the effects of different inflation rates. For example, assume that the exchange rate between the United Kingdom and the United States is 2 pounds to the dollar. The purchasing power parity predicts that an item costing 2 pounds in the United Kingdom will cost one dollar in the United States. Remember, this assumes that the items are equivalent. One other important assumption is that the supply and demand for the items are relatively equal between the two nations. If there is a surplus of the item, its price will drop: a high demand will cause its price to increase. If we assume that the items are traded internationally, we can safely assume that the item is traded to a level to reach international equilibrium.

d. Changes in Tastes and Preferences. Changes in tastes and preferences can include changes due to perceived improvement in quality, as well as the obvious shifts due to changes in a nations' society.

e. Change in Income. As the income of a nation increases, demand for goods purchased increases. This increase in demand will occur for products that are imported, as well as manufactured domestically. How the relative trade balance is affected can cause a change in the nation's exchange rate.

FACTORS AFFECTING EXCHANGE: WHY DO EXCHANGE RATES VARY?

Exhibit 14.0 summarizes the variables that might have an effect on the exchange rates of a currency.

Exhibit 14.0

Name of Variable (Factor)	Effect of Currency (Exchange Rate)
Inflation (rises)	Currency drops
Interest rate (rises)	Currency drops
Political Stability (rises)	Currency strengthens
Labor conditions improve	Currency strengthens
Government spending (rises)	Currency drops
Speculation that currency will increase in value	Currency strengthens

If a nation appreciates its currency in relation to other national currencies, what will be the effect on other nation's exports and imports? On the willingness of that nation's citizens to invest abroad?

If a nation appreciates its currency, its imports will tend to increase while its exports will tend to decrease. This means that other nations will tend to see an increase in their exports and a reduction in their imports from the country whose currency has been appreciated.

Shifts in Exchange Rates: Devaluation and Revaluation

Changes in gold backing are called devaluation and revaluation. Devaluation refers to a country's reducing its gold backing to lower the price of its currency to others. Revaluation refers to a country's increasing its gold backing to raise the price of its currency to others.

Devaluation

Devaluation results in a lower price for currency and an increase in the demand for products of the devaluating country. Consider the following example. To begin with, the U.S. defines the dollar as 1/20 of an ounce of gold, and Germany defines the mark as 1/80 of an ounce of gold. The exchange rate is one dollar equals four marks. It takes four marks to purchase one dollar. If an American car cost 10,000 dollars, it takes 40,000 marks to purchase it.

If the United States devalues its currency, it backs the dollar with less gold. Let us assume it is lowered to 1/40 of an ounce of gold. With the mark still at 1/80 of an ounce, the exchange rate is now two marks for one dollar. The dollar is now cheaper for person buying with marks. The 10,000 dollar car now costs only 20,000 marks.

The result of devaluation to foreigners is two-fold. First, the price of the currency being devalued decreases. Second, the lower price of currency reduces the price of goods to foreigners, thus, stimulating trade.

The result of devaluation to domestic consumers is to make foreign currency and foreign goods more expensive. To begin with, at 1/20 of an ounce of gold for the dollar and 1/80 of an ounce of gold for the mark, the exchange rate was four marks for one dollar, or a mark costing 25 cents. With the new backing of 1/40 of an ounce of gold for the dollar, the exchange rate is four marks for one dollar, or a mark costing 50 cents. Under the old exchange rate of four marks per dollar, a German car costing 40,000 marks costs 10,000 dollars (40,000/4 = 10,000). Now the same care costs 20,000 dollars (40,000/2 = 20,000).

If the United States were to devalue, it would mean better exchange rates and lower prices for foreigners, but worse exchange rates and higher prices for Americans. Devaluation would tend to *increase* exports and *decrease* imports.

Revaluation

Revaluation occurs when a nation increases the gold backing its currency. The results are the opposite of the ones when a country devalues. That is, a currency is priced above equilibrium.

To foreigners, the currency and goods denominated in it will cost more. To people in that country, foreign currencies and goods will be cheaper. Revaluation tends to *reduce* exports and *increase* imports.

If, to begin with, the dollar is defined as 1/20 of an ounce of gold and the mark is 1/80 of an ounce, the exchange rate is four marks per dollar. If the U.S. revalues the dollar to 1/10 of an ounce of gold, the exchange rate is eight marks per dollar. To people with marks, the dollar is now twice as expensive. To people with dollars, they can now buy twice as many marks. The effect, therefore, will be to discourage the purchase of American goods and to encourage the purchase of foreign goods.

Depreciation and Appreciation of the U.S. Dollar

Currency appreciation is an increase in the value of the country's currency relative to other currencies as a result of a decrease in its supply relative to the demand for it.

A depreciation of the U.S. dollar versus the yen occurs when the demand for Japanese imported cars rises in the United States.

Depreciation or appreciation of the U.S. dollar will affect the relative prices of foreign and domestic goods.

Changes in the exchange rate will change relative prices of foreign currencies and domestic products, altering import and export levels. Specifically, depreciation of the dollar will lower imports to the United States. Appreciation of the dollar will have the opposite effect.

In this context, appreciation of the dollar means that a dollar can buy more units of a foreign currency. Appreciation can reduce the price of foreign goods in the United States and increase the price of domestic goods abroad. The demand for internationally traded goods is downward sloping, which means that appreciation of the dollar will give rise to more imports and fewer exports.

A depreciation of the dollar means that a dollar is able to buy fewer units of the national currency. The change in exchange rates will affect the relative prices of foreign and domestic goods. Hence, the goods are downward sloping. This means that depreciation of the dollar will give rise to fewer imports and more exports.

Example: If the Italian lira is listed at an exchange rate in the U.S. dollar equivalent of $0.001, that means that 10,000 lira would trade for $10, a bushel of U.S. wheat costing $2.50 would cost 2,500 lira, and a liter of olive oil costing 12,000 lira would cost $12.

Exchange rate differences do not mean that one country is better or stronger than another, only that they measure value on a differently proportioned scale.

Developed vs. Developing Countries

The process of economic growth is different for countries in different stages of development. Countries can be classified into three types: first world countries, second world countries, and third world countries.

The first world countries include the non-communist industrialized countries. Included would be the countries of Western Europe, the United States, Australia, Canada, New Zealand, and Japan. The second world includes Eastern Europe, Russia, the People's Republic of China. The Third world consists of the developing countries. These countries are referred to as the less developed countries (LDCs).

Less Developed Countries

Less developed countries are the poorest countries. They are attempting to develop, but face critical problems of overpopulation, food shortages, lack of educational facilities, poverty, and lack of capital and motivation. These countries have very low living standards and little hope for change in the near future.

Areas

The less developed countries are found in Latin America, Africa, and Asia. All of Latin America is included. All the African countries, except the Union of South Africa, are included. Because of the resources in South Africa, such as gold and diamonds, the country has a high per capita living standard. Some of the Asian countries are also classified as less developed countries, ones with low per capita living standards.

Barriers to Doing Business in Less Developed Countries (LDC)

International trade for the United States has been mainly with the developed nations and not with the less developed nations. Proponents of free trade see an increase in welfare for all parties in a trade agreement, but the low incomes in the less developed countries and the barriers to doing business in these countries have resulted in little trade. The barriers in less developed countries are not as apparent as tariffs and import quotas. They take more subtle forms that are specifically addressed by the risk of dealing with the country itself which may prevent payment for goods and services and potentially jeopardize the financial investment and personnel involved.

Political

A political risk may be defined as the impact of changes in national and international political forces on business operations, physical assets, personnel and management. Political forces will cause drastic changes in a country's business environment that affect the profit and other goals of a particular business enterprise. Assessments are needed in pre-investment decisions where political risk is integrated with studies of marketing, production, logistics and finance.

Sources of political risk are:

    a. Social unrest and disorder.

    b. Nationalism.

    c. Armed conflicts.

d. Internal rebellions for political power.

   e. Terrorism.

   f. New international alliances.

A governmental goal to attract foreign investment and reinvestment over the long term would be furthered by creating an atmosphere of business confidence and stability. Whether a particular government will encourage or discourage U.S. firms will depend on its success in maintaining the political stability of the country. Political stability is the most important determining factor in establishing and maintaining good business relations. Government stability can have two dimensions: the simple ability of the government to maintain power; and 2) the continuation and consistency of government policies toward business.

It is difficult to do business in those countries where regional, national or international politics perpetuate trading hostilities. Examples are given of the long-standing Arab-Israeli, Vietnam-Cambodia and South African hostilities. Hostilities can be perpetuated due to long-lived ideological, racial and political differences between countries or ethnic groups.

There are five areas of major concern when measuring political risk:

   a. Impetus toward national control over the economy.

   b. Performance of the macroeconomy.

   c. Political stability in the host country.

   d. International autonomy / dependence of the host country.

   e. Obsolescing of bargains between the host government and foreign firms.

Excessive Government Intervention in Business

Most governments commonly offer incentives to attract some foreign investors; they also maintain controls over the entry of others. The U.S., for example, prohibits foreign investment in a very limited list of industries, such as coastal shipping; however other industries are open to investment, and there is no need for negotiations with the federal government. France is likely to consider each proposal on its own merits; only after negotiations and analysis will the government grant permission to the foreigner to invest, and the permission is likely to be accompanied by a condition that is tailored to the individual case.

In some countries, governments have imposed so-called performance requirements on foreign investors, whether already established in the country or applying for admission. These requirements are designed to increase the benefits of the investors' projects to the host country. Some requirements are:

   a. Foreign investors must purchase or produce locally a certain proportion of units needed in the manufacturing process.

   b. Foreign investors must share ownership with local investors.

Failure to create incentives for entry into a country can slow investment into a less developed country. The lack of use of government sponsored market research, tax incentives, deferrals or credits as well as instances of failure to show active support curtails investment.

Restrictions on Majority Ownership

Some countries regard local ownership as an important national objective. (Foreign investors must establish foreign identity in accordance with the rules and regulations of the host country.) In some countries, managers may not have the full range of choices, or, if they do they are very limited. It is very important for the business person to research the investment laws in the country he/she will be doing business in.

Through pre-investment study of a country, the interested parties can find practices and policies that will affect ownership with the goal to increase the influence of the host country on the operations.

　　a. Mandatory local-ownership provisions in which local share varies from a minority to majority position (100 percent local ownership represents a nationalized situation).

　　b. Insistence that local citizens hold responsible managerial positions by designating certain positions that must be held by local citizens or by establishing limits on values of salaries that may be paid to expatriate managers.

　　c. Establishment of rules that carefully delimit the subsidiary's ability to operate.

Exchange and Remittance Controls

Many firms throughout the world convert vast quantities of money from one currency into another. The manager cannot operate for very long in the international arena without encountering some problems entailing the international movement of money. In handling such problems, a manager is exposed to a set of institutions and a group of risks that his or her domestic counterpart ordinarily does not encounter. In one country you may be able to bring in more currency and take more out than in another country.

Doing business across international borders always involves risks related to finance. However, avoiding or controlling risk in global trade is an everyday occurrence for importers and exporters. The government of a country can determine the exchange rate value. A floating exchange rate is determined by the market forces. In contrast to the floating rate, a country can establish a fixed-rate system which determines the value of the currency against other currencies. Fixed rates can be adjusted frequently or infrequently as determined by the government of a country. A frequently used tool of developing countries is exchange controls. This allows the government to protect the value of the currency through control of the supply of the money and reduce the demand for foreign currency. More than one exchange rate can be used in an effort to influence trade transactions. Payments can be delayed by the less developing country in anticipation of a reduction of currency value, which would be at the expense of the seller. The process of hedging is the attempt to offset the effects of risk resulting from future changes in the value of foreign currency through the balancing of assets and liabilities in the foreign currency, thus reducing exposure.

Host countries can establish a ceiling on the amount of monies repatriated from their business activities. Usually, if the activities occur in a sector deemed to be highly important to the economy, the ceiling can be lowered, with greater requirements for reinvestment in capital.

Economic Barriers

The economic assessment should include several variables: economic size, income levels, growth trends, sectoral trends, external dependence and economic integrations, price level forecasts, balance-of-payments forecasts, foreign exchange earnings prospects, and foreign exchange needs.

Nationalization and Expropriation

Nationalization refers to the government taking over all operations or properties of a business. Expropriation is the ultimate host-country control over foreign enterprises. The firm is forced to give up assets and profitable operations for which it has risked capital. The compensation following expropriation has usually been less than the value of the business. The amount of nationalization since World War II has been significant.

Expropriation has been described as a "useful policy" to increase the rate of economic modernization in an effort to grow with the population and its needs. The host government can use the practice of nationalization as a shifting of the blame for past failures to the dominance of foreign influence and exploitation with the implied promise of greater national prosperity through increased control.

The following are factors that contribute to the precarious situation of foreign capital in LDCs:

- Limited upward social mobility in the developing countries, which will produce frustration among large numbers of the population.

- Nationalism directs political choices against foreigners and in favor of groups within the host country.

- The central planning and rapid development ethic, fueled and aided in part by the developed countries themselves, stimulates a bias toward statism among Third World governing elites.

- Conspicuous consumption and the investments of local elites as well as foreign firms will affect the structure of the national regime for foreign investment.

- Increased governmental capability in the twentieth century relative to the resources available to the modernizing monarchs of early modern Europe makes direct state control of economic activity more viable.

- Informal confiscation was an aspect of western expansion (secularizing church properties, taking land and resources from the indigenous populations of the western hemisphere) and many of the developed states have public corporations in sectors vital to national security and welfare, such as aerospace, electricity, and transportation.

- The decline in the deference shown to private property is having a powerful negative effect on the ability of foreign investors to justify their existence and protect their assets.

- The populations in the less developed nations are too highly mobilized and aware of the consumption patterns of the national and international elites to willingly reduce their own meager consumption in the interests of a development program with high short-run and deferred benefits. Justifiably, they want to see concrete improvements in their condition now.

There are no guaranteed solutions to nationalization risk. However, the Overseas Private Investment Corporation (OPIC) was created by the Foreign Assistance Act in 1969 to mobilize and facilitate the flow of U.S. capital and skills to friendly countries and areas of the developing world, thereby complementing the development assistance objectives in the United States. OPIC assists U.S. investors in this effort through two principal programs: (1) the issuance of insurance against certain political risk and (2) the financing of such enterprises through direct loans and/or guarantees. OPIC operates in approximately 100 developing countries around the world. Insurance, financing and other forms of investment assistance are available for new ventures or the expansion of existing enterprises. In all instances, the investment projects supported by OPIC must assist in the social and economic development of the host country, and be consistent with the economic interests of the United States.

Investment Program: OPIC insures investments in qualified projects in less developed friendly countries in which there are political risks. The risks that OPIC's statute authorized it to insure against are:

   a. Inability to convert into dollars local currency received by the investor as profits or earnings or return on the original investment.

b. Loss of investment due to expropriation, nationalization, or confiscation by action of a foreign government. Loss of income and loss due to political violence, i.e. war, revolution, insurrection, or civil strife.

   c. Special Programs: OPIC offers highly flexible and innovative coverage for investment in mineral explorations and development (including processing where it is an integral part of a development project): for oil and gas exploration, development and production; for construction and other contracting projects; for cross-border lease transactions and for institutional loans.

   d. Financial Services: The major objectives of OPIC's finance program are to promote and finance economically viable projects in the developing world which are sponsored by U.S. business. OPIC financing may be in the form of either direct loans to a project or loan guarantees issued to private U.S. financial institutions. The OPIC loan guarantee is an all-risk guaranty for the prompt payment of principal and interest. OPIC financing is based on the project's economic and financial viability and usually does not involve a U.S. sponsor's guaranty of the project.

Trade Policy

The importation of certain products, usually to protect infant industries or established industries under marketing pressure from foreign countries, is controlled by quotas. Less Developed Countries are sensitive to the effects of imports. A chief concern is that the imports would cause the failure on the part of the local industries to develop capital goods industries. An inability to compete with more developed countries generates the perceived need to assess barriers focused on imports that reduce domestic control of productivity, thus allowing for greater demand of locally produced goods. Specific legislation establishes quotas for this control. In the U.S., import quotas are divided into two types: absolute and quantitative quotas; that is, no more than the amount specified may be permitted during the quota period. Quantities entered in excess of the quota for the period are subject to higher duty rates. As a rule, countries apply the same tariff rate for a given product or products from a specific sector of production.

Theoretically, in free trade, greater welfare would be experienced when items produced with greater efficiency elsewhere would be imported and the resources once used in their production would be transferred to the production of items in the areas of comparative advantage. This trade-off is difficult in both the developing and developed countries. Pressures from displaced workers and firms would be felt in the political arena as demands to prevent shifts in productions to new areas.

Communication

Although nothing substitutes for personal contact when developing an international marketing structure, this might not always be possible. Depending upon what country you are doing business in, as technology improves, more alternative forms of communication become available. Recent developments in computer software are allowing the translation of transmissions into parent company language, thus improving communication. Successful importing and exporting depends on reliable two-way communication.

The transmission and receipt of information can be facilitated through the host country's investment in the hardware necessary for communication, electronic telephone exchanges, fax machines, copiers, and paper. In addition to the hardware of communication, the country's receptiveness to open communication from outside sources can increase the transmission of scientific and technological information which will aid in the development of greater domestic expertise in local factors. The ability to travel freely would help to gain greater access to higher level skills and information which is freely disseminated between and within industries. Understanding that resources for expenditures of this nature are limited, it is imperative that the developing country acknowledge the future benefits of this type of investment.

Distribution Infrastructure

You can have the best logistics plan, in which your product is moved from the manufacturer in one country to the customer in another. What if the circumstances say otherwise? Yes, it looks good on paper, but if you can't distribute your product, your plan is no good. There are many physical elements that may slow down or even prohibit the distribution of your product. Transportation and insurance costs are an increasing barrier to trade. The lengthy time needed to transport goods can compromise the quality of perishable goods, and bulky items can increase the costs to a point of making the transaction too expensive to be beneficial. The concept of value added can be seen in the process of getting the product to market. A weak distribution network characterized by inadequate warehousing facilities and road systems, as well as poor modes of transportation such as a lack of truck fleets, boats, developed harbors and material handling equipment, will prevent the product from reaching its market.

The experience in the Philippine islands can help to exemplify problems of distribution. One major contributing factor to the problem was the geography of this island nation. The dispersion of the population over many islands has caused the need for companies to locate regional offices on the various islands with the headquarters located in Manila. Poorly constructed roads slowed the travel of trucks from the regional distribution centers. Under Ferdinand Marcos' rule, the latter half of the 1970s witnessed an increase in commercial truck hijacking on some of the islands. Failure to protect and properly regulate distribution is as great a hindrance to getting product to market as the physical lack of infrastructure.

Recruiting Locals

The search for qualified personnel requires extensive use of personal contact acquired over time. Job advertising will be relatively non-existent in most less developed countries. Job history analysis, testing and other recruitment methods must be accommodated to the cultural norms of the country, such as company loyalty to employees and manager's obligations to relatives and friends. The recruitment must take into consideration the effect the new technology will have on present jobs.

An important consideration of hiring is the level of education necessary to perform the required tasks. A less developed country is more apt to have a low literacy rate due to the inequality and poor quality of the educational system, which reduces the quality of the labor pool. Literacy rates, minimum educational requirements, and the percentage of the population deemed literate are normally lower in less developed countries. Greater ability to manage production factors, advancement of applied sciences and technology, and greater economic growth can be the result of an educated population.

Training

Training must be customized to the capabilities and needs of trainees in the local situation. The following are recommendations to achieve successful training in the host country.

    a. Training groups should consist of people with similar backgrounds. Training must be meaningful from the perspective of the trainee.

    b. Earn the respect and trust of the labor force.

    c. Adjust to learning habits and yield to differences in thinking patterns.

    d. Modify instructional materials for the local culture.

    e. Make rewards appropriate to the motivational systems.

    f. Show an interest in learning the culture and customs of your trainees. Cultural understanding enables one to conduct business and relate to people without constantly analyzing situations and without making too many mistakes.

The ease of training local recruits can be traced back to the educational level of the new employees. The higher the level of educational accomplishment, the greater the opportunity to train new skills. It would lessen the need to teach rudimentary requirements to perform the task and allow progress in attaining higher levels of proficiency in a shorter period of time.

On the other hand, not all barriers to trade originate in the less developed countries. Following are examples of barriers established by the United States government.

Foreign Corrupt Practices Act (FCPA)

This U.S. law has created debates and confusion among those U.S. firms which are engaged in international business. It prohibits U.S. citizens/firms from bribing or using "questionable" payments to get export contracts. No other country has such a law. In West Germany, the U.K., and Denmark, bribery payments are legally allowed and a tax-deductible business expense. Certain ambiguities in the interpretation of FCPA provisions include the definition of "grease" payments which are permitted. Many people believe the FCPA has retarded the growth of U.S. export trade. The ethical dilemma resulting from the passage of FCPA has been viewed as a failure on the part of the American government to recognize practices viewed as entirely acceptable and ethical in other countries. The legislation precludes the company proposing entry into the country from participating in the ritual of business and implies that local customs are unsavory and unacceptable.

Antitrust

American companies are not allowed to join forces and bid on large projects in other countries under U.S. antitrust laws. The Sherman Act and the Clayton and Federal Trade Commission Acts were written to protect small business and control mergers in order to restrict firms from becoming dominant and/or predatory. A dominant firm may not be a monopoly but can enjoy the power over price and control over production quantity leading to higher profits. Mergers with local firms can produce monopolies or a dominant firm with resulting economies of scale and lower costs of production. Only one manufacturer may be needed to supply the product to a smaller market, thus reducing competition. Yet the previously held belief that greater market power is inherently bad is waning. Increasingly, attention is paid to the intent of the merger and the consequence in respect to the effect on the sellers', as well as buyers', market.

The Export Trading Company Act of 1982 was signed into law to allow the formation of Export Trading Companies. These ETC's can apply for antitrust immunity in an attempt to become more competitive. The antitrust laws prevent entry into the less developed countries on the same ground upon which business from other industrialized countries can operate, thus creating a barrier from the originating country, not from the less developed country. The American laws in effect prevent the increase of market power and the achievement of greater economic efficiency.

WHAT MAKES A COUNTRY POOR?

Two-thirds of the world's population live in non-industrialized countries. These countries are referred to by various designations, the most common and inclusive being Less Developed Countries (LDCs).

Studies have shown that the major problems facing LDCs in their efforts to grow and develop include:

   a. Low income, which restricts the ability of countries to save and invest.

   b. Overpopulation and relatively high rates of population. Families are usually large. Children are viewed as important resources that can be readily used in the farm economy. There are programs through the UN for population control that combine education in family planning and birth control clinics with some governmental incentives and community pressure for small families.

c. Ethical systems that do not value business and efficiency as much as traditional aspects of life (i.e. family cohesion, religion, etc.) may cause people to reject development.

d. Class structure based on caste, politics, religion, or sex may inhibit educational growth and restrict the population's overall productivity.

e. Government priorities may not be in accord with the most favorable development practices; i.e., the industrial countries placed the highest possible value on economic efficiency, even if it led to differentials in income or unemployment. By contrast, LDCs are more willing to tolerate inefficiency for the following reasons: equality of income, social order and full employment.

f. Economic policies: government strategies that have undermined their economic development in the long run. Examples:

- Exploitation of agriculture to provide cheap food for the growing urban populations.

- Lower agricultural prices resulted in a decrease in agricultural output, so that countries which historically were self-sufficient had to begin importing food.

- Protectionist measures are enacted to keep out imported manufactured goods, leaving the market to high-cost domestic producers. This results in inflation and inefficient production.

Major Characteristics of Less Developed Countries (LDCs)

a. Political instability

b. Per Capita Income is less than $2000. There are wide differences among the LDCs; most of the world's population is found in countries with a per capita income of only a few hundred dollars a year.

c. Health problems

d. Technology is minimum; small and inefficient manufacturing sectors

e. Low saving rate

f. Seventy percent of the population engaged in agriculture; malnutrition

g. High illiteracy rates

h. Hard topography and difficult climate

14.1 Learning Practice and Solutions

If the Italian Lira is listed at an exchange rate in the U.S. equivalence of $0.001, that means 10,000 Lira would trade for $10.00; hence, a bushel of U.S. wheat costing $2.50 would cost 2500 Lira. A liter of olive oil costing 12,000 Lira would cost U.S. $12.00.

14.2 LEARNING PRACTICE AND SOLUTIONS

Suppose that a typical Brazilian worker can produce 9 pounds of coffee or 3 skirts in one hour, while a typical Mexican worker can produce 12 pounds of coffee or 4 skirts in one hour. Assume that these are the only two goods produced, will it pay Mexico to trade with Brazil?

Because the opportunity cost to Brazil and Mexico of producing (1) pound of coffee is (3) skirts, neither nation has a competitive advantage in producing coffee and skirts. Therefore, it doesn't pay for Mexico to trade with Brazil, or vice versa.

CHAPTER SUMMARY

1. Foreign trade constitutes 10 percent of the U.S. GNP.

2. The United States exports more goods to Canada and Japan than to other countries.

3. The major exports of the U.S. are: machinery, transport equipment, chemicals, crude materials, foods, and manufactured goods.

4. The largest amount of U.S. imports come from Japan and Canada.

5. The major imports of the U.S. are: mineral fuels, machinery, transport equipment, and manufactured goods.

6. The terms of trade measures the relationship between the prices a country gets for its exports and the prices it pays for imports over a period of time.

7. The reasons for trade are: cost advantages, greater variety of goods, greater choice, expansion of markets for domestic goods, and political reasons.

8. The free-trade theory states that other countries should specialize in products in which they have an advantage and then trade free from barriers for the products they don't produce.

9. Protectionist theory states that countries should diversify and restrict trade with other countries by: tariffs, quotas, orderly marketing agreements, local content laws, anti-dumping rules, and subsidies, etc.

10. The main arguments for protection are: infant industry argument, national defense argument, protect jobs argument, high wages argument, diversity argument, and retaliation argument.

11. The consequences of a tariff are: higher prices, more domestic products, less foreign goods, and more tax revenue.

12. The exchange rate is the price of one currency in terms of another. It is the rate at which one currency is exchanged for another.

13. Absolute advantage refers to a country being able to produce something faster, cheaper, and more efficiently than other countries.

14. The determination of exchange rates is simply an application of the laws of supply and demand. Other factors which determine the exchange rate of a nation under the flexible exchange rate system include (a) the nation's interest rates, (b) the nation's economic strength and performance, (c) purchasing power parity (PPP), (d) changes in tastes and preferences, and (e) changes in income.

15. Flexible exchange rates is an international monetary system in which foreign exchange rates are allowed to adjust to reflect changes in the supply and demand for money.

16. Fixed exchange rates do not fluctuate with the supply and demand for money in a particular country.

17. Most of the foreign trade of the United States is with developed countries.

18. The sources of political risk are: social unrest, nationalism, armed conflicts, internal rebellions, terrorism, and new international alliances.

19. The five areas of major concern when measuring political risk are: national control over the economy, performance of the macroeconomy, political stability, international autonomy of the host country, and obsolescing of bargains.

20. The factors that contribute to the precarious situation of foreign capital in LDCs are: limited upward social mobility, nationalism, central planning, conspicuous consumption, direct state control, economic activity, informal confiscation, decline in private property, and unwillingness to reduce consumption.

21. Successful importing and exporting depend on reliable two-way communication and an effective distribution infrastructure.

22. The training of locals must be customized to the capabilities and needs of trainees in the local situation.

23. U.S. laws prevent American firms from bribery to get export contracts and from joining forces to bid on large projects in other countries.

24. The major problems facing less developed countries are: low incomes, overpopulation, ethical systems that do not value development, class structure, economic policies, and protectionist policies.

25. The Bretton Woods System worked reasonably well for nearly two decades. The system officially dissolved for several reasons.

Chapter 14
Key Concepts

Absolute Advantage—Being able to produce more of a particular product from the input used.

Ad Valorem tariff—The tax is computed as a percentage of the value of the item.

Appreciation—Refers to an increase in the value of a currency under floating exchange rates.

Bretton Woods System—Established exchange rates in terms of the price of an ounce of gold. The exchange rate for a country was to be based on the equilibrium price of its currency.

Comparative Advantage—Arises from countries having different opportunity costs of producing particular goods. This creates the opportunity for all nations to gain from trade.

Currency Devaluation—A reduction of a nation's exchange rate.

Depreciation—Refers to a decrease in the value of a currency under floating exchange rates.

Devaluation—Results in a lower price for domestic currency, and an increase in the demand for products of the devaluing country.

Distribution Infrastructure—The system of product and supplies distribution.

Dumping—Selling a product in a foreign country at a price that is below the price charged in the home country, or below the cost of production.

Exports—Goods sold to foreign countries.

Fixed Exchange Rate—Rates do not fluctuate with the supply and demand for money in a particular country (based on government intervention).

Flexible Exchange Rate—A floating international monetary system in which foreign exchange rates are allowed to adjust to reflect changes in the supply and demand for money.

Foreign Corrupt Practices Act—Prohibits U.S. citizens and firms from bribing or using "questionable" payments to get export contracts.

Foreign Exchange Market—Refers to when money is traded for money. The largest exchange markets in the world are located in New York and London.

Forward Market—The forward market rates are the costs of today for a commitment by one party to deliver to or take from another party an agreed amount of currency at a fixed future date.

Imports—Goods purchased from foreign countries.

Less Developed Country—The countries with the lowest per capita standard of living.

Local Content Requirement—A certain percentage of a product's total value would have to be produced domestically.

Local Ownership Provision—Foreign investors must establish foreign identity.

Nationalization—The host country taking ownership of all activities or properties.

Orderly Marketing Agreement—Negotiated agreements among nations to institute voluntary marketing export quotas.

Overseas Private Investment Corporation—To mobilize and facilitate the flow of U.S. capital and skills to friendly countries and areas of the developing world.

Performance Requirement—Requirements to increase the benefits of the investor's projects to the host country.

Political Risk—The impact of changes in national and international political forces and business operations, physical assets, personnel, and management.

Political Stability—The ability of the government to maintain power and the continuation and consistency of government policy toward business.

Protectionist Theory—Keep foreign goods out of a country to protect domestic firms and labor.

Quota—Limits on the number of items, or the value of items, to be imported.

Revaluation—Occurs when a nation increases the gold backing its currency.

Specific Tariff—A fixed amount of tax is charged for every item imported.

Spot Market—Permits the buying and selling of foreign exchange for immediate delivery (although technically they can take up to 2 days to clear).

Subsidy—Government granting sums of money to help business.

Tariff—A tax on imports.

Terms of Trade—Measures the relationship between the prices a country gets for its exports and the prices it pays for imports over a period of time.

DISCUSSION QUESTIONS

1. What is flexible exchange rate and what are the difficulties associated with it?
2. What is a fixed exchange rate?
3. Explain briefly the variables that might have an effect on the exchange rates of a currency.
4. Compare and contrast:
   a. The gold standard and the Bretton Woods System, and
   b. The fixed exchange rate system and the flexible rate system.
5. Explain the following: Revaluation, Devaluation, Depreciation and Appreciation
6. What are the spot and forward markets?
7. Discuss the factors which determine the exchange rate.
8. Discuss the advantages to a country that engages in international trade.
9. Distinguish between the free-trade theory and the protectionist theory of trade.
10. Explain absolute and comparative advantage.
11. Discuss some of the tools of protectionism.
12. Discuss the reasons for government restrictions on trade.
13. Discuss the sources of political risk in investing in less developed countries.
14. Explain performance requirements imposed on foreign investors.
15. Discuss the purpose of a pre-investment study.
16. Discuss the economic barriers to trade in less developed countries.
17. Discuss some of the factors that contribute to the precarious situation of foreign capital in less developed countries.
18. Discuss the purpose of the Overseas Private Investment Corporation and the risks it insures against.
19. Discuss the effect of a weak distribution network.
20. List some recommendations for training locals to work in foreign plants.
21. Should the U.S. allow companies or executives to accept bribes?
22. List some factors which make less developed countries poor.

14.2 LEARNING PRACTICE

Use the following table, answer questions a through d.

Output Per Worker

Country	Tons of Steel	Number of Televisions
A	15	45
B	10	20

a. Which country has the comparative advantage* in the production of steel?

b. If trade opens up between Country A and Country B, which product should Country A's firm specialize in?

c. Which country has the absolute advantage in the production of steel and which country has the absolute advatange in the production of televisions?

d. Calculate the opportunity cost of producing one ton of steel in Country A.

---

*If a country has a comparative advantage in the production of good X, then it can produce X at the lowest opportunity cost.

Chapter 15

Government: Taxation and the Economy

LEARNING OBJECTIVES

After you have studied this chapter in the text, and attended class lectures regularly, you will be able to:

1. Identify the important functions of government in the economy: the stabilization function, the allocation function, and the distribution function.

2. Understand the goals to be achieved by the government for the economy: full employment, price stability, economic growth, and favorable balance of payments.

3. Construct and explain the Lorenz curve.

4. Discuss the meaning of taxes and the effects of taxes on the economy.

5. Recognize the major sources of government revenue: printing money, taxing, and borrowing.

6. Identify the federal government receipts and expenditures and the importance of various categories of spending and sources of revenue in the U.S. in recent years.

7. Understand the basic classification of taxes.

8. Distinguish between the three types of income taxes: regressive, proportional, and progressive taxes.

9. Identify the twin deficits and the burden of the debt.

10. Understand ways to cut the deficits.

11. Understand the economic system of the United States.

Government, Taxation, and the Economy

Government and Mixed Economy

The economy of the U.S. is classified as a mixed economic system. An economy is based on private ownership, property rights, and free economic competition among individuals and businesses. A mixed economy is one in which economic decisions are made both by the private sector and by the government.

However, minimum wage laws, child labor laws, and environmental regulations are a few examples of government restrictions on the functioning of the marketplace.

Government is essential to a civilized society. Its tasks are to ensure a peaceful society, to provide for the national defense, and to secure basic freedoms. Government at all levels—national, state, and local, but especially the national government—plays a much larger role in the life of the average member of the society than it did during President Washington's Administration or even during President Lincoln's time. Its actions affect people all over the globe.

Government refers to the institution and processes by which groups achieve order and control in society. Government is thus seen as a necessary element in society, as no other institution would be able to achieve order.

In the United States, there are three different levels of government. At the top is a national government divided into three main jurisdictions: executive, legislative, and judicial. The President serves as the head of government, the chief executive along with his cabinet. Congress is composed of two houses, the House of Representatives and the Senate, and serves as the legislative section. A court system, ending in the Supreme Court, constitutes the judicial system.

Beneath the federal government are 50 state governments which conduct the affairs of the state. The Tenth Amendment to the U.S. Constitution states: "The powers not delegated to the United States by the Constitution, nor prohibited by it to the States, are reserved to the States respectively, or to the people."

Since states reflect different people and needs, state laws, taxing policies, and spending policies are different.

At the lowest level are cities, counties, townships, and other local political divisions. These divisions are under direct state control. The United States' system of government is, therefore, a three-tiered structure with many divisions—a complex system. This results in differences in laws from division to division and delays in achieving needed legislation.

Functions

There are three main functions of a government in an economy. They are:

    a. the allocation function,

    b. the distribution function, and

    c. the stabilization function.

a. Allocation Function

The allocation function refers to the government directing resources and funds to the production of public goods. Public goods differ from private goods, first, in that no one is excluded from their consumption. If a consumer buys an orange, he takes it and consumes it. No one else can also consume it. National defense, however, is available to all citizens. No one is excluded, not even if he or she doesn't pay taxes.

Secondly, public and private goods differ in that private goods are paid for by the consumer out of disposable personal income. Public goods are paid for out of tax revenues.

Some of the examples of public goods are: highways, sewer systems, water systems, parks, and education.

b. Distribution Function and the Lorenz Curve

The distribution function of government refers to the use of taxes and welfare to affect the incomes of individuals in the economy. The concern is with income inequality, which essentially refers to a small sector of the economy controlling a larger portion of income, and a large sector of the economy controlling a smaller portion of income.

The Lorenz Curve

The Lorenz Curve is a convenient means of visualizing the degree of income inequality. The more the curve bows away from the straight line, the greater is the inequality in income distribution.

The degree of income inequality can be seen through the Lorenz Curve shown in Figure 15.1. Here we *cumulate* the "percentage of families" on the horizontal axis and the "percentage of income" on the vertical axis. The theoretical possibility of a completely equal distribution of income is represented by the diagonal straight line because such a line indicates that any given percentage of families receives that same percentage of income. That is, if 20 percent of all families receive 20 percent of total income, 40 percent receive 40 percent, 60 percent receive 60 percent, and so one, then all these points will fall on the diagonal line.

We locate the Lorenz curve to visualize the actual distribution of income. Observe that the bottom 20 percent of all families received about 4.6 percent of the income, as shown by point *a*; the bottom 40 percent received 15.4 percent (=4.6 + 10.8) as shown by point *b*; and so forth. The white area, determined by the extent to which the resulting Lorenz Curve sags away from the line of perfect equality, indicates the degree of income inequality. The larger this area or gap, the greater the degree of income inequality. If the actual income distribution were perfectly equal, the Lorenz Curve and the diagonal would coincide, and the gap would disappear.

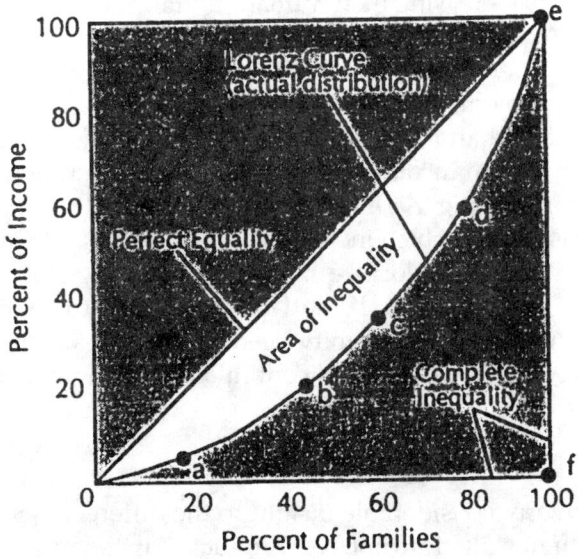

The Lorenz Curve is a convenient means of visualizing the degree of income inequality. Specifically, the white area between the line of perfect equality and the Lorenz Curve reflects the degree of income inequality.

Figure 15.1
The Lorenz Curve

Poverty and Inequality

The rewards of a market system are linked to productivity, and some households in every society are not as productive as other households.

For this reason, household income will differ, or the distribution of income will be unequal. Some will have more and some will have less.

Poverty and inequality are related issues about which many people feel very strongly. But the issues of *poverty* and *inequality* are *different*.

In simplest terms, poverty means the state of people with very low incomes. A more appropriate measure of poverty might be a relative measure that compares poverty to what is necessary or relative to what others have.

This poverty concept is subject to disagreement. There are many alternative ways of defining poverty and drawing lines. The U.S. government method of obtaining poverty statistics by pricing frugal food budgets and multiplying by three is only one such system. Some define the lower 10 or 20 percent of the population as living in poverty simply by reason of their relative position in the income distribution. Another possible criterion is the receipt of less than half the median income of the society in question.

According to the official Census Bureau statistics, the percentage of the population in the U.S. now considered to be living in poverty is about 14 percent. Poverty may be one of the most apparent and severe shortcomings of capitalism.

Who are the poor? The people in certain segments of society who are particularly apt to be living below the poverty line are the very old, the very young, the uneducated, the black, the physically or mentally handicapped, and the families headed by a single female.

Helping the Poor—Investment in Human Capital

Educational and job-training programs also rely on the labor market to help the poor. Human capital comprises various skills that a worker has obtained through education, and job training is one source of income inequality. Provisions for educational opportunities and job training attempt to make the poor more self-sufficient by increasing their human capital, and, consequently, improving their wages.

In a competitive labor market, demand depends on the value of workers' marginal product—the amount by which an extra dollar will supplement the firm's revenue. Employees with little human capital are likely to be less productive than those with substantial training and experience. Consequently, these workers are less able to increase the firm's revenue, resulting in low demand for their labor and low wages. By increasing these worker' human capital through education and job training, their productivity is raised, which increases both demand and wages for these workers. Therefore, in a technologically-driven world, quality and flexibility of its human resources will determine a nation's competitive position. If the United States is to continue to prosper, business, government, and the educational community need to develop a comprehensive human investment strategy, which begins before birth and continues throughout a person's life.

Primary Causes of Poverty

The following should provide cause of poverty considerable insight to the differences in ability and training workers who are uneducated or unskilled are not over productive in today's economy, and their wages reflect that fact. Those who are physically or mentally handicapped are also at a disadvantage.

- Statistical evidence suggests that sexual and racial discrimination also contribute to poverty.

- Low aggregate demand (AD) or total spending in the economy brings recession, unemployment, and therefore poverty.

- Differences in job tastes. Poverty sometimes stems from a person's lifestyle. Some people prefer job satisfaction more than monetary reward, while others may speculate in the pursuit of high incomes and fail.

- The issue of the "deserving" versus "undeserving" poor—if a person becomes poor through his or her own behavior, for example, taking drugs, having dozens of children, catching venereal disease through promiscuous sexuality, and so on.

How Does the Government Try to Reduce Poverty?

In the U.S., redistribution and the attempt to correct poverty are accomplished through taxation and a number of government transfer programs. The largest of these programs are Social Security, public assistance, unemployment compensation, Medicare and Medicaid, food stamps, and various public housing programs.

Tax Policy

One approach to reducing poverty is to provide people with enough income to bring them above the poverty level. Funds used to supplement the incomes of the poor must come from somewhere. Many societies adopt a Robin Hood approach, taking from the rich to give to the poor. Income taxes can influence income distribution through their impact on after-tax income. Taxes may be progressive, proportional, or regressive. (Social security taxes are regressive.)

A progressive income tax is a tax the percentage of which rises as income rises—the marginal tax rate increases as income increases.

A proportional tax is a tax whose rate does not change as the tax base changes. The rate of a proportional income tax remains the same at every level of income.

A progressive tax rate tends to reduce income inequality; a proportional tax does not affect income distribution; and a regressive tax increases inequality. A progressive tax takes larger percentages of wealth from high-income members of society than it takes from low-income members.

This tends to equalize after-tax incomes. In the United State, the income tax is slightly progressive.

- Social Security is the largest social insurance program. It helps a family replace income that is lost when a worker retires, becomes disabled, or dies. Two thirds of the aged rely on Social Security for more than half their income.

- Unemployment Insurance provides temporary benefits to regularly employed people who become temporarily unemployed. Benefits usually amount to 50% of normal wages.

- Aid to Families with Dependent Children is the largest cash welfare program. The average benefit is $300 a month for a family headed by a woman with two small children. Saving and earnings are limited.

- Supplemental Security Income—65% of SSI recipients are blind or otherwise disabled. The rest are over 65 years of age. Recipients of SSI must meet certain disability requirements, or be of a certain age, or have incomes lower than $4,500.

Why Has *Inequality* Been Growing in the United States?

a. Tax rates have declined for high-income groups since the 1970s, and benefits for the poor have not kept pace with inflation.

b. In terms of demographics, large numbers of less experienced and less skilled "baby boomers" have entered the labor force along with a large number of unmarried or divorced women with children. Groups with less experience and fewer skills have lower incomes.

c. Import competition has reduced the demand for unskilled workers who used to command high wages in manufacturing industries.

d. The demand for highly skilled workers has increased significantly, which raises the incomes of these groups.

c. Stabilization Function

Early economists felt that the economy was self-correcting if disruptions in employment occurred. According to the business cycle, recessions were always corrected and unemployment reduced, as shown in Figure 15.2.

At boom (a), the economy has reached a new high level. At this point, however, something happens, and the economy begins to slide down. Perhaps it is a lessening of confidence or, simply, the fact that people have what they want. Consumption is reduced. As that happens, new orders are reduced, production is reduced, employment drops, income drops, and consumption drops from there. This is called a downswing. The economy slides into a recession.

At this point, consumers begin to need replacements for goods beginning to wear out. Confidence builds and spending increases. This is called an upswing. As this happens, new orders pick up, production increases, employment increases, and income increases. This causes further increases in consumption, pushing the economy to a level higher than before.

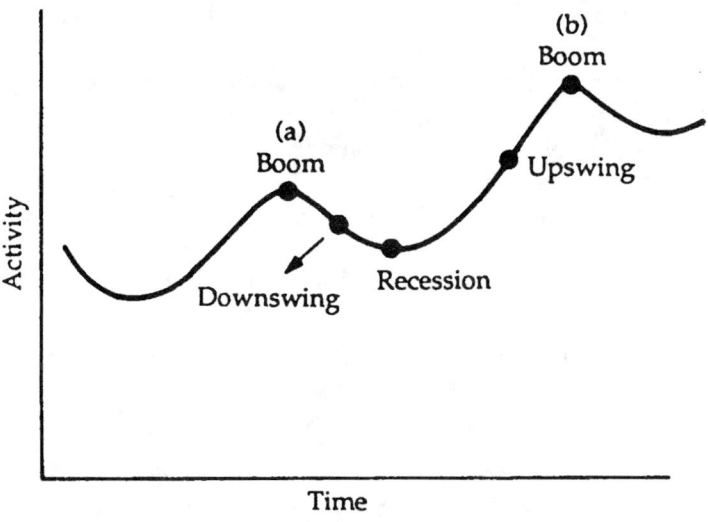

Figure 15.2
Business Cycle

As the above demonstrates, all of this happened independently of any outside (government) intervention. The business cycle corrects itself. The Great Depression, however, was very severe, and indications were that it could not self-correct. This led John Maynard Keynes to propose government action in the form of tax changes and spending changes to turn the economy around. John Maynard Keynes developed what is called macroeconomics.

Government Goals

The government strives to achieve four goals for the economy:

   a. Full employment—to have 96 percent of the labor force employed.

   b. Price stability—to have minimal inflation—3 percent or less.

c. Favorable balance of payments—to have more money entering the country than leaving.

   d. Economic growth—to have an increase in Gross Domestic Product (GDP) sufficient for the increased needs and wants of the economy.

ECONOMIC GROWTH

We will provide an introduction to the topic of economic growth and development. *Economic growth occurs when the real GDP of a nation expands.*

Economic development is characterized by such things as a high level of consumption, broadbased educational achievement, adequate housing, and access to high quality health care. Achieving these goals can only come after long periods of sustained, high-level economic growth.

One approach to deficit reduction is to rely on economic growth to increase tax revenues. However, to promote further growth, former President Bush relied on capital-gains tax cuts, whereas President Clinton relies on government investment. In economic terms, the deficit resulting from the ill-advised tax cuts of the early 1980s are dissavings. They have lowered the total national savings available to finance long-term investment in the economy, which is the source of productivity gains and economic growth.

According to Adam Smith, the wealth of nations is dependent on gains from the following: specialization and trade, expansion in the size of the market, and the discovery of more productive ways of doing things. Also a government that respects property rights and follows monetary and fiscal policies consistently, with a stable price level, helps to provide the framework for the creation of wealth. Hence, economic growth can be described graphically as an *output shift in a nation's production possibilities curve (PPC).*

Economic growth is a complex process and is determined by several factors such as open economy, gains from trade, competition among firms, convertibility of domestic currency, investment and efficient use of capital, tax rates, stable money and prices.

Determinants of Economic Growth

In defining economic growth and development we are referring to the progress a nation makes in its productive capabilities with regards to the provision of goods and services. Growth usually is indicated by a higher standard of living by material comfort.

In providing any developmental model it is appropriate to note that behind all theories development is the basic premise that any economic system grows in terms of output of goods and services due to either an increase in productive inputs (land, labor, and capital) and/or an increase in the productiveness concerning the usage of these inputs. The faster the growth of inputs and the productiveness of usage of these inputs occurs, the faster the economic system will grow in material terms. This relationship holds for any and all economic systems and will govern our review of the basic factors determining economic development and the rate of growth.

Basic Factors Determining Level of Development and Rate of Growth

The basic explanation of economic development, or a growth model, includes the following components or determining factors:

   a. Basic resource endowments.

   b. Development of human capital as resource.

   c. Savings and investment.

   d. Institutional and structural support.

e. Domestic competitive pressures and existence of private property and markets.

f. Degree of integration in the world trade and finance markets.

g. Political and social factors, including economic policy implications.

Each of these components influences the level, speed, and directions of economic development.

Nevertheless, economic growth is not only a new idea, it is also a good idea.

Growth Size

The government has greatly increased in size and scope in the 20th century.

In 1900, the share of GNP which dealt with government expenditures was about 8 percent. By 1995 this share grew to 35 percent. This is explained by several causes.

a. Growth in population. As the population grew, so did the demand for public services.

b. War. During this time period, there were two major world wars and several smaller wars. These wars increased the demand for national defense and war expenditures. The Cold War between the U.S.A. and the communist countries maintained a large demand for defense expenditures.

c. Urbanization. During this time period, there was a trend for the population to shift to living in cities and not rural areas. This has resulted in an increased need for city services, such as sewers, streets, parks, etc.

d. The automobile. The major forms of transportation in the U.S. are the car, bus, and truck. This has resulted in a need for streets, roads, and highways.

e. Education. During this time period, the importance of education for the economy was recognized. Local governments developed K-12 school systems and community colleges. States developed colleges and universities to provide more people with advanced education. In 1900, an eighth grade education or less was sufficient. In 1990, thousands of people were pursuing advanced degrees and, even then, were having difficulty finding jobs.

f. Welfare. During the 1900s, many public support programs have been developed to help people left out of the market system. These include: agricultural subsidies, social security, disability income, aid to families with dependent children, unemployment benefits, etc.

GOVERNMENT REVENUES

There are three major sources of government revenue: *printing money, taxing,* and *borrowing*. Printing money would dump large amounts of new money into circulation, causing resources to flow to the government. As a result, prices would rise since there would be no increase in goods or services. This would be the situation of excess demand, limited supply, and rising prices.

Income taxes are a source of revenue for government. There are three types of income taxes: progressive, proportional, and regressive.

A progressive tax is one where the tax rate increases as income increases. Higher income has higher rates, as shown in Figure 15.3.

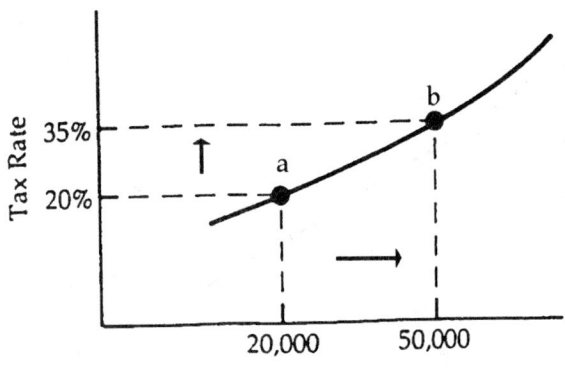

Figure 15.3
Progressive Income Tax

In Figure 15.3 a household with a $20,000 income would pay a 20 percent tax rate, whereas a $50,000 household would pay a 35 percent tax rate. This would be progressive. An example would be the United States Federal Income Tax.

A proportional tax is one where the tax rate remains the same, regardless of the household income. This is shown in Figure 15.4.

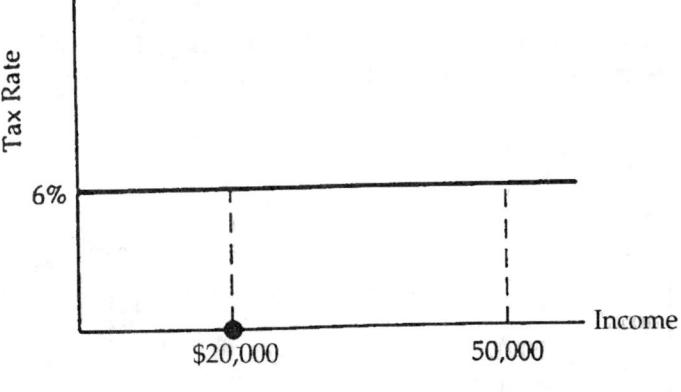

Figure 15.4
Proportional Tax

In Figure 15.4 a household with a $20,000 income would pay the same tax rate as a household earning $50,000. This would be classified as a proportional tax. An example would be many state income taxes, where all people are taxed the same percentage.

A regressive tax is one where the tax rate decreases as income increases. Households with higher incomes are taxed less than households with lower incomes. This is shown in Figure 15.5.

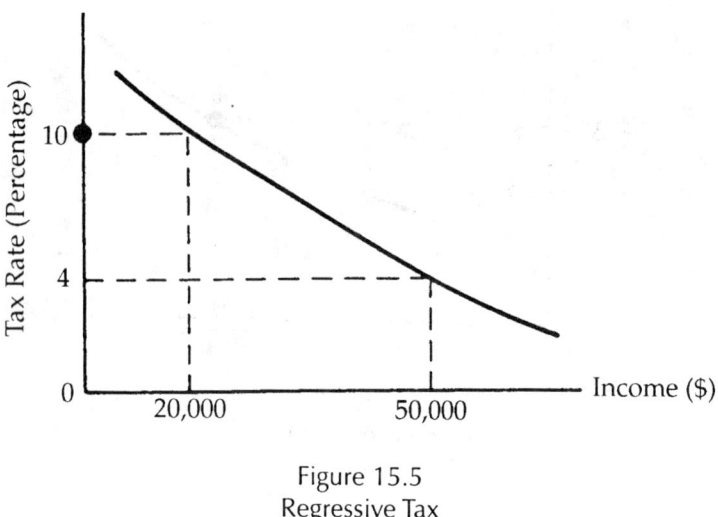

Figure 15.5
Regressive Tax

Example: Social Security Contribution.

A household with a $20,000 income would be taxed at the rate of 10 percent, whereas a household with a $50,000 income would be taxed only 4 percent. This type of tax would be called regressive. A regressive tax is one which affects low-income households more than high-income households.

Low-income families tend to spend a greater portion of their disposable income, whereas higher income households save more, as shown in Figure 15.6.

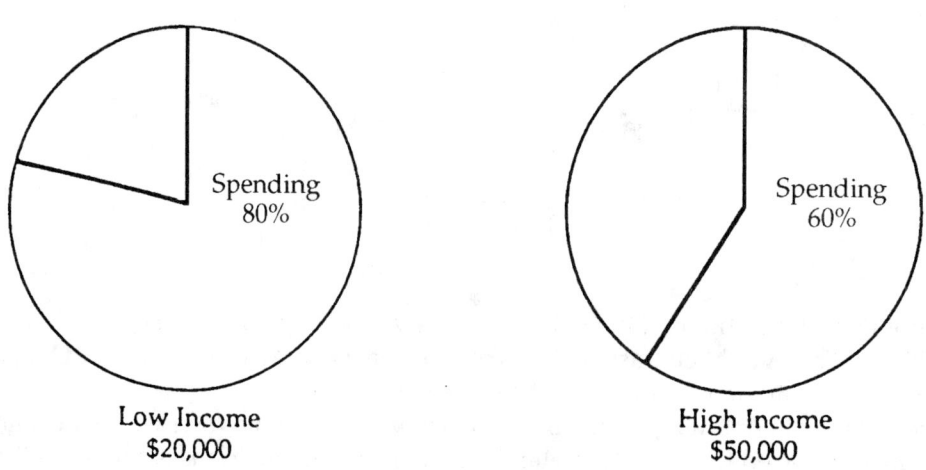

Figure 15.6
Spending Percentage

Borrowing

The main source of government revenue is from income taxes. Usually, not enough revenue is generated this way, and the government must borrow. The government does this by selling bonds. In this way, all government expenditures are covered.

Borrowers want funds that they do not immediately possess. A government that seeks to borrow does so because its tax revenues are not sufficient to finance all the expenditures that it has budgeted. Budget deficit = Gov. Rev. − Gov. Exp.

Two major problems result from the government's borrowing. The first is that the debt is never paid off, and each year adds to the national debt, making it grow. This results in an interest burden to the taxpayer.

A second problem is that this borrowing tends to crowd out other investments, as the government pays higher interest to attract lenders. (Crowding out takes place when the government budget deficit reduces domestic investment.)

The Burden of the Government Debt on Future Generations

a. People worry that their children will have to pay back the debt that past generations have accumulated

b. But U.S. citizens own most government bonds, so future generations will just be paying themselves

c. However, there could be a burden, because if tax rates have to be raised in the future to pay off the debt, the higher tax rates could be discretionary

d. Also, since bondholders are richer on average than nonbondholders, when the debt was repaid there would be a large transfer from the poor to the rich

e. Finally, government deficits reduce national saving according to many economists

- If so, with lower saving there will be lower investment
- Lower investment means a smaller capital stock
- A smaller capital stock means less output in the future
- So the future standard of living will be lower

However, over the last 30 years, conventional wisdom held that budget deficits stimulated economic growth. Initially, most economists assumed that economic growth would generate sufficient tax receipts to lead to budget balance over the business cycle. But as deficits persisted even during boom times, policy makers worried that deficit reduction would cause a recession and therefore was too costly a policy to pursue. Today, conventional wisdom holds that the large stock of federal debt has crowded out private investments that would have boosted the trend rate of economic growth.

Fair Tax

Taxes are commonly accepted as necessary to finance the expenditures of the government. It is also commonly believed that the tax rate should be fair. In discussing fairness, two criteria have developed; horizontal and vertical equity.

Horizontal equity refers to individuals earning the same income, regardless of how it is earned, paying the same tax. A sole proprietor, a corporate executive, and a garbage collector all earning 36,000 dollars would be taxed the same rate.

Vertical equity refers to persons with different incomes being taxed different rates. Thus a person earning 50,000 dollars would be taxed differently than a person earning 20,000 dollars. In order to achieve vertical equity, two principles are presented: the ability-to-pay principle and the benefits-received principle.

According to the ability-to-pay principle, the tax rate should increase as a person's income increases. Accordingly, a person earning 50,000 dollars would pay a higher rate than a person earning 20,000 dollars. This principle is used in the progressive income tax.

According to the benefits-received principle, a person should be taxed in proportion to the benefits received from government expenditures. An example would be the federal and state gasoline tax, which is used to build and repair highways. The people who use these highways receive the benefits and pay the tax on gasoline. The people who do not use the highways receive no benefits and don't pay the tax since they don't buy gasoline.

Negative Income Tax

The negative income tax is a plan to replace the welfare system with a single cash payment based on a household's level of income. A break-even level of income would be determined based on current economic conditions. Households with incomes above the break-even level would be subject to the regular tax rates.

Households with incomes below the break-even level would receive a payment based on their incomes. A household with no income would receive a guaranteed annual income, the maximum amount. Households with some income would receive a reduced payment based on a pre-established formula.

To explain this concept we will present several examples. We will assume the break-even level of income to be $20,000. This is the income a household would need to adequately make it through the year. The guaranteed income will be $10,000. The tax rate will be 25% based on the difference between the break-even income and the household's earned income.

Given:	Break-even level of income	$20,000
	Guaranteed income	$10,000
	Tax rate on difference of earned and guaranteed income	25%

Example 1 Household income $00,000.
The household would receive a payment of the full $10,000.
Disposable income, $10,000

Example 2 Household income $6,000
The household would receive a payment of $3,500.
Break-even level minus earned income, times 25 percent.
$20,000 − $6,000 = $14,000 x .25 = $3500
Disposable income $9,500.

Example 3 Household income $15,000
The household would receive a payment of $1,250.
Break-even level minus earned income, times 25 percent
$20,000 − $15,000 = $5,000 x .25 = $1,250.

Example 4 Household income $20,000
The household would not receive a payment.
Break-even level minus earned income, times 25 percent
$20,000 − $20,000 = 0 x .25 = 0.

Example 5 Household income $30,000.
The household would pay tax of $2,500.
Break-even level minus earned income, time 25 percent
$20,000 − $30,000 = $10,000 x .25 = $2,500.

The above examples are based on only one possible formula. The advantages of the negative income tax system are that it would cut the large administrative costs of the welfare system. To apply for the negative income tax form all a household would have to do is file a tax form and payments would be sent to the household or payment would be made by the household. The major disadvantage is that some households may choose not to work and to collect the guaranteed income. Like all other programs, the benefits will have to be compared with the costs to determine whether the United States should adopt such a program.

Negative Income Tax (NIT): Another Approach

Another approach to the negative income tax has been developed by Dr. Rabboh, co-author of this text. In this approach there are four provisions.

1. Families are guaranteed a minimum income.
2. There is a cash transfer based on the amount of the family's income.
3. The cash transfer decreases as the family's income increases.
4. Families below certain earnings would receive a cash transfer. Families above certain earnings would pay tax.

Example 1.

If the family has no earnings, it will receive the full amount of the guaranteed minimum income. If the guaranteed amount is $10,000, this family will receive the full amount of $10,000 as a cash transfer.

Example 2.

If a family has earnings of $6,000, the cash transfer will be reduced. The cash transfer will decrease based on the negative income tax rate. If the rate is 30%, the cash transfer will be reduced by $.30 for every dollar earned. If the family earns $6,000 its $10,000 transfer will be reduced by $6,000 x .30 or $1,800. The cash transfer will be $8,200 ($10,000 – 1,800). Thus the family's total income (DPI) will be $6,000 in earnings plus $8,200 in transfers for a total of $14,200.

Example 3.

If the family earns $10,000, the cash transfer will be $10,000 – 3,000 = $7,000. The total income will be $10,000 + 7,000 = $17,000.

Example 4.

If the family earns $20,000, the cash transfer will be $10,000 – 6,000 – $4,000. The total income will be $20,000 + 4,000 – $24,000.

Example 5.

If the family earns $30,000, the cash transfer will be $10,000 – 9,000 = $1,000. The total income will be $30,000 + 1,000 = $31,000.

Example 6.

If the family earns $40,000, the cash transfer will be $10,000 – 12,000 = – $2,000. This family would not receive a cash transfer but would have to pay tax of $1,200. Families below certain earnings would collect a cash transfer; Families above certain incomes would pay tax.

Uses of Taxes

There are six uses of taxes that we will cite in this section.

1. Raise Revenue. The government needs revenue to carry out the functions of the executive, legislative, and judicial branches.

2. Provide Public Goods. The government provides highways, schools, police protection, fire protection, sewage systems, parks, and other goods. The alternative to financing these goods by taxes is to charge for them as they are used. This would mean tuition for schools, tolls for highways, entrance fees to parks, fees for the police to recover a stolen car, and fees for the fire department to put out a fire.

3. Redistribute Income. Income inequity can exist in a country. This means a small percentage of people control a large percentage of income. The means to correct this is to tax higher incomes higher tax rates. This will reduce the income controlled. The tax money can be redistributed to the lower incomes by welfare.

4. Provide Stabilization. The two main macroeconomic problems faced by a nation are inflation and unemployment. Inflation can be caused by excessive demand. Raising taxes will reduce disposable income and thereby reduce demand. Unemployment can be caused by too-low demand. Lowering taxes will increase disposable income and thereby increase demand.

5. Discourage Foreign Trade. The United States has been faced with a balance of trade deficit for many years. A balance of trade deficit results when imports exceed exports. To discourage imports, a tax can be charged, called a tariff, to raise prices and reduce the quantity of imports demanded.

6. Punish Sin. There are certain products that much of society at times considers undesirable, such as alcohol and cigarettes. To discourage consumption (punish), a tax can be placed on the item so the consumer (sinner) has to pay a higher price (be punished).

Tax Computation Form

Taxes tend to be classified as specific or as ad valorem. Specific refers to a set charge or tax on an item. An example would be cigarettes or gasoline. There might be a tax of 60 cents per pack on cigarettes. If a person buys one pack, the tax is 60 cents. If the person buys two packs, the tax would be 1.20 dollars.

An ad valorem tax is one based on the value of the item. An example would be a sales tax. If the tax is 5 percent and an item is priced at 1 dollar, the tax is 5 cents. If, however, the item is priced at 10 dollars, the tax would be 50 cents. As the value or price of the item increases, the amount of the tax increases.

Direct—Indirect

An important question in the discussion of taxes is "who pays the tax?" Sometimes the tax can be shifted to someone else, who then pays it. Usually, taxes on the household, such as income taxes, sales taxes, and property taxes, are paid for by the household. These are called direct.

Taxes on businesses, however, such as business property taxes, corporation income taxes, and other business taxes, are passed on to the consumer in the form of higher prices. The consumer or the household assumes most taxes in the United States. These taxes are called indirect.

General—Specific

Taxes can be classified as general or specific, depending on the intended use of the tax revenue. A general tax will eventually be spent on government activity, but there is no specific purpose in mind when the tax is collected. A specific tax, however, is intended for a specific purpose. An example would be a tax on gasoline, where the funds are intended for highway construction or repair.

Tax Base

There are three traditional bases for taxes: income, wealth, and a commodity. Income is the major source of tax revenue today in developed countries. Wealth taxes would refer to property taxes, estate, and inheritance taxes. Commodity taxes tend to take the form of sales taxes.

TAXATION IN THE UNITED STATES

Taxes have been a way of life for hundreds, if not thousands of years. As the old adage goes, "the only two sure things in life are death and taxes." They are the primary source of revenue for operating our governments.

Taxes are generally assessed at three levels: federal, state, and local (which may include city, county, township, etc.). The major types of taxes include: business franchise or capital value taxes, income taxes, sales and use taxes, property taxes, inheritance taxes (including estate and gift taxes), intangibles taxes, employment security taxes, alcoholic beverage taxes, cigarette taxes, insurance taxes, admissions and amusement taxes, and real estate transfer taxes.

Income Taxes

The federal income tax, as we know it today, began in 1913, with the enactment of the 16th Amendment of the Constitution. There have been many new laws enacted within recent years, yielding a proliferation of new legislation. From 1913–78, there were 61 bills affecting income taxation laws. In the last 10 years, there have been 40 pieces on income tax legislation, including certain legislation which drastically changed our tax laws. Historically, tax relief legislation has followed when federal revenues, as a percentage of gross national product (GNP), approach/reach 20%. This was the situation prior to the enactment of new tax relief legislation in 1948, 1975, 1977, 1978, 1981, and 1986.

State Income Taxes

Income taxes are also a major source of revenue for the states, many of which "piggyback" on the federal system of taxation as shown in Table 15.2.

Sales/Use Tax

Sales and use taxes are generally levied at the state and local levels, and are a primary source of revenue for the states. For example, in Michigan, during 1988, the sales tax accounted for 17.2 percent of all state and local tax revenues. This compares to the national average of 24.3 percent. Sales taxes are imposed on the purchase of items in a tax jurisdiction: use taxes are collected on items bought in another jurisdiction but used in the taxing jurisdiction, and are imposed on the privilege of ownership of possession, storage, use, or consumption of goods in a jurisdiction. The use tax is generally complementary or supplemental to the sales tax. States vary as to which party in the transaction bears the responsibility for paying the tax. In some states, it is the responsibility of the seller, in others, the consumer. This tax is generally a flat rate with state rates ranging from 3 percent to 8.25 percent.

Property Taxes

Property taxes are the largest source of revenue for cities and municipalities. Property taxes are direct taxes, and are also referred to as "ad valorem" taxes. Property taxes may be assessed on real property, tangible personal property, or intangible personal property.

Other Taxes

Inheritance taxes are taxes paid in order to transfer wealth to beneficiaries. They are imposed, generally, at the federal and state levels.

Many of the other taxes are excise taxes, levied on certain products. These may include such items as alcoholic beverage taxes and cigarette taxes (commonly referred to as "sin" taxes), as well as gasoline and severance taxes (energy related taxes). These taxes are sometimes levied for a specific purpose, e.g., maintenance of highway systems or to help cover costs of administering special programs. These taxes are frequently levied at both the state and federal levels.

As demonstrated above, there are taxes designed to cover almost any purpose. They are there to generate revenue to operate our government. Unfortunately, however, the number of different taxes we are required to pay and the complexity of the tax laws are ever-increasing.

FEDERAL & STATE EXPENDITURES

To see the overall picture of government spending, we usually combine Federal, State, and local government spending. But the composition of Federal government budget is quite different from state and local government budgets.

a. Federal Government Expenditures

According to the *First Annual Report of the United States 1995*, the tax dollar is spent as follows:

Social Security	$0.22
Defense	$0.19
Interest on debt	$0.14
Welfare	$0.14
Medicare	$0.10
Health	$0.08
Transportation, research, and housing	$0.04
Education	$0.03
Agriculture and resources	$0.03
Veterans' Benefits	$0.03
TOTAL	$1.00

b. State and Local Revenues and Expenditures

The main sources of tax revenue for state and local governments are: property taxes, sales and gross receipts taxes, individual income taxes, corporation net income taxes, and revenue from the federal government.

The three main expenditures are: education, highways, and public welfare. The category All Other includes: libraries, hospitals, police protection, fire protection, sewage treatment, garbage collection, parks, and others.

Table 15.2
State and Local Government Revenues

General Revenue by Source
Property Taxes
Sales and Gross Receipts Taxes
Individual Income Taxes
Corporation Net Income Taxes
Revenue from the Federal Government
All Other
TOTAL
General Expenditures by Function
Education
Highways
Public Welfare
All Other
TOTAL

Source: Economic Report of the President 1995

c. Revenues & Expenditures for the State of Michigan

Michigan's general governmental operations are accounted for in the General Fund and 32 Special Revenue Funds. Total revenue and other sources of funds for general governmental operations for fiscal year 1998 were $32.9 billion. The two largest revenue components include taxes of $20.6 billion and revenues from the federal government comprising another $7.7 billion.

Expenditures and other uses of funds for governmental operations totaled $32.4 billion, or $3,298 per person, of which $11.5 billion supports K-12 and higher education and $6.8 billion supports health services.

Overall, Michigan's financial management of its revenues and expenditures is in very good condition. The February 1999 issue of *Governing* magazine gave the state an "A-" rating for its financial management capabilities—one of the best records in America.

The graphs in this article show the breakdown of fiscal year 1998 revenues and expenditures, including transfers to and from other funds, and other sources and uses of funds.

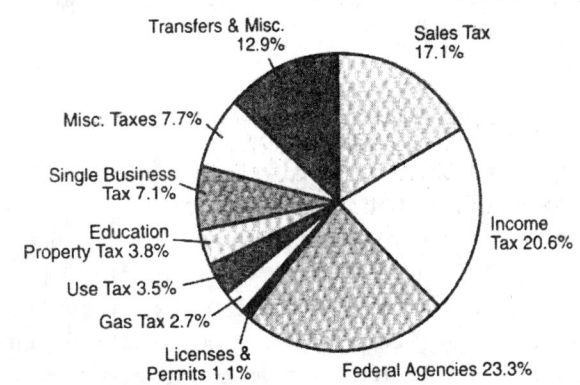

FY 1998 Revenues

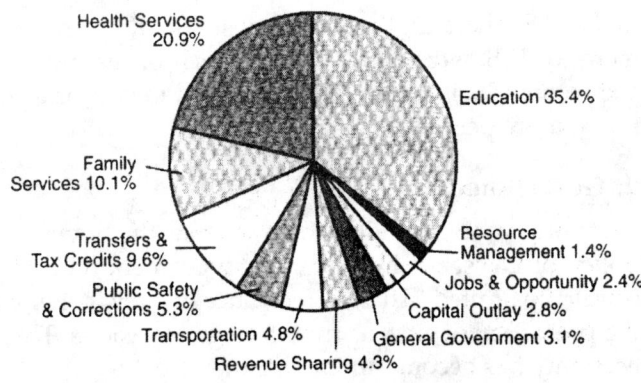

FY 1998 Expenditures

Source: State of Michigan

THE ECONOMIC SYSTEM OF THE UNITED STATES

The U.S. is the best example of a capitalist market economy with democracy. However many changes have occurred over time, as government has sought to modify the working of the free market. Democracy is the greatest way mankind has ever known to live by and follow. It gives everyone freedom of speech and religion and an equal opportunity to do the things they wish. Democracy also issues reasonable regulations over the social and economic capitalism and free enterprise. Capitalism and private enterprise are the greatest social and economic ways mankind has discovered for getting things done. They encourage optimum production of the things that mankind needs for a good life: great joy and accomplishments.

Benefits of market capitalism:

- more choices for market participants
- more efficient ⇒ higher standard of living
- more equity ⇒ distribution proportional to contribution of resource suppliers
- more opportunity for achieving progress, efficiency improvements, and upward social mobility
- less discrimination

a. Private Enterprises

Private Enterprise is one of the basic institutions of the U.S. economy. There is very little government ownership of industry. Anyone with an idea and capital is free to start his or her own business. There is the right to succeed and the right to fail. The U.S. consists of small enterprises and large corporations.

b. Large Corporations

Large corporations may also be global enterprises. As modem technology has increased, it has become an internationally marketable commodity because it is readily transferable through the operations of global corporations. This has resulted in the globalization of production. In the 1920's, corporate largeness was stimulated by changes that were occurring in the economy—particularly the mass production of automobiles. World War II contributed to the trend toward largeness. Large corporations produced the airplanes and tanks used by the U.S. during the 1940's and 1950's. The trend increased, facilitated by a new type of merger called the conglomerate. Today, the globalization of markets for goods and services, the global corporations do business all over the world.

c. Small Enterprises

In the U.S., there are thousands of small and medium sized business firms that provide employment for U.S. workers as well as much of the innovation necessary for global competitiveness. Today, the U.S. is a more services-oriented economy: opportunities have increased for consulting firms; more people are also self-employed.

d. Government

For many years, the idea has been that the government of a capitalist system should follow a policy of Laissez-Faire. That is, government had a limited role to play in society. Its activities should be limited to the performance of a few general functions. Examples are public works, and the protection of citizens from foreign invasions. The appropriate role of government in the U.S. economy has become an important subject.

e. Public Finance

Public finance is an indicator of the extent of government participation in a modified market economy. Taxes serve two purposes: they provide government with a source of revenue, and they can be used to effect a redistribution of income to the Federal Government, the sales tax is the most important source of income to the states, and local governments rely on property taxation. The following are the seven principal categories of the Federal Government Taxes.

1. Individual income tax
2. Corporate income tax
3. Excise taxes
4. Social Insurance taxes and contribution
5. Custom duties
6. Estate and gifts taxes
7. Deposit of Earnings by Federal Reserve System

However, the three most important types of the Federal Government Expenditures are: direct benefits payment to individuals, national defense, and interest payment on the national debt.

f. Economic Stabilization Policies

Government intervention includes fiscal and monetary policies that are implemented by the use of taxation and transfer payments, by its purchase of goods and services, and by the Federal Reserve's control of the money supply and interest rates. *Fiscal policy* refers to the manipulation of government spending and raises for the purpose of stabilizing domestic output, employment, and the price level. Its object is to increase or decrease the level of aggregate demand through changes in the level of government expenditures and taxation. *Monetary policy* is used by Federal Reserve to control the level of national income and the price level through variations in the money supply. The fundamental role of the Federal Reserve is to control the supply of money in the economy. Effects on interest rates are a product of this control. Monetary policy influences interest rates in two distinct ways, depending on whether or not the monetary policy affects inflation. The central bank controls the money supply through open-market operations, buying and selling bonds. If it wishes to increase the money supply, it buys bonds on the open market. To buy these bonds it must induce us to sell them by bidding up their price. This resize in the price of bonds means that the interest coupon on a bond is now a lower percentage payment. That is, the interest rate falls. Similarly, if the central bank wishes to decrease the money supply, it sells bonds on the open market. To sell bonds it must make them attractive to potential buyers by offering a higher interest rate, accomplished by selling the bonds at a lower price.

In marking Monetary Policy plans, the Federal Reserve and the open market operations are involved in a complex, dynamic process in which monetary policy is only one of many forces affecting employment, output, and prices.

The government's budgetary policies influence the economy through the changes in tax and spending programs. Shift in business and consumer confidence and a variety of other market forces, also affects saving and spending plans of business and households. Changes in expectations about economic prospects and policies, through their effects on interest rates and financial conditions, can have significant influence on the outcome for jobs, output and prices. According to the Federal Reserve Bank of New York 1998, Monetary Policy formulation is not a simple technical matter. It is clearly an art in that it greatly depends on experience, expertise, and adjustments.

g. Government Regulation and Control of Business

The regulations and control of business is considered necessary for several reasons, all of which are associated with some failure of the market systems. One failure is its inability to furnish society or its members with a satisfactory means for achieving certain wants, for example, the desire for a cleaner environment. Initiative for a cleaner environment therefore falls to public agencies, which use controls that have major impact on the operation of business firms. The distribution of income and wealth can be considered as a few in the market systems. Large income often accrues to individuals, not on the basis of their contribution to output but through inherited wealth or the exercise of special privilege. Antitrust is the American name for laws, agencies, and actions to protect and promote competition. Antitrust laws were first developed in the late 1800's to put an end to the growth abused of the trust. Americans antitrust laws are encapsulated in the Sherman and Clayton Acts. The Sherman Act prohibits the formation of monopolies and other business combinations that restrain interstate or foreign trade.

It also prohibits various anticompetitive business practices such as group boycotts and price fixing. The Clayton Act prohibits mergers whose end result is to substantially lessen competition and prohibits price discrimination whose intent is to ruin competitors. The Clayton Act also restricts the arrangement of interlocking directorates: It provides that no person shall be a director in two or more corporations if they are competitors.

h. Social Regulations

The government engages in social regulation of business in such matters as hiring the disabled, occupational safety, consumer protection, environmental protection, and affirmative action. The rationale for social regulations is that the market system does not work to solve such problems as sex and race discrimination.

i. The National Debt

President Clinton will probably be regarded as one of the most popular presidents of this century. For the first time in over 30 years, the United States is experiencing a surplus budget. Significantly, during the Reagan Administration, the U.S. experienced a massive increase in the Federal debt, an increase in equality and wealth, and budget deficits. The Federal debt, which was less than a trillion dollars in 1980, was $4.9 trillion by the end of 1995.

j. Merchandise Trade

The merchandise trade account measures the trade deficit or surplus. Its balance is derived by subtracting merchandise imports from merchandise exports. An export is considered positive because it results in a flow of outflow abroad; and import is considered negative because it results in outflow of money paid abroad. The merchandise trade account is part of a country's current account that consists of the following:

1. Merchandise Account (Imports and exports of physical goods)
2. Service Accounts (Tourist expenditures for hotel services, or services of an insurance/travel agent)
3. Net Investment income (Payment made for past investments, such as dividends)
4. Net Transfer Account (Payment in and out of the country such as a gift to a person living abroad)

The balance of payments record all movements of money in and out of a country. A debt is recorded whenever money leaves a country, and a credit is recorded whenever money enters the country.

The U.S. imported a whopping $817 billion worth of goods and services in the first nine months of 1998, according to the U.S. Bureau of the Census, which collects U.S. trade statistics. During the same period, the U.S. exported $694 billion worth of goods and services, resulting in a $123 billion international trade deficit for the January through September 1998 period.

Table 1
Imported Commodities by the U.S.
(January - September 1998)

Commodity	Value (in billions of U.S. $)
Computer Accessories	47,953
Crude Oil	28,969
Semiconductors	25,494
Cotton Apparel and Household Goods	20,546
Non-wool and non-cotton Apparel and Textiles	16,368
Electric Apparatus	15,524
Toys, Games, and Sporting Goods	14,283
Telecommunications Equipment	13,626
Pharmaceutical Preparations	12,454
Other Household Goods	11,906

Source: Bureau of the Census, Foreign Trade Division. 1999

k. Foreign Direct Investment

Direct investments are real investments in factories, capital goods, land and inventories where both capital and management are involved and the investor retains control over use of the invested subsidiary or taking control of another firm. In international multinational corporations engaged in manufacturing, resource extraction or services. Direct investment is now the principal channel of international private capital flows.

The motives for direct investment abroad are generally the same as for portfolio investments. It is an attempt to earn higher returns, maybe because there are higher growth rates abroad, more favorable tax treatment or greater availability of infrastructures. It is also done in order to diversify risk. It has been found those firms with strong international orientation, either through exports or through foreign production and sales facilities are more profitable and have a much smaller variability in profits than purely domestic firms. The question is, when residents of a nation do not borrow from other nations and make real investments in their own nation, rather than accept direct investments from abroad. There are several possible explanations. Most importantly, many large corporations want to retain direct control. The corporation will make direct investments abroad while involving production abroad of a differentiated product that is also produced at home.

Another important reason for direct foreign investments is to obtain control of a needed raw material and thus ensure an uninterrupted supply at the lowest possible cost. Some other reason for direct foreign investments are to avoid tariffs and other restrictions that nations impose on imports or to take advantage of various government subsidies to encourage direct foreign investments.

The United States is the world's largest homogeneous market offering a large and varied demand for high quality products and services, so some of the reasons for foreign direct investment in the U.S. would be that science and technology are highly regarded and the U.S. Society is generally responsive to innovations; political, economic and societal freedom guarantees foreign investors that they can operate on an equal footing with domestic producers; business atmosphere is flexible and dynamic—you can trim and integrate a company faster than you can anywhere else; operating costs in comparison to many other countries are fairly small and taxes are also lower than others; the United States provides a relative high rate of return on direct investment; and depending on the strength of the dollar, the exchange rate can also provide a strong incentive.

l. Strengths of the U.S. Economy

A close look at the U.S. economy reveals the following: The United States has many strengths; Its standard of living, as measured by real per capita GDP, is the highest in the world. Its unemployment rate as of the spring of 1999 is the lowest of all (G8) countries. The average productivity of U.S. industries and workers as a whole is at the top compared to the industrialized nations. The U.S. has the leadership position in industries once considered lost to the Japanese, including the automobile industry. The U.S. position as a provider of services, such as consulting, is by far the strongest of any country and will increase in the future. Finally, the economic growth for the United States is the highest among the industrialized countries.

In addition, U.S. houses generally are more affordable and offer more amenities than housing in other countries. In the United States the average price of a home is around 3 times the average annual salary of the U.S. worker compared to multiples of 8.6. in Japan, 6.4 in Italy, 6.1 in the United Kingdom, and 4.9 in Canada. America's opportunities, diversity, rich resources, advancement, technology, and power are unlimited. In 1997, the United States of America created more employment for its citizens than did the entire continent of Europe in a decade.

CHAPTER SUMMARY

1. Governments provide and finance goods and services in a way that differs from the way that business firms make them available.

2. Some of the examples of public goods are: national defense, highways, sewer systems, water systems, fire stations, and education.

3. Government plays an important role in an economic system. Economists identify at least three important functions of government: stabilization function, allocation function, and the distribution function.

4. The stabilization function involves an attempt to maintain a reasonable level of employment, price stability, and economic growth.

5. The allocation function refers to the government's directing resources and funds to the production of public goods.

6. The distribution function of the government refers to the use of taxes and welfare to affect the income of individuals in the economy. The concern is with income inequality.

7. The Lorenz curve is used to indicate the amount of income inequality in a country.

8. There are three major sources of government revenue: printing money, taxing, and borrowing.

9. There are three types of income tax: progressive, proportional and regressive. A progressive income tax is one where the tax rate increases as income increases. A proportional tax is one where the tax rate remains the same, regardless of the household income. A regressive tax is one where the tax rate decreases as income increases.

10. Government deficits are financed by borrowing. Reducing government deficits requires either increased taxes or reduced spending.

11. Individual and corporate income taxes are used at the federal, state, and local levels. Social security taxes are imposed by the federal government. Sales and property taxes are imposed at the state and local levels, although the federal government has imposed some excise taxes.

12. A tax is said to be fair if there is horizontal and vertical equity. Horizontal equity means that people with the same income are taxed the same. Vertical equity means that person with different incomes are taxed different rates.

13. The ability-to-pay principle states that persons with higher incomes should pay higher tax rates.

14. The benefits-received principle states that a person should be taxed according to the benefits received from government expenditures.

15. The uses of taxes are to: raise revenue, provide public goods, redistribute income, provide stabilization, discourage foreign trade, and punish sin.

16. The negative income tax is a plan to replace the welfare system by paying households a cash payment if their income falls below the established break-even level.

17. The three main sources of revenue for the federal government are: the individual income tax, the social security tax, and the corporate income tax. The main area of federal expenditures are: national defense, social security, interest, income security, and Medicare.

18. The three main sources of revenue for state and local governments are: property taxes, corporation net income taxes, and revenue from the federal government. The main expenditures are: education, highways, and public welfare.

19. The United States has been troubled by twin deficits, the domestic spending deficit, and the foreign payments deficit.

Chapter 15
Key Concepts

Ability-to-Pay Principle—The tax rate increases as a person's income increases.

Ad Valorem Tax—A tax based on the value of an item.

Allocation Function—Government directing resources and funds to the production of public goods.

Balanced Budget—Revenue equaling expenditures.

Benefits-Received Principle—A person should be taxed based on the benefits the person receives from government expenditures.

Boom—A high point on the business cycle.

Business Cycle—The volume of economic activity goes through periods of expansion and contraction.

Deficit—Spending exceeds revenue.

Deficit Budget—Planned revenue less than planned expenditures.

Direct Tax—A tax paid by the first party billed.

Distribution Function—The use of taxes and welfare to affect the incomes of individuals in the economy.

Excise Tax—A tax levied on certain products such as alcohol and cigarettes.

General Tax—To be spent on any governmental activity.

Horizontal Equity—Individuals earning the same income, regardless of how it is earned, pay the same tax.

Indirect Tax—A tax that is shifted to a second person to pay—as a tax on business being included in the price paid for by the consumer.

Lorenz Curve—A curve used to indicate the amount of income inequality in a country.

National Debt—The debt incurred by the federal government by its borrowing to finance expenditures.

Negative Income Tax—A welfare replacement plan in which households earning below a break-even level of income would receive a cash payment, and households with incomes above the break-even level would pay taxes.

Omnibus Budget Reconciliation Act—An act to reduce the federal deficit by imposing caps.

Private Goods—Goods purchased by consumers.

Progressive Income Tax—The tax rate increases as income increases.

Property Tax—A tax on the ownership of property.

Proportional Income Tax—The tax rate is the same for all incomes.

Regressive Income Tax—The tax rate decreases as income increases.

Sales Tax—A tax imposed on the purchase of an item in a tax jurisdiction.

Specific Tax—A tax intended for a specific purpose—as a gas tax to pay for highway repairs.

Surplus Budget—Government revenue exceeds government expenditures.

Stabilization Function—The government setting goals of reducing inflation and unemployment.

Upswing—An increase in economic activity bringing the economy out of a recession.

Use Tax—Imposed on items purchased in another tax jurisdiction, but used in the tax jurisdiction imposing the tax.

Vertical Equity—Persons with different incomes being taxed different rates.

DISCUSSION QUESTIONS

1. Explain the allocation function of government.
2. Explain the distribution function of government.
3. Discuss the stabilization function of government.
4. Explain what is shown by the Lorenz curve.
5. How can government reduce income inequality?
6. Present the parts of the business cycle.
7. What are the four goals of the U.S. economy?
7. Distinguish between progressive, regressive, and proportional taxes.
8. Discuss how a tax can be fair.
9. Present the uses of taxes.
10. Explain the concept of the negative income tax.
11. Compare the sources of revenue for the federal and state and local governments.
12. Compare the functions of the expenditures of the federal and the state and local governments.
13. Why has inequality been growing in the United States?
14. Discuss the primary cause of poverty.
15. Explain the importance of government.
16. Present the concept of economic growth and economic development.

Index

A
Absolute Advantage, 354
AFL-CIO Merger, 289
Agreement, 264
Agricultural Prices, 86
Allocation Function, 388
American Federation of Labor, 288
Analysis of Regulation, 311
Anti-Monopoly Legislation, 320
Antitrust, 379
Antitrust Philosophy, 315
Arabic Tradition & Muslims, 47
Areas, 373
Arguments for Deregulation, 314
Arguments against Deregulation, 315
Assignment of Property Rights, 345
Average Product of Labor (APL), 282

B
Basic Antitrust Laws, 316
Bonds, 170
Borrowing, 397
Bretton Woods System, 368
Budget Constraints, 154

C
Cartel, 263
Cause and Effect Fallacy, 10
Causes of Changes in Supply and Demand, 83
Ceteris Paribus, 10
Changes in Demand and Supply of Currency, 364
Changes in the Market Price, 79
Characteristics, 103
    Characteristics of Indifference Curves, 151
    Characteristics of Monopoly, 285
    Characteristics of Pure Competition, 198
Cheating, 264
Choices, 34
Civil Rights Act, 291
Clayton Act, 290, 317
Collective Bargaining and Wage Rates, 292
Collusion, 262
Common and Preferred Stocks, 170
Communication, 377
Comparative Advantage, 355
Competitive Firm's Short Run Supply Curve, 202
Competitive Labor Market, 280
Complementary Good, 117
Composition Fallacy, The, 11

Concerns and Benefits from Immigrants, 300
Congress of Industrial Organization (CIO), 289
Consequences of Advertising, 246
Constant Returns to Scale, 184
Consumer's Maximization of Utility, 156
Corporation, 169
Cost Advantage, 357
Cost-Benefit Analysis, 336
Cournot Model, 268
Cross Elasticity of Demand, 115

D
Demand, Cost, Revenue, and the
    Profit Maximization, 200
Depreciation and Appreciation
    of the U.S. Dollar, 372
Deregulation, 314
Derivation of the Demand Curve, 158
Determinants of Income, 297
Devaluation, 371
Diamond-Water Paradox, The, 146
Direct Regulation, 345
Direct—Indirect, 400
Discrimination, 299
Diseconomies of Scale, 183
Distribution Function and the Lorenz Curve, 389
Distribution Infrastructure, 378
Dominance, 264
Dumping, 230

E
Economic Approach, The, 4
Economic Efficiency, 332
Economic Growth, 42, 393
Economic Stabilization Policies, 405
Economic Systems, 46
Economics, 2
Economics of Agriculture, 209
Economics Statistics, 24
Efficiency, 44
Elasticity, 98
Entry, 264
Equilibrium, 74
Evaluating Monopolistic Competition, 252
Exchange Rates, 368
Expansion of Markets for Domestic Goods, 357
Externalities, 333

F

Factors Affecting the Demand for Labor, 300
Fair Tax, 397
Federal Government Expenditures, 402
Federal Trade Commission Act, 320
Firm's Supply, 66
Fixed Exchange Rate (FER), 368
Flexible Exchange vs. Managed Floating Exchange Rates, 368
Foreign Corrupt Practices Act (FCPA), 379
Foreign Direct Investment, 407
Foreign Exchange Markets, 363
Forward Market, 363
Functions, 388

G

Game Theory, 268
General—Specific, 401
Gold Standard, 367
Government, 404
Government Goals, 392
Government Regulation and Control of Business, 406
Government Revenues, 394
Greater Choice, 357
Growth Size, 394

H

Health and Safety Regulation, 321

I

Immigration, 299
Implicit Costs, 172
Income Elasticity, 112
Income Elasticity of Demand, 111
Income Taxes, 401
Independent Good, 118
Indifference Curve Analysis, 146
Industry Supply Curve, 202
Interdependence, 260
Internalizing, 342

K

Kinked Demand Curve Model, 266

L

Landrum-Griffin Act, 290
Large Corporations, 404
Legislations Concerning Labor, 297
Less Developed Countries, 373
Long Run Equilibrium Condition in the Monopolistic Competition, 250
Lorenz Curve, 389
Luxury Items, 114

M

Marginal Benefit (MB), 331
Marginal Cost, 330
Marginal Private Costs (MPC), 335
Marginal Product of Labor (MPL), 283
Marginal Rate of Transformation, 41
Marginal Rates of Substitution (MRS), 150
Marginal Social Costs (MSC), 335
Marginal Utility, 140
Market Demand, 64
Market Failure, 333
Market Power, 232
Market Structures, 198
Market Success, 330
Market Supply, 72
Mastering Economics, 22
Maximizing Total Utility, 143
Merchandise Trade, 406
Mergers, 261
Minimum Wage Controversy, 313
Minimum Wages, 86
Mixed Market Structure, 49
Monopolistic Competition, 244
Monopoly, 218
Monopsony, 283
Monopsony in the Market for Nurses, 285

N

National Debt, 406
Negative Income Tax, 398
Neutral Good, 115
New-Wave Regulation, 321
Non-Price Competition, 224, 245
Normal Goods, 113
Norris-LaGuardia Act, 290

O

Opportunity Costs, 37. 172

P

Partnership, 168
Perfectly Elastic Demand, 105
Perfectly Elastic Supply, 123
Perfectly Inelastic Demand, 107
Political Reasons, 357
Pollution, 339
Post-Civil War, 288
Poverty and Inequality, 390
Pre-Civil War, 287
Price Ceiling, 87
Price Controls, 85
Price Controls: Agricultural Price Support, 312
Price Discrimination, 229
Price Elasticity, 98
Price Floor, 85

Price Rigidity, 261
Price Searcher, 224
Prices, 339
Pricing Policies, 266
Primary Causes of Poverty, 390
Principle of Diminishing
    Marginal Utility (DMU), 141
Principle of Diminishing Returns, 180
Prisoner's Dilemma, 269
Private Enterprises, 404
Product Differentiation, 244
Production Possibilities, 38
Profit Maximization Principle:
    Unit Cost Minus Unit Revenue, 203
Profit Rule, 204
Property Taxes, 402
Protectionism Theory, 358
Public Finance, 405
Public Policy of the 19th Century, 289
Purely Competitive Firm in
    Long Run Equilibrium, 208

Q
Quantity Demanded and Demand, 84
Quantity Supplied and Supply, 84

R
Racial Discrimination, 299
Rationale for Regulation, 311
Reasons for Trade, 356
Regulatory Process, 310
Relatively Elastic, 100
Relatively Elastic Supply, 120
Relatively Inelastic, 101
Relatively Inelastic Supply, 122
Resource Allocations, 234
Revaluation, 372
Robinson-Patman Act, 319

S
Sales/Use Tax, 401
Scarcity, 32
Sex Education, 338
Sherman Act, 316
Short Run Profit Maximization
    Under Pure Competition, 203

Short-Run Conditions: Profits and Loss, 248
Slope, 18, 110
Small Enterprises, 404
Social Regulations, 323, 406
Social Sciences, 2
Sole Proprietorship, 168
Sources of Pollution, 341
Spot Market, 363
Stabilization Function, 392
State and Local Revenues and Expenditures, 402
State Income Taxes, 401
Strengths of the U.S. Economy, 408
Substitute Good, 117
Sunk Cost, 172
Supply Curve, 247
Supply Curve of the Monopolist, 222

T
Taft-Hartley Act, 290
Tax Computation Form, 400
Tax Policy, 391
Terms of Trade, 353
The Rational Consumer, 140
Total Fixed Costs, 173
Total Product of Labor (TPL), 282
Total Revenue Method, 121
Total Utility, 140
Total Variable Costs, 174
Trade Policy, 377
Training, 379

U
Unitary Elastic, 104
Unitary Elastic Supply, 126
Uses of Taxes, 400
Utility Consumer Behavior, 143

V
Variety of Goods, 357

W
Wage Differentials, 295
Wagner Act, 290

Z
Zero Profits in Industry, The Meaning of, 250